Annual Review
of Irish Law 1994

Raymond Byrne
B.C.L., LL.M., Barrister-at-Law
Lecturer in Law, Dublin City University

William Binchy
B.A., B.C.L., LL.M., Barrister-at-Law
Regius Professor of Laws, Trinity College Dublin
Formerly, Research Counsellor, The Law Reform Commission

ROUND HALL SWEET & MAXWELL
DUBLIN

The typesetting for this book was produced by
Gough Typesetting Services, Dublin for
ROUND HALL SWEET & MAXWELL
4 Upper Ormond Quay, Dublin 7.

A catalogue record for this book
is available from the British Library.

ISBN1-85800-075-0

ISSN 0791-1084

Printed by
Hartnolls, Cornwall

Content

Preface

In this eighth volume in the Annual Review series, our purpose continues to be to provide a review of legal developments, judicial and statutory, that occurred in 1994. In terms of case law, this includes those judgments which were delivered in 1994, regardless of whether they have been (or will be) reported and which were circulated up to the date of the preface. Once again, it is a pleasure to thank those who made the task of completing this volume less onerous.

Mr Justice Brian Walsh (who, as we have mentioned in previous volumes, was the originator of the concept of an Annual Review of Irish Law) continues to be most supportive and we remain very grateful for this. Once again, we are in the debt of a number of people for providing access to library facilities. In particular, Ms Peggy McQuinn, of the Office of the Supreme Court, Ms Margaret Byrne and Ms Mary Gaynor, of the Library of the Incorporated Law Society of Ireland, and Mr Johnathon Armstrong and Ms Therese Broy, of the King's Inns Library, were as helpful as ever with a number of difficult queries from the authors. And once again, Ms Jennifer Aston, Librarian in the Law Library, Four Courts, was also especially helpful in facilitating access to statutory material which is otherwise very difficult to source.

We would also like to express our heartfelt thanks to the staffs of the Dublin City University and Trinity College libraries for their assistance in the research for this volume. This seventh volume in the Annual Review series also marks a departure from previous years. The authors are delighted to have had the benefit of specialist contributions on Company Law, Communications, Contract Law, Equity and Land Law included in the volume. The authors continue to take final responsibility for the overall text as in the past, but are especially grateful for the contributions of David Tomkin and Adam McAuley in Company Law, Eamon Hall in Communications, Eoin O'Dell in Contract Law, Hilary Delany in Equity and Paul Coughlan in Land Law.

Eoin O'Dell would like to thank Barry Doherty for his help with material in the discussion of *RGDATA v Tara Publishing* [1995] 1 IR 89; [1995] 1 ILRM 453 (High Court, Murphy J), below, pp. 151-7) and for access to drafts of his PhD thesis: *Competition Law in Ireland* (TCD in progress).

Finally, we are very grateful to Round Hall Sweet & Maxwell and Gilbert

Gough, whose professionalism ensures the continued production of this series.

Raymond Byrne and William Binchy,
Dublin

November 1996

Table of Cases

Other Tables

CONSTITUTIONAL PROVISIONS

STATUTES

Ireland

England

STATUTORY INSTRUMENTS

ANNUAL REVIEW OF IRISH LAW 1994

Administrative Law

APPROPRIATION

The Appropriation Act 1994 provided as follows. For the year ended December 31, 1994, the amount for supply grants was £9,623,592,000 and for appropriations-in-aid was £908,852,000. A shortfall for the year 1991, amounting to £5,807 in respect of the appropriation-in-aid to the State Laboratory, was also included (see also the 1993 Review, 3). The 1994 Act came into effect on its signature by the President on December 27, 1994.

COMPTROLLER AND AUDITOR GENERAL

The Comptroller and Auditor General (s. 6) Order 1994 (SI No. 196 of 1994), made under the Comptroller and Auditor General (Amendment) Act 1993 (1993 Review, 147-50) requires health boards to submit annual accounts to the Comptroller and Auditor General and to the Houses of the Oireachtas. Similarly, the Comptroller and Auditor General (s. 7) Order 1994 (SI No. 197 of 1994) requires Vocational Education Committees to submit annual accounts to the Comptroller and Auditor General and to the Houses of the Oireachtas.

DIPLOMATIC RELATIONS

Diplomatic immunity: WTO The WTO (Designation and Immunities) Order 1994 (SI No. 329 of 1994) enabled diplomatic immunity to be conferred on the World Trade Organisation (WTO) and its officials pursuant to the Diplomatic Relations and Immunities Act 1967 in order to meet the requirements of the 1994 Marrakesh Agreement that provided for the establishment of the WTO by way of replacement for the General Agreement on Tariffs and Trade (GATT). The General Agreement on Tariffs and Trade (Designation and Immunities) Order 1994 (SI No. 465 of 1994) enabled diplomatic immunity to be conferred on GATT and its officials and also the staff of the Interim Commission for the International Trade Organisation which preceded the formal establishment of the WTO.

NATIONAL MONUMENTS

The National Monuments (Amendment) Act 1994, as the Explanatory Memorandum to the Bill as published stated, establishes the State's right to ownership of all archaeological objects with no known owner found after the enactment of the Act. 1994 Act extends the statutory protection and preservation of archaeological objects to include the concept of treasure trove and provides for the payment of rewards to the finders of archaeological objects. It also put in place procedures for reporting any find of such objects and also their initial preservation. The Act also creates offences relating to the possession, sale, or acquisition of unreported archaeological objects found since 1930. To that extent, the 1994 Act can be seen as a belated legislative response to the decision of the Supreme Court in *Webb v Ireland* [1988] IR 353; [1988] ILRM 565 (1987 Review, 104-107), in which the Court had held that the ancient prerogative of treasure trove had not survived the enactment of the Constitution of Ireland 1937. In addition to these elements of the 1994 Act, provision is also made for the extension and amendment of the National Monuments Acts 1930 to 1987 in respect of, *inter alia*, the recording and preservation of all monuments, the acquisition of monuments and increasing the penalties for offences under these Acts. All provisions of the 1994 Act, except s. 17, came into effect on November 21, 1994: National Monuments (Amendment) Act 1994 (Commencement) Order 1994 (SI No. 337 of 1994). S. 17 of the Act came into effect on March 1, 1995: National Monuments (Amendment) Act 1994 (Commencement) (No. 2) Order 1994 (SI No. 338 of 1994).

As to the detail of the 1994 Act, s. 2 expressly establishes the State's right to ownership of all archaeological objects (subject to a right to waive this in s. 3) which have no known owner found in the State after the Act came into effect. 'Owner' is defined as the person who is entitled to the actual possession of the object, which is similar to the existing definition in the National Monuments Acts 1930 to 1987. Ss. 4 and 5 create a number of offences relating to the retention of possession of an archaeological object found in the State or to engage in the sale, exchange or disposal of such object. This extends the existing law, in particular s. 23 of the National Monuments Act 1930, which only required the finder of an archaeological object to report such finding to the Director of the National Museum. In this respect s. 19 of the 1994 Act amends s. 23 of the National Monuments Act 1930 and revises and extends the procedures for reporting the finding of archaeological objects. The forms required for these purposes are contained in the National Monuments (Prescription of Form) Regulations 1994 (SI No. 339 of 1994) and the National Monuments (Prescription of Form) (No. 2) Regulations 1994 (SI No. 340 of 1994).

S. 7 provides for the seizure and forfeiture of unauthorised detection devices and diving equipment found at the site of a national monument. S. 7 also extends the and replaces s. 2(6) of the National Monuments (Amendment) Act 1987 which had, *inter alia*, restricted the use and possession of detection devices in places protected under the National Monuments Acts 1930 to 1987. S. 8 provides for inspections and excavations of national monuments to be carried out by the Director of the National Museum, while s. 9 authorises the Director to take possession on behalf of the State of archaeological objects. S. 10 provides for the payment of a reward by the Director to a person finding an archaeological object as well as to the owner or occupier of the land where the object is retained by the State. Payments require the consent of the Minister and the Minister for Finance. No right to a reward is created by s. 10, but s. 10(3) sets out the criteria to be used by the Director of the National Museum, namely, the intrinsic value and importance of the object, the circumstances of its finding and amounts paid in other comparable cases. While the Act creates no right to a reward, the concept of legitimate expectation referred to in the *Webb* case would appear to support a very strong sense of entitlement. Nonetheless, s.10(4) expressly provides that there is no obligation on the Director of the National Museum to pay any reward unless satisfied that it is in the public interest to do so.

S. 11 provides for the acquisition either by agreement or compulsorily of national monuments by the Commissioners of Public Works. This replaces s. 6 of the National Monuments (Amendment) Act 1987 which had provided for the acquisition of national monuments, parts thereof and lands in their vicinity, whereas s. 11 of the 1994 Act extends this to rights, easements or other interests. S. 12 provides for the first time for the establishment by the Commissioners of Public Works of a list of all monuments as well as other places where they believe monuments are located. Significantly, s. 12(3) provides that an owner or occupier of a monument or place listed under s. 12 shall not carry out any work on the monument or place so recorded unless he gives prior notice in writing to the Commissioners. Except in the case of urgent necessity, work may not commence until two months have elapsed following the giving of the notice. The requirements concerning exhibition of maps and listed monuments are set out in the National Monuments (Exhibition of Record of Monuments) Regulations 1994 (SI No. 341 of 1994).

A number of other important administrative improvements are also included in the 1994 Act concerning the protection of national monuments and the preservation of archaeological objects. Finally, we may note that s. 13 provides for penalties on conviction for the new offences created under the Act. The maximum penalty on summary conviction is £1,000 and/or twelve months imprisonment and on conviction on indictment £50,000 and/or five years imprisonment.

JUDICIAL REVIEW

Bias In *O'Reilly v Cassidy (No. 2)* [1995] 1 ILRM 311, Flood J accepted the applicant's claim that a decision of the respondent judge of the Circuit Court fell foul of the bias rule.

The applicant was the holder of a seven-day intoxicating liquor licence in respect of a public house. Various persons objected to the renewal of the applicant's licence on the grounds that she did not operate or have control over the premises and that she was not a fit person to hold a licence as she had done nothing to deal with the many cases of disorderly conduct on the premises and the adjacent street during the past twelve months. These were rejected in the District Court. On further appeal to the Circuit Court, counsel for one of the objectors was also the daughter of the first named respondent judge of the Circuit Court. No objection was taken prior to or at the commencement of the proceedings to her appearing for the objector or to the first named respondent presiding over the appeal. However, counsel for the applicant referred to the relationship in the course of submissions concerning the admissibility of evidence. The hearing was adjourned in order to facilitate the examination of documents requested by the applicant. At the adjourned hearing, the respondent declined to allow a further adjournment to allow the applicant inspect documents produced in court on the morning of the adjourned hearing. After exchanges between counsel for the applicant and the respondent judge counsel withdrew from the hearing. Subsequently, the respondent made an order which allowed the objections to the renewal of the applicant's intoxicating liquor licence.

The Supreme Court [1995] 1 ILRM 306 (see 10-11, below) gave liberty to the applicant to apply by way of judicial review for an order of *certiorari* quashing the order of the respondent. In the High Court, Flood J quashed the first named respondent's order of May 3, 1994 and remitted the matter to the Circuit Court to rehear and determine the appeal.

Before dealing with the question of bias, Flood J considered the respondent's refusal to grant an adjournment at the resumed hearing. He pointed out that the adjournment of a case is a matter for the discretion of the trial judge, but that it must be exercised within constitutional parameters so that a fair balance is struck between the importance of the matters in issue for the applicant and the procedural discipline which must be maintained if the court is to discharge its business with reasonable dispatch. In the instant case, the applicant had failed to take any steps to inspect the documents which may have existed and were germane to the matters in issue during the period of five weeks from the service of the notice to produce to the date of the resumed hearing. However, since the renewal of the intoxicating liquor licence was clearly a matter of fundamental financial importance to the applicant, fair procedures demanded that indulgence must be granted to the applicant and her legal advisers. Consequently, he concluded that the refusal to grant an adjournment constituted a breach of the fair procedures to which the applicant had a constitutional right.

Turning to the issue of bias, Flood J emphasised that there was no question of actual bias in issue as the applicant had expressly abandoned any suggestion of bias being displayed by the respondent judge. Here the appropriate test was whether a person in the position of the applicant, being a reasonable person, might reasonably fear that the probable outcome of the case as matters stood, having regard to the evidence tendered, might be contributed to and worsened by the fact that the counsel for the second named respondent was a daughter of the presiding judge. Flood J considered that the mere fact that a judge's daughter was briefed before him was not sufficient to give rise to the possibility that a reasonable man would consider that bias would follow. To accept such a proposition, he said, would be to derogate the oath which was made and subscribed to by every judge on being appointed pursuant to the Constitution to a totally empty formula.

In addition to the relationship, there must exist some element which could, not would, give rise to a fear in the mind of a reasonable man that in the circumstances the relationship between counsel and the judge could affect the outcome of the case. In the circumstances, Flood J concluded that the complaint by the applicant as to the relationship between the objector's counsel and the respondent judge became so inextricably entangled with other factors that there was a real possibility that the end product would give rise to a fear in a reasonable person that the outcome of the proceedings could be affected by the relationship between counsel and judge. In those circumstances, the case for bias had been established.

By contrast, in *McNally v Martin* [1995] 1 ILRM 350, the Supreme Court rejected another claim of bias, in this instance concerning a judge of the District Court. The applicant had been charged in the District Court before the respondent judge with feigning a heart attack with the intention of frustrating a prosecution under s. 49 of the Road Traffic Act 1961, contrary to s. 18(3) of the Road Traffic (Amendment) Act 1978, as amended by s. 5 of the Road Traffic (Amendment) Act 1984, and with failing to give the necessary blood or urine sample to a designated medical practitioner contrary to s. 13(3) of the Road Traffic (Amendment) Act 1978, as amended by the Road Traffic (Amendment) Act 1984. At the hearing there was an essential gap in the prosecution's proofs in relation to the s. 13 charge as there was no evidence that the doctor called by the prosecution was a registered medical practitioner at the time when she examined the applicant at the Garda station. Counsel for the applicant sought to rely on the decision of the High Court in *Director of Public Prosecutions v O'Donoghue* [1991] 1 IR 448, but was not permitted to do so by the respondent who said: 'I know the case and the point raised in the case and will refuse it or any other point you make'. The applicant was convicted on both charges.

The applicant sought an order of *certiorari* in the High Court to quash the convictions. In the High Court, Murphy J quashed the conviction under s. 13 as the applicant had been deprived of his basic rights of justice at his trial. However, as to the s. 18 charge, he held that it was open to the respondent to convict on that charge and that in the circumstances a reasonable person present in the courtroom throughout the hearing of the case would not have inferred bias on the part of the respondent. The applicant appealed against the latter element of the decision but the Supreme Court (Hamilton CJ, O'Flaherty and Denham JJ) dismissed the appeal.

Delivering the only reasoned judgment, O'Flaherty J stated that the error in relation to the s. 13 charge did not affect the hearing of the case in relation to the s. 18 charge. He considered that the respondent judge had behaved impeccably in hearing the evidence and submissions of the appellant in relation to the s. 18 charge. Quoting with approval the views of Hederman J in *Sweeney v Brophy* [1993] 2 IR 202 (1992 Review, 268-70), O'Flaherty J stated that the circumstances in which a conviction would be quashed by way of *certiorari* are to be strictly confined to a breach of the fundamental tenets of constitutional justice. He did not consider that such had occurred in the instant case.

Certiorari of local authority auditor's charge   In *Downey v O'Brien* [1994] 2 ILRM 130, the facts of which are discussed in more detail in the Local Government chapter, 339-42, below, Costello J (as he then was) considered certain procedural aspects of an application for an order of *certiorari* under s. 12 of the Local Government (Ireland) Act 1871 seeking to quash a charge made by a local government auditor. He held that, in such an application, neither party can adduce fresh evidence and that the court must base its decision on the materials which were before the local government auditor. However, he added that affidavit evidence could be adduced in order to establish or explain what material was before the auditor. Costello J acknowledged *certiorari* proceedings under s. 12 of the 1871 Act could not be regarded as an appeal by way of rehearing. However, following *The State (Raftis) v Leonard* [1960] IR 381, he concluded that, unlike ordinary *certiorari* proceedings, the Court could come to a different conclusion on the evidence which had been before the auditor and was not confined to merely considering whether there was evidence to support the auditor's findings of fact.

Cross-examination at hearing In *Gallagher v Revenue Commissioners and Ors (No. 2)* [1995] 1 ILRM 241, Morris J and, on appeal, the Supreme Court upheld the right of the applicant to require direct evidence as to the substance of disciplinary charges made against him and to cross-examine the persons making the allegations against him. Although the Supreme Court decision in this case was delivered in January 1995, we consider it here for the sake of completeness. The applicant was an officer of customs and excise in charge of a mobile customs patrol unit. Among his duties was the task of identifying vehicles which had been imported illegally into the State and, in certain cases, determining the value of the particular vehicle so that the outstanding duty could be paid and the vehicle released. A number of allegations were made against the applicant to the effect that between May 1984 and June 1985 he had deliberately undervalued vehicles and thereby caused a loss of revenue to the State. The applicant was suspended in January 1988 and the respondents sent written details of the allegations to him in January 1989. It was claimed that he had failed to name the importers of certain vehicles correctly, deliberately undervalued vehicles, failed to transmit certain forms to the Gardaí and failed to obtain the counter-signature of importers or owners on official receipts. The applicant opted for an oral inquiry into the allegations. The Revenue Commissioners refused to permit him legal representation, or allow him to see in advance the statements of the two customs officers who had investigated the case against him or transcripts of interviews which they had with him. The applicant instituted judicial review proceedings and in the course of discovery the statements and transcripts were made available to him. In 1991, Blayney J held [1991] ILRM 632 (1991 Review, 8-10) that the applicant was entitled to legal representation at the inquiry. An oral hearing commenced in February 1992. It was chaired by the personnel officer of the Revenue Commissioners. The applicant's legal advisers indicated that the applicant wished to confront and cross-examine the persons whose evidence was said to be adverse to him. When it was indicated that these witnesses were not going to be called, the applicant and his legal advisers withdrew from the inquiry and it proceeded in their absence. Subsequently, a recommendation was made that the applicant be dismissed from the Civil Service and this was given effect to in February 1992.

The applicant then instituted the instant judicial review proceedings in which he sought, *inter alia*, an order of *certiorari* quashing the decision to dismiss him. In the High Court, Morris J granted the relief sought, ordered that the applicant should be reinstated and directed that he be paid his arrears of salary. The respondents appealed, but the Supreme Court (Hamilton CJ, O'Flaherty and Denham JJ) dismissed the appeal.

Delivering the leading judgment, Hamilton CJ stated that, in view of the consequences for the applicant in the event of a decision adverse to him, the personnel officer was obliged to act judicially and adopt procedures which were fair and reasonable. Citing the decision of the Court in *Kiely v Minister for Social Welfare* [1977] IR 267, he stated that while tribunals exercising quasi-judicial functions are given a certain latitude in the exercise of their functions, and in determining the requirements of natural justice and fair procedures in the circumstances of the case, they may not act in such a way as to imperil a fair hearing or a fair result.

As to the attendance of witnesses, he referred with approval to the leading decision of the English Court of Appeal in *R. v Board of Visitors of Hull Prison, ex parte St. Germain* [1979] 1 WLR 1401 to the effect that mere administrative difficulties in securing the attendance of witnesses before a tribunal or inquiry is not a sufficient ground for depriving a person charged before the tribunal of the right to cross-examine witnesses as to facts which are essential to the establishment of the charges against him. In any event, he noted that there was no suggestion in the instant case that anyone had been asked to come from outside the jurisdiction to give evidence and had refused to do so. He stated that the failure of the personnel officer to require direct evidence as to the valuation of the vehicles involved in the instant case deprived the applicant of the opportunity of hearing this evidence and challenging it by means of cross-examination. This, he concluded, was contrary to the requirements of natural justice and the requirements of fair procedures. Finally, the Supreme Court also held that the inquiry had suffered from a fundamental defect in that no proper evidence had been adduced as to the value of the vehicles and only hearsay accounts had been considered. In addition, the cases concerning particular vehicles were very old so that the recollection of events, whether by documentation or hearsay accounts, for what they were worth, was dimmed. Furthermore, the cases related to a commodity the price of which varied widely according to factors such as the condition of the vehicle, the geographical location of the point of sale, the character of the parties and their willingness to buy or sell. As already indicated, the Court upheld the decision in the High Court to quash the dismissal.

Leave to apply In *O'Reilly v Cassidy* [1995] 1 ILRM 306, the Supreme Court (Finlay CJ, O'Flaherty and Blayney JJ) granted the applicant leave to seek judicial review where she alleged that the respondent judge of the Circuit Court had acted contrary to fair procedures in refusing to allow an adjournment and where it was also alleged that the respondent was in breach of the rule against bias. As we have already seen, the application was ultimately successful in the High Court on one of these points only (see *O'Reilly v Cassidy (No. 2)* [1995] 1 ILRM 311, discussed 6-7, above), but regardless of the outcome the decision of the Supreme Court is of great interest on the general principles to be applied in such cases.

In delivering the leading judgment, Finlay CJ stated that when considering an application for leave to seek judicial review the sole concern of the court is that the bringing of proceedings should not be permitted if there is not an arguable case and it was not appropriate for the court to express any view on whether the grounds alleged are strong or weak.

In the instant case, there had been a refusal by the Circuit Court judge to allow an adjournment so that the applicant's legal advisers could read documents which had been produced in court: see further 6, above. Finlay CJ held that this raised an arguable ground of unfair procedures, and we might note in this respect that the applicant was ultimately successful on this aspect of the case: see 7, above.

As to the suggestion of bias, which centred on the fact that counsel for one of the parties was the daughter of the respondent judge, Finlay CJ stated that, where there is no initial objection to this there is no impropriety in the judge continuing to hear the case. In the instant case, there was no allegation that bias had been displayed at any stage by the Circuit Court judge, but Finlay CJ accepted that, in light of the applicant's very considerable stake in the decision and the fact that she instructed her counsel to object to the relationship, it was arguable that the Circuit Court judge should have discontinued the case and either arranged for another judge to hear it or taken some other step. As we have already seen, 7, above while the applicant was ultimately successful on this point, it was not on the general principle of kinship between the judge and counsel but rather the particular circumstances in which that might have been seen.

Unreasonableness In *Madigan v Radio Telefís Éireann* [1994] 2 ILRM 472, Kinlen J rejected the applicant's claim that the respondent had acted unreasonably within the meaning of the Supreme Court decisions in *The State (Keegan) v Stardust Victims' Compensation Tribunal* [1986] IR 642; [1987] ILRM 202 and *O'Keeffe v An Bórd Pleanála* [1993] 1 IR 39; [1992] ILRM 237 (1991 Review, 16-8). The applicant, an independent candidate in the 1994 European Parliament election, had challenged the policy by which the respondent, the State broadcasting body, had allocated broadcast time to those involved in the election. Kinlen J held that the policy, which took into account past electoral participation but also had regard to the needs of independent candidates, was consistent with the respondent's statutory duty to ensure impartiality pursuant to s. 18 of the Broadcasting Authority Act 1960 as amended.

Agriculture

ANIMAL DISEASES

General   The European Communities (Control of Infectious Animal Diseases) Regulations 1994 (SI No. 317 of 1994) gave effect to Directives 92/35/EEC and 92/119/EEC and laid down control measures for the diseases referred to in Reg. 2 of the Regulations, namely, African horse sickness, blue tongue, epizootic haemorrhagic disease in deer (see also below), goat pox, lumpy skin disease, peste des petits ruminants, Rift Valley fever, Teschen disease and vesicular stomatitis.

Avian influenza   The European Communities (Avian Influenza) Regulations 1994 (SI No. 172 of 1994) gave effect to Directive 92/40/EEC on the control of avian influenza.

Epizootic haemorrhagic disease in deer   The Diseases of Animals (Notification of Infectious Diseases) Order 1994 (SI No. 2 of 1994) made epizootic haemorrhagic disease in deer a notifiable disease under the Diseases of Animals Act 1966.

Greyhound movement   The Transit of Animals (Amendment) Order 1994 (SI No. 258 of 1994), made under the Diseases of Animals Act 1966, amended the Transit of Animals Order 1973 so that it applied to the transport of greyhounds. It also revoked and replaced the Transit of Greyhounds Order 1954.

Newcastle disease   The European Communities (Newcastle Disease) Regulations 1994 (SI No. 226 of 1994) gave effect to Directive 92/66/EEC on the control of Newcastle disease.

Sheep scab and sheep dipping   The Sheep Scab (Ireland) Order of 1905 (Amendment) Order 1994 (SI No. 290 of 1994) and the Sheep Dipping Order 1965 (Amendment) Order 1994 (SI No. 291 of 1994) enable the use of both dip and non-dip sheep scab treatments pursuant to the Sheep Scab (Ireland) Order of 1905 and also provided for the abolition of compulsory sheep dipping contained in the Sheep Dipping Order 1965.

Trade in animals and animal products   Regulations listed below, 20-22, also contain provisions concerned directly with the preventive measures concerned with animal disease.

ANIMAL PEDIGREE REGISTRATION

General   The European Communities (Registration of Pedigree Animals) Regulations 1994 (SI No. 150 of 1994) gave effect to Directive 91/174/EEC and provide for the approval and recognition of organisations which maintain registers for pure-bred animals and related matters concerning their marketing. The 1991 Directive and the 1994 Regulations apply to all animals covered by Annex II to the EC Treaty, except sheep, goats, cattle, water buffalo, pigs and equidae, for which separate arrangements are made under other Directives. On the arrangements for sheep and goats, see SI No. 16 of 1994, and for pigs, see SI No. 151, both referred to below. On cattle and water buffalo, see SI No. 297 of 1994, 22, below.

Breeding pigs   The European Communities (Breeding Pig Herd-Book and Register) Regulations 1994 (SI No. 151 of 1994) gave effect to Directive 88/661/EEC, 90/118/EEC and 90/119/EEC and provide for the approval and recognition of organisations which maintain herd-books and registers for breeding pigs and related matters concerning their marketing.

Pure-bred sheep and goats   The European Communities (Pure-Bred Sheep and Coat Flock-Book) Regulations 1994 (SI No. 16 of 1994) gave effect to Directive 89/361/EEC and provide for the approval and recognition of organisations which maintain flock-books for pure-bred sheep and goats and related matters concerning their marketing.

ANIMAL PROTECTION AND WELFARE

Animal vivisection and experiments   The European Communities (Amendment of Cruelty to Animals Act 1876) Regulations 1994 (SI No. 17 of 1994) amended the Cruelty to Animals Act 1876 (which prohibits vivisection and other painful experiments on living animals subject to certain exceptions) by inserting a new s. 12A into the 1876 Act in order to give effect to Directive 86/609/EEC.

Deer farming   The Welfare of Deer Regulations 1994 (SI No. 267 of 1994), made under the Protection of Animals Kept for Farming Purposes Act 1984, prohibited the removal of deer antlers while the deer are in live velvet except in certain limited circumstances.

Penalties The Protection of Animals Act 1911 (Section 1) (Variation of Fines) Regulations 1994 (SI No. 148 of 1994) increased the maximum fine on summary conviction for cruelty to animals under s. 1 of the 1911 Act (as amended by s. 20 of the Control of Dogs Act 1986) from £500 to £1,000. The increased penalties apply to offences committed after May 19, 1994, when the Regulations were made: see Regulation 2(2).

ANIMAL REMEDIES

Consultative committee The Animal Remedies Consultative Committee (Prescribed Organisations) Regulations 1994 (SI No. 175 of 1994) prescribed the list of organisations entitled to nominate candidates for appointment to the Animal Remedies Consultative Committee as required by the Animal Remedies Act 1993 (see the 1993 Review, 35).

Manufacturing controls The European Communities (Animal Remedies and Medicated Feedingstuffs) Regulations 1994 (SI No. 176 of 1994) implemented the detailed requirements of Directive 90/167/EEC. Although made under the European Communities Act 1972, the 1994 Regulations should be read in conjunction with the Animal Remedies Act 1993, from which a number of definitions were taken for the purposes of the 1994 Regulations.

COMMON AGRICULTURAL POLICY

Audit of transactions The European Communities (Common Agricultural Policy) Scrutiny of Transactions) Regulations 1994 (SI No. 274 of 1994) deal with the scrutiny of transactions forming part of financing by the Guarantee Section of the European Agricultural Guidance and Guarantee Fund (FEOGA) as required by Council Regulation No. 4045/89) and provide for the establishment of an Audit Committee to monitor the application of the 1989 Council Regulation.

Milk quota The European Communities (Milk Quota) Regulations 1994 (SI No. 70 of 1994) laid down updated and detailed administrative arrangements for the operation of the CAP milk quota system in Ireland, in accordance with Regulations 3950/92, 536/93, 2055/93 and 2562/93. Subject to transitional arrangements, the 1994 Regulations also revoked the European Communities (Milk Levy) Regulations 1985.

FOOD PROMOTION BOARD

The An Bord Bia Act 1994 established An Bord Bia, the Irish Food Board, which will act as a State Food Promotion Board. The Explanatory And Financial Memorandum published when the An Bord Bia Act 1994 was presented as a Bill indicated that the 1994 Act followed from the Report of the Expert Group on the Food Industry, which reported to the Minister for Agriculture, Food and Forestry in 1993. The Expert Group recommended the establishment of a single food promotion body whose functions would comprise those formerly exercised by Coras Beostoic agus Feola (CBF), the food marketing and promotion functions of An Bord Trachtala (ABT) and the export market development functions of An Bord Iascaigh Mhara (BIM) and An Bord Glas. Except in so far as it relates to BIM that recommendation was accepted by the Government and the purpose of the 1994 Act was to give effect to the Expert Group's Report. The 1994 Act made consequential provision for the dissolution of the CBF and the transfer of its staff, assets and liabilities to An Bord Bia, for the establishment of separate Subsidiary Boards to deal with the main product sectors, for an appropriate transfer of ABT staff to the new body. The Act also continues the provision of industry funding for the Bord by way of fees or levies on livestock and agricultural products: this function had formerly been performed by CBF. The Act fully came into force with the formal establishment of An Bord Bia on 1 December 1994: An Bord Bia Act 1994 (Establishment Day) Order 1994 (SI No. 394 of 1994). As a consequence, the Coras Beostoic agus Feola Acts 1979 and 1988 and s. 55 of the Abattoirs Act 1988 stood repealed from that date: see s. 6(5) of the Act.

HORSERACING INDUSTRY

The Explanatory And Financial Memorandum published when the Irish Horseracing Industry Act 1994 was published as a Bill noted that the Act came against the background that, in October 1992, the Minister for Agriculture, Food and Forestry had announced proposals for the re-organisation of the Irish Horseracing Industry. It appeared that substantial agreement had been reached with the industry to these proposals, and industry involvement in the preparation of the legislation was continued through the appointment by the Minister of a representative committee.

The 1994 Act provided, *inter alia*, for the establishment of a Horseracing Authority to replace the Racing Board and to take on a wider role in relation to the horseracing industry. The Authority was conferred with functions concerning all matters relating to the overall administration of horseracing, including the authorisation and regulation of racecourses, prize-money and starting prices, the establishment and operation of racecourses, the operation of totalisator (Tote) betting, the establishment of a special subsidiary by the Authority to operate as bookmaker, subject to the consent of the Minister for Agriculture, Food and Forestry and the Minister for Finance.

The Authority is not, however, responsible for the enforcement of the rules of racing or for the provision of integrity services for racing. The 1994 Act assigned these functions to another new body entitled the Racing Regulatory Body, comprising the Turf Club and the Irish National Hunt Steeplechase Committee In addition to the implementation of the rules of racing and the provision of integrity services, this body is empowered to determine whether race-fixtures may be held having regard to the condition of the track and the safety of horses and jockeys. The 1994 Act provides that the Authority will guarantee the costs of integrity services provided that the Regulatory Body agrees its budget in advance with the Authority.

The 1994 Act continued existing arrangements for bookmaking at race-courses and for the Appeal Committee to deal with appeals in relation to such permits. However, two significant new provisions were included in the Act: the possible introduction of on-course betting offices to be regulated for by the Authority, and that the revenue (by way of levy) from all bets placed at racecourses will go to the Authority, including bets on races or any other events taking place other than at the racecourse at which the bet is placed. The latter category of bet will be subject to a rate of levy equivalent to the rate of excise duty which would otherwise have applied to such a bet — at present 10%. It should be noted that the Finance Act 1994 included a provision to remove the excise duty on such bets placed at racecourses.

The 1994 also provided for the dissolution of the Racing Board, the repeal of the Racing Board and Racecourses Acts 1945 and 1975, as well as for minor amendments to the Totalisator Act 1929, the Betting Act, 1931 and the Licensing Acts 1833-1995, the latter to provide an appropriate regime for the granting of liquor licences at race meetings. The Act fully came into force with the formal establishment of the Irish Horseracing Authority on December 1, 1994: Irish Horseracing Industry Act 1994 (Establishment Day) Order 1994 (SI No. 391 of 1994) and Irish Horseracing Industry Act 1994 (Part IX) (Commencement) Order 1994 (SI No. 392 of 1994).

MILK SUPPLY

The Milk (Regulation Of Supply) Act 1994 provided for the establishment of the National Milk Agency and for the consequent dissolution of the Cork and Dublin District Milk Boards. This was necessary because the functions of the Cork and Dublin Boards were deemed invalid under EC law and there was a consequent need to put in place alternative arrangements to ensure a year-round supply of drinking milk in the country as a whole.

In effect, the 1994 Act also sets down standards for milk supply. Thus, s. 5 of the Act prohibits the sale of heat-treated milk for liquid consumption unless it has been prepared from raw milk produced on foot of a registered contract or else on the processor's own farm. Penalties for contravention of this provision are also laid down. S. 6 deals with the conditions for the registration of contracts by the Agency. It provides that the contract period must be for a minimum 12 month period; that the contract specifies that the untreated milk supplied by the producer must meet at least such quality standards as may, from time to time, be prescribed by law; that the contract provides for all year round supply by the producer of raw milk with a specified minimum percentage of the producer's production being supplied during the winter months or for supply during the winter months only; that the contract, in the opinion of the Agency, provides adequate compensation to the producer for raw milk supplied under the contract throughout the year, in particular for milk supplied in the winter months. The section also provides for the continued registration of the contract to be dependent on the submission annually of a supplement to the contract which must satisfy the Agency that adequate compensation will be offered to the producer for the supply of milk during the following winter months.

S. 7 of the Act provides that the Agency shall maintain a register of contracts, a register of producers and a register of processors, while s. 8 provides for the payment of a levy by milk processors to the Agency. Other provisions provide that the Agency will act as a Milk Inspectorate, with substantial powers of entry, inspection and enforcement.

The Act provided for the repeal of the Milk (Regulation of Supply and Price) Acts 1936 to 1967, the existing legislation dealing with the District Milk Boards' operations. The Milk (Regulation of Supply) (Establishment of National Milk Agency) Order 1994 (SI No. 409 of 1994) brought the 1994 Act fully into force by establishing the National Milk Agency as and from December 30, 1994. The Cork and Dublin District Milk Boards were abolished by the Milk (Regulation of Supply) (Abolition of the Cork District Milk Board) Order 1994 (SI No. 410 of 1994) and the Milk (Regulation of Supply) (Abolition of the Dublin District Milk Board) Order 1994 (SI No. 411 of 1994).

PLANT HEALTH

Cereal seed The European Communities (Cereal Seed) (Amendment) Regulations 1994 (SI No. 281 of 1994) further amended the Regulations of 1981 of the same title by revising the fees for cereal crop inspection and certification of cereal seed required under the Regulations.

Fertilizers The European Communities (Marketing of Fertilizers) Regulations 1994 (SI No. 162 of 1994) amended the 1991 Regulations of the same title to give effect to Directive 93/69/EEC. The European Communities (Sampling and Analysis of Fertilizers) Regulations 1993 (SI No. 257) implemented Directive 93/1/EEC concerning the analysis of fertilizers for trace elements of boron, cobalt, copper, iron, manganese, molybdenum and zinc.

Fodder plants The European Communities (Seed of Fodder Plants) (Amendment) Regulations 1994 (SI No. 212 of 1994) prescribed new fees for the certification and testing of fodder plant seed in accordance with the Regulations of 1981 to 1993 of the same title.

Organisms harmful to plants or plant products The European Communities (Introduction of Organisms Harmful to Plants or Plant Products) (Prohibition) (Amendment) Regulations 1994 (SI No. 47 of 1994) and the European Communities (Introduction of Organisms Harmful to Plants or Plant Products) (Prohibition) (Amendment) (No. 2) Regulations 1994 (SI No. 280 of 1994) implemented Directives 93/106/EC, 93/110/EC, 94/3/EC and 94/13/EC, which involved amendments to the Principal Directive in this area 77/93/EEC. The 1977 Directive was implemented by the European Communities (Introduction of Organisms Harmful to Plants or Plant Products) (Prohibition) Regulations 1980, as amended.

Pesticide residues Both the European Communities (Pesticide Residues) (Fruit and Vegetables) (Amendment) Regulations 1994 (SI No. 189 of 1994) (which amended 1989 Regulations of the same title) and the European Communities (Pesticide Residues) (Products of Plant Origin, including Fruit and Vegetables) Regulations 1994 (SI No. 190 of 1994) implemented Directive 93/58/EEC, which laid down further maximum pesticide residue limits for a number of substances in fruit and vegetables and other products of plant origin.

Plant propagating products: manufacturing controls The European Communities (Marketing of Vegetable Propagating and Planting Material, other than Seed) Regulations 1994 (SI No. 159 of 1994), the European Communities (Marketing of Fruit Plant Propagating Material and Fruit Plants intended for Fruit Production) Regulations 1994 (SI No. 160 of 1994 and SI No. 198 of 1994) and the European Communities (Marketing of Ornamental Plant Propagating Material and Ornamental Plants) Regulations 1994 (SI No. 161 of 1994 and SI No. 199 of 1994) gave effect to a number of Directives laying down minimum standards largely concerning plant propagating material, such as rootstock and other materials intended to assist the propagation of plants. Provisions were included in the three sets of Regulations to ensure there is no unnecessary overlap with the requirements of the European Communities (Introduction of Organisms Harmful to Plants or Plant Products) (Prohibition) Regulations 1980 to 1994 (see above). The three sets of Regulations came into force on June 1, 1994.

Plant protection products: manufacturing controls The European Communities (Authorization, Placing on the Market, Use and Control of Plant Protection Products) Regulations 1994 (SI No. 139 of 1994) implemented the detailed requirements (the Regulations run to over 330 pages) of Directive 91/414/EEC concerning the standards required in the manufacture of plant protection products. In that respect, the Regulations have an environmental as well as purely agricultural element to them. The Regulations also contain provisions to ensure that there is no unnecessary overlap with the provisions of the European Communities (Classification, Packaging and Labelling of Pesticides) Regulations 1994 (SI No. 138 of 1994), discussed in the Safety and Health chapter, 394, below.

Seed potatoes The European Communities (Seed Potatoes) (Amendment) Regulations 1994 (SI No. 288 of 1994) amended the 1980 Regulations of the same title and gave effect to Directive 93/35/EEC and 93/17/EEC.

PROPRIETARY PLANT RIGHTS

The Plant Varieties (Proprietary Rights) (Amendment) Regulations 1994 (SI No. 393 of 1994) extended the plant breeders' rights available under the Plant Varieties (Proprietary Rights) Act 1980 to an additional eight specified genera or species.

RETIREMENT OF FARMERS

The European Communities (Retirement of Farmers) Regulations 1994 (SI No. 246 of 1994) provided for a further increase in the annuity payable to retiring farmers under the terms of the 1974 Regulations of the same title.

TRADE IN ANIMALS, PRODUCTS AND BY-PRODUCTS

Beef carcass classification   The European Communities (Beef Carcass Classification) Regulations 1994 (SI No. 8 of 1994) put in place the administrative arrangements required to give effect to a range of Community Regulations on the labelling, stamping and classification of adult bovine animals slaughtered at meat export premises. They revoked the European Communities (Beef Carcass Classification) Regulations 1982 and 1991 and came into effect on January 28, 1994.

Disposal and processing of animal by-products   The European Communities (Disposal, Processing and Placing on the Market of Animal By-Products) Regulations 1994 (SI No. 257 of 1994) implemented Directive 90/667/EEC, as amended by Council Directive 92/118/EEC, and Commission Decision 92/562/EEC laying down the veterinary rules for the disposal and processing of animal by-products, for their placing on the market and for the prevention of pathogens in feedingstuffs of animal or fish origin. As with SI No. 289 of 1994, below, the Regulations provide for powers of authorised officers and prosecution of offences and are stated to be in addition to any provisions contained in the Diseases of Animals Act 1966. The Regulations came into force on September 1, 1994.

Feedingstuffs   The European Communities (Feedingstuffs) (Tolerances of Undesirable Substances and Products) (Amendment) Regulations 1994 (SI No. 34 of 1994) amended the European Communities (Feedingstuffs) (Tolerances of Undesirable Substances and Products) Regulations 1989 to 1993 (see the 1993 Review, 39) in order to implement Directive 92/88/EEC. The European Communities (Protein Feedingstuffs) (Amendment) Regulations 1994 (SI No. 50 of 1994) amended the European Communities (Protein Feedingstuffs) Regulations 1986 and 1991 to give effect to Directives 93/26/EEC and 93/56/EEC. The European Communities (Additives in Feedingstuffs) (Amendment) Regulations 1994 (SI No. 55 of 1994) amended the European Communities (Additives in Feedingstuffs) Regulations 1989 to give effect to Directives 93/27/EEC and 93/55/EEC. The European Communities (Marketing of Feedingstuffs) (Amendment) Regulations 1994 (SI No. 143 of 1994) amended the European Communities (Marketing of Feedingstuffs) Regulations 1984 to 1993 to give effect to Directive 93/28/EEC. The European Communities (Feeding Stuffs) (Methods of Analysis) (Amendment) Regulations 1994 (SI No. 269 of 1994) amended the European Communities (Feeding Stuffs) (Method of Analysis) Regulations 1989 to 1993 (see the 1993 Review, 39) in order to implement Directive 93/70/EEC and 93/117/EEC.

Import of animals and animal products from non-EC States   The European Communities (Importation of Animals and Animal Products from Third Countries) Regulations 1994 (SI No. 255 of 1994) implemented Directive 90/675/EEC on the organisation of veterinary checks on animal products entering the EC from third countries and Directive 91/496/EEC on the organisation of veterinary checks on animals entering the EC from third countries. They also provide for the ports and airports through which agricultural products covered by the Regulations must be imported; approval of authorised officers to implement and enforce the Regulations and the prosecution of offences. The Regulations came into force on August 2, 1994.

Import of dogs and cats   The European Communities (Importation of Dogs and Cats) Regulations 1994 (SI No. 261 of 1994) implemented Article 10.3 of Directive 92/65/EEC and specify the conditions under which dogs and cats (excluding pets) may be brought into the State from EC Member States other than the United Kingdom. The form of notices concerned with the prevention of rabies is also prescribed. The Regulations supplement the provisions of the Dogs and Cats Orders 1929 to 1970 and came into force on August 2, 1994.

Minced meat and meat preparations   The European Communities (Minced Meat) Regulations 1994 (SI No. 215 of 1994) are referred to in the Safety and Health chapter, 401-2, below.

Pig carcass grading   The European Communities (Pig Carcass Grading) Regulations 1994 (SI No. 216 of 1994) amended the European Communities (Pig Carcass Grading) Regulations 1988 to 1993 in order to implement various Commission Decisions concerning the calculation of lean meat percentage of pig carcasses. They came into effect on July 25, 1994.

Trade in animals and animal products   The European Communities (Trade in Animals and Animal Products) Regulations 1994 (SI No. 289 of 1994) implemented Directive 89/662/EEC on veterinary checks in intra-

Community trade and Directive 90/425/EEC on veterinary and zootechnical checks applicable in intra-Community trade in certain live animals and products. They also provide for: (i) the application of the requirements of EC Directives on veterinary and zootechnical trade in agricultural products with other EC Member States; (ii) the registration of consignees and other persons involved in trade with other EC Member States; (iii) approval of authorised officers of the Department of Agriculture to implement and enforce the Regulations and (iv) the prosecution of offences. The Regulations came into force on October 1, 1994.

Trade in bovine breeding animals, semen, ova and embryos   The European Communities (Trade in Bovine Breeding Animals, their Semen, Ova and Embryos) Regulations 1994 (SI No. 297 of 1994) implemented Directives 93/52/EEC and 93/60/EEC and Decisions 94/113/EC and 94/515/EC which deal with veterinary conditions relating to trade in and assessment for breeding of bovine breeding animals, their semen, ova and embryos. The Regulations, which are in addition to any provisions of the Diseases of Animals Act 1966, also prescribe the form of certificates to be used in the trade of the genetic subject-matter of the Regulations and they came into force on their signing on September 20, 1994. As with SI Nos. 257 and 289 of 1994, above, the Regulations provide for powers of authorised officers and prosecution of offences The 1994 Regulations revoked and replaced the European Communities (Trade in Bovine Breeding Animals, their Semen, Ova and Embryos) Regulations 1993 and 1994 (SI No. 259 of 1993 and SI No. 152 of 1994).

WILDLIFE

Nature reserve   The Nature Reserve (Knocksink Wood) Establishment Order 1994 (SI No. 58 of 1994) recognised certain parts of land in Knocksink Wood, County Wicklow as a nature reserve under s. 15 of the Wildlife Act 1976 in order to preserve the woodland ecosystem it represented. To similar effect was the Nature Reserve (Cummeragh River Bog) Establishment Order 1994 (SI No. 116 of 1994), which concerned an area in County Kerry.

Wild birds: special protection areas   The European Communities (Conservation of Wild Birds) (Amendment) Regulations 1994 (SI No. 59 of 1994) and the European Communities (Conservation of Wild Birds) (Amendment) (No. 2) Regulations 1994 (SI No. 349 of 1994) amended the Schedule to the European Communities (Conservation of Wild Birds) Regulations 1985 (which had implemented Directive 79/409/EEC) by adding 12 new areas as special protection areas for wildbirds to the existing list.

Aliens and Immigration

COMMITTAL

The Aliens (Amendment) (No. 3) Order 1994 (SI No. 193 of 1994) amended the Aliens Order 1946 so that a person may be committed to the Central Mental Hospital, Dundrum, pending determination of an application for permission to remain in the State.

ENTRY AND LANDING

Particular person prohibited   The Aliens (No. 2) Order 1994 (SI No. 94 of 1994), made under s. 5 of the Aliens Act 1935, prohibited a named person, a citizen of South Africa, from landing in or entering the State.

VISA REQUIREMENTS

Transit visa: additional specified States   The Aliens (Amendment) Order 1994 (SI No. 9 of 1994) amended the Aliens Order 1946 so that a citizen of Romania requires a transit visa when transiting the State. Similarly, the Aliens (Amendment) (No. 5) Order 1994 (SI No. 326 of 1994) amended the 1946 Order so that a citizen of Cuba requires a transit visa when transiting the State.

Visa   The Aliens (Amendment) (No. 4) Order 1994 (SI No. 311 of 1994) amended the Aliens Order 1946 so that a citizen of Sierra Leone requires a visa in order to enter the State.

Arts and Culture

RETURN OF CULTURAL OBJECTS

The European Communities (Return of Cultural Objects) Regulations 1994 (SI No. 182 of 1994) implemented Directive 93/7/EC on the return of cultural objects unlawfully removed from the territory of a Member State on or after January 1, 1993. Regrettably, the Regulations do not reproduce the definition in the 1993 Directive of the term 'cultural object', but it extends to national treasures of artistic, historic or archaeological value, certain objects for which various thresholds of value in order for the Regulations to apply are set down, as well as objects on the inventory of a public collection or ecclesiastical institution. Under the Directive and Regulations, a Member State is empowered to apply to the competent authority of another Member State for the return of objects covered by the 1993 Directive. The Minister for Arts, Culture and the Gaeltacht was designated as the competent authority for the purposes of the Directive and Regulations. The Minister is authorised to apply to the High Court to seek the enforcement measures, including search and seizure orders, specified in the Regulations. The Minister is also empowered to act as intermediary in a dispute, where the parties involved consent, and the parties may also opt for arbitration rather than court proceedings by consent. The 1994 Regulations are, of course, without prejudice to any criminal proceedings that may ensure from unlawful removal of such objects.

Commercial Law

COMMERCIAL AGENTS

The European Communities (Commercial Agents) Regulations 1994 (SI No. 33 of 1994) gave effect to Directive 86/653/EEC on Self-Employed Commercial Agents, but this was done in an entirely unsatisfactory manner. Contrary to accepted practice, much of the actual text the 1986 Directive, running to over 20 substantive Articles, was not 'transposed' in the 1994 Regulations and one is thus required to read the text of the Directive alongside the 1994 Regulations in order to understand the impact of the Directive and the 1994 Regulations on Irish law. The 1986 Directive amounts to a 'codification' with amendments of some of the main elements of the law of agency, at least concerning commercial agents involved in buying and selling goods. Significant changes to existing law were also effected by the 1986 Directive, notably a substantial modification to the common law principles concerning the non-payment of commission after the end of the period of a commercial agency. Other less obvious elements of the Directive concern the law on restraint of trade. It is most unsatisfactory that such radical transformations of prior law should be done virtually *sub rosa*.

Implementation and retrospective effect Regulation 2(3) gives laconic effect in Irish law to the 1986 Directive as follows:

> The [1986] Directive shall, subject to these Regulations, apply to the relations between commercial agents and their principals from January 1, 1994.

Although the Regulations were made by the Minister for Enterprise and Employment on February 21, 1994, the retrospective element of the 1994 Regulations was required since Article 22 of the 1986 Directive required its terms to be implemented by January 1, 1994 and that the implementing legislation must apply to existing contracts. For criticism of a similar retrospection element in the European Communities (Unfair Terms in Consumer Contracts) Regulations 1995 (SI No. 27 of 1995) (which we will discuss in the 1995 Review), see Finbarr Murphy's article 'The Unfair Contract Terms Regulations 1995: A Red Card for the State' (1995) 14 *ILT* 156.

In fact, most Member States were required to implement the 1986

Directive by January 1, 1990, with a 'transition' period for existing agency contracts up to January 1, 1994. However, the two Common Law Member States were given until January 1, 1994 to put in place the necessary legal machinery because, as one of the recitals to the Directive stated, they 'have to make a particular effort to adapt their regulations, especially those concerning indemnity for termination of contract between the principal and the commercial agent'. As we will see, the specific point on which the Directive allowed this extension for Ireland is nowhere alluded to in the 1994 Regulations. The reality is, therefore, that far from making a 'particular effort', no effort whatsoever would appear to have been made to adapt existing Irish law to the new regime provided for in the 1986 Directive.

Commercial agent in goods, not real property   Although the 1994 Regulations are largely uninformative on the substantive content of the 1986 Directive, they provide a comprehensive definition of 'commercial agent'. Thus, Regulation 2(1), replicating in this respect Article 1.2 of the 1986 Directive, defines 'commercial agent' as:

> a self-employed intermediary who has continuing authority to negotiate the sale or purchase of goods on behalf of another person, hereinafter called 'the principal', or to negotiate and conclude transactions on behalf of and in the name of the principal.

Thus the general scope of the 1986 Directive and the 1994 Regulations extend to self-employed commercial agents dealing in goods. While the Directive and Regulations are therefore extremely wide-ranging, encompassing what might formerly have been called 'commercial travellers', they do not extend, for example, to estate agents or to solicitors when either are engaged in the sale of real property. As to what is comprised by the word 'goods', in the absence of a definition in the 1994 Regulations, the definition in s. 1(1) of the Sale of Goods Act 1893 might prove to be persuasive.

Other excluded categories   In addition to the restriction to agents dealing in goods and, by implication, the exclusion of real property transactions, the 1994 Regulations also exclude the following categories of agents from their scope, in accordance with Article 1.3 and 2 of the 1986 Directive:

(a) a person who, in the capacity of an officer of a company or association, is empowered to enter into commitments binding on that company or association;

(b) a partner who is lawfully authorised to enter into commitments binding on the partners;

(c) a receiver, and receiver and manager, a liquidator or an examiner, as defined in the Companies Acts 1963 to 1990, or a trustee in bankruptcy;

(d) a commercial agent whose services are unpaid;

(e) a commercial agent operating on commodity exchanges or in the commodity market; or

(f) a consumer credit agent or a mail order catalogue agent for consumer goods, 'whose activities . . . are considered secondary', Regulation 1(2) specifying that there is a presumption that such activities are secondary, unless the contrary is established.

While most of these categories of excluded persons are relatively straightforward, the final category merits further comment. Article 2.2 of the Directive provided that the Member States were empowered to exclude persons 'whose activities as commercial agents are considered secondary by the law of that Member State'. This option was exercised in the 1994 Regulations, and the nature of what is 'secondary' thus remains for elucidation in case law.

Turning to the substance of the changes effected in Irish law by the 1994 Regulations, we must revert to the terms of the 1986 Directive, in particular Articles 3 to 21. In fact, much like a domestic Act of the Oireachtas, the 1986 Directive is divided into Chapters, though they are not all of similar size. Thus, Chapter 2 of the Directive, which concerns the rights and obligations of the principal and agent, comprises Articles 3 to 5; Chapter 3 of the Directive, which deals with remuneration, covers Articles 6 to 12; and Chapter 4 of the Directive, which deals with the conclusion and termination of the agency contract, covers Articles 13 to 19.

Rights and obligations of the agent   Article 3.1 of the 1986 Directive provides that, in performing his or her activities a commercial agent must 'look after his principal's interests and act dutifully and in good faith.' Article 3.2 adds that, in particular, a commercial agent must: (a) make proper efforts to negotiate and, where appropriate, conclude the transactions he or she is instructed to take care of; (b) communicate to his principal all the necessary information available to him; and (c) comply with reasonable instructions given by his principal. Subject to some minor variation in language, this in effect amounts to a 'codification' of existing agency law in Ireland, in particular concerning good faith and the disclosure of material information.

Rights and obligations of the principal   As to the principal, Article 4.1 of the 1986 Directive provides that in his relations with his commercial agent, a principal must also act 'dutifully and in good faith'. Article 4.2. adds that, a principal must in particular: (a) provide his commercial agent with the necessary documentation relating to the goods concerned; (b) obtain for his commercial agent the information necessary for the performance of the agency contract, and in particular notify the commercial agent within a reasonable period once he anticipates that the volume of commercial transactions will be significantly lower than that which the commercial agent could normally have expected. Article 4.3 requires that a principal must, in addition, inform the commercial agent within a reasonable period of his (the principal's) acceptance, refusal, and of any non-execution of a commercial transaction which the commercial agent has procured for the principal.

Non-exclusion of duties and obligations of principal and agent   Article 5 of the 1986 Directive provides that the parties may not derogate from the provisions of Articles 3 and 4.

Remuneration generally   Article 6.1 of the 1986 Directive provides that, in the absence of any agreement on this matter between the parties, a commercial agent 'shall be entitled to the remuneration that commercial agents appointed for the goods forming the subject of his agency contract are customarily allowed in the place where he carries on his activities.' This general principle is stated to be 'without prejudice to the application of any compulsory provisions of the Member States concerning the level of remuneration'. In addition, if there is no customary practice in the sector, a commercial agent 'shall be entitled to reasonable remuneration taking into account all the aspects of the transaction.'

Commission defined   Article 6.2 of the 1986 Directive provides that any part of the remuneration which varies with the number or value of business transactions shall be deemed to be commission within the meaning of the Directive. This definition of commission is by way of introduction to Articles 7 to 12, which deal in detail with the payment of commission, because Article 6.3 provides that Articles 7 to 12 shall not apply if the commercial agent is not remunerated wholly or in part by commission.

Right to commission during currency of agency   Article 7.1 of the 1986 Directive provides that a commercial agent shall be entitled to commission on commercial transactions concluded during the period covered by the agency contract:

(a) where the transaction has been concluded as a result of his or her action; or

(b) where the transaction is concluded with a third party whom he or she has previously acquired as a customer for transactions of the same kind.

Article 7.2 provides that a commercial agent shall also be entitled to commission on transactions concluded during the period covered by the agency contract: either (i) where he or she is entrusted with a specific geographical area or group of customers; or (ii) where he or she has an exclusive right to a specific geographical area or group of customers, and where the transaction has been entered into with a customer belonging to that area or group. Article 7.2 goes on to provides that 'Member States shall include in their legislation one of the possibilities referred to in [(i) and (ii)]'. In this respect, Regulation 4 of the 1994 Regulations took up this option by providing that:

> a commercial agent shall be entitled to commission on commercial transactions concluded during the period covered by the agency contract only where the agent has an exclusive right to a specific geographical area or group of customers and where the transaction has been entered into with a customer belonging to that area or group. (emphasis added)

Thus, under the 1994 Regulations, an agent is not entitled to commission merely where he or she is entrusted with a specific geographical area or group of customers.

Right to commission after termination of agency   Article 8 of the 1986 Directive provides that a commercial agent shall be entitled to commission on commercial transactions concluded after the agency contract has terminated: (a) if the transaction is mainly attributable to the commercial agent's efforts prior to the termination of the agency contract and if the transaction was entered into within a reasonable period after that contract terminated; or (b) if, in accordance with the conditions referred to in Article 7, above, the order of the third party reached the principal or the commercial agent before the agency contract terminated. As already indicated, Article 8 modifies substantially the common law principles concerning the non-payment of commission after the end of the period of a commercial agency. In *Ward v Spivack Ltd* [1957] IR 40, the Supreme Court had held that, in the absence of an express term providing for continuing payments after the termination of an agency, the courts would not imply such a term into a contract. The 1986 Directive, as implemented by the 1994 Regulations, reversed the effect of the *Ward* case.

Sharing commission   Article 9 of the 1986 Directive provides that a commercial agent shall not be entitled to commission if that commission is payable, pursuant to Article 8, to the previous commercial agent, 'unless it is equitable because of the circumstances for the Commission to be shared between the commercial agents.'

When commission becomes due Article 10.1 of the 1986 Directive provides that the commission becomes due as soon as one of the following circumstances obtains:

> (a) the principal has executed the transaction; or (b) the principal should, according to his agreement with the third party, have executed the transaction; or (c) the third party has executed the transaction.

The reference to the 'third party' in this context is, of course, a familiar one in agency. Article 10.2 goes on to provide that the commission shall become due at the latest when the third party has executed his part of the transaction or should have done so if the principal had executed his part of the transaction. Article 10.3 provides that the commission shall be paid not later than the last day of the month following the quarter in which it became due. Article 10.4 prohibits any exclusion from the requirements of Article 10.2 and 10.3 by providing that '[a]greements to derogate from paragraphs 2 and 3 to the detriment of the commercial agent shall not be permitted.' The somewhat awkward language of Article 10.4 cries out for suitable 'translation' into domestic law, though no doubt its intent is clear enough.

Extinguishment of right to commission Article 11.1 of the 1986 Directive provides that the right to commission can be extinguished only if the following two circumstances arise: (a) it is established that the contract between the third party and the principal will not be executed; and (b) the non-execution 'is due to a reason for which the principal is not to blame.' Article 11.2 provides that any commission which the commercial agent has already received shall be refunded if the right to it is extinguished. As with Article 10, Article 11.3 provides that agreements to derogate from Article 11.1 'to the detriment of the commercial agent shall not be permitted.'

Statement of commission due Article 12.1 requires the principal to supply the commercial agent with a statement of the commission due, not later than the last day of the month following the quarter in which the commission has become due. This statement must set out the main components used in calculating the amount of commission. Article 12.2 provides that a commercial agent is entitled to demand that he be provided with all the information, and in particular an extract from 'the books', which is available to the principal and which the agent needs in order to check the amount of the commission due. Again, Article 12.3 provides that agreements to derogate from Article 12.1 and 2 'to the detriment of the commercial agent shall not be permitted.' Finally, Article 12.4 provides that the terms of the Directive are without prejudice to ('shall not conflict with') any legislative provisions in the Member States which already recognised the right of a commercial agent to inspect a principal's books.

Written terms of contract   Article 13.1 of the 1986 Directive provides that each party shall be entitled to receive from the other, on request, a signed written document setting out the terms of the agency contract, including any terms subsequently agreed. Again, the Directive prohibits any exclusion of this by providing that '[w]aiver of this right shall not be permitted.' Article 13.2 goes on to provide that '[n]otwithstanding paragraph 1 a Member State may provide that an agency contract shall not be valid unless evidenced in writing.' In accordance with this provision, Regulation 5 of the 1994 Regulations provides that '[t]he agency contract shall not be valid unless it is evidenced in writing.'

Conversion from definite to indefinite period   Article 14 of the 1986 Directive provides that an agency contract for a fixed period which continues to be performed by both parties after that period has expired 'shall be deemed to be converted into an agency contract for an indefinite period.'

Notice of termination of agency contract   Article 15.1 of the 1986 Directive provides that, where an agency contract is concluded for an indefinite period either party may terminate it by notice. Article 15.2 provides that (in other cases) the relevant notice periods shall be:

> one month for the first year of the contract, two months for the second year commenced, and three months for the third year commenced and subsequent years.

As with other similar protective provisions of the 1986 Directive, Article 15.2 adds that the parties 'may not agree on shorter periods of notice.'
Article 15.3 goes on to provide as follows:

> Member States may fix the period of notice at four months for the fourth year of the contract and subsequent years. They may decide that the parties may not agree to shorter periods.

In the absence of any provision in the 1994 Regulations on this issue, it seems that the three month maximum notice in Article 15.2 would apply to the fourth and subsequent years. However, given the 'minimalist' text of the 1994 Regulations, it remains to be seen whether an Irish court would conclude that no view had been formed by the 'Member State' on this point and that the court itself (perhaps as an 'emanation of the State') would revert to the text of the Directive and, using the teleological interpretive technique, imply a four month notice period in an appropriate case. Such 'breathing of life' into Article 15.3 might be supported by the terms of Article 15.4.

Article 15.4 provides that, if the parties agree on longer periods 'than those laid down in Article 15.2 and 3', the period of notice to be observed by the principal must not be shorter than that to be observed by the commercial agent. Article 15.5 provides that, unless otherwise agreed by the parties, the end of the period of notice must coincide with the end of a calendar month. Finally, Article 15.6 provides that Article 15 itself shall apply to an agency contract for a fixed period where it is converted under Article 14 into an agency contract for an indefinite period, subject to the proviso that the earlier fixed period must be taken into account in the calculation of the period of notice.

Immediate termination   Article 16 of the 1986 Directive provides that nothing in the Directive is to be taken as affecting the application of the law of the Member States where these provide for the immediate termination of the agency contract either: (a) because of the failure of one party to carry out all or part of his obligations; or (b) where exceptional circumstances arise.

Indemnification and/or compensation of agent by principal   Article 17 of the 1986 Directive obliges the Member States take the measures necessary to ensure that the commercial agent is, after termination of the agency contract, either indemnified in accordance with Article 17.2 or else compensated for damage in accordance with Article 17.

Indemnification   As to indemnification, Article 17.2.(a) provides that the commercial agent shall be entitled to an indemnity where the following two conditions are met:

> [i] he has brought the principal new customers or has significantly increased the volume of business with existing customers and the principal continues to derive substantial benefits from the business with such customers; and [ii] the payment of this indemnity is equitable having regard to all the circumstances and, in particular, the commission lost by the commercial agent on the business transacted with such customers.

Article 17.2.(a) goes on to provide that Member States may provide that an indemnity is also required in circumstances involving 'the application or otherwise of a restraint of trade clause, within the meaning of Article 20 [of the Directive']. This option was not taken up in the 1994 Regulations.

Article 17.2.(b) provides that the amount of the indemnity may not exceed a figure equivalent to an indemnity for one year calculated from the commercial agent's average annual remuneration over the preceding five years and, if the contract goes back less than five years, the indemnity must be calculated on the average for the period in question. Finally, Article 17.2(c) provides that the existence of an indemnity shall not prevent the commercial agent from seeking the alternative remedy of damages.

Compensation for damage Turning to that alternative remedy, Article 17.3 provides that the commercial agent is entitled to compensation for any damage he suffers as a result of the termination of his relations with the principal. Crucially, the 1986 Directive goes on to specify a presumption of damage ('[s]uch damage shall be deemed to occur') where the termination occurs in the following circumstances:

> depriving the commercial agent of the commission which proper performance of the agency contract would have procured him whilst providing the principal with substantial benefits linked to the commercial agent's activities, and/or which have not enabled the commercial agent to amortise the costs and expenses that he had incurred for the performance of the agency contract on the principal's advice.

Death of principal Article 17.4 goes on to provide that entitlement to the indemnity and/or compensation for damage also arises where the agency contract is terminated as a result of the commercial agent's death.

Loss of right to indemnity and/or compensation for damage Article 17.5 of the Directive contains a form of limitations statute, by providing that the commercial agent shall lose the entitlement to the indemnity and/or compensation for damage if, within one year following termination of the contract, he has not notified the principal that he intends pursuing his entitlement. In addition, Article 18 provides the indemnity or compensation will not be payable in any of the following three situations:

> (a) where the principal has terminated the agency contract because of default attributable to the commercial agent which would justify immediate termination of the agency contract under national law; (b) where the commercial agent has terminated the agency contract, unless such termination is justified by circumstances attributable to the principal or on grounds of age, infirmity or illness of the commercial agent in consequence of which he cannot reasonably be required to continue his activities; (c) where, with the agreement of the principal, the commercial agent assigns his rights and duties under the agency contract to another person.

In keeping with other provisions of the 1986 Directive, Article 19 provides that the parties may not derogate from Articles 17 and 18 to the detriment of the commercial agent.

Restraint of trade clauses   Article 20 deals with restraint of trade clauses, which it defines as any agreements 'restricting the business activities of a commercial agent following termination of the agency contract.' Article 20.2 provides that a restraint of trade clause shall be valid only if it complies with the following conditions:

(a) it is concluded in writing;

(b) it relates to the geographical area or the group of customers and the geographical area entrusted to the commercial agent and to the kind of goods covered by his or her agency under the contract;

(c) it is for a period of no more than two years after termination of the agency contract.

Article 20.4 goes on to state that these provisions are without prejudice to ('shall not affect') any provisions of national law which impose other restrictions on the validity or enforceability of restraint of trade clauses or which enable the courts to reduce the obligations on the parties resulting from such an agreement. In this respect, it would appear that the 1986 Directive is certainly more specific and, in some instances, would be more stringent than the 'reasonableness' test applied heretofore in Irish law: see generally, Clark, *Contract Law in Ireland*, 3rd ed. (Sweet & Maxwell, 1991). Notwithstanding that the 1986 Directive is limited to self-employed commercial agents, Article 20 represents a significant change in the substantive law of restraint of trade in the State. It also remains to be considered to what extent the 1986 Directive is consistent with the broad terms of the Competition Acts 1991 and 1996, though the principle *generalia specialibus non derogant* might give priority to the Directive.

Confidentiality and disclosure of information   Article 21 of the 1986 Directive is a confidentiality provision to the effect that '[n]othing in this Directive shall require a Member State to provide for the disclosure of information where such disclosure would be contrary to public policy.' Again, in the absence of any substantive provision on this point in the 1994 Regulations, one is left to assume that Article 21 may be directly effective in Irish law.

COMPETITION

Non-competition clause: trade magazine   In *RGDATA v Tara Publishing*

Co. Ltd [1995] 1 ILRM 453, Murphy J rejected a claim that a non-competition clauses in an agreement concerning the transfer of an undertaking connected with a retail trade magazine was in breach of the Competition Act 1991 or the EC Treaty. The background was as follows.

The magazine 'Retail News' was published for circulation among independent grocers who were members of RGDATA. In the early 1980s the magazine was printed and published as a joint venture between the plaintiff and the defendant, the profits being divided equally between them. The profits were derived solely from advertising fees paid by suppliers who advertised in the magazine. By an agreement made in 1985, the plaintiff sold to the defendant the plaintiff's interest in the title and ownership of the publications 'Retail News' and 'Retail News Yearbook'. The agreement contained two restrictive covenants. Clause 2 provided that, for the duration of the agreement the plaintiff would not publish any other publications in the Republic of Ireland, and 'Retail News' was to be the only official publication of RGDATA. Clause 7 provided that the agreement was to remain in force for 20 years.

The plaintiff sought a declaration that clause 2 of the 1985 agreement was void by virtue of s. 4(1) of the Competition Act 1991, which prohibits agreements between undertakings, decisions by associations of undertakings and concerted practices which have as their object or effect the prevention, restriction or distortion of competition in trade in goods or services in the State or part thereof, including those which limit or control production, markets, technical development or investments. The defendant accepted that the wide scope and long duration of the covenants which were in restraint of competition could not be justified if the sale related just to the goodwill and assets in the title of a newspaper or magazine. However, it claimed that the agreement related to a publication long established as the official publication of the plaintiff association and circulated to all its members with the assurance that it was the official magazine of the association serving the independent grocer.

The defendant counterclaimed for damages, alleging a breach of the agreement by the plaintiff in publishing a document 'How to manage your shop', which had been described as 'An RGDATA publication'.

Murphy J refused the plaintiff's application and allowed the defendant's counterclaim and awarding it damages.

As to the plaintiff's claim, he took the view that while RGDATA members were a clearly defined and valuable market, it was not a market which the plaintiff had a monopoly in exploiting through the magazine. Nevertheless, he accepted that there was a particular relationship between the plaintiff and its members and that an important consideration for both parties to the 1985 agreement was the reasonable expectation among potential suppliers to the grocery industry that RGDATA members were more likely to read the official publication of their own organisation in preference to other publications. He thus concluded that the plaintiff was selling to the defendant not only a well-established title but also the right to represent the title as the official publication of the plaintiff association.

Murphy J found it surprising that when the plaintiff granted to the defendant the right to represent the magazine as the official publication of the association, it did not expressly reserve any control over the content or quality of the magazine or impose any specific obligations on the defendant in relation to its publication or circulation. However, he agreed that such terms were to be inferred.

He went on to hold that the inclusion in an agreement of non-competition clauses for the sale of an undertaking was not of itself sufficient to remove such clauses from the scope of Article 85(1) of the EC Treaty. Applying the principles in the Court of Justice's decision in *Remia BV v Commission* [1985] ECR 2545, Murphy J noted that non-competition clauses had the merit of ensuring that the transfer had the effect intended and they contributed to the promotion of competition as they led to more undertakings in the relevant market. Nevertheless, he held that they had to be necessary to the transfer of the undertaking and their duration and scope had to be limited to that purpose but that where these conditions were satisfied, the clauses were not prohibited by Article 85(1).

Murphy J went on to note that the matter could be viewed at three levels. First, if a vendor was selling the goodwill attached to a named publication, the vendor could be required to covenant against competing in the same business for a reasonable period to ensure that the purchaser achieved the goodwill in the undertaking purchased. Second, where a particular title was purchased, covenants could be included precluding the vendor indefinitely from publishing a comparable magazine under that title. Finally, where a purchaser acquired, as here, not just the right to the goodwill in a magazine under a particular title, but also the right to represent the magazine as the only official publication of the vendor to its members, this would also be a concluded property transaction which might be lawfully sustained by covenants precluding the vendor from purporting to publish any other comparable magazine, either under the same title or under any other title as 'the official publication of RGDATA'.

However, he also pointed out that such covenants could not lawfully prevent the vendor from publishing after a reasonable time any other magazine, provided it did not offend in either of those respects. In the instant case, although the plaintiff would be precluded from publishing a magazine under or with a particular title or accolade could in theory restrict competition, but only in the sense that the plaintiff could not reclaim and exploit the asset which it had alienated. Murphy J concluded that the covenant precluding the publication of magazines generally should be severed from the covenant contained in clause 2, as it was too extensive, and was in breach of common law principles, the 1991 Act and the EC Treaty. However, the plaintiff was free to publish only if the publications were not described or represented or held out to be official publications of RGDATA. Finally, on the defendant's counterclaim, he was of the clear view that the publication by the plaintiff of the document with the description 'An RGDATA publication' constituted a breach of the 1985 agreement. He assessed damages at £7,500 as a sum that would compensate the defendant for the loss in advertising revenue which flowed from the unlawful competition.

Trade association: safety In *Donovan and Others v Electricity Supply Board* [1994] 2 ILRM 325, Costello J(as he then was) held that a non-statutory requirement that electrical contract work had to be certified by an inspector employed by a trade association did not infringe domestic or European competition law. The case arose against the following background.

The Electro-Technical Council of Ireland (ETCI) was a body established in 1972 to promote and develop safety standards in electrical work. To this end, it approved and published National Wiring Rules, which were amended from time to time. Where an electrical contractor installs electrical an installation or equipment, a completion certificate certifies, in effect, that the work has been done in accordance with the relevant ETCI National Wiring Rules. In 1991, a private company called the Register of Electrical Contractors of Ireland Ltd (RECI) was established, the members being the ETCI, two trade associations and the defendant, the latter being the State-owned body with responsibility for electricity generation, distribution and supply. A self-regulatory system was proposed and a register of electrical contractors was compiled. From September 1992, the defendant Board would only supply electrical power to installations covered by a completion certificate signed by either a RECI-registered contractor or, if the work was carried out by a non-registered contractor, a RECI inspector. While registered contractors could sign their own completion certificates, a non-registered contractor was required to pay a fee of £85 in order to have the installation inspected by a RECI inspector who would then sign the certificate if satisfied it complied with ETCI Rules. The defendant Board mounted a promotional campaign in which the public was urged to use the services of registered contractors to ensure that they got a good service and in which it was suggested that unregistered contractors were 'cowboys'.

As in the RGDATA case, above, the instant case revolved around the Competition Act 1991. As we have already seen, s. 4(1) of the 1991 Act prohibits anti-competitive agreements between undertakings, decisions by associations of undertakings and concerted practices. S. 5(1) prohibits any abuse by one or more undertakings in a dominant position. The Competition Authority is empowered by s. 4(2) and (4) to grant licences or issue certificates which, respectively, exempt acts otherwise contrary to s. 4(1), or certify that no breach of s. 4(1) has occurred. There is no power to grant licences or issue certificates in relation to s. 5. An application for a licence or certificate is made by way of a notification to the competition authority under s. 7. Where a licence or certificate is sought in respect of a s. 4(1) agreement, decision or concerted practice which was in existence when s. 4 came into force, s. 7(2) provides that a notification must be made within one year of the commencement of s. 4. A right of action for breach of s. 4(1) or s. 5 is conferred by s. 6. S. 6(7) suspends this right of action in respect of claims under s. 4(1) where a notification has been made under s. 7(2) and a final decision is still pending.

In September 1992 the defendant Board notified the Competition Authority pursuant to s. 7 of the 1991 Act of the arrangements in question. In October 1992 the plaintiffs, non-RECI electrical contractors, instituted proceedings challenging the validity of the arrangements under the 1991 Act and/or Articles 85 and 86 of the EC Treaty. It was agreed that, under the 1991 Act, the Board's notification suspended the plaintiffs' right of action for any breach of s. 4(1) of the 1991 Act and limited the claim to one under s. 5. In November 1992 Lardner J granted the plaintiffs an interlocutory injunction restraining the implementation of the regime and it was subsequently amended.

The plaintiffs claimed that the original RECI regime, as it existed in September 1992, involved, *inter alia*, an abuse by the defendant of its dominant position in the market for the supply and was thus in breach of s. 5 of the 1991 Act and sought appropriate declaratory and injunctive relief. Costello J refused the relief sought and found that the arrangements were justified.

Given that the defendant had a virtual monopoly of generation, distribution and supply it was hardly surprising that Costello J held that the defendant Board was in a dominant position for the supply of electrical contracting services. Thus, if it could be shown that the defendant had acted in breach of s. 4(1), in that the effect of the RECI regime was to restrict or distort competition by non-registered competitors, this would amount to the imposition of unfair trading conditions and an abuse of the defendant's position.

He accepted that the effect of the RECI regime, including the promotional campaign and the inspection fee, was to restrict competition by non-registered contractors and that it was well established under European Community law that rules of admission to trade associations should be based on objective criteria with a proper appeal procedure.

In relation to the original RECI regime, Costello J held that the lack of objective standards for registration, the arbitrary power to refuse enrolment, the absence of any appeal procedure, and the requirement that the applicant should have suitable premises, which had nothing to do with the considerations of safety which had prompted the establishment of the register, constituted unjustifiable restrictions affecting enrolment on the RECI register. Costello J went on to state that, while securing membership of RECI would have enabled non-registered contractors to overcome the competitive disadvantage which they faced, the unjustifiable restrictions on membership gave rise to restrictions on competition in the electrical contracting trade. Thus he concluded that, from September 1992 until the grant of the interlocutory injunction, the defendant had unintentionally abused its dominant position by imposing unfair trading conditions contrary to s. 5.

However, he went on to state that the subsequent amendments to RECI's memorandum, articles of association and rules for registration overcame the defects in the original regime so that the rules relating to enrolment no longer constituted a barrier to entry and competition was no longer distorted or restricted. From the date of the amendments, therefore, it could not be said that the defendant was abusing its dominant position.

As to the defendant Board's notification to the Competition Authority under s. 7 of the 1991 Act, he pointed out that it had been expressed as being for the purpose of obtaining a certificate or, in the event of refusal, a licence and it could not, therefore, be regarded as an application for a licence. Since the defendant would have been entitled to modify or amend the agreements to which the notification related to ensure the grant of a certificate at any time before the Competition Authority. made an adjudication, the Board did not abuse its dominant position by introducing new conditions of supply before any such adjudication.

The decision of Costello J is of great interest, being the first decision of the High Court outlining the circumstances in which considerations concerning public policy factors such as public safety may be brought into account in determining the scope of the Competition Act 1991. As Costello J himself acknowledged, this approach is consistent with the jurisprudence developed under Article 85 and 86 of the EC Treaty.

INSURANCE

Non-life The European Communities (Non-life Insurance) Framework Regulations 1994 (SI No. 359 of 1994) gave effect to the Third Non-life Insurance Framework Directive (92/49/EEC) which institutes a single authorisation system of supervision of insurance undertakings operating in the

EC Member States. Insurance undertakings transacting business on either a cross-border or branch basis are now subject to the overall supervisory control of the supervisory authority where their head offices are located. The 1994 Regulations require non-life insurance undertakings to furnish information and statistical documents necessary for supervision purposes to the Minister for Enterprise and Employment. The Regulations also introduce revised rules for the valuation of underwriting liabilities and assets and revised requirements for localisation of assets. The Regulations provide that any significant increase or decrease in shareholdings in an insurance undertaking must be notified in advance to the Minister. The Regulations also include certain information requirements which insurance undertakings must disclose to policyholders when an insurance contract is being effected. Insurers underwriting third party motor insurance will continue to be subject to existing requirements including the necessity for services insurers to appoint a claims representative in the State to handle third-party insurance claims. The Regulations incorporate a number of consumer protection measures, in particular Regulation 24, which oblige insurance undertakings to comply with the 'general good' requirements of the Member State, such as complying with the terms of the Consumer Information Act 1978, the Sale of Goods and Supply of Services Act 1980 and the Health Insurance Act 1994 (on the latter, see the Health Services chapter, 284-7, below). Regulation 24 also requires insurers to comply with 'provisions contained in consumer credit legislation adopted by the State', which general phrase was, it may be assumed, intended to cover legislation such as the Consumer Credit Act 1995 (which we will discuss in the 1995 Review). The 1994 Regulations have the effect of amending or modifying certain provisions of the Insurance Acts 1909 to 1989 and previous Insurance Regulations made under the European Communities Act 1972, including the European Communities (Non-life Insurance) (Amendment) Regulations 1991 (see the 1991 Review, 32). The 1994 Regulations came into force on December 8, 1994.

Life   The European Communities (Life Assurance) Framework Regulations 1994 (SI No. 360 of 1994) gave effect to the Third life Assurance Framework Directive (92/96/EEC). As with SI No. 359 of 1994, above, these Regulations instituted a single authorisation system of supervision of insurance undertakings operating throughout the EC Member States whereby insurance undertakings transacting business on either a cross-border or branch basis will be subject to overall supervisory control of the supervisory authority where their head offices are located. The Regulations also implement relevant provisions of the Second Life Assurance Freedom of Services Directive (90/619/EEC). The Regulations require life assurance undertakings to submit statutory returns to the Minister for Enterprise and Employment in the format set out in the Schedules to the Regulations. They also require an actuarial investigation to be carried out annually and introduce revised rules for the valuation of underwriting liabilities and assets and revised requirements for localisation of assets and the treatment of reinsurance. The Regulations provide that any significant increase or decrease in shareholdings in an insurance undertaking must be notified in advance to the Minister. The Regulations introduce a mandatory 15 day 'cooling off' period for policyholders taking out most types of life assurance. The Regulations also introduce disclosure requirements for insurers obliging them to furnish information about the insurance company as well as information about the commitment and pertinent changes during the term of the insurance contract. Again, as with SI No. 359, above, the Regulations contain provisions which oblige insurance undertakings to comply with the 'general good' requirements of the State as specified. They also provide for reciprocity measures regarding life assurance activities in third countries. We again note that these Regulations have the effect of amending or modifying certain provisions of the Insurance Acts 1909 to 1989 and previous Insurance Regulations made under the European Communities Act 1972, including the European Communities (Life Assurance) Regulations 1984 and the European Communities (Life Assurance Accounts Statements and Valuations) Regulations 1986. The 1994 Regulations came into force on December 8, 1994.

INTELLECTUAL PROPERTY

Copyright: computer programs In *News Datacom Ltd, British Sky Broadcasting Ltd and Sky Television plc v Lyons and Ors* [1994] 1 ILRM 241 Flood J considered the European Communities (Legal Protection of Computer Programs) Regulations 1993 (1993 Review, 56) in the context of an application for an interlocutory injunction: see the Equity chapter, 242, below.

Copyright: performing rights *Phonographic Performance (Ireland) Ltd v Cody and Princes Investments Ltd* [1994] 2 ILRM 241, a case concerning the enforcement of performing rights pursuant to the Copyright Act 1963, raised the question of proof of infringement by affidavit: see the discussion in the Practice and Procedure chapter, 366-9, below.

INTERNATIONAL TRADE

Trade sanctions: removal The Financial Transfers (Haiti) (Revocation) Order 1994 (SI No. 452 of 1994) gave effect to UN Security Council

Resolution No. 944 of 1994 and removed the financial trade sanctions which had been imposed on by the Financial Transfers (Haiti) Order 1993 (1993 Review, 49).

Trade sanctions: scope of power to impound In *Bosphorus Hava Yollari Turizm Ve Ticaret Anonim Sirketi v Minister for Transport, Energy and Communications and Ors* [1994] 2 ILRM 551, Murphy J held that the respondent Minister had acted ultra vires in impounding the applicant company's aircraft pursuant to the European Communities (Prohibition of Trade with the Federal Republic of Yugoslavia (Serbia and Montenegro)) Regulations 1993 (see the 1993 Review, 63).

The case arose against the background of the UN and EC trade sanctions imposed on Serbia and its ally Montenegro in the context of the war in former Yugoslavia. The UN Security Council Resolution 820/1993 had been followed by the EC's Council Regulation No. 990/93, which prohibited the export to or the importation from the Federal Republic of Yugoslavia (Serbia and Montenegro) of any commodities or products. The recitals to the Council Regulation noted the adoption of the UN Security Council's Resolution and indeed its terms were reflected in Article 8 of the Regulation itself, which provided that 'all vessels . . . and aircraft in which a majority or controlling interest is held by a person or undertaking in or operating from the Federal Republic of Yugoslavia . . . shall be impounded by the competent authorities of the Member States'. The European Communities (Prohibition of Trade with the Federal Republic of Yugoslavia (Serbia and Montenegro)) Regulations 1993 were made in June 1993 to give effect to the administrative arrangements required to comply fully with the Council Regulation. The respondent Minister was constituted the 'Competent Authority' for the purposes of Article 8 of the Council Regulation.

The applicant was a company incorporated under Turkish law in which all shares were held by Turkish nationals. By a lease agreement made in April 1992, Yugoslav Airlines (JAT), described as 'the lessor', leased two of its aircraft to the applicant, described as 'the lessee', for a period of 48 months. The lease provided for a monthly rental and a deposit to be paid for each aircraft, and expressly provided that ownership stayed with the lessor but that the lessee had the right to inscribe the aircraft into the Turkish Register of Civil Aviation with notification that the lessor was the owner. Subsequent to delivery, the applicant had complete control of the aircraft and the cabin and flight crew were employees of the applicant. The aircraft were registered with the Turkish Ministry of Transport and Communications General Directorate of Civil Aviation. The relevant certificates identified JAT as the owner of the aircraft and the applicant as the operator. Expert evidence was given that the certificates were conclusive evidence that the aircraft were of Turkish nationality and under the control of the applicant, and that it was possible to register aeroplanes in only one jurisdiction under the Convention on International Civil Aviation. Neither aircraft had returned to Yugoslavia or any of the states of the former Yugoslavia since their delivery to the applicant. One of the aircraft arrived in Dublin in April 1993 for maintenance by the fourth named respondent. The Irish government issued instructions in May 1993 that 'the aircraft was to be stopped'. The respondent Minister then ordered that the aircraft be impounded pursuant to Council Regulation 990/93. The Minister had been advised by the United Nations Sanctions Committee that the aircraft fell within the terms of Resolution 820/1993.

The applicant sought a declaration that the aircraft did not come within the terms of Article 8 of Council Regulation 990/93 and that the first named respondent was not empowered to impound the aircraft. As already indicated, Murphy J found that the Minister was not empowered to impound the aircraft in question.

Murphy J noted that, while UN Resolutions did not form part of Irish domestic law, Security Council Resolution 820/1993 had provided the genesis for Article 8 of Council Regulation 990/93 and thus any judicial or academic commentary on its terms could be of assistance in interpretation. However, in the absence of such commentary, he considered that the unexplained conclusion of the UN Sanctions Committee was of no value to the court.

Moving to the EC element of the case, Murphy J held that the appropriate interpretive technique to adopt was the teleological or schematic approach, which he acknowledged as a fundamental principle of interpretation to be applied to EC Regulations and Directives. He accepted in this respect that the express purpose of Council Regulation 990/93 was to deter the Federal Republic of Yugoslavia (Serbia and Montenegro) from engaging in activities leading to unacceptable loss of human life and material damage. The Regulation was thus intended to operate as a punishment, deterrent or sanction against the Federal Republic's people or government. However, the Regulation was not, he felt, intended to punish or penalise peoples or countries that had not caused or contributed to what he described as the tragic events in the former Yugoslavia. He concluded that, although Article 8 of the Regulation failed to distinguish between the nature, as opposed to the degree or percentage, of the interest held by the Yugoslav person or undertaking in the asset, the relevant 'interest' was the possession or the right to enjoy control or regulate the use of the asset, rather than the right to any income derived from it. On this understanding, the majority and controlling interest in the aircraft was held by the applicant alone and so the respondent Minister had not been empowered to impound the aircraft in the circumstances.

Subsequent to this decision, it was held that the Minister was required to compensate the applicant company for the delay in releasing the aircraft in question: see *Bosphorus Hava Yollari Turizm Ve Ticaret Anonim Sirketi v Minister for Transport, Energy and Communications and Ors (No. 2)*, High Court, January 22, 1996. We will return to this aspect of the case in the 1996 Review. The European Communities (Prohibition of Trade with the Federal Republic of Yugoslavia (Serbia and Montenegro)) Regulations 1993 themselves were later revoked having regard to subsequent events in the former Yugoslavia, in particular the lifting of full sanctions on Serbia and Montenegro.

WTO We merely note here the establishment of the World Trade Organisation (WTO), by the Marrakesh Agreement signed on April 15, 1994. While in general outside the scope of this Review (but see 3, above, in the Administrative Law chapter), the Marrakesh Agreement (and the conclusion of the Uruguay Round under its predecessor, GATT) is likely to have an enormous impact in the future on trade emanating from the State.

PUBLIC SUPPLY AND WORKS CONTRACTS

Further steps in implementing the EC-based requirement that public service, public supply and public works contracts be open to bids from commercial undertakings in all Member States were given effect in 1994. On previous Regulations, see the 1992 Review, 46, and the 1993 Review, 66.

Review procedure The European Communities (Review Procedures for the Award of Public Supply, Public Works and Public Services Contracts) (No. 2) Regulations 1994 (SI No. 309 of 1994) consolidated the arrangements already in place in this area by specifying that the High Court is designated as the review body in respect of these contracts and may quash any contract which has been awarded in breach of the terms of the relevant Directives. They also revoked previous Regulations in this area, the European Communities (Review Procedures for the Award of Public Supply and Public Works Contracts) Regulations 1992 (1992 Review, 46) and the European Communities (Review Procedures for the Award of Public Supply, Public Works and Public Services Contracts) Regulations 1994 (SI No. 5 of 1994).

Supply contracts The European Communities (Award of Public Supply Contracts) (Amendment) Regulations 1994 (SI No. 292 of 1994) amended the European Communities (Award of Public Supply Contracts) Regulations 1992 (1992 Review, 46) in order to give effect to Directive 93/36/EEC, which had consolidated previous Directives on the award of public supply contracts. The 1994 Regulations did this in a rather unsatisfactory manner by providing merely that any references in the 1992 Regulations to the previous Directives should be taken as a reference to the 1993 Consolidating Directive 'in accordance with the correlation table set out in Annex IV to the [1993] Council Directive.'

Works contracts In tandem with SI No. 292 of 1994, above, the European Communities (Award of Public Works Contracts) (Amendment) Regulations 1994 (SI No. 293 of 1994) purported to amend the European Communities (Award of Public Works Contracts) Regulations 1992 (1992 Review, 46) in order to give effect to Directive 93/37/EEC, which had consolidated previous Directives on the award of public works contracts, including building and civil engineering works. However, not only do these Regulations suffer from the same 'scissors and paste' defect as SI No. 292 of 1994, above, but the printed A5 version of SI No. 293 of 1994 suffers from the additional defects that Reg. 1 miscites them as the 'European Communities (Award of Public Supply Contracts) (Amendment) Regulations 1994' and Reg. 3 purports to adapt the 'European Communities (Award of Public Supply Contracts) Regulations 1992' (though it does refer to the correct SI No., namely SI No. 36 of 1992). This defect did not occur in the original A4 version of SI No. 293 of 1994, but unfortunately it is the A5 version that becomes the 'permanent' record of the Regulations in the bound volumes of Statutory Instruments. In any event, this merely serves to underline the limitations to the method of 'amendment' chosen in both SI No. 292 of 1994 and SI No. 293 of 1994 in what is a significant regulatory element concerning a large part of the Irish economy.

WEIGHTS AND MEASURES

Summer time and winter time The Winter Time Order 1994 (SI No. 395 of 1994), which gave effect to Directive 94/21/EC, varied the periods of winter time (and consequently summer time) as provided for in the Standard Time (Amendment) Act 1971, in respect of the years 1995, 1996 and 1997. The Order had the effect of causing summer time to begin one week later in 1995 and two weeks later in each of the following two years. Summer time ended one week earlier in 1995. The Order also provides that the change from one period of time to another will be at 1 a.m. and not at 2 a.m. as was previously the case.

Communications

Dr Eamonn G. Hall

Communications law in 1994 reflected the increasing significance of modern communications facilities in the development of the life of the individual and the welfare of the nation. Central to communications law is the right to communicate. The right to communicate is not only a necessary goal in a democratic society but represents a basic human need and is a vital component of all social organisation. The right to communicate represents, subject to qualifications, the right to speak, the right to hear and be heard, and the right to reply. 1994 was the tenth anniversary of the reporting of the judgment of Costello J (as he then was) in *Attorney General v Paperlink Ltd* [1984] ILRM 373. In *Paperlink*, Costello J stated that as the act of communication is the exercise of such a basic human faculty, a right to communicate must inhere in the citizen by virtue of his human personality and was one of those personal unspecified rights of the citizen protected by Article 40.3.1° of the Constitution.

Communications law in Ireland (as in other spheres of law) is being influenced increasingly by case law and developments emanating from Ireland's membership of the European Communities and the European Union. The EU Council Resolution of February 7, 1994 (94/C 48/01 OJEC No. C48/1, 16.2.94) on universal service principles in the telecommunications sector reflected the concerns of the Council of the European Union in relation to the greater facilitation of the right to communicate. The Council recognised that the maintenance and development of a universal telecommunications service, ensured through adequate financing, was a key factor for the future development of telecommunications in the European Community. The principles of universality, equality and continuity were stated to be the basis for such a service so as to permit access at an affordable price to a defined minimum service of a specified quality to all users everywhere in the light of specific national conditions.

In its Resolution of February 7, 1994, the EU Council noted that common principles for the provision of universal service will be necessary in order to achieve a balanced and fair regulatory environment throughout the Community, taking account of specific national conditions regarding regulatory and market aspects. Specifically, the Council recognised that in pursuing the objective of maintaining and developing a universal telecommunications service, account will be taken of the specific circumstances of the peripheral regions with less developed networks and of very small networks and the role which the appropriate Community support framework may play having regard to national priorities. The concept of the right to communicate relates not only to the telecommunications carrier services but also has a significance for broadcasting and other media of communication.

The concept of a universal telecommunications services entitling persons to exercise their right to communicate is recognised in Ireland in the context of the carrier service in s. 14 of the Postal and Telecommunications Services Act 1983 which specifies the principal objects of the national telecommunications company known as Telecom Éireann. The objects, *inter alia*, are:

(a) to provide a national telecommunications service within the State and between the State and places outside the State; and

(b) to meet the industrial, commercial, social and household needs of the State for comprehensive and efficient telecommunications services and, as far as Telecom Éireann consider reasonably practicable to satisfy all reasonable demands for such service throughout the State.

BROADCASTING

Broadcasting Complaints Commission   The fifteenth annual report of the Broadcasting Complaints Commission published in 1994 contains details of complaints considered and decided by the Commission. The Commission was established pursuant to ss. 18A to 18C of the Broadcasting Authority Act 1960 as inserted by s. 4 of the Broadcasting Authority (Amendment) Act 1976. The chairperson of the Commission for the year under review was Ms. Geri Silke, barrister. The Commission's function pursuant to the Broadcasting Authority Act 1960 as amended, is to adjudicate upon complaints relating to news, current affairs, ministerial prohibitions, invasion of privacy, advertising and certain published matters broadcast by both RTE and other sound broadcasting services.

In the year under review, seven complaints were examined by the Commission. Six of these complaints referred to programmes broadcast by RTE and one by Midlands Radio 3. In the *Complaint of the Workers' Party* (1994 Annual Report) the complaint related to the alleged exclusion of the legitimate viewpoint of the Workers' Party from the national airwaves, i.e. RTE radio and television. The complaint referred to a news broadcast on August 26, 1992 concerning a peaceful march outside Government Buildings by the Workers' Party to protest at the lack of Government action to create jobs. In correspondence to the Workers' Party, RTE had stated that the

Workers' Party could not be given the same prominence that would normally be afforded to bigger political parties and that the activities of the Workers' Party were covered in RTE's broadcasting service in the context of it being a small party in size and representation. The Commission found that there was no breach of s. 18(1)(a) of the Broadcasting Authority Act 1960 as amended by the Broadcasting Authority (Amendment) Act 1976 concerning objectivity and impartiality.

Several of the complaints to the Commission related to RTE's coverage of the disturbances in Northern Ireland. In the *Complaint of Mr Karl Martin* (1994 Annual Report), the complainant argued that RTE in specific programmes was biased in favour of the Nationalist/Roman Catholic community in Northern Ireland and against the Unionist/Protestant community there. RTE rejected that thesis. It was also argued that RTE had engaged in double standards when describing deaths arising from the activities of the IRA and the actions of the security forces in Northern Ireland. It was alleged that RTE had reported deaths in Northern Ireland 'in IRA's terms' and that the nature of RTE news reporting had played into the hands of subversives. RTE had stated that its news coverage of the Northern Ireland situation over the past two decades had been generally recognised as being fair and impartial. Regarding the terminology used by RTE in describing deaths at the hands of the IRA or arising from the actions of the UK security forces, RTE had a policy of not using the word 'murder'. RTE instead used the expression 'killed', 'shot dead', or other relevant descriptions. RTE in its response to the complaint stated that they were concerned by Mr. Martin's allegation that RTE's broadcast reports could be construed as in some way serving the propaganda interests of subversives. RTE rejected such a serious allegation made against it and its staff. The complaints were dismissed by the Commission.

In the context of complaints in relation to the broadcasting services, it is of note, that pursuant to European influences, (Council Directive of 3 October 1989 (89/552/EEC OJEC No. L 298/23, 17.10.89)) s. 8 of the Broadcasting Act 1990 empowers the Broadcasting Complaints Commission to award a powerful remedy to a limited category of complainant. In addition to publication of a decision in the printed media, where the Commission finds in favour, in whole or in part, of a complainant in relation to a broadcast of inaccurate facts or information in relation to a person which constituted an attack on that person's honour or reputation, the relevant broadcasting service must (unless the Commission considers it inappropriate) broadcast the Commission decision at a time and in a manner corresponding to that in which the offending broadcast took place.

Digital video broadcasting Digital technology is considered to offer significant benefits for the future of television and for the future electronic information highways. Common standards are considered an essential pre-requisite for such an approach. In Council Resolution of June 27, 1994 on a framework for Community policy on digital video broadcasting (94)/ C/181/02 OJ EC 2.7 94) the Council of the European Union declared that the preferred way to achieve the objective of harmonious market development of digital video broadcasting would be by means of a consensus approach involving all relevant economic agents including broadcasting organisations. The Council raised the issue of introducing regulatory measures if the requirements of fair and open competition, consumer protection or other significant public interests so demanded in order to facilitate the achievement of this objective and the protection of those interests.

Election broadcasts The decision of Kinlen J in *Madigan v Radio Telefís Éireann* [1994] 2 ILRM 472 is outlined in the Administrative Law chapter, 11, above.

Guidelines in relation to character and content of RTE programming on radio and television On January 20, 1994, RTE issued guidelines on the observance of s. 18(1) of the Broadcasting Authority Act 1960 as amended by s. 3 of the Broadcasting Authority (Amendment) Act 1976 in relation to requirements concerning the character and content of RTE pro-gramming on radio and television. In effect, the Guidelines set out the policy of RTE in its approach to, and interpretation of, the legislation regulating the content of the broadcast media.

The Guidelines quote Article 40.6.1.i of the Constitution concerning freedom of speech and Article 10 of the European Convention for the Protection of Human Rights and Fundamental Freedoms and state that broadcasting must generally reflect the mores and respect the values of the society in which it operates, acknowledging its standards of taste, decency and justice. The Guidelines note that broadcasting cannot be just a channel for any and all opinions nor can it be neutral in its basic philosophy and attitudes. It must, however, be impartial. The Guidelines note that broadcast-ing must seek to widen and deepen the knowledge of the audience in programming which includes such critical examination of public issues as is considered necessary to fulfil the needs of impartial and objective enquiry. RTE interprets the statutory obligation of objectivity as the setting forth of an actual external situation uncoloured by the feelings or subjective views of the broadcaster. In the context of the statutory obligation to be impartial, RTE interpreted that concept 'as being fair and just in reporting and presenting the facts without favouring any particular interest or interests involved'.

On current affairs, the statutory requirements in s. 18 of the Broadcasting

Authority Act 1960, as amended, of being 'fair to all interests' is interpreted by RTE as requiring the programme-makers to present in an equitable manner the views of persons or interests involved in a significant way in a particular issue. It was stated that all who appear on radio and television were regarded as agreeing to face 'penetrating questions' but were entitled to courtesy and fair play. RTE does not assume any right 'to place any person on trial before the nation by aggressive questioning or otherwise'.

RTE personnel were advised that care should be taken to avoid unfairness to those who, for any reason, are unable to present their own case and to those who are unorganised or inarticulate. The Guidelines also state that RTE accepted that any organisation or any person, whether in private or in public life, had a right to decline an invitation to participate in a programme. The programme makers were directed not to draw any conclusions from such a refusal nor, particularly, where a named person is involved, make a reference to it. Only in exceptional circumstances and where it would be essential to establish publicly the intent of the programme to be comprehensive, impartial and fair to all significant interests concerned would programme-makers be regarded as justified in stating that an invitation had been declined.

The Guidelines deal with the statutory prohibition on promoting or inciting to crime or undermining the authority of the State set out in s. 18(1A) of the Broadcasting Authority Act 1960, as amended. In the context of members of certain organisations which are unlawful in the State or pro-scribed in Northern Ireland, it was stated that any approach to a person belonging to such an organisation in contemplation of a broadcast must have the express approval of the Director General and any item to be broadcast must have been referred by the relevant Divisional Head to the Director General whose express approval would be required before any material is broadcast. The Guidelines noted that statements from these organisations, or from a spokesperson for them, on significant developments including the acceptance or denial of responsibility for violence or other unlawful activity may be reported. Details are also set down in relation to interviews with Sinn Féin and Republican Sinn Féin representatives.

The Guidelines also consider the issue of the privacy of the individual which is implicitly recognised in a statutory sense in s. 18(1B) of the Broadcasting Authority Act 1960, as amended, which provides that the RTE Authority shall not, in its programmes and in the means employed to make such programmes unreasonably encroach on the privacy of an individual.

Guidelines for IRTC sound broadcasting services Guidelines were also issued by the Independent Radio and Television Commission (IRTC) in relation to sound broadcasting services with effect from January 20, 1994. The Commission noted that it would be prudent for independent broadcasting contractors to familiarise themselves specifically with the Offences Against the State Act 1939, the Defamation Act 1961 and the Prohibition of Incitement to Hatred Act 1989. Having cited relevant provisions of the Radio and Television Act 1988, the IRTC 1994 Guidelines contain some noble expressions on freedom of speech. In a statement of principles, the Guidelines outline the importance of communication in a democracy and state that there should be a strong presumption against prior restraint or censorship of subject-matter and more particularly 'points of view' as transmitted by the media. Freedom of speech was stated to be an essential democratic right and while it was not absolute, the conditions of permissible interference by the State should be interpreted with caution.

The IRTC Guidelines state that there should be no arbitrary limits imposed on the free discussion and debate of political points of view or ideas. In general, the statement of principles in the Guidelines favours a policy of post-facto rebuttal or correction over one of prior restraint. In particular, the Guidelines refer to the statutory expression 'likely to promote or incite to crime' and state that this prohibition should be taken to refer to utterances that can reasonably be held to lead to identifiable criminal harm 'that is to trigger an immediate and direct criminal action on the part of one or more people'.

In a noble statement of principle, the IRTC noted that the presumption in a democracy is that viewers or listeners can decide responsibly how they should respond to what is said via the media in general including the broadcast media. It noted that interviewers should be at liberty to ask political spokespersons to justify political policies and actions, even where these relate to the use of violence for political ends. Implicit in this is the liberty to respond.

The Guidelines state that in this as in all matters of major political interest or controversy the need to deal with issues in a balanced way and to ensure that the opportunity of rebuttal exists is particularly acute.

The IRTC Guidelines noted that if a decision to interview members of unlawful organisations was being considered, extreme caution should be adopted and broadcasts completed 'in exceptional circumstances only'. The Guidelines noted that in news programmes relating to unlawful organisations it was permissible to report factual material and statements. However, extreme caution should be adopted in the use of sound recordings. The Guidelines noted that in all matters of sensitivity, political or otherwise, broadcasters should adopt a careful approach in the use of live material and, where the programme format allows, should pre-record material. The Guidelines noted that especially where live interviews were being considered it was appropriate to ensure that only senior journalists should be charged with the responsibility involved. It was noted that 'senior' in this context does not refer to age necessarily 'but to experience, status or ability'. These Guidelines were still extant in July 1996.

POSTAL COMMUNICATIONS

Pursuant to s. 70 of the Postal and Telecommunications Services Act 1983 with the consent of the Minister for Transport, Energy and Communications, An Post enacted the Inland Post (Amendment) (No. 51) Scheme 1994 (SI No. 98 of 1994) which provided for increases in the parcel post rates charged for An Post's courier service. The Foreign Parcel Post (Amendment) (No. 29) Scheme 1994 (SI No. 99 of 1994) made pursuant to s. 70 of the Postal and Telecommunications Services Act 1983 authorised An Post to change the fees that may be charged for the courier services for items being sent to destinations outside the State.

TELECOMMUNICATIONS CARRIER SERVICES

Appeals process S. 111(2A) of the Postal and Telecommunications Services Act 1983 (No. 24 of 1983) as amended by the European Communities Telecommunications Services) Regulations 1992 (SI No. 45 of 1992) provides that the Minister for Transport, Energy and Communications may grant a licence for certain telecommunications services on the basis of a declaration by the applicant for the licence that the telecommunications service in respect of which the licence is being sought complies with service conditions prescribed by the Minister.

There is provision in the European Communities (Telecommunications) Services Regulations 1992 for an appeal against a refusal of the Minister to grant a licence, a decision to revoke, or a decision to suspend a licence under that Act. A person may within 21 days of the relevant notification appeal in the prescribed manner to the District Court against such a decision. The European Communities (Telecommunications Services) (Appeals) Regulations 1994 (SI No. 398 of 1994) prescribe the procedure to be followed in an appeal to the District Court where an application for a licence under s. 111(2A) of the Postal and Telecommunications Services Act 1983, as amended, is refused or a licence granted under that section of the Act is suspended or revoked.

Cellular digital land based mobile communications (GSM) The European Communities (Co-ordinated) Introduction of Public Pan-European Cellular Digital Land Based Mobile Communications – GSM) Regulations

1994 (SI No. 416 of 1994) give effect to Council Directive No. 87/372 EEC on the frequency bands designated for the co-ordinated introduction of a public pan-European cellular digital land-based mobile communications systems (GSM) in the Community. This Directive provides for the exclusive designation of certain frequency bands conforming to the European Tele-communications Standard (ETS) developed by the GSM (Global Special Mobile) Technical Committee of the European Telecommunications Stand-ards Institute (ETSI) whereby users provided with a cellular telecommuni-cations service in one Member State may gain access to the service in any other Member State. The Directive acknowledges however that some interim analogue cellular systems operate in certain radio frequency bands. The public cellular radio service provided in each Member State must conform to the European Telecommunications Standard (ETS) drawn up by the GSM (Global Special Mobile) Technical Committee of the European Telecommu-nications Standards Institute (ETSI).

Digital cordless communications   The European Communities (Digital European Cordless Telecommunications – DECT) Regulations 1994 (SI No. 168 of 1994) give effect to Council Directive No. 91/287/EEC on the frequency bands designated for the co-ordinated use of Digital European Cordless Telecommunications (DECT) within the Community. With effect from July 1, 1994 a specified frequency band is dedicated exclusively for DECT. The digital European cordless telecommunications system must conform to the European Telecommunications Standard (ETS) developed by the European Telecommunications Standards Institute (ETSI).

European Radio Communications Office   In 1990, the European Radio Communications Committee established a European Radio Communications Office as a centre of expertise on radio communications issues. A convention to establish the Office was opened for signature on June 23, 1993 at The Hague and was signed on behalf of the State on that day.

S. 42(A) of the Diplomatic Relations and Immunities Act 1967 as amended by the Diplomatic Relations and Immunities (Amendment) Act 1976 provides that the Government may by order make provisions to enable international organisations, communities or bodies, their institutions or organs and their property, and persons to have and enjoy in the State any inviolability, exemptions, facilities, immunities, privileges or rights provided for in relation to them by an international agreement to which the State is or intends to become a party.

Pursuant to the European Radio Communications Office (European Radio Communications Office) (Privileges and Immunities) Order, 1994 (SI No. 186 of 1994) the Government provided that the European Radio Communications Office shall have legal personality and shall enjoy full capacity necessary for the exercise of its function and the achievement of its purposes and may in particular: (a) enter into contracts; (b) acquire, lease, hold and dispose of movable and immovable property; (c) be a party to legal proceedings and (d) conclude agreements with States and international organisations.

General terms and conditions in relation to provision of telecommunications services The Telecommunications Scheme, 1994 (SI No. 177 of 1994), containing 111 articles and 5 schedules, consolidated with amendments the provisions of all existing schemes relating to the telecommunications services provided by Telecom Éireann other than the telemessage and foreign telegram services. This 1994 Scheme was made pursuant to s. 90 of the Postal and Telecommunications Services Act 1983 which empowers Telecom Éireann to make schemes in relation to its charges and other terms and conditions, save in so far as may otherwise be agreed between Telecom Éireann and a person availing of any such service.

The 1994 Scheme contains terms and conditions which are incorporated into the contract of each customer of Telecom Éireann and deals with such matters, *inter alia*, as suspension of service, termination of contract volume discounts, *force majeure* and other such matters.

Article 28 of the 1994 Scheme, in particular, deals with the use of telecommunications services and provides that no telecommunication service shall be used:

(a) for the transmission of any message or other matter which is grossly offensive or of an indecent, obscene, or menacing character whether addressed to a telecommunications exchange operator or any other person;

(b) for the persistent making or attempted making of calls for the purpose of causing annoyance, inconvenience or needless anxiety to any person;

(c) for the transmission of any message or other matter, which the sender knows to be false, for the purpose of causing annoyance, inconvenience or needless anxiety to any person; and, or

(d) in any manner which, in the opinion of Telecom Éireann, may adversely affect the use of any telecommunications service by other customers or which may adversely affect any telecommunications service as a whole.

The Telecommunications (Amendment) Scheme 1994 (SI No. 11 of

1994) was revoked by SI. No. 177 of 1994. The Telecommunications (Amendment) (No. 2) Scheme 1994 (SI No. 272 of 1994) provided for the introduction of an Eirpac access charge and made certain modifications to the Telecommunications Scheme 1994. 'Eirpac' is the name assigned by Telecom Éireann to its packet switched data network service.

Internal market for telecommunications services   Council Directive 90/387/EEC of 28 June 1990 on the establishment of an internal market for telecommunications services through the implementation of open network provision, provided that the Council would adopt specific open network provision conditions for leased lines. Leased lines relate to the offer of transmission capacity between network termination points and which do not include what may be termed 'on demand switching' i.e. 'switched' service offered to the public. Council Directive 92/44/EEC of June 5, 1992 as amended by Commission Decision 94/439/EC, July 15, 1994 (application of open network provision to leased telecommunications lines) was given effect to in Irish law in European Communities (Application of Open Network Provision to Leased Lines) Regulations 1994 (SI No. 328 of 1994).

Leased lines were specifically defined in the 1994 Regulations as meaning telecommunications facilities provided in the context of the establishment, development and operation of the public telecommunications network, which provide for transparent transmission capacity between network termination points and which do not include on-demand switching (switching functions which the user can control as part of the leased line provision).

The National Regulatory Authority for telecommunications, in this instance the Minister for Transport, Energy and Communications, is obliged by the 1994 Regulations to publish in an appropriate manner details of licensing and declaration requirements and conditions for the attachment of terminal equipment in respect of users of leased lines.

Telecom Éireann is obliged, pursuant to the Regulations, to provide information in respect of the technical characteristics, tariffs, supply and usage conditions of leased lines in a format to be published in accordance with the requirements set out in Annex II to the Regulations. Users have the right of appeal to the National Regulatory Authority in the event of a dispute concerning a termination date in relation to the withdrawal of a particular type of leased line. Access to and usage of leased lines were to be restricted only to ensure compliance with certain essential requirements.

VIDEO RECORDINGS

Implementation of the Video Recordings Act 1989   Several sections of
the Video Recordings Act 1989, an Act providing for the control and
regulation of the supply and importation of video recordings were made in
1994. Pursuant to the Video Recordings Act 1989 (Commencement Order)
1994, (SI No. 133 of 1994), May 12, 1994 was fixed as the day on which
certain provisions of the Video Recordings Act 1989 came into operation.
These provisions related, *inter alia*, to the certification of video works by the
Official Censor.

S. 3 of the 1989 Act came into operation on May 12, 1994 and sets out
the criteria for determining whether a supply certificate should be granted
for a video by the Official Censor. Pursuant to s. 3 of the 1989 Act the Official
Censor has a discretion to declare that a video is unfit for viewing because,
inter alia, the viewing of it would be likely to cause persons to commit crimes
whether by inciting or encouraging them to do so or by indicating or
suggesting ways of doing so or of avoiding detection. Other grounds include
criteria such as that the viewing of the video would be likely to stir up hatred
between a group of persons in the State or elsewhere on account of
their race, colour, nationality, religion, ethnic or national origins, membership of the travelling community or sexual orientation or, would tend by
reason of the inclusion in it of obscene or indecent matters, to deprave or
corrupt persons who might view it or, depict acts of gross violence or cruelty
(including mutilation or torture of humans or animals). See generally,
annotation by Professor Kevin Boyle of the Video Recordings Act 1989 in
ICLSA.

The Video Recordings Act 1989 (Supply Certificate and Labelling)
Regulations 1994 (SI No. 134 of 1994) made provision pursuant to ss. 12
and 31 of the Video Recordings Act 1989 in relation to applications for
supply certificates, labels and the labelling of video recordings by the Official
Censor. There are several classifications. The first classification provides that
the video is fit for viewing by persons generally; the next classification is fit
for viewing generally but in the case of a child under 12 years only in the
company of an responsible adult. The next category is fit for viewing by a
person aged 15 years or more. The final category (apart from refusal to grant
a supply certificate) is fit for viewing by persons aged 18 years or more.

The Video Recordings Act 1989 (Appeals) Regulations 1994 (SI No. 135
of 1994) prescribe the manner of appeals under s. 10(1) of the Video
Recordings Act 1989 against a prohibition order and under s. 10(2) against
a classification granted.

The Video Recordings Act 1989 (Registers) Regulations 1994 (SI No.
136 of 1994) prescribe the form of the Register of Certificated Video Works

and the Register of Prohibited Video Works under ss. 14 and 15 of the Video Recordings Act 1989.

The Video Recordings Act 1989 (Fees) Regulations 1994 (SI No. 137 of 1994) prescribe the fees to be charged in relation to applications for supply certificates under s. 3, appeals under s. 10 and for licences issued s. 18 of the Video Recordings Act 1989.

PUBLICATIONS

Censorship issues and issues associated with freedom of expression in the context of broadcasting were reflected in scholarly articles published in 1994. See, in general, Editorial, 'The lifting of section 31' (1994) 12 *ILT* 49, Colum Kenny 'Section 31 and the Censorship of Programmes (1994) 12 *ILT* 50; Desmond M. Clarke, 'Section 31 and Censorship: A Philosophical Perspective' (1994) 12 *ILT* 53; Kevin Boyle 'Freedom of Expression and Democracy', in Heffernan, ed., *Human Rights, A European Perspective* (The Round Hall Press, 1994); Eoin O'Dell 'Speech in a Cold Climate: "The Chilling Effect" of the Contempt Jurisdiction' in *Human Rights, a European Perspective*, above; and Gerard Quinn, 'Extending the Coverage of Freedom of Expression to Commercial Speech: A Comparative Perspective' in *Human Rights, A European Perspective*, above.

Company Law

Dr David Tomkin and Adam Mc Auley
of Dublin City University Business School

Lifting the corporate veil *Lac Minerals Ltd v. Chevron Mineral Corporation of Ireland Ltd & Ors.* [1995] 1 ILRM 161, High Court, Murphy J. Two companies, A. and B. entered into a joint venture. In order to circumvent the pre-emption clause in this joint venture agreement, A. transferred his interest in the joint venture to another company which thereupon contracted to sell it to C.

A dispute arose over the interpretation of the pre-emption clause in the joint venture agreement. It went to arbitration. The arbitrator decided that the complex arrangement had not successfully circumvented the pre-emption clause and, as part of his award, required A. to offer its interest to B. B. eventually agreed to accept A.'s offer.

C. however argued that the time limit in the pre-emption clause had expired when B. sought to accept A.'s offer. C. initiated proceedings. C. was a stranger to the joint venture agreement and had to show that it possessed some identifiable interest in it. In order to do this, *inter alia*, C. invited the court to lift the corporate veil and expose the underlying ownership interests.

In the High Court Murphy J said that since at some stage all the participants had disregarded their independent status, they could not seek now to rely on their separate legal identities.

Murphy J said that for a court to lift the corporate veil over companies in a group, two things were required. First, that the decisions of one company were so dominated by another as to refute the existence of separate identities. Second, that the interests of justice would be served by lifting the veil.

Murphy J held that B. had accepted A.'s offer within the prescribed time, and dismissed C.'s claim.

Company seal *Safeera Ltd v Wallace and O'Regan*, High Court, July 12, 1994, Morris J. Where a company's memorandum and articles prescribe how a company seal must be affixed and who must countersign, these requirements must be strictly observed if the deed sealed is to be valid.

This case does not conflict with *In re McCabe (a Bankrupt)*, Supreme Court, May 7, 1993, O'Flaherty, Egan, Denham JJ. The difference is that in *Safeera* the countersignatures on the deed were not those of two directors.

This was apparent from the discrepancy between the sealed document, the provisions of the memorandum and articles and the company resolutions. In *McCabe* the discrepancy was not obvious. The sealing provisions were on the face of it valid. *Turquand* (1856) 6 E. & B. 327 obviates the necessity of inquiry into the internal procedures anterior to compliance with the requirements in question.

Companies and *in camera* proceedings   *In the Matter of Countyglen plc (Under Investigation) and in the Matter of the Companies Act 1990 and in the Matter of an application pursuant to s. 7(4) of the Companies Act 1990: Frank Clarke (applicant)*, High Court [1995] 1 ILRM 213 (October 28, 1994). This case revisits the principles governing the hearing of company law cases *in camera*. Article 34 of the Constitution requires that the administration of justice shall be conducted in open courts by judges. Article 34 allows for *in camera* proceedings in limited and special cases.

In this case, the applicant was appointed by the High Court to investigate the affairs of the company. The inspector sought directions from the High Court. Specifically, he looked for authority to engage a firm of solicitors in Guernsey to make an application under the Criminal Justice (Fraud Investigation) (Bailiwick of Guernsey) Law 1991. This was to require the Guernsey Procurer to investigate the affairs of Dykstra Holdings Ltd (Dykstra). The inspector also sought an order extending the time for delivery of his report.

The inspector sought to have both applications heard *in camera*. Counsel for the inspector argued that this application to hear both these issues was concerned not with the administration of justice but with administrative matters. Therefore, Article 34 did not apply, and the court could hear the applications *in camera*.

In the High Court, Murphy J held that the hearing of an inspector's application by a High Court judge did not of itself constitute the administration of justice. In other company law areas, many orders are made which are merely administrative directions, not the administration of justice.

Murphy J points out that an inspector investigating a company is not engaging in the administration of justice. Therefore, a judge who gives guidance or directions as to how the inspector is to effect his investigation is likewise not engaging in the administration of justice. Seeking directions from the court enables the inspector to confirm his own position, and the propriety of his own actions.

Murphy J granted the order to the inspector to allow the matters to be heard *in camera*.

Aspects of this case are discussed by D. Tomkin & A. Dignam (1994) 'Investigations and Inspections under the Companies Act 1990', *ILT*, Vol. 12, No. 1, 26; and by D. McGrath (1993) 'Investigations Under the Companies Act 1990', *ILT*, Vol. 11, No.12, 264-268. McGrath's article examines investigations under part II of the Companies Act 1990. It examines specifically whether the Minister's stated objective of placing investigations under the auspices of the courts has been successful. The author concludes that the system has been vindicated and that the courts have dealt with investigations in a competent and expeditious manner.

Oppression: measure of damages & valuation of shares   *Irish Press plc v Ingersoll Irish Publications Ltd*, High Court, May 13, 1994, Barron J. In December 1993, Barron J found that the defendants had committed 'oppression' within the meaning of s. 205 of the Companies Act 1963. He remitted the matter for a further hearing to deal with the quantum of damages, and the value to be placed on the shares of two of the companies in the Irish Press Group. Accordingly, he delivered this judgment on these two issues.

Barron J held that the principles of assessment of damages in a s. 205 case were the same as those which apply in every tort case. The function of such damages is to put back the petitioner in the position he would have been, but for the oppression.

Barron J held that this should be achieved by replacing any assets of the undertaking lost through the period of the oppression so that the assets of the undertaking should be as near as possible or the same as they were at the commencement of the oppression.

Barron J considered that the measure of damages should be computed by reference to two factors. The first was the amount necessary to restore the assets to the figure at which they were before the oppression commenced. The second was the drop in value of the undertaking of the company since that date, measured as of the date of judgment 'on this issue': that is to say, not the date on which the s. 205 action was determined (16-21 December 1993) but rather the date of the instant judgment (May 13, 1994). The reason for Barron J's holding might be that he found that aspects of the oppression had continued even after judgment was delivered on December 21, 1993.

It may be objected, however, that Barron J lumps together two different matters: the wrong done to the company, and the oppression of its shareholders. Barron J here attempts to remedy both the wrong done to the company, and put an end to the wrong done to the shareholders.

The Supreme Court overturned the basis of Barron J's order of December 1993. It held that an award of damages cannot be made under s. 205. The function of the court under s. 205 is to make such an order as will bring the oppression complained of to an end. The Supreme Court held that when the order was made for the transfer of the shares, this ended the oppression complained of.

Receivership: charges *In The Matter of Chipboard Products Ltd (in liquidation) and in the Matter of the Companies Act 1963*, High Court, October 20, 1994, Barr J. A company created certain charges over its assets. Some of the charges were in favour of the Bank of Ireland, others in favour of the Minister for Finance. The Minister appointed a receiver. Subsequently, and by agreement with the Minister's officials, a liquidator was appointed. He arranged to look after the Minister's interests.

The liquidator claimed that because the Minister had agreed to this course of action, the Minister was not be entitled to interest in respect of sums due after the commencement of the liquidation. Barr J decided that the appointment of the liquidator as agent of the Minister for the purposes of recovering sums to due to him in such circumstances did not operate to disentitle the Minister to interest after the date of the presentation of the petition.

Payment of receiver pursuant to Conveyancing Act 1881 *In the Matter of City Car Sales Ltd (in Receivership and Liquidation) and in the Matter of the Companies Acts 1963 to 1990*, High Court [1995] 1 ILRM 221 concerns the computation and assessment of a receiver's costs. On May 27, 1983 City Car Sales Ltd (the company) issued a debenture to Allied Irish Banks plc. The company went into receivership and by deed of appointment dated March 31, 1989 a receiver and manager was appointed over the undertaking and all the assets and property of the company. The debenture expressly incorporated the provisions of ss. 19-24 of the Conveyancing Act 1881.

S. 24(6) of the Conveyancing Act 1881 entitles a receiver to retain a proportion of moneys received by him, for defrayment of his costs and expenses. The section allows a receiver to retain as remuneration a maximum of 5% on the gross amount of money received. However, if a receiver wants more than 5%, permission of the court is necessary. The receiver here retained more than 5%. The company subsequently went into liquidation.

The liquidator asked the court to exercise its statutory discretion under s. 318 of the Companies Act, 1963 to fix the amount of the receiver's fees and expenses.

First, the receiver submitted that as the receivership was not one pertaining to the income of mortgaged property, the provisions of the 1881 Act did not apply. Alternatively, he argued that if his construction of the debenture was incorrect, he would apply pursuant to s. 24(6) for the court to fix a higher rate of remuneration. Geoghegan J in the High Court held that the provisions of the 1881 Act were not confined solely to receivers of income. S. 19(2) of the 1881 Act permitted the parties to extend the provisions of that Act to other types of receivership.

In this case, the deed of appointment clearly intended the provisions of the 1881 Act to apply. The receiver's remuneration was therefore governed by s. 24(6) of the 1881 Act. This deed of appointment did not specify any rate of commission. In such a case, the receiver was entitled to retain a 5% commission, without applying to court. Here the receiver had retained more than 5% and this without court sanction.

Geoghegan J then deliberated upon what the court shall allow as remuneration. He found that the receiver had fixed his remuneration on a normal accounting basis and had acted at all times *bona fide*. The fact that the receivership had come to an end did not prevent the receiver making an application to the court to fix a higher amount in respect of his remuneration. The judge agreed that a literal construction of s. 318 of the 1963 Act gives the court a power to permit a higher amount in respect of remuneration than would otherwise have been allowed by the debenture. He noted that the purpose of s. 318 was to curb excessive remuneration being retained by a receiver.

In this case Geoghegan J found that the remuneration was clearly not excessive, and made an order under s. 24(6) of the 1881 Act. This allowed the receiver to retain what he had already taken.

The effects of an examinership on book debts, and the purpose of examinership generally   *In the Matter of The Companies (Amendment) Act 1990 and in Re Holidair Ltd* [1994] 1 ILRM 481; [1994] 1 IR 416. This case, which has attracted a large amount of commentary and criticism, returns to one of the main themes of company law, the creation of book debts, the effect of court protection on the secured creditors and their book debts, and a wider question, the role, purpose and function of an examiner.

In the *Holidair* case, two banks had lent substantial sums to companies in the Kentz group. Their lending was secured by debentures which included fixed charges over book debts. Each charge to the bank was described as a first fixed charge. The charges creating the book debts contained two important provisions. These were designed to 'freeze' the book debts. The first condition was that the borrower could not deal with the book debts in any way without the lender's prior written consent. The second condition was that the borrower had to pay the proceeds of the book debts into designated bank accounts.

The companies fell into massive arrears. The bank appointed receivers and managers on January 19. On January 21, 19 companies in the Kentz Group petitioned for court protection. The group owed huge sums of money to various creditors. The High Court dismissed the receiver and manager. It appointed an interim examiner over the group that day. The interim examiner was confirmed as examiner of the Kentz Group on January 27. On January 31 and February 3, the banks sought to use their power to nominate 'book debts receivable accounts' in AIB Clonmel.

The examiner subsequently sought leave of the High Court to exercise the borrowing powers of the directors to keep the companies functioning on a short term basis, whilst seeking to formulate proposals for a restructuring, including seeking investment. The High Court allowed the examiner to certify the sums borrowed as expenses under s. 10 of the Companies (Amendment) Act 1990. This gave him the power to borrow.

The question arose: could the examiner use the book debts as security? If he could, he would only have to raise £1.3 million to keep the group viable. If not, the examiner would have to borrow £3 million, to keep it viable.

In the High Court, Costello J dealt with whether the charges over the book debts were fixed or floating. He was faced with a plethora of Irish cases which looked at charged book debts and which came to different conclusions: see *Re Keenan Bros Ltd* [1985] IR 501, *Re Wogans (Drogheda) (No. 1)* [1993] 1 IR 157 (noted by Dr D. Tomkin & Dr A. Dignam in the 1992 Annual Review, 53-5). See on this point and generally see G. McCormack (1993) 'Company Law – Fixed or Floating: Another Charge Conundrum', *DULJ*, Vol. 15, 55; Dr J. Breslin (1995) 'Company Charges over Book Debts After Holidair and New Bullas Trading', *CLP*, Vol. 2, No. 2, 32-5).

Costello J, in the light of these authorities, held that the description of the charge in the document is not conclusive. It must be supported by conditions in the document which restrict the borrower from dealing with the charged assets in a manner 'incompatible with the essence of a floating charge'.

Costello J then considered the conditions in each of the charges. The first condition was that the borrower could not deal with the book debts in any way without the lender's prior written consent. The second condition was that the borrower had to pay the proceeds of the book debts into designated bank accounts. Costello J held that these conditions restricted the borrower from dealing with the charged assets in a manner 'incompatible with the essence of a floating charge'. The charges were therefore fixed.

The fact that the banks only designated a book debts receivable account some days after the examiner was appointed, did not affect Costello J's conclusion.

Costello J was bound by the Supreme Court's decision in *Re Wogans* (see the 1992 Annual Review, 53-5) which decides that a court may not construe a deed by reference to the subsequent conduct of the parties.

The fact that the bank designated the book debts receivable account at a very late stage represented a concession on its part to the borrowers. This non-designation in no way affected the status of the charge.

Secondly, were the debenture holders prohibited either by s. 5(2)(d) of the Companies (Amendment) Act 1990 or by an estoppel from withdrawing consent to use by the companies of the charged book debts? Costello J said that under s. 5(2)(d), no action may be taken to realise the whole or any part of property secured by a charge without the consent of the examiner.

Costello J held that by nominating specific book debts receivable accounts, each bank was taking steps to 'preserve [its] property' as opposed to taking action to 'realise [its] security'.

Before the examinership the companies were permitted the use of the book debts. Were the banks now estopped from issuing directions? Costello J held that no estoppel arose as no representation had been made to the borrowers that the banks were not going to rely upon their legal rights. The *Wogan* decision permitted a debenture holder to grant flexibility — and withdraw it — as the deed so specified. The banks could thus insist that the book debts be lodged to designated accounts. The borrowing powers accorded by the court to the examiner were no different from those exercised by the directors. This meant that the examiner would have to obtain the consent of the bank before borrowing. The companies and the examiner appealed.

In the Supreme Court, Blayney J dealt with the first question whether the book debts charge was fixed or floating. The rest of the court concurred with his decision. Blayney J agreed with Costello J that the description of the charge was not conclusive. He agreed with Romer LJ's factors *In Re Yorkshire Woolcombers' Association Ltd* [1903] 2 Ch 284. Three characteristics usually found in a floating charge are:

(a) a charge on a class of assets present and future;
(b) the class of assets is one which, in the ordinary course of the business of the company, would be changing from time to time; and,
(c) such that it is contemplated that, the company can continue to use the class of assets in its business in the ordinary way until some future step is taken by or on behalf of the charge holder.

Blayney J held that the *Holidair* charges satisfied criteria (a) and (b).

The remaining issue was whether the conditions in the debenture permitted the companies to continue to use these book debts in its business in the ordinary way. First, Blayney J considered the two restrictions on dealing with book debts contained within the debenture. The first prohibited the company 'without the prior consent in writing of the [bank] sell, factor, discount or otherwise charge or assign or dispose of the same'. This restriction only applied to the book debts themselves. It did *not* apply to cash received in respect of these book debts. The second condition required the companies to pay the proceeds of book debts into a designated account which the bank 'may from time to time select'. The banks attempted to argue that this clause empowered them to require the borrowers to lodge the proceeds of the book debts to any account the banks nominated.

Blayney J held that this interpretation was inconsistent with the purpose specifically set out in the debenture, to allow the companies to carry on trading 'in proper and efficient manner'. Thus the borrowers had to be able to use the book debts in the ordinary course of the company's business. This meant that the discretion to designate bank accounts was restricted to the companies' *own* bank accounts. This satisfied the third of Romer LJ's tests in *In Re Yorkshire Woolcombers' Association Ltd* [1903] 2 Ch 284. Each such charge was a floating charge.

Blayney J said that in *Keenan* and in *Wogan*, the respective debenture either nominated or provided for the nomination of a specific bank account in a bank or lending institution into which the proceeds of the book debts were paid. In addition, the debentures restricted withdrawals without prior consent of the lender therefrom. These clauses hence created fixed charges over book debts.

In *Holidair*, the debenture only covered the book debts and not the proceeds. Furthermore, there was no similar provision which nominated or provided for the nomination of a specific bank account in a bank or lending institution into which the proceeds of the book debts were to be paid. Determining that the charge was a floating charge did not change the fact that the charge had crystallised upon the appointment of a receiver and manager on January 19.

Did they de-crystallise on the appointment of an examiner? Blayney J held yes, for three reasons. One: on appointment of the examiner, the receiver could no longer act. It would accordingly have been pointless to keep the book debts frozen. Two: the purpose of the examinership was to facilitate the protection of the company and consequently of its shareholders, workforce and creditors. It would be wholly inconsistent with that purpose for the company to be deprived of the use of its book debts. They were absolutely essential for its survival during the period of protection. Blayney J went further, and in an argument scarcely calculated to appeal to the commercial sense of bankers, suggested that it was no injustice to the banks to allow the examiner to deal with the book debts. In so doing, the examiner would replace old book debts with new ones. Three: s. 5(2)(d) of the Companies (Amendment) Act 1990 prohibits the receiver from insisting that the book debts remain crystallised.

Finlay CJ's judgment deals with the examiner's power to pledge the book debts. He looked to the purpose of the Act. He stated that the Act provides a period of protection for the formulation of some scheme of arrangement, rather than an immediate liquidation or receivership of the company. He relied on McCarthy J's judgment in *Re Atlantic Magnetics (In Receivership)* [1993] 2 IR 561 at 578:

[i]t is, I believe, of great importance to bear in mind in the application of the Act that its purpose is protection — protection of the company and consequently of its shareholders, workforce and creditors. It is clear that parliament intended that the fate of the company and those who depend upon it should not lie solely in the hands of one or more large creditors who can by appointing a receiver pursuant to a debenture effectively terminate its operation and secure as best they may the discharge of the monies due to them to the inevitable disadvantage of those less protected, the Act is to provide a breathing space albeit at the expense of some creditor or creditors.

Finlay CJ identified another purpose to the 1990 Act. It was to give the company a breathing space during the relatively short protection period, if possible and appropriate.

These considerations had to be borne in mind when any ambiguity or doubt arose concerning the construction of the Act. Finlay CJ went on to examine the scope of s. 9 and s. 7 of the 1990 Act as they applied to the *Holidair* facts. He held that s. 9(1), (2) and (3) permitted the court to give powers to the examiner which the directors could have enjoyed. S. 9(4) permitted the court to transfer to the examiner other broader powers (including those of a liquidator) which directors could never enjoy.

The order made by Costello J which allowed for the examiner's borrowing was expressly made under to ss. 9 (1)-(3) and not subs. (4). The examiner had the same powers to borrow as the board of directors. As the directors were precluded from borrowing without the consent of the bank, so too was the examiner.

Finlay CJ then considered s. 7(5) of the 1990 Act, which empowers the examiner to take steps to rectify any actual or proposed detrimental acts or omissions of the company or its officers, employees, members, or creditors in relation to, *inter alia*, income and assets: the section expressly includes contracts. Finlay CJ said that the use of the words 'actual or proposed' applies to contracts already in existence prior to the examinership. He considered that the requirement to seek the banks' consent and their stated intention not to agree constituted a contract which is likely to be detrimental to the company. Therefore the examiner in this case could take rectifying steps by borrowing without the banks' permission.

Finlay CJ then considered the bank's request that proceeds of the book debts should be lodged to a nominated bank account, and that no withdrawals be permitted without the consent of the bank.

Finlay CJ held that this request and the restriction constituted an attempt to realise the bank's security and thereby a breach of s. 5(2)(d) of the 1990 Act.

The question then arose of payment of costs and expenses in an examinership. S. 29 (3) of the 1990 Act allows the examiner to certify the costs and expenses of the examinership. S. 10 provides that such certified costs if sanctioned by the court, must be paid first of all. Considering this aspect of the *Holidair* case, Finlay CJ affirmed his own judgment in *Re Atlantic Magnetics*. He held that this allows the court to sanction the payment of remuneration, costs and expenses in priority to any secured or unsecured creditor. If the unsecured assets are insufficient to meet these costs, the court may direct that these be paid out of secured assets. The Supreme Court allowed the appeal.

Two conclusions follow. First, debentures should constrain the powers of lenders to deal with book debts by ensuring that the borrower:

(a) is prohibited from selling, factoring, discounting, charging, assigning, disposing of, pledging, alienating or setting off the book debts in every fashion, so that the only way in which the borrower can deal with the book debts is to collect the entire proceeds of all of them, and,

(b) is obliged to pay these proceeds in their entirety into a designated book debts receivables account specifically in the lender's name.

The lender should ensure that other clauses in the debenture do not contradict or negate the effect of such restrictions.

Second, a misconception may arise that Finlay CJ's comments support the proposition that examiners may borrow to secure the long term viability of the company. This is not so. Cases such as *Re Edenpark* and *Re Don Bluth* (see the 1993 Annual Review, 95-7) stresses that when an examiner borrows money, such borrowings must be incurred for the purpose of keeping the company going *for the period of the examinership*. The borrowings are not justifiable by reference to the long term viability of the company.

See M. Connaughton (1994) *CLP*, Vol. 1, No. 4, 110-3; A. Campbell & K. Garrett, *Insolvency Law* (1996) 16 February, p. 12-8; M.J. Walsh, *Insolvency Law & Practice* (1995) Vol. 11 No. 5, 145-147; L. MacDermott (1994), *International Company & Commercial Law Review*, Vol. 5, No. 8,. 162-3; P.R. Dobbyn & P. Reid (1994), *Journal of International Banking Law*, Vol. 9 No. 8, 321-7; B. Judge (1994), *European Financial Services Law*, Vol. 1, No. 1, 29. For a full discussion of the entire subject see the important text book by John L. O'Donnell, *Examinerships: The Companies (Amendment) Act 1990* (Oak Tree Press, Dublin, 1994).

Examinership: certification of costs *Re Don Bluth Entertainment Ltd* [1994] 2 ILRM 436 turns on how 'paid in full' is defined in the context of examinerships and s. 29(3) of the Companies (Amendment) Act 1990. The facts of this case are set out in the 1993 Annual Review, 95. There the High Court, *inter alia*, considered an examiner's certification of a loan for $1,050,000 under ss. 10 and 29 of the Companies (Amendment) Act 1990. The lender appealed to the Supreme Court solely on the ground that the judge erred in fixing the date upon which the loan was repayable.

The High Court had directed that the sum be converted from US dollars to Irish pounds as of the date of the commencement of the liquidation of the company. The lender argued that the conversion should be calculated on the date of payment. By performing the conversion at the date of the winding up's commencement, the lender stood to lose £200,000 as a result of currency fluctuation. The Supreme Court allowed the appeal.

The question turned on whether the loan would be 'paid in full' as specified in s. 29(3) if the High Court decision stood. Blayney J held that it would not. He stated that on the date of repayment, the company would have to hand over sufficient number of Irish pounds to enable the lender to purchase $1,050,000. If the liquidator were to carry out the High Court order there would be a shortfall of some £200,000. The loan would therefore not be 'repaid in full'.

The High Court judge had erred in applying *Re Lines Bros. Ltd* [1983] Ch 1. This case concerned an unsecured debt in a foreign currency due to a creditor in a liquidation. The debt had to be paid *pari passu* with other unsecured debts. This case was distinguishable from the present case. The debt in this case was not an ordinary unsecured debt. It was a debt which under s. 29(3) is to be paid in full 'before any other claim, secured or unsecured'.

Transforming a members' voluntary winding up into a Court winding up of a quasi-Partnership Company   *In the Matter of the Companies Acts 1963-1990 and the Matter of Gilt Construction Ltd (In Voluntary Liquidation)* [1994] 2 ILRM 456. This case discusses when and if a members' voluntary winding up should be converted into a court winding up.

The company in question was a private 'quasi-partnership' company. A resolution had been passed to wind it up voluntarily, and a liquidator had been appointed. In the course of the winding up, the two shareholders of the company fell out. One of them applied to court to have the voluntary liquidation halted, and transformed into a court liquidation. He alleged that the other shareholder and the liquidator were conspiring to manipulate the assets of the company for the shareholder's own benefit.

In the High Court, O'Hanlon J expressed himself unable to determine whether or not this allegation was well-founded. He stated that essentially this was not relevant to the main issue. O'Hanlon J held that a court must be slow to dislodge a voluntary liquidator who has been validly appointed. The judge placed weight on the following three considerations. First, a voluntary liquidation was essentially simple. The transformation into a court winding up would be complex and time consuming. Second, the size of the company was relevant. This was a small company, with inconsiderable assets. The transformation would be expensive. It might dissipate all the company funds. Third, O'Hanlon J pointed out that in voluntary liquidations, there already exists a mechanism for dealing with complaints such as those of the petitioner, who was a creditor. The Act provides that the liquidator or any contributory or creditor in a voluntary winding up may apply to court in respect of any unexpected complexities which might arise in the course of such a winding up. The order was consequently refused.

Winding Up: Advertisement of the Petition *Clandown Ltd v Brid Davis* [1994] 2 ILRM 536. When is the presentation of a winding up petition an 'abuse of the court'?

The *Clandown* case involved a former director, employee and shareholder who was injuncted from advertising for a winding up petition, and proceeding further with it. She claimed the company owed her in excess of £50,000. The company disputed the debt.

In the High Court, Morris J held, here following the earlier authorities, that a winding up petition is not a legitimate means of seeking to enforce payment of a debt which is *bona fide* disputed. The amount of the claim has to be clear and incapable of dispute.

Morris J was careful not to prejudge the disputed claim, and indicated that he had no function to decide upon it. He did however conclude that on the evidence of the affidavits filed, he was not satisfied that the defendant's claim was clear and incapable of dispute. Morris J granted an injunction restraining the proceedings and the advertisement of the petition. This did not prevent the petitioner commencing proceedings for the debt, and pursuing her remedy in the ordinary way.

This case reiterates the point that the winding up process is not to be availed of in respect of disputed debts. It deals with a larger policy conflict. It balances the rights of a creditor to put an end to trading of an insolvent company, against the right of a company to avoid the importunate claim of a disgruntled or impatient creditor.

This case must be compared with Keane J's decision in *Truck and Machinery Sales Ltd v. Marubeni Komatsu Ltd*, High Court, February 23, 1996, noted by T.B. Courtney (1996), *CLP*, Vol. 3, No. 4, 106-7. This decision appears to suggest that once the petitioner has established that £1,000 or some greater sum is due, the court will grant the petition.

Statutory Changes to Company Law: 1994: Investment Limited Partnerships Act 1994 (1994 No. 24) The purpose of this Act is to provide an appropriate scheme for externally based investors to make inward investment in Ireland. It constitutes and provides for the regulation of the investment limited partnership as a vehicle for such investment.

The Act sets out a legal structure for investment limited partnerships. It provides for their regulation by the Central Bank. It excludes the application of the Limited Partnership Act 1907 to investment limited partnerships. Part II of the Act regulates the constitution of such entities. Part III regulates their formation. Part IV controls the administration of such partnerships. Part V accords specific powers to the Central Bank in connection with the regulation of investment limited partnerships. Part VI provides for the dissolution of these partnerships. The legislation is discussed in detail by D. Murphy in his annotation in *ICLSA*, 1994, 24-01, and by the same author in his article (1994) 'Investment Limited Partnerships', *CLP*, Vol. 1, No. 10, 287-94.

European Communities (Single Member Private Limited Companies) Regulations 1994 (SI No. 275 of 1994) As a result of the 12th EU Directive on Company Law, it is now possible to form a 'one person company'.

The regulations relates to all private companies limited by shares or companies limited by guarantee and having a share capital and empowers such companies to continue or to be formed as single member private companies. The statutory instrument provides for consequential alterations to, *inter alia*, the annual general meeting (for which a written decision substitutes) and to the quorum requirements. Though the Statutory Instrument permits companies to be formed or carry on business with a single member, it does not remove pre-existing requirements for there to be at least two directors. This seriously limits the value of this attempted reform. The statutory instrument modifies s. 36 of the Companies Act 1963, which relates to a private company which carries on business with less than the minimum of two members. S. 36 provided that after six months the remaining member became personally liable without limitation of liability for the company's debts. This provision is obviously now inapplicable to one-person companies. SI No. 306 of 1994 provides for the requisite forms for the conversion of a private limited company of the traditional sort to the new one-person company, and vice versa. SI No. 275 of 1994 (which came into force on October 1, 1994) is discussed by T.B. Courtney & B. Hutchinson (1994), 'The Single Member Private Company Regulations: Perpetuating an Anomaly', 1994, *CLP* Vol. 1, No. 11, 307-15.

Companies (Forms) Order 1994 (SI No. 100 of 1994) The Companies (Forms) Order, 1994, SI No. 100 of 1994, brought into law on April 27, 1994, sets out the requisite forms which must now be used in order to return information under Part XI of the Companies Act 1963 and the European Communities (Branch Disclosures) Regulations 1993.

New publications Thomas B. Courtney with G. Brian Hutchinson, *The Law of Private Companies* (Butterworths (Ireland) Ltd, 1994); and Thomas B. Courtney, *CLR* (Brehon Publishing Ltd, 1994).

The *Law of Private Companies* analyses and digests the major aspects of Irish company law legislation and case-law, and is an addition to the growing number of texts on Irish commercial law. The 1994 (and 1995) edition(s) of Thomas B. Courtney's *CLR* serve to update the text-book, and also abstract relevant material from *CLP* of which Courtney is the editor, and which is a forum for the discussion of company law issues.

Conflicts of Law

ADMIRALTY PROCEEDINGS

In the 1989 Review 69-73, we analysed the Jurisdiction of Courts (Maritime Convention) Act 1989, which incorporated into Irish law the Brussels Arrest Convention 1952. The Act fell for consideration in The *MT 'Marshal Gelovani'; Intergraan B.V. v The Owners and All Persons Claiming an Interest in the MT 'Marshal Gelovani'*, High Court, June 2, 1994. A Netherlands company in dispute with a Georgian shipping company in relation to an alleged breach of a charter party relating to a vessel owned by the shipping company, was given liberty by Kinlen J to arrest another vessel owned by the shipping company, which was discharging cargo at an Irish port. The shipping company later successfully sought the release of the vessel.

Georgia is not a party to the Convention. The nett issue in the case was whether the plaintiff was entitled under the Convention to arrest a ship in respect of an alleged breach of charter party by a sister ship where both vessels flew the flag of a non-contracting state and were in the same ownership. It seemed clear to Barr J that the plaintiff would be so entitled if the Republic of Georgia was a contracting state, under Article 3, read in conjunction with Articles 1(1) and 8(1). Article 8(2), dealing with the arrest of ships flying the flag of a non-contracting state, provides as follows:

> A ship flying the flag of a non-contracting state may be arrested in the jurisdiction of any contracting state in respect of any of the maritime claims enumerated in Article 1, or of any other claim for which the law of the contracting state permits arrest.

Article 3 provides that:

> [a] claimant may arrest either the particular ship in respect of which the maritime claim arose or any other ship which is owned by the person who was, at the time when the maritime claim arose, the owner of the particular ship.

The question requiring resolution was whether Article 8(2) opened the door to Article 3 and permitted the arrest of a ship in connection with a maritime claim against a sister ship where both vessels fly the flag of a non-contracting state. Barr J thought that the answer had to be in the negative. Although the Oireachtas had legislative power to provide for the sister ship arrest of a vessel within Irish jurisdiction which was flying the flag of a non-contracting state, no such power had in fact been conferred by the 1989 Act or any other statutory provision.

In seeking to interpret Article 8(2), Barr J derived much support from the fact that the Convention, being an international treaty, was a creature of public international law and bound by public international law principles. It was a long-established general principle, enshrined in the Vienna Convention on the Law of Treaties 1961, that any state not party to an international treaty or Convention could not be bound by it. Therefore it would not have been lawful for the contracting states to incorporate into the Convention a provision, such as the right to arrest a sister ship, applicable to the ships of non-contracting states, where some individual contracting states had had no such provision in their domestic law previously. Subject to marginal widening of the range of maritime claims in Article 1, Article 8(2) was essentially no more than a restatement of pre-existing maritime law whereby a ship flying the flag of a non-contracting state might be arrested in the jurisdiction of a contracting state in respect of the same maritime claims for which the ships of contracting states might be arrested — those enumerated in Article 1 but also extended to included any other claim for which the law of the contracting state permitted arrest. Barr J considered that the fact that arrest of ships registered in contracting and non-contracting states was dealt with in separate subsections of Article 8 was strongly supportive of this interpretation:

> It could not have been otherwise having regard to the general principles of public international law . . . with which the framers of the Convention were obliged to conform.

CHILD ABDUCTION

The matter of child abduction fell for discussion in several decisions in 1994, as the courts continued to give guidance on the scope of several crucial concepts in the Hague and Luxembourg Conventions, which were given legal effect in Ireland by legislation in 1991: see the 1991 Review, 81-6.

The Hague Convention Under Article 13(b) of the Hague Convention, the court is not bound to order the return of a child who was wrongfully removed from the state of his or her habitual residence where there is a grave risk that the return would expose the child to physical or psychological harm or otherwise place the child in an intolerable situation. The Irish courts have endorsed the test laid down by the Court of Appeal in *Re A. (a minor) Abductions* [1988] 1 FLR 365: cf. *In re Y.A.A., a infant; M.A. v P.R. (otherwise known as P.A.)*, High Court, Flood J., July 23, 1992, *C.K. v C.K.* [1994] 1 IR 25 (Supreme Court, affirming High Court (Denham J), 1992). The question of harm is inevitably one of degree. In *M.D.P. v S.M.B.*, High Court, July 8, 1994 (reversed on another issue, *sub nom, In re R. (a minor); P. v B.* [1994] 3 IR 507), Budd J had to deal with allegations of 'incidents of physical violence' by the father, apparently on the mother of the child. The mother, who had been living with the father in Spain before bringing the child back to her home in Ireland, also alleged that the father drank to excess and smoked in the presence of the child, who was aged two at the time of her removal.

Budd J referred to other Irish cases on the issue. He described *In re Y.A.A., a infant; M.A. v P.R. (otherwise known as P.A.)*, above (analysed in the 1992 Review, 110-2) as 'a very strong case indeed.' There the mother had fled from the father, stricken with fear for her own safety and that of her child. In *R.G. v B.G.*, High Court, November 12, 1992, analysed in the 1992 Review 112, there had been very strong evidence of instances of violence towards the children by the father when he had taken drink. Costello J had accepted that the mother had left home in a state of fear for the safety of the children and that she was very frightened of the father's violence towards herself and the children.

In the instant case, whilst Budd J, on the basis of the evidence of a clinical psychologist, admitted to having 'a real apprehension and anxiety' about the mother returning to Spain so far as her health and welfare might be affected, his apprehension was 'nowhere near' a feeling that there was a grave risk to the child. Accordingly he held that Article 13(b) did not apply. This finding was not appealed.

It should be noted that the clinical psychologist's assessment was based on what the mother had told her; this witness was not in a position, therefore, to assist the court as to what had happened when the parties had cohabited in Spain. Budd J did not expand on the allegations of incidents of physical violence by the father. Both the father and the mother had given oral evidence. All the reader of the judgment can do is note that these allegations were not established to Budd J's satisfaction.

In *H. v Ireland*, Supreme Court, May 19, 1994, the question of a potential clash of jurisdictions arose. The Supreme Court had earlier made an order that, if a minor who was the subject-matter of the proceedings was returned to the State, the Garda Síochána should bring him before the High Court as soon as possible. A fortnight later, the English Court of Appeal, relying on

Article 13 of the Hague Convention, had refused to return the minor to Ireland, had made him a ward of court, placed him in the interim care and control of named relations, given the father visiting access and ordered that the minor was not to be removed from the jurisdiction or from the care and control of his relations, save with the leave of the court. The minor's mother was ordered not to make contact with the relations.

The minor's mother sought orders declaring that, by virtue, *inter alia*, of the Supreme Court's earlier order, the minor should be no longer deemed to be in her custody and directing the Director of Prosecutions to prosecute the minor's father in relation to the abduction of the minor from the State. Barron J ordered that the matter be adjourned generally with liberty to re-enter when the minor returned to the jurisdiction. The Supreme Court affirmed.

As to the first order sought by the appellant, Denham J stressed the inappropriateness of making an order on the issue of the minor's custody while he was in England:

> If he returns to Ireland the [earlier] order of the Supreme Court . . . will operate. As long as the minor remains in England these proceedings are a moot, and in view of the well established jurisprudence of this Court on the subject of moots, together with the fundamental concept in matters relating to children that their welfare is the paramount concern of the court and that circumstances change and require different solutions as children's lives evolve, it is not appropriate now to make an order on the issue of the custody of the minor.

The Supreme Court declined to order the Director of Public Prosecutions to prosecute the minor's father on the basis, first, that the Director is independent in the performance of his duties (cf. *H. v Director of Public Prosecutions*, Supreme Court, May 19, 1994) and secondly that the minor's mother had made no previous complaint to the Gardaí and the minor's father and the minor was out of the jurisdiction.

In *In re P.K. and A.K., infants; N.K. v J.K.* [1994] 3 IR 483, Morris J considered the meaning of acquiescence in the retention of children within the jurisdiction for the purposes of Article 13 of the Hague Convention. The parties had been married in England in 1985. There were two young sons, aged eight and four. The husband had taken them to Ireland in June 1993, after unhappy differences had arisen between the spouses. The wife sought their return.

The first question was whether there had been a wrongful removal or retention of the boys, within the meaning of Article 3 of the Hague Convention. Morris J rejected the wife's contention that her consent to their *removal* had not been voluntary. The evidence in the case, including her instructions to her solicitors, the stance she had taken in earlier litigation and the language that she had used on a postcard addressed to her children (where she had written 'Sorry' and 'Please forgive me') suggested to the Judge that she had not acted under duress even though the parties during their married life together 'had displayed violence to one another'.

Morris J went on to hold that the husband had wrongfully *retained* the children in Ireland since, when the mother visited the children in Ireland in September 1993, the husband had made clear to her that she could have full access to them only if she agreed to live with her husband and children as part of the family. This constituted a denial of her rights under England's Children's Act 1989.

As to acquiescence, Morris J accepted as a correct statement of the manner in which a court should approach the question Waite J's observations in *W. v W. (Child Abduction: Acquiescence)* [1993] 2 FLR 211, at 217 to the effect that:

> [t]he gist of the definition can, perhaps, be summarised in this way. Acquiescence means acceptance. It may be active, arising from express words or consent, or passive, arising by inference from silence or inactivity. It must be real in the sense that the parent must be informed of his or her general right of objection, but precise knowledge of legal rights and remedies and specifically the remedies under the Hague Convention is not necessary. It must be ascertained on a survey of all relevant circumstances, viewed objectively in the round. It is in every case a question of degree to be answered by considering whether the parent has conducted himself in a way that would be inconsistent with his later seeking a summary order for the child's return.

In the instant case, apart for one reference in a letter in June 1993 from her solicitors, there was 'no hint or suggestion' that the wife had retreated from the agreed position that the children would return to Ireland with their father until he was served with the proceedings in April 1994. She had confirmed in writing to her husband in July 1993 that she had no intention of trying to get the boys back from him at that time. Morris J was of the view that it was probably in early October 1993 that the wife had decided to take steps to get the children back. She had not learned of the Hague Convention until the following November or December. Morris J considered that the four-month period from June to October constituted acquiescence in the children's removal and retention. In these circumstances, the court was not bound to order the return of the children but was left with a discretion. Morris J adjourned the proceedings to enable him to hear evidence as to how he should exercise that discretion.

In *In re R. (a minor); P. v B.* [1994] 3 IR 507, to which we have already referred, the Supreme Court also endorsed Waite J's observations in *W. v W. (Child Abduction: Acquiescence)* [1993] 2 FLR 211, at 217 on the meaning and scope of 'acquiescence' under the Hague Convention. Denham J (Hamilton CJ and Egan J concurring) also quoted, with apparent approval, Lord Donaldson MR's observations in *In re A. (Minors) (Abduction: Acquiescence)* [1992] 2 FLR 14, at 29 that:

> [i]n context, the difference between 'consent' and 'acquiescence' is simply one of timing. Consent, if it occurs, precedes the wrongful taking or retention. Acquiescence, if it occurs, follows it. In each case it may be expressed or it may be inferred from conduct, including inaction, in circumstances in which different conduct is to be expected if there were no consent or, as the case may be, acquiescence. Any consent or acquiescence must, of course, be real.

In the instant case, an Irish woman, who had been living for three years in Spain with a Spanish man, had brought their two-year old daughter home with her to Ireland. The mother's father had come to Spain to accompany her and her child home because she was poorly. He had assured the child's father that the mother was only going home to recuperate, the inference being that she would in due course return to Spain. The mother had come home on other previous occasions with the child and later had returned to Spain. On this occasion, the child's father had been informed immediately of the safe arrival in Ireland of the mother and the child. He had phoned her a number of times and she had told him that she 'needed time' to sort herself out. The child's father was under the impression that she would return in due course because she had previously done so. When time moved on, without her returning, the father 'set the wheels in motion for a return to be requested and for legal steps to be taken' (*per* Budd J in the High Court proceedings). Nearly nine months elapsed between the departure of the mother and child and the issuing of proceedings in the High Court.

Budd J considered that, the father could not be blamed for any delay in consulting a lawyer or for any delay that might have arisen thereafter. The Supreme Court agreed. Denham J concluded that there had been 'no long term acceptable of a state of affairs.' In all the circumstances, applying the correct test to the evidence, it was clear that there had been no acquiescence by the father.

In this case, the Supreme Court addressed the important question of undertakings given, or required to be given, where a court is ordering the return of a minor to the state from which he or she has wrongfully been abducted. Whilst the matter arose for consideration in the context of the

Hague Convention, it seems clear that what the Court had to say would apply with equal force to proceedings under the provision of the Luxembourg Convention.

The phenomenon of undertakings is not a new one. In *C.K. v C. K.* [1994] 1 IR 250, Denham J accepted an undertaking in relation to the Hague Convention: see the 1993 Review 128-9; and in *R.J. v M.R.* [1994] 1 IR 271, analysed in the 1993 Review, 131, the Supreme Court had accepted undertakings in proceedings under the Luxembourg Convention. English courts have acted similarly.

Denham J (Hamilton CJ and Egan J concurring) was satisfied that undertakings might be given by a party to proceedings under the 1991 Act and accepted by the court. They were 'entirely consistent' with the Act and the Hague Convention, since they were for the welfare of the child during the transition from one jurisdiction to another. Undertakings might be of particular relevance to very young children. Undertakings were compatible with international law and, when for the welfare of the child, were in accord with the child's constitutional protection. Undertakings might also protect parents in their roles and in the exercise of their rights under the Constitution.

In the instant case, the father, who was seeking the return to Spain of his daughter, had given undertakings to the High Court that he would pay the mother a weekly sum worth £190, by way of maintenance for herself and the child, that he would lodge five months' maintenance in the mother's account and that he would pay rent on the parties' apartment, giving the mother the entitlement to select alternative accommodation up to the value of £250 per month.

Denham J was satisfied that these conditions were reasonable in the circumstances to protect the young child on her return to the jurisdiction of the Spanish courts. They did not in any way usurp the jurisdiction of the Spanish courts to determine the questions of custody and access.

In the High Court Budd J had accepted these conditions but he had also addressed the long-term education and maintenance of the child and the question of bi-annual visits of the child to Ireland. In doing so, he had, in Denham J's opinion, considered matters more appropriately determined by the Spanish courts. In adjourning the proceedings pending the resolution of issues such as the provision of a car for the mother and the type of residence she and her child should have, Budd J, with the best of motives, had lost sight of the necessity in law to act expeditiously to return the child to the country of her habitual residence. The Hague Convention envisaged a summary process to ensure the prompt return of children after wrongful removal.

Accordingly the Supreme Court held that the child should be returned to Spain on the basis of the reasonable undertakings that it had identified.

Luxembourg Convention   In *In re A., a minor; (a Minor); S.M. v A.J.B.* [1994] 3 IR 491, Morris J addressed a number of issues relating to the Luxembourg Convention on the Recognition and Enforcement of Decisions Concerning the Custody of Children and the Restoration of Custody of Children, which was given effect in Irish law by the Child Abduction and Enforcement of Court Orders Act 1991. See the 1991 Review, 81-6. The plaintiff, the mother of a minor born in 1984, sought the return of the child to England. The minor had been residing there with the defendant, his father, pursuant to an order of a magistrates' court in England. The plaintiff had been given access rights by that court. The father had later taken the child with him to Ireland.

The plaintiff claimed that the child should be returned to the jurisdiction of the English courts, on the basis of Article 1, which provides that:

> [a] decision relating to custody given in a contracting state shall be recognised and, where it is enforceable in the state of origin, made enforceable in every other contracting state.

Under Article 1(c), an order relating to access is included within the definition of a 'decision relating to custody'. The defendant argued first that the plaintiff's proofs were defective in that the plaintiff's affidavit of laws had failed to state that the order of the magistrates' court was enforceable in the state of origin. Morris J had little hesitation in rejecting this submission. He did 'not consider that it represented a realistic or proper approach to the consideration of the effect of a court order made in England, valid on its face and made with apparent jurisdiction'. Morris J had no greater sympathy for the defendant's contention that the affidavit of laws had failed to establish an improper removal of the minor within the meaning of Article 1(d); once there was factual evidence before the court which led the court to conclude that a wrongful removal had occurred, it was unnecessary for the affidavit of laws to deal with the matter.

The defendant next argued that the obligation resting on the Irish court to recognise and enforce the order of the magistrates' court did not necessarily require that the child be returned to England: Article 11(2) gave the court competence 'to fix the conditions' for the implementation and exercise of the rights of access. Morris J rejected this argument. He pointed to the provisions as to access which were set out in the English order: these were that the plaintiff was to have contact with the minor in Oldham, Lancashire 'on Saturday between 10 a.m. and 6 p.m.' and that the minor was to be transported by taxi or through a third party to avoid any contact between the parents. Morris J did not accept that the Irish High Court had any jurisdiction to interfere with these arrangements. To do so would contravene Article 9(3), which provides that 'in no circumstances may the foreign decision be reviewed as to its substance'.

Even if the arrangements relating to transportation by taxi or by a third party could be varied on the basis that this amounted to no more than fixing the conditions for the implementation and exercise of the right of access in accordance with Article 11(2), Morris J did not see, from a practical point of view, that there was any method whereby the minor could be made available to the plaintiff on Saturdays in Oldham between 10 a.m. and 6 p.m. Any such arrangement, he thought, 'would be . . . wildly impractical and unrealistic'. The only way in which the provisions relating to the plaintiff's access to the minor could be implemented was by returning him to the jurisdiction of the English Courts.

The defendant unsuccessfully invoked Article 10(1)(b), which authorises the refusal to recognise and enforce the order of a foreign court:

> if it is found that by reason of a change of circumstances, including the passage of time, not including a mere change in the residence of the child after an improper removal, the effects of the original decision are manifestly no longer in accordance with the welfare of the child.

The defendant contended that the only evidence relevant to this aspect of the case was that contained in his affidavit, to the effect that he and the minor had been subjected to threats from the plaintiff's boyfriend. Morris J interpreted this evidence differently:

> Assuming that every word . . . is correct, then what is happening is that the plaintiff's boyfriend . . . is threatening the defendant with violence if he goes near the plaintiff or the [parties' two girls, residing with the plaintiff]. There is nothing to suggest that the [minor] is not welcome to be in contact with the plaintiff. There is nothing which would indicate that it is in the best interests of the [minor] to discontinue this association with the plaintiff. . . .

Nothing that the minor had said to Morris J (who had sought to ascertain his view, as Article 14(1)(a) required) supported the defendant in advancing his case under Article 10(1)(b).

The defendant argued that, in exercising his discretion under Article 10, Morris J should take into account several factors which leant against ordering the child's return. These were the *lapse of time* before the plaintiff had activated the court, the *reasons* why the child had been removed from the jurisdiction, the child's *age* and *means by which access might be provided* other than in accordance with the method prescribed in the original order.

Morris J acknowledged the essential relevance of these factors but considered that they were not the only matters to be taken into account. He stressed the fact that the defendant had to show that the original decision was 'manifestly no longer in accordance with the welfare of the child'. He quoted in aid Finlay CJ's statement in *R.J. v M.R.* [1994] 1 IR 271, at 289 to the effect that the insertion of this word must indicate that the standard of proof was 'something more than the probability appropriate for the ordinary proof in a civil action.' (cf. our criticism of this strategy: 1993 Review, 131-5.) He considered that the Chief Justice's approach was reflected in Booth J's remarks in *Re L. (Child Abduction; European Convention)*, December 12, 1991 that:

> [w]here orders have been made the purpose of the Act is to enable the court to give effect to them. Only in circumstances where it is clear that such a return would be manifestly — and that is the word used in Article 10(1)(b) — against the interests of the child and that the original decision is manifestly no longer in accordance with the welfare of the child should the court exercise its discretion not to comply with the spirit and terms of the Act and Convention.

Morris J expressed his agreement with this statement which, incidentally, overstates the burden on the party opposing the return of the child. There is no express requirement to establish that the *return* would be manifestly against the interests of the child. Such a conclusion no doubt flows almost automatically from what *is* required to be established but nonetheless, in expressing as two separate hurdles what should properly be reduced to one, Booth J misstated the true burden resting on the party opposing the child's return.

At all events, Morris J made an order declaring that the minor had been wrongfully removed from the jurisdiction of the English courts and directing that he be returned to that jurisdiction.

DEFAMATION

The M.V. 'Anton Lopatin': Scofish International Ltd v The Owners and All Persons Claiming an Interest in the M.V. 'Anton Lopatin', High Court, October 18, 1994 concerned an international dispute between the plaintiffs, Scottish and Latvian companies, and the defendant, a New York company, arising from the chartering of a fishing vessel. The plaintiffs claimed that the defendant was in breach of contract in purporting to sell fish from the vessel to a third party; the defendant sought to counterclaim, alleging that the plaintiffs had induced a breach of contract and were guilty of wrongful arrest of the vessel; the defendant also claimed damages for libel based on a letter written by one of the plaintiffs which alleged that the defendant had not been lawfully entitled to sell the fish.

The parties by written agreement mutually accepted the exclusive jurisdiction of the Irish courts to try the dispute that had arisen regarding the plaintiffs' claim for damages for breach of contract. This agreement also provided that the parties agreed that the proper law of the contract was Irish law and that the dispute should be tried according to Irish law. It said nothing about counterclaims.

The plaintiffs sought under O. 21, r.14 of the Rules of the Superior Courts 1986 to have the counterclaims excluded. Barr J held that the counterclaims alleging inducing breach of contract and wrongful arrest of the vessel should not be excluded since they all arose out of the same business relationship which was the subject-matter of the plaintiffs' claim. He excluded the counterclaim alleging libel, however.

Barr J appeared to concede that the issue of defamation stood or fell on the court's findings as to the plaintiffs' claim and the defendant's other counterclaims since, if the contract had been frustrated, as the defendant alleged, then the defendant would have been lawfully entitled to sell the fish as it had done and the complaint would have been defamatory. (The judgment contains no discussion of whether the defence of qualified privilege would have arisen; that issue was clearly consequential and subsidiary to the primary question of the *prima facie* defamatory quality of what had been written.) The reason for excluding the defendant's counterclaim for libel was that the plaintiffs had a *prima facie* right to have the issue of defamation tried by jury. The other issues were not justiciable by jury. If the defendant wished to persist in bringing an action for defamation against the plaintiffs, it should await the outcome of the existing action. If that was decided in its favour, it seemed to Barr J that it must succeed in establishing defamation by the plaintiff who wrote the letter as it would be bound by the judgment of the High Court as *res judicata* that the defendant had been lawfully entitled to sell the fish. On that basis, the defamation action would be likely to be in essence an assessment of damages.

Accordingly, Barr J held that the defendant's claim for defamation should not proceed in the instant action by way of counterclaim but, if taken, should be the subject matter of a separate action. Barr J added that:

[t]his in turn would have to be brought in another jurisdiction unless the parties again agree to accept the jurisdiction of this court in that regard.

The result is surely less than satisfactory, though this is not in any way the responsibility of the judge. The parties' choice of the Irish courts as having exclusive jurisdiction to deal with their dispute is seriously compromised by having elements of that dispute detached and left to the vagaries of an unregulated jungle of competing states' laws, compounded by an equally impenetrable thicket of choice of law rules. All of these difficulties flow from the fact that certain issues in Irish law are disposed of by the judge, others by the jury. This problem can be dealt with satisfactorily within the domestic system. The idea that the defendant's counterclaim for libel should have been cast outside the Irish legal system is unfortunate.

There are strong arguments why the *res judicata* principle should not apply transnationally. Outside the context of conventions which address the problem, it is a matter of contingency whether the laws of evidence of another jurisdiction take the view that *res judicata* should extend to the prior determination of the issue by a *foreign* court. Certainly Irish law is not so generous. A desirable solution might have been that the counterclaim for defamation be heard, in separate proceedings with a jury, by the Irish High Court.

FOREIGN DIVORCE

In the 1993 Review, 201, we discussed the case of *W. v W.* [1993] ILRM 294, where the Supreme Court held that the doctrine of the domicile of dependency of married women had not survived the promulgation of the Constitution and, further, that the traditional rule whereby a foreign divorce would be recognised if obtained in the country of the common domicile of the spouses should be replaced by a rule affording recognition to a foreign divorce obtained in the country of domicile of one of the spouses. A change on these lines had been effected prospectively by the Domicile and Recognition of Foreign Divorces Act 1985.

The same issue fell for consideration in *Clancy v Minister for Social Welfare*, High Court, February 18, 1994. The case involved a refusal by the defendant to give a widow's pension to the plaintiff, who had gone through a ceremony of marriage in England with a man whose domicile was at all stages Irish, the man having formerly married in Ireland and been divorced by his wife in England. The refusal was based on the legal view in the Department of Social Welfare that, even if the first wife's domicile would be regarded as English, ignoring the doctrine of dependent domicile, the divorce could not be recognised under Irish law as it had not been obtained in the country of the *common domicile of the spouses*.

In an extensive judgment, Budd J laid great emphasis on Barr J's judgment in *M. (C.) v M. (T.)* [1988] ILRM 456, which we analyse in the 1988 Review, 73-80, 112-3. He nonetheless accepted that Barr J's holding that the domicile of dependency had not survived the enactment of the Constitution did raise certain problems:

> It involves the resulting effect that the number of the pre-1986 foreign divorces entitled to recognition has been increased and there must also be implications in respect of rights of remarriage, succession, mainte- nance and adoption. One can readily envisage situations in which new legal relationships have already been entered into in reliance on the old common law domicile principle: for instance, citizens may have been advised that their spouse's foreign divorce is not entitled to recognition because of the former wife's dependent domicile rule and now this advice may no longer be correct. In some cases the position of a spouse whose legal entitlements depend on the non-recognition of a foreign divorce may have disimproved.

Budd J also noted that the manner in which certain children's domicile of origin was determined by 'where the child's mother is married' might now have to be altered:

> [F]or example, if the father has an Irish domicile and the mother has a French domicile, then the child will no longer have the Irish domicile by virtue of the mother's dependent domicile on her husband's domi- cile.

Budd J's anxieties are worthy of close attention. They represent the first judicial acknowledgment of the concern we expressed in the 1988 Review, 73-7, that retrospective legislative or judicial abolition of the domicile of dependency of married women must logically impact on the traditional rules relating to the domicile of children, which are infected with the same discriminatory bias against married women.

In his review of earlier decisions on recognition of foreign divorces, Budd J evinced some unease about the lack of certainty in its application of the ground for non-recognition formulated by Barrington J in *L.B. v H.B.*, High Court, July 21, 1980. There Barrington J had held that the collusion between the parties in obtaining a divorce in France based on false facts relating to the ground for a decree had amounted to 'a substantial defeat of justice', which warranted the denial of recognition by the Irish courts to the decree, even though there had been no misrepresentation as to the *jurisdictional* competence of the French divorce court. Budd J speculated that the possible rationale of the decision in *L.B. v H.B.* had been that the extent of the deception practiced on the French court had been such that the parties' conduct had gone 'beyond that line which divides mere impropriety from a substantial defeat of justice and accordingly [that] it would be contrary to Irish public policy to recognise such a foreign divorce'. While recognising the need for this judicial discretion, Budd J counselled that it should be 'confined to extreme cases'. There was, he thought:

> a peril in the widening of the area of judicial discretion on foot of notional doctrines of public policy which can lead to uncertainty with regard to marital status. It is vital that in matters of determination of marital status, lawyers should be able to ascertain the law with certainty so that they may give an answer to the client's question: 'Am I married or not?'

Budd J expressed the view that, 'if a divorced spouse were given a right to maintenance and ancillary relief in appropriate cases and such rights could be enforced in this State, then this might obviate some of the very real practical injustices that are caused after a decree of divorce or legal separation.' (This has since taken place: see Part III of the Family Law Act 1995.)

Budd J considered that he was not required to address the argument, advanced by counsel for the plaintiff, that it was not material to the validity in the State of the foreign marriage that the earlier divorce decree was not recognised here, provided it was a valid divorce decree under the laws of the State that granted it. Whilst declining to resolve the issue, Budd J did allow himself the observation that:

> in general it would seem preferable to avoid limping marriages and the situation which could arise in which a person could be regarded as a bigamist in one jurisdiction and a married person in another jurisdiction.

It must be admitted that the public policy underlying the courts' approach to the question of recognising, or denying recognition to, foreign divorces has been in disarray since the Supreme Court's decision in *W. v W.* The willingness of the courts to identify the *desideratum* of avoiding limping marriages cannot be reconciled with the protection of lifelong marriage which Article 41 contained prior to the introduction of divorce in 1995. *W. v W.* and *Clancy* were, of course, decided before this fundamental constitutional transformation. It must be obvious that states with a no-fault divorce regime, far from adopting restrictive private international law rules relating to recognition of foreign divorces and subsequent marriages, will tilt towards recognising the latest relationship, formalised as marriage, for the time being. The desire to afford recognition to the most recent relationship has led the English courts to recognise a second (or subsequent) marriage, valid according to the *lex domicilii*, even where it was preceded by a divorce that was not recognised under the rules of English private international law. The contemporary English propensity to recognise the later marriage has the effect of withdrawing recognition to the earlier marriage whose ongoing validity could not have been contested. This withdrawing of recognition is based essentially on a premise of the capacity to enter into bigamous (or plural) marriages, since the trigger for recognition of the later marriage is not connected in any way with the earlier divorce: the fact that the divorce was not recognised under English private international law was of no relevance.

For Irish courts, prior to the introduction of divorce into Irish law, to consider themselves obliged to chase after these developments, in the name of avoiding limping marriages, would seem misconceived.

FOREIGN PENAL LAW

In *'The Antelope'* 10 Wheaton (1825) 66, at 123, Marshall CJ observed that 'the courts of no country execute the penal laws of another'. The broad thrust of this statement remains true today, though debate naturally takes place as to what qualities are essential to make a law a penal one for these purposes. In the Privy Council case of *Huntington v Attrill* [1893] AC 150, at 157, Lord Watson quoted with approval what Gray J had said in the US Supreme Court decision of *Wisconsin v Pelican Insurance Co.* (1888) 127 US (2) Davis 265, 32 L Ed 239, at 243:

> The rule that the courts of no country execute the law of another applies not only to prosecutions and sentences for crimes and misdemeanors, but to all suits in favour of the State for the recovery of pecuniary penalties for any violation of statutes for the protection of its revenue or other municipal laws, and to all judgments for such penalties.

Lord Watson then commented:

> A proceeding, in order to come within the scope of the rule must be in the nature of a suit in favour of the State whose law has been infringed. All the provisions of municipal statutes for the regulation of trade and trading companies are presumably enacted in the interest and for the benefit of the community at large; and persons who violate these provisions are, in a certain sense, offenders against the State law, as well as against individuals who may be injured by their misconduct. But foreign tribunals do not regard these violations of statute law as offences against the State, unless their vindication rests with the State itself, or with the community which it represents. Penalties may be attached to

them, but that circumstances will not bring them within the rule, except in cases where these penalties are recoverable at the instance of the State. . . .

The matter fell for consideration in *Bank of Ireland v Meeneghan* [1994] 3 IR 111. The defendant had been charged in England with being knowingly concerned in the fraudulent evasion of Value Added Tax. The English High Court had made a restraint order under Part VI of the British Criminal Justice Act 1988, restraining him from disposing or dealing with his assets in any way save for a weekly allowance to cover legal and living expenses. He was admitted to bail but whilst his trial was pending he absconded. Warrants for his arrest were then issued.

For some years previously the defendant had been a customer of the English-registered plaintiff bank, which carried on business in Ireland and in England and was registered in England. The proceedings were concerned with one of his accounts, which was in the branch office of the bank in Castlebar. The restraint order had specifically referred to this account and restrained the defendant from dealing with it. The order provided that, in so far as the order purported to have extra-territorial effect, no person would be affected by it unless he or she was subject to the jurisdiction of the Court, had been given notice of the order and was able to prevent acts outside the jurisdiction of the Court which would assist in the breach of the terms of the order. The defendant applied to the Bank for payment of the sums he held in the Castlebar deposit. The Bank, concerned about the legal effect of the restraint order, instituted interpleader proceedings as to whether the money on deposit was the property of the defendant or of Britain's Commissioners of Customs and Excise.

The Commissioners did not make any proprietary claim to the monies in the Castlebar deposit. They accepted that they could not establish that it represented VAT to which they were by law beneficially entitled. Their claim was based on the restraint order; they asserted that its effect was that the defendant could not lawfully require the bank to pay him the money it owed him on this account.

Costello J closed examined the relevant provisions of the 1988 Act. Part VI of the Act gave powers to both the Crown Courts and Magistrates' Courts to make confiscation orders. Under s. 71 the court had power to make a confiscation order against an offender where:

(a) he was found guilty of any offence to which Part VI applied; and
(b) it was satisfied —

(i) that he had benefited from that offence or from that offence taken

together with some other offence of which he was convicted in the
same proceedings . . . and

(ii) that his benefit was at least the minimum (specified) amount.

The section defined the offences to which Part VI applied as well as the
'minimum amount' referred to in s. 71. No confiscation order had been made
in the instant case. Under s. 77, the High Court might by order prohibit any
person from dealing with any 'realisable property', subject to such conditions
and exceptions as might be specified in the order. The power to make a
restraining order could be exercised only in accordance with s. 76, that is,
where:

(a) proceedings had been instituted in England and Wales against the
defendant for an offence to which Part VI applied;

(b) the proceedings had not been concluded, and

(c) either a confiscation order had been made or it appeared to the court
that there were reasonable grounds for thinking that a confiscation order
might be made in them.

S. 77(5) provided that a restraint order could be made only on the application
of the prosecutor, and s. 77(6) provided that it should be discharged when
proceedings for the offence were concluded. After it had made a restraint
order the court had power to appoint a receiver to take possession of any
realisable property (s. 77(8)), and sums realised by a receiver on the sale of
property might be applied towards the satisfaction of a confiscation order if
one was subsequently made (s. 81(1)).

Costello J drew particular attention to the following features of s. 77
restraint orders:

(a) a restraint order was made prior to a confiscation order and in order
to make it efficacious;

(b) it could only be made at the instance of the prosecutor;

(c) it could only be made after criminal proceedings had been instituted
and either a confiscation order had been made or there were reasonable
grounds for thinking that a confiscation order would be made.

The Commissioners submitted, first, that the restraint order was not a
penal order. Next, they argued that a distinction should be made between the
'recognition' of a foreign penal law and its 'enforcement'. They made a third
argument, which Costello J ultimately did not consider he was called on to
address, to the effect that the public policy considerations justifying the rule
against non-enforcement of 'foreign revenue claims' had no application

where claims for VAT were made because VAT was a tax subject to the law of the European Union and portion of the proceeds of the tax was payable by each member State of the Union, in contrast to other taxes levied in member States.

Costello J derived much assistance from the English Court of Appeal decision of *United States of America v Inkey* [1989] 1 QB 255. There Purchas LJ had reviewed the authorities and concluded that they established the following propositions:

(1) The consideration of whether the claim sought to be enforced in the English courts is one which involves the assertion of foreign sovereignty, and is to be determined according to the criteria of English law;

(2) regard will be had to the attitude adopted by the courts of the foreign jurisdiction, which will always receive serious attention and may on occasions be decisive;

(3) the category of the right of action, i.e. whether public or private, will depend on the party in whose favour it is created, on the purpose of the law or enactment in the foreign State on which its based and on the general context of the case as a whole;

(4) the fact that the right, statutory or otherwise, is penal in nature will not deprive a person, who asserts a personal claim depending thereon, from having recourse to the courts of this country; on the other hand, by whatever description it may be known, if the purpose of the action is the enforcement of a sanction, power or right at the instance of the State in its sovereign capacity, it will not be entertained;

(5) the fact that in the foreign jurisdiction recourse may be had in a civil forum to enforce the right will not necessarily affect the true nature of the right being enforced in this country.

Returning to the facts of the instant case, Costello J noted that the Commissioners' claim was not for a sum of money owed by a person sued within this jurisdiction but the assertion of a claim that by virtue of the 1988 Act and the High Court order made thereunder the bank could lawfully pay the debt it owed a person within this jurisdiction. Applying the criteria established by the cases to which he had referred he had 'no doubt' that the claim was based on a penal law. It was one derived from a criminal statute under which the courts in England might make an order *confiscating* a convicted person's assets. Quite clearly in the absence of appropriate legislation (which, as Costello J noted, was coincidentally under consideration in the Oireachtas) the Irish courts could not enforce such an order. But the *restraint* order on which the claim was based was an order made to *make effective a future proposed confiscation order* and was therefore itself penal in character. Furthermore, the restraint imposed by the English court pursuant to the 1988 Act was imposed 'not for the benefit of a private individual but at the instance of an organ of the State as part of the process to recover a penalty on behalf of the State.' Costello J therefore held that the Irish courts could not enforce the law on which the Commissioners relied.

Costello J then turned to the Commissioners' alternative argument that they were seeking not enforcement, but merely *recognition* of the foreign penal law. He noted that in *Buchanan v McVeigh* [1954] IR 89, the argument had been advanced that the rule against non-enforcement meant that the court could not even inform itself or the revenue provisions of the law of another country. This extreme view had been rejected by Kingsmill Moore J (*id.*, at 100), who held that the court could inform itself as to the provisions of a foreign law in order to determine the question whether a foreign transaction was or was not fraudulent and void according to the law of the foreign country. This view was upheld in the Supreme Court where the Chief Justice observed that the Irish courts could take notice of the revenue law of a foreign country in order to ascertain whether according to that law a party's conduct had been honest or dishonest. In Costello J's view, this distinction did not help the Commissioners:

> They asked the court to do a great deal more than merely to take note of the existence of the [restraint] order . . . and the statute under which it was made: they asked the court to act on the knowledge it has thus obtained and give effect to it by refusing to allow the bank to pay the money it owes to the defendant. This seems to me to amount to the 'enforcement' of the order and so is contrary to the rule.

Costello J noted that the English decisions accepted that the concept of 'recognition' might be used in a *different* sense. This could arise when no question of the direct or indirect enforcement of a foreign penal law was involved. It had been explained in Dicey & Morris's *Conflict of Laws* (12th ed., 1993, p. 99) as follows:

> Where a direct or indirect enforcement does not arise, a foreign law of a type falling within Rule 3 (1) will be recognised if it is relevant to the issue and provided it is not contrary to public policy. For example, a contract invalid according to a penal or revenue law of its applicable law, or performance of which is prohibited by a penal law of the place

of performance, may be held to be invalid or unenforceable; and the English court will refuse to restrain trustees from acting in compliance with foreign fiscal legislation forming part of the proper law of the trust. Likewise trustees will be entitled to be indemnified out of an estate in England in respect of such sums which they have been personally compelled to pay abroad in satisfaction of a foreign government's claim for estate duty upon that estate even though the claim would have been unenforceable in this country.

The Commissioners could not rely on this principle. The issue for determination was whether the bank was precluded by law from paying the debt it owed the defendant. This issue could be determined only under Irish law and no conflict rule had been suggested which would require the Irish court to apply the law of England to this dispute. The restraint order could have legal effect in Ireland only if the court was permitted by law to enforce it. The instant case was one, therefore, of the direct enforcement of a foreign penal law and not merely the 'recognition' of a foreign penal law which was to be applied under Irish conflict rules.

As the Commissioners' claim amounted to the enforcement of a foreign penal law, Costello J considered it unnecessary for him to consider the submission that the rule against non-enforcement of foreign *revenue* laws did not apply where the claim was for the enforcement of a VAT claim.

Costello J made an order determining that the money in the account was the property of the defendant and that the bank was entitled to pay it to the defendant forthwith.

Perhaps it would have been beneficial to have had the Commissioners' argument relating to the distinct position of a VAT claim resolved. Foreign revenue claims have traditionally not been enforced because their penal law status has not been in serious controversy. The Commissioners were seeking to argue that VAT was not in this traditional category. The merits of their case might with benefit have been tested, since they were not seeking to challenge the traditional rule but rather to argue that it was not applicable in relation to VAT.

FORUM NON CONVENIENS

In *Doe v Armour Pharmaceutical Co. Inc.* [1994] 1 ILRM 416, the Supreme Court confronted the relatively unusual situation of a plaintiff's assertion of *forum non conveniens*. The matter was one of some human poignancy. The plaintiffs were all hemophiliacs who were HIV positive or the personal representatives of deceased hemophiliacs who had contracted AIDS. The defendants were manufacturers of a blood clotting factor which, the plaintiffs alleged, had brought about their condition. The proceedings were for alleged negligence in the manufacture and preparation of the product.

The plaintiffs had initially commenced proceedings in the courts of New York State. The defendants had there sought to have the actions dismissed on the ground of *forum non conveniens*. The New York judges, in two separate proceedings, had dismissed the proceedings but subject to the important conditions that the defendants consent to suit filed by the plaintiffs in Ireland and waive any statute of limitation defence that might have arisen. Proceedings were then launched in Ireland. Later the plaintiffs sought to have the proceedings stayed on the basis that they would more conveniently and properly be tried in New York. Flood J refused this application and the Supreme Court dismissed the plaintiffs' appeal.

Blayney J was the only member of the court to deliver a judgment, Finlay CJ, O'Flaherty, Egan and Denham JJ concurring. The first step was to ascertain what test would have been applied if the application was 'the normal one', that is, one made by a defendant. He referred to a number of English authorities as well as the Supreme Court decision in *Joseph Murphy Structural Engineers Ltd. v Manitowoc (UK) Ltd*, July 30, 1985. In almost all of the cases to which he referred, including the Irish decision, the test had been formulated in such a way that it could be applied only to cases in which the applicant for the stay was the defendant. In *MacShannon v Rockware Glass Ltd* [1978] 1 All ER 625, however, Lord Salmon had formulated the test in broader terms, capable of embracing an application by a plaintiff or a defendant. He had observed (at 636) that 'the real test depends on what the court in its discretion considers that justice demands.' The English Court of Appeal had adopted a very similar test in *Attorney General v Arthur Andersen & Co.* [1989] ECC 224, where the applicant for a stay was the plaintiff. Mustill LJ had said:

> In the end, counsel found themselves unable to dispute this way of stating the issue. This is hardly surprising, since there must be something wrong with a procedural rule which would deny that, if a way of conducting the proceedings is found to be the most fair way, then that is the way in which they ought to be conducted.

> Nor am I convinced that a solution to the present problem is much advanced by talking in terms of burden of proof. Naturally, if a plaintiff has thought fit to commence an action, with all the hardship to the defendant which this involves in terms of expense, worry and disruption, he should in general be made to face up to the situation which he has chosen to create, and should not be permitted to conduct the action

to a timetable which corresponds only to his own whimsy. Having put his hand to plough he should continue to the end of the furrow. This is only fairness and common sense. But the same considerations must demand that in some instances the approach should be different. The question for the learned judge, and for us also when reviewing this decision, is to my mind no more than this, whether the good management of the concurrent sets of proceedings clearly requires the English court, in charge of one set of those proceedings, to decree that a temporary halt should be called — temporary, because we must wait to discover what the American court is going to do.

Blayney J adopted this test, regarding it as 'in effect the same test' as enunciated by Lord Salmon in *MacShannon v Rockware Glass Ltd*. The question, therefore, in the instant case was whether justice required that the plaintiff's action should be stayed. Blayney J had regard to the fact that, when initiating their proceeds, the plaintiffs had chosen to bring them in the State of New York. It seemed quite clear that they could have initiated them in Ireland, but they chose not to do so.

The New York courts had plainly wanted to ensure that there would be no obstacle to the plaintiffs bringing their actions here. There was only one contingency which could result in an obstacle that they could not control: that the Irish courts might decline to accept jurisdiction. Obviously they could not direct the High Court to hear the cases so, to deal with this contingency, they had restrained the defendant from acting to prevent the plaintiffs from returning to the New York court if the Irish court should decline to accept jurisdiction.

On these facts, Blayney J was 'firmly' of the view that justice did not require that the proceedings be stayed. It seemed to him in the first place that it was unjust that the defendants should have had to face again a trial of the issue of what was the appropriate forum for the case. That issue had been decided in the proceedings in New York which had been instituted by the plaintiffs, which had held that New York was *forum non conveniens*. If the plaintiffs were dissatisfied with that decision, they could have appealed it, but they had not. In seeking a stay on the grounds of Ireland's being *forum non conveniens*, they were in effect asking the High Court 'rather than the New York appellate court' to reverse the decision of the New York court.

Blayney J's second reason for concluding that justice did not require the granting of a stay was based on the form of the judgments and orders of the New York court. The judgments in effect decided that Ireland was the proper forum for the cases and the orders giving effect to them imposed conditions for the benefit of the plaintiffs to ensure that their actions would get a hearing in Ireland. It was extremely unlikely that the conditions imposed by the New

York court for the benefit of the plaintiffs could be construed as entitling the plaintiffs to apply to the High Court to decline jurisdiction. Whatever might be the correct meaning to be given to the phrase 'if the Irish court should decline to accept jurisdiction' it could hardly be construed as an invitation to the plaintiffs to bring the motion to stay the proceedings in Ireland.

Even if there were no objection by the defendants to the actions coming back before the New York court, there would still remain the question of what that court would do:

> Could it reverse its decision that it is *forum non conveniens* and hear the actions, or would it, or a superior court, extend the time for the plaintiffs to appeal against that decision? The only thing that is certain is that there would be bound to be further delays and having regard to the nature of these actions and the length of time that has already elapsed since they were commenced it would not be just to either side to permit such a situation.

It is true, of course, that jurisdictional issues should not be considered in isolation. The Supreme Court, in *Grehan v Medical Incorporated* [1986] IR 528 recognised the importance of the choice-of-law implications of a selection of any particular forum as having jurisdiction. This is especially significant where the differing legal systems competing for jurisdiction approach the issue of liability, causation and damages in radically different ways. In the context of product liability, the European Directive of 1985 (implemented by the Liability for Defective Products Act 1991: see the 1991 Review, 204) goes some way to bringing Irish law into harmony with the law of the United States, but important differences still remain. For a comprehensive analysis of these implications, see Mark Cole and David Tomkin, '*Doe v Armour – Forum (non) Conveniens* or political decision?' (1994) 12 *ILT* 267.

JURISDICTION

Domicile In *Deutsche Bank Aktiengesellschaft v Murtagh*, High Court, December 19, 1994, Costello J addressed a number of issues of general importance in private international law. The plaintiff claimed one million Deutchmarks, allegedly due on guarantees executed by the defendants, the contracts of guarantee having been executed in Germany and subject to German law. Neither of the defendants was an Irish citizen. The jurisdictional basis of the plaintiff's proceedings against the defendants was challenged by the defendants. Their argument was in essence that s. 13 of the Jurisdiction of Courts and Enforcement of Judgments (European Communities) Act 1988 should be interpreted as requiring not only that the defendants be ordinarily resident in the State but also that they have an Irish domicile in accordance with well established common law principles.

Under Article 2 of the Brussels Convention, persons domiciled in a contracting state may be sued in the courts of that state, whatever their nationality. 'Domicile' is not defined but Article 52 provides that, in order to determine whether a party is domiciled in the contracting state whose courts are seized with the matter, 'the Court shall apply its own internal law'. S. 13 of the 1988 Act provides that:

> [s]ubject to Article 52, Part 1 of the Fifth Schedule to this Act shall apply in relation to the text of the English language of the 1968 Convention . . . in order to determine for the purposes of the 1968 Convention and this Act whether an individual is domiciled in the State. . . .

Part 1 of the Fifth Schedule provides that an individual is domiciled in the State, or in a state other than a contracting state, if, but only if, he or she is ordinarily resident in the State or in that other state.

When acceding to the Convention, Ireland and Britain undertook that in their implementing legislation they would provide for a concept of domicile that would depart from the traditional rules and would tend to reflect more the concept of *domicile* and understood in the original states of the E.E.C.: Schlosser Report, para 73. The defendants nonetheless contended that the phrase '[s]ubject to Article 52 of the Convention' in s. 13 had the effect of maintaining the vitality of the traditional rules; otherwise the section would have read '[t]o give effect to Article 52 of the Convention' or '[i]n pursuance to Article 52 of the Convention' or words of similar effect.

Not surprisingly Costello J rejected this interpretation. His language was robust:

> S. 13 is quite clear — in order to determine for the purposes of the 1968 Convention and the 1988 Act whether an individual is domiciled in the State the court must apply the provisions of the 5th Schedule to the Act. This means that the traditional common law principles relating to the concept of domicile are not to be applied; instead the court will consider whether the defendant is 'ordinarily resident' in the State. If he is and if he is a national of a contracting state then the court has jurisdiction in accordance with the Convention and the Act.

Accordingly the question narrowed its focus to whether the defendants were ordinarily resident here. Costello J took guidance from Maguire CJ's observations in *State (Goertz) v Minister for Justice* [1948] IR 45, at 55:

> Cases have been cited to us in which the meaning of the words, 'resident' and 'ordinarily resident', have been considered. In my view they are of very little help. They are of assistance, however, in showing that the word 'resident', not being a term of art, must be construed by reference to the statute in which it is found. The cases of *Levene v Inland Revenue Commissioners* [1921] AC 217 and *Lysaght's* case [1928] AC 234 which deals with the meaning of the term in the Income Tax Act 1918, afford no sure guidance as to the meaning of the term in the Act under consideration here. Neither does the interpretation placed on the term, 'resident', in cases under the Children Act 1908 of which *Stoke-on-Trent Borough Council v Cheshire County Council* [1915] 3 KB 699 is an example. Still less is it to be got from the case of *Berkshire County Council v Reading Borough Council* [1921] 2 KB 787 which is a case concerning the meaning of the term in the Mental Deficiency Act 1913. In these cases 'ordinarily resident', should be construed according to their ordinary meaning and with the aid of such light as is thrown upon them by the general intention of the legislation in which they occur and, of course, with reference to the facts of the particular case.

Costello J considered that he was therefore obliged to give to the words 'ordinarily resident' in the 1988 Act their ordinary meaning 'in the light of the general intention of the 1988 legislation.'

The facts in this case were not in dispute. In an affidavit sworn by Mr Murtagh on 24 October 1994 it was stated:

> I am a British citizen and have been born and raised in the United Kingdom and I hold a British Passport. I have lived much of my adult life in Germany and have moved backwards and forwards between the United Kingdom and Germany a number of times. While I have been living with my family (my wife and four children) in Terryglass for the last twelve months I cannot say with any certainty that I would remain in Terryglass or even in Ireland. As in the past, it is likely that, should a business opportunity arise in Germany the United Kingdom or else-where, I will move my family to that country in order to exploit such opportunity. My wife is a German national and I believe and hope that it is her intention to reside where I reside.

Neither of the defendants had suggested that they had any residence outside Ireland and it had been clearly established that since October 1993 the defendants had been resident in a substantial property (which they valued at £300,000) at Terryglass and they had no other residence in any of the other contracting states. Furthermore, the defendants' children attended school in the State and the defendants had a number of bank accounts in the State. Costello J did not attach weight to the first defendant's adverting to the possibility that he might change his residence should a suitable business opportunity arise. This state of mind might be relevant if the court was determining whether the defendant had acquired an Irish domicile of choice according to common law principles, but it was not relevant on the facts of the case when the court was deciding whether the defendant is ordinarily resident in the State.

Giving the words 'ordinarily resident' their ordinary meaning and bearing in mind the context in which they appeared in the 1988 Act, Costello J held that it had been established that when the proceedings were instituted the defendants were 'ordinarily resident' in the State and they continued to be 'ordinarily resident' here. It followed therefore, that the Irish courts had jurisdiction to adjudicate on the plaintiff's claim.

On October 17, 1994, the plaintiff had sought an order restraining the defendants from dealing with assets held by them in the jurisdiction and in particular the property known as Terryglass. On October 24 the first defendant had sworn an affidavit in which he stated that the property was subject to a charge to secure a loan of £50,000 and that it was also subject to a further charge securing a loan of £200,000. Instead of an order being made on the plaintiff's motion the defendants gave undertakings and the motion was adjourned. One of the undertakings was to swear an affidavit identifying their assets within the jurisdiction. The affidavit sworn pursuant to this undertaking disclosed that the second charge was a charge 'in favour of John Mansfield of 140 Borough Road, Middlesboro, England in the sum of STG £200,000' ranking in priority behind the Building Society's mortgage. The plaintiff was concerned to learn about the second charge as it had written a letter of demand on the October 7, five days before the charge had, apparently, been executed and the charge was not in favour of a financial institution but of a private individual. Accordingly, it successfully applied for an interim injunction on November 22 restraining the defendants from dealing outside the State with monies received in consideration for the execution of the second charge. A motion for an interlocutory injunction seeking a similar order until the trial of the action followed and ancillary orders were also sought.

Costello J was satisfied that the plaintiff was entitled to the relief it claimed. In his opinion the court had jurisdiction to restrain the dissipation of extra-territorial assets where such an order was warranted by the facts. The basis on which a *Mareva* injunction was granted was to ensure that a defendant did not take action designed to frustrate subsequent orders of the court. It was well established in England that a *Mareva* injunction might extend to foreign assets and Costello J believed that the Irish courts had a similar power in order to avoid the frustration of subsequent orders it might make. The court had ancillary powers also and in suitable cases it might grant a disclosure order requiring a defendant to swear an affidavit in respect of assets outside the jurisdiction. Costello J cited *Derby & Co. Ltd v Weldon (Nos. 3 and 4)* [1989] 2 WLR 412 in support.

Accordingly Costello J made an order restraining the dealing, outside the jurisdiction, with any money, assets or other valuable things received in consideration of the execution of the second charge. He also made an order requiring the defendants to disclose on affidavit information concerning the making of the loan secured by the second charge and how its proceeds had been utilised.

Jurisdiction agreements   Article 17 of the Brussels Convention, as originally drafted, provided that:

> [i]f the parties one or more of whom is domiciled in a contracting state have, by agreement in writing or by an oral agreement confirmed in writing, agreed that a court or courts of a contracting state are to have jurisdiction to settle any disputes which have arisen or which may arise in connection with a particular legal relationship, that court or those courts shall have exclusive jurisdiction.

When Ireland, Britain and Denmark were adopting the Convention, the Accession Convention amended Article 17 to provide (in part) as follows:

> If the parties one or more of whom are domiciled in a contracting state have agreed that a court or the courts of a contracting state are to have jurisdiction to settle any disputes which have arisen or which may arise in connection with a particular legal relationship, that court or those courts shall have exclusive jurisdiction. Such an agreement conferring jurisdiction shall be either in writing or evidenced in writing or, in international trade or commerce, in a form which accords with practices in that trade or commerce of which the parties are or ought to have been aware.

The Court of Justice jurisprudence on Article 17, in its original manifestation, was to the effect that the requirements must be strictly construed and that an alleged consensus must be clearly and precisely demonstrated. In *Estasis Salotti v Ruwa* [1976] ECR 1831, the Court of Justice, emphasising these principles, went on to say that, if the jurisdiction clause is on the back of a contract, the requirement of Article 17 is fulfilled only where the contract signed by both parties contains an express reference to those general conditions.

In *Tilly Rus v Nova* [1984] ECR 2417, the Court of Justice examined the validity of a jurisdiction clause in a bill of lading. It considered that, where a jurisdiction clause appeared in the conditions printed on a bill of lading signed by the carrier, the requirement of an 'agreement in writing' was satisfied only if the shipper had expressed in writing its consent to the conditions containing that clause either in the document itself or in another document. The mere permitting of a jurisdiction clause on the reverse of a bill of lading did not satisfy the requirements of Article 7 since this gave no guarantee that the other party had actually consented to the clauses derogating from the ordinary jurisdictional rules of the Convention.

These two decisions were, of course, before the change brought about to Article 17, which includes, in international trade and commerce, an agreement conferring jurisdiction in a form that accords with practices in that trade or commerce of which the parties were or ought to have been aware. In his Report to the 1978 Accession Convention, in para. 179, Professor Peter Schlosser states that the Courts' interpretation of Article 17 had not catered adequately for the customs and requirements of international trade:

> In particular the requirement that the other party to a contract with anyone employing general conditions of trade has to give written confirmation of their inclusion in the contract before any jurisdiction clause in those conditions can be effective is unacceptable in international trade. International trade is heavily dependent on standard conditions which incorporate jurisdiction clauses. Nor are those conditions in many cases unilaterally dictated by one set of interests in the market; they have frequently been negotiated by representatives of the various interests. Owing to the need for calculations based on constantly fluctuating market prices, it has to be possible to conclude contracts swiftly by means of a confirmation of order incorporating sets of conditions. These are the factors behind the relaxation of the formal provisions for international trade in the amended version of Article 17. This is, however, as should be clearly emphasised, only a relaxation of the formal requirements. It must be proved that a consensus existed on the inclusion in the contract of the general conditions of trade and the particular provisions. . . .

The matter arose in *Hanley t/a Seapoint Navigation v Someport-Walon and GEC Alsthom*, High Court, December 20, 1994. Carroll J ordered the setting aside of service of notice of a plenary summons on the defendants,

French companies, by a carrier who asserted a place of business in Ireland. The dispute concerned problems encountered in connection with loading one of the plaintiff's vessels in Antwerp. The plaintiff sought to rely on a choice of jurisdiction clause contained in clause 3 of the Carrier Bill of Lading Form, which constituted general conditions printed on the reverse of the initial page of the Online Booking Note, which the plaintiff had employed. On the evidence, Carroll J concluded that, even taking into account the relaxation of the formal provision for international trade in the amended version of Article 17, the plaintiff had not proved a consensus on the inclusion in the contract of the particular provision conferring jurisdiction. A director of the first defendant was not specifically aware of clause 3 and, in the circumstances of the case, Carroll J was of the opinion that it could not be said that he ought to have been aware of it. The first defendant had not received a copy of the printed general conditions until after the plenary summons had been issued.

We should note briefly a separate ground for setting aside service of notice of the plenary summons, which was that the plaintiff had not strictly proved its principal place of business.

Tort The courts have been less than confident in their analysis of the juridical attributes of the action for breach of constitutional rights. What seemed incontrovertible when stated for the first time in *Meskell v Córas Iompair Éireann* [1973] IR 121 has become the subject of judicial puzzlement, if not embarrassment, in later cases. What precisely is the nature of the action? Is it a tort? Is it a supplement to the common law and statutory system of remedies? Or is it an entirely novel action, with its own distinct principles relating to such matters as the mental disposition of the defendant, causation, remoteness and quantum of damages and limitation of actions? Cf. Binchy, 'Constitutional Remedies and the Law of Torts', in J. O'Reilly ed., *Human Rights and Constitutional Law: Essays in Honour of Brian Walsh* (1992).

In *Hayes v Ireland* [1987] ILRM 651, Carroll J held that the action for breach of constitutional rights was not a tortious action for the purposes of s. 4 of the Trade Disputes Act 1906, which conferred wide-ranging immunity of trade unions in respect of tortious liability. See our comments in the 1990 Review, 350-1. In *Schmidt v Home Secretary of the Government of the United Kingdom* [1995] 1 ILRM 301, Geoghegan J was called on to determine whether the action for breach of constitutional rights and actionable breaches of Community law giving rise to damages are 'matters relating to tort' within the meaning of Article 5 of the Convention. He observed:

> It was as a result of judge-made law that breach of statutory duty became regarded as a tort. If breach of statutory duty is a tort, I cannot see any

reason why breach of a constitutional right or breach of European Community law in circumstances where the respective breaches give rise to claims of damages should not be characterised as torts.

Geoghegan J considered that, in the instant case, 'the harmful event' for the purposes of Article 5(3) had to be regarded as having occurred in Ireland. He set aside an earlier High Court order granting liberty to the plaintiff to serve proceedings out of the jurisdiction on the defendants, under O. 11 of the Rules of the Superior Courts 1986. The proper procedure was prescribed by r. 4 of the 1989 Rules, inserting a new O. 11A.

We must wait for a future case to analyse in detail the broader questions that follow from this characterisation. At a jurisdictional level difficult issues will arise as to the extra-territorial remit of the protection of constitutional rights. In *Handelskwekerij G. J. Bier B.V. v Mines de Potasse d'Alsace S.A.* [1976] ECR 1735, at 1746, the Court of Justice held that:

the meaning of the expression 'place where the harmful event occurred' in Article 5(3) must be established in such a way as to acknowledge that the plaintiff has an option to commence proceedings either at the place where the damage occurred or at the place of the event giving rise to it.

When one is dealing with certain breaches of constitutional right it may seem easy to identify *one* place where 'the damage occurred'. Thus, for example, if a traffic accident occurred in England, in which the plaintiff received injuries, England would surely be regarded, for the purposes of a tort claim, as being the place where the damage occurred, and it might be considered equally obvious that it should be similarly characterised for the purposes of a claim for breach of the plaintiff's constitutional rights of health and bodily integrity.

The difficulty, at a conceptual level, is that there is a difference, on the one hand, between wrongfully *harming* someone, which is a robust description of the essence of a tort, and, on the other hand, breaching (or otherwise infringing) a person's constitutionally protected rights. Constitutional rights tend to be capable of being exercised over an indefinite (sometimes lifelong) period. *Breaching* a constitutional right thus can extend over a period of time. A tort usually is complete once the plaintiff has sustained an injury; what happens to the plaintiff later will normally be regarded as raising issues as to the consequences rather than the commission of the tort. (We need not here concern ourselves with the relatively rare instances of an ongoing tort, such as continuing trespass (cf. McMahon & Binchy, *Irish Law of Torts* (2nd ed., 1990) 438-440) or a case where a plaintiff is exposed to insidious injury, in the workplace or in the wider environment, and his or her physical condition gradually deteriorates over a long period of time.)

Could it be argued that where an Irish national, domiciled and resident in Ireland, is injured in a traffic accident in England, his or her constitutional rights of bodily integrity and health are breached, not only in England but also in Ireland, since the entitlement to exercise these rights over a long period is undoubtedly compromised in Ireland, where the plaintiff's life is centred? And, if the accident was a serious one and the plaintiff was obliged to live the rest of his or her days in a wheelchair in Ireland, could Article 5(3) be invoked in an Irish court in relation to infringement of the plaintiff's right of associate? The right to associate necessarily contemplates a period of time for its exercise. This sense of continuity does not easily harmonise with the notion of single moment in which damage 'occurs'.

MAINTENANCE ENTITLEMENTS

Maintenance Act 1994   The Maintenance Act 1994 enables the State to ratify two important international conventions designed to assist claimants to recover financial support from maintenance debtors living in another country. The social policy inspiring the legislation is well described by James Martin and Caoímhín Ó hUigínn in para. 1 of their Report on the E.C. Rome Convention, which was finalised during the Irish Presidency of the Council of Ministers in 1990:

> The task facing a maintenance creditor who wishes to recover mainte-nance payments from abroad is daunting. By definition a maintenance creditor lacks financial independence and will not normally have the resources necessary to pay for the legal and other assistance necessary to enforce a maintenance judgment abroad. The maintenance debtor (or his assets) has be to located. The maintenance judgment and supporting documentation have to be transmitted to that Member State. The docu-mentation may have to be translated into the language of that state. An application has to be made to have the maintenance judgment recog-nised as enforceable in that state. There may be an appeal against such a decision Even after judgment has been declared enforceable there may be difficulties in enforcement. Maintenance judgments will often be for the periodic payment of relatively small sums of money. Therefore, unlike judgments for liquidated sums, the execution or enforcement of the maintenance judgment will not be a once off act but a continuous process. The maintenance debtor initially may make the payments due but subsequently may default and enforcement procedures may be required. The problem of enforcement, therefore, continues as long as

the maintenance judgment lasts. There is also the added problem that if circumstances change the original maintenance judgment may be varied and the whole process may have to be repeated. At each stage in the process there is potential for delay whereas the vital interests of the maintenance creditor demand speedy enforcement procedures.

Traditionally, under the rules of Irish private international law, our courts would not recognise or enforce a foreign maintenance order because it was not regarded as final and conclusive — the qualities of a foreign judgment meriting recognition and enforcement — since the maintenance order could be varied, as regards future payments, by the foreign court that granted it. Costello J's judgment in *McC. v McC.* [1994] 1 ILRM 101 (High Court, 1993) which we analysed in the 1993 Review, 135-61, displaced the traditional policy by affording recognition to foreign maintenance orders, on the basis that a future prospect of variation did not affect the finality or conclusiveness of orders already made. Nonetheless, this decision had little or no impact on the several elements of difficulty identified in the Martin/Ó hUigínn Report.

The Act enables the State to ratify, not merely the *Rome Convention* of 1990 but also the United Nations' *New York Convention* of 1956. Both conventions provide for the establishment of a central authority by each of the contracting states. This central authority is charged with the responsibility of handling the practical aspects of the maintenance application: it completes the necessary documentation and sends it to the central authority of the state where the maintenance debtor is residing. That central authority then takes responsibility for processing the claim and for ensuring that maintenance payments are transmitted to the claimant. Section 4(1) of the Act provides that, pending appointment of the Central Authority by the Minister for Equality and Law Reform, the Minister is to exercise these functions. It is worth noting that the Department of Equality and Law Reform has replaced the Department of Justice as the Central Authority for the Child Abduction and Enforcement of Custody Orders Act 1991: Family Law Act 1995, s.45.

The 1994 Act does not affect the operation of the Maintenance Orders Act 1974, which gives effect to an international agreement between Ireland and Britain and which has a model closely similar to that of the 1994 Act, based on the Brussels Convention: see W. Binchy, *Irish Conflicts of Law* (1988), 310-17, A. Shatter, *Family Law in the Republic of Ireland* (3rd ed., 1986), 461-6.

When the Rome Convention was being prepared, consideration was given to the question whether jurisdiction to interpret it should be conferred on the Court of Justice but it was decided ultimately that this would be neither necessary nor appropriate:

The Convention does not lay down a legal framework governing the relationship between private parties involved in litigation. On the contrary it imposes general obligations on Member States, who will retain a certain discretion in deciding exactly how these should be implemented, and puts in place arrangements which are generally administrative in character. Many of the legal aspects (e.g. jurisdiction, recognition) are already covered by the Brussels Convention and the Court of Justice has jurisdiction in these fields. In any event the existence of the Standing Committee [set up under the terms of Article 8] should ensure a reasonably uniform application in all the Member States. (Martin/Ó hUigínn Report, para. 4.)

It is clear that the Rome Convention is permissive rather than mandatory so far as the maintenance creditor's options are concerned (Article 1, paragraph 1), but the Central Authority is required to process all applications in accordance with the provisions of the Convention.

The New York Convention is in force in over forty states, including several with a large Irish population, such as Australia and New Zealand, but not the United States of America. It is based on the central authority system of transmission and enforcement, going further than the Rome Convention in that it does not require the claimant to have first obtained a maintenance order in his or her own state.

Part II of the Act deals with the recognition and enforcement of maintenance orders from 'reciprocating jurisdictions'. In order to be a reciprocating jurisdiction, a state must be a contracting party to either the Brussels or the Lugano Convention (cf. the 1993 Review, 118) and must operate a central authority system to assist maintenance creditors. Ireland's central authority may utilise the procedures for recognition prescribed by the Jurisdiction of Courts and Enforcement of Judgments Acts 1988 (cf the 1988 Review 90-104) and 1993 (cf. the 1993 Review, 118-25) when it receives an application from another state pursuant to Part II. This means that the Master of the High Court has an important role, as he or she does under the 1974, 1988 and 1993 Acts.

The District Court is given power to enforce *foreign* lump sum maintenance orders: (ss. 9-12), as it now has in relation to *domestic* maintenance orders: Family Law Act 1995, s. 42. The District Court's jurisdiction in relation to the enforcement of foreign maintenance orders is based on the maintenance debtor's place of residence or the place of residence of the person (or seat of the company) who (or which) is the maintenance debtor's employer if the maintenance debtor does not reside in the State: s. 11(6). The domestic procedure for the transmission of payments through the district court clerk and for attachment of earnings orders under the Family Law

(Maintenance of Spouses and Children) Act 1976 (as amended) is paralleled in Part II.

Part III of the Act deals with applications for the recovery of maintenance from designated jurisdictions — jurisdictions that are contracting parties to the New York Convention. S. 13(1) enables the Minister for Foreign Affairs to declare by order that any other state is a 'designated jurisdiction'. Thus, if, for example, an agreement with the United States were be made, all that would be necessary to give it effect in our law would be a ministerial order.

S. 14 sets out the procedure that the Irish Central Authority must adopt on receipt of a request from a central authority of a designated jurisdiction on behalf of a claimant for the recovery of maintenance from a person residing in the State. If the request is accompanied by an order of a court in a Contracting State (within the meaning of the 1988 and 1993 Acts) — such as France or Germany, for example — the Central Authority should transmit the request to the *Master of the High Court* for enforcement in accordance with s. 15 of the 1988 Act, and Part II of the 1994 Act accordingly applies. If the request is accompanied by an order made by any other court and the Central Authority is of opinion that it may be enforceable in the State, it should apply to the District Court for the enforcement of the order. If the request is not accompanied by a court order (or enforcement of the order is refused), then the Central Authority should apply to the District or Circuit Court (depending on the quantum of the claim, on par with the jurisdictional criteria of the Family Law (Maintenance of Spouses and Children) Act 1976): s. 14 (1) of the 1994 Act. In this context, if the request is for a relief order under s. 24 of the Family Law Act 1995, the Central Authority should apply to the Circuit Court: s. 45(c) of the 1995 Act.

The Minister for Law Reform and Equality, Mr Taylor, summarising the effect of these provisions, explained that:

> European Union and EFTA states — other than Austria and Ireland — will be both reciprocating jurisdictions for the purposes of Part II . . . and designated jurisdictions for the purposes of Part III. How this will operate in practice is as follows. Applications for recognition and enforcement in Ireland of maintenance orders which were made in those countries will be dealt with under Part II because they come within the scope of the Brussels and Lugano Conventions. However, where there is no actual order, these conventions will not apply and an application from one of those countries will be dealt with under Part III. (444 *Dáil Debates*, col. 790 (June 24, 1994)).

S. 15 deals with applications for maintenance brought by persons residing in the State against persons residing in a designated jurisdiction. The claimant applies to the Central Authority to have the claim transmitted to the central authority of a foreign state. She (or he) may give evidence on sworn deposition before the District Court as to the facts relating to the claim. The Court, if satisfied that the deposition sets forth facts from which it may be determined that the respondent owes a duty to maintain the claimant, may certify accordingly.

S. 18 enables the High Court, on application by the Central Authority, to grant provisional, including protective, measures in respect of a request made to the Central Authority by a central authority of a designated jurisdiction under Part III. S. 11 of the 1988 Act contains a similar provision in relation to such applications under Part II: cf. the *Explanatory Memorandum*, para. 25. These orders include *Mareva* injunctions.

Part IV of the Act contains provisions common to both reciprocating and designated jurisdictions. S. 20 enables the Central Authority to obtain information from any public office holder or body (subs. 1) or, on successful application to the District Court, any other person or body (subs. 2) as to the whereabouts, place of work or location and extent of the assets of a maintenance debtor. Thus, for example, the Department of Social Welfare or the revenue authorities may be required to disclose these details.

Part V contains miscellaneous provisions. S. 22(a) gives statutory effect to Costello J's decision in *McC. v McC.* [1994] 1 ILRM 101, to which we have already referred, that recognition or enforcement of a foreign maintenance order (other than a provisional order) may not be refused by reason only of the fact that the court that made it had power to vary or revoke it. S. 22(b) goes further. It provides that recognition or enforcement of a foreign maintenance order (again other than a provisional order) may not be refused on the ground that, under the rules of Irish private international law, the foreign court had not jurisdiction because the respondent was not resident or present there at the date of the commencement of the relevant proceedings, *provided that on that date the claimant was resident there*. Cf. Binchy, *op. cit.*, 304, 589-91.

S. 23(1) provides that payments under foreign maintenance orders are to be in Irish currency. The exchange rate for converting the amount due is that prevailing on the date the Irish court makes the order for enforcement of the foreign order. The Minister pointed out (*op. cit.*, col. 793) that '[a] maintenance order for periodic payments could have a different exchange rate for each periodic payment and that would result in a totally unmanageable situation.'

SOVEREIGN IMMUNITY

In the 1991 Review 90-2, we examined *Government of Canada v Employment Appeals Tribunal* [1992] 2 IR 484; [1992] ILRM 325, where the Supreme Court held that the Government of Canada was entitled to claim sovereign immunity in unfair dismissal proceedings taken against it by a chauffeur formerly employed in the Canadian Embassy. The judgments of McCarthy and O'Flaherty JJ accepted that there was 'restrictive' immunity attaching to foreign states, which did not extend to claims based on activities of a trading, commercial or otherwise private law character, in which the state had chosen to engage.

A broad assault on this case failed in *McElhinney v Williams* [1994] 2 ILRM 115. The plaintiff issued proceedings against a corporal of the British army resident in Northern Ireland for alleged assault in attempting to fire a loaded gun at him. The conduct was alleged to have occurred within the State. The claim was also made against the Secretary of State for Northern Ireland, on the basis of responsibility for the actions of members of the British army based in the North. On the basis of the hierarchical rules of precedent generally (though far from invariably) obeyed by the Irish courts, the plaintiff had a difficulty : unless he could distinguish the *Government of Canada* case, his action would fail on the basis of sovereign immunity. Clearly the restrictions on sovereign immunity relating to commercial activities had no relevance to his case. The plaintiff sought to limit the Supreme Court decision to unfair dismissal proceedings but Costello J, was understandably was unreceptive; had the decision been so restricted, he was 'sure that this would have been made clear in the judgments'.

The plaintiff next contended that, since his claim was one for the infringement of a constitutionally protected right, the principle of sovereign immunity should not be applied as to do so would itself be an infringement of this right. Costello J did not agree:

> I think it is true that the principle of international law which I am applying bears on a different right, namely, the right to claim redress in the courts. But the principle of international law which I am applying does not infringe that right either; it regulates it, as the Constitution permits, because of the recognition given specifically to the principles of international law.

Costello J, in following the Supreme Court precedent, did not consider it necessary to address two other interesting arguments put forward by the plaintiff. The first was that international law did not now recognise the principle of sovereign immunity *in respect of torts committed within the jurisdiction of the forum state*. Counsel for the plaintiff referred to an array of legislation in Britain, the United States and Canada over the previous two decades incorporating this limitation, as well as the European Convention on Sovereign Immunity 1972 and draft conventions on state immunity prepared by the International Law Association and the International Law Commission.

The second argument rendered moot by the principle of precedential hierarchy was that the court should act on the principle of reciprocity. The plaintiff claimed that this is a well-established principle of international law and that the Irish courts should not grant immunity to the British government in the instant case because Britain's State Immunity Act 1978 would not grant sovereign immunity to Ireland if Ireland was sued in Britain for a tort committed in Britain in circumstances similar to those in the instant case.

Costello J rejected the contention that Murphy J's decision in *Schmidt v Home Secretary of the Government of the United Kingdom*, High Court, January 19, 1994 had been *per incuriam*. In *Schmidt*, Murphy J, invoking *Government of Canada v Employment Appeals Tribunal*, had held that proceedings for, *inter alia*, trespass to the person and breach of constitutional rights against the Home Secretary, the first defendant in the litigation, were not maintainable on the ground of sovereign immunity. Subsequently the second and third defendants, the Commissioner of the Metropolitan Police and an individual police constable, also sought to invoke sovereign immunity: [1995] 1 ILRM 301. Geoghegan J acceded to their application. Both defendants were officers of the Crown, carrying out Crown's policy. There was nothing commercial in their activities. Geoghegan J was 'quite satisfied that what happened was an exercise of the British Crown's sovereignty through the Crown's agents'. Accordingly sovereign immunity applied.

Geoghegan J admitted to having had some doubts about the position of the third defendant in view of O'Byrne J's observation in *Saorstát and Continental Steamship Co. Ltd v De Las Morenas* [1945] IR 291, at 301, to the effect that there was no authority for the proposition that a government should be impeached 'merely because its agent was sued'. Geoghegan J distinguished *Saorstát* from the instant case on the basis that the acts of which the plaintiff complained formed part of the direct execution of British Crown policy in a public rather than a commercial domain. Undoubtedly this distinction was accepted by O'Byrne J, whose remarks were made in the context of a Spanish army colonel's activities, purchasing Irish horses on behalf of the Spanish Government and contracting to transmit them in one of the plaintiff company's vessels: see Binchy, *op. cit.*, 175-6.

Constitutional Law

ACCESS TO COURTS

Limitation of actions In *Tuohy v Courtney and Ors* [1994] 2 ILRM 503, the Supreme Court upheld the constitutional validity of the six-year limitation period concerning contract and tort claims contained in ss. 11(1)(a) and 11(2)(a) of the Statute of Limitations 1957. We consider this decision in the Limitations of Actions chapter, 336-8, below.

ADMINISTRATION OF JUSTICE

Company investigation: whether administration of justice In *In re Countyglen plc* [1995] 1 ILRM 213, Murphy J considered whether a hearing before an inspector appointed to investigate the affairs of a company pursuant to the Companies Act 1990 must be held in public or could be held *in camera*. He thus considered whether such a hearing constituted the administration of justice within the meaning of Article 34.1 see the discussion in the Company Law chapter, 59-60, above.

Judicial bias In *Dublin Wellwoman Centre Ltd and Ors v Ireland and Ors* [1995] 1 ILRM 408, the Supreme Court accepted a claim of an appearance of bias where a High Court judge had declined to recuse herself from hearing a particular case. In 1992, Carroll J was the chairwoman of the Second Commission on the Status of Women. In that capacity she wrote a letter to the Taoiseach in which she indicated that it was the view of the Commission that women should have the right to avail of counselling and information in relation to abortion, as well as the right to travel abroad in order to obtain an abortion. In a separate statement to the government, the Commission expressed the view that the amendment to the protocol to the Maastricht Treaty proposed by the government, which would provide for the right of freedom to travel (see the 1992 Review, 199-205), was too narrow and should also provide for freedom of information and counselling.

The Fourteenth Amendment of the Constitution Act 1992 amended Article 40.3.3°, which guarantees the right to life of the unborn child, so as to provide, *inter alia*, that it did not limit freedom to obtain or make available in the State, subject to such conditions as may be laid down by law, information relating to services lawfully available in another state. In its final report the Commission expressed the view that legislation designed to implement this amendment should not contain unreasonable restrictions.

The plaintiffs brought proceedings seeking a declaration that in the light of Article 40.3.3°, they could make available within the State information relating to abortion services lawfully available in another member state of the European Union and could inform pregnant women as to the identity, location and means of communicating with clinics providing such services. In October 1994 the plaintiffs' application came on for hearing before Carroll J. The third named defendant requested Carroll J to recuse (that is, discharge) herself from hearing and determining the application on the grounds that her activities as chairwoman of the Commission on the Status of Women created a reasonable apprehension of bias. Carroll J refused to do so because she was satisfied that she was not biased. An order of the High Court dated 12 October 1994 recited that an application to the judge to discharge herself had been made and refused. The third named defendant successfully appealed to the Supreme Court (Hamilton CJ, Egan, Blayney, Denham and Costello JJ).

Delivering the leading judgment, Denham J dealt first with whether the refusal by Carroll J to recuse herself was a 'determination' within Article 34.4.3° of the Constitution in respect of which an appeal lay to the Court. Denham J stated that, in refusing to discharge herself, Carroll J had made a determination on an issue that affected the interest of one of the parties before the court. The determination was concerned with the issue of bias and so constituted a decision on a matter of constitutional justice. It bore all the characteristics of a decision in that the issue was raised before the court, arguments were submitted by the opposing parties, reference was made to the law and the Constitution, and the trial judge reserved her decision and gave a written judgment setting out the reasons why she would not discharge herself. The fact that it was an issue preliminary to a trial did not divest it of the status of a decision within the meaning of Article 34.4.3°.

Moving to the substantive issue raised in the case, Denham J stated it was essential to the administration of justice that there should not be actual or subjective bias, and furthermore no objective bias in the sense of the circumstances giving rise to an apprehension on the part of a reasonable person that there might be bias. In the instant case, Denham J emphasised that there was no suggestion of actual bias. The only issue raised concerned the objective test and so it had to be asked whether a person in the position of the third named defendant, being a reasonable person, would apprehend that his chance of a fair and independent hearing of the question at issue did not exist by reason of the previous non-judicial position, statements and actions of the trial judge on issues which constituted the kernel of the case.

Denham J concluded that Carroll J had erred in that she did not address the question of objective bias. It was not a question of whether the trial judge considered that she was or was not biased, or whether the third named defendant considered that she was or was not biased. The real point was that the interpretation which the plaintiffs were seeking to have placed on Article 40.3.3° might correspond with the views of the Commission on the Status of Women and so in the circumstances Carroll J should have discharged herself.

For two other examples where judicial bias was raised, see *O'Reilly v Cassidy (No. 2)* [1995] 1 ILRM 311 and *McNally v Martin* [1995] 1 ILRM 350, discussed in the Administrative Law chapter, 6-8, above.

Judicial immunity from suit In *Deighan v Ireland and Ors* [1995] 1 ILRM 88, Flood J rejected a claim that the common law judicial immunity from suit could be challenged: see the discussion in the Torts chapter, 463-5, below.

ASSOCIATION

In *Clancy v Irish Rugby Football Union* [1995] 1 ILRM 193, Morris J considered the right to association under Article 40.6.1 of the Constitution in the context of restrictions on a Rugby Union club member: see the discussion in the Sport and Law chapter, 436-8, below.

CITIZENSHIP

Foreign births entry The Explanatory Memorandum to the Irish Nationality and Citizenship Act 1994 when it was published as a Bill explained that its purpose was to regularise the citizenship rights of persons whose applications for inclusion in a Foreign Births Entry Book or the Foreign Births Register were received before the time limit of December 31, 1986, which had been provided for in the transitional provision of the Irish Nationality and Citizenship Act 1986 but which had not been processed by that date.

The Memorandum explained that persons of Irish descent born abroad may become Irish citizens by registration in circumstances set out in the Irish Nationality and Citizenship Acts 1956 and 1986. These Acts, *inter alia*, allow a person born outside Ireland to register if he/she has a grandparent, or in certain circumstances a great grandparent, who was born in Ireland. Citizenship is obtained by registering the applicant's birth with the Department of Foreign Affairs or with Irish Diplomatic Missions and Consular Offices.

Under the 1956 Act, the right to citizenship by descent was very wide. The 1986 Act tightened up the provisions contained in the 1956 Act by providing, *inter alia*, that the fourth generation applicant, that is, a person with a great grandparent born in Ireland, can be registered only if the parent through whom he/she is claiming Irish descent was already registered at the time of his/her birth. The 1986 Act provided for a six months grace period, ending on 31 December 1986, during which the previous provisions continued to apply. The period related not to the receipt of applications but to registration.

It would appear that, during the grace period, the number of applications for registration of foreign births increased substantially. Despite measures taken to deal with these applications, a significant number remained unregistered at the end of that period, that is, December 31, 1986. The 1994 Act accordingly enabled such applicants to be registered on the same conditions as if they had been registered on July 1, 1986. The Act came into force on May 1, 1995 on its signature by the President. The relevant detailed procedures were set out in the Foreign Births (Amendment) Regulations 1994 (SI No. 155 of 1994).

ELECTIONS

The Electoral Act 1992 (Section 165) Regulations 1994 (SI No. 132 of 1994) made certain provisions to facilitate the taking of polls for the Dáil by-elections, the European Parliament elections (see the European Community chapter, 136 below) and the Údarás na Gaeltachta elections (see the Irish Language and Gaeltacht chapter, 293, below) on the same day.

FAMILY

Judicial separation In *F. v F., Ireland and the Attorney General* [1995] 2 IR 254; [1994] 2 ILRM 401 (HC); [1994] 2 ILRM 572 (SC), the High Court and, on appeal, the Supreme Court upheld the validity of, *inter alia*, a number of key provisions in the Judicial Separation and Family Law Reform Act 1989. We consider the judgments in this important case at 263, below.

Social Welfare In the 1989 Review, 96-8, we analysed Carroll J's judgment in *Mhic Mathúna v Ireland*, High Court, 27 January 1989, dismissing the plaintiffs' challenge to the constitutional validity of certain provisions of the income tax and social welfare codes. The Supreme Court dismissed the appeal: [1995] 1 ILRM 69.

The plaintiffs, spouses and parents of a large family, were concerned at the gradual reduction of tax free allowances for dependent children over the years from 1978 to 1987. They contended that his reduction, in conjunction with the financial State support given to unmarried mothers who were no co-habiting, constituted invidious discrimination against them and was a failure on the part of the Oireachtas to discharge its duties to them under Article 41, as a married couple and as a family.

Carroll J held that the discrimination had not been invidious since the position of a single parent, whether widow, widower, separated married woman or unmarried women was different from that of two married parents living together in that the functions with them were performing were different and that it was a justifiable part of social policy to see their needs as different. Moreover, the Court had no function in directing the Oireachtas to enact legislation in any form. She rejected the plaintiff's argument based on the suggestion that the preferential treatment of unmarried persons would be an inducement not to marry, thus undermining the authority of marriage, on which the family was based.

Finally, Carroll J concluded that the courts, in the administration of justice, had no function in determining taxation policy.

The plaintiffs conducted the appeal without legal representation. This is unfortunate for the broader development of constitutional law. However competent they may have been — and the Supreme Court commended them for their clarity and the careful preparation of the case — it would have been helpful to have had the contribution of counsel experience in constitutional jurisprudence.

The Supreme Court, in dismissing the appeal, stated that it was satisfied that the reasons for which Carroll J had reached her decision were correct. It invoked Keane J's judgment in *Somjee v Minister for Justice* [1981] ILRM 324, at 327, in support of the proposition that when a court condemns an impugned statutory provision, it is not entitled to direct the Oireachtas to enact new and different provisions. The Court also referred to its earlier decision in *Madigan v Attorney General* [1986] ILRM 136, where O'Higgins CJ, pronouncing the judgment of the Court had said that, when examining the constitutionality of a taxation law:

> the Court does not enter into the area of taxation policy, nor concern itself with the effectiveness of the choices made by the Government and the Oireachtas; all such matters relating to this object and range of taxation are matters of national policy which cannot be considered by the courts. The courts' concern relates solely to the question whether what has been done affects, adversely, constitutional rights, obligations and guarantees.

Finally, the Court derived support from Costello J's judgment in *O'Reilly v Limerick Corporation* [1989] ILRM 181, analysed in the 1988 Review, 114-5, 304-6, to the effect that claims relating to distributive justice in the allocation of public resources 'should, to comply with the Constitution, be advanced in Leinster house rather that in the Four Courts'.

The Court agreed with Carroll J that there were 'abundant grounds for distinguishing between the needs and requirements of single parents and those of married parents living together and rearing a family together'. Once such justification for disparity arose, the Court was satisfied that it could not interfere by seeking to assess what the extent of the disparity should be with regard to the provisions of Article 41. This was not a case in which such a total removal of support or absence of support could be supported. What was asserted in the instant case was that the measure of support over a period had become insufficient.

It was clear that the provision of the social welfare allowance for children of married parents living together was not by any means the only form of financial suport provided by the State for one upbringing of children by married parents:

> Such matters as the contributions of the State to free primary and secondary education, provisions of free or assisted medical services and other matters would all go into the question as to whether the support was a proper discharge of the constitutional duty. Added to that would be the vital question as to whether it was a proper discharge of the constitutional duty of the State under Article 41 bearing in mind the other constitutional duties of the State and the other demands properly to be made upon the resources of the State.

These were peculiarly matters within the field of national policy to be decided by a combination of the executive and the legislature that could not be adjudicated upon by the courts.

The result in *Mhic Mathúna* was not greatly surprising: our courts have been very slow to rewrite the tax and social welfare codes in response to constitutional requirements. Nonetheless one could not help feeling a certain sympathy with the plaintiffs in sensing that the Supreme Court failed to confront the substance of their case. There is a strong association between marriage and on ongoing viable relationship between the spouses, in contrast to the absence of such a strong association in the case of unmarried parents — even taking into account the increase in marital breakdown and in unmarried cohabitations. The failure of the tax and social welfare codes to have distinctive regard to the social reality which reflects this difference was at the heart of the plaintiff's complaint.

JUDICIAL INDEPENDENCE

Pension arrangements   *McMenamin v Ireland* [1994] 2 ILRM 151 was a partially successful challenge to the validity of certain deficiencies in the pensions arrangements made for judges of the District Court. The case arose as follows.

Paragraph 8 of the Schedule to the Courts (Supplemental Provisions) Act 1961 provides that a judge of the District Court who, having reached the age of 65, vacates his office after at least 20 years' service shall be granted a pension for life of two-thirds of his remuneration at the time of such vacation of office. S. 2 of the Courts of Justice and Court Officers (Superannuation) Act 1961 applies to any person appointed as a judge of the Supreme Court, High Court, Circuit Court or District Court. S. 2(2)of that Act provides that on the grant of a pension to any person to whom the section applies, there shall be granted to that person a gratuity equal to one and one-half times the yearly amount of the pension as reduced under s. 2(5). S. 2(3) provides that if a judge of the Supreme Court, High Court, Circuit Court or District Court dies while in office after having served as such for five years or more, there shall be granted to his personal representative a gratuity equal to the yearly amount of his salary. S. 2(5) provides that the pension payable to a person to whom s. 2 applies shall be reduced by one-fourth. The applicant was appointed as a judge of the District Court on March 1, 1983 and was due to retire on 4 February 1997. Keane J granted him leave to bring an application for judicial review so as to challenge the pension and gratuity arrangements provided for in the Courts of Justice and Court Officers (Superannuation) Act 1961. The applicant claimed that given the disparity between the benefits received by way of gratuity and the proportion by which the pension was reduced by s. 2(5), the scheme had been irrational from its inception, or alternatively had become irrational as a result of changes in economic circumstances since its enactment. It was also argued that the scheme was invalid having regard to Article 40.1 of the Constitution in that Circuit Court judges qualified for a full pension after 15 years' service, while 20 years' service was required in the case of District Court judges.

Geoghegan J granted a declaration that the State, in permitting a gross inequality to arise as between the reduction in the pension of District Court judges and the cost of lump sum gratuities intended to be met by such reduction, was in breach of its constitutional duty to secure pension rights for district judges which were not irrational or wholly inequitable.

He considered that the Courts of Justice and Court Officers (Superannuation) Act 1961 did not alter the notional pension right of two-thirds, but effected a compulsory reduction of the amount payable by one fourth in order to meet the cost to the State of the new benefits by way of retirement gratuity and death gratuity which judges were to receive under s. 2 of the Act. He stated that the expert evidence adduced by the State established that the reduction in pension effected in the light of the gratuity arrangements had not been devised in an arbitrary and irrational fashion or by means of a mere rule of thumb. The reduction had clearly been designed to finance the retirement and death gratuities which were introduced at the same time. Accordingly, the plaintiff's claim that the retirement gratuity was irrational from the outset failed.

However, Geoghegan J went on to hold that, as a consequence of changed circumstances, the 25% reduction in the notional two-thirds pension was, in the context of the statutory scheme, no longer rational or equitable. At the date of his judgment in 1994, the appropriate reduction for the purpose of financing existing benefits would be 22%. Stated in a different way, a reduction of 25% in the amount of the notional two-thirds pension should result in a gratuity of 1.9 times the reduced pension, instead of one which was 1.5 times the reduced pension, as was the case in 1994. This meant that a lump sum of approximately twice the pension, rather than one and a half times the pension, would have been appropriate in 1994 if the original rationale of the statutory scheme was applied.

Geoghegan J held that it was implicit in the Constitution that judges must receive salaries and pension benefits quite apart from any recruitment considerations; otherwise, the essential independence of the judges would be undermined. He did not consider that this constitutional obligation was discharged by making salary or pension arrangements for judges which are irrational or wholly inequitable. Article 36 could not, in his view, be interpreted as conferring on the Oireachtas an unfettered right to fix salaries and pensions for judges without regard to rationality. Rather, the State was under a constitutional obligation to provide salary and pension arrangements for judges of the District Court which at any given time, and not just at the time of the relevant enactment, are not unreasonable in the sense of being irrational or inherently inequitable. Geoghegan J added that, even if external circumstances had the effect of removing the equality so that the benefits have a value substantially less than the compulsory reduction from pension intended to pay for them, the State would be in breach of its constitutional obligation to secure pension arrangements for judges which are not irrational or wholly inequitable.

As to the argument on Article 40.1, this case proved no less stony ground than many others. Applying the general principles in *Quinn's Supermarket Ltd v Attorney General* [1972] IR 1, he considered that the equality provision applies only where there is a *prima facie* case of unfair discrimination and that even if a differentiation could be categorised as unfair, it would not necessarily contravene Article 40.1 which requires only equality as human persons. In the instant case, the evidence established that the average age of judges appointed to the District Court was considerably less than that of judges appointed to the Circuit Court and this negatived any suggestion of unfair discrimination. In addition, legitimate recruitment considerations might also justify the differential. In any event, he concluded that the inequality in qualification for full pension as between District Court and Circuit Court judges was not an inequality between judges as human persons.

Geoghegan J then turned to the question of appropriate relief in view of his earlier conclusion that s. 2(5) of the Courts of Justice and Court Officers (Superannuation) Act 1961 had resulted in impermissible discrepancies. He noted that if s. 2(5) of the 1961 Act was declared unconstitutional while the rest of s. 2 was left intact an anomalous and unjust situation would arise in that judges would be entitled to lump sums in addition to receiving full two-thirds pensions. This would give judges a benefit far in excess of what would be normal in the private or public sector. However, he considered that the entire section could not be regarded as unconstitutional simply because of changed events and the mere fact that there may be a constitutional obligation to alter and update the mechanism of a statutory scheme does not render the enactment unconstitutional.

He concluded that declaratory relief was the most appropriate in these circumstances. In any event, nothing beyond a declaratory order could be made in this case as amending legislation would be required to remove the anomaly and, given the separation of powers provided for in the Constitution, the court had no jurisdiction to order that any particular form of legislation should be introduced.

LOCUS STANDI

In *Tuohy v Courtney and Ors* [1994] 2 ILRM 503, the Supreme Court considered the plaintiff's standing to challenge certain provisions of the Statute of Limitations 1957: see the Limitations of Actions chapter, 336-8, below.

OIREACHTAS

Allowances and salaries to members The Oireachtas (Allowances to Members) (Amendment) Act 1994 updated the arrangements concerning allowances to members to take account of the changed Committee system in the Oireachtas. S. 2 of the 1994 Act provided that the Government may, by Order, provide for the payment of an annual allowance, out of moneys

provided by the Committees of the Oireachtas, to every member of the
Oireachtas who is chairman of an Oireachtas Committee. It is worthy of note
that the definition of 'Oireachtas Committee' includes not merely a Committee appointed by order of either or both of the Houses of the Oireachtas but
also the British-Irish Inter-Parliamentary Body. S. 3 of the 1994 Act provides
for a similar annual allowance to the Leader of the House in Seanad Éireann.
The first such Order was the Oireachtas (Allowances to Members) (Amendment) Act 1994 (sections 2 and 3) Order 1994 (SI No. 302 of 1994). Finally,
s. 6 of the 1994 Act provides for amendment to the travelling allowances of
members of the Oireachtas who reside in their constituencies. The 1994 Act
came into effect on July 10, 1994 on its signature by the President, but some
of its provisions also had retrospective effect. The Members of the Oireachtas
and Ministerial and Parliamentary Offices (Allowances and Salaries) Order
1994 (SI No. 303 of 1994) gave effect to increases in the general payments
and salaries for members of the Oireachtas, Government Ministers, other
office holders (including the Attorney General) and Opposition leaders in
line with Report No. 35 of the Review Body on Higher Remuneration in the
Public Sector of January 1992. Thus, for example, with effect from May 1,
1995, the salary for the Taoiseach was £95,279 (comprising TD salary of
£32,059 and additional salary of Taoiseach of £63,220). This salary was less
than that granted, for example, to the Chief Justice (whose salary rose to
£95,920 in 1995) under the marginally more generous implementation of
Report No. 35 for the judiciary contained in SI No. 273 of 1994: see the
Practice and Procedure chapter, 380, below. Finally, the Oireachtas (Allowances to Members) (Travelling Facilities) (Amendment) Regulations 1994
(SI No. 343 of 1994) consolidated the travelling expenses regime for members of the Oireachtas; and, although the word 'Amendment' appears in the
title of the 1994 Regulations, they replaced and revoked the prior Regulations
in this area, the Oireachtas (Allowances to Members) (Travelling Facilities)
Regulations 1983 and the Oireachtas (Allowances to Members) (Travelling
Facilities) (Amendment) Regulations 1990.

Elections: by-election petition   In *Dudley v An Taoiseach and Ors* [1994]
2 ILRM 321, Geoghegan J declined to order that a writ be moved to hold a
by-election to fill a vacancy in Dáil Éireann though he did grant certain other
relief in the case. The case arose against the background that s. 39(2) of the
Electoral Act 1992 provides that where a vacancy occurs in the membership
of the Dáil otherwise than in consequence of a dissolution, the Ceann
Chomhairle of the Dáil shall, as soon as he is directed by the Dáil to do so,
direct the Clerk of the Dáil to issue a writ to the returning officer of the
constituency where the vacancy has occurred directing the returning officer
to cause an election to be held of a member of the Dáil to fill the vacancy.

The applicant was a student residing in the Dublin South Central constituency. A former Dáil deputy for that constituency had resigned his seat almost fourteen months earlier. No writ to hold a by-election in the constituency had been moved in the Dáil, despite a number of efforts which were opposed by the Taoiseach and the government. The applicant applied for leave to institute judicial review proceedings on the grounds that his rights to vote at common law, by statute and under the Constitution were being infringed. Geoghegan J granted leave to institute judicial review proceedings as against the government of Ireland and the Attorney General and directed that Ireland should be joined as a respondent.

He held that, having regard to Article 16(7) of the Constitution, there was an arguable case that there is a constitutional obligation to hold a by-election within a reasonable time of a vacancy occurring and that a reasonable time had elapsed in this case. However, he held that declaratory relief was not obtainable as against Dáil Éireann because such relief should only be granted where it could be followed up by an enforceable order. Such an order could not, in his view, be made as the courts could not grant an order of *mandamus* compelling the body of members of the Dáil to vote in a particular way on a particular motion. Geoghegan J considered that the Taoiseach was not under a personal responsibility in relation to any of the matters complained about and so leave to institute judicial review proceedings against him was refused.

A particular point in the applicant's favour was that since Dáil Éireann could not move a writ of its own motion, Geoghegan J felt there was an arguable case that the government had a constitutional obligation to set down and to support motions for the issue of a writ for the holding of a by-election after a reasonable time has elapsed from the vacancy arising. As judicial review of a Minister in the exercise of his powers and functions could lie, he concluded that there must be an arguable case that the judicial review of the conduct of the government could be granted in the circumstances of this case.

Oireachtas committees: privileges   The Select Committee On Legislation And Security Of Dáil Éireann (Privilege And Immunity) Act 1994 provided for the same privileges and immunities for any person appearing before the Select Committee on Legislation and Security of Dáil Éireann established under the Act as if that person were a witness before the High Court. In addition, the Act provided for complete immunity from criminal prosecution in connection with any evidence given by such a person. The Committee had been established pursuant to an Order of Dáil Éireann of 6 December 1994 to enquire into the events surrounding the fall of the Government in November 1994. The Committee reported on this matter in February 1995. The report is considered in Casey, *The Irish Law Officers* (Round Hall Sweet and Maxwell, 1996).

Pension scheme   The Houses of the Oireachtas (Members) (Pensions Scheme) (Additional Allowances) (Deduction of Contributions) Regulations 1994 (SI No. 218 of 1994) made some further amendments to the 1992 Scheme (1992 Review, 209-9) to take account of the Oireachtas (Allowances to Members) (Amendment) Act 1994, discussed above, 117.

PRIVACY

In *M. v Drury and Ors* [1994] 2 IR 8; [1995] 1 ILRM 108, O'Hanlon J rejected claims that certain newspaper coverage of the circumstances surrounding the breakdown of the plaintiff's marriage was in conflict with her right of privacy under the Constitution.

The plaintiff had instituted proceedings against her husband for a judicial separation. The five children of the marriage lived with the plaintiff in the family home. The husband contended that the breakdown of the marriage was attributable to the plaintiff forming an adulterous relationship with a priest. The plaintiff made numerous counter charges of infidelity against her husband. The trial judge in the judicial separation proceedings, O'Hanlon J, found that both spouses had established ample grounds for a judicial separation.

However, the husband continued his claim that the plaintiff's affair with a priest was the sole cause of the breakdown of the marriage and expressed an intention of instituting proceedings seeking damages against authorities in the Roman Catholic Church for their alleged failure to intervene when allegations of misconduct against the priest were brought to their attention. He contacted the press to obtain maximum publicity for the allegations he was making against his wife and the priest, and negotiated a lucrative contract for the sale of this story to the Mirror Group, who were the publishers of The Daily Mirror newspaper. As a result, a series of reports appeared in the press. While these reports referred to an Irish architect, the father of five children, who was demanding compensation because a priest had had an affair with his wife, they did not contain names or other descriptive details which would identify the parties involved. However, in May 1994 a reporter and photographer from The Star newspaper called to the plaintiff's home while she was absent and represented to three of her children, who were all minors, that they were friends of their father and requested a photograph of him. A photograph was produced and then some photographs of the children were taken. The men returned later and took a further photograph of the plaintiff without her consent. The plaintiff made a complaint to the editorial staff of the newspaper and was assured that if photographs had been taken without permission they would not be used. Later in May 1994 more detailed stories were published by The Daily Mirror and The Star newspapers.

The plaintiff became aware that The Daily Mirror proposed to publish an extended front page feature about these matters and Kinlen J granted the plaintiff an interim order preventing publication or distribution of the issue of that newspaper which contained the article. On the same day an application was made to O'Hanlon J on behalf of the Mirror Group to discharge the interim order. A further interim order was made by O'Hanlon J restraining the publication of all material taken from the hearing of the judicial separation proceedings, but otherwise permitting the publication of the article. On June 2, 1994 The Daily Mirror carried a front page containing the story followed by four further pages of narrative and photographs. The story was given similar prominence in The Star newspaper which appeared on the same day.

The plaintiff applied for an interlocutory injunction restraining the defendants from publishing or communicating to any person any matter or fact particular to the family life of the plaintiff and relating to the intimate family relationship between herself and her husband or of any matter concerning the plaintiff and her children arising from the judicial separation proceedings, which had been held *in camera*, save such matters as might lawfully be disclosed in such proceedings. However, O'Hanlon J held that the plaintiff had not established that there was a fair question to be tried and that the balance of convenience favoured the refusal of the relief sought.

O'Hanlon J noted that the case was not concerned with the intimacies of married life or the marital communications between a husband and a wife. Instead, it involved allegations made by a husband of an extra-marital liaison entered into by his wife which he was anxious to publicise for the purpose of giving vent to his anger against the third party involved, and also possibly for the purpose of reaping some financial reward for himself. He sated that the courts would intervene in an appropriate case to prevent publication pending trial if the truth of the allegations were seriously challenged. The law of libel could also be invoked in aid of such a claim. Furthermore, injunctive relief could be obtained pursuant to the various legislative provisions, such as the Judicial Separation and Family Law Reform Act 1989, where there had been a breach of the *in camera* rule. In the instant case, though, O'Hanlon J concluded that nothing in Articles 40 and 41 of the Constitution established that there was a fair question to be tried as to whether some right of the plaintiff would be breached if further revelations of the kind which had already appeared in print were repeated in the future.

He accepted that while the courts had a jurisdiction to intervene for the protection of an infant, and also to guard the interests of a ward of court, there was a marked reluctance to exercise this jurisdiction in a manner which would entrench on the freedom of expression enjoyed by the media merely to avoid the distress which would be caused by the publication of matters which show a parent in a sordid or unfavourable light. However, he did state that there were extreme cases where the constitutionally protected right to privacy may require intervention by the courts, for example where confidential communications between a husband and a wife during their married life together would be protected against disclosure. But he thought that it should be left to the legislature and not to the courts to decide on such exceptions to principle of freedom of speech.

Where, as here, the court had been asked to intervene to restrain the publication of material, the truth of which had not yet been disputed, in order to prevent distress to the children, it would represent a new departure in the law for which no precedent had been shown and for which there was no constitutional basis, especially having regard to the Constitution's strongly expressed guarantees in favour of freedom of expression. While this view might be seen as being quite favourably disposed to the media in general, O'Hanlon J made it clear that the court had little sympathy for the section of the press which sought to exploit the human tragedy of others in order to promote their sales. However, he also accepted that the balance of convenience should also take into account the undesirability of holding up the publication of material in circumstances where the ultimate decision was likely to be that it was quite lawful to publish. Otherwise the interlocutory injunction could be used to encroach in a significant manner on the freedom of the press.

In those circumstances, as already indicated, he refused the plaintiff the very general relief sought. However, it is worthy of note that this be seen in the context of the concession made in the case by the defendants, namely that photographs of the plaintiff and the children, which had been taken by Star reporters without their permission, would not be included in any future stories. That concession may very well prove critical to an assessment of the general significance of the case itself.

REFERENDA

As stated in the Explanatory Memorandum to the Referendum Act 1994 when it was first published as a Bill, the purpose of the 1994 Act was to amend and consolidate the law relating to the taking of a referendum. Existing law on the subject was contained Referendum Act 1942, but this had subsequently been amended on eight occasions. The 1994 Act repealed the 1942 Act, as amended. The 1994 Act applies to a referendum to amend the Constitution, of which there have been many since 1937, as well as to a referendum held pursuant to Article 27 of the Constitution for any other purpose, of which there have been (at the time of writing) none since 1937.

The 1994 Act applies to referenda, with necessary modifications, the provisions of the Electoral Act 1992 (1992 Review, 141-4) in relation to matters such as postal voting, special voting, taking the poll at polling stations, arrangements for the counting of votes and electoral offences. The passing of the Referendum Act 1994, along with the Electoral Act 1992 two years before, represents a major updating of all legislation in the electoral area. Some of the principal features of the 1994 Act, and the changes effected by it to the existing law on referenda, are outlined below. For a comprehensive discussion, see Thomas John O'Dowd, *Annotation, ICLSA*.

Constitutional referendum v 'ordinary' referendum We have already noted that the 1994 Act applies to a referendum to amend the Constitution as well as to an 'ordinary' referendum held pursuant to Article 27 of the Constitution, the latter including a referendum to approve, or disapprove, a Bill which has been passed by both Houses of the Oireachtas. While the arrangements for both would be broadly similar, one matter concerning the list of electors is of great importance. Thus, s. 17 of the 1994 Act requires each registration authority to send to the referendum returning officer details of the number of presidential electors on the register of electors not later than 5 days before the polling day at an ordinary referendum. Unlike the position at a constitutional referendum, where the issue is decided by a majority of the votes cast, the question of whether a Bill, which is the subject of an ordinary referendum, is vetoed is settled by reference to the proportion of the total electorate who vote against it.

Form of ballot paper Pursuant to s. 24 of the 1994 Act, the Minister for the Environment may provide, by Order, approved by both Houses of the Oireachtas, for the inclusion of a descriptive heading on the ballot paper at a referendum where this is considered necessary. Similar provision was made in primary legislation on a number of occasions in the past where the polls at two or more referenda were taken on the same day. The 1994 Act now provides that this may be done without the need for primary legislation.

Transfer of vote By s. 31 of the 1994 Act, an elector employed by a local returning officer may be authorised to vote in the polling station at which he or she is employed even if the station is outside his/her own constituency.

Counting the votes The 1994 Act omits the requirement in previous law for Ministerial approval for the appointment of a deputy local returning officer and for the provision of a counting centre outside the constituency. In addition, under s. 34, the local returning officer is enabled to record on the ballot paper the effect of his or her ruling on a 'doubtful' ballot paper.

Recount of votes cast at a referendum   Under s. 36 of the 1994 Act the referendum returning officer is empowered to direct a complete re-examination and recount of the votes cast in every constituency. Under the 1942 Act, as amended, a recount could be demanded in an individual constituency but there was no provision for a complete recount of the votes in all the constituencies. The Explanatory Memorandum explained that this provision was 'intended to deal with a situation where the overall result of the voting might be very close and a recount would be desirable to put the matter beyond doubt, thus avoiding the necessity for a time-consuming and expensive referendum petition.' It is of interest to note that in the first referendum held after the passing of the 1994 Act, the 1995 referendum to remove the constitutional ban on divorce (which we will discuss in the 1995 Review), the result was exceptionally close and the returning officer ordered a complete recount as provided for in the 1994 Act. While this recount confirmed the original outcome, a referendum petition nonetheless resulted, *Hanafin v Minister for the Environment*, High Court, 1 March 1996; [1996] 2 ILRM 61 (SC), which we will also discuss in the 1995 Review. It may be that, contrary to the expectations of the drafters of the 1994 Act, a close referendum result may, perhaps more than a clear one, would result in a petition.

Referendum petitions   The Explanatory Memorandum stated that the provisions relating to referendum petitions were being tightened up under the 1994 Act and certainly this was true in a formal sense. Thus, under s. 42 of the 1994 Act, leave of the High Court to present a petition must be sought within 7 days of the publication of the provisional referendum certificate rather than 10 days as provided under previous law. In addition, the petition must be presented within 3 days of the grant of leave by the High Court, whereas under the previous system a petition could be presented within 21 days of the publication of the provisional referendum certificate. While the 1994 Act is more stringent in this area than under the 1942 Act, the 1994 Act did not in any way prove a deterrent to the presentation of the *Hanafin* petition in the wake of the first referendum held after the passing of the 1994 Act. In our discussion of the *Hanafin* case in the 1995 Review, we will also discuss the grounds on which a referendum petition may be presented pursuant to s. 43 of the 1994 Act. The grounds on which a petition may be based are limited by s. 43 to any one of four matters where is alleged that 'the result of the referendum as a whole was affected materially': (a) the commission of electoral offences under the Electoral Act 1992, (b) obstruction of 'or interference with' the referendum (the words in quotation marks being the subject of particular analysis in the *Hanafin* case), (c) failure to conduct the referendum in accordance with the 1994 Act or (d) any mistake or irregularity in the conduct of the referendum.

REMEDIES

Injunction: interlocutory In *Colmey v Pinewood Developments Ltd* [1995] 1 ILRM 331, Carroll J declined to grant an interlocutory injunction to the plaintiff preventing the District Court exercising its powers in ejectment proceedings.

The defendant had acquired property as a commercial investment in 1989. The plaintiff in the first case had resided in that property as a weekly tenant for approximately 19 years. She was served with a notice to quit in May 1994 and ejectment proceedings in the District Court were served in August 1994. She sought a declaration from the High Court that those proceedings were offensive to the Constitution on the grounds that her health would be imperilled by having to leave the premises. The plaintiffs in the second case claimed, *inter alia*, a constitutional property right entitling them to remain in undisturbed possession as long as they observed the conditions of the contract with the landlord. Carroll J refused the relief sought in both cases.

She held that, in determining whether there is a fair issue to be tried, it was not for the courts to hold that the plaintiff would probably not succeed and once the claim was not frivolous or vexatious, the plaintiff was entitled to have her claim decided in a full action. She went on, however, that the District Court should not be injuncted from exercising the jurisdiction conferred on it by statute and the Court must assume that the District Court judge would administer justice in accordance with the law. Thus, she concluded that the balance of convenience lay in preserving free access to the District Court.

Perpetual injunction In *Lovett t/a Lovett Transport v Gogan t/a PS Travel and Ors* [1995] 1 ILRM 12, the Supreme Court confirmed that a private individual may enforce legislation by means of injunctive relief, particularly where it is established that there has been a breach of that person's constitutional rights.

The case arose against the background of long-running litigation concerning road transport legislation. The plaintiff held an occasional passenger licences under the Road Transport Act 1932 allowing him to operate road passenger services on Fridays and Sundays to and from certain points in Dublin and County Clare. The first and fifth named defendants, who did not hold such licences, operated similar services with coaches hired from other persons. The plaintiff sought *inter alia* injunctive relief restraining the defendants from operating their services on Fridays and Sundays. In the High Court, Costello J held that the defendants were operating 'an occasional road passenger service' and made an order permanently restraining the first and fifth named defendants from operating or participating in the operation of any regular coach service between points in Dublin and County Clare other than a passenger road service within the meaning of the Road Transport Act 1932 carried on in accordance with a licence granted under that Act. On appeal by the first and fifth named defendants, the Supreme Court (Finlay CJ, Egan and Denham JJ) upheld this decision.

Delivering the leading judgment, Finlay CJ agreed with Costello J that the first and fifth named defendants were operating a road passenger service as defined in the 1932 Act for which a licence was required. Distinguishing the instant case from *Director of Public Prosecutions v Go-Travel Ltd* [1992] 2 IR 1 (1991 Review, 464-5), he stated that there was nothing in the 1932 Act, and in particular in the conditions which the Minister for Transport could impose under s. 12, which would confine the granting of a licence to the person who owned the bus concerned.

Turning to the relief claimed, the Chief Justice stated that the plaintiff was entitled to an injunction to restrain the defendants' unlawful act or continued commission of an offence under s. 7 of the 1932 Act. In particular, he cited with approval the judgment of O'Hanlon J in *Parsons v Kavanagh* [1990] ILRM 560 (1988 Review, xv-xvii) to the effect that where criminal offences are being committed contrary to statute which have the effect of infringing an individual's constitutional right to earn a livelihood by lawful means, such an individual is entitled to seek redress against those persons who have infringed that right. In the instant case, Finlay CJ considered that, in accordance with the jurisprudence of the Court as outlined in *Meskell v Coras Iompair Éireann* [1973] IR 121, the granting of an injunction was appropriate where the plaintiff can establish that it is the only way of protecting him from the threatened invasion of his constitutional right, especially where the fine which could be imposed on the defendants under the Road Transport Act 1932 was minimal.

On the criteria to be applied in determining whether to grant an injunction to protect the invasion of an individual's constitutional rights, Finlay CJ made a number of important comments. He considered that the matter should not be considered on the basis of the criteria governing the discretion of the court to grant the equitable remedy of an injunction or the equitable doctrine that a plaintiff seeking such relief must come to court with clean hands. Instead, the test to be applied by the court is whether the plaintiff has a constitutional right and if that right is being threatened. In the instant case, that issue had been established in the plaintiff's favour.

SEPARATION OF POWERS

Howard and Ors v Commissioners of Public Works in Ireland and Ors (No. 2) [1994] 2 ILRM 301, in which the constitutionality of the State Authorities (Development and Management) Act 1993 was upheld, is discussed in the Local Government chapter, 356-8, below.

TRIAL OF OFFENCES

Binding to the peace In *Gregory and Ors v Windle and Ors* [1995] 1 ILRM 131, O'Hanlon J rejected constitutional challenges to the long-standing power of judges to bind person to keep the peace. The plaintiffs had been convicted by a judge of the District Court of using threatening or abusive or insulting behaviour with intent to provoke a breach of the peace or whereby a breach of the peace might be occasioned, contrary to s. 14(13) of the Dublin Police Act 1842. The case had arisen against the background of long-standing disputes concerning casual trading licences in the city of Dublin, and it is notable that the first plaintiff was at the time of the offence (and is at the time of writing) a member of Dáil Éireann who supported those protesting against the casual trading arrangements. All those involved in the instant proceedings were bound over to the peace by the defendant judge of the District Court with a requirement that they enter recognisances and provide a solvent surety, in the sum of £1,000 as regards two of the plaintiffs, and in the sum of £500 as regards the third. The judge also directed that,in default of entering the recognisance or providing a surety, they would be imprisoned. Each plaintiff subsequently failed to enter the recognisance and a warrant was issued for their arrest and imprisonment.

Each plaintiff was granted leave to challenge the validity of the District Court order and warrant of committal by way of judicial review.

S. 54 of the Courts (Supplemental Provisions) Act 1961 provides that:

> The jurisdiction formerly exercised by justices of the peace to make an order binding a person to the peace or to good behaviour or to both the peace and good behaviour and requiring him to enter a recognisance in that behalf may be exercised by . . . (c) a [judge] of the District Court within the district to which he is for the time being assigned.

The plaintiffs sought, *inter alia*, declarations that the common law powers of magistrates to bind to the peace were not carried over on the enactment of the Constitution, and that s. 54 of the Courts (Supplemental Provisions) Act 1961 was repugnant to the Constitution. On behalf of the first and second named plaintiffs it was pointed out that their offence was committed during a protest by street traders and that no evidence was adduced indicating a likelihood or propensity on their part to engage in conduct likely to disturb the peace in the future. One of the plaintiffs also averred that he had no access to any person who could come forward as a solvent surety in the sum of £1,000. Ultimately, while O'Hanlon J dismissed the challenge to the constitutional validity of the orders, he quashed them having regard to lapse of time.

O'Hanlon J reviewed the history of the jurisdiction to bind to the peace and to require sureties, originating from common law, the justices' commission and a statute enacted in 1360 of Edward III, 34 Edwd III, c.1, and he referred to the discussion of this history in *R. (Feehan) v Queens Co. JJ* (1882) 10 LR Ir 294 and *Ex parte Tanner MP*, August 8, 1889, reported in *Judgments of the Superior Courts in Ireland* (Stationery Office, 1903). On this basis, he felt that there was at least *prima facie* support for the validity of the orders.

As to the Constitution, the plaintiffs relied on the decision of the Supreme Court in *The People v O'Callaghan* [1966] IR 501 as frowning on any jurisdiction that appeared to authorise preventative detention. However, O'Hanlon J compared the power to bind to the peace with that concerning contempt of court. Having referred to the decisions in *Keegan v de Burca* [1973] IR 223 and *The State (Commins) v McRann* [1977] IR 78, he concluded that the Constitution does not prevent the continuance in force of the jurisdiction of the courts to bind to the peace and to be of good behaviour and to provide sureties for such undertaking, under penalty of committal to prison for a fixed and limited period if default is made in complying with the order of the court, and on the basis that the person concerned is to be released from detention upon complying with the order of the court at any time before the fixed period of detention has expired. In this respect, he considered that the liberty of the individual is sufficiently safeguarded by the supervisory role exercised by the superior courts in respect of the orders made by courts of limited and local jurisdiction, particularly where there is an abuse of authority or where the amount of security fails to bear a relation to the quality and quantity of the offence or to the situation and circumstances of the party.

As to the instant case, however, O'Hanlon J was of the view that as a number of years had elapsed since the making of the orders by the judge of the District Court, and there was no evidence to suggest that the plaintiffs had not continued to keep the peace and to be of good behaviour, the purpose of the orders had become spent. In the circumstances, he concluded that the correct course was to quash the orders.

Right to silence In *Heaney and McGuiness v Ireland and the Attorney*

General [1994] 2 ILRM 420, Costello J (as he then was) rejected the claim that the Constitution had extended the scope of the right to silence, or the right against self-incrimination, beyond that which existed at common law.

Under s. 52(1) of the Offences Against the State Act 1939, a member of the Garda Síochána may demand that a person detained under Part IV of the Act should give a full account of his movements and actions during any specified period and all information in his possession in relation to the commission or intended commission by another person of any offence under the Act or any scheduled offence. S. 52(2) provides that a person who fails or refuses to give such account or any such information, or gives an account or information which is false or misleading, shall be guilty of an offence and be liable on summary conviction to imprisonment for a term not exceeding six months. S. 52 is contained in Part V of the 1939 Act and applies only when that part of the Act is in force. By virtue of s. 35, this requires a proclamation to the effect that the government is satisfied that the ordinary courts are inadequate to secure the effective administration of justice and the preservation of peace and order.

The plaintiffs, who were suspected of being members of the IRA and of being involved in a bomb attack, were arrested by the Gardaí under s. 30 of the 1939 Act. During their detention both were asked, pursuant to s. 52, to account for their movements. Both refused to do so or to answer any questions which were put to them. Each was charged with being a member of the IRA, and failing to account for his movements pursuant to s. 52. The Special Criminal Court acquitted them of the charges of IRA membership, but convicted them in respect of the offences under s. 52 and sentenced them to six months' imprisonment. The plaintiffs instituted proceedings in which they claimed a declaration that s. 52 was invalid on the ground that it infringed the constitutionally protected right to silence. Costello J refused the relief sought.

First, he dealt with a preliminary objection by the defendants that the plaintiffs had no locus standi to challenge s. 52 on the basis that they had not asserted that any answers they would give would incriminate them: an argument which, if successful, would have presented the plaintiffs with an interesting dilemma. However, Costello J rejected this argument, and held that where the right to remain silent exists it is enjoyed by both the guilty and the innocent so that a plaintiff who challenges the constitutional validity of a statutory provision on the ground that it infringes the right is not required to assert, in order to establish *locus standi*, that he would have incriminated himself had he acted as required by the statute.

Turning to the nature of the common law right to silence itself, Costello J referred with approval to the speech of Lord Mustill in *R. v Director of Serious Fraud Office, ex parte Smith* [1993] AC 1 that it does not denote a single right but comprises 'a disparate group of immunities'. From this, Costello J formed the following important conclusions which are worth quoting in full:

> The right to silence can arise in a variety of different circumstances. The nature and scope of the right and the reasons why it was conferred by law can differ in significant ways and will depend on the circumstances in which it is conferred and exercised. . . . When a person is arrested as a suspect and subsequently charged with an offence two discrete immunities are conferred by the common law: . . . (a) the immunity against self-incrimination of a suspect and (b) an immunity against self-incrimination of an accused person during his trial. The suspect's immunity was developed in order to avoid the risk of untrue confessions being obtained from a person whilst in police custody. The law does not prohibit a suspect from confessing to a crime - nor does it prohibit the questioning of a suspect in custody. It provides, however, that a suspect should not be required to answer questions on pain of punishment should he not wish to do so, that he is free to remain silent should he so choose and that he should be informed of his right to do so. An accused's immunity was developed by the common law courts in response to the abuses arising from court procedures involving the judicial interrogation of accused persons. As a result, an accused cannot be required to give evidence at his own trial or compelled to adduce evidence on his own behalf and is entitled to remain silent during it, and not to be questioned either by the prosecution or the presiding judge.

Costello J then went on to consider the constitutional context within which the common law right to silence was to be considered. In this respect, he rejected the argument by the State that Article 38.1 of the Constitution, which provides that no person shall be tried on any criminal charge save in due course of law, implies more than the simple assertion that trials are to be held in accordance with laws enacted by the Oireachtas. Affirming mainstream constitutional jurisprudence on this, he held that Article 38.1 comprises a guarantee that criminal trials will be conducted in accordance with basic principles of justice. Those basic principles may be of ancient origin and part of the long established principles of the common law, or they may be of more recent origin and widely accepted in other jurisdictions and recognised in international conventions as the basic requirements of a fair trial. Of the long-established principles, he cited the presumption of innocence, that an accused cannot be tried for an offence unknown to the law, or charged a second time with the same offence, that the accused must know the case he or she has to meet and that evidence obtained illegally will, generally, be inadmissible.

Turning to the right to silence, Costello J accepted that the immunity of an accused at his trial, by virtue of which he is not obliged to give evidence or required to adduce evidence on his own behalf, and cannot be questioned against his will, was of such long standing and so widely accepted as basic to the rules under which criminal trials are conducted that it should be regarded as one of the rights which come within the terms of the guarantee of a fair trial contained in Article 38.1. It is notable that he cited with approval the decision of the European Court of Human Rights in *Funke v France* (1993) 16 EHRR 297 to the effect that this right was inherent in the right to a fair hearing in Article 6(1) of the European Convention on Human Rights and Fundamental Freedoms. While the precise right in the instant case was concerned not with the right to silence at trial but the right to silence while in police custody, Costello J was prepared to accept that this was also protected under the general umbrella of Article 38.1. He commented that the fairness of a trial may be compromised by what happens prior to it, for example where unfairly obtained evidence may be ruled inadmissible at trial. Accordingly, he concluded that the suspect's common law immunity against self-incrimination is protected under Article 38.1.

However, he was also of the view that this did not determine the matter in the plaintiffs' favour. Costello J stated that the right to silence may in certain circumstances be abridged by the Oireachtas. In determining whether such a restriction was constitutionally permissible, he held that a test of proportionality, as described by the Supreme Court in *Cox v Ireland* [1992] 2 IR 503 (1991 Review 105-7) and the Supreme Court of Canada in *Chaulk v R.* [1990] 3 SCR 1303, should be applied so as to balance the exercise of protected rights and the exigencies of the common good in a democratic society.

Turning to s. 52 of the 1939 Act, Costello J noted that the purpose of the Offences against the State Act 1939 was to make provision, mainly in terms of arrest, trial and punishment, for acts and conduct calculated to undermine public order and the authority of the State. The main object which s. 52 was designed to achieve was to assist the Gardaí in their investigation of serious crimes of a subversive nature involving the security of the State. While it imposed a restriction on the right to silence of a suspect arrested under s. 30, he concluded that it could not be said that it was arbitrary or based on irrational considerations. What had to be considered was whether the restrictions impaired the rights of the suspect as little as possible and were such that their effects were proportionate to the objective which s. 52 sought to achieve.

Looking at the detriment to the right holder which the restriction on the exercise of the right imposed, a law which requires a suspect to give information under pain of punishment if he refuses to do so increases the risk that he may wrongfully confess to having committed a crime. However, he noted that the law afforded other protections to minimise this risk and provided safeguards against any possible abuse of the statutory power, and he cited the passage from the judgment of Finlay CJ in *The People v Quilligan (No. 3)* [1993] 2 IR 305, which described the rights of a suspect in custody and which we quoted in the 1992 Review, 236-7. Bearing these protections in mind, Costello J concluded that the restrictions on the right to silence imposed by s. 52 of the 1939 Act could not be regarded as excessive and the provision was proportionate to the objective which it was designed to achieve.

Costello J also rejected two further claims concerning s. 52. First, that it infringed the presumption of innocence. He considered that although compliance with s. 52 might result in the production of evidence which could be used at a subsequent trial to establish guilt this did not infringe the legal presumption of innocence which the accused would continue to enjoy. Like the statutory provisions on the collection of fingerprints, now contained in the Criminal Justice (Forensic Evidence) Act 1990 (see the 1990 Review, 206-7), Costello J held that s. 52 was concerned with the gathering of evidence and not with the legal presumption which both a suspect and an accused would continue to enjoy. The other challenge rejected by Costello J was that s. 52 replaced the well established adversarial nature of the criminal trial with an inquisitorial system. But Costello J rejected this in the following important passage:

> The right to silence enjoyed by an accused at his trial is based on the law's rejection of an inquisitorial type of criminal trial. The requirements of [s. 52] do not bear on trial procedures. The right to silence of a suspect in custody is derived from different principles. He may be questioned whilst in custody provided he gets the proper caution from his interrogator and is informed of his right to silence. A law which requires him to give specified information does not, in my opinion, alter the essential features of either his custody as a suspect or of any subsequent trial he may undergo as an accused.

One might cavil with this portion of Costello J's judgment. In particular, it is notable that he appears to be of the view that existing procedural safeguards are sufficient to protect the right to silence in police custody and to 'reject' the inquisitorial model. While this may be a tempting approach to take, it seems to ignore the argument of those who suggest that existing safeguards are, in fact, inadequate and that an 'informal' inquisitorial system has been created. This would appear to be supported by the assertion by a former Commissioner of the Garda Síochána that a global figure, not confined to Ireland, is that 'something in the order of 80% of all crime solved is achieved by questioning suspects': see McLaughlin, 'Legal Constraints in Criminal Investigation' (1981) 16 Ir Jur(ns) 217 at p.220. While it may be the case that all such confessions were obtained by fair procedures and compliance with existing procedural protections, it does seem to cast some doubt over whether the right to silence has sufficient protection. One might query whether the types of procedural protections available at trial for the right to silence are comparable to those available in police custody. On the debate, for example, over access to a solicitor while in police custody, see the discussion of *The People v Healy* [1990] 2 IR 73; [1990] ILRM 313 in the 1989 Review, 137-9 and of the adequacy of the procedural protections outlined in *The People v Quilligan (No. 3)* [1993] 2 IR 305, see the 1992 Review, 237-9.

For completeness, we note two other arguments dealt with by Costello J in *Heaney*. He rejected the suggestion that s. 52 breached the guarantee of equality before the law contained in Article 40.1, holding that the Oireachtas had valid grounds for legislating in respect of the serious crimes referred to in the 1939 Act in a manner different to that in which it legislates for other types of crimes. Nor was he prepared to hold that the right to silence was an unenumerated personal right within the meaning of Article 40.3.1°. He held that its protection was confined to that under Article 38.1, although he concluded that, in any event, even if the right to silence was protected by Article 40.3.1°, there could be no breach because the restrictions imposed by s. 52 were constitutionally permissible.

We note here that the Supreme Court upheld Costello J's decision in July 1996. We will return to this in the 1996 Review.

Contract Law

Eoin O'Dell, Law School, Trinity College, Dublin

Clark and Clarke, *Contract, Cases and Materials* (Gill & Macmillan) is an important new work on the subject published in 1994.

FRUSTRATION

The doctrine of frustration It was once the case that, at common law, contractual obligations were absolute, in the sense that a party who failed to perform was strictly liable for breach even if the reason for his failure to perform arose from an event beyond his control (*Pardine v Jane* (1647) Aleyn 26; 82 ER 897). However, it has long been recognised and accepted that such supervening events can have the effect of discharging the contract (*Taylor v Caldwell* (1863) 3 B&S 826; 122 ER 309). In such circumstances, it is now said that the contract has been frustrated. The doctrine is often invoked as a defence: a party who, as a consequence of the supervening event, can no longer perform his obligations under the contract, seeks to rely on the frustration as having discharged the contract so as to resist an action for specific performance. It should also be noticed, however, that benefits have often been transferred under such frustrated contracts, and, in certain circumstances, such benefits may be recovered back (see, *e.g.* *Fibrosa v Fairbairn* [1943] AC 32 where a contract was frustrated by the outbreak of the second world war, and the plaintiff recovered an advance payment as money paid on a consideration which had failed). Thus, if a contract has been discharged by a supervening event, the doctrine of frustration is a defence to an action to enforce the contract, and can constitute the facts from which a cause of action in restitution (for failure of consideration) may be generated. Note, however, that Ireland is one of the few common law jurisdictions not to have made legislative provision for remedies for frustrated contracts (on the success or otherwise of such provision, see Stewart and Carter (1992) 51 *CLJ*; McKendrick, 'Frustration, Restitution, and Loss Apportionment' in Burrows (ed.), *Essays on the Law of Restitution* (Oxford, 1991), 147)).

As a matter of Irish law, frustration occurs 'whenever the law recognises that without default of either party a contractual obligation has become incapable of being performed because of some intervening illegality or because the circumstances in which performance is called for rendered it something radically different from that which was undertaken by the contract' (*Bates v Model Bakery* [1993] 1 IR 359, 369; [1993] ILRM 22, 29 *per* O'Flaherty J holding that a strike after notice does not frustrate a contract of employment; following *Becton, Dickinson Ltd v Lee* [1973] IR 1; see the 1992 Review, 403-5). That it is extraordinarily difficult for a party to maintain a plea of frustration, even so defined, is illustrated by the decision of the Supreme Court in *Neville v Guardian Builders* [1995] 1 ILRM 1 overruling the decision of Murphy J in the High Court [1990] ILRM 601; (see 1991 Review, 130-131)).

The parties had entered into a contract by which *Neville* would construct houses on a plot of land owned by Guardian. The plot of land was adjoined by a strip of land owned by the council, which was in turn adjoined by an hotel. In March 1987, Guardian granted Neville a licence to enter onto the plot for that purpose. To complete its agreement with Neville, Guardian sought to buy the council strip and to obtain planning permission for the combined site. Planning permission for the Guardian plot with an access road over the council strip was obtained in May 1988. However, by October 1988, Guardian had failed to acquire the strip from the council. Neville sued for specific performance of its contract with Guardian, and Guardian sought to argue that the failure of the negotiations with the council frustrated its contract with Neville. This argument succeeded in the High Court but failed in the Supreme Court.

As to the negotiations between Neville and the council, a 1984 agreement that the council would sell their strip was unenforceable since Guardian had failed to comply with its conditions. The 1987/1988 negotiations had broken down since the council had already granted to the hotel in 1983 a planning permission to extend its car park with an exit over the council strip. This 1983 permission to the hotel and the 1988 permission to Guardian were inconsistent, the council insisted that it would not change the position of the hotel exit without the permission of the hotel, and it was not prepared to sell the strip to Guardian unless the position of the hotel's exit were left unchanged or Guardian could come to an arrangement with the hotel. The alleged frustration therefore consisted in Guardian's failure to purchase the council strip.

In the High Court, Murphy J reaffirmed the modern orthodoxy that the juridical basis of frustration is a matter of the operation of law upon construction of the contract rather than being based upon an implied term, and held that since both parties expected a successful outcome to Guardian's negotiations with the council, which expectation had been frustrated, he would refuse specific performance. For Professor Clark, a consequence of this decision is that '[t]he failure of a contemplated event may just as much frustrate a contract as a cataclysmic occurrence. The crucial fact to note is that even though the parties, objectively, could have anticipated difficulties in obtaining permission, the contract did not contain a provision dealing with the contingency'. (Clark, *Contract Law in Ireland* (3rd ed., 1992) p. 427). However, 'there is considerable support both in principle and in the authorities for the view that foresight or foreseeability of the supervening event excludes frustration.' (Treitel, pp. 801-802). To the extent that it was not clear that the negotiations with the local authorities in respect of roads and access points would be successfully concluded, it may be arguable that failure to agree these matters was at least objectively foreseeable if not necessarily actually foreseen by the parties. That being so, the doctrine of frustration would be excluded.

Consequently, it may be that to stretch the doctrine of frustration as far as Murphy J did may be to stretch it beyond its limits. *Krell v Henry* [1903] 2 KB 740 upon which he relies, rests on very shaky ground (see Treitel, *The Law of Contract* (8th ed., 111), p. 784). Further, in *Amalgamated Investments v Walker* [1977] 1 WLR 164, the legitimate actions of a public body in listing property the subject matter of the sale so as to render impossible the proposed development was held not to amount to a frustration. By analogy, here it may be that the legitimate actions of the public body in respect of access points so as to render impossible the proposed development could be said not to amount to a frustration. Furthermore, in this context, it is clear that a party cannot rely on self-induced frustration (Treitel, pp. 803-804). Thus, in *Herman v Owners of the SS Vicia* [1946] IR 138, the failure of owners to obtain the documents necessary to gain access to English ports, though it might be described as frustration, was self-induced, and did not frustrate their contracts with their crew.

It may very well be that any frustration on the facts is self-induced, at least in so far as the absence of any agreement with the council was the result of Guardian's failure so to secure by any of the means mentioned in the judgment (negotiations with the hotel, an indemnity, *etc.*). Swanton comments that a 'satisfactory rationale of the rule regarding self-induced frustration will usually be that a person cannot take advantage of his own wrong, since normally it will be the "inducer" who will be seeking to avoid the contract on the grounds of frustration' ('The Concept of Self-Induced Frustration' (1990) 2 *JCL* 206, 226). This is precisely the case here, and for that reason, it should not have been held that the contract was frustrated.

It may be that it would have been better for Guardian to argue that the contract was conditional (albeit that the condition of availability of access is implied rather than expressed), the condition being unfulfilled, the contract would thereby be unenforceable. Or it may he that Murphy J's decision would have been supportable on the basis that what was being claimed by Neville was an order for specific performance, an equitable order at the discretion of the judge. Although case law has bounded that discretion, it could be exercised to refuse the order for specific performance even if a plea of frustration could not be sustained. This would seem a much sounder basis for the conclusion flowing from Murphy J's assertion that no Court would 'compel Neville's to build houses on land to which they could gain access as a matter of right'. It is a cardinal principle that 'Equity will not specifically enforce that which cannot be done' (Meagher, Gummow and Lehane Equity, *Doctrines and Remedies* (3rd ed., 1992) para. 2028, p. 511). It is clear that Guardian could not grant access over the land, and therefore, so the argument would run, equity should not specifically enforce the agreement to that effect with Neville. Of course, the discretion not to grant specific performance would not amount to a complete defence; the court could order damages in lieu if it declines to order specific performance.

Frustration and specific performance In the context of the claim for specific performance, it had been 'urged that the plaintiffs were entitled to obtain an order for specific performance of so much of the agreement as could be performed and either to waive performance of the remaining terms or to be compensated for their breach' and Murphy J did 'not doubt the correctness of that contention' in an appropriate case. It is submitted that Murphy J should have doubted it: 'when the Court cannot compel specific performance of the contract as a whole, it will not interfere to compel specific performance of part of a contract'. (Meagher, Gummow and Lehane, p. 510, para. 2026 citing *Ryan v Mutual Tontine Westminster Chambers Association* [1893] 1 Ch 116, 123 *per* Lord Esher MR). Keane J, writing extra-judicially has reached the same conclusion (*Equity and the Law of Trusts in the Republic of Ireland* (1988) p. 247, para. 16.08). In the event, nothing turned on this point, even in the Supreme Court, where the decision of Murphy J was overruled, and specific performance ordered. For Blayney J (Finlay CJ and Denham J concurring), it was clear that it was part of the agreement between Neville and Guardian that Guardian had undertaken to allow Neville access to the plot over the council strip. While Guardian did not at the time own the council strip, they nonetheless agreed to give access to Neville over it, being satisfied that they would be able to acquire title from the council to enable them to do this. Thus, as Murphy J had at first instance, Blayney J considered a frustration to be an event which so significantly changes the nature of the outstanding contractual rights and/or obligations from what the parties could reasonable have contemplated that it would be unjust to hold them to the literal sense of its stipulations in the new circumstances (citing *National Carriers Ltd v Panalpina* [1981] AC 675, 700 *per* Lord Simon; 717 *per* Lord Roskill; *cp. Bates supra*)).

No such event had occurred here: '[n]o event supervened which significantly changed the nature of Guardian's obligation to provide access to the licence plot which involved constructing the access road. . . . The only unexpected problem that Guardian had was the council insisting that the position of the exit from the hotel car park to the access road should not be altered, but this could not by any means be termed a supervening event which significantly changed the nature of Guardian's obligation under the licence agreement. It made it more onerous, but that was all'. With respect, this must be correct, in its own terms and for the reasons given above as to why the judgment of Murphy J was questionable (especially with regard to self-induced frustration).

Frustration and contracts of employment   It is now unchallengeable that a strike after due notice will frustrate a contract of employment (*e.g.*, *Bates, supra*). This principle informs the background to a quite extraordinary case, *Browne v Bank of Ireland* (District Court, unreported, January 17, 1994, Judge Ballagh). In early 1992, during a period of industrial action, some bank employees (members of the Irish Bank Officials' Association) refused to sign a loyalty pledge to their employer; and also refused to work overtime or to collect charges on certain transactions. As a consequence, the banks paid their employees' salaries less 20% which broadly represented the amount lost in uncollected charges. The four plaintiffs did not sign the pledges, were not in a position to work overtime, and had no contact with the public, but still had their salaries deducted. They sued the defendant banks to determine whether the banks would be liable to pay the deduction. The amount of each individual plaintiff's claim was very small (£235 to £538), but the potential liability on the part of the banks if they lost, due to their consequential liability to those of their employees who had refused to sign the pledges, was enormous. Thus could arise the extraordinary spectacle of senior and junior counsel briefed on both sides in the lowest court in the hierarchy, and of the judge in that court taking the time to prepare a lengthy written judgment. In the event, Judge Ballagh held that the plaintiffs were entitled to recover the unpaid salaries.

First, the failure to sign the loyalty pledges did not constitute a breach of contract on the part of the employees. Thus, 'the banks had no right to make the deductions' (*Welborn v Australian Postal Commission* [1984] VR 257, 267-268 *per* Fullagar J considered and followed). Further, the action was more properly to be regarded as action in debt rather than in contract, approving the views expressed by Napier [1984] *CLJ* 337.

Second, Judge Ballagh distinguished possible contrary authorities on the facts, in two (*Miles v Wakefield UDC* [1987] ICR 368; [1987] AC 539 and *Ticehurst v BT* [1992] IRLR 219) 'there was an actual withdrawal of labour', in the other two (*Henthorn v CEGB* [1980] IRLR 361 and *Wiluszynski v*

London Borough of Tower Hamlets [1989] IRLR 259) there was 'at the very least, limited industrial action which meant that the plaintiffs were in breach of contract'. Implicit in this is Judge Ballagh's acceptance that the plaintiffs here were not in breach of contract. However, although a strike, preceded by due notice, does not amount to repudiation or frustration of the contract of employment *Browne* does not address the logical corollary that more limited industrial action not amounting to strike likewise does not amount to repudiation or frustration. Twomey, '"Macho Management", Moral Outrage and the IBOA: Limited Industrial Action and the law' (1993) 3 *ISLR* 131 had made precisely this argument in the context of this dispute well before *Browne* was heard, and, though the issue would have been addressed in a further wave of cases arising out of the dispute, none seems to have been taken.

The award included interest at the Courts Act rate, emphasising the finding that it was an action in debt. It is important to characterise the basis of that debt. Even though the action was not for damages for breach of contract, it could still have been a contractual debt by virtue of the distinction between an action for an agreed (or liquidated) sum and one for damages (an unliquidated sum), (see *e.g.* Treitel, p. 895). On the other hand, if the consequence of Judge Ballagh's conclusion that action arose in debt rather than in contract is that it is a non-contractual debt, then the only non-contractual reason for liability in Judge Ballagh's judgment seems to lie in his earlier finding that the banks 'accepted without comment or complaint the work performed by all the plaintiffs', whereupon the action becomes restitutionary, and the basis of the cause of action would seem to be the banks' 'free acceptance' of the plaintiffs' work. Although controversial (see, *e.g.* Birks, 'In Defence of Free Acceptance' in Burrows (ed.), *supra*), the essence of this cause of action has recently been neatly summed up by Aldous J: 'why should a man who receives and uses a service, knowing that it is not being rendered free, not pay for it?'. (*BAGS v Gilbert* [1994] FSR 723, 743). Where a plaintiff confers a benefit upon a defendant, and the defendant, with the opportunity to reject, fails to exercise that opportunity, the defendant comes under a duty to make restitution to the plaintiff in the amount of the benefit so conferred. *Gilbert* is an excellent example of a defendant who exercised his opportunity to reject. The plaintiff provided a service which those in the defendant's trade (bookmakers) found beneficial.

> Furthermore, the evidence established that Gilbert had received demands for payment for many years and therefore knew that BAGS believed that it should be paid and was entitled to payment. If those had been the complete facts, there would be a persuasive argument that Gilbert should pay based upon . . . unjust enrichment. Why should a

man who receives and uses a service, knowing that it is not being rendered free, not pay for it? However, the facts of this case are different.

BAGS knew that Gilbert did not want the BAGS service. BAGS knew that if the service was provided to Gilbert, it would not pay. . . . Does the law impose a duty upon a person to pay, when he receives and uses a service knowing that it is not being offered free: when he makes it clear to the provider of a service that he does not want the service and that he will not pay for it? The answer is, I believe, no. . . .

When a party makes it clear to the provider of a service that he will not pay for it or does not want it, then it cannot be against the conscience of that man that he should refuse to pay for the service.

Similar reasoning explains the decision in *Allied Discount Card v Bord Fáilte Éireann* [1991] 2 IR 185 (Lynch J). On the facts of *Browne*, however, the banks wanted the services being provided by their employees, and took no opportunity to reject them. Thus, a cause of action in restitution would seem to arise. (*Cp. Mead* (1991) 11 Leg Stud 172; *cf. Birks An Introduction to the Law of Restitution* (1988) p. 305; Sales (1988) 8 *OJLS* 301; all discussing *Miles v Wakefield UDC* [1987] AC 539).

GOOD FAITH

In *Lac Minerals v Chevron Mineral Corporation of Ireland and Ivernia* [1995] 1 ILRM 161 (HC, Murphy J) (below, pp. 146-8) Murphy J 'advert[ed] . . . to a principle well-established in the law of that state but unknown in Ireland, namely, that is to say 'the covenant of good faith and fair dealing' which is readily implied in contracts governed by New York law. This covenant requires that parties must act in good faith consistently with the intent expressed in the objectively discernible terms of the contract.' As to whether that covenant is in fact entirely unknown in Ireland, see the 1993 Review, pp. 177-8.

MISREPRESENTATION

Definition   'A misrepresentation is made when one contracting party has uttered a statement of fact which is untrue.' (Clark, p. 228). Since it is only statements of fact which in principle are actionable, neither statements of opinion (*Bissett v Wilkinson* [1927] AC 177; *Smith v Lynn* (1954) 85 ILTR 57) nor representation as to the future will be. However, a statement of intention 'like one of opinion, may amount to a misrepresentation of fact (though it was honestly made) if it involves an implied assertion that the representor has reasonable grounds for his opinion or belief' (Treitel, p. 309). This definitional matter figured in the decision of O'Hanlon J in *Donnellan v Dungoyne* [1995] 1 ILRM 388 (HC).

Here, the Circuit Court had found that a misrepresentation on the part of the defendants' estate agent that all of the units of a shopping centre would be occupied before the following Christmas had induced the plaintiff to take a lease of shop in the centre in late 1991, and had awarded damages of £20,000. The defendants appealed, and sought to argue that the statement of the estate agent was not a statement of fact, but merely 'sales talk' (which, being a statement of opinion, or, on the facts, a representation as to the future, would not be actionable). O'Hanlon J accepted that a letting agent must do a certain amount of optimistic talking up of the prospects of the property, and continued that:

> press releases which were published from time to time, the very colourful and informative brochures prepared for the preview, and for the official opening, and the encouraging remarks attributed to the developer . . . were all of a character which were will within the bounds of what was permissible in the important task of attempting to 'sell' the centre to potential tenants.
>
> At no relevant stage, however, was the centre fully-let or well on the way to being fully-let, and I am satisfied that the information available to the letting agents . . . was at no stage of a character which could have justified them in making a firm forecast that the entire, or almost the entire Centre would be occupied and trading by a particular date in the near future.

For O'Hanlon J, the letting agents had traversed that line; 'in their enthusiasm to secure the best possible result not only for the clients, the developers, but also for all the tenants in the centre, . . . [the agents] allow[ed] themselves too much latitude in the description they gave of the progress of the efforts to let these remaining units, and the degree of success that had been achieved.' Thus, O'Hanlon J sustained the judgment of the Circuit Court that some degree of negligent misrepresentation had taken place and was a contributing factor in inducing the plaintiffs to take the lease.

Remedies A plaintiff may seek to make the defendant liable in contract or in tort. If he seeks a remedy in contract, he will seek to rescind the contract, to set it aside 'for all purposes, so as to restore, as far as possible, the state of things which existed before the contract' (Treitel, pp. 341-342). Recission is usually granted unless a recognised bar (such as affirmation, laches, the intervention of third party rights, or the impossibility of restitution) is present. If, however, the plaintiff seeks a remedy in tort, his claim is that the misrepresentation amounted to the tort of deceit (fraudulent misrepresentation) or to the tort of negligence (negligent misrepresentation), the loss on the contract being the loss caused by the tort. In such cases, the plaintiff recovers damages for the tort. 'He can generally do this whether he rescinds the contract or not, though he cannot pursue both remedies if this results in his recovering twice for the same loss' (Treitel, p. 318).

In considering the appropriate relief in *Donnellan v Dungoyne*, O'Hanlon J was not prepared to accept the plaintiffs' evidence that:

> but for the giving of this assurance in early November 1991 they would not have entered into a letting of the unit. Had they been given a more accurate picture of the situation . . . I believe from all the previous history of the negotiations between the parties, that they would still have been prepared to go ahead, but would in all probability have held out for even greater inducements . . .

> On this basis, I am of opinion that a case has not been made out for recission of the lease . . . but merely for damages for breach of warranty, and negligent misrepresentation, as happened in *Esso v Mardon* [1976] 1 QB 801 and *McAnarney v Hanrahan* [1993] 3 IR 492 . . . .

Although O'Hanlon J refused to rescind the contract, (with the consequence that the lease between the parties would have remained on foot had it not otherwise terminated), his reason for so doing is not one of the recognised bars to recission. It may be nevertheless be observed that since recission for misrepresentation is, however, an equitable remedy, it is, therefore discretionary; and that all O'Hanlon J did was to exercise his discretion to refuse such relief. However, that characterisation of the remedy of recission for misrepresentation may not be accurate. Thus, in respect of fraudulent misrepresentation, a plaintiff may rescind *at law*; recission is equitable only where the misrepresentation is innocent (which for these purposes simply means non-fraudulent, and thus includes negligence). Again, 'pre-contractual . . . misrepresentation . . . *prima facie* confers an unqualified right of recission' (Atiyah, *An Introduction to the Law of Contract* (Oxford, 1995), p. 400). In an attempt to add flexibility to this rule, the legislature has provided that a court may in its discretion refuse recission 'declare the contract subsisting and award damages in lieu of recission', but only if the misrepresentation is not fraudulent, and only in respect of contracts for the sale of goods or the supply of services (Sale of Goods and Supply of Services Act, 1980; s. 45(2)). (In England, s. 2(2) of the Misrepresentation

Act 1967 is in equivalent terms, though it is not limited to sales or services contracts). Prior to the legislative provision of such a power, it did not theretofore exist, and still does not exist outside of the special statutory context. Given that the contract here was not a sale of goods or a supply of services, the 1980 Act does not apply, and there would seem to be no basis for this aspect of O'Hanlon J's decision. He did, however, by citing *Mardon* and *McAnarney*, indicate that the basis of liability was in tort, and not in contract; and since recission is not a precondition of liability in tort, his refusal of recission is ultimately of little moment (*quaere*, however, whether relief in tort was claimed by the plaintiff and/or granted in the Circuit Court?).

On the calculation of damages, O'Hanlon J held that the misrepresentation caused only part of the losses suffered by the plaintiff, observed that when another tenant who raised the issue of the agent's misrepresentation with the developers of the shopping centre was given six months rent free in settlement, and awarded damages in the amount of seven months rent, £12,000. Why damages should have been confined to seven months rent is unclear, especially since he found as fact that 'had the plaintiffs been given the full picture . . . and had simultaneously been offered not five months but a year's period free of rent, they would have gone ahead with the proposal to take a lease'. If damages in tort represent the plaintiff's loss, and if the plaintiff here lost the opportunity to use the premises rent-free for a year, then the loss is equivalent to twelve and not seven months rent.

OFFER AND ACCEPTANCE

It was once a commonplace in England to say of some matter universally acknowledged that 'every schoolboy knows' it. In the realm of the law of contract, the basic rules of offer and acceptance are surely such that every student (and every lawyer) knows them. Thus, such legally significant acts as offers, acceptances, rejections and revocations are in general not valid until they have been successfully communicated; thus in the case of negotiations by post, they are not valid until they have arrived. But, as every student knows, to this rule there is an exception: the postal rule, by which an acceptance by post is effective as soon as it is posted (Winfield (1939) 55 *LQR* 509; Evans (1966) 15 *ICLQ* 553; Gardner (1992) 12 *OJLS* 170). Though entirely anomalous and arbitrary, it stands as a constant reminder that many rules of law, which owe little to logic and much to history, survive because they exhibit the supposed virtue of certainty. So universally is the postal rule acknowledged that it has now become itself a commonplace. Thus, in *Kelly v Cruise Catering* [1994] ILRM 394 (SC) a contract of employment had been signed by the defendant-employer in Oslo, and sent to the plaintiff-employee in Dublin, who signed it and returned it by post. For Blayney J (O'Flaherty and Egan JJ concurring), it was:

> clear on these facts that the contract was made by post so that the well-settled rule as enunciated by Denning LJ in *Entores v Miles Far East Corporation* [1955] 2 QB 327, 332 applies:
>
>> When a contract is made by post it is clear law throughout the common law countries that the acceptance is complete as soon as the letter is put into the post box, and that is the place where the contract is made.
>
> Accordingly, the plaintiffs' acceptance was complete when, in Dublin, he posted the signed contract to the first defendant and where the signed contract was posted, which was Dublin, was the place where the contract was made.

So far, at least, so certain. (Similarly *Sanderson v Cunningham* [1919] 2 IR 234). And, though certainty is often achieved at the expense of justice, the postal rule has withstood assaults launched against it under the battle-cry of 'injustice'. It did so again in the present case:

> It was contended by counsel for the first named defendant that this rule could on occasion cause injustice. It was possible, for example, that the acceptance might be lost in the post and in such cases it would be unjust to hold a party to a contract when he had never received the acceptance. That is no doubt correct but it is not a relevant consideration in the present case where the signed contract was received by the first named defendant. There are no circumstances here calling for any divergence from the well-established rule.

It may be thought, however, that Blayney J's concession — that it would be unjust to hold to a contract an offeror to whom an acceptance had never arrived — has dented the absoluteness of the rule. But even here the rule holds: in *Household Fire and Carriage Accident Insurance Co. v Grant* (1879) 4 Ex D 216, it was held the letter of acceptance was effective even though it never arrived. Thus, when 'a contract is made by post, one of the parties may be prejudiced if a posted acceptance is lost or delayed; for the offeree may believe that there is a contract and the offeror that there is none, and each may act in reliance on his belief. The post[al] rule favours the offeree, and is sometimes justified on the ground that an offeror who chooses to start negotiations by post takes the risk of delay and accidents in the post;

or on the ground that the offeror can protect himself by expressly stipulating that he is not to be bound until actual receipt of the acceptance. . . .' (Treitel, p. 24).

Nevertheless rules also supposedly based on certainty, and of equal vintage, have crumbled: thus, it is no longer the law that a mistake of law is not an actionable mistake (see [1993] *Restitution Law Review* 140, 141-142; *Air Canada v British Colombia* (1989) 59 DLR (4th) 161; *David Securities v Commonwealth Bank of Australia* (1992) 175 CLR 353; in *Pine Valley v Minister for the Environment* [1987] IR 23, Henchy J in the Supreme Court held that although a payment 'was paid under a mistake of law, . . . in my opinion it would be recoverable no less than if it had been paid under a mistake of fact' (at p. 42)). They are usually abrogated not only because they are unjust but also because the presence of exceptions undercuts the very basic of the rules, or the rules are inconsistent with or are not justified by their rationales, or the rules do not fit with other cognate aspects of the law. As to exceptions, it must be reasonable in the circumstances to use the postal service (Treitel, p. 23; see *e.g. Apicella v Scala* (1931) 66 ILTR 33), and in *Holwell v Hughes* [1974] 1 All ER 161, Lawton LJ held that the rule does not apply in all cases of purported acceptance by post:

> [f]irst, it does not apply when the express terms of the offer specify that it [the acceptance] must reach the offeror . . . Secondly, it probably does not operate if its application would produce manifest inconvenience and absurdity [. . . doubting *Household Fire Insurance v Grant* (*supra*), and these] factors of inconvenience and absurdity are but illustrations of a wider principle, namely that the rule does not apply, if having regard to all the circumstances, including the nature of the subject matter under consideration, the negotiating parties cannot have intended that there should be a binding agreement until the party accepting the offer . . . had in fact communicated the acceptance . . .

Whither certainty with so vague an exception? As to rationales, the postal rule is often justified on the bases that (i) there is a *consensus ad idem* and thus an agreement when the acceptance is posted; (ii) that without the certainty achieved by the rule the offeror would have to notify the offeree that the acceptance had arrived, and that the offeree would have to so notify the offeror, and so on; (iii) that the post office is the agent of the offeror or the common agent of both parties; and (iv) the rule minimises difficulties of proof, (at least in Victorian times, when there was a postal book in every office recording outgoing mail; see Clark, p. 18). But none of these will work; (i) if a consensus ad idem is reached at the very moment an offer is accepted, why the need for any communication, but if communication is necessary, why single out communication by post: 'any other proof of intention to accept equally well show that the parties were in agreement' (Treitel, p. 24); (ii) the infinite regression, even if it were a valid fear, could just as easily be broken by a rule which predicated effectiveness on the arrival as on the despatch of the letter; (iii) when the recipient had to pay for mail, it may have been valid to regard the post office as the agent of the recipient/offeror, but when, as now, the sender pays for the mail, it must surely be equally as valid to regard the post office as the agent of the sender/offeree: in which case there is no basis for deeming the acceptance to have arrived; and to say that the post office is the agent for both, whilst possible, is simply to justify one arbitrary rule on the basis of another, and not on the basis of logic; (iv) there is little to be said for this rationale: to justify a rule for commerce on the brink of the twenty-first century on the basis of a commercial reality which was extant at the in the early nineteenth century but which is long since gone is little short of absurd. As to cognate areas, we are back to what every student knows, that absent the postal rule, offers, revocations, rejections, and acceptances other than by post, are effective only upon arrival.

In truth, then, little justifies the postal rule, other than its antiquity (it is traced back to *Adams v Lindsell* (1818) 1 B & Ald 681; 106 ER 250, and, as such, this exception probably antedates the general rule to which it is now the exception) and its supposed certainty. Even then, a rule that an acceptance by post is effective only when it has arrived is equally certain. Thus, there is much more to be said against the postal rule than merely that it would on occasion cause injustice. And yet the postal rule is one which every student knows, and after *Kelly v Cruise Catering*, it is still a commonplace.

PRINCIPLES OF INTERPRETATION

In the interpretation of contracts, it is well settled that a court should attempt to give meaning to every provision of the contract; so that where there is an irreconcilable inconsistency between two terms that a term of the contract should be rejected. This principle formed the basis of the decision of Murphy J in *Lac Minerals v Chevron Mineral Corporation of Ireland and Ivernia* [1995] 1 ILRM 161 (HC, Murphy J), Chevron held mineral mining licences and concluded a joint venture agreement with Ivernia to exploit the licences. A section of the agreement allowed any party to the agreement to assign its interest, subject to pre-emption by the other parties; in one place, the agreement gave such other parties 45 days to exercise these pre-emption rights, in another it gave 60. Chevron entered into negotiations to sell its interest to Lac, and gave Ivernia notice of its intention to sell. 56 days later, Ivernia sought to pre-empt. In this action, Lac contended that the pre-emption period in the Chevron-lvernia contract was to be construed as 45 days, and, were it to be construed as 60 days that this should be rectified to 45 days.

Arguably, the conflict was so severe that *both* clauses could be said to have been rendered void for uncertainty, and could therefore have been severed, thus leaving a pre-emption process without a timetable. Either that would have been unworkable, in which case the entire process would have fallen, Chevron's pre-emption would have been ineffective, and Lac's purchase secure; or, the Court could have implied that the pre-emption was to be exercised in a reasonable time, and then considered whether the exercise after 56 days would have been reasonable in the circumstances. However, this point was not taken.

For Murphy J, 'the essential problem [was] . . . whether these two apparently irreconcilable time limits can be harmonised and, if not, which should be rejected'. He held that there was a manifest and irreconcilable inconsistency between those two terms, and on its proper interpretation, the agreement gave Ivernia 60 days. As to Murphy J's approach to this problem, first, it is important note his *dictum* that 'the authority of *Forbes v Git* [1922] 1 AC 256' 'that an earlier provision in a document' should be preferred to a later one' was 'questionable'. Second, as to the clause (s. 15.3.1) which requires an intending assignee to give notice to the other parties to the contract of this intent, that written notice was described as an 'offer', but in Murphy J's view, 'it is not correct to equate this written notice with an offer in the sense in which that word is used in the general law of contract. The written notice prescribed by s. 15.3.1 is not an originating offer. It is merely machinery' for the operation of the pre-emption. Having rejected these two interpretative strategies, Murphy J observed:

> that the rights of a recipient of the notice (an offeree) are set out in the agreement, and 'the most important of those rights is stated unequivocally in the following terms:
>
> > The offeree shall have the right and option for the period of 60 days after receipt of the offer [*etc.*] . . .
>
> In the circumstances it seems that, notwithstanding the fact that the offeror is required to state in the notice to be delivered by him that the offer is open for acceptance for a period of 45 days, the actual right of the offeree to exercise the right and option extends for a period of 60 days from the receipt of the notice.

Consequently, he was prepared to hold that the proper period for the exercise of the pre-emption rights was 60 days.

RECTIFICATION

In *Lac Minerals v Chevron Mineral Corporation of Ireland and Iventia* [1995] 1 ILRM 161 (HC, Murphy J3 (immediately above), Murphy J held that a contract between Chevron and Ivernia gave Ivernia 60 days to exercise a right to pre-empt Chevron's sale of its interest to Lac. In this action, Lac contended that this should be rectified to 45 days. However, on this issue, Murphy J held that Lac, whose claim derived solely from its agreements with Chevron, could not maintain a claim for the rectification of the Chevron-Ivernia contract, to which they were not parties and under which they derived no estate. Consequently, a party not privy to a contract may seek rectification of that contract provided there is some nexus between that party and that contract. For example, if two parties erroneously reduce an agreement to writing, and then one party sells or assigns his interest to a third party, that third party is privy to or affected by the same mistake in such a way that it would be unconscionable for the defendant to seek to rely on the document which erroneously recorded or mistakenly implemented the true agreement. For these propositions, Murphy J relied upon *Majestic Homes Property v Wise* [1978] QdR 225 and *Shepheard v Graham* (1947) 66 NZLR 654. In those cases, 'if relief had not been granted the defendants would have retained a wholly unconscionable benefit to the detriment of the plaintiff in the action rather than his predecessor in title.' The crucial distinction between those cases and *Lac Minerals v Chevron*, 'is the fact that the mistake between Chevron and Ivernia was in no sense repeated or extended to Lac.'

From those cases, it seems that where there is a contract between A. and B. in respect of certain subject matter by which, as a consequence of mistake, A. has profited at B.'s expense, and then there is a contract between B. and C. in respect of the same subject matter, so that A.'s profit is now at C.'s expense, a court can rectify both agreements or deem that A. holds such profit on trust for C., to ensure that he does not so profit. Thus, in *Majestic Homes Property v Wise*, where A. (the Wises) received a greater leasehold period than intended in the lease from B. (Hamilton), and B. then assigned the lessor's interest to C. (Majestic), it was held in an action between the new parties to the lease that it should be rectified to reflect the agreement between the former parties to the lease, and, in the alternative, that A (the Wises) held the surplus interest on trust for B. and C. (Hamilton and his successors in title, Majestic). Again, in *Shepheard v Graham*, A. (Mrs Graham) intending to sell certain property to B. (Lady Clifford), misdescribed it so that the conveyance related only to a portion of the property; B. then sold on to C. (Shepheard). Both B. and C. occupied the entire property, and when C. discovered the misdescription, sought rectification of the transfer from A. to B. and of that from B. to C. As to the first conveyance, it was held that A.

held the surplus interest 'merely as trustee' for B. and her assignee C. If the trust in such circumstances is understood as a direct action by C. against A. to prevent A.'s unjust enrichment at C.'s expense, then the rectification action is unnecessary.

In this context, consider Murphy J's *dictum* that '[t]itle acquired by mistake is held on trust', a *dictum* he derived from *Majestic Homes v Wise* following *Craddock v Hunt* [1923] 2 Ch 136, 155 where Lord Sterndale MR: 'could see no conscience or honesty in the defendant's claim, and I think he should he declared a trustee for the plaintiff's land to which he has by mistake got a title which he knew had been knocked down to them and which he never thought was intended to be sold to him or had been bought by him.' There is clearly some notion of unjust enrichment at work in the treatment of *Majestic Homes* and *Shepheard* (actions which were justified as preventing a defendant acquiring 'a wholly unconscionable gain'). It is submitted, therefore, that this trust is best understood as a direct action by C. against A. to prevent A.'s unjust enrichment at C.' s expense, and the *dictum* that title acquired by mistake is held on trust must be understood simply as the consequence of, and confined to, that action. Finally, since on the facts of *Lac Minerals v Chevron*, above, there was nothing in the transaction of A. (Ivernia) being enriched at the expense of B. (Chevron), and B. and C. contracting so that A. is now enriched at the expense of C. (Lac), Lac was properly held unable to rely on *Majestic Homes* and *Shepheard*.

More generally, Murphy J began his analysis of rectification by reference to the principle that the 'burden falling on a party claiming rectification . . . of a document on the basis of mutual mistake is a heavy one', derived from the decision of the Supreme Court in *Irish Life Assurance Co. v Dublin Land Securities*:

> . . . bearing in mind the heavy burden of proof that lies on those seeking rectification, the question to be addressed is whether there was convincing proof, reflected in some outward expression of accord, that the contract in writing did not represent the common continuing intention of the parties on which the court can act, and whether the plaintiff can positively show what that common intention was in relation to the provisions which the appellant says were intended to exclude the vacant lands at Palmerstown ([1989] IR 253, 263).

Nevertheless, since he held that the remedy was not in principle available to Lac, Murphy J did not need to go into the sufficiency of the evidence Nevertheless, he did so, and found, on the balance of probabilities, that an agreement was probably reached that the rights of pre-emption would subsist only for 45 days, but nevertheless thought it unlikely that if a party to the contract had sought rectification on this basis, 'the courts exercising what is described as their "equitable jurisdiction" would have ordered the rectification of the [agreement] to substitute the figure of 45 days for 60 days' in the relevant clause.

Two points deserve mention here. First, the holding in *Irish Life* (above) represents the Irish acceptance that the clear proof required to rectify a contract is proof of a 'common continuing intention' and not necessarily the more rigid requirement of proof that 'formalities apart, there must have been a concluded contract? (*Rose v Pim* [1953] 2 All ER 739, *per* Delming LJ). The former test has been adopted and the latter rejected in England in a line of authority beginning with *Joscelyne v Nissen* [1970] 1 All ER 1213 and in Ireland in *Irish Life* (above; see the 1989 Review, pp. 230). Second, it provides a good example of a case in which a court will, in its discretion, decline to order rectification (see Delany, *Equity and the Law of Trusts in Ireland* (1995) p. 471).

Finally, it may be that rectification, even if available, would have been inappropriate here. It has been written that '[p]roceedings for rectification ought not to be brought if whatever mistake appearing in the written document is of a kind that the true meaning of the document could be ascertained as a matter of construction without recourse to extrinsic evidence' (Meagher, Gummow and Lehane, para. 2608, p. 675). Since Murphy J first interpreted the contract and came to a conclusion as to its true meaning, that process should have precluded rectification, at least if the observation above is accepted.

REMEDIES FOR BREACH OF CONTRACT

If P. and D. enter into a contract, by which D. will not do something (such as grant a charge or execute a mortgage over certain property) without first gaining the permission of P., and D. nevertheless does so (as by granting a charge or mortgage in favour of T.), P.'s remedies are on his contract with D. only; they are not against T., and do not affect the validity of the transaction between D. and T. (*cp* the treatment of the negative pledge clause in *Welch v Bowmaker (Ireland)* [1980] TR 251 (SC)).

Section 18 of the Conveyancing Act 1881 gives a power *prima facie* to a mortgagor in possession to grant a lease without joining in the mortgagee-bank. If the bank nevertheless stipulates that such a lease cannot be granted without its consent, and, as in the hypothetical, the mortgagor nevertheless purports to grant a lease, then the bank's remedy would only be on its contract with the mortgagor. However, s. 18(13) provides that the section 'applies only if and in so far as a contrary intention is not expressed . . . in writing', so the general rule is displaced. Consequently, in *ICC Bank v Verling* [1995] 1 ILRM 123, where a mortgagor purported to execute a lease without the consent of the bank and in breach of a contract which expressly stipulated otherwise, s. 18(13) was held to render the lease void. However, on the facts, counsel for T. contended that the bank had notice of the assignment and thus were estopped from disputing it. No such estoppel arose: the plaintiffs had 'never acquiesced in or recognised the lease by any express or positive conduct such as by demanding or accepting rent thereunder in place of the first defendant.' Indeed, it was held that whereas the mortgagee-bank was entitled to rely on the consent clause, it was T. who took with (constructive) notice of bank's interest!

Measure of damages The proper measure of damages for breach of a non-compete clause arose in *RGDATA v Tara Publishing* [1995] 1 IR 89; [1995] 1 ILRM 453 (HC, Murphy J) (immediately below; on this issue, see p. 157).

RESTRAINT OF TRADE

In *RGDATA v Tara Publishing* [1995] 1 IR 89; [1995] 1 ILRM 453 (HC, Murphy J), the plaintiffs had sold a magazine title to the defendants, and in breach of a valid non- compete clause had published a rival magazine. On the plaintiffs' application for a declaration that the non-compete clause was void, the offending part of the clause was severed; and the defendants' counterclaim for damages for breach of the (valid portion of the) clause succeeded.

The case was the first opportunity presented to the High Court to determine whether or not the rules on restraint of trade at common law have survived the enactment of the Competition Act 1991 (on which see Bolger, "Restraint of Trade Law in Ireland" (1996) *Gazette* 245).

Restraint of trade At common law, a clause in restraint of trade is void, unless reasonable, and the test of such reasonableness is two-fold: (i) whether the restraint is reasonable as between the parties, having regard to the length of time, geographical extent, and subject matter of the restraint, and (ii) whether it is reasonable in the public interest (see *e.g. McEllistrim v Ballymacelligott Co-op* [1919] AC 548; *Esso v Harpers* [1968] AC 269). Where a clause would on this test be void, however, it is possible to sever the offending clause and leave the remainder of the contract untouched, and it is possible even to sever words from the restraint of trade clause so as to render it reasonable (*e.g. Attwood v Lamont* [1920] 3 KB 571; *Skerry v Moles* (1907) 42 ILTR 46).

The restraint of trade doctrine has been rationalised on the basis that it is necessary to prevent the unfair taking advantage of an inequality of bargaining power as between the parties (*Schroeder Music v Macauley* [1974] 3 All ER 616, 623 *per* Lord Diplock. In *Kerry Co-Op v An Bord Bainne*, O'Flaherty J approved *Schroeder*, and McCarthy J wrote that '[t]he doctrine of restraint of trade is a classic instance of the application of public policy . . . . It is desirable from the standpoint of the public good to protect the right to work of weaker parties from abuse and to gain the economic benefits of preventing such abuses.' ([1991] ILRM 851, 869) If that is the reason for the doctrine of restraint of trade, then there must be inequality of bargaining power which is unfairly taken advantage of, and the term in restraint of trade is the index of this abuse of inequality of bargaining power.

European law   As is so often nowadays the case, the winds of change blowing over the common law in this area come from Brussels. Article 85 of the Treaty of Rome provides that agreements 'which have as their object or effect the prevention, restriction or distortion of competition' are void. However, in an important series of cases, the ECJ has held that certain restrictions on conduct need not necessarily amount to restrictions on competition incompatible with Article 85. (See *e.g. Green* (1988) 9 ECLR 190; Whish and Sufrin (1987) 7 *OxYEL* 1). Thus, in Case 42/84 *Remia and Nutricia v Commission* [1985] ECR 2545, the Court held that restrictive covenants imposed on the vendor of a business and goodwill could fall outside Article 85 if they were necessary having regard to the length of time, geographical extent, and subject matter of the restraint (Whish, *Competition Law* (3rd ed, 1993), pp. 463-4).

The Competition Act 1991   (See, generally, Doherty, *Competition Law in Ireland* (M.Litt thesis, TCD, 1995) to which the treatment here is indebted); Article 85 is reflected in s. 4 of the Competition Act 1991, an Act the long title of which states its aim as seeking 'to prohibit, by analogy with' Article 85 anti-competitive practices. There thus arises the issue of the status, in the interpretation of s. 4, of the decisions of the ECJ and of Court of First Instance and of the Commission. (See generally Cooke, 16 *ICEL* 45, Shanley, 16 *ICEL* 79; Cooke, 20 *ICEL* 82). Such judicial consideration of the issue as there has been is mixed. In *Deane v VHI* [1992] 2 IR 319 the Supreme Court interpretation of a phrase in s. 4 having its origin in Article 85 was based on old English (rather than recent EC) authorities. More open to the European way are the decisions of Costello J in *Donovan v ESB* [1994] 2 ILRM 325 and *Masterfoods v HB Ice Cream* [1993] ILRM 145.

Nevertheless, even where reference to European caselaw is appropriate, caution must be exercised. For example, Article 85, in common with the other competition sections in Title V of the Treaty, subserves the ends of Articles 2 and 3 of the Treaty (as amended). Thus, while Article 3(g) (formerly Article 3(f)) requires a competitive market, Community-wide, Articles 2 and 3(c) posit (progressive) market integration. As a result, the ECJ has held that partitioning of markets into national sectors by seeking to prevent parallel imports impeded such market integration and was thus in breach of Article 85(1): joined cases 56 & 58/64 *Consten and Grundig v Commission* [1966] ECR 299. Thus some of the EC case law is based on a market integration ethos, whereas the Irish Competition Act is based entirely on an ethos of a competitive national market. Thus for Keane J the analogy with EC law referred to in the Preamble to the 1991 Act is 'necessarily incomplete, since one of the principal objectives of the Treaty (some would say the paramount objective) is the establishment of a single integrated market in the Community, whereas such a market already exists in the State' (*Callinan v VHI* [1994] 3 CMLR 796). Therefore, decisions reached on the basis of considerations appropriate in the ECJ as a consequence of Articles 2 and 3 could therefore be inappropriate in Ireland where those articles do not colour the interpretation of s. 4 of the 1991 Act. That having been said, however, no such inappropriate considerations are to be found in *Remia*, and in the absence of any other authorities, it should be considered at least persuasive in the interpretation of s. 4.

The Act and restraint of trade clauses (Bergeron (1990-93) 9 *JISLL* 57; and Reid (1990-93) 9 *JISLL* 80). The Competition Act 1991, established a Competition Authority to ensure that the objectives of the Act were realised, and it soon concerned itself embroiled in matters these matters, in both its first decision and its first notice (respectively: *Nallen/O'Toole* (April 2, 1992) and 'Employee Agreements and the Competition Act', *Iris Oifigiúil*, 14 September 1992; on the enforceability of such notices, see Hyland (1993) 11 *ILT (ns)* 240.) But here, an important distinction drawn by the Competition Authority emerges. The doctrine of restraint of trade applies in many instances, including restraints on departing employees and restraints on the vendors of a business and goodwill. Under the Act, however, the Competition Authority seems to apply different rules to each of these two situations.

As to employee restraints, in its individual decisions, the Authority has tended to apply a test under s. 4 considering issues such as the temporal, geographical and subject matter limits of the restrictions, much as the Commission does under Article 85 after *Remia*. On the length of the restriction, the Authority has tended to limit it to two years, or even less (*e.g. Apex/Murtagh* (June 10, 1993) (one of the few cases to date in which the Authority has refused a licence); *Cambridge/Imari* (June 21, 1993)). Again, it is only when the departed employee becomes an 'undertaking' for the purposes of s. 4 that the Act can apply, and it seems that this will happen where the former employee starts up a new business, but not where he simply takes up employment with a new employer. (*Peter Mark/Stapleton* (18 February 1993); Hogan 20 *ICEL* 96).

As to restrictions on the sale of a business, the Authority's approach was outlined in *Nallen/O'Toole*: again, the Authority begins from a presumption against restraints longer than two years, but allows extensions to three years where the vendor is locally significant and will remain in the business, and to five years where know-how is transferred. But here, jesuitical distinctions between departing employees who are or are not undertakings are so significant, since the Authority will usually regard both the vendor and the purchaser as undertakings, (even in the case of a purchaser who becomes an undertaking by virtue of the purchase: *Fortune/Budget Travel* (September 14, 1992).

The treaty, the statute and the common law   It will thus be seen that the approach of the common law to issues of restraint of trade is significantly different than the approach of the ECJ and of the Competition Authority to the interpretation of Article 85 (EC) and s. 4 of 1991 Act. For example, at common law, the test requires an analysis of reasonableness *both* as between the parties (taking into account the temporal, geographical and subject-matter scope of the clause) and in the public interest. The fact that the ECJ in *Remia* (above) also stressed the temporal, geographical and subject-matter scope of such a clause could make it easy to conclude that the common law and the law under Article 85 are the same. But such an easy conclusion would be misconceived, as it misses the second limb of the common law test, the emphasis on the public interest. On a very important level, therefore, the tests are different.

If it is assumed that the test properly to be applied under s. 4 is that set out in *Remia*, then it follows that the tests at common law and under the statute are different, because of the addition of the element of the public interest at common law. And, in the view of at least one commentator, the practice of the Irish courts on this issue in the past (*e.g. Macken v O'Reilly* [1979] ILRM 79 (SC)) gives little reason to believe that the encouragement of competition is a legitimate matter of public interest (Behrens (ed.), *The Application of EEC Competition Rules by the Member State Courts. Volume 2: Benelux and Ireland* (1994) p. 248 (Maher)). Even if it is or becomes so, there is nothing in the notion of public policy here to confine it to the encouragement of competition; certainly, the rationale identified above as underlying the doctrine, that of preventing inequality of bargaining power at most protects the interests of consumers or competitors rather than the process of competition (*e.g.* Whish, pp. 14-15, 29; to the observation that preventing such inequality sounds like preventing an abuse of a dominant position, it may be answered that this is aim of Article 86 (EC) and of s. 5 of the Act, whereas we are here concerned with Article 85 (EC) and s. 4 of the Act.) Furthermore, if Article 85 is now added to the picture, given that it can be influenced by the policies stated in Articles 2 and 3, where it is, there is no reason to suppose that the outcome or reasoning at EC level would be the same as it would be under the Act or the same as it would be at common law: the underlying policies could pull in different directions.

Again, on its application of the its understanding of s. 4, the Authority has departed quite significantly from the common law. The common law does not have different sets of rules for restraints on departing employees and restraints on the vendors of a business and goodwill; the Competition Authority does. Again, the common law is not committed to as inflexible a rule as a two-year limit, but can accommodate restrictions of 25 years or more (*e.g. Nordenfelt v Maxim Nordernfelt* [1894] AC 535 (HL)), nor is the doctrine in the employment context confined to situations where the employee starts up a new business, but is capable of restraining him in his new employment with a subsequent employer.

As a matter of statutory interpretation, it is presumed that express words are needed to displace a common law rule; and, while a statute may, exceptionally, impliedly amend the common law, the courts lean heavily against such a conclusion (*e.g. Smith v Director of the SFO* [1992] 3 All ER 456 (HL): clear words needed to displace common law rule of privilege against self-incrimination). So, here, without such express or necessarily implied amendment of the common law, Irish law would seem to be left with two tests for determining the validity of restraints of trade, one at common law and one under statute; presumably, if it fails just one of these, then it is invalid. (This raises the interesting (appalling?) spectre of a restraint which, under the Act, the Authority has validated, but which later fails the common law test in a Court).

The impact of *RGDATA*   All of these issues are to be found in Murphy J's decision in *RGDATA v Tara Publishing (supra)*. The plaintiffs, a retailers' representative association, had sold to the defendants the title and ownership of the 'official publications' of the plaintiff association. The contract of sale included clauses precluding RGDATA publishing in Ireland, for at least 20 – and possibly 25 – years, anything except press releases and photographs. Nevertheless, thereafter, the plaintiffs published a rival magazine, and later sought a declaration that the clauses were void either under the common law doctrine of restraint of trade or under s. 4 of the Competition Act 1991. The defendants resisted this claim, and counter-claimed for breach of the agreement. Murphy J had little difficulty in concluding that a 20 to 25 year restraint went far beyond what was necessary to preserve the goodwill of the title (though *cf. Mulligan v Corr* [1925] 1 IR 169, 177 (restraint valid, though unlimited as to time, where geographical and subject matter restrictions were reasonable) and *Nordenfelt (supra)* world-wide ban for 25 years reasonable in the circumstances). Consequently, he severed a portion of that restraint of trade clause, and allowed the defendants' counterclaim for damages.

As to the validity of the restraint of trade clause at common law and under the Act, counsel for each party accepted that the applicable legal provisions were correctly stated in *Remia* (above), thus obviating the need for much of the discussion above. Nevertheless, there are hints in Murphy J's judgment that he perceived both similarities and differences between the two positions. First, there is the passage which probably forms the *ratio* of the case:

> The fact that . . . RGDATA in the present case would be precluded from publishing a magazine under a particular title or with a particular accolade may in theory restrict competition but only in the sense that the vendor cannot reclaim and exploit the asset of which he has disposed. Any additional restriction which would impose wider restrictions of a lengthy nature would offend the Treaty of Rome, the Act of 1991 and at common law. 97/460

If not ambiguous on the issue, the last sentence seems to treat the tests established in those three sources as interchangeable. It seems from the nature of the last sentence, and especially from the failure to differentiate the offence as between the Treaty of Rome, the Act of 1991, and the common law, that it would offend all three for similar or the same reasons. Thus, it would seem that Murphy J regarded the tests as the same under all three heads, and in particular, that the test of a clause in restraint of trade is the same as the test of a clause which is anti-competitive within the meaning of s. 4 of the 1991 Act. However, as has been demonstrated above, the tests are in fact quite different. Again, he concluded that in 'accordance with the principles well established at common law and recognised in the Act of 1991, I conclude that I should sever the covenant precluding publication of magazines generally . . . [allowing the plaintiffs to publish magazines] if but only if the magazines . . . are not described, represented or held out to be the official publications of RGDATA' (97/460). This passage clearly indicates that on the issue of severance at least, Murphy J thought that the common law applied equally under the Act.

On the other hand, in dealing with prior question of whether and to what extent the clause was invalid, he clearly envisaged differences in the standards set at common law and under the Act; thus: 'Counsel on behalf of Tara rightly and necessarily accepted that the apparently wide ranging and long running covenants in restraint of competition . . . could not be justified *even* under the common law principles established prior to the enactment of the Competition Act, 1991, if the sale related simply to goodwill and assets consisting in the title of a newspaper or magazine' (93/457 emphasis added). That 'even' suggests that he sees the rules at law and under the Act as different, though it is ambiguous as to whether the Act has *displaced* the 'prior' common law. Ultimately, the most revealing factor is that Murphy J determined the validity of the clause expressly by reference to the Act, and only referred to the common law by way of comparative analogy rather than as law binding in the circumstances. But this would be an unsatisfactory basis upon which to conclude that the Act has displaced the common law in this context.

Two issues must be separated and addressed: (i) are the tests for the validity of restraint of trade clauses at common law and under the statute the same, (ii) if not has the common law test been displaced by the statutory test. Unfortunately, *RGDATA* provides little clear guidance on this question.

The measure of damages In the event, in *RGDATA*, the clause after severance was enforceable, and was breached by plaintiffs' publication. For that breach of contract, Murphy J awarded damages 'computed on the basis that advertising revenue was lost as a result of the competition from the RGDATA publication. That loss was assessed by Tara ... at some £15,000. Counsel on behalf of Tara conceded that this was not specific computation of special damages but rather an indication of the loss which flowed from the unlawful competition. I think in the circumstances that if I assessed damages at £7,500 it would meet the justice of the case' (98/461).

In *Hickey v Roches Stores* (High Court, 14 July 1976; now reported [1993] *RLR* 196) Finlay J allowed the plaintiffs to claim the profits which the defendants had made by their breach of an exclusive distribution agreement. Likewise, such damages in the restitution measure could have been sought and awarded here, and this would have resulted in a much more satisfactory measure of damages than the rough and ready calculation in the case itself. It is doubtful, however, whether such damages would be available in England after the much criticised *Surrey Co. Co. v Bredero Homes* [1992] 3 A11 ER 302 (Ferris J); [1993] 3 All ER 705 (CA) and *Jaggard v Sawyer* [1995] 1 WLR 269 (CA); though *dicta* in *Samson v Proctor* [1975] 1 NZLR 655 and *Hospital Products v US Surgical Corporation* (1984) 156 CLR 41 suggest that they would be available respectively in New Zealand and Australia.

Criminal Law

CONTEMPT OF COURT

The Law Reform Commission's *Report on Contempt of Court* (LRC 47–1994) proposes a wide range of changes in the law on this subject. It does so in a period of changing attitudes and practices: criticisms of the judiciary has become more robust, the *sub judice* protection has shrunk in the face of a more assertive media policy and the claim for journalistic privilege to protect sources has gained support.

On the latter issue, the Commission is divided. President Hederman and Commissioners Buckley and O'Leary are satisfied that the broad powers available to the court under the Constitution, as decided in *In re O'Kelly* (1974) 108 ILTR 97, 'should not and cannot be limited or restricted in any way' (para. 4.39). They are content to be bound by the *O'Kelly* decision and would not consider a non-specific approach, such as was adopted by s.10 of Britain's Contempt of Court Act 1981, to be any advance by way of clarification or otherwise on the present law. The minority, Commissioners Duncan and Gaffney, favour legislation similar to s. 10, but with a stricter test of 'necessity'. They recommend that the court should not be permitted to order disclosure unless it is established that disclosure is clearly necessary to prevent injustice, or in the interest of national security or to prevent disorder or crime. In their view, this approach gives 'appropriate, though admittedly not absolute, recognition to the public interest in the protection of journalistic sources.' (Para. 4.38). They drew support from the decision of the European Commission of Human Rights in *Goodwin v The United Kingdom* (Application No 17488/91, Report adopted March 1, 1994).

On the question of the courts' jurisdiction to attach for contempt, there is again division, here relating to the interpretation of the existing law rather than to how best the law should be changed. The (unidentified) majority acknowledges that the common law of contempt can be altered or codified by statute but that such legislation could not have any effect on the courts' inherent jurisdiction in the area. On that basis it is scarcely surprising that the majority does not recommend any new legislation in respect of contempt in the face of the court.

The constitutional argument against the existing law on *in facie* contempt is that it is ill-defined in its scope, requiring the judge to act, not merely as a judge , but also as a witness and prosecutor. The majority's response to this criticism is less than fully convincing:

> Whereas the principles of natural justice require that no one should act
> as judge in his own cause, the cause in question in the context of
> contempt *in facie* is the proper administration of justice, a cause in which
> every citizen has an equal interest. The cause is not the judge's personal
> exclusion, cause. If it is so considered, from any point of view, contempt
> *in facie*, an offence *sui generis*, must constitute an exception to the
> relevant principles of natural justice (para. 4.5).

The minority is not happy with the lack of clarity in the existing law and
recommends that a court's power to deal summarily with *in facie* contempt
should be limited to measures necessary to maintain the orderly, efficient and
dignified conduct of court proceedings. It accepts the need to maintain the
summary procedure to enable a presiding judge to remain in control of
proceedings; it notes also that judges have not abused their powers in this
area and have done no more by way of summary procedure than is absolutely
necessary to maintain order. In the minority's view, it is appropriate that the
new legislation should reflect this healthy state of affairs and that further
legitimacy should be given to the judicial powers to deal effectively with *in
facie* contempt Tby a more precise formulation of what those powers are'
(para. 4.9.). Accordingly the minority recommends that the common law
offence of in facie contempt be replaced by a statutory offence with the
following elements:

> (a) it would embrace any disruptive or other conduct that threatens the
> orderly, efficient and dignified conduct of the court's proceedings;
> (b) the procedure would be necessary;
> (c) the court would have power to order the offender's removal and or
> detention in custody for up to a month, subject by the general principle
> that any sanction imposed should be no more than necessary to enable
> the court to continue proceedings in an orderly manner.

All of the Commissioners are agreed that, where a party or witness or a legal
representative of one of the parties fails to attend the court without reasonable
excuse and with the intention of interfering with the administration of justice
(or reckless in that context), that person should be guilty of an offence
punishable by the maximum available summary punishment.

On the question of the use of tape recorders (or other sound recorders) in
court, the Commission, resiling from the position it provisionally adopted in
its *Consultation Paper on Contempt of Court*, published in 1993, takes the
view that the legislation should not give the presiding judge the discretion to

permit or refuse leave to use recorders in court. Its argument in favour of this change of mind scarcely goes so far as justifying the removal of judicial discretion on the matter:

> The Constitution requires that justice be administered in public and it is regarded as a natural consequence of this that media reporters, and any other persons who may wish to do so, may take notes of the proceedings and do not require permission from the judge or any one also so to do. Their use would, of course, be undesirable if they disrupted the court proceedings to any significant extent, but there is nothing to indicate that this is the case. It is true that recorders may be replayed to coach a person who is yet to give evidence. It is also the case that some witnesses might feel intimidated by the knowledge that their evidence is being recorded. These seem, however, to be weak arguments for requiring the use of sound recorders to be regulated by the court.

On photographs, television and video recordings, the Commission kicks to touch, recommending that an advisory committee be established to review the arrangement for, and legal provision relating to, the recording and broadcasting of court proceedings by the media. Part of the responsibilities of this committee would be to devise and monitor projects involving research and the actual broadcasting of civil and criminal trial and appellate proceedings.

On the subject of scandalising the court, the Commission, modifying the proposals provisionally put forward in its Consultation Paper, recommends that the common law offence of contempt by scandalising the court should consist in:

(i) imputing corrupt conduct to a judge or court, or
(ii) publishing to the public a false account of legal proceedings.

A person would be convicted of this offence only here there is a substantial risk that the administration of justice, the judiciary or any particular judge or judges will be brought into serious disrepute. As regards *mens rea*, a person would be guilty of the offence only where he or she knew that there was a substantial risk that the publication would bring the administration of justice, the judiciary or any particular judge or judges into serious disrepute or was recklessly indifferent in that regard. In the case of a publication of a false account, criminal responsibility would similarly arise only where the defendant intended to publish a false account or was recklessly indifferent as to whether it was false.

The *truth* of a communication would render it law. The onus of proof of the truth of an implication of corrupt judicial conduct would rest on the defence; the onus of proving the falsity of an account of legal proceedings published (or provided for publication to the public or a section of the public would rest on the prosecution.

As regards the liability of editors, media proprietors and others for scandalous publications, the Commission recommends that the same principles should apply as apply in respect of *sub judice* contempt. Abuse of the judiciary, even if scurrilous, would not constitute an offence. The Commission recommends that there should be no legislative interference with the court's power to attack summarily for contempt by scandalising. Finally in this context, the Commission proposes that a court should be empowered to order the publication of an apology and/or a correction in cases of scandalising, similar to the orders it recommended in its *Report on the Civil Law of Defamation* (LRC 38–1991).

On the *sub judice* rule, the Commission modifies some of the recommendations tentatively advanced in the Consultation Paper. It notes that these were criticised as being unduly restrictive of media freedom to comment on matters of public interest and as having a dangerous tendency to curtail knowledge by the people of wrongdoing in many areas, including spheres where the public interest is directly involved. It rejects these criticisms robustly, noting that:

> while it would be a manifestly unfair and distorted view of the submissions from the media to say that they overlook, still less disregard, the vital public interest in the proper and fair administration of justice, we remain convinced that it is not given sufficient weight/and perhaps understandably so in the submissions advanced by them or on their behalf. In particular we remain sceptical of the suggestion that the unquestionably greater freedom of comment enjoyed by the media in the United States, particularly in the period approaching a criminal trial (as is evidenced by the publicity being given to the O.J. Simpson case at the moment), is a desirable model to be followed in this jurisdiction. We think it cannot be emphasised too strongly that, particularly in the case of criminal proceedings, the powerful effect of coverage by the press, radio and television may, if not subjected to reasonable safeguards, have potentially serious effects for the proper administration of justice and may result in the imprisonment for lengthy periods of innocent people. In contrast, the public interest in the free flow of information is by no means wholly interrupted by a careful observance of the *sub judice* rule, since, at worst, the inhibition on unrestricted commend and publication of allegedly relevant facts is of a temporary nature only (para. 6.4).

The Commission considers that the best approach would be to prescribe that the *sub judice* rule applies to any publication that creates a substantial risk that the course of justice in the proceedings in question may be seriously impeded or prejudiced. It proposes that the legislation should include an *illustrative* test of statements capable of constituting such a 'substantial risk' in the case of criminal proceedings. These are statements to the effect, or from which it could reasonable inferred, that:

the accused is innocent or is guilty of the offence, or that the jury should acquit or should convict;

the accused has one or more prior criminal convictions;

the accused has committed or has been charged or is about to be charged with another offence, or is or has been suspected of committing another offence, or was or was not involved in an act, omission or even relating to the commission of the offence, or in conduct similar to the conduct involved in the offence;

the accused has confessed to having committed the offence or has made an admission in relation to the offence;

the accused has a good or bad character, either generally or in a particular respect;

the accused, during the investigation into the offence, behaved in a manner from which it might be inferred that he or she was innocent or guilty of the offence;

the accused, or any person likely to provide evidence at the trial (whether for the prosecution or the defence), is or is not likely to be a credible witness;

a document or thing to be addressed in evidence at the trial of the accused should or should not be accept as being reliable;

the prosecution has been undertaken for an improper motive.

The Commission rightly disdains the possibility of drawing up a similar list for civil proceedings; the circumstances that can arise in civil proceedings lack the common denominator of criminal prosecutions.

On the important question of the requisite *mens rea* in proceedings for *sub judice* contempt, the Commission adheres to the proposal made tentatively in the Consultation Paper that the test should be that of *negligence*. It rejects the suggestion, made by the media, that only intentional or reckless conduct should be penalised. In its view such a test would tilt the balance unfairly against the interests of those concerned in civil or criminal litigation.

The Commission also adheres to its tentative proposal that *sub judice* liability should arise, not only where proceedings are active but also earlier than this, where the publisher is actually aware of facts which, to his or her knowledge, render the publication certain, or virtually certain, to cause serious prejudice to a person whose imminent involvement in criminal or civil proceedings is virtually certain.

With the exception of President Hederman, the Commissioners recommend that the *sub judice* rule should not apply to appellate proceedings, which are invariably decided by non-jury courts. They consider that, if the rule applied to appellate cases, this would, in effect, reverse the decision of the Supreme Court in *Cullen v Toibin* [1984] ILRM 577, commenting that:

> [w]hile some of us share the opinion of Barrington J, the judge of the High Court in *Cullen v Toibin*, that judges can be prejudiced judges by their training and experience are more accustomed to having to take objective positions than a jury and a line has to be draw somewhere (para. 6.14).

With respect, drawing the line so as to render it *impossible* to control *sub judice* contempt at the appellate stage is unwise. It would seem mistaken to interpret the decision of *Cullen v Toibin* as going so far; although some broad statements were made in the Supreme Court, it is clear that the particular facts of the case were in the minds of the judges. It is not hard to envisage cases where the prejudice can be so subtle and insidious, or alternatively so blatant and intimidatory, as to have an effect on an appellate court.

On the related question of whether the *sub judice* rule should apply to judicial review proceedings, the majority of the Commissioners, again with the President dissenting, recommend that it should not, echoing O'Hanlon J's approach in *Desmond v Glackin* [1992] ILRM 490. One may wonder whether it is sensible to assume that judges are so impervious to all influences. The logic of the majority's position is that the *sub judice* rule should have no application to any function of the judicial process conducted by a judge rather than a jury.

As to possible *defences*, the Commission adheres to its uncontroversial recommendation, made tentatively in the Consultation Paper, that there should be a defence of reasonable necessity to publish. Far more controversially, but in our view correctly, it adheres to its earlier proposal that it should not be a defence that the offending material was published incidentally to a discussion of public affairs. In spite of considerable opposition to this proposal, the Commission stays firm, emphasising that this does not mean that public discussion of issues of public interest relevant to an imminent case is *automatically* stifled:

> It means no more than that the discussion must be conducted in a manner which does not offend the *sub judice* rule. Moreover, if other recommendations we have made are implemented, the position of the media will be eased significantly in that liability will attack only where the publisher ought reasonably to have appreciated that the publication created a substantial risk of causing serious prejudice to particular legal proceedings. On balance, we think that may result in the occasional discussion of public affairs is a relatively small price to pay for securing justice to those engage in criminal and civil legal proceedings (para. 6.25).

In the Consultation Paper, the Commission recommended tentatively that the present law should be clarified by providing an express statutory defence to contempt proceedings for fair and accurate reports of proceedings in the Oireachtas contemporaneously with or shortly after the proceedings. The Commission also proposed that the Ceann Comhairle of the Dáil and Cathaoirleach of the Seanad should be entitled to prohibit publication of any specific portion of the proceedings on the basis that it might offend against the *sub judice* rule. This latter proposal met with strong objection from the media, which accused the Commission of attempting to roll back hard-won press freedoms and of assigning to politicians the right to conceal wrongdoing that had been exposed on the floor of the Oireachtas. The Commission in its Report comments acidly that:

> [s]o far as we are aware, no commentator in the media expressed any concern at the possibility that criminal trials might be put in jeopardy by the irresponsible use of parliamentary privilege, although a graphic illustration of its potential for mischief had been afforded in England in recent times in a case which was extensively reported in the same media (para. 6.28).

The case to which the Commission is here referring is of course that of the Rev Patrick Ryan, whose extradition to Britain was refused by the Attorney General, Mr John Murray, on the basis of the prejudice that had been engendered in Britain: see *The Irish Times*, December 14, 1988 and our comments in the 1988 Review 155-6.

The Commission, while remaining unconvinced that its proposal would represent any serious intrusion into press freedom, accepts that it would present serious practical difficulties, since it would not be possible to prevent the live transmission of offending material on radio or television. It is also satisfied, on further consideration, that it was probably inappropriate to entrust powers of this nature to politicians who, however experienced they might be in questions of parliamentary procedure, were not necessarily equipped with legal training. Accordingly it abandons its recommendation in relation to the Ceann Comhairle and Cathaoirleach, whilst reiterating its proposal as to the statutory defence relating to reports of proceedings in the Oireachtas.

The Commission sets out detailed recommendations regarding the liability that should attack to the various categories of persons responsible for the publication of material in breach of the *sub judice* rule. Of particular interest is the proposal that those in control of newspapers and other media, such as editors, should be capable of being criminally responsible for *sub judice* contempt to the extent that by the exercise of that control they ought to have prevented the publication of the offending material. Also of significance is the recommendation that the proprietors of newspapers should be liable for *sub judice* contempt published in their newspapers on the vicarious liability principle but that only fines should be imposed on personal owners by way of punishment.

The Commission recommends that there should be a provision on the lines of s.4(2) of the British legislation of 1981, giving the court power to order the *postponement* of publication of any report of its proceedings where it appears necessary for avoiding a substantial risk of prejudice to the administration of justice in those, or other imminent or pending, proceedings. It follows the advice of the Boyle/McGonagle submission on behalf of the National Newspapers of Ireland that the legislation should incorporate a provision on the lives of an English Practice Director requiring that the order be formulated in precise terms, committed to writing by the judge personally or by the registrar or clerk of the court under the judge's direction and a permanent record kept.

The Commission makes several recommendations relating to acts interfering with the administration of justice other than *in facie* contempt, scandalising or offences against the *sub judice* rule. It proposes a generic offence extending to conduct creating a substantial risk of serious interference with the administration of justice. The *mens rea* test attaching to this offence would require proof of intention or recklessness, both as to the physical act in question and the consequential risk of serious interference.

The Commission proposes that it should be an offence to make or offer payment to any person who is, or is likely to be, a party, a witness or a juror in legal proceedings where, in the particular circumstances, the making or offer of the payment creates a substantial risk of injury to the administration of justice or to the constitutional or other rights of any person. Making reasonable payments for expenses sustained by the witness or party in giving the interview would not be unlawful.

The Commission goes on to recommend that threatening reprisals against a party, intending thereby to publish that party for having participated in civil legal proceedings should be an offence, if done without reasonable excuse. It acknowledges the wide-ranging implications this proposal may have in the context of industrial relations.

In relation to the secrecy of the jury-room the Commission proposes that it should not be contempt to disclose offences committed in the jury-room or miscarriages of justice that occurred there, to the extent that they do not offend against the exclusionary rule. *Bona fide* research into the manner in which juries arrive at their verdict would be permitted subject to the approval and control of the Chief Justice, the President of the High Court or the President of the Circuit Court, an appropriate intentional or reckless disclosure of the voting score in a acquittal after the judge has informed the jury of their right to come to a majority verdict would constitute contempt as would, more generally, any intentional or reckless disclosure of other arbitration as to what took place in the jury room, where this creates a risk of detriment to the liberty, reputation or physical or financial interests of a party to litigation.

In relation to civil contempt, the Commission recommends the continuation of open-ended imprisonment as a sanction, with fines also having a role. Contempt proceedings would continue to apply to family litigation, with imprisonment being retained as a sanction for wilful refusal or culpable neglect to obey a court order to support one's family. One spouse's contemptuous defiance of a court order would not be capable of being 'traded off' against the breach of another order by the other spouse. It should, however, continue to be a *factor*, to be given such weight as the court considers appropriate in any subsequent proceedings brought by a spouse seeking to vary or discharge an order respecting that other spouse's obligation relating to the family.

The Commission makes detailed proposals in relation to contempt in the context of tribunals. In summary, it recommends that the contempt model should not be adopted and that instead the matter should be dealt with by a series of statutory offences. In regard to the question of disclosure, the Commission recommends that the legislation should provide that a person may be required to disclose the source of information contained in a publication for which he or she is responsible only if it is established to the satisfaction of a tribunal of inquiry that disclosure is absolutely necessary for the purpose of the inquiry or to protect the constitutional rights of any other person.

On jurisdiction, the Commission proposes that the District and Circuit Courts should enjoy the same jurisdiction in relation to *criminal* contempt as is presently enjoyed by the High Court, and the same in *civil* contempt also, save for the fines imposed to encourage compliance with an order, which would be limited to a maximum of £200 *per day* or a single fine of up to £5,000 in the case of the District Court, the equivalent maxima for the Circuit Court being £600 and £15,000 respectively.

The Commission reiterates its tentative view that it would be better to leave to the Supreme Court the task of clarifying the problems left unresolved by its decision in *State (DPP) v Walsh* [1981] IR 412, rather than risk the possibility of introducing legislative changes that might turn out to be unconstitutional. A similar caution leads the Commission to recommend no change to the law of civil contempt in so far as jury trial is not permitted. Undoubtedly, the *Walsh* decision was a severe disappointment in its apparent lack of concern for the due process entitlements of those who are accused of criminal contempt. It is particularly unfortunate that the Supreme Court's pronouncements were made in a case of alleged scandalising of the court, where judicial sensitivities would be at their most intense. One can only hope that the Court will revisit the subject in the near future.

DEFENCES

Insanity and automatism In *The People v Courtney*, Court of Criminal Appeal, July 21, 1994, the Court declined to overturn a jury verdict based on a direction in which the trial judge had, in effect, rejected a plea by the defendant that the effects of post traumatic stress disorder were equivalent to the effects of insanity and/or automatism.

The defendant had been charged with murder, having made a statement to the Gardaí in which he gave the following account. He stated that, at 4 a.m. on the date in question, as he and his girlfriend were walking home in Dublin city, a car stopped and the woman driving it asked them for directions to a house in the area. The defendant said he attempted to give her directions and then offered to show her the way. They dropped the defendant's girlfriend at her flat before driving on towards the address the driver was seeking. The defendant said there was some general conversation in the car between him and the victim, following which she said, 'you never know who you pick up in a car at this time of night' and 'I could get you done for attacking me, if I went to the police it would only be your word against mine'. The defendant said that she was laughing at him, and that he 'blew a fuse and went mad'. He said he punched her several times in the face, rendering her semi-conscious. He then changed places with her, and drove the car

towards the mountains. As he was driving, the woman regained conscious-
ness and started to scream. There was a struggle and she fell out of the
passenger door. As she was lying on the ground kicking and struggling, the
defendant said he hit her several times with a rock on the head and face. The
defendant said he then took her clothes off and threw them in a field. He then
drove back into the city and abandoned the car before returning to his flat.

The defendant claimed he had no plan nor did he intend to kill the victim,
and that he had acted in a panic and without any control. He gave evidence
concerning his tours of duty with the Defence Forces in Lebanon, where a
number of shooting incidents had caused him considerable distress. A
psychiatrist and two psychologists gave evidence for the defence to the effect
that the defendant had a vulnerable personality and was suffering from a
post-traumatic stress disorder since 1988, with a marked exacerbation of
symptoms in 1990 when the killing had occurred. At the end of the trial, the
judge left two questions to the jury: (1) whether the accused was acting under
the influence of an irresistible impulse caused by a defect of reason due to
mental illness, which debarred him from refraining from killing the victim;
and (2) whether they were satisfied beyond a reasonable doubt that the
presumption that the accused intended to kill or cause serious injury to the
deceased had not been rebutted. He indicated that the possible verdicts were
(1) guilty but insane; (2) guilty of manslaughter, if they found that the accused
had not proved insanity on the balance of probabilities but the jury were not
satisfied that the intention had not been rebutted; and (3) guilty of murder.
The jury unanimously rejected the defence of insanity and, by a majority,
found the defendant guilty of murder.

As already indicated, the Court of Criminal Appeal (O'Flaherty, Johnson
and Geoghegan JJ) refused the application for leave to appeal and affirmed
the conviction. On the trial judge's direction in relation to the defence of
insanity, the Court found that the defence complaint that he had sought to
'trivialise' the defendant's claim had not been made out. The Court noted
that the question left to the jury on the point of irresistible impulse had been
agreed by counsel for the prosecution and defence. The Court t commented
that the 'trial judge painstakingly explained to [the jury] what was required
to be dealt with in regard to providing an answer to this question.' Indeed,
the Court noted that the approach adopted in the case conformed precisely
to that set out by Griffin J in his judgment in *Doyle v Wicklow County Council*
[1974] IR 66. Ultimately, it may be said that the decision in *Courtney* turned
on whether the trial judge's directions should be disturbed by an appellate
court. However, more widely it also confirms that the defence options
available to a person who claims to have been acting under an irresistible
impulse, automatism or post traumatic stress disorder are relatively limited.
In the absence of a defence of diminished responsibility, the defendant was

left with the narrow boundaries of insanity, albeit as expanded by the decision in *Doyle v Wicklow County Council* [1974] IR 66. For a fuller discussion of the different elements involved in the *Courtney* case, see Una Ní Raifeartaigh's comments in (1995) 5 *ICLJ* 105-107.

Self-defence In *The People v Clarke* [1995] 1 ILRM 355, the Court of Criminal Appeal considered a claim of self-defence in the context of a manslaughter charge. The defendant had been indicted on the charge of murder, tried in the Central Criminal Court and convicted of manslaughter, for which he was sentenced to ten years' penal servitude. In the statement which he made to the Gardaí on the day after the killing, he claimed that he had been playing pool in a hotel when the deceased repeatedly assaulted him and threatened to kill him and his family. When the fight was broken up the deceased indicated that he was going to return with a hatchet and kill the defendant. The defendant went home, obtained his father's shotgun and later met the deceased who was on his way home from the hotel. The defendant claimed that he had merely intended to frighten the deceased with the shotgun, but when confronted the deceased lunged at him and threatened to kill him. The defendant claimed that he had intended to fire a shot over the deceased's head, but the shot hit the deceased and killed him. The defendant did not give evidence at his trial. In charging the jury, the trial judge O'Hanlon J indicated that they could either convict the defendant of murder, acquit him completely or find him guilty of manslaughter. He also drew the attention of the jury to the fact that instead of calling the Gardaí after being attacked by the deceased, the applicant had returned to his own house and armed himself. O'Hanlon J then observed that while the jury 'could in theory' acquit the applicant of all responsibility, the facts hardly admitted of the possibility of an acquittal as there had been ample time to avoid the confrontation and call the Gardaí. As regards the statement made by the applicant to the Gardaí, O'Hanlon J indicated to the jury that this was not the equivalent of a person giving oral evidence under oath in court which could be heard by the jury and tested by cross-examination. Thus the statement was merely evidence of what the defendant had said to the Gardaí on the day after the killing. The defendant sought leave to appeal against his conviction on the grounds, *inter alia*, that O'Hanlon J had erred in directing the jury that the acquittal of the defendant by virtue of the defence of self-defence was a theoretical possibility, and that O'Hanlon J had misdirected the jury in relation to statements made by him to the Gardaí and, in particular, had unfairly contrasted exculpatory portions of the statements with sworn testimony so as to subvert the right of an accused not to give evidence at his trial. The Court of Criminal Appeal (O'Flaherty, Keane and Carney JJ) allowed the appeal and ordered a retrial. Delivering the Court's judgment, O'Flaherty

J considered that O'Hanlon J had erred in two respects, for concerning the 'theoretical possibility' of an acquittal and. secondly, concerning the evidential weight to be attached to the statement by the defendant to the Gardaí.

As to the trial judge's comment on the possibility of an acquittal, O'Flaherty J stated that this part of the charge had set at nought the previous impeccable charge on the three options where self-defence is raised. He quoted with approval the views of Walsh J in *The People v Quinn* [1965] IR 366, that, where self-defence was raised the onus rested on the prosecution to disprove the matter and that a jury must be directed that in order to convict they had to be satisfied beyond reasonable doubt that the applicant had killed the deceased and beyond reasonable doubt that the prosecution had negatived the issue of self-defence. O'Flaherty J continued:

> To say to a jury that something is only theoretically possible is in effect to invite them not to consider it at all; whereas it was accepted by [O'Hanlon J] at the outset of his charge and was accepted by counsel for the prosecution . . . that the defence of self-defence had been raised to the extent necessary for consideration by a jury. Once raised, a charge along the lines described in the *Quinn* case was required . . . [O'Hanlon J] went beyond commenting upon the particular facts of the case; his direction was bound to be taken by the jury as a direction on a matter of law, and that really amounted to a direction to them not to consider in any realistic way the defence of self-defence.

The Court reiterated the view of the Court itself in *The People v Crosbie* (1961) 1 Frewen 231 that, once a statement is put in evidence it becomes evidence in the real sense of the word, not only against the person who made it, but for him, as to facts contained in it which are favourable to his defence. A jury is not bound to accept such favourable facts as true, even if unrefuted by contrary evidence, but they should be told to receive, weigh and consider them as evidence.

As to the effect of a 'mixed' statement such as that made by the accused to the Gardaí, where it consisted both of inculpatory and exculpatory elements, the Court adopted the approach taken recently in England, exemplified by the decision of the Court of Appeal in. *R. v Duncan* (1981) 73 Cr App R 359, subsequently approved by the House of Lords in *R. v Sharp* (1987) 86 Cr App R 274.

In the instant case, O'Hanlon J had drawn a distinction between the incriminating parts and exculpatory parts of the applicant's statement to the Gardaí. In line with the recent English cases, this approach should not be adopted, although the Court acknowledged that O'Hanlon J's approach had once held sway. While a trial judge was entitled to comment unfavourably

on certain changes that had subsequently been made in regard to the applicant's original statement, the Court also held that there was an obligation on
the trial judge when dealing with the statement to remind the jury that the
accused had clearly raised the defence of self-defence in the course of his
first statement and thus they had to consider that defence. O'Flaherty J added:

> It would have been appropriate, too, to point out that that statement was
> made at a very early stage before the accused had got any legal advice
> and was made spontaneously to the Gardaí. It was necessary to remind
> the jury that the accused had never departed from the essential stance
> that he had taken as regards why he had shot the deceased. The jury
> might well have believed that explanation or disbelieved it and, either
> way, might still have held against the accused. But his explanation
> should have been laid before the jury as part of the evidence in the trial.

As already indicated, on both these grounds the Court allowed the appeal
and ordered a re-trial.

DELAY

Indictment trials: fraud   In *Cahalane v Murphy and Director of Public
Prosecutions* [1994] 2 ILRM 383 and *Hogan v President of the Circuit Court*,
Supreme Court, June 21, 1994, the Supreme Court considered the application
of the principles enunciated in *The State (O'Connell) v Fawsitt* [1986] IR
362; [1986] ILRM 639 and in *Director of Public Prosecutions v Byrne* [1993]
ILRM 475 (HC); [1994] 2 ILRM 91 (SC) (1993 Review, 223-6) in the context
of trials on indictment concerning complex frauds.

In *Cahalane*, the applicant had been charged in September 1991 with a
number of tax offences. All but one of these offences were alleged to have
been committed in the years 1986 and 1987. The charges arose out of an
investigation conducted by the Revenue and Customs authorities between
1986 and 1991 into an alleged scheme in the Cork region whereby an alcohol
based animal rub manufactured by the applicant – and for which purpose he
had access to large quantities of duty-free alcohol – was being treated and
sold on to publicans as whiskey and vodka for human consumption, thereby
resulting in large losses to the Revenue in unpaid excise duties. As a result
of these investigations, a file was prepared and sent to the Director of Public
Prosecutions in November 1989. A direction to prepare a case for trial on
indictment against the applicant was issued by the Director in October 1990.
He was charged in September 1991 and a book of evidence was served in
December 1991. However, an order returning him for trial was not made until

January 1993 owing to delays caused by the taking of depositions from prosecution witnesses and the preparation of the book of evidence. The applicant sought an order of prohibition and an injunction restraining his trial from taking place on the grounds that the delay involved in bringing his case to trial was both excessive and unconscionable and that there had been a failure on the part of the State to vindicate his right to a speedy trial. The applicant also claimed that any defence he might have to these charges had been prejudiced as a result of the death of two potential witnesses.

In the High Court, Carney J granted the relief sought in respect of all but one of the charges on the grounds that the Director of Public Prosecutions had failed to exercise reasonable expedition in dealing with the applicant's case and that the applicant would have been prejudiced in his defence as a result of the deaths of the two potential witnesses. In relation to a charge of knowingly and wilfully submitting an incorrect return of income tax, which was alleged to have occurred in 1990, Carney J held that there had been no unreasonable delay in bringing the matter on for trial and that the applicant had not established prejudice in that respect.

The Director of Public Prosecutions appealed against the decision of the High Court to prohibit the trial on the majority of the charges, but the Supreme Court (Finlay CJ, O'Flaherty, Egan, Blayney and Denham JJ) dismissed the appeal.

Delivering the only reasoned judgment, Finlay CJ confirmed the view of the Court in *The State (O'Connell) v Fawsitt* [1986] IR 362 and *Director of Public Prosecutions v Byrne* [1994] 2 ILRM 91 that the right to an expeditious trial is an important positive constitutional right. In the instant case, he concluded that the evidence as established showed a failure on the part of the Director of Public Prosecutions to vindicate that right.

The Chief Justice accepted that charges of conspiracy frequently involved proving matters of considerable complexity and intricacy and that the facts and circumstances of the instant case indicated that there were matters of complexity involved which called for careful and detailed investigation. However, notwithstanding the difficulties associated with investigating the charges at issue in the instant case, the Director had failed to offer any explanation for the long periods of delay totalling 22 months which had occurred between the time when the file was sent to his office and directions to charge were given, and when the accused was actually charged.

Finlay CJ held that the procedure whereby depositions were taken in the District Court by the Director based on considerations of convenience to the judge of the District Court and the availability of court accommodation were wholly inconsistent with the obligation on the part of the State authorities to vindicate the right of the applicant to an expeditious trial. On this basis, the Court agreed with the view expressed by Carney J that the trial on the charges in question should be prohibited.

The second case in this area was *Hogan v President of the Circuit Court*, Supreme Court, June 21, 1994. In this case the applicant had been arrested and charged in December 1992 on 49 counts of larceny, falsification of accounts and forgery, alleged to have occurred in the period 1978 to 1982. The offences were related to the management of the affairs of a registered friendly society, the Transport Employees Tontine and Beneficial Society. The society had been founded by the applicant's father and the applicant had worked in the society from 1969 until its collapse in 1984. The Gardaí had first become involved in the case in December 1984, and between then and December 1992, when the applicant was charged, they and inspectors appointed by the Registrar of Friendly Societies had been involved in investigating the case. The applicant sought an order of prohibition on the ground that there had been excessive delay on the part of the prosecution in bringing the charges to hearing, that he would be prejudiced in the preparation and presentation of his defence, and that he had been denied his constitutional right to a fair and speedy trial. The prejudice alleged was that one of the prosecution witnesses, the applicant's father, was now 95 years of age and his memory was defective, and that two of the witnesses the applicant proposed to call had died.

In the High Court, Morris J granted the order sought by the respondent and this was upheld by the Supreme Court (Finlay CJ, O'Flaherty, Egan, Blayney and Denham JJ). It was argued on behalf of the Director of Public Prosecutions that the death of the two witnesses had occurred at a time when even without unjustifiable delay the case might not have concluded, and that the applicant's father was a witness for the prosecution and there was no concrete evidence that he was incapable of giving evidence. Attention was also drawn to the gravity of the crimes involved and the great number of persons who must have suffered as a result of the collapse of the society, and it was argued in a case such as this prosecution should not be prohibited except in the event of clearly established irremediable prejudice to the defence at the trial.

Delivering the leading judgment, Finlay CJ stated that the accused's constitutional right to an expeditious trial was not confined to a consideration of the period between the date of charge and the date of trial. Applying the principles in *Cahalane v Murphy* [1994] 2 ILRM 383, above, he stated that, quite apart from any question of prejudice to the defence, there was clear evidence that the authorities had disregarded their obligation to provide for and protect the constitutional right of an accused person to an expeditious trial. Finally, the fact that a considerable number of people had undergone considerable financial suffering and distress must not, in his view, deter the Court from according to the applicant his constitutional rights.

Indictment trial: sexual offence In *G. v Director of Public Prosecutions* [1994] 1 IR 374 and *O'Connor v Smith*, High Court, November 17, 1994 the courts considered the general principles concerning delay in the context of prosecutions for sexual offences, particularly in what are generally described as child sexual abuse cases. Such cases involve the particular problem that a formal complaint may not emerge until some considerable time after the events involved in the alleged offences.

Summary trials We have already noted that the decision of the Supreme Court in *Director of Public Prosecutions v Byrne* [1994] 2 ILRM 91 was discussed in the 1993 Review, 223-6.

DRUG TRAFFICKING

The Criminal Justice Act 1994 contains significant provisions aimed at tackling the growing incidence of international drug trafficking and associated activities such as money laundering. The Explanatory Memorandum to the 1994 Act when it was originally published as a Bill noted that it had been increasingly recognised that the traditional methods of dealing with drug trafficking in particular were not sufficient and that what was required was a means of depriving persons who obtain large profits from crime of those profits. The 1994 Act attempted to tackle this by providing, *inter alia*, for the seizure and confiscation of the proceeds of drug trafficking and other serious offences, the creation of an offence of money laundering and other measures to give effect to a number of international instruments on drug trafficking, money laundering and mutual assistance in criminal matters. The Criminal Justice Act 1994 (Commencement) Order 1994 (SI No. 324 of 1994) brought into force the measures in the 1994 Act allowing for the confiscation of the proceeds of drug trafficking and enforcement powers in respect of trafficking offences at sea with effect from November 14, 1994. The Criminal Justice Act 1994 (Commencement) Order 1995 (SI No. 55 of 1995) brought into effect the provisions on money laundering on dates between March 6 and May 2, 1995.

Confiscation and enforcement Parts II and III of the 1994 Act (ss. 4-30) deal with the confiscation of proceeds and consequential enforcement matters. Prior to the 1994 Act, the courts had only limited power to order the seizure and confiscation of criminal proceeds. S. 4 of the 1994 Act (which deals specifically with drug trafficking) and s. 9 (which deals with other offences) extended that power to all cases where a person is convicted of an offence on indictment. S. 19 of the 1994 Act deals with the enforcement of confiscation orders by the Director of Public Prosecutions. Other sections deal with related matters such as the forfeiture of property used in criminal offences. In this respect, the 1994 Act took into account the recommendations made by the Law Reform Commission in its report *The Confiscation of the Proceeds from Crime* (LRC 35-1991), discussed in the 1991 Review, 132-4.

Money laundering Part IV of the 1994 Act (ss. 31 and 32) made provision for anti-laundering measures in line with Directive 91/308/EEC on the prevention of the use of the financial system for the purpose of money laundering. In particular, s. 32 requires financial institutions (described in the Act as 'designated bodies') to take 'reasonable measures' concerning transactions which may involve the activities covered by the Act. Detailed Regulations have been made to describe the measures required of financial institutions under the 1994 Act: the Criminal Justice Act 1994 (s. 32(10)(a)) Regulations 1995 (SI No. 104 of 1995), the Criminal Justice Act 1994 (Section 32(10)(b)) Regulations 1995 (SI No. 105 of 1995), the Criminal Justice Act 1994 (s. 32(10)(d)) Regulations 1995 (SI No. 106 of 1995) and the Criminal Justice Act 1994 (s. 32(10)(d)) (No. 2) Regulations 1995 (SI No. 324 of 1995).

Drug trafficking at sea and international co-operation Part V of the 1994 Act (ss. 33-37) deals with drug trafficking offences at sea and gives effect, in part, to the United Nations Vienna Convention against Illicit Traffic in Narcotic Drugs and Psychotropic Substances (1988) (on other aspects of the 1988 Convention, see the 1993 Review, 243-4). Finally, we note here that Part VII of the 1994 Act (ss. 46 to 56) provides for international co-operation in relation to criminal matters in accordance with the Council of Europe Convention on Mutual Assistance in Criminal Matters (1959), the Council of Europe Convention on Laundering, Search, Seizure and Confiscation of the Proceeds of Crime (1990) and the Vienna Drugs Convention (1988). We note briefly that, where proceedings are served on a person outside the State, s. 50(7) of the 1994 Act repeals s. 24 of the Extradition Act 1870 and s. 5 of the Extradition Act 1873, with a consequential repeal of the provisions in the ss. 3 and 4 of the Extradition (European Convention on the Suppression of Terrorism) Act 1987. The provisions in the Acts of 1870 and 1873 were the only parts of the previous legislation on extradition that had not been repealed by the Extradition Act 1965. Consequential repeals to s. 3 of the Genocide Act 1973 were also made by s. 50 of the 1994 Act.

EVIDENCE

Accomplice   In *The People v Hogan* [1994] 2 ILRM 74, the Court of Criminal Appeal (O'Flaherty, Geoghegan and Kinlen JJ) considered whether a trial judge's warning as to the danger of convicting an accused on the basis of the uncorroborated evidence of an accomplice had been defective.

The case concerned an armed robbery in which a woman was held up by a masked man who had a hand gun who forced her to drive her car to a nearby forest where they were joined by another masked man. The woman was robbed of £627. Another vehicle appeared and the two men made their escape. These two men were convicted following guilty pleas. The applicant was tried and convicted in the Dublin Circuit Criminal Court on charges of robbery, possession of a firearm with intent to rob, false imprisonment and common assault. It was the prosecution case that the applicant drove the vehicle that appeared on the scene after the robbery. The woman who had been robbed was unable to identify the robbers or the vehicle in which they escaped. At the applicant's trial one of the convicted men testified that the applicant supplied the gun, the mask and the get-away vehicle. Counsel for the defence emphasised that on appeal this witness had obtained a reduction of his sentence on the basis that he had co-operated with the Gardaí. It was also pointed out that this witness was likely to have known of the presence in the applicant's house of a gun and a mask.

In the course of his charge to the jury, the trial judge warned them of the danger of convicting on the uncorroborated evidence of such a witness. He went on to say that if they believed the evidence of the accomplice they were entitled to convict on it. He explained that:

> the kind of corroboration which is required is not confirmation by independent evidence of everything which the accomplice has sworn to because his evidence would be entirely unnecessary if that was so. What is required is some independent testimony which affects the accused by tending to connect him with the crime. That is to say evidence, either direct or circumstantial which implicates the accused, which confirms in some particular, not only the evidence given by the accomplice that the crime has been committed, but also the evidence that the accused committed it.

The Court of Criminal Appeal (O'Flaherty, Geoghegan and Kinlen JJ) upheld the defendant's conviction.

Delivering the Court's judgment, O'Flaherty J accepted the argument by counsel for the defendant that the purpose of pointing out the need for corroboration is not to confirm the accomplice's account of the events, but to find whether the alleged corroborative evidence implicates the accused in the crime with which he is charged as the Court in *The People v Phelan* (1950) 1 Frewen 98 had indicated. However, in the instant case, the Court held that the trial judge's warning in relation to accomplice evidence was as complete as the circumstances of the case required: he had warned the jury of the danger of acting on the uncorroborated evidence of an accomplice, he furnished them with a full description of what corroboration meant in law and correctly set out the matters in the case which were capable of being corroborative. It was very clear, the Court held, that it was for the jury to decide whether any of those matters were so capable of affording such corroboration and any reference to confirmation of the accomplice's evidence was merely an aside.

The Court considered that the reference by counsel for the defence to the reduction in sentence obtained by the accomplice and his likely knowledge as to the location of the gun and the mask made it abundantly clear to the jury why the warning in relation to accomplice evidence was required and the fact that the trial judge did not expand further as to the reasons for the warning did not render his charge to the jury defective. The Court also found significant that the trial judge was not requisitioned by counsel for the defence to elaborate in any respect on his charge regarding accomplice evidence and that, indeed, it had been accepted that he had given a correct direction to the jury on the question of corroboration.

Complaint of sexual assault The circumstances in which a complaint of sexual assault is admissible were considered in two Court of Criminal Appeal decisions in 1994, *The People v Kiernan*, Court of Criminal Appeal, March 11, 1994 and *The People v McD.*, Court of Criminal Appeal, July 27, 1994 (also referred to below, 226). In both cases, the Court applied the principles outlined by the Court in *The People v Brophy* [1992] ILRM 709 (1992 Review, 253). In each case, the issue arose as to whether, in accordance with the *Brophy* criteria, the complainants had made a complaint of sexual assault at the first opportunity available to them, or 'as soon as was reasonably possible. This form of 'complaint' is, of course, different from a formal complaint to the Garda Síochána. For other cases on this area, see further the 1992 Review, 252-5.

'Mixed' statement to Gardaí: evidential value In *The People v Clarke* [1995] 1 ILRM 355, which we discuss above, 169-71, the evidential effect of a 'mixed' statement made by an accused to the Gardaí, consisting both of inculpatory and exculpatory elements, was considered.

EXTRADITION

Statutory reform The Extradition (Amendment) Act 1994 effected further important reform to the extradition arrangements, particularly with regard to political offences. The 1994 Act thus amended a number of provisions of the Extradition Act 1965 and the Extradition (European Convention on the Suppression of Terrorism) Act 1987. The overall effect of the Act was to clarify and extend the range of offences not to be regarded as political offences, fully implementing the European Convention on the Suppression of Terrorism and giving effect to the requirements relating to extradition in the United Nations Convention Against Illicit Traffic in Narcotic Drugs and Psychotropic Substances (1988) (as to which, see also the Criminal Justice Act 1994 discussed above, 174-5). The 1994 Act also made a number of changes in the administrative arrangements concerning extradition, including the centralisation of proceedings in the Dublin Metropolitan District Court and reserving decisions on the granting of bail in extradition cases to the High Court. The 1994 Act came into force on August 22, 1994: Extradition (Amendment) Act 1994 (Commencement) Order 1994 (SI No. 220 of 1994).

Political offences It will be recalled that the Extradition Act 1965 provides that extradition will not be granted for an offence which is a political offence or an offence connected with a political offence. The general definition of what constituted a political offence was, originally, largely a matter for the courts, but the substantial criticism of a number of these decisions, as well as the requirements of recent international instruments, has resulted in substantial statutory intervention in the area. S. 3 of the 1965 Act provided that 'political offence' did not include the taking or attempted taking of the life of a Head of State or a member of his family but otherwise left the matter undefined. S. 3 of the Genocide Act 1973 provided that no offence which if committed in the State would be punishable as genocide or as an attempt, conspiracy or incitement to commit genocide shall be regarded as a political offence or an offence connected with a political offence for the purposes of extradition. However, the first major intervention in this area was the Extradition (European Convention on the Suppression of Terrorism) Act 1987 (see generally the 1987 Review, 130). S. 3 of the 1987 Act provided that the following offences cannot be regarded as political offences or as. offences connected with a political offence (a) an offence under the Hague Convention for the Suppression of Unlawful Seizure of Aircraft (1970), (b) an offence under the Montreal Convention for the Suppression of Unlawful Acts against the Safety of Civil Aviation (1971), (c) a serious offence involving an attack against the life, physical integrity or liberty of an internationally protected person, (d) an offence involving kidnapping, the taking of a hostage or serious false imprisonment, (e) an offence involving the use of an explosive or an automatic firearm, if such use endangers persons and (f) any offence of attempting to commit or being an accomplice in relation to any of the foregoing offences.

S. 4 of the 1987 Act also provided that, in addition to the offences listed in s. 3, any serious offence involving an act of violence against the life, physical integrity or liberty of a person or involving an act against property if the act created collective danger for persons, and any offence of attempting to commit, or being an accomplice in relation to, any of the foregoing offences shall not be regarded as a political offence or an offence connected with a political offence if the court, or the Minister for Justice as the case may be, is of opinion that the offence cannot properly be so regarded. In determining whether or not such offences are or are not to be regarded as political, consideration must be given to any particularly serious aspect of the offence including, that it created a collective danger to the life, physical integrity or liberty of persons, that it affected persons foreign to the motives behind it, or that cruel or vicious means were used in the commission of the offence. In *Sloan v Culligan* [1992] 1 IR 223, *sub nom. Magee v Culligan* [1992] ILRM 186 (1991 Review, 155-160), the Supreme Court held, inter alia, that the 1987 Act should be strictly construed and that it did not prevent possession of an M60 machine gun and ammunition with intent to endanger life or cause serious injury to property being regarded as political for the purposes of extradition. The 1994 Act deals with what were thus considered as loopholes in the 1987 Act (see the 1991 Review, 160) and it amends both the 1965 and 1987 Acts so that offences involving explosives or firearms, all offences of the type envisaged by the Convention on the Suppression of Terrorism, are not to be regarded as political offences for the purposes of extradition. The opportunity was also taken, as indicated, to specify that drugs offences would not be regarded in any cases as political offences for extradition purposes.

Political offences: terrorism S. 2 of the 1994 Act, which amends s. 3 of the Extradition (European Convention on the Suppression of Terrorism) Act 1987, is the key section on the political offence exception The 1987 Act had implemented Article 1 of the European Convention on Terrorism by providing that certain specified offences shall never be regarded as political. S. 2 if the 1994 Act takes advantage of Article 2 of the Convention, which provides that States may decide not to regard as political certain serious offences of kinds described in that Article and not covered by Article 1. While s. 4 of the 1987 Act had implemented Article 2 to some extent, the courts had, under the 1987 Act, retained the type of discretion to have regard to particular circumstances in determining the issue which had led to the conclusions in the *Sloan* case, above. S. 3 of the 1987 Act, as now amended by s. 2 of the 1994 Act provides that the offences described in Article 2 of the Convention, namely any serious offence involving (a) an act of violence, other than one covered by Article 1, against the life, physical integrity or liberty of a person, or (b) an act against property other than one covered by Article 1, if the act created a collective danger for persons are added to the existing list of offences which may never be regarded as political offences. In addition to reversing certain aspects of the decision in Sloan, these changes also have the effect of reversing the political offence element of the decision of Flood J in *Magee v O'Dea* [1994] 1 ILRM 540, discussed below, 186-8.

One aspect of a decision of the courts that has been confirmed by the 1994 Act is that in *Ellis v O'Dea (No. 2)* [1991] ILRM 346 (1991 Review, 217-20), where extradition was sought and granted in respect of a charge of conspiracy to cause an explosion. The Supreme Court decided there that, although the 1987 Act explicitly provided that if the substantive offence cannot be regarded as political then an attempt to commit such an offence or being an accomplice to such an offence cannot be a political offence either but was silent on the question of conspiracy to commit an offence where the substantive offence cannot be regarded as political, conspiracy was covered by the Act. The 1994 Act confirms this by explicitly adding conspiracy.

Drugs offences   S. 3 of the 1994 Act amended s. 3 of the Extradition Act 1965, the effect of which is to exclude an offence within the scope of Article 3 of the United Nations Vienna Convention Against Illicit Traffic in Narcotic Drugs and Psychotropic Substances (1988) from the scope of 'political offence' and 'revenue offence', so that the extradition of a person in connection with a drug offence covered by Article 3 of the Vienna Convention cannot be refused on the grounds that the offence in question is a political offence or a revenue offence. This alteration to Irish law, together with the passage of the Criminal Justice Act 1994 (see 174-5, above), permitted the State to ratify the 1988 Vienna Convention.

Centralisation of proceedings   S. 3(b) and s. 4 of the 1994 Act provided for the centralising of extradition proceedings in the Dublin Metropolitan District Court for all purposes for which the District Court has jurisdiction under Parts II and III of the 1965 Act. It was proposed that a panel of judges from the Dublin Metropolitan District will be nominated by the President of the District Court and they will deal with all extradition cases. The intention was to ensure greater continuity in extradition cases and allow the judges in question to develop expertise in extradition matters.

Granting of bail by High Court   S. 5 of the 1994 Act inserted a new section

7A into the Extradition Act 1965 providing that a person arrested under Parts II or III of the 1965 Act may only be admitted to bail by order of the High Court. Prior to the 1994 Act, the District Court had jurisdiction to grant bail in most criminal proceedings including extradition.

Arrest and handing over procedures The remaining sections in the 1994 Act effect a number of other important administrative changes. We will note two of these here. S. 6 of the 1994 Act allows the arrest of a person for extradition purposes although the arresting Garda does not have the extradition warrant in his possession at that time. However within 24 hours of the arrest, the warrant issued must be produced and a copy given to the person arrested. The other provision we note is s. 12, which amends s. 47 (1) of the 1965 Act. In *The State (Holmes) v Furlong* [1967] IR 210, the Supreme Court had held that s. 47(1) of the 1965 Act required, in effect, that the District Court, when making an order for delivery of a person, must specify in the order a particular point of departure from the State at which that person is to be delivered into the custody of the police force of the requesting jurisdiction. It was felt that the fact that the point of departure is known in advance can give rise to security difficulties. S. 12 of the 1994 Act restates s. 47(1) of the 1965 Act, but with the deletion of the reference to 'at some convenient point of departure from the State' and inserts a new s. 47(1)(A) which provides that a person in whose case an order is made shall be brought by the Garda Síochána as soon as may be to a point of departure from the State and there delivered into the custody of a member of the police force of the place in which the warrant has been issued for conveyance to the place.

We now turn to examine the case law on extradition in 1994.

Constitutional rights: whether in danger In *Larkin v O'Dea* [1994] 2 ILRM 448 (HC); [1995] 2 ILRM 1 (SC), Morris J and, on appeal, the Supreme Court declined to order the applicant's extradition on the ground that his rights as a citizen would not protected if extradited to a jurisdiction where evidence obtained in violation of his constitutional rights might be given. Although the Supreme Court decision in the case was delivered in January 1995, we consider it here for the sake of completeness.

The applicant, an Irish citizen, was arrested and taken to Dundalk Garda Station in connection with the alleged murder of a person in Northern Ireland. The applicant was detained under the provisions of s. 4 of the Criminal Justice Act 1984. His detention was extended for a period of six hours, after which he was released from custody without charge.

Under s. 10(1) of the Criminal Justice Act 1984, any further arrest is prohibited unless a district judge is satisfied on the information supplied to him on oath by a member of the Garda Síochána not below the rank of superintendent that further information has come to the knowledge of the Gardaí since the person's release as to his suspected participation in the offence for which his arrest was sought. An application was made in which a superintendent indicated that further information had come into the possession of the Gardaí since the date of the applicant's original release and that further inquiries had been made to establish the author of the alleged crime. The district judge granted a warrant authorising the re-arrest of the applicant. The applicant was arrested and subsequently released. However, it was alleged that during this period of detention the applicant made incriminating admissions regarding the alleged murder. The applicant was arrested for a third time and brought before the District Court where he was remanded in custody and subsequently an order was made for his extradition to Northern Ireland to face trial for the alleged murder. It was submitted on behalf of the applicant that the court should refuse to sanction the order for extradition of the applicant on the grounds that any alleged admissions made by him in violation of his constitutional rights would be inadmissible in this jurisdiction and if such evidence was admissible in Northern Ireland, then the extradition would be a failure on the part of the court to vindicate the applicant's constitutional rights. It was submitted on behalf of the respondent that the court should not concern itself with the rules of practice and procedure which would govern a hearing in Northern Ireland because, it was submitted, the hearing in that jurisdiction would be fair. In particular, under article 76 of the Police and Criminal Evidence (Northern Ireland) Order 1989, the Northern Ireland court could refuse to admit evidence on which the prosecution sought to rely if it appeared to the court that, having regard to all the circumstances, including the manner in which the evidence was obtained, its admission would have such an adverse effect on the fairness of the proceedings that the court ought not to admit it. Morris J ordered the release of the applicant.

He held that s. 10 of the 1984 Act required that the information supplied on oath to a District Court judge must indicate that further information relating to a person's suspected participation in the offence for which the arrest is sought had come to the knowledge of the Gardaí since the release of the person previously arrested. He held that the District Court judge in the instant case could not have been satisfied that the matters referred to in s. 10 existed as nothing in the information sworn by the superintendent indicated that the further information or inquiries established that it was the applicant who was the author of the alleged murder. Accordingly he held that the warrant purporting to authorise the re-arrest of the applicant was invalid and the statements obtained during the period of this detention were inadmissible. In considering whether it was appropriate to extradite the applicant, Morris J held that the issue was whether the court would fulfil its obligation to vindicate a citizen's constitutional rights if it ordered his extradition to a jurisdiction where evidence obtained in violation of his constitutional rights might be admissible. Morris J discharged the extradition order and ordered the release of the applicant because the respondent could not give an undertaking that inadmissible evidence would not be made available to the prosecuting authorities in Northern Ireland. The respondent unsuccessfully appealed, and the Supreme Court (Hamilton CJ, Costello P, O'Flaherty, Blayney and Denham JJ) confirmed the approach of Morris J.

Delivering one of the leading judgments, Hamilton CJ cited with approval the judgment of Henchy J in *Shannon v Ireland* [1984] IR 548; [1985] ILRM 449 to the effect that there was an obligation on all organs of state, and in particular the judicial arm, to ensure that in the operation of the provisions of the 1965 Act the constitutional rights of persons affected were defended and vindicated. The Chief Justice also confirmed dicta in the Shannon case that, since the 1965 Act did not deal with the procedures to be followed by the prosecution in the requesting state, it was impossible to guarantee in advance that the prosecution of the person extradited would necessarily accord with Irish constitutional requirements. but that there was a presumption that the 1965 Act would not be operated in violation of the constitutional rights of those affected by its operation. If it was shown in a particular case that the provisions of the Act were being used in a manner inconsistent with such rights, the Chief Justice pointed out that the courts would be bound to refuse to give effect to these provisions.He went on to state that '[i]t is well established that every extradition case must be decided in the light of its own particular facts and circumstances.' In the instant case, the Court was concerned with the violation of the constitutional rights of the applicant within the jurisdiction of this State and not whether the applicant would get a fair trial in Northern Ireland. In this respect, he said that there was a clear legislative policy that when a correct application for extradition was made, the individual concerned should be extradited subject to the provisions of the 1965 Act.

In a concurring judgment, Denham J noted that the duty on the courts to vindicate the constitutional rights of citizens obliged it to refuse to extradite the applicant. Here, it was clear that as the warrant authorising the further arrest of the applicant was bad, and the statements which were obtained by the servants or agents of the State were inadmissible in this jurisdiction, as indicated in the decision of the Court in *The People v Kenny* [1990] 2 IR 110 (1990 Review, 202-5), notwithstanding that there might have been no deliberate attempt to breach the applicant's rights. Although for this reason the statements would be admissible in the prosecution of the applicant in Northern Ireland, the Court would be giving effect to an unconstitutional act in that the fruit of such an act could be used against the applicant in another jurisdiction and would thus be failing in its constitutional obligation to defend and vindicate the constitutional rights of the applicant if it were to give effect to the provisions of the 1965 Act and permit the extradition of the applicant to Northern Ireland. On this basis, as already indicated, the Supreme Court declined to extradite the applicant.

Discovery: third party In *Fusco v O'Dea* [1994] 2 ILRM 389, the Supreme Court declined to order third party discovery under O.31, r.29 of the Rules of the Superior Courts 1986 against a party outside the jurisdiction in the context of an extradition case: see the discussion in the Practice and Procedure chapter, 376-8, below.

Extra-territoriality In *Aamand v Smithwick and Attorney General* [1995] 1 ILRM 61, the Supreme Court, in confirming that the Extradition Act 1965 must be strictly construed, declined to extradite the applicant as the offence for which his extradition was requested, smuggling cocaine on the high seas, did not correspond to an offence under Irish law.

Article 7(2) of the European Convention on Extradition 1957 provides that when the offence for which extradition is requested has been committed outside the territory of the requesting state, extradition may only be refused if the law of the requested state does not allow prosecution for the same category of offence when committed outside its territory or does not allow extradition for the offence concerned. S. 10(1) of the Extradition Act 1965 provides that extradition shall be granted only in respect of an offence which is punishable under the laws of the requesting country and of the State by imprisonment for a maximum period of at least one year or by a more severe penalty and for which, if there has been a conviction and sentence in the requesting country, imprisonment for a period of at least four months or a more severe penalty has been imposed. S. 10(3) provides that in s. 10 references to an offence punishable under the laws of the State shall be construed as including references to an act which, if it had been committed in the State, would constitute such an offence.

The applicant was detained pursuant to an order by the first respondent judge under s. 29(1) of the Extradition Act 1965, his extradition having been requested by Denmark in relation to two offences of smuggling cocaine on the high seas.

The applicant argued (i) that having regard to the provisions of Article 7(2) of the 1957 Convention, his extradition was prohibited because the offences in respect of which the request for extradition had been made were alleged to have been committed outside Denmark and Irish law does not allow prosecution for that category of offence when committed outside the territory of Ireland; and (ii) that by reason of the fact that no offence was known to Irish law of the smuggling or handling of prohibited drugs if committed by an Irish citizen outside the territory of Ireland, the offences in respect of which extradition was requested were not offences which were punishable under the laws of the State and that his extradition was accordingly prohibited by virtue of the provisions of s. 10 of the 1965 Act.

As already indicated, the Supreme Court (Finlay CJ, O'Flaherty, Egan, Blayney and Denham JJ) held that the Extradition Act 1965 and the Extradition Act 1965 (Part II) (No. 23) Order 1989 (which incorporated into Irish law the European Convention on Extradition constituted a penal statutory code involving penal sanctions on an individual and must therefore be strictly construed. Accordingly, an individual should not be subjected to detention and extradition unless the legislation provides so unambiguously.

Turning to the instant case, Finlay CJ stated that the combined effect of s. 8(1) and s. 8(5) of the 1965 Act was to incorporate the 1957 Convention into domestic law. The fact that some provisions of the Convention were repeated in the 1965 Act did not, in his view, indicate that the legislature intended to exclude provisions not so expressly repeated as to do so would give s. 8(5) of the 1965 Act, which provides that every extradition agreement shall have the force of law, no meaning since the Convention was an extradition agreement within the definition contained in s. 8(1).

He went on to state that the provisions of Part II of the 1965 Act not only applied the dominant statutory provisions where they were inconsistent with the terms of an extradition agreement but also constituted a set of basic requirements and guidelines for cases where the government, being satisfied that appropriate reciprocal facilities will be afforded by another country, applies Part II of the Act to a request for extradition in a case where no convention, extradition treaty or agreement exists. Finlay CJ considered that s. 10(3) of the 1965 Act was not inconsistent with Article 7(2) of the Convention. If it were intended to be so, he felt that there would be some reference to extra territorial offences in the requesting country which are not extra territorial offences in this State. Indeed, Finlay CJ explained s. 10(3) of the 1965 Act as ensuring that where the offence named in the request from the requesting country cannot be matched by any offence of a similar name in Ireland, but the acts constituting that offence would constitute an offence punishable in Ireland, the provisions of s. 10(1), which refer to an offence punishable under the laws of the requesting country and of the State, could not be too narrowly construed.

By virtue of Article 7(2), Finlay CJ held that the applicant's extradition was prohibited since the offence for which extradition was requested had been alleged to have been committed outside the requesting country's territory and the law of Ireland did not allow prosecution for such an offence when committed outside the territory of Ireland.

While the *Aamand* case raised some mundane issues concerning extra-territoriality and correspondence of offences under the 1965 Act, it can also be seen in the wider context of the international enforcement of drug control legislation. In that respect, the decision indicates some of the inadequacies in the 1965 Act and the 1957 Convention on Extradition on which it was based. For some perceptive criticisms of the regime in that respect, see Michael Forde's article, 'Extradition and extraterritorial crimes: safe havens for drugs traffickers?'(1994) 4 *ICLJ* 160. For other attempts to deal with international drug trafficking and its associated money laundering operations, see the discussion of the Criminal Justice Act 1994, 174-5 above.

Political offence: collective danger to life   In *Magee v O'Dea* [1994] 1 ILRM 540, Flood J considered the original terms of s. 4(1)(a) of the Extradition (European Convention on the Suppression of Terrorism) Act 1987, which provides that, where an offence does not fall within s. 3 of the 1987 Act, a Court has a discretion to determine whether an offence is to be regarded as a political offence or as an offence connected with a political offence if the court, having taken into account, *inter alia*, that it created a collective danger to the life, physical integrity or liberty of persons, is of the opinion that the offence cannot properly be regarded as a political offence or as an offence connected with a political offence. As we have already mentioned, s. 4(1) of the 1987 Act has been greatly restricted by the additions made to s. 3 of the 1987 Act by the Extradition (Amendment) Act 1994: see discussion of the 1994 Act, 178-81, above. In that respect, while the outcome of the Magee case would be different in the wake of the 1994 Act, it remains of interest not only for the application of the general approach taken by Flood J to the discretion under s. 4 of the 1987 Act (which remains of some significance even after the 1994 Act) but also because he dealt with the separate issue of the impact of adverse pre-trial publicity in an extradition case.

The background was that, in 1993, a warrant for the arrest of the plaintiff was issued in England, alleging that he had murdered a sergeant in the British army. The warrant was transmitted to the defendant, an Assistant Commissioner of An Garda Síochána who backed the warrant and authorised its execution within the State. The plaintiff was detained pursuant to s. 30 of the Offences Against the State Act 1939, and was charged before the District Court with failing to give his name when requested to do so contrary to that Act. He was remanded in custody and, on the remand date, whilst in custody in the courthouse in Limerick, was introduced to a solicitor who had been retained on his behalf. The proceedings under the 1939 Act were struck out, but on leaving the court the plaintiff was arrested on foot of the extradition warrant. A few minutes later the extradition case was called. The District

Court judge did not invite the defence solicitor to seek an adjournment. Having heard the evidence he withdrew, but came back into court to recall of his own motion a witness as to the identity of the plaintiff. He did so without informing either the plaintiff's solicitor or the State Solicitor of what he intended to do. The District Court judge made an order pursuant to s. 47 of the Extradition Act 1965, directing the plaintiff's delivery into the custody of the relevant English Constabulary. He also informed the plaintiff of his rights under s. 50 of the 1965 Act and of his right of appeal.

The plaintiff applied to the High Court seeking an inquiry under Article 40 of the Constitution and made an application for his release pursuant to s. 50 of the Extradition Act 1965.

Before dealing with the two issues already mentioned, Flood J dealt with the procedures adopted by the District Court judge. He accepted that the judge had a right to recall a witness of his own motion, but noted that this practice should be used sparingly in criminal cases as otherwise it might appear that the judge was becoming partisan. In the instant case, given that the defence solicitor was engaged only minutes before the case came on, the district judge should have invited him to apply for an adjournment to enable him to investigate and prepare his defence properly and examine the documentation. In addition, the speed with which the matter was dealt with, the failure of the judge to ensure that the defence solicitor had an opportunity to consider all aspects of the case and the failure to advise the defence solicitor of his intention to recall the witness who had given evidence of identity amounted to the use of unfair procedures in a matter where strict proof was required. He thus concluded that the order of the District Court was invalid and that the plaintiff's detention was not in accordance with law.

Flood J then considered (the unamended: see 179-80, above) s. 4(1)(a) of the Extradition (European Convention on the Suppression of Terrorism) Act 1987. He was of the view that while there were members of the public in the area at the time of the killing, there was no recorded instance of a member of the public feeling endangered, nor of a member of the public having dispersed as a result of panic induced by the shooting. He stated that the attack was a planned operation which related to a specific individual so that, judged by an objective test, the killing did not therefore create a collective danger to the life, physical integrity or liberty of persons within the meaning of s. 4(1)(a) of the 1987 Act. The offence in question was therefore a political offence and he concluded that an order for extradition could not be made. As already indicated, this element of the decision was, in effect, reversed by the Extradition (Amendment) Act 1994.

As to adverse pre-trial publicity, Flood J applied the principles in *D. v Director of Public Prosecutions* [1994] 1 ILRM 435 (discussed below, 200-1). He stated that before the court could conclude that adverse publicity had made it impossible to hold a fair trial, the plaintiff had to show that there was a real or serious risk that the trial would be unfair if it were allowed to proceed. In this instance, he held that coverage by a number of newspapers in England, and in particular the use of photographs of the plaintiff, had undoubtedly been prejudicial. Whilst this coverage would have 'faded' in the public recollection during the intervening two years, and whilst a trial judge would strongly and properly charge a jury to ignore such coverage, there was, on the balance of probabilities, a serious risk of unfairness. Accordingly he concluded that extradition should be refused on this ground also.

Rule of specialty   The Extradition (Rule of Specialty and Re-Extradition for Purposes of Part III of Extradition Act 1965) Order 1994 (SI No. 221 of 1994), which was made under s. 3 of the Extradition (European Convention on the Suppression of Terrorism) Act 1987, modifies the provisions of ss. 20, 21 and 39 of the Extradition Act 1965 (which deal with the rule of specially and with re-extradition) for the purposes of the 'backing of warrants' form of extradition that applies between the State and the United Kingdom under Part III of the 1965 Act. The Order came into force on 22 August 1994, the same date on which the Extradition (Amendment) Act 1994 entered into effect: see SI No. 220 of 1994. Although not directly linked to the contents of the 1994 Act, it had been indicated during the course of the passage of the 1994 Act that the rule of specialty would apply to extraditions between the State and the United Kingdom, and the 1994 Order gives effect to this.

FIREARMS AND OFFENSIVE WEAPONS

Joint possession   In *The People v Foley*, Court of Criminal Appeal, July 18, 1994, the Court (O'Flaherty, Budd and Kinlen JJ) considered the question of joint possession in the context of a prosecution for possession of firearms. The case arose against the following background.

During a search of a room conducted by a number of Gardaí on foot of a search warrant, a shotgun was found on the bed, a revolver was found on a heater, and a hold-all with the butt of a shotgun visibly protruding and various items of electronic surveillance equipment were also found There were three men present in the room at the time, including the defendant, who was sitting on the bed in close proximity to the shotgun. The defendant was charged on two counts, possession of firearms in suspicious circumstances and possession of ammunition in suspicious circumstances, both contrary to s. 27(A)(I) of the Firearms Act 1964, as inserted by s. 8 of the Criminal Law

(Jurisdiction) Act 1976 and as amended by s. 14(4) of the Criminal Justice Act 1984. He was convicted on both counts in the Special Criminal Court. One of his co-accused was also convicted of the same offences and the other co-accused, who gave evidence at the trial that he had merely called in for a short visit, did not know the defendant and was not aware of the presence of the firearms, was acquitted. The Special Criminal Court found that the two convicted men were in joint possession of the guns and ammunition.

The defendant's application for leave to appeal to the Court of Criminal Appeal was ultimately dismissed. Delivering the Court's decision, Budd J accepted that its function was to determine whether the trial had been conducted in accordance with constitutional standards of fairness, to review rulings on matters of law, to review the application of the rules of evidence in the course of the trial and to consider whether any inferences of fact drawn by the court of trial can be supported by the evidence.

The Court also accepted that the mere presence of an article in close proximity to an accused person will not always raise the inference of possession. However, circumstances could arise where an inference of knowledge and control could be drawn. In the instant case, the trial court's inference that the defendant had been in possession of the firearms and ammunition had been reasonable and not perverse. The Court thus distinguished the instant case from that in *R. v Whelan* [1972] NI 153, where a firearm had been found concealed under a bundle of clothes on top of a chest of drawers in a bedroom shared by three people. In that case, all three denied knowledge of the firearm and the Northern Ireland Court of Appeal had held that all three must be acquitted. However, in the *Foley* case, the Court rejected the defendant's argument that it was not possible to say whether one man of the three in the room in particular was in possession of the firearms. Although the Court upheld the conviction in this case, Budd J made approving references to the decisions in *Sweet v Parsley* [1970] AC 132 and *Gammon (Hong Kong) Ltd v Attorney General for Hong Kong* [1985] AC 1 in support of the proposition that some element of *mens rea* is required in a prosecution for possession of firearms.

INSANITY

Insanity and automatism   We discuss above, 167-9, the decision in *The People v Courtney*, Court of Criminal Appeal, July 21, 1994, in which the Court, in effect, rejected a plea by the defendant that the effects of post traumatic stress disorder were equivalent to the effects of insanity and/or automatism.

Post-trial review   In *Gallagher v Director of the Central Mental Hospital*, High Court, 16 December 1994, Barron J dealt with some elements of the post-trial procedures put in place in the early 1990s to deal with persons found guilty but insane. Indeed, these arrangements arose, in part, from previous litigation initiated by the applicant in the instant case.

The applicant had been found guilty but insane at his trial for murder and was sentenced to be detained in the Central Mental Hospital until the pleasure of the Government of Ireland was made known: on the origin of this form of order, see the 1990 Review, 160-2. In *Application of Gallagher* [1991] 1 IR 31, *sub nom The People v Gallagher* [1991] ILRM 339 (1990 Review, 164-6), the Supreme Court held that the question of the applicant's release was a matter for the Government rather than the courts. Arising from this decision, an Advisory Committee was set up by the Minister for Justice to advise on applications for the release of persons found guilty but insane. An initial application to this Committee by the applicant was rejected. In a second review of his case in March 1994, the Advisory Committee was of the view that the applicant was still suffering from a personality disorder and would be a potential danger to the public if released; that he was progressing despite the absence of help in the hospital; that he should be given structured training and that his case be reviewed after one year.

The applicant sought an enquiry pursuant to Article 40.4.2° of the Constitution as to the legality of his detention on the ground that a personality disorder did not constitute mental illness and thus did not justify his detention in the Central Mental Hospital. The consultant forensic psychiatrist attached to the Central Mental Hospital confirmed that the applicant was not suffering from a mental illness but rather a personality disorder but that there was a serious and substantial risk that the applicant would repeat his crimes if he were released. Barron J ordered that the matter be remitted to the Government for its further consideration.

He noted that, in light of the Supreme Court decision in the previous application by the applicant, the question of his release was not a matter for the courts but rather for the Government acting on the recommendation of the Advisory Committee. He accepted that the courts retained jurisdiction to review the procedures of the Committee in order to ensure that the rules of natural and constitutional justice are observed. In the instant case, he held that the Committee had given the applicant a fair hearing. However, he also held that its recommendations were subject to some potential defects for two reasons. In the first place, the institution in which the applicant was detained did not have the facilities the Committee envisaged for training. Second, some of the views expressed by the forensic psychiatrist were in conflict with the verdict of the jury at the trial. On this basis, he concluded that the matter should be remitted to the Government for its further consideration.

It may be noted that the proceedings in this case illustrate the urgent necessity to introduce legislation to deal with the upshot of the 'guilty but insane' verdicts. The *Gallagher* cases and also other cases in this area, such as the *Courtney* case discussed above, 167-9, illustrate the need for a defence of diminished responsibility. At the time of writing (August 1996), it is reported that legislation to introduce such a defence and to place on a statutory footing the current arrangements are at an advanced state of preparation.

JUDICIAL REVIEW

Quash or re-trial The question whether the quashing of a criminal conviction on judicial review amounts in effect to an acquittal or may result in an order for a re-trial arose again in *Grennan v Kirby and Director of Public Prosecutions* [1994] 2 ILRM 199.

Before the applicant's trial in the District Court, his solicitor applied to the first named respondent for an adjournment of the proceedings on the grounds that he was seeking to retain the services of a particular barrister. The prosecuting Garda consented to the adjournment but it was refused by the first named respondent who proceeded with the hearing that led to the applicant's conviction.

The applicant applied to the High Court to have his conviction quashed. The Director of Public Prosecutions agreed that *certiorari* should issue against the conviction. The only matter which had to be decided was whether the proceedings should be remitted to the District Court.

Murphy J quashed the conviction and remitted the matter to the District Court. He began by referring to the leading authorities in this area, including *The State (Keeney) v O'Malley* [1986] ILRM 31 and *Sweeney v Brophy* [1993] 2 IR 202; [1993] ILRM 449 (the latter discussed in the 1992 Review, 268-70). From these, he concluded that where a court or tribunal which has the nominal or formal power to determine a particular issue engages in misconduct or commits an error which could be described as a routine mishap the correct remedy is an appeal and *certiorari* is not available, but that if the misconduct or error of the court or tribunal amounts to a breach of the fundamental tenets of constitutional justice the decision should be quashed by *certiorari*. However, he also accepted that, in certain situations, the order of *certiorari* should be granted on the basis that the defendant would be entitled to plead *autrefois acquit* because the misconduct or error did not deprive the court or tribunal of its jurisdiction.

Applying the principles in *The State (Tynan) v Keane* [1968] IR 348, he stated that if a court or tribunal makes an order without jurisdiction, either because it never had jurisdiction or it subsequently lost jurisdiction, the principle of *autrefois convict* cannot apply to any order made by it nor can the principle of *autrefois acquit* be raised in respect of the order of *certiorari* which quashed it. However, if the error or misconduct is sufficiently fundamental, Murphy J accepted that the court or tribunal cannot be treated as thereafter continuing to act within jurisdiction and any order made by it must be treated as having been made outside its jurisdiction.

In the instant case, he held that the action of the District Court judge in refusing to adjourn the trial with the consent of the prosecution to enable the applicant's solicitor to instruct counsel was of such a nature as to deprive him of jurisdiction to enter upon the hearing of the matter. As the order and conviction were a nullity, he concluded that there was nothing to prevent the matter being proceeded with in the District Court. By way of some consolation to the applicant, Murphy J held that he was entitled to his costs as the proceedings were necessary to correct the error of the District Court judge.

LAW REFORM COMMISSION REPORT ON NON-FATAL OFFENCES AGAINST THE PERSON

The Commission's Report contains comprehensive recommendations for reform of the law of non-fatal offences against the person. The subject is one of the current controversy internationally, raising important issues, on the one hand, as to possible new areas of protection by the criminal law against unwarranted intrusion and, on the other, as to the possible *removal* of criminal sanction from harmful, consensual physical conduct.

The Commission's recommendations fall into three categories : see the *Summary of the Report*, published in February 1994. These are:

- (a) reforms that simplify;
- (b) reforms that fill gaps in the law;
- (c) reforms that codify the law.

(a) *Simplification* As to simplification, the Commission unsurprisingly recommends that the vast tapestry of common law Victorian legislative offences relating to assault should be dismantled and replaced by a statutory model of assault, in the following terms:

(1) A person is guilty of assault who, without lawful excuse, intentionally or recklessly —

(a) causes physical hurt, or directly or indirectly applies force to or causes an impact on the body of another; or
(b) causes another to believe on reasonable grounds that he or she is likely immediately to be subjected to any such force or impact,

without the consent of the other.

(2) For the purposes of subs. (1)(a), 'force' includes:

(a) application of heat, light, electric current, noise or any other form of energy and
(b) application of matter in solid, liquid or gaseous form.

This offence would be tried summarily. The Commission proposes similar models for more serious assaults, triable on indictment.

It is clear that under this proposed summary offence, a person could be convicted of causing hurt indirectly, by way of a booby trap, for example. What is less clear is the Commission's statement (paras 9.54-5), in relation to paragraph (1)(b), that:

[t]he requirement of immediacy and the rule that words alone cannot constitute an assault are abandoned in favour of a requirement of reasonableness as to the apprehension of force or violence.

The reasonableness of the belief will in all cases be a matter of evidence, so that words or conduct, including conditional threats, which would not lead a person of reasonable firmness to apprehend such force, and threats of violence which are too remote in time, will be excluded.

This inclusion in subs. (1)(b) of the word 'immediately' seems inconsistent with this analysis. Nor does it appear that words alone are incapable of constituting an assault under the proposed offence, provided, of course, the District Judge is permitted to assess the impact of the words in the context in which they are spoken: cf. Mahon & Binchy, *Irish Law of Torts* (2nd ed., 1990), 406.

As regards the related indictable offences, the Commission proposes that intentional or reckless assault causing harm should warrant up to five years imprisonment or a fine of £5,000 (or both) and that intentional or reckless assault causing *serious* harm should warrant up to life imprisonment or a fine of £100,000 (or both). 'Serious harm' should be defined as 'injury which causes a substantial risk of death or which causes permanent disfigurement or protracted loss or impairment of the mobility of the body as a whole or of the function of any particular bodily member or organ'.

To ease the task of the prosecution, the Commission proposes that the legislation should include a provision similar to that in s. 10 of the Misuse of Drugs Act 1984, for proof of harm or serious harm by a doctor's certificate. It calls in aid the legislative precedents in relation to blood alcohol level and drugs, where, guided by the Supreme Court's *dicta* in *Maher v Attorney*

General [1973] IR 140, a certificate signed by an officer of the Forensic Science Laboratory of the Department of Justice is evidence of any fact thereby certified until the contrary is proved.

The Commission defends its recommendation as follows:

> The proof of harm or serious harm in the context of offences against the person would appear to be even less potentially controversial than proof of whether a particular substance was a prohibited drug. The defendant can always challenge the evidence if he or she deems it proper or relevant to do [so]. The provision in s. 10 of the Misuse of Drugs Act 1984 has operated smoothly and without controversy to the convenience of all. Medical evidence of actual bodily harm is not always a necessary proof.

One can sympathise with the Commission's desire to shed from the process of criminal trials redundant, time-consuming oral evidence where it is plain that the matter could have been fairly and more expeditiously handled by documentary evidence which would not be contested by the accused save in the rarest of cases. Nevertheless the Commission's reasoning in this particular context can be questioned. The Commission notes that in practice, under the present regime of offences, the issue whether injury constitutes actual bodily harm or grievous bodily harm is 'usually obvious, straightforward and uncontested.' The problem for the Commission is that, although the Criminal Justice Act 1984 provides for modes of agreeing evidence in advance of a trial, the Code of the Criminal Bar is not favourable to this practice. An experienced Senior Counsel (unidentified in the Report) wrote a submission to the Commission on pre-trial review of evidence with a view to shortening trials, in which he or she expressed the view to shortening trials, favouring the approach that 'the onus of proof rests on the prosecution, and the defence should not, by way of sanction or otherwise, be obliged to assist in any respect the prosecution in presenting its case'.

The Commission's motivation in proposing that a doctor's certificate be evidence of harm or serious harm is therefore designed to achieve a policy thwarted at present by the Code of the Criminal Bar. There are good reasons why our legislators should hesitate before taking this course: a cumulative process of legislative changes, each of them modest when viewed in isolation, could gradually transform the libertarian principles underlying the requirement of proof beyond reasonable doubt. More specifically in relation to the proposed offences, it is hard to see how a doctor could give a certificate on a question so lacking in scientific definition as whether 'harm' or 'serious harm' has been caused. It is one thing for a measurement of blood alcohol or an investigation as to the presence of a particular drug to be made and reported on; it is quite another for a doctor to assert that a particular condition constitutes 'harm' when the Commission itself (para. 9.65) states that it is 'not disposed to define "harm" as the law operates satisfactorily without a definition at the moment.' Moreover, the Commission's proposed definition of 'serious harm' is lacking in scientifically measurable criteria. At what point does a 'substantial' risk of death arise? Does the answer depend on the degree of *likelihood* or the degree of *immediacy* of this outcome? Is a 50% risk of death within months more or less substantial than a 70% risk that the injury caused by the defendant will shorten the victim's life, in the long term, by some years? At what point does a permanent disfigurement become 'protracted'? Particular doctors no doubt have their own views on those questions but their answers have no greater relevance to the guilt or innocence of the accused than those of any other randomly chosen members of our community and certainly are not in the realm of science.

The Commission recommends that the felony of kidnapping should be repealed on the basis that it is superfluous since the offence of false imprisonment, punishable by life imprisonment, extends to all takings or detentions by force or threat of force and gives rise to no difficulties in practice.

The Commission also recommends the abolition of the common law offence of public nuisance, subject to a proviso that this should not affect any existing power of a public authority to take steps to abate public nuisances or other conduct injurious to public health. The vast array of legislation relating to sanitary services, roads, pollution and planning has resulted in a situation where, as the Commission observes (para. 9.262), 'there can hardly be any example of behaviour that endangers public health and safety which is not punishable as a specific offence.'

(b) *Reforms that fill gaps* The Commission proposes the enactment of a new statutory offence of torture, thereby facilitating Ireland's accession to the United Nations' *Convention against Torture and Other Cruel, Inhuman or Degrading Treatment or Punishment*, adopted by the U.N. General Assembly in December 1994. The creation of such a specific offence in domestic law, while not necessitated by existing international obligations, 'would give concrete effect to the principle that torture constitutes a serious violation of the right to bodily integrity which warrants special prohibition and punishment in the criminal law' (para. 9.306).

The Commission recommends that consideration be given in favour of establishing an offence of hostage-taking, as envisaged by Articles 1 and 2 of the International Convention against the Taking of Hostages, adopted by resolution of the United Nations General Assembly in 1979. Although the Convention entered into force on June 3, 1983, Ireland has not yet signed it. The Commission envisages that 'it may be thought desirable' to extend jurisdiction to all acts of hostage-taking, irrespective of the nationality of the offender and of the country where the offence is committed. As a safeguard, it postulates that all prosecutions could be made subject to the consent of Director of Public Prosecutions.

Under present law (Conspiracy and Protection of Property Act 1875, s. 7) it is an offence to intimidate by means of *threats of violence*. The Commission considers that *any* acts of harassment that interfere seriously with a person's right to a peaceful and private life should be captured by the criminal law. It recommends that:

> a person who, without lawful authority or reasonable excuse, harasses another by persistently following, watching or besetting him or her in any place, by use of the telephone or otherwise, should be guilty of an offence. A person would harass another when his or her acts seriously interfered with another's peace or privacy.

It seems that the second sentence is designed to address the *effect on the victim* that the prosecution must prove, in *addition* to the requirements established in the first sentence rather than constituting some alternative definition of the *actus reus*. Certainly the second sentence lacks sufficient specificity to make it appropriate as a definition of the *actus reus*: the spectre of unconstitutional vagueness would arise.

The Commission recommends the creation of a new statutory offence of endangerment where a person intentionally or recklessly engages in conduct which 'creates a substantial risk of death or serious harm to another person'. It would, in the first place, cover 'the gap in existing law' arising from the fact that a person who recklessly creates a risk of serious injury commits no offence although he or she may be prosecuted for attempt where he or she does so intentionally or for causing serious injury where such injury results. In certain cases, where the evidence of intent is insufficient, the proposed offence might 'provide a valuable alternative to a charge of attempted murder or attempting to cause serious injury' (para. 9.238).

Once again prosecutorial preferences seem to have prevailed over broader questions of justice. No doubt a prosecutor who is sure of the guilt of an accused will feel aggrieved when the evidence turns out to be insufficient to warrant a conviction; but that feeling of grievance should not be assuaged by the creation of an entirely different offence. The 'gap' in the existing law is not the result of some legislative anomaly or thoughtlessness on the part of judges or legislators over the years. Instead it represents a judgment that criminal responsibility should be narrowly defined and certainly not used as a pragmatic device to shore up prosecutions for substantive consummated offences where the evidence is too thin to sustain a conviction.

It is, however, true that there are several specific offences of endangerment in the present law. Some of these are part of the Victorian fetish for dealing separately and in minute detail with every manifestation of human weakness but others, such as dangerous and careless driving and the reckless discharge of a firearm, encapsulate a sound policy which few people would question. Again pragmatic concerns for prosecutorial success raise their head. The Commission argues that its proposed generic offence of endangerment

> would provide a useful supplement to existing specific offences of endangerment. In this connection, the general offence would not be designed to replace all such offences, which in many cases would be the subject of greater penalties on account of the special hazards of the conduct sought to be prevented, but would provide instead for a residual generic offence (para. 9.239).

The Commission considers that its proposed offence 'would have the particular advantage of removing some anomalies which arise from the operation of existing law'. (*Id.*) Yet the primary example it proffers scarcely advances its case: a builder causing obvious danger to the lives of others in the course of demolishing a building would commit a serious offence under the Commission's proposed offence of malicious damage, which it recommended in its *Report on Malicious Damage* (LRC 26–1988) para. 40, but he would be guilty of a far less serious offence under the Safety, Health and Welfare at Work Act 1989 if he created a similar degree of danger in the course of constructing new building. Two comments seem appropriate. First, this 'anomaly' is entirely hypothetical, since the Commission's proposal in its earlier Report was not in fact incorporated into Irish law in the Criminal Damage Act 1991, though it is part of England's law: Criminal Damage Act 1971, s. 1(2)(a). One finds here an overreliance analysis by English commentators on weaknesses in English legislation (cf. E.g. Smith, 'Liability for Endangerment: English And Hoc Pragmatism and American Innovation' [1983] *Crim L Rev* 127), resulting in having to assume, unconvincingly, that Irish law will inevitably follow English anomalies which our legislators have already rejected. Secondly, the specific problem of the builder does not need to be resolved by creating a generic offence; all that is necessary is to fine-tune the 1989 Act if its provisions are considered to fall marginally short of the desirable scope of criminal responsibility.

(c) *Reforms that codify* The most difficult issue addressed by the Commission in this report is that of consent. Generally consent is a defence to prosecutions for non-fatal offences against the person but should it *always* be so? For example, should professional boxing or other violent sports render the participants subject to criminal prosecution in spite of the willing participation of those involved? In considering these questions should people who engage in sado-masochistic acts, consensually, be prosecuted? The Commission had the benefit of the decision of the House of Lords in *R. v Brown* [1993] 2 All ER 75. The Commission, after a detailed examination of the issue, recommends that, rather than resort to an artificial ascription of assault to consensual conduct, the better approach is for the legislation to include a specific offence relating to consensual infliction of serious harm, on the following lines:

> A person who causes serious harm to another with another's consent shall be guilty of an offence unless that harm is inflicted:
>
> (a) with the purpose of benefiting another person, or
> (b) in pursuance of a socially beneficial function or activity,
>
> and, in either case having regard to the intended beneficial purpose, function or activity, the inflictions of that harm was reasonable.

It is worth recording the Commission's reflections on the philosophical dimensions of this issue:

> The pattern that emerges from the common law on this subject is that there is a societal interest in the protection of life and bodily integrity as values in themselves. The taking of a person's life even with consent involves the destruction of a thing of value. Similarly the infliction of bodily hurt or mutilation involves interference with a thing of human value. In this latter case, context is vital. The purpose of the infliction of the injury is crucial. At the core of this subject is the question of the normative dimensions of the relationship between one person and another person's disposition of his or her body, health or life. If individual autonomy is such that we are morally free to have done to our body, health or life as we please, then it may seem difficult to justify a criminal sanction on another person for doing that to which we freely consent. The philosophy underlying the present law is that individual autonomy does not run so far: our life and health are not our playthings to use or abuse as we wish. Human life is a thing of value, even if we do not in fact treat it as such. Society has a legitimate interest in protecting this thing of value against abuse, just as it may legitimately protect other things of value which are under individuals' control. To regard human life and bodily integrity as devoid of value which generates a legitimate social interest in their protection save in cases where people choose to respect that value is a controversial approach which is out of harmony with the central principles of criminal law (para. 9.138).

This analysis harmonises well with the values underlying the fundamental rights provisions of the Constitution and is in striking contrast with two more recent decisions of the Supreme Court: *In re the Regulation of Information (Services Outside the State for Termination of Pregnancies) Bill* [1995] 2 ILRM 81 and *In re a Ward of Court* [1995] 2 ILRM 401.

The Commission goes on to propose that, without prejudice to the generality of its recommendation in relation to consensual, seriously harmful, conduct, the consensual infliction of serious harm should not be unlawful if it occurs in the playing of a *bona fide* sport where the act causing the injury is done within the rules of the sport. It notes (para. 9.141) that the inclusion of the reference to the bona fide quality of the sport 'is designed to prevent bogus characterisations.' One may wonder, whether the concept of a *'bona fide* sport' is too heavily affected by sociological bias.

On the questions of medical treatment afforded to minors, the Commission recommends that the legislation include a provision similar to s. 8 of England's Family Law Reform Act 1969. This provides as follows:

(1) The consent of a minor who has attained the age of sixteen years to any surgical, medical or dental treatment which in the absence of consent, would constitute a trespass to his person, shall be as effective as it would be if he were of full age and where a minor has by virtue of this section given an effective consent to any treatment it shall not be necessary to obtain any consent for it from his parent or guardian. . . .

(3) Nothing in this section shall be construed as making ineffective any consent which would have been effective if this section had not been enacted.

The Report does not contain any detailed analysis of the constitutional dimensions of this issue. It notes that the English decision of *Gillick v West Norfolk and Wisbech Area Health Authority* [1986] AC 112 'might or might not be followed by our Supreme Court in a civil case but in criminal cases should be imported, where possible . . .' (para. 9.169). The Commission offers little clear supporting argument for this conclusion. The reality on the ground, of course, is that any child capable of reaching up to a machine that dispenses contraceptives has legal access to contraception but the issue is surely worthy of deeper reflection extending beyond this specific context.

The Commission analyses the question of parental chastisement of children in some detail. While making it plain that it would favour making it an offence for a parent to administer any physical chastisement to a child in any circumstance, it considers it important that change be made in stages. The sudden introduction of criminal liability for any assault into the home without more education and information would be inimical to good reform and the interests to children. Foundations have to be laid with prudence. Without proper guidance in effective, enlightened, non-violent parenting, parents will feel lost, resentful and resistant to change (para. 9.211).

Accordingly the Commission recommends that:

[w]hereas it would be premature to abolish the common law chastise-ment exception immediately, the re-education of parents should proceed without delay and the exception should be abolished at the right time (para. 9.214).

PRE-TRIAL PUBLICITY

As we mentioned in the 1993 Review, 242, the effect of media coverage on pending proceedings, and its potential to prejudice court proceedings has been considered by the Supreme Court in two decisions in the context of the right to a trial in due course of law under Article 38.1 of the Constitution, *D. v Director of Public Prosecutions* [1994] 1 ILRM 435 and *Z. v Director of Public Prosecutions* [1994] 2 ILRM 481. In the context of the *Z.* case in particular, the Supreme Court declined to prohibit a trial on sexual assault charges which had been attended by unprecedented media attention. For a comprehensive discussion of the issues in the cases, see Gordon Duffy's article, (1994) 4 *ICLJ* 113.

In *D. v Director of Public Prosecutions* [1994] 1 ILRM 435, the applicant had been charged with indecently assaulting a young girl in a boat off the Donegal coast on a date unknown between April and November 1988. His trial on this charge came on for hearing before the Dublin Circuit Criminal Court on July 27, 1992. As a result of inaccurate reporting in two of the national daily newspapers of the evidence adduced at the trial, the jury was discharged and the editors of these papers summoned to court to explain their conduct. At this hearing, counsel for the Director of Public Prosecutions remarked that as a result of this inaccurate reporting, a 'patently guilty man had gone free.' The combination of these events ensured that the case received widespread publicity, with one Sunday newspaper in particular running a series of highly charged feature articles on the case. The applicant sought to prohibit the Director from proceeding with a re-trial on the basis that the likely prejudice engendered in anyone who read these articles was such as to make it impossible for him to receive a fair trial and also that, by reason of the delay which had occurred from the time of the date of the commission of the alleged offence and any subsequent re-trial, he was prejudiced in the preparation of his defence to this charge. In the High Court, Carney J granted the relief sought and held that anyone who had read these articles would not be suitable for jury service in any trial and that it would be impossible to say that the passage of time could cure or diminish the likelihood of prejudice in the case on account of the unusual location in which the incident was alleged to have occurred and the improper publicity generated by the discharge of the jury. However, on appeal, a majority of the Supreme Court (O'Flaherty, Blayney and Denham JJ; Finlay CJ and Egan J dissenting) held that the re-trial could proceed.

Delivering the leading judgment for the majority, Blayney J accepted that the right of an accused to a fair trial is of fundamental constitutional importance, and the question which the court must answer is whether there is a real risk that the applicant would not obtain such a fair trial because of the coverage of the case in the media. Citing the well-known extradition case *Finucane v McMahon* [1990] 1 IR 165 (1990 Review, 212-16), he stated that the appropriate burden of proof on an applicant in establishing the likelihood of an unfair trial is to show that there is a real or serious risk that there will be an unfair trial.

In the instant case, he stated that while it was possible that a member of the jury would remember reading the article and associate it with the instant case and feel sympathy towards the victim, the applicant had failed to show that there was a real or serious risk that the jury would be prevented from returning an impartial verdict in the case. The majority considered that to hold otherwise would be to imply that jurors would ignore their oath and duties as jurors as well as the charge of the trial judge to well and truly decide the case on the evidence adduced during the course of the trial alone and not to allow themselves to be influenced by any matters extraneous to the trial itself.

In a concurring judgment, Denham J opined:

> A court must give some consideration to the community's right to have this alleged crime prosecuted in the usual way. However, on the hierarchy of constitutional rights, there is no doubt that the applicant's right to fair procedures is superior to the community's right to prosecute.

In the *D.* case, of course, it might be said that the court was engaged in some form of unacknowledged balancing of 'rights', although it might be more accurate to speak of a community's 'interest' rather than right.

The question of pre-trial publicity returned to the Supreme Court shortly afterwards in *Z. v Director of Public Prosecutions* [1994] 2 ILRM 481, a case arising out of *Attorney General v X.* [1992] ILRM 401; [1992] 1 IR 1 which in turn had given rise to an on-going national debate concerning abortion that rarely lost sight of the *X.* case (see the 1992 Review, 159-186).

The applicant had been returned for trial in the Dublin Circuit Criminal Court and was awaiting trial in respect of a number of sexual offences. He applied for judicial review seeking a declaration that the nature and extent of the pre-trial publicity arising from the *X.* case and the alleged facts and surrounding circumstances which gave rise to the pending prosecution had irreparably prejudiced the prospect of the applicant obtaining a fair trial. In particular it was contended that publicity surrounding the alleged taking of samples for DNA testing and references in newspapers to such tests as having yielded conclusive proof as to the guilt of the applicant rendered a fair trial impossible or gave rise to a very real risk of an unfair trial. The book of evidence served on the applicant revealed that evidence as to DNA tests was being tendered. The applicant made it clear that he would challenge both its admissibility and probative value at the trial. The applicant also sought a declaration that the published findings of fact made by the High Court and the Supreme Court in the course of judgments in *X.* had similarly prejudiced the prospect of a fair and impartial trial.

A preliminary point arose in the judicial review application, namely whether it should be heard otherwise than in public pursuant to s. 45(1)(a) of the Courts (Supplemental Provisions) Act 1961 which provides that justice may be administered otherwise than in public in applications of an urgent nature for relief by way of habeas corpus, bail, prohibition or injunction. In the High Court, Hamilton P (as he then was) ordered the hearing to be in public He held that s. 45(1)(a) of the 1961 Act applied only to such applications which were, because of their nature, so urgent that they had to be made before a judge in his home or some place to which the public did not directly have access and did not apply to applications of that nature made in court. On the question of public hearings, see *In re R. Ltd* [1989] IR 126 (1989 Review, 55-8) and *Irish Press Ltd v Ingersoll Publications Ltd* [1993] ILRM 797 (1993 Review, 89).

Moving to the main issue raised in the application, Hamilton P noted that the essential ingredient of a trial of a criminal offence was that it took place before a court which had the power to punish in the event of a guilty verdict; that such proceedings were accusatorial and involved a prosecutor and an accused; and that the sole purpose of the verdict was, in the case of an acquittal, to form the basis for the discharge of the accused from the jeopardy in which he stood or, in the case of a conviction, for his punishment in respect of the crime which he had committed. He considered that none of these features were present in the earlier civil proceedings, and thus they did not constitute an invasion of the right to trial by jury on a criminal charge. As to the findings of fact referred to in the High Court and Supreme Court judgments, he pointed out that these did not prejudge the findings of fact to be made in the hearing of the criminal charges and thus the decisions of the High Court and Supreme Court did not determine the issue of guilt or innocence.

Hamilton P noted that the right of an accused to receive a fair trial was entrenched in the legal system along with the fundamental principle that no person shall be convicted of a criminal offence otherwise than after a fair trial according to law and in this regard Article 38 of the Constitution recognised the fundamental role of juries in the criminal justice system. He considered that it was the duty of a jury to act with complete impartiality and detachment and it was the obligation of the trial judge to instruct them accordingly. He felt that the accused's rights could be protected by appropriate procedural controls, whether adjournments or other interlocutory orders, by rulings on the presumption of innocence, the onus of proof, the admissibility of evidence and by directions to the jury designed to counteract any prejudice which the accused might otherwise suffer.

In the instant case, he did not consider that any insuperable obstacles existed that would prevent a trial in due course of law under Article 38.1 of the Constitution. However, he did state that, having regard to the nature and extent of the pre-trial publicity that had taken place, particular care would have to be taken in empanelling the jury and in the conduct of the trial, including the giving of directions to the jury.

On further appeal, this view was unanimously upheld by the Supreme Court (Finlay CJ, O'Flaherty, Egan, Blayney and Denham JJ).

Delivering the leading judgment, Finlay CJ stated that an accused who seeks an order prohibiting his trial on the ground that circumstances have arisen which would render it unfair must establish that there is a real risk by reason of those circumstances that he could not obtain a fair trial. He added that the applicant must also establish that it is not possible to avoid such unfairness by the trial judge giving appropriate directions and rulings to the jury.

Quoting with approval the views of Denham J in *D. v Director of Public Prosecutions* [1994] 1 ILRM 435, above, he stated that while a court must give some consideration to the community's right to have alleged crimes prosecuted in the usual way, the accused's right to fair procedures is superior to the community's right to prosecute. In this respect, he stated that the right to a fair trial is one of the most fundamental constitutional rights and that if there was a real risk that an accused person would not receive a fair trial, there would be no question of his right to a fair trial being balanced against the community's right to have crimes prosecuted.

The Chief Justice accepted that, as a matter of practical probability, it would not be possible to empanel a jury consisting of persons who would be unaware that the charges against the accused concerned the girl who was the respondent in the *X.* case and that this had to be borne in mind when considering whether the applicant would receive a fair trial given what he described as the 'saturation publicity' that had occurred.

Finlay CJ acknowledged that in certain cases a trial judge seeking to prevent pre-trial publicity from damaging the prospect of a fair trial may be faced with a dilemma. If he points out to the jury that they must ignore such publicity and confine their deliberations to the sworn evidence before them, he may remind them of the publicity or of a link between it and the case they are trying of which they had been unaware. No such danger existed in this case as the trial judge would be able to point out in a specific and detailed way to the jury that the pre-trial publicity, in particular that concerning the case of *Attorney General v X.*, was wholly irrelevant and must be put out of their minds. A jury so instructed would be able to bring an impartial mind to the case and would be scrupulous in preventing themselves from deciding the case based on any view arising from the general publicity which had occurred.

The Chief Justice stated that if the applicant's objections to the DNA test evidence were overruled by the trial judge and the evidence was presented to the jury, there would not be a real risk of an unfair trial as the trial judge would direct the jury to concentrate on the sworn evidence and ignore the publicity concerning the tests. On the other hand, if the prosecution decided for any reason not to tender the results of the DNA tests in evidence, or if they were tendered but were ruled inadmissible, the trial judge would be able to avoid any potential unfairness. He stated that if there was a risk that the jury might conclude from the fact that the DNA evidence was not adduced that they were being deprived of some important evidence and that they would then try the question of guilt or innocence more on their memory of the publicity associated with such tests, it would be proper for the trial judge to point out to them that, having regard to the presumption of innocence, they must try the case on the presumption that whatever DNA testing took place did not implicate the accused in the offences with which he was charged.

In all the circumstances, therefore, the Court concluded that there was no basis on which the trial should be prohibited. As Gordon Duffy has noted in his article (1994) 4 *ICLJ* 113, 141, while the decisions in both *D.* and *Z.* are welcome, their effect is that 'in pitching the test [of prejudice] as high as they have . . . the Supreme Court has effectively killed off the prospect of any further cases coming before the courts in the future.' (*ibid.*, at p.159).

PROCEDURE

Addition of charges to indictment after sending forward In *O'Connell v Director of Public Prosecutions* [1994] 1 ILRM 21, the Supreme Court (Finlay CJ, Blayney and Denham JJ) upheld the validity of the power of the Director under s. 18 of the Criminal Procedure Act 1967 to add further charges to an indictment where an accused has been sent forward for trial.

The applicant had been charged before the District Court with the commission of three indictable offences relating to the alleged importation of cannabis resin into the State. The statement of charges made reference to the contravention of Regulation 4(1)(c) of the Misuse of Drugs Regulations 1979. As these Regulations had been repealed and replaced by the Misuse of Drugs Regulations 1988, at the preliminary examination the District Judge discharged the applicant in respect of these charges and sent him forward for trial in the Circuit Court on the remaining charge of unlawful possession of a controlled drug. In exercise of his powers under s. 18 of the 1967 Act, the Director included four further charges in the indictment. These were the possession of a controlled drug for the purpose of supplying it to another, importing a controlled drug into the State, conspiring to import a controlled drug into the State, and importing a controlled drug into the State for the purpose of selling it or otherwise supplying it to another. The charges of unlawfully importing a controlled drug into the State and conspiring to import a controlled drug into the State were expressed to be in contravention of article 4(1)(c) of the Misuse of Drugs Regulations 1988. The applicant initiated judicial review proceedings seeking an order of *certiorari* quashing the indictment in whole or in part and an order of prohibition preventing the second named respondent from proceeding with the trial. An undertaking was given that the charge of possession of a controlled drug for the purpose of supplying it to another would be withdrawn when the matter came to trial in the Circuit Court. In the High Court, Keane J held that the addition to the indictment of the charges of unlawfully importing a controlled drug into the State and conspiring to import a controlled drug into the State was an attempt to render nugatory the decision of the District Judge to discharge the applicant in respect of these charges. Accordingly, Keane J granted a declaration that the addition of these counts was *ultra vires* the Director's powers under s. 18. In relation to the addition of the charge of importing a controlled drug into the State for the purpose of selling it or otherwise supplying it to another, Keane J held that as the district judge had not discharged the applicant in respect of such a charge, the Director was entitled to include it in the indictment under s. 18 of the 1967 Act. On further appeal, the Supreme Court held in the Director's favour on both issues.

The Court held that the fact that the District Court judge did not exercise his power under s. 8(2) of the 1967 Act to have the accused tried for an offence other than that charged did not mean that he had found that the offence in respect of which he had sent the applicant forward for trial was the only offence supported by the evidence. The Court thus concluded that it remained open to the Director to add counts based on the documents and exhibits considered by the district judge at the preliminary examination.

The Court went on to hold that the counts in the indictment concerning the charges of unlawfully importing a controlled drug into the State and conspiring to import a controlled drug into the State in contravention of the 1988 Regulations were not technically the same as those expressed in the statement of charges to be in contravention of the 1979 Regulations and that. Distinguishing the instant case from the power in s. 62 of the Courts of Justice Act 1936 (which had been declared unconstitutional in *Costello v Director of Public Prosecutions* [1984] IR 436), the Court held that the addition of these counts by the Director amounted to the exercise of a purely executive or administrative function. It did not conflict with the exercise of the judicial powers of the District Judge as he had not discharged the applicant in respect of these counts. In conclusion, citing dicta in *O'Shea v Director of Public Prosecutions* [1988] IR 655, it was noted that the Director did not determine any issue but merely placed issues before the courts for determination. As Una Ní Raifeartaigh commented on the case ((1994) 4 *ICLJ* 73-4):

> Two lines of reasoning make their appearance in the judgments of the Supreme Court. The first takes the view that there has been no discharge in respect of the disputed counts in the indictment on the basis that the original charges were technically different from those counts. Thus the reference to the correct Regulations is deemed to transform the counts sufficiently for the purpose of the Costello principle. The second line of reasoning, evident in the judgment of Blayney J, is effectively in the alternative, as it proceeds on the basis that there has been a discharge in respect of the same counts or charges in the District Court. Blayney J draws a distinction between a discharge based on insufficiency of evidence and discharge based on the invalidity of the charge.

While she described Blayney J's distinction as 'unusual', she noted that it 'may prove useful to the prosecution in future cases.'

Duplicity of charges   In *O'B. v Pattwell* [1994] 2 ILRM 465, the Supreme Court upheld a decision of the O'Hanlon J [1993] ILRM 614 (see the 1992 Review, 292-3) to the effect that no duplicity of charges within the meaning of s. 14 of the Interpretation Act 1937 was involved where a person is charged with both common law rape and unlawful carnal knowledge of girl under 15 years of age.

S. 14 of the Interpretation Act 1937 provides:

Where any act, whether of commission or omission, constitutes an offence under two or more statutes or under a statute and at common law, the offender shall, unless the contrary intention appears, be liable to be prosecuted and punished under either or any of those statutes or at common law, but shall not be liable to be punished twice for the same offence.

S. 8(2) of the Criminal Procedure Act 1967 provides:

If the [judge of the District Court] is of opinion that there is a sufficient case to put the accused on trial for some indictable offence other than that charged, he shall cause him to be charged with that offence and . . . send him forward for trial.

The applicant was served with a statement of charges containing three charges: (i) indecent assault contrary to common law and s. 10 of the Criminal Law (Rape) Act 1981; (ii) unlawful carnal knowledge of a girl under the age of 15 years, contrary to s. 1(1) of the Criminal Law (Amendment) Act 1935 and (iii) unlawful carnal knowledge of a named female forcibly and against her will contrary to common law. After a preliminary examination, the first named respondent sent the accused forward for trial on the three charges and an additional offence of buggery contrary to s. 61 of the Offences Against the Person Act 1861.

The applicant commenced proceedings by way of judicial review seeking to quash the order returning him for trial. On his behalf it was submitted that s. 14 of the 1937 Act meant that it was not permissible to send the applicant forward on both the second and third charges, and that the prosecution should be put to its election. It was also submitted that the first named respondent had no power to add the buggery charge, except in substitution for one of the charges already brought.

In the High Court, O'Hanlon J held that the act of commission alleged in the second and third counts did not constitute 'the same offence' at common law and under statute, and that even if this were not so, the prohibition contained in s. 14 of the Act of 1937 was directed only against the possibility of double punishment in respect of the same incident. He also held that a District Court judge exercising his powers under the 1967 Act was not precluded from adding charges in addition to those already contained in the statement of charges.

In appealing to the Supreme Court, the applicant further argued that since s. 3 of the 1935 Act permitted a person charged with rape to be found guilty of an offence under s. 1(1) of that Act, it was not permissible to include an express account of that charge on the indictment in addition to the count of rape. The Supreme Court (O'Flaherty, Egan and Denham JJ) dismissed the appeal.

Having reviewed the decisions of the Court of Criminal Appeal in *The People v Coughlan* (1968) 1 Frewen 325 and *The People v Dermody* [1956] IR 307, O'Flaherty J, delivering the leading judgment for the Court, concluded that they should be overruled. He stated that the offence of rape at common law, in which force or a lack of consent was an element, was different from the 'statutory rape' offence of unlawful carnal knowledge of a young girl in s. 1(1) of the 1935 Act, where the issue of consent was irrelevant. They were thus not the 'same offence' for the purposes of s. 14 of the 1937 Act.

On the procedural side, O'Flaherty J stated that, when charging the jury the trial judge should point out that if there is a conviction in respect of rape it will then be unnecessary for the jury to go further in relation to the 1935 Act count, but if they are not satisfied that there has been rape they should consider whether the offence under the 1935 Act was committed. While s. 3 of the 1935 Act provided that an accused person charged with rape could, as an alternative, be found guilty of an offence under s. 1(1), O'Flaherty J did not consider that this precluded the inclusion of an express count in the indictment. Nor, he said, was there any requirement in s. 8(2) of the 1967 Act that a new charge which a district judge proposed to add had to be in substitution for an existing charge. He suggested that, in any event the point was academic as s. 18 of the 1967 Act expressly permitted the Director of Public Prosecutions to add an additional count.

Finally, O'Flaherty J referred to certain dicta of Haugh J delivering the judgment of the Court of Criminal Appeal in *The People v Coughlan* (1968) 1 Frewen 325. In that case, the Court had suggested that, in cases involving young girls, prosecutors should consider whether it was appropriate to proceed with only the count of unlawful carnal knowledge of a girl under 15 and thereby avoid the necessity of exposing the complainant to the ordeal of appearing in order to prove the issue of force or lack of consent. O'Flaherty J opined that, while this might very often (O'Flaherty J's emphasis) be appropriate, it should not be the invariable policy and there would be cases where the prosecution should insist that the more serious charge of rape should proceed.

Prosecutorial discretion: failure to initiate prosecution In *H. v Director of Public Prosecutions and Garda Commissioner* [1994] 2 ILRM 285, the Supreme Court refused to quash a decision by the Director of Public Prosecutions in which he had declined to initiate a criminal prosecution involving sexual offences against children. The applicant had commenced a private prosecution against her husband T.T.M. and his brother J.M. in which she alleged that they had committed various sexual offences against her son N.H. This followed the refusal of the Director to initiate such a prosecution in his name.

The applicant then sought liberty to apply for judicial review to obtain orders compelling the director to initiate a prosecution against T.T.M. and J.M. or alternatively to provide reasons to the applicant as to why he had failed to do so, and further to supply her with any statements taken by the Gardaí and other documentation in his possession to enable her to pursue her independent prosecution.

In the High Court, Barron J held that a decision by the Director in relation to a prosecution could only be challenged if it was demonstrated that he had reached the decision *mala fides*, or was influenced by an improper motive or improper policy. However he also took the view that once an adverse decision was challenged by a person with *locus standi* to challenge it, the Director was obliged to give reasons. However, in the instant case he refused the applicant relief, as in the circumstances it was unlikely that N.H. who was now in England, would ever be willing to testify.

The applicant appealed to the Supreme Court. The Director of Public Prosecutions also appealed seeking a variation of the decision of Barron J that he was obliged to give reasons for a decision not to prosecute. The Supreme Court (O'Flaherty, Egan and Denham JJ) dismissed the applicant's appeal, and also allowed the variation sought by the Director. The Court agreed with Barron J that the instant case was not an appropriate one in which to order the Director to bring a prosecution, as it was unlikely that the alleged victim would testify in any event.

In his judgment, O'Flaherty J commented that if the Director was subjected to frequent applications by discomfited persons for *mandamus* seeking to compel him to bring prosecutions, it would stretch his office beyond endurance.

The Court confirmed that, in accordance with its decision in *The State (McCormack) v Curran* [1987] ILRM 225, the Director's discretion in relation to prosecutions can only be reviewed if it is demonstrated that he reached a decision *mala fides* or was influenced by an improper motive or improper policy. The Court distinguished the Director's functions from those discussed in *International Fishing Vessels Ltd v Minister for the Marine* [1989] IR 149 (see the 1989 Review, 18) in which the Court held that the Minister was required to give reasons for his refusal to grant a sea-fishing licence. The Court in H. would appear to have viewed the International Fishing Vessels case as being based on the conclusion that the giving of reasons was 'an essential prerequisite to ensure fair procedures' and that the refusal by the Minister to give reasons placed a serious obstacle in the way of judicial review. This narrow interpretation of that decisions would appear to confirm that the courts are reluctant to extend the notion of a right to be given reasons: see the case law discussed in the 1993 Review, 30-33. Finally, the Court concluded that the applicant had failed to make out a *prima facie* case of *mala fides* against the respondents and accordingly the case was not one where the Director should be obliged to give his reasons for not bringing a prosecution. There remains, of course the possibility that the mala fides test will permit o judicial review, at least in some circumstances. However, the history of judicial reluctance to review the functions of the Director is such that this appears a remote possibility.

Summary trial: advance information   In *Director of Public Prosecutions v Doyle* [1994] 1 ILRM 529, the Supreme Court (Finlay CJ, O'Flaherty, Egan, Blayney and Denham JJ) provided invaluable guidance on the circumstances in which the prosecution might be required to furnish information in advance of trial to a person accused of an indictable being tried summarily.

The defendant had elected for summary trial in the District Court in respect of four indictable offences with which he had been charged and to which he had pleaded not guilty. The accused's solicitor requested copies of all statements taken by the Gardaí. He was furnished with a copy of a statement which the accused had made and told that no other statements had been taken. At the trial a Garda gave evidence as to an interview which he had conducted with the accused and the statement which the accused had made. The Garda stated that he had interviewed the injured parties but had not taken a written statement from any of them. It also emerged that none of the Gardaí involved in the investigation had made written statements. The accused's counsel objected on the grounds that the Director of Public Prosecutions had failed to furnish the accused with statements from all witnesses whose evidence was crucial to the prosecution case.

On a case stated, the Supreme Court held that where an indictable offence is being disposed of by way of summary trial in the District Court, there is no general obligation to furnish, on request, the statements of the proposed witnesses for the prosecution. Delivering the only judgment on behalf of the Court, Denham J held that there was no intermediate level of procedure between the District Court and a court hearing a trial on indictment.

However, while stating this general rule, the Court also held that, as a matter of fair procedures and in the absence of legislation on the matter, the appropriate test for the District Court judge was whether, given the facts of the particular case, it would be in the interests of justice that the accused should be furnished, before the trial, with the statements on which the prosecution case would proceed.

The Court held that the furnishing of statements or other relevant documents before the trial may be unnecessary in many minor cases, but that in serious or complex cases it may be required in order to inform the accused of the accusation so that he might prepare his defence. In deciding whether or not constitutional justice requires statements or documents to be furnished before the trial, Denham J was of the view that the District Court judge could take into account, *inter alia*, the following factors:

(a) the seriousness of the charge,

(b) the importance of the statements or documents,

(c) the fact that the accused has already been informed of the nature and substance of the accusation and

(d) the likelihood that there is no risk of injustice in failing to furnish the statements or documents in issue to the accused.

She went on to state that a request by an accused that statements should be furnished before the trial was not conclusive as to whether or not such statements should be made available to the accused though it too was a factor which the District judge could take into account. Where a statement or document is sought by the accused before the trial, she stated that the appropriate procedure is to send a letter to the prosecution requesting the statement or document. If this request is refused the matter should then be listed before the district judge so that it can be determined.

Denham J also noted that the nature of a summary trial in the District Court is such that an adjournment can be effected more easily than in the case of a trial on indictment before a jury. If it transpired at any stage during the course of a trial in the District Court that the accused, his solicitor or counsel, needed time in the interests of justice to consider a statement or document of which he has no prior notice and which is material to the action, she stated that it was for the District Judge to decide whether or not an adjournment would be reasonable.

Finally, Denham J stated that if no statements have been taken by the Gardaí in the course of the investigation of the offence, it is for the District Judge to determine whether or not it is necessary, in the interests of justice and fair procedures, for the accused to be furnished with information as to proposed evidence before the trial.

In the later case *O'Driscoll v Wallace*, High Court, August 17, 1994, the applicants had been charged with assault occasioning actual bodily harm, and indictable offence triable summarily under s. 2 of the 1951 Act. Here the applicants sought the type of disclosure from the prosecution prior to their election to be tried summarily and, in that context, the respondent judge of the District Court held they were not entitled to such disclosure. However, on judicial review, O'Hanlon J quashed the decision and, in accordance with the principles laid down in *Director of Public Prosecutions v Doyle* [1994] 1 ILRM 529, above, he held that the applicants were entitled to the information sought. Of some interest is that O'Hanlon J took the view that, in the absence of formal rules of court on the disclosure of material in these cases, the procedure set out in the English rules of court, the Magistrates' Courts (Advance Information) Rules 1985, should be taken as guideline rules. While this is, of course, a somewhat unusual course to adopt, O'Hanlon J's pragmatic approach points up the enormous gap in the rules of court in the wake of the *Doyle* decision. At the time of writing, no formal rules have yet been made in the State to take account of *Doyle*, so the advice of O'Hanlon J would appear to be the best indication of 'best practice'.

PUBLIC ORDER OFFENCES

The Criminal Justice (Public Order) Act 1994 provides for a number of connected matters: the updating of the law in relation to public order offences, the creation of an offence specifically aimed at racketeering and updating the law on demanding money with menaces, arrangements for the organisation of crowd control at large public events and, finally, by way of addition at a late stage, the regulation of advertising for brothels. Although the 1994 Act involved some welcome updating of largely outdated laws on public order, the vague nature of some of the provisions proposed in the Criminal Justice (Public Order) Bill 1993 as originally published resulted in substantial amendments to the legislation as it proceeded through the Oireachtas. The provisions of the 1994 Act on public order generally arose in part from recommendations made by the Law Reform Commission in two reports: *Report on Offences under the Dublin Police Acts and Related Offences* (LRC 14-1985) and *Report on Vagrancy and Related Offences* (LRC ll-1985). Those on racketeering derive from recommendations in the Commission's Report, *The Law Relating to Dishonesty* (LRC 43-1992) (discussed in the 1992 Review, 275-850. The provisions on public events involved the implementation of certain recommendations made by the Hamilton *Committee on Public Safety and Crowd Control* (on the latter see the 1990 Review, 476). Finally, those on advertising of brothels were included to redeem a commitment to legislate on this topic made during the passing of the Criminal Law (Sexual Offences) Act 1993 (discussed in the 1993 Review, 266). In accordance with s. 1(3) of the 1994 Act, the Act came into force on April 3, 1994, that is one month after its signature into law by the President.

Intoxication in public places   S. 4 of the 1994 Act creates an offence of intoxication in a place public, but only where the person is intoxicated to such an extent as would give rise to a reasonable apprehension that he might either be a danger to himself or any other person in the vicinity, subject to a maximum fine of £100. The section also empowers the Gardaí to confiscate intoxicating substances where they suspect with reasonable cause that an offence is being committed.

Disorderly and threatening behaviour   S. 5 of the 1994 Act, which deals with disorderly or offensive conduct in a public place, was the most contro-versial provision of the Act. It initially proposed to make it an offence for any person 'to engage in any shouting, singing or boisterous conduct in a public place.' This was criticised for being vague and, as finally enacted s. 5 creates an offence of engaging in offensive conduct, which is defined as 'any unreasonable behaviour which, having regard to all the circumstances, is likely to cause serious offence or serious annoyance to any person who is, or might reasonably expected to be, aware of such behaviour.' While the section remains quite wide is scope the use of words such as 'reasonable' would appear to render it constitutionally permissible. The maximum penalty is a fine of £500. S. 6, which creates an offence of engaging in threatening, abusive or insulting behaviour in a public place with intent to provoke a breach of the peace, was seen by the drafters as a more serious than that in s. 5 of the 1994 Act. A person guilty of an offence under s. 6 is liable on summary conviction to a maximum fine not exceeding £500 and/or to six months imprisonment. Finally, s. 7 of the 1994 Act created an offence of distributing or displaying any writing, sign or visible representation which is threatening, abusive, insulting or obscene with intent to provoke a breach of the peace. The penalties are the same as provided for in s. 6 of the Act. In his annotation to the 1994 Act, *ICLSA*, Gerard Hogan notes that concerns expressed by civil liberties opponents to this provision may have been borne out in the immediate wake of its coming into effect when an anti-abortion campaigner handing out pictures of aborted foetuses was arrested under the 1994 Act and informed she would be charged under s. 7.

'Moving on'   S. 8 of the 1994 Act creates a 'moving on' offence. It empowers the Gardaí to direct a person who is acting in a manner contrary to the provisions of sections 4, 5, 6, 7 or 9 or is loitering in circumstances that give rise to a reasonable apprehension for the safety of persons or property or for the maintenance of the public peace to desist from the behaviour in question or else to 'leave immediately the vicinity', that is to 'move on'. The maximum penalties on summary conviction are a fine of £500 and/or six months imprisonment. S. 8 of the 1994 Act in effect replaces 'loitering with intent' in s. 4 of the Vagrancy Act 1824, which had been found unconstitutional in *King v Attorney General* [1981] IR 233. S. 9 of the 1994 Act creates a new statutory offence of wilful obstruction, defined as a situation where a person wilfully prevents or interrupts the free passage of any person or vehicle in any public place. A maximum fine of £200 is provided for, and s. 9 replaces s. 13(3) of the Summary Jurisdiction (Ireland) Act 1851.

Assaults   S. 10 of the 1994 Act increased the penalty for common assault or battery in s. 11(2) of the Criminal Justice Act 1951 to a fine not exceeding £1,000 (up from £50) and/or imprisonment for a term not exceeding 12 months (up from 6 months). S. 18 of the 1994 Act provides that it shall be an offence to assault a person with intent to cause bodily harm or commit an indictable offence. A person guilty of an offence under s. 18 will be liable on summary prosecution to a maximum fine of £1,000 and/or 12 months imprisonment. On indictment, the penalties are an unlimited fine and/or 5 years imprisonment. S. 19(1) deals with assaults on a 'peace officer' acting in the execution of his duty or assault any other person acting in the aid of a peace officer or assault any other person with intent to resist or prevent the lawful apprehension or detention of himself or of any other person for any offence. S. 19(6) defines a peace officer as a member of the Garda Síochána, a prison officer or a member of the Defence Forces (as originally drafted, a sheriff or a traffic warden were also included, but this was dropped from the final version of s. 19). A person guilty of an offence under s. 19(1) will be liable on summary conviction to a maximum fine of £1,000 and/or 12 months imprisonment and, on indictment, to an unlimited fine and/or imprisonment for a term not exceeding 5 years. The right of a person to elect for either summary trial or trial on indictment has been retained in connection with offences under s. 19(1): the Criminal Justice (Public Order) Bill 1993 had proposed to remove the right to elect for jury trial, but this was dropped after objection was raised as to whether this infringed the right to jury trial in Article 38.5 of the Constitution. S. 19(3) deals with resisting or wilfully obstructing a peace officer or a person assisting a peace officer, and prosecutions here would be summary only, where the maximum penalties are a fine of £500 and/or six months imprisonment. S. 19 replaces and modernises the equivalent offences in s. 38 of the Offences Against the Person Act 1861, which has been repealed.

Trespass-related offences   S. 11 creates an offence of entering a building or its curtilege as a trespasser with intent to commit an offence. A person guilty of an offence under this section will be liable (on summary conviction) to a fine not exceeding £1,000 and/or to imprisonment for a term not exceeding 6 months. S. 12 amended s. 4 of the Vagrancy Act 1824 to take account of the other amendments to the 1824 Act effected by the 1994 Act. Gerard Hogan provides a most helpful updated text of the extant s. 4 in his Annotation to the 1994 Act. S. 13 of the 1994 Act provides that it shall be an offence for a person to trespass on any dwelling or curtilege in such a manner as causes or is likely to cause fear in another person. The penalties as for under s. 11.

Riot, violent disorder and affray S. 14 replaces the common law offence of riot. S. 14(1) provides that when 12 or more persons who are present together at any place (whether that place is a public place or a private place or both) use or threaten to use unlawful violence for a common purpose, and the conduct of those persons, taken together, is such as would cause persons 'of reasonable firmness' present at that place to fear for his or another person's safety then each of the persons using unlawful violence for the common purposes shall commit the offence of riot. Prosecutions can only take place on indictment, where the maximum penalties are an unlimited fine and/or 10 years imprisonment. S. 14(4) provides for the formal abolition of the common law offence of riot. S. 15 replaces the common law offences of rout and unlawful assembly with an offence of violent disorder. This applies when three or more persons are present together at any place (whether that place is a public place or a private place or both) use or threaten to use unlawful violence and the conduct of those persons, taken together, is such as would cause a person of reasonable firmness present at that place to fear for his or another person's safety, then each of the persons using or threatening unlawful violence shall commit the offence of violent disorder. This is thus a lesser form of the riot offence described in s. 14 of the 1994 Act. As with riot, only prosecutions on indictment can arise, and the maximum penalties are identical, though a person cannot be convicted without proof of an intention to use or threaten violence or is aware that his or her conduct may be violent or threaten violence. S. 15(6) provides for the formal abolition of the common law offences of rout and unlawful assembly. S. 16 of the 1994 Act deals with the third offence in this general category, affray. This arises where two or more persons at any place (whether that place is a public place or a private place or both) use or threaten to use violence towards each other; the violence so used or threatened by one of those persons is unlawful and the conduct of those persons is such as would cause a person of reasonable firmness to fear for his or another person's safety. Again, prosecutions are on indictment only, where the maximum penalties are an unlimited fine and/or five years imprisonment. S. 16(4) formally abolishes the common law offence of affray.

Blackmail, extortion and demanding money with menaces   S. 17 of the 1994 Act provides that it is an offence for any person who, with a view to gain for himself or another or with intent to cause loss to another, make any unwarranted demand with menaces. Prosecutions will be by indictment, with maximum penalties of an unlimited fine and/or 14 years imprisonment. S. 17 is aimed specifically at the problem of racketeering, and it replaces existing offences in ss. 29-31 of the Larceny Act 1916, which were repealed. These changes follow the Law Reform Commission's 1992 Report, The Law Relating to Dishonesty, referred to above. S. 3 of the Criminal Damage Act 1991 also covers some of this ground.

Crowd control at public events   Ss. 20, 21 and 22 of the 1994 Act deal with the control of access to large public events, such as sports events and concerts and, as already indicated, implement certain recommendations of the 1990 Hamilton Committee Report on Public Safety and Crowd Control. S. 21 authorises the erection by Gardaí of barriers on any road, street, lane or alley not more than one mile from where an event is taking place. A Garda is also empowered to divert persons and, where possession of a ticket is required for entrance to the event, to prohibit people who have no tickets from passing the barrier. S. 22 of the 1994 Act empowers the Gardaí to search for — and seize — intoxicating liquor or any disposable container or any other article which could be used to cause injury. The maximum penalty under both sections is a £500 fine.

Advertising of brothels and prostitution   As already indicated, s. 23 of the 1994 prohibits the advertising of premises as brothels and the services of a prostitute. The section includes advertisements where the 'circumstances or manner give rise to the reasonable inference that the premises is a brothel or that the service is one of prostitution.' The maximum penalty on summary conviction is a fine of £1,000, which rises to £10,000 on conviction on indictment.

Arrest without warrant   S. 24 of the 1994 Act authorises the Gardaí to arrest without warrant people committing offences under the following sections of the 1994 Act: ss. 4, 6, 7, 8, 11, 13 and 14 to 19. S. 24(2) authorises a Garda to demand the name and address of persons suspected of committing offences under the sections listed and a power of arrest without warrant when a person fails to give his name or address.

ROAD TRAFFIC

The Road Traffic Act 1994 deals with the following major items: it restated and strengthened the law relating to drink driving, reducing the permitted level of alcohol from 100 to 80 milligrams per 100 millilitres of blood and increasing the penalties attaching to convictions; and it introduced many new measures intended to secure better enforcement of the Road Traffic Acts. The Road Traffic Act 1994 (Commencement) Order 1994 (SI No. 222 of 1994) brought much of the 1994 Act, except Part III, into effect from July 22, 1994. The Road Traffic Act 1994 (Commencement) (No. 2) Order 1994 (SI No. 350 of 1994) brought Part III of the 1994 Act into effect from December 2, 1994. Included in Part III were the provisions dealing with the drink driving offence. The Road Traffic Act 1994 (Commencement) Order 1995 (SI No. 86 of 1995) brought ss. 40, 41 and 47 of the 1994 Act into effect from April 19, 1995 and s. 43 into effect from June 1, 1995. At the time of writing, ss. 25, 35, 36 and 49 of the 1994 Act had not been brought into force.

Medical Bureau of Road Safety   Part II of the 1994 Act (ss. 5 to 8) deal with the Medical Bureau of Road Safety. S. 5 amends s. 27 of the Road Traffic Act 1968 and contains definitions of terms relevant to the Medical Bureau. S. 6 re-enacts, with modifications, s. 38 of the 1968 Act and sets out the functions and duties of the Medical Bureau of Road Safety. The principal change is to allow the Bureau to test for the presence of drugs in blood specimens in addition to testing for the presence of drugs in urine. S. 7 re-enacts, with modifications, s. 39(2) of the 1968 Act and sets out the functions of the Director of the Medical Bureau. The Director is charged in general terms with responsibility for managing the business of the Bureau and for general supervision of the performance by it of its functions.

Driving offences   Part III of the 1994 Act (ss. 9 to 24) deals with driving offences generally, but in particular drink driving offences. S. 10 re-enacts, with amendments and additions, s. 49 of the Road Traffic Act 1961, dealing with the offence of driving or attempting to drive a mechanically propelled vehicle in a public place while under the influence of an intoxicant. The principal amendment is a reduction in the maximum permissible alcohol level at which a person is permitted to drive, or attempt to drive, a vehicle from 100 to 80 milligrams of alcohol per 100 millilitres of blood and from 135 to 107 milligrams of alcohol per 100 millilitres of urine. In addition, the Minister for the Environment is empowered for the first time to vary by Regulations (subject to prior approval by both Houses of the Oireachtas) the levels of alcohol permissible in a person's blood, urine or breath and set different limits for different classes of drivers. It had originally been proposed that the section would also include a power for a member of the Garda Síochána to enter on private property to secure an arrest for an offence under the section. However, this was dropped from the final version of s. 10 of the 1994 Act on the basis that it was regarded as being potentially unconstitutional. Instead, s. 39 of the 1994 Act provides for a modified power of entry, varying with the offence for which the power is used. For offences under ss. 49 and 50 of the 1961 Act, as amended, s. 39(2) of the 1994 Act provides that a Garda may:

> enter without warrant (if need be by the use of reasonable force) any place (including the curtilege of a dwelling but not including a dwelling) where the person is or where a member, with reasonable cause, suspects him to be.

For discussion of the powers of entry prior to the 1994 Act, see *Director of Public Prosecutions v McCreesh* [1992] 2 IR 239 (1991 Review, 131-2).

The maximum penalty for offences under s. 49 of the 1961 Act, as amended by s. 10 of the 1994 Act, remain unchanged: a maximum fine of £1000 and/or 6 months imprisonment. However, the increases in the mandatory consequential disqualification from driving provided under s. 26 of the 1994 Act for an offence under s. 49 of the 1961 Act were to prove controversial. We have already noted that Part III of the 1994 Act came into effect in December 1994. Arising from the Christmas 1994 drink-driving campaign, the prospect of mandatory disqualifications for offenders (particularly those charged the 'morning after' with an offence under s. 49 of the 1961 Act) led to modifications in the disqualification provisions in the 1994 Act. The Road Traffic Act 1995 substituted a 'sliding scale' regime of disqualification for a conviction under s. 49, an arrangement which had apparently been rejected for the 1994 Act as being in potential conflict with the judicial discretion on sentencing. It remains to be seen whether the sliding scale arrangement of the 1995 Act will be challenged on this ground.

S. 11 of the 1994 Act re-enacts, with amendments and additions, s. 50 of the Road Traffic Act 1961 and relates to the offence of being in charge of a mechanically propelled vehicle in a public place while under the influence of an intoxicant, It contains provisions corresponding to those in s. 10 but provides for increased penalties: a maximum fine of £1,000 and/or 6 months imprisonment, thus bringing it into line with the s. 49 offence.

S.12 of the 1994 Act re-enacts, with modifications, s. 12 of the 1978 Act obliging a person to provide a preliminary breath specimen if requested by a member of the Garda Síochána. New provisions provide that a Garda may require a driver to accompany him to a nearby place, including a vehicle, to provide a breath specimen and may require the driver to remain at that place in his presence or in the presence of another member of the Garda Síochána for up to one hour until a breath testing apparatus becomes available. The penalty for refusing or failing to provide a preliminary breath specimen is unchanged:. a maximum fine of £1,000 and/or 6 months imprisonment.

S. 13 of the 1994 Act replaces ss. 13 and 14 of the 1978 Act and obliges certain persons to provide a breath, blood or urine specimen following arrest. It extends the requirement in the 1978 Act to give a breath/blood/urine specimen following arrest for driving and/or being in charge of a vehicle while under the influence of an intoxicant to the offences of dangerous driving and taking a vehicle without authority. The requirement to provide a specimen of breath has been extended to a requirement to provide two specimens of breath for evidential purposes, to comply with new procedures in s. 17 of the 1994 Act. The penalty for refusing or failing to provide a specimen remains unchanged: a maximum fine of £1,000 and/or 6 months imprisonment.

S. 14 of the 1994 Act re-enacts s. 17 of the 1978 Act with minor amendments. It empowers a Garda to require a person in charge of a mechanically propelled vehicle where the Garda is of the opinion that the person is under the influence of drugs to accompany the Garda to a Garda station and, once at the station, that a blood or urine specimen be provided by a person. The penalty for refusing or failing to provide a specimen remains unchanged: a maximum fine of £1,000 and/or 6 months imprisonment.

S. 15 of the 1994 Act provides a new power for both a Garda and a designated doctor to enter a hospital to take a blood or urine specimen from a driver suspected of being involved in a traffic accident. It provides that it is an offence for such a person to refuse or fail to provide a specimen unless the doctor in the hospital in charge of the person refuses to permit the taking of the specimen on medical grounds. The penalty for refusing or failing to provide a specimen is a maximum fine of £1,000 and/or 6 months imprisonment.

S. 16 of the 1994 Act provides a new power for a Garda to detain an intoxicated driver who has been arrested where the release of the driver could be a threat to the safety of themselves or of other persons, subject to a number of safeguards to protect the rights of a driver detained and a maximum period of detention of 8 hours.

S. 17 of the 1994 Act provides for the procedures following the taking of a breath specimen under s. 13 of the 1994 Act. Where a person has provided two specimens of breath under s. 13, the specimen with the higher reading is to be disregarded. The statement of the concentration of alcohol in the person's breath to be used in evidence will be the printout from the breath testing apparatus and the person concerned will be supplied with a copy of the statement. S. 18 re-enacts, with minor modifications, s. 21 of the

1978 Act on the procedures to be adopted following the taking and provision of specimens of blood or urine. S. 19 of the 1994 Act re-enacts, with minor modifications and additions, s. 22 of the 1978 Act on the procedure to be followed by the Medical Bureau of Road Safety regarding specimens. S. 20 re-enacts, with minor modifications, s. 18 of the 1978 Act, providing that it is an offence to take alcohol with a view to frustrating a prosecution under ss. 49 or 50 of the 1961 Act and provides that the Court will disregard any evidence of having consumed intoxicating liquor between the time of the alleged offence and the giving of a specimen. The maximum penalty is unchanged: a maximum fine of £1,000 and/or 6 months imprisonment. S. 21 re-enacts s. 23 of the 1978 Act with amendments. The section gives evidential value to the statement, form and certificate provided for in ss. 17 to 19 of the 1994 Act. The section also provides for presumptions that certain persons are 'doctors' for the purposes of prosecutions. See also the terms of the Medical Practitioners (Amendment) Act 1993, discussed in the 1993 Review, 253.

S. 23 of the 1994 Act re-enacts, with amendments, s. 19 of the 1978 Act and provides a defence for the refusal or failure to permit the taking of a blood specimen. S. 23 extends the defence clause to the taking of breath specimens. However, in all cases, the defence that there was a special and substantial reason for the refusal or failure is conditional on the person providing a specimen in an alternative form.

The forms to be completed under Part III of the 1994 Act are contained in the Road Traffic Act 1994 (Part III) Regulations 1994 (SI No. 351 of 1994).

Driving licences   Part IV of the 1994 Act (ss. 25 to 29) concerns driving licences. S. 25 replaces s. 40 of the Road Traffic Act 1961 which required that a person produce a driving licence if demanded by a Garda, subject to a period of ten days within which to produce a driving licence at a nominated Garda Station. S. 25 of the 1994 Act provides that a driving licence must be produced immediately and effectively requires a driver to carry a driving licence at all times when driving a vehicle; however a Garda now retains an option to require production of a driving licence within ten days.

S. 26 of the 1994 Act replaced s. 26 of the Road Traffic Act 1961 and set out new disqualification periods for drink driving and other road traffic offences. The section provides that a person found guilty of an offence listed in the Second Schedule to the 1961 Act (as inserted by the 1994 Act) will be automatically disqualified from holding a driving licence and gives the Court the option to impose a disqualification until a driving test or a certificate of fitness is obtained. S. 26(3) introduced a new requirement that a person found guilty of an offence of driving while under the influence of an intoxicant (under s. 49 of the 1961 Act, as amended by the 1994 Act) or being in charge of a mechanically propelled vehicle while under the influence of an intoxicant (s. 50 of the 1961 Act, as amended) or dangerous driving (s. 53 of the 1961 Act, as amended) or any of the 'refusal' offences in ss. 13 to 15 of the 1994 Act was, in addition to the minimum period of disqualification, automatically disqualified until the person passes a driving test and produces a driving licence. The mandatory disqualification periods on conviction for the following offences are also increased to two years in the case of a first offence and to four years in the case of a second or any subsequent offence: of driving while under the influence of an intoxicant, being in charge of a vehicle while under the influence of an intoxicant, dangerous driving where the contravention caused death or serious bodily harm to another person or refusing or failing to provide a specimen. Other new mandatory disqualification periods were also introduced by s. 26 of the 1994 Act but, as already indicated, those for drink-related offences proved contentious and were replaced by a 'sliding scale' arrangement in the Road Traffic Act 1995.

Speed limits Part V of the 1994 Act (ss. 30 to 34 amend the existing statutory provisions concerning the setting of mandatory speed limits. Thus, s. 31 inserted a s. 44B into the Road Traffic Act 1961 to provide a specific statutory basis in primary legislation for a motorway speed limit, currently set at 70 mph. S. 33 replaces s. 46 of the Road Traffic Act 1961 and transfers responsibility from the Minister for the Environment to local authorities for speed limits. in built-up areas.

Traffic regulations Part VI of the 1994 Act (ss. 35 to 38) deal with new arrangements for making Traffic Regulations. S. 35 facilitated the amalgamation of Traffic and Parking Regulations under the control of the Minister for the Environment. S. 36 introduced new arrangements for the application and management of local parking controls. It empowers road authorities (county councils, county borough and borough corporations and urban district councils) to make bye-laws governing the type of parking controls to apply in their areas e.g. meter parking or disc parking. Under the bye-laws, the road authorities will have responsibility for determining the places where parking is to be subject to the payment of fees and for determining the level of fees and the conditions to be applied. Before making bye-laws under s. 36, road authorities must consult the Garda Commissioner, give public notice of their intention to make the bye-laws and consider any observations or objections which result from this process.

Miscellaneous Part VII of the 1994 Act (ss. 39 to 49) deal with a number of miscellaneous matters. We have already discussed s. 39 of the 1994 Act, above, 218. Of the other sections in this Part, we should mention s. 41, which empower a Garda to detain vehicles for motor tax or motor insurance offences or where the driver is too young to hold a driving licence. The detailed provisions governing the operation of the impounding provisions are set out in the Road Traffic Act 1994 (Section 41) Regulations 1995 (SI No. 89 of 1995). S. 43 amends s. 103 of the Road Traffic Act 1961 to provide that 'on-the-spot fines', such as those for parking offences, can be paid to civilians authorised by the Minister for Justice at a named Garda station or at some other named location.

SENTENCING

Lenient sentence In *The People v Byrne, sub nom Director of Public Prosecutions v Byrne* [1995] 1 ILRM 279, the Court of Criminal Appeal considered its function in reviewing a sentence claimed to be unduly lenient pursuant to the Criminal Justice Act 1993: see 224-6, below.

Manslaughter In *The People v Gallagher*, Court of Criminal Appeal, 4 March 1994, the Court (Denham, Barr and Morris JJ) considered a number of previous cases in which sentences for manslaughter had been imposed. The defendant had pleaded guilty to manslaughter, having driven a car onto the footpath where the deceased had been standing and struck her. He had consumed between 10 and 15 pints of beer and had driven home directly, realising only the next morning what had occurred. He had immediately gone to a Garda Station and reported the matter. The defendant had 15 previous convictions, though none concerned drink-related driving offences. Having pleaded guilty, he was sentenced to seven years imprisonment and disqualified from holding a driving licence for life. He appealed against the severity of sentence and was, at least in part, successful.

It had been argued on his behalf that the trial judge had not given sufficient weight to the applicant's remorse, his personal circumstances, his alcoholism and attempts to deal with it since the offence, and his plea to the offence at the earliest opportunity. Having heard counsel for the applicant refer to two cases in which the sentences for manslaughter in similar circumstances had been lighter, the Court adjourned the application to enable counsel to seek further material on sentencing in cases of dangerous driving causing death and manslaughter arising from driving a motor vehicle. The result was that five other cases were put before the Court.

Having considered these, delivering the Court's judgment, Denham J stated that the sentence of seven years adequately reflected the serious nature of the offence and the circumstances surrounding the event. However, the Court concluded that three years of the sentence would be suspended on condition that during his period of imprisonment the applicant would attend the AA programme for alcoholics and other rehabilitation programmes which the prison authorities might require him to attend. For a previous example in which the Court was prepared to examine a wide range of previous cases of a type similar to that before the Court, see *The People v Egan (L.) (No. 2)*, Court of Criminal Appeal, February 4, 1991 (1991 Review, 180), a case concerning rape.

Sexual assault: buggery In *The People v M.* [1994] 2 ILRM 541, the Supreme Court considered the application of the sentencing principles it had established in *The People v Tiernan* [1988] IR 250 (1988 Review, 181-4) in the context of the offence of buggery.

The appellant, a brother in a religious order, had pleaded guilty to a number of counts involving assaults on young boys at a school where he had been teaching. He was sentenced as follows: on three counts of buggery with a male person contrary to s. 61 of the Offences Against the Person Act 1861, 18 years penal servitude; on two counts of sexual assault contrary to s. 4 of the Criminal Law (Rape) (Amendment) Act 1990, 18 years imprisonment; on two counts of indecent assault on a male person contrary to s. 62 of the Offences Against the Person Act 1861, nine years imprisonment; and on a count of indecent assault contrary to s. 2 of the Criminal Law (Rape) (Amendment) Act 1990, four years imprisonment.

He appealed to the Supreme Court against the severity of the sentence. On his behalf it was submitted that the sentences were excessive and inappropriate to the circumstances of the case, and that the trial judge had erred in law in finding himself constrained in the circumstances of the case by the decision of the Supreme Court in the *Tiernan* case. The Supreme Court (Finlay CJ, O'Flaherty, Egan, Blayney and Denham JJ) reduced the 18 year sentences to 12 years, the nine year sentences to seven years and the four year sentence to three.

The judgments delivered by Blayney and Denham JJ emphasised that sentences must be proportionate, first of all to the crime, but also to the personal circumstances of the offender and that an accused person has a constitutional right which guarantees that his trial will not shut out a sentence appropriate to his degree of guilt and relevant personal circumstances. They pointed out that the general impact of a crime on a victim is a factor in sentencing, but the nature of the offence and the offender's personal circumstances are the key issues, as criminal law is an action between the State and the offender, rather than between the offender and the victim. This approach clearly puts in context the 'victim impact reports' which are now part of the sentencing process, as required by the Criminal Justice Act 1993 (see the 1993 Review, 264).

In the instant case, the Court held that the most important mitigating factor was that the appellant had admitted his guilt promptly and pleaded guilty at his trial. In keeping with the Tiernan case, the Court accepted that a guilty plea is an important mitigating factor in rape cases and the situation was similar here where the young boys involved were spared the considerable worry of giving evidence in court. In addition, the defendant's personal circumstances constituted a further relevant factor: he had had a life of personal isolation; he had joined the religious order at the age of 13 and since then had minimal contact with his family, persons of the opposite sex and the community in general. Another relevant factor for the Court was the likelihood of a recurrence of misconduct on release. The Court noted that the defendant's superiors at his religious community had undertaken that he would never teach again and that they would look after his welfare on release, whether he returned to religious life or not.

A further factor was the prospect of rehabilitating the offender so that he may re-enter society wherever this is reasonably possible, and the Court again applied well-established principles in holding that this included the maintenance of an element of hope or a 'light at the end of the tunnel', citing *The People v O'Driscoll* (1972) 1 Frewen 351 and *The People v Poyning* [1972] IR 402. Thus the age at which a sentenced person would re-enter society is a relevant consideration and in the instant case the defendant was aged 50, and would be in his mid-60s on release, even with remission. The Court also noted that there was no evidence or suggestion of brutality or violence in the case, and whilst it was a serious one, the Court felt that the trial judge's assessment of the appropriate sentence had been coloured by a very extreme view of the case.

The Court considered that a reduction of sentence in mitigation should not always be calculated in relation to the maximum sentence applicable, and that a sentencing judge should look first at where on the range of penalties a particular case would lie and then make an appropriate reduction based on the mitigating circumstances. While the trial judge had imposed nine year sentences in respect of counts where a maximum sentence of ten years was permissible, the Court felt that a reduction of 10% was not a sufficient recognition of the requirement to mitigate.

Clearly, the reference to the 10% reduction in mitigation does not indicate that the Supreme Court in *M.* was suggesting a tariff approach to sentencing, since the Irish courts have tended to avoid such an approach. Nonetheless, the approach since Tiernan itself has been to indicate that a gradient of reduction must be appropriate in virtually all cases, subject of course to the need for individualised sentences as in the instant case.

Sexual assault: rape   *The People v Byrne, sub nom Director of Public*

Prosecutions v Byrne [1995] 1 ILRM 279 was the first opportunity for the Court of Criminal Appeal to consider its function in reviewing a sentence claimed to be unduly lenient pursuant to the Criminal Justice Act 1993. As we noted in the 1993 Review, 255, s. 2(1) of the Criminal Justice Act 1993, provides that the Director of Public Prosecutions may apply to the Court of Criminal Appeal to review a sentence he believes was 'unduly lenient'.

The defendant had been sentenced in the Central Criminal Court to ten years' penal servitude in respect of two counts of rape and to ten years' imprisonment on one count of buggery contrary to s. 4 of the Criminal Law (Rape) Act 1990. The sentences were to run concurrently. The sentences related to the rape at knifepoint of a woman and the rape and buggery of a 77 year old widow. The defendant had a previous conviction in 1985 in relation to indecent assault. He had been detained under s. 4 of the Criminal Justice Act 1984 and had confessed to the Gardaí. He signed guilty pleas in the District Court and affirmed these written signed pleas in the Central Criminal Court. The trial judge heard reports from a psychiatrist on the impact of the attacks on the two women, from another psychiatrist who gave evidence as to his examination of the accused, and from a probation and welfare officer who had made a report on the accused. In sentencing, the trial judge said he took into account the victim impact reports and the confession of the accused. He said that in the absence of a guilty plea he would have felt a sentence of 14 years appropriate, but because of the way in which the accused had approached the case, he felt that a sentence of 10 years was a fair and reasonable one.

The Director of Public Prosecutions made an application under s. 2 of the 1993 Act for a review of the sentence. It was submitted that the sentence was not 'unduly lenient' in relation to the first woman having regard to the mitigating factors. However it was argued that the imposition of concurrent ten year sentences in relation to the offences committed in respect of the second woman was unduly lenient as the effect was that no additional penalty was imposed in respect of those offences, particularly having regard to the offence against the first woman. The Court of Criminal Appeal (O'Flaherty, Geoghegan and Kinlen JJ) dismissed the application. Delivering the Court's judgment O'Flaherty J stated that the Director of Public Prosecutions bears the onus of proving that a sentence called into question was 'unduly lenient' under the 1993 Act. On hearing the application, the Court considered it should afford great weight to the trial judge's reasons for imposing the sentence as he hears the evidence at first hand and may detect nuances that may not be as readily discernible to an appellate court. In particular, where a trial judge has kept a balance between the particular circumstances of the commission of the offence and the relevant personal circumstances of the person concerned, his decision should not be disturbed.

Thus, the inquiry to be made by a court on this type of application is to determine whether a sentence was 'unduly lenient'. Nothing but a substantial departure from what would be regarded as the appropriate sentence would justify the intervention of the reviewing court. It is notable in this context that the Court drew a clear distinction between its approach on an appeal by a convicted person and one by he Director. In an important passage, the Court stated:

> [I]t is in the view of the court unlikely to be of help to ask, if there had been imposed a more severe sentence, would it be upheld on appeal by an appellant as being right in principle? And that is because . . . the test to be applied . . . is not the converse of the enquiry the court makes where there is an appeal by an appellant.

In the instant case, the sentence of ten years was a substantial one and *prima facie* could not be categorised as 'unduly lenient'. While the offences in this case had to be looked at as being in the higher range on the scale of rapes because of the aggravating factors, the Court also felt it should look at the accused's situation, and in particular his early confession and plea of guilty. Applying the principles laid down in *The People v Tiernan* [1988] IR 250 and *The People v G.* [1994] 1 IR 587 (1993 Review, 263), the Court pointed out that an early admission of guilt in a rape case, followed by a subsequent plea of guilty, can be a significant mitigating factor insofar as it spares the victim from the ordeal of coming to court. Here the trial judge had indicated that without the guilty plea the appropriate sentence would have been fourteen years. In those circumstances, the Court concluded that the trial judge had brought all the correct principles to bear, and it had not been suggested that he took into consideration anything he should not have taken into consideration and for that reason the Court, as already indicated, dismissed the Director's application. For an informative discussion of the decision in the case, see Tom O'Malley's article. 'The First Prosecution Appeal Against Sentence' (1994) 4 *ICLJ* 192.

SEXUAL OFFENCES

Rape: belief as to consent In *The People v McD.*, Court of Criminal Appeal, July 27, 1994, the Court (O'Flaherty, Keane and Lavan JJ) considered the effect of s. 2(2) of the Criminal Law (Rape) Act 1981, which provides that if, at a trial for rape, 'the jury has to consider whether a man believed that a woman was consenting to sexual intercourse, the presence or absence of reasonable grounds for such a belief is a matter to which the jury is to have regard, in conjunction with any other relevant matters, in considering whether he so believed.' The Court applied the principles previously established in *The People v F.*, Court of Criminal Appeal, May 27, 1993 (1993 Review, 266) and *The People v Creighton* [1994] 1 ILRM 551 (1993 Review, 267) that s. 2(2) of the 1981 Act did not apply where there was a direct conflict of evidence between the complainants and the defendant.

STOP AND SEARCH

Stopping vehicles: extent of power In *Director of Public Prosecutions (Stratford) v Fagan* [1993] 2 IR 95 (HC); [1994] 2 ILRM 349 (SC), the Supreme Court upheld the power to establish checkpoints for the purposes of the Road Traffic Acts.

S. 109(1) of the Road Traffic Act 1961, as amended by the Road Traffic Act 1968, provides that a person driving a vehicle in a public place shall stop the vehicle on being so required by a member of An Garda Síochána and shall keep it stationary for such period as is reasonably necessary in order to enable such member to discharge his duties. The defendant was charged with driving a motor vehicle in a public place while there was present in his body a quantity of alcohol in excess of the permitted level. In the District Court the prosecuting Garda gave evidence that while on checkpoint duty in a public street, he had seen a car being driven along that street and had signalled to the driver to stop. He stated that when the car stopped and he spoke to the driver, he noticed a smell of intoxicating liquor from the driver's breath, that his speech was slurred and that on stepping out of the car the driver seemed to be very unsteady. Having formed the view that the driver was under the influence of intoxicating liquor, the Garda informed him of this opinion and arrested him under s. 49(6) of the Road Traffic Act 1961, as amended. At the conclusion of the prosecution case the defendant submitted that unless the Garda had suspected that a criminal offence had been committed, he had no power to stop a vehicle in a public place and that no evidence to this effect had been given in this case. On a case stated, the High Court(Carney J) held that s. 109(1) of the 1961 Act authorised a Garda to stop a vehicle in order to ascertain whether there was a contravention of s. 49 of the 1961 Act. It was also held that a Garda had a common law power to operate random road traffic checks, including checks in relation to drunk driving, which involved the stopping of vehicles even though there might be no immediate suspicion that an offence had been committed. The defendant appealed but the Supreme Court (Finlay CJ, O'Flaherty, Egan and Blayney JJ; Denham J dissenting in part) dismissed the appeal.

The Court held that since the Gardaí are under a common law duty to detect and prevent crime, it followed that if they find it necessary to require motorists to stop in order adequately to detect and prevent crime, they have full power to do so at common law. The Court held that the Gardaí were under a clear duty to do everything in their power to detect and prevent the crime of drunk driving and that the widespread operation of random checkpoints designed to combat this offence fell within the common law power of the Gardaí to detect and prevent crime. The Court added that the establishment of a checkpoint in the vicinity of licensed premises, at a time of night when such premises are being closed, in order to identify persons who may be committing breaches of the laws relating to driving while under the influence of alcohol, was a proper exercise of the common law powers of the Gardaí.

The Court added, however, that the power of the Gardaí to stop a vehicle had to be exercised in a *bona fide* manner and if a Garda were to exercise the power in a capricious, arbitrary or improper manner it would be wholly illegal. Thus it was open to a member of the public to ask the Garda concerned as to why he has been stopped and, if subsequently charged with any offence, to raise the question of the propriety of being stopped in that context.

As to the statutory position. the majority of the Court held that s. 109(1) of the 1961 Act does not give the Gardaí any power to require a motorist to stop. Rather, approving the analysis of the English Court of Appeal in *Steel v Goacher* [1983] RTR 98, the Court held that it merely imposed an obligation on the driver of a vehicle to stop when required to do so by a Garda and its purpose was to avoid the dangerous uncertainty and disorder which might otherwise arise if a motorist was unsure as to whether he should stop for a Garda.

Finally, we may note that, in dissent, Denham J considered that the authority of the Gardaí to stop a person in a vehicle or restrict liberty in any way should be clear and certain, and have a precise statutory basis. Since she considered that s. 109(1) of the 1961 Act did not fall into this category, she concluded that the Gardaí did not possess the powers which the majority was prepared to ascribe to them.

STRICT LIABILITY OFFENCES

In *Maguire v Shannon Regional Fisheries Board* [1994] 2 ILRM 253, Lynch J held that certain offences concerning water pollution constituted offences of strict liability in respect of which it was not necessary to establish *mens rea*.

The case involved s. 171(1)(b) of the Fisheries (Consolidation) Act 1959, which provides that any person who throws, empties, permits or causes to fall into any waters any deleterious matter shall, unless such act is done under and in accordance with a licence granted by the Minister for the Marine, be guilty of an offence. S. 42 of the Local Government (Water Pollution) (Amendment) Act 1990 provides that a person found guilty of such an offence on indictment can be sentenced to a fine of up to £25,000 and/or five years' imprisonment.

The defendant operated a piggery near to a river. A pipe which formed part of the piggery's feeding system fractured and some of the whey which it was carrying escaped into the river. Tests subsequently carried out by the respondent's officers revealed that the river had been polluted. The defendant was charged in the District Court with causing deleterious matter to fall into waters contrary to s. 171(1)(b) of the 1959 Act. The District Court judge found as a fact that the appellant had taken all reasonable steps to prevent the accident at considerable expense and that the staff at the piggery had done everything in their power to prevent the flow of whey into the river. However, he concluded that s. 171(1)(b) created an offence of strict liability and convicted the appellant as he had caused the flow of whey into the river. On a case stated to the High Court, Lynch J upheld the finding that the offence was one of strict liability.

Lynch J accepted, in accordance with the leading decision in *Sherras v De Rutzen* [1895] 1 QB 918, that *prima facie, mens rea* is required for every criminal offence, whether common law or statutory.

However, he concluded that s. 171 of the 1959 Act provided for an offence of strict liability. Quoting with approval extracts from the leading decisions in *Gammon (Hong Kong) Ltd v Attorney General of Hong Kong* [1985] AC 1 and *Alphacell Ltd v Woodward* [1972] AC 824, he stated that s. 171 was regulatory in nature and did not create an offence which would be regarded as being of a truly criminal character. The creation of strict liability in respect of the pollution of rivers and streams, coupled with provision for heavy penalties for such offences, promoted, he considered, the objects of the 1959 Act by encouraging greater vigilance to prevent the commission of the prohibited act. He also noted that, if proof of *mens rea* was required it would be very difficult to establish that an offence had been committed.

In the instant case, while the immediate or proximate cause of the flow of whey into the river was the fracture of the pipe, the activities of the appellant in running his piggery close to the river caused the whey to be present in the pipe and therefore to escape into the river. On the basis of the test of liability laid down in *Alphacell Ltd v Woodward*, therefore, he concurred with the view expressed by the trial judge that the defendant was guilty of an offence.

The decision in *Maguire* was expressly approved by Murphy J in

Shannon Regional Fisheries Board v Cavan County Council, High Court,
December 21, 1994. This was also a prosecution under s. 171 of the Fisheries
(Consolidation) Act 1959, as amended. However, in this instance, the defendant was a local authority required by statute to receive public sewage and
the offences related to discharges from sewage treatment works operated by
the defendant in its capacity as sanitary authority. The sewage treatment
works had been constructed in 1951 and were designed to cater for a
population of 700 persons. As a result of population increase and the
improved domestic sanitary facilities in the area, as well as the increase in
the per capita of population volume of effluent requiring treatment since
1951, the sewage treatment works had become inadequate for their purpose.
The defendant Council had made efforts to up-grade or replace the existing
works but the capital needed for such projects were only available to a local
authority from the Department of Environment.

The District Court judge concluded that the defendant Council had taken
all reasonable care to prevent the entry of deleterious matter into the areas in
question. However, on a case stated to the High Court, Murphy J, as already
indicated, approved the decision of Lynch J in *Maguire v Shannon Regional
Fisheries Board* [1994] 2 ILRM 253, above, and held that the offence created
by s. 171(1)(b) of the 1959 Act, as amended, was one of strict liability in
which mens rea, negligence and/or knowledge were not essential ingredients.
In that respect, the District Court judge was obliged to proceed to convict the
defendant. Murphy J rejected the contention by the defendant that, to convict
it in circumstances where it was without the resources needed to comply with
its statutory duties would be in breach of the fundamental right to basic justice
as elaborated in *The State (Healy) v Donoghue* [1976] IR 325.

However, Murphy J also added some comments on the application of the
Probation of Offenders Act 1907 and on the payment of costs which are of
some interest and which, to some extent, address the argument arising from
The State (Healy) v Donoghue. He held that the 1907 Act applied to the
offences in the 1959 Act and that the invocation or otherwise of the Probation
of Offenders Act 1907, and indeed the penalty, was a matter wholly within
the discretion of the trial judge. As to the evaluation of the question of costs
and expenses, this was also within the trial judge's discretion, but he
considered that it would be premature to consider the issue until after the
charges had been disposed of and taking account of the reasons advanced by
the defendant for being relieved of the prima facie liability to pay costs and
expenses. This discretionary approach may have dealt with the immediate
issue in the instant case, but it must surely be a 'stop gap' approach. Many
provisions of 'regulatory' criminal law that provide for strict liability, such
as the 1959 Act, also tend to include provisions which provide that failure to
remedy the matter causing the offence is itself a 'continuing' offence. One

must question whether the discretionary approach suggested by Murphy J could be employed indefinitely in a situation where a local authority were, in effect, to shrug its shoulders and point to central government. Of course, an alternative might be for the local authority to suggest that a Government Department be prosecuted as being the 'causative factor' in the offence. Such an option is another common feature of such 'regulatory' criminal laws. Whether the courts would be content to see such 'buck passing' taken to this level remains to be seen. Could one be faced, ultimately, with the prospect that the Minister for the Environment might wish to 'point the finger' at the budgetary constraints imposed by the Minister for Finance who would, in turn point to the limitations imposed by the economic convergence criteria required for Economic and Monetary Union under the Maastricht Treaty on European Union? In different contexts, the courts have been prepared to considered certain budgetary realities: see *O'Reilly v Limerick Corporation* [1989] ILRM 181 (1988 Review, 114-5), but by contrast no reference was made to such factors in *The State (Healy) v Donoghue* [1976] IR 325 or in the context of the maintenance of courthouses in *Hoey v Minister for Justice* [1994] 1 ILRM 334 (1993 Review, 443). Whether any such issues arise in the future in the context of prosecutions against local authorities remains to be seen, but it seems unlikely that the courts would accept a full defence of financial inability to comply. In the meantime, the discretionary approach suggested by Murphy J in the *Shannon Regional Fisheries Board* case would appear to be the only available solution.

TIME LIMITS

Indictable offence prosecuted summarily In *Director of Public Prosecutions v Logan* [1994] 2 ILRM 229, the Supreme Court held that a summary prosecution for assault contrary to common law was subject to the six-month time limit prescribed by s. 10(4) of the Petty Sessions (Ireland) Act 1851, notwithstanding that such offence was capable of being brought on indictment.

S. 42 of the Offences Against the Person Act 1861, as amended by s. 11 of the Criminal Justice Act 1951, provided that a charge of assault contrary to common law can be prosecuted summarily. S. 46 of the 1861 Act provides that if the assault or battery complained of was accompanied by an attempt to commit a felony, or the District Court is of the opinion that it is a fit subject for a prosecution on indictment, the District Court shall abstain from adjudicating upon it. S. 47 of the 1861 Act provides that a person convicted on indictment in respect of a common assault may be imprisoned for a term not exceeding one year. S. 7 of the Criminal Justice Act 1951 provides:

paragraph 4 (which prescribes time-limits for the making of complaints in cases of summary jurisdiction) of s. 10 of the Petty Sessions (Ireland) Act 1851, shall not apply to a complaint in respect of an indictable offence.

The defendant had been charged in the District Court with assault contrary to common law, s. 42 of the 1861 Act and s.11 of the 1951 Act. The District Court judge dismissed the charges on the ground that the application for the issue of a summons had not been made within the period of six months from the date of the alleged offence in circumstances where the prosecution had decided to deal with the charge summarily. The judge stated a case to the High Court where it was held that as an assault at common law could be prosecuted on indictment it was an indictable offence and thus s. 7 of the 1951 Act applied. This meant that the six-month period laid down by s. 10(4) of the 1851 Act did not apply and the District Court judge had been incorrect in dismissing the charges. However, on the defendant's further appeal to the Supreme Court (Finlay CJ, Blayney and Egan JJ) the view of the District Court judge was upheld. In so doing, the Court overruled the High Court decision in *McGrail v Ruane* [1989] ILRM 498 (1988 Review, 186).

Delivering the only reasoned judgment, Blayney J held that the phrase 'complaint in respect of an indictable offence' in s. 7 of the 1951 Act referred to a complaint in respect of an indictable offence which was a scheduled offence, as defined by s. 2 of the 1951 Act, and could be tried summarily by the District Court under s. 2(2), provided that the conditions set out in that subsection were satisfied. As s. 7 provided that s. 10(4) of the 1851 Act shall not apply, he interpreted it as dealing with a situation in which s. 10(4) would otherwise apply, or otherwise might apply. Hence it could only be taken to apply to a complaint in respect of an indictable offence which the District Court had jurisdiction to try summarily under s. 2(2) of the 1951 Act.

Since the offence of assault contrary to common law was not a scheduled offence within the meaning of s. 2 of the 1951 Act, but was a common law offence which may be prosecuted summarily under s. 42 of the 1861 Act or tried on indictment under s. 47 of the 1861 Act, s. 7 of the 1951 Act did not apply to prosecutions under s. 42 of the 1861 Act for assault contrary to common law. Furthermore, as a matter of construction, Blayney J concluded that the words 'complaint in respect of an indictable offence' in s. 7 were capable of a reasonable and sensible application because they clearly referred to a complaint of an indictable offence set out in the First Schedule to the 1951 Act. He felt that there was no need to extend them to the offence of assault contrary to common law triable summarily under the 1861 Act because that offence also happened to be triable on indictment under s. 47 of the 1861 Act. There was thus no reason to extend the words to provide that

s. 10(4) of the 1851 Act should no longer apply to a prosecution under s. 42.

We note here that the Criminal Justice (Public Order) Act 1994 has updated certain aspects of the law on assault, retaining the right to elect for summary trial: see the discussion above, 214.

WARRANTS

Bench warrant *Walsh v Ireland*, Supreme Court, November 10, 1994 will be considered in the 1995 Review.

Search warrant In *Director of Public Prosecutions v Dunne*, High Court, October 14, 1994, Carney J ruled invalid a search warrant concerning the defendant private dwelling.

Members of An Garda Síochána had carried out a search of the defendant's dwelling house pursuant to a warrant obtained from a Peace Commissioner under s. 26 of the Misuse of Drugs Acts 1977, as amended. S. 26 requires that the Peace Commissioner issuing the warrant is satisfied that drugs are on the premises to which the warrant relates. On the printed form of the search warrant in the instant case, the words 'is on the premises' had inadvertently been deleted. The defendant was prosecuted for resisting the Gardaí under s. 21(4) of the Misuse of Drugs Act 1977 as amended by s. 6 of the Misuse of Drugs Act 1984. In the District Court, the validity of the warrant to search was challenged. On a case stated to the High Court, Carney J held that the warrant was flawed. He held that the constitutional protection given in Article 40.5 of the Constitution to the dwelling house is one of the most important, clear and unqualified protections given by the Constitution to the citizen. If a printed form is to set aside that protection, it must, he stated, be clear, complete, accurate and unambiguous. In this respect, the warrant in the instant case did not make sense without relying on the words that had been crossed out and accordingly it was not an effective authority for breaching the constitutional inviolability of the defendant's dwelling house.

Education

Governing body elections and gender balance   The Dublin Institute of Technology (Amendment) Act 1994 amended s. 6 of the Dublin Institute of Technology Act 1992 (see the 1992 Review, 309) in respect of matters relating to the appointment of governing bodies to the DIT Colleges. In the case of academic staff elections, the 1994 Act provides that the electorate shall include not only permanent full-time staff but also those part-time staff who teach for not less than 280 time-tabled hours in an academic year. Provision is also made to enable the Minister for Education to vary the number of hours from time to time. Provision for gender equity in the academic staff elections was also made, by requiring that the two staff positions on the Governing Body be filled by one man and one woman. In the case of non-academic staff, provision was made to include in the electorate all permanent full-time staff and those part-time staff who work at least 50%. of the hours of a full-time staff member. As in the case of academic staff elections, the Minister may vary the number of hours of work in the Institute which are necessary to enable a person to participate in these elections.

The 1994 Act also amends the provisions relating to student elections for governing body positions. The 1992 Act had provided for elections among students for these positions. The 1994 Act provided that the two registered students shall be chosen according to regulations made by the governing body. Gender equity is also provided for in respect of the two members selected to represent students.

Finally, the 1994 Act alters the procedure for selection of other interests to the Governing Body. Under the 1992 Act, the Dublin Vocational Education Committee (VEC) was required to select five organisations and accept the nominations of these. The 1994 Act requires the VEC to seek nominations from any number of relevant organisations and to select their recommendations to the Minister for Education from these nominations. In making such recommendations, the VEC is obliged to ensure a gender balance and also to implement any directives laid down by the Minister for Education. The 1994 Act came into effect on December 7, 1994 on its signature by the President.

LEGAL EDUCATION

The statutory provisions concerning the Law Society of Ireland's examinations, and in particular the changes effected by the Solicitors (Amendment) Act 1994, are referred to in the Solicitors chapter, 417-35, below.

MINISTERIAL CONTROL OF APPOINTMENTS

In *Minister for Education v Regional Technical College, Letterkenny (Morrow, Notice Party)* [1995] 1 ILRM 438, the Supreme Court considered the role of the Minister for Education in the context of the appointment of the financial controller of a Regional Technical College (RTC). While the Court held that the Minister had little power to have an appointment quashed, some important comments were made on the statutory provisions in this area, contained in the Regional Technical Colleges Act 1992. s. 11(1) of the Regional Technical Colleges Act 1992 provides that a college may, subject to the approval of the Minister for Education given with the concurrence of the Minister for Finance, appoint such persons to be its officers and servants as its governing body thinks proper. s. 11(1)(b) of the 1992 Act provides that the selection of officers and servants shall be a function of the college in accordance with procedures which may be determined by the Minister for Education. In March 1993 a document was sent to the Director of Letterkenny RTC from the Department of Education which set out the procedures by which RTCs should select their staff. The selection procedures provided that the job description and requirements for each post should be determined by the Director, in consultation with the relevant head of function, of each RTC. The procedures also required that the Director should screen the applications to ensure that only candidates who met the requirements for the posts were considered by the selection board. The Council of Directors of the regional technical colleges drew up a draft document setting out the job description and qualifications for the post of secretary/financial controller. This document was approved by all of the directors and the Minister's representatives. It stated that the successful candidate would have a relevant degree with first or second class honours and/or professional qualifications, together with at least five years' post-qualification senior management experience.

Advertisements for the post of secretary/financial controller in Letterkenny RTC were published in May 1993. Although they did not specify the criteria mentioned in the job description, applicants were informed of the qualifications and experience required. In June 1993, the Notice Party, Mr Morrow, forwarded to Letterkenny RTC an application form in relation to this post. It stated that he was employed by Donegal County Council as an administrative officer and that he had obtained a pass in the Leaving Certificate examination. He had not attended university or obtained any third level education and did not have any professional qualifications. The Director of Letterkenny RTC consulted with the chairman of the selection board and Mr Morrow's name was sent forward to the selection board. The board interviewed 27 candidates, including Mr Morrow. It recommended to the governing body of the college that he should be appointed. In July 1993 the governing body appointed Mr Morrow and he accepted the post. The Director of the college did not inform the Minister or the Department of Education of Mr Morrow's appointment. The Department subsequently requested information relating to the appointment and in September 1994 a copy of Mr Morrow's application form was forwarded to it. The Director was informed that as Mr Morrow did not have the academic or senior management experience required by the job description, his appointment could not be approved by the Minister.

The Minister then instituted proceedings seeking an order of *certiorari* quashing the appointment of Mr Morrow on the grounds that the appointment had been made in contravention of s. 11(1) of the 1992 Act and that the college had acted *ultra vires*. It was argued that the appointment was made without the approval of the Minister and that the College had failed to follow the selection procedures determined by the Minister. In the High Court, Costello J (as he then was) granted an order of *certiorari* quashing the appointment of Mr Morrow and, in lieu of directing that the order should issue, ordered that the college should send before the Court for the purpose of being quashed all records and entries relating to the appointment. The College and Mr Morrow appealed. It was submitted that the Minister's approval was required for the creation of the position of secretary/financial controller, but was not required for the appointment of any person to that office. It was also submitted that as the requirements for that office were a matter for the Director of the college, he was entitled to alter them. It was submitted by Mr Morrow that it would be unjust and improper in all the circumstances to grant the orders sought because he had resigned his former position in order to take up the post with the College. The Supreme Court (Hamilton CJ, O'Flaherty, Egan, Blayney and Denham JJ) unanimously allowed the appeal and vacated the order of the High Court.

Delivering the only reasoned judgment for the Court, Hamilton CJ held that there was a clear difference between the power of appointment of officers and servants by the colleges, and the power of selection of those officers and servants. He considered that s. 11(1)(a) of the 1992 Act concerned the creation of such positions and required the approval of the Minister for Education, with the concurrence of the Minister for Finance, but that once the posts had been created, different considerations applied and the process of selection was the function of the college, although it had to be made in accordance with such procedures as may be determined by the Minister.

As to qualifications, Hamilton CJ held that it was a matter for the director of the college, after appropriate consultation, to determine the requirements and qualifications for the post of secretary/financial controller and this was expressly recognised in the selection procedures drawn up by the Minister. s. 11(1)(a) of the 1992 Act did not, he felt, give the Minister any power to determine the qualifications for the post. The Chief Justice stated that, when the applications were screened the requirements for the post were those which had been agreed by the Directors of the colleges and the Minister. He accepted that, in the instant case, these requirements were not adhered to as Mr Morrow did not have any relevant degree or professional qualification. However, since the Director had the power to determine the requirements for the position, and this necessarily included the power to alter them, it could not be said that once he had fixed the requirements for a particular post they were absolutely immutable and could not be changed under any circumstances.

On the remedies available, Hamilton CJ concluded that, as the original requirements which were communicated to all the applicants were not adhered to, it was possible that an unsuccessful applicant could challenge Mr Morrow's appointment, but it was not open to the Minister to challenge the validity of the appointment. He went on to state that even if it had been open to the Minister to challenge the appointment, the court would have to be satisfied that it would be just and proper in all the circumstances to grant the orders sought. In this respect, Mr Morrow had resigned from his previous position to take up the post with the College and therefore, if his appointment were quashed he would be without employment. On this basis, he concluded that, in the circumstances it would not be just and proper to make the orders sought by the Minister.

While the Minister was thus unsuccessful in seeking relief in the case, the comments by the Supreme Court on the respective roles of the Minister and the RTC will be of wider interest. Although the Letterkenny case concerned the particular terms of the 1992 Act, its provisions may be relevant in a wider context in view of the Department of Education's 1995 White Paper on Education which aims to put in place an Education Act for the educational sector generally in the near future. Thus, the Letterkenny case may be required reading, particularly for those engaged in the drafting of an Education Act, with a view to defining the respective roles of the Minister for Education and those in executive positions in the various schools, colleges and Universities who would be affected by such an Act.

NCEA DESIGNATION OF COLLEGES

The National Council for Educational Awards Act 1979 (Designation of Institutions) Order 1994 (SI No. 25 of 1994) designated the Mid West Business Institute, Limerick and the HSI College, Limerick as institutions to which the 1979 Act applied, and they thus came within the remit of the NCEA. The National Council for Educational Awards Act 1979 (Designation of Institutions) (No. 2) Order 1994 (SI No. 49 of 1994) designated Skerry's College, Cork as an institution to which the 1979 Act applied, and it thus also came within the remit of the NCEA. The National Council for Educational Awards Act 1979 (Designation of Institutions) (No. 3) Order 1994 (SI No. 334 of 1994) designated the Burren College of Art, St. Nicholas Montessori College Ireland and the American College, Dublin as institutions to which the 1979 Act applied, and they thus also came within the remit of the NCEA.

RECOGNITION OF QUALIFICATIONS

Pharmacy   The European Communities (European Economic Area) (Recognition of Qualifications in Pharmacy) Regulations 1994 (SI No. 438 of 1994) amended the European Communities (Recognition of Qualifications in Pharmacy) Regulations 1987 to 1991 (see the 1991 Review, 187) as well as s. 22A of, and Schedule 2 to, the Pharmacy Act 1875 (as previously amended by the Regulations of 1987 to 1991) to give effect to the recognition of qualifications of pharmacists from those EFTA States who are also members of the EEA (as to which see the 1993 Review, 307).

Veterinary medicine   Similarly, the European Communities (European Economic Area) (Recognition of Qualifications in Veterinary Medicine) Regulations 1994 (SI No. 268 of 1994) amended the European Communities (Recognition of Qualifications in Veterinary Medicine) Regulations 1980 to 1992 (see the 1992 Review, 312) as well as s. 31 of the Veterinary Surgeons Act 1931 to give effect to the recognition of qualifications of veterinary surgeon from those EFTA States who are also members of the EEA.

REGIONAL TECHNICAL COLLEGES

Governing body elections and gender balance   The Regional Technical Colleges (Amendment) Act 1994 performs the same role for regional Technical Colleges (RTCs) as the Dublin Institute of Technology (Amendment)

Act 1994 performed for the DIT and amends the Regional Technical Colleges Act 1992 (1992 Review, 307) in respect of matters relating to the appointment of governing bodies. The 1994 Act came into effect on December 2, 1994 on its signature by the President.

VOCATIONAL EDUCATION

The Vocational Education (Grants for Annual Schemes of Committees) Regulations 1994 (SI No. 464 of 1994), made under the Vocational Education Act 1930, provided for the additional, supplemental and special grants to Vocational Education Committees for 1994.

Electricity and Energy

MINERAL EXPLORATION

The Minerals Development (Amendment) Regulations 1994 (SI No. 319 of 1994) amended the Minerals Development Regulations 1979 (SI No. 340 of 1979) and the Minerals Development Regulations 1989 (SI No. 44 of 1989) by providing that applications for prospecting licences must be made in a revised form and be accompanied by an increased fee of £150 which is also the new increased fee for an ancillary rights licence or preservation of support order. The requirement for all applicants for prospecting licences to give a specific security to the Minister for Transport, Energy and Communications was abolished. The 1994 Regulations came into effect on November 1, 1994.

PETROLEUM

Whitegate offtake The Fuels (Petroleum Oils) (Amendment) Order 1994 (SI No.170 of 1994) amended the substantive provisions of the Fuels (Petroleum Oils) Order 1983, which requires petroleum fuel importers to purchase a proportion of their products from the State-owned Irish National Petroleum Corporation Ltd's refinery in Whitegate, Cork. The 1994 Order extended the scope of the 1983 Order by reducing the threshold at which the regime applies from 20 tonnes to 5 tonnes and also extended the product range to which the obligation to purchase applies. The 1994 Order came into effect on July 1, 1994. The Petroleum Oils (Regulation or Control of Acquisition, Supply, Distribution or Marketing) (Continuance) Order 1994 (SI No.423 of 1994) continued through to the end of 1995 the regime outlined in the 1983 Order.

Equity

Hilary Delany, Trinity College Law School

EQUITABLE MAXIMS

'Equity looks on that as done which ought to be done' Where a specifi-cally enforceable obligation exists, equity regards the parties as being in the position in which they would have been had the obligation been performed, and their legal rights and duties are assessed by reference to this position. The most frequently cited example of the operation of this maxim is that, in equity, a specifically enforceable contract for a lease is treated as being equivalent to a lease and the rights and duties of the parties are regarded as being the same as if the lease had actually been executed (see *Walsh v Lonsdale* (1882) 21 Ch D 9). Traditionally, a qualification to the operation of this maxim was recognised as set out in *Snell's Equity* (29th ed., 1990, Baker and Langan, p.40), namely that 'Equity treats a contract to do a thing as if the thing were already done, though only in favour of persons entitled to enforce the contract specifically and not in favour of volunteers', and this principle has been accepted recently in England by Scott J in *Davis v Richards and Wallington Ltd* [1990] 1 WLR 1511.

However, this requirement does not appear to have been enforced by Carroll J in *Shanahan v Redmond*, High Court (Carroll J) June 21, 1994. The deceased named his cousin as sole beneficiary of a trust, the assets of which comprised a life insurance policy. The parties fell out and the deceased attempted unsuccessfully to exercise a power of appointment over the trust funds in his own favour. Subsequently, he instructed the insurance company to cancel the policy and to replace it with a similar one under which he would be the sole beneficiary. Although this direction had not been carried out when the testator died, Carroll J applied the maxim that 'equity looks on that as done which ought to be done' and held that the existing policy should be treated as if it were a substitute policy in which the deceased was named as sole beneficiary. Thus it would appear that the maxim may benefit not merely persons entitled to enforce a contract specifically but also volunteers.

EQUITABLE REMEDIES

Interlocutory injunctions There were a number of judgments delivered during this year dealing with the grant of interlocutory injunctions and to a large extent, established principles were applied (see e.g. *Colmey v Pinewood Developments Ltd* [1995] 1 ILRM 331 and *Howard v Clare County Council*, High Court, Costello J, March 3, 1994). However, several points of interest may be noted. *An Post v Irish Permanent plc* [1995] 1 ILRM 336 concerned an application by the plaintiff for an interlocutory injunction to restrain alleged passing off in relation to the use of the term 'savings certificate' by the defendant to describe a financial savings product which it was issuing in competition with the plaintiff. Kinlen J granted an interlocutory injunction as he was satisfied that there was a serious question to be tried and that the balance of convenience favoured the granting of the order. In doing so he rejected the argument that the fact the matter was likely to be tried quickly was an important consideration, so it would appear that the fact that a trial is likely to take place within a relatively short space of time of the application for the interlocutory order is not one of the factors which should influence the exercise of the court's discretion. A further issue raised in this case was whether the court could take into account the wider question of public convenience in deciding whether to grant or refuse an interlocutory injunction. However, Kinlen J said that he would express no view on this matter at the interlocutory stage as it was one more properly to be determined at trial. (It should be noted that the case was settled prior to trial with the defendant giving an undertaking that it would not sell products bearing the name 'savings certificates'.)

Another case concerning the grant of an interlocutory injunction was *News Datacom Ltd v Lyons* [1994] 1 ILRM 450 which concerned an application to restrain an alleged breach of copyright in software and smart cards used to decode scrambled satellite television signals. Flood J commented that the mere fact that the conduct of one of the parties, in this case the defendant, might be questionable as a matter of ethics or morality was not a reason to grant relief in the absence of any other accepted grounds for making the order sought. Despite his apparent acceptance of the test in *Campus Oil*, namely, that a person seeking the grant of an interlocutory injunction must show that there is a fair question to be tried, Flood J stated that to raise a fair question to be tried in cases of alleged breach of copyright the plaintiff must tender some positive evidence 'which at minimum gives rise to an implication that copying has taken place and which rescues the court from the doldrums of unadulterated speculation though falling far short of an established probability'. It is arguable that such an approach bears some resemblance to the now discredited '*prima facie* test' and in the circumstances, Flood J refused to grant the interlocutory injunction sought. The decision is under appeal and it remains to be seen whether the Supreme Court will apply a more orthodox form of the *Campus Oil* test in deciding this question.

Mareva injunctions The fact that *Mareva* injunctions may be made on a worldwide basis has recently been confirmed by the High Court in *Deutsche Bank Atkiengesellchaft v Murtagh* [1995] 1 ILRM 381. The plaintiff bank, which had brought proceedings against the defendants seeking to recover monies which it claimed were due on foot of a guarantee, sought an order restraining the defendants from dealing with certain assets outside the State. While the extra- territorial Mareva injunction has been recognised in England since the landmark decision of the Court of Appeal in *Babanaft International Co. SA v Bassatne* [1990] Ch 13, the validity of such orders was still untested in this jurisdiction. Costello J stated that he was satisfied that 'the court has jurisdiction to restrain the dissipation of extra-territorial assets where such an order is warranted by the facts'. He said that it was well established in England that a *Mareva* injunction may extend to foreign assets and that he believed the Irish courts had similar powers to avoid frustration of subsequent orders. In his view the basis on which a Mareva injunction is granted is to ensure that a defendant does not take any steps which may have the result of frustrating orders which the court may subsequently make. Costello J also stated that the court has an ancillary power to grant a disclosure order requiring a defendant to swear an affidavit detailing the assets which he holds outside the jurisdiction, which may be of significance if the *Mareva* order is to be of any real practical value. [It should be noted that the *Mareva* injunction granted a month later by Murphy J in *Countyglen v Carway* [1995] 1 ILRM 481 — this case will be considered in the 1995 Annual Review — was confined to assets within the jurisdiction, but this was the extent of the order sought by the plaintiffs. His comment that a *Mareva* injunction should be restricted to assets within the jurisdiction of the court must be viewed as purely *obiter* and it is unlikely that such an approach would be followed if an appropriate case arose for an order of greater scope, given the unequivocal approval of Costello J to orders of an extra-territorial nature.]

Frustration A contract may be rendered impossible to perform by reason of frustration and the circumstances in which this may occur have recently been considered by the Supreme Court in *Neville & Sons Ltd v Guardian Builders Ltd* [1995] 1 ILRM 1. The plaintiff and defendant entered into an agreement whereby the plaintiff contracted to build houses on a site owned by the defendant. It was accepted that the only effective means of access to the site would be by the construction of a new roadway which involved the acquisition of a strip of land owned by the county council, although difficulties arose in acquiring this land. The plaintiff sought specific performance of the agreement and the defendant contended that by reason of the difficulties which had arisen in relation to access to the site, performance of the contract had been rendered impossible or possible only in circumstances so different from those contemplated that both parties were relieved from any further obligations. Murphy J accepted that performance of the contract had been frustrated by intervening circumstances and held that the plaintiff was not entitled to specific performance (see [1990] ILRM 601). However, this decision was reversed by the Supreme Court and in the course of his judgment Blayney J considered the circumstances in which frustration of a contract will take place. He quoted with approval from the judgment of Lord Simon in *National Carriers Ltd v Panalpina (Northern) Ltd* [1981] AC 675, 700 to the effect that when a supervening event occurs, without the fault of either party and for which the contract makes no adequate provision, which so significantly changes the nature of the outstanding contractual rights and obligations from what the parties could reasonably have contemplated at the time of its execution, it would be unjust to hold them to the terms of the contract in the new circumstances. Applying this principle, Blayney J concluded that what had transpired could not be termed a supervening event which significantly changed the nature of the defendant's obligations and while it made performance of the contract more onerous, he was satisfied that the defence of frustration should fail.

Rectification　It emerges from the decision of Murphy J in *Lac Minerals Ltd v Chevron Mineral Corporation of Ireland* [1995] 1 ILRM 161 that a claim for rectification cannot succeed where it is not made by either of the parties involved in the original agreement, but by a party who although undoubtedly affected by it was in no sense privy to the manner in which it was negotiated, or the circumstances in which the error occurred. The first and second named defendants had entered into a joint venture agreement to exploit mineral rights. The agreement gave a right to either party to transfer its interest to a third party provided that the other was given a right of pre-emption in respect of that interest. The plaintiff, who had entered into an agreement for the indirect acquisition of the first named defendant's interest, claimed that the time within which the right of pre-emption could be exercised was limited to a period of 45 days and that as this period had expired, the second named defendant could no longer exercise the right. It sought rectification of the joint venture agreement to provide for a period of 45 days on the basis that the period of 60 days which had been included in the agreement was recorded by mistake. Murphy J concluded that the case law in the area demonstrated that while an action for rectification does not require that parties to litigation should be privy to the same contract, 'they must be privy to or affected by the same mistake in such a way that it would be unconscionable for the defendant in such proceedings to seek to rely on the document which erroneously recorded or mistakenly implemented the true agreement,' and on this basis dismissed the plaintiff's claim.

Tracing in Equity The question of whether it is possible to trace into an overdrawn bank account has recently been considered in both England and Ireland. The view put forward by Hobhouse J in *Westdeutsche Landesbank v Islington London Borough Council* (1993) 91 LGR 323 was that 'the mere fact that a bank account or group of accounts may not be in credit does not mean that the right of a beneficiary to trace through the assets of a fiduciary has been lost'. However, the better view is that accepted by the Court of Appeal in *Bishopsgate Investment Management Ltd v Homan* [1994] 3 WLR 1270 that an equitable tracing remedy could not be pursued through an overdrawn and therefore non-existent fund. The same conclusion was reached by Murphy J in *PMPA v PMPS*, High Court (Murphy J) June 27, 1994 in which the plaintiff had made an *ultra vires* payment of £450,000 to the defendant which the latter had lodged in an overdrawn account. Murphy J was satisfied that the plaintiff could not pursue a tracing remedy as the monies had been dissipated and no longer existed as such, although he concluded that the defendant had had no right to these monies in the first instance and that the plaintiff was entitled to restitution. It would seem therefore that once the balance in an account falls below a certain level or becomes overdrawn, the capacity to trace is limited to the lowest intermediate balance and in the case of an overdrawn account, ceases altogether.

TRUSTS

Certainty of objects While the House of Lords took the opportunity to reformulate the test of certainty of objects for modern discretionary trusts in the landmark case of *McPhail v Doulton* [1971] AC 424, and held that the trust is valid if it can be said with certainty that any given individual is or is not a member of the class, there was good reason for supposing that in this jurisdiction, to ensure validity it was necessary that the whole class of potential beneficiaries could be ascertained (see *Re Parker* [1966] IR 308, 318 *per* Budd J). These alternative approaches have recently been considered, albeit in an *obiter* context, by Murphy J in *O'Byrne v Davoren* [1994] 3 IR 373. The testatrix's will provided that the residue of her estate should be held on trust for the post primary education of such members of a class consisting of the children, grandchildren and direct descendants of named persons whom the trustees in their discretion should decide would be most likely to benefit therefrom. Murphy J was satisfied that the gift was sufficiently certain but held that it was void because it infringed the rule against perpetuities and the rule against perpetual trusts. Nevertheless, it is interesting to compare the view which he expressed on the question of certainty with those put forward by the House of Lords in *McPhail v Doulton*. Murphy J commented that not only was the judgment of Budd J in *Re Parker* [1966] IR 308 a precedent of greater authority than that of the House of Lords but he also preferred the reasoning in the former case, namely that an imperative trust for the division of income between such members of a class as the trustees may select is invalid unless the whole class of potential beneficiaries can be ascertained. Murphy J also said that he approved Budd J's view to the effect that difficulties in interpretation should not be sufficient to render a gift void for uncertainty; as Budd J had said 'to be void for this reason it must be utterly impossible to put a meaning on it'. So Murphy J concluded that the court should endeavour to resolve ambiguities and uncertainties where this was compatible with the expressed or implied wishes of the testator and concluded that this view would have been of decisive importance in upholding the validity of the residuary bequest if the class of relatives had been confined to those living at the date of the testatrix's death.

It is unlikely that as a result of the comments of Murphy J the courts in this jurisdiction will feel compelled to follow the *Parker* approach irrespective of the nature of the discretionary trust involved. From a practical perspective, the requirement of the need for equal division which seems to lie behind *Parker* is far from suitable in the case of many modern discretionary trusts and it is likely that the court would also give some consideration to the question of how it would exercise its discretion should the trustees fail to do so. Where the testator's intentions are likely to be fulfilled by equal division amongst all the potential beneficiaries, clearly the certainty requirement laid down in *Parker* is to be preferred. However, as the judgment of Lord Wilberforce in *McPhail* made clear, this is no longer the case in relation to many modern discretionary trusts which are designed to benefit a much wider class of beneficiary and it is difficult to fault the conclusion reached in the latter case on the basis of the nature of the trust involved. Therefore, the observations of Murphy J in *O'Byrne v Davoren* should be read with a certain degree of caution and the courts should be encouraged to consider the nature of the discretionary trust at issue before laying down any rigid test in relation to certainty of objects.

Resulting trusts   Often a joint deposit account is opened in a manner which allows the transferor or depositor alone to retain dominion over the money in the account during his lifetime but which shows the intention that the balance should go to the other party should he survive him. Where such an arrangement is put in place the question arises whether the money which remains in the account on the depositor's death should be subject to a resulting trust in favour of his estate or whether it can be paid over to the other party. Traditionally the approach adopted in this jurisdiction, as laid down by the Supreme Court in *Owens v Greene* [1932] IR 225 was that in these circumstances a resulting trust arose in favour of the transferor's estate. While O'Hanlon J arrived at the same conclusion in *Lynch v Burke* [1990] 1 IR 1, there were definite signs in his judgment that he was unhappy with the reasoning in the earlier Supreme Court decision. As he stated (at p. 13):

> I consider that in the present case I am bound to follow and apply [*Owens v Greene*] but having regard to the fact that it is a decision which appears to conflict with the interpretation of this branch of the law in so many other common law jurisdictions it might well be a case where the Supreme Court would be disposed to review again the correctness of that decision, if a suitable opportunity arose for so doing.

This statement was quoted with approval by Morris J in *AIB Finance Ltd v Sligo County Council* [1995] 1 ILRM 81 although once again the result in that case was in line with that reached in *Owens v Greene*. The deceased, a priest who wished to benefit his home town in Co. Sligo, had lodged a sum of money in a bank account in the joint names of himself and Sligo County Council with the intention that the money should be used to carry out a specific project under an urban renewal scheme. The priest died and the question arose whether his executor or the county council was entitled to the monies in the account. Although the mandate executed in favour of the bank contained a provision that these monies should be paid to the county council as survivor on the priest's death, there was evidence that the deceased had intended to and had in fact retained control over these funds during his lifetime. Morris J concluded that there was at most an incomplete gift and that the relationship of trustee and beneficiary had not existed as between the deceased and the county council. Therefore he found that a resulting trust in favour of the deceased's executor arose.

While in the circumstances it was not necessary for Morris J to decide whether the reasoning in *Owens* was correct as there was insufficient evidence to rebut the presumption of a resulting trust in favour of the deceased's estate, the fact that he saw fit to expressly approve of O'Hanlon J's *dicta* in *Lynch* set out above was of interest and this issue has finally been laid to rest by the Supreme Court in its judgment in *Lynch v Burke* [1996] 1 ILRM 81. (This decision will be examined in the 1995 Annual Review).

European Community and European Union Law

ACCESSION OF NEW MEMBERS

The European Communities (Amendment) Act 1994 enabled the State to ratify the Accession Treaty under which Austria, Finland and Sweden acceded to membership of the European Union. The 1994 Act achieved this by including that Accession Treaty in s. 2 of the European Communities Act 1972. In keeping with previous practice, the 1994 Act amended s. 2 of the 1972 Act by means of providing a consolidated list) of the Treaties and other documents (including the various Accession Treaties) which are a part of Irish domestic law by virtue of Community membership. The 1994 Act came into effect on 1 January 1995 in accordance with the timetable for the three States to accede to Union membership: European Communities (Amendment) Act 1994 (Commencement) Order 1994 (SI No. 455 of 1994).

EUROPEAN PARLIAMENT ELECTIONS

The European Parliament Elections (Voting and Candidature) Regulations 1994 (SI No. 14 of 1994) were referred to in the 1993 Review. The European Parliament Elections (Forms) Regulations 1994 (SI No. 75 of 1994) specified the forms to be used at the European Parliament elections of 1994.

LEGISLATIVE IMPLEMENTATION OF EC REQUIREMENTS IN IRISH LAW

The following Regulations and Orders made in 1993 pursuant to the provisions of s. 3 of the European Communities Act 1972, or other statutory powers, involve the implementation of Community obligations.

Air Pollution Act 1987 (Sulphur Content of Gas Oil) Regulations 1994: see the Safety and Health chapter, 396, below.
District Court (Service Abroad of Documents in Civil or Commercial Matters) Rules 1994: see the Practice and Procedure chapter, 385, below.
Double Taxation Relief (Taxes on Income) (Adjustment of Profits of Associated Enterprises) (European Community) Order 1994.

Environmental Protection Agency Act 1992 (Urban Waste Water Treatment) Regulations 1994: see the Safety and Health chapter, 399, below.

European Communities (Active Implantable Medical Devices) Regulations 1994: see the Safety and Health chapter, 403, below.

European Communities (Additives in Feedingstuffs) (Amendment) Regulations 1994: see the Agriculture chapter, 20, above.

European Communities (Amendment) Act 1993 (section 2) (Commencement) Order 1994: see the 1993 Review, 309.

European Communities (Amendment) Act 1993 (section 6(1)) Order 1994: see the 1993 Review, 310.

European Communities (Amendment) Act 1994 (Commencement) Order 1994: see 248, above.

European Communities (Amendment of Cruelty to Animals Act 1876) Regulations 1994: see the Agriculture chapter, 13, above.

European Communities (Animal Remedies and Medicated Feedingstuffs) Regulations 1994: see the Agriculture chapter, 14, above.

European Communities (Application of Open Network Provision to Leased Lines) Regulations 1994: see the Communications chapter, 55, above.

European Communities (Asbestos Waste) Regulations 1994: see the Safety and Health chapter, 396, below.

European Communities (Authorization, Placing on the Market, Use and Control of Plant Protection Products) Regulations 1994 see the Agriculture chapter, 19, above.

European Communities (Avian Influenza) Regulations 1994: see the Agriculture chapter, 12, above.

European Communities (Award of Public Supply Contracts) (Amendment) Regulations 1994: see the Commercial Law chapter, 45, above.

European Communities (Award of Public Works Contracts) (Amendment) Regulations 1994: see the Commercial Law chapter, 45, above.

European Communities (Batteries and Accumulators) Regulations 1994: see the Safety and Health chapter, 395, below.

European Communities (Beef Carcass Classification) Regulations 1994: see the Agriculture chapter, 20, above.

European Communities (Breeding Pig Herd-Book and Register) Regulations 1994: see the Agriculture chapter, 13, above.

European Communities (Cereal Seed) (Amendment) Regulations 1994: see the Agriculture chapter, 18, above.

European Communities (Classification, Packaging, Labelling and Notification of Dangerous Substances) Regulations 1994: see the Safety and Health chapter, 392, below.

European Communities (Classification, Packaging and Labelling of Pesticides) Regulations 1994: see the Safety and Health chapter, 394, below.

European Communities (Combined Transport of Dangerous Goods) Regulations 1994: see the Transport chapter, 468, below.

European Communities (Commercial Agents) Regulations 1994: see the Commercial Law chapter, 25, above.

European Communities (Common Agricultural Policy) Regulations 1994: see the Agriculture chapter, 14, above.

European Communities (Control of Infectious Diseases in Animals) Regulations 1994: see the Agriculture chapter, 12, above.

European Communities (Conservation of Wild Birds) (Amendment) Regulations 1994: see the Agriculture chapter, 22, above.

European Communities (Conservation of Wild Birds) (Amendment) (No. 2) Regulations 1994: see the Agriculture chapter, 22, above.

European Communities (Construction Products) (Amendment) Regulations 1994: see the Safety and Health chapter, 402, below.

European Communities (Co-ordinated Introduction of Public Pan-European Cellular Digital Land-based Mobile Communications-GSM) Regulations 1994: see the Communications chapter, 52, above.

European Communities (Dangerous Substances and Preparations) (Marketing and Use) Regulations 1994: see the Safety and Health chapter, 393, below.

European Communities (Digital European Cordless Telecommunication-DECT) Regulations 1994 see the Communications chapter, 53, above.

European Communities (Disposal, Processing and Placing on the Market of Animal By-Products) Regulations 1994: see the Agriculture chapter, 20, above.

European Communities (Environmental Impact Assessment) (Amendment) Regulations 1994: see the Safety and Health chapter, 397, below.

European Communities (European Economic Area) (Recognition of Qualifications in Pharmacy) Regulations 1994: see the Education chapter, 238, above.

European Communities (European Economic Area) (Recognition of Qualifications in Veterinary Medicine) Regulations 1994 see the Education chapter, 238, above.

European Communities (Extraction Solvents in Foodstuffs) (Revocation) Regulations 1994 see the Safety and Health chapter, 400, below.

European Communities (Feedingstuffs) (Methods of Analysis) (Amendment) Regulations 1994: see the Agriculture chapter, 21, above.

European Communities (Feedingstuffs) (Tolerances of Undesirable Substances and Products) (Amendment) Regulations 1994: see the Agriculture chapter, 20, above.

European Communities (Infant Formulae) Regulations 1994: see the Safety and Health chapter, 401, below.

European Communities (International Carriage of Goods by Road) Regulations 1994 see the Transport chapter, 470, below.

European Communities (Introduction of Organisms Harmful to Plants or Plant Products) (Prohibition) (Amendment) Regulations 1994: see the Agriculture chapter, 18, above.

European Communities (Introduction of Organisms Harmful to Plants or Plant Products) (Prohibition) (Amendment) (No. 2) Regulations 1994: see the Agriculture chapter, 18, above.

European Communities (Importation of Animals and Animal Products from Third Countries) Regulations 1994: see the Agriculture chapter, 21, above.

European Communities (Importation of Dogs and Cats) Regulations 1994: see the Agriculture chapter, 21, above.

European Communities (Labelling, Presentation and Advertising of Foodstuffs) (Amendment) Regulations 1994: see the Safety and Health chapter, 401, below.

European Communities (Life Assurance) Framework Regulations 1994: see the Commercial Law chapter, 40, above.

European Communities (Low Voltage Electrical Equipment) (Amendment) Regulations 1994: see the Safety and Health chapter, 402, below.

European Communities (Machinery) Regulations 1994: see the Safety and Health chapter, 403, below.

European Communities (Marketing of Feedingstuffs) (Amendment) Regulations 1994: see the Agriculture chapter, 21, above.

European Communities (Marketing of Fertilisers) Regulations 1994: see the Agriculture chapter, 18, above.

European Communities (Marketing of Fruit Plant Propagating Material and Fruit Plants intended for Fruit Production) Regulations 1994: see the Agriculture chapter, 19, above.

European Communities (Marketing of Ornamental Plant Propagating Material and Ornamental Plants) Regulations 1994: see the Agriculture chapter, 19, above.

European Communities (Marketing of Ornamental Plant Propagating Material and Ornamental Plants) (Amendment) Regulations 1994: see the Agriculture chapter, 19, above.

European Communities (Marketing of Vegetable Propagating and Planting Material, other than Seed) Regulations 1994: see the Agriculture chapter, 18, above.

European Communities (Materials and Articles intended to come into Contact with Foodstuffs) (Amendment) Regulations 1994: see the Safety and Health chapter, 401, below.

European Communities (Materials and Articles intended to come into contact with Foodstuffs) (Amendment) (No. 2) Regulations 1994: see the Safety and Health chapter, 401, below.

European Communities (Milk Quota) Regulations 1994: see the Agriculture chapter, 14, above.

European Communities (Minced Meat) Regulations 1994: see the Agriculture chapter, 21, above.

European Communities (Mechanically Propelled Vehicle Emission Control) Regulations 1994: see the Transport chapter, 469, below.

European Communities (Medical Devices) Regulations 1994: see the Safety and Health chapter, 403, below.

European Communities (Motor Vehicles Type Approval) Regulations 1994: see the Transport chapter, 469, below.

European Communities (Newcastle Disease) Regulations 1994: see the Agriculture chapter, 12, above.

European Communities (Non-automatic Weighing Instruments) (Amendment) Regulations 1994: see the Safety and Health chapter, 403-4, below.

European Communities (Non-life Insurance) Framework Regulations 1994: see the Commercial Law chapter, 39, above.

European Communities (Personal Protective Equipment) (Amendment) Regulations 1994: see the Safety and Health chapter, 404, below.

European Communities (Personal Protective Equipment) (CE Marking) Regulations 1994: see the Safety and Health chapter, 404, below.

European Communities (Pesticide Residues) (Fruit and Vegetables) (Amendment) Regulations 1994: see the Agriculture chapter, 18, above.

European Communities (Pesticide Residues) (Products of Plant Origin, including Fruit and Vegetables) Regulations 1994: see the Agriculture chapter, 18, above.

European Communities (Pig Carcass (Grading)) (Amendment) Regulations 1994: see the Agriculture chapter, 21, above.

European Communities (Protection of Outside Workers from Ionising Radiation) Regulations 1994: see the Safety and Health chapter, 406, below.

European Communities (Protein Feedingstuffs) (Amendment) Regulations 1994: see the Agriculture chapter, 20, above.

European Communities (Pure-Bred Sheep and Coat Flock-Book) Regulations 1994: see the Agriculture chapter, 13, above.

European Communities (Registration of Pedigree Animals) Regulations 1994: see the Agriculture chapter, 13, above.

European Communities (Retirement of Farmers) Regulations 1994: see the Agriculture chapter, 20, above.

European Communities (Return of Cultural Objects) Regulations 1994: see the Arts and Culture chapter, 24, above.

European Communities (Review Procedures for the Award of Public Supply, Public Works and Public Services Contracts) Regulations 1994: see the Commercial Law chapter, 44, above.

European Communities (Review Procedures for the Award of Public Supply, Public Works and Public Services Contracts) (No. 2) Regulations 1994: see the Commercial Law chapter, 44, above.

European Communities (Safety of Toys) (Amendment) Regulations 1994: see the Safety and Health chapter, 404, below.

European Communities (Seed of Fodder Plants) (Amendment) Regulations 1994: see the Agriculture chapter, 18, above.

European Communities (Seed Potatoes) (Amendment) Regulations 1994: see the Agriculture chapter, 19, above.

European Communities (Single-Member Private Limited Companies) (Forms) Regulations 1994: see the Company Law chapter, 70, above.

European Communities (Single-Member Private Limited Companies) Regulations 1994 see the Company Law chapter, 70, above.

European Communities (Supervision and Control of Certain Shipments of Radioactive Waste) Regulations 1994: see the Safety and Health chapter, 407, below.

European Communities (Telecommunications Services) (Appeals) Regulations 1994: see the Communications chapter, 52, above.

European Communities (Trade in Animals and Animal Products) Regulations 1994: see the Agriculture chapter, 21, above.

European Communities (Trade in Bovine Breeding Animals, their Semen, Ova and Embryos) (Amendment) Regulations 1994: see the Agriculture chapter, 22, above.

European Communities (Trade in Bovine Breeding Animals, their Semen, Ova and Embryos) Regulations 1994: see the Agriculture chapter, 22, above.

European Communities (Transfrontier Shipment Waste) Regulations 1994: see the Safety and Health chapter, 399, below.

European Parliament Elections (Forms) Regulations 1994: see 248, above.

European Parliament Elections (Voting and Candidature) Regulations 1994: see above, 248.

Food Standards (Fruit Juices and Fruit Nectars) (European Communities) (Amendment) Regulations 1994: see the Safety and Health chapter, 401, below.

Genetically Modified Organisms Regulations 1994: see the Safety and Health chapter, 397, below.

Health (Emulsifiers, Stabilisers, Thickeners and Gelling Agents in Food) Regulations 1994: see the Safety and Health chapter, 400, below.

Local Government (Water Pollution) Act 1977 and 1990 (Control of Carbon Tetrachloride, DDT and Pentachlorophenol Discharges) Regulations 1994: see the Safety and Health chapter, 399, below.

Local Government (Water Pollution) Acts 1977 and 1990 (Control of EDC, TRI, PER and TCB Discharges) Regulations 1994: see the Safety and Health chapter, 399, below.

Medical Preparations (Labelling and Package leaflets) (Amendment) Regulations 1994: see the Health Services chapter, 287, below.

Medical Preparations (Licensing, Advertisement and Sale) (Amendment) Regulations 1994: see the Health Services chapter, 287, below.

Quality of Bathing Waters (Amendment) Regulations 1994: see the Safety and Health chapter, 399, below.

Quality of Shellfish Waters Regulations 1994 see the Safety and Health chapter, 400, below.

Safety, Health and Welfare at Work (Biological Agents) Regulations 1994: see the Safety and Health chapter, 404, below.

Safety, Health and Welfare at Work (Chemical Agents) Regulations 1994 : see the Safety and Health chapter, 405, below.

Safety, Health and Welfare at Work (Pregnant Employees Etc.) Regulations 1994: see the Safety and Health chapter, 406, below.

Sea Fisheries (International Waters) (Driftnet) Order 1994: see the Fisheries chapter, 278, below.

Social Welfare (Health and Safety Benefit) Regulations 1994: see the Social

Welfare chapter, 414, below.

Tobacco Products (Control of Advertising, Sponsorship and Sales Promotion) (Amendment) Regulations 1994 see the Safety and Health chapter, 407, below.

Winter Time Order 1994 : see the Commercial Law chapter, 45, above.

In addition, the following Acts, or parts thereof, also involved the implementation of Community obligations:

European Community (Amendment) Act 1994;

Finance Act 1994;

Fisheries (Amendment) Act 1994;

Health Insurance Act 1994;

Maternity Protection Act 1994;

Milk (Regulation of Supply) Act 1994;

Terms of Employment (Information) Act 1994.

Family Law

ADOPTION

Parental failure   In the 1988 Review, 246-51, we analysed the provisions of the Adoption Act 1988, which introduced the principle of compulsory adoption. The Supreme Court, on an Article 26 Reference, upheld the constitutional validity of the legislation: [1989] ILRM 266; [1989] IR 656. In *In re J.C. and C.C. Minors; Mid Western Health Board v An Bord Uchtála*, High Court, July 5, 1994, (*ex tempore*), Budd J held that the necessary proofs required under s. 3(1) of the Adoption Act 1988 had been established and accordingly he granted to the prospective adoptive parents custody of two minors pending the making of an adoption order by An Bord Uchtála. The short judgment does not contain a detailed recitation of the facts but the overall picture emerges nonetheless. The parents had separated in 1981. The father was faced with 'the impossible situation' of having to look after five children ranging in age from six to one. On the advice of the local curate he made arrangements for two of the children to be looked after by a family and for the other three children to be looked after in a convent.

The two minors whose prospective adoption was in issue were placed with one family for a time before being placed with the prospective adopters, with whom they had been residing for many years at the time of the application to the court. They were aged seventeen and sixteen at this time. There was no doubt about the quality of the care that they had received. The prospective adopters were 'obviously two decent and honourable people' whose lives were inextricably intertwined with those of the two minors whom they were rearing as long-term foster children. The minors were 'obviously two well brought up, healthy and good-looking youngsters'.

What is not so clear is the question of the parental failure required by s. 3(1) as a pre-condition of adoption under the 1988 Act. It will be recalled that it must be established that the parents have failed in their duty to the child whose prospective adoption is in question and that it is likely that the failure will continue until the child reaches the age of eighteen. In the instant case Budd J's gentle and discreet discussion of this aspect of the case makes it difficult to identify parental failure of the intensity that the Act envisages. He mentioned the lack of contact between the parents and the children during the period the children were with the prospective adopters. In the case of the father, where the gap was seven years, Budd J noted that 'for a number of very understandable reasons' the father had not made contact.

The father was not opposing the adoption; on the contrary he said to the court that he was aware of the strong bond between his children and the prospective adopters, that he knew the children wanted to be adopted and that adoption would give them security. Budd J observed that the father's support for the adoption was '[t]he happiest feature' of the case.

The tenor of the judgment is one that favours adoption with the consent of a married parent where adoption offers advantages for the child. This is evident from a number of passages. Thus, for example, Budd J observed:

> As our Constitution puts emphasis on the family, I think it is entirely natural that a change in the law has been brought about after very considerable effort by the then Attorney General, among others, because there were perhaps eight hundred or more children of lawful marriages in institutions in this country, children who were being deprived of the chance of having the loving relationships which a family unit can provide.

Budd J went on to observe that it seemed to him that there were:

> obvious advantages in adoption: the fact that the two minors do not have to go into explanations when they are going for job interviews or going to third level institutions as to why they have one name on their birth certificates and are known by another name. There is also the advantage that they are obviously treated as the son and daughter of the household in which they are living and, in the normal way, one would hope that some of this world's goods may pass to them, but this is not in any way a thought on the part of the two minors. I think that they regard themselves as owing love and affection to [the prospective adopters] for bringing them up in a loving home, and it is quite clear that they both desire to be adopted and to treat [the prospective adopters] as their parents.

Budd J noted that, because of the wording of the Constitution, the 1988 Act had been drafted with considerable care and he was 'therefore obliged to make certain findings to enable the Adoption Board to process the application.' Having heard what the advantages of adoption were to the two minors and taking into account the fact that they wished to be adopted and that adoption would have to take place before their eighteenth birthdays, it seemed to him that he 'should grasp the nettle at this stage and make findings so that the adoption of both minors may be processed'.

Budd J had great sympathy for both parents and could readily understand the hurt and distress which the father must have felt on visiting the children's foster home. It 'must have been a very great wrench from his point of view' to have to ask for assistance in their upbringing. Budd J thought that 'it required considerable self-sacrifice on his part to do what he did'; he as 'sure that he acted out of knowing what was in the best interests of his children.' In the ensuing years, the father had felt that he could become distressed if he visited the children and that his distress would communicate itself to them and would cause a feeling of insecurity on the part of the foster parents and the children. In this respect also Budd J thought that the father had acted with considerable self-sacrifice.

Nonetheless Budd J found that the requirements of s. 3 had been complied with. The only element of parental failure that he mentioned was the failure to keep in contact with the children, which, in the case of the father, Budd J attributed to 'a number of very understandable reasons'.

It is hard to interpret this decision otherwise than as one based on a belief in the desirability of adoption in the circumstances, untroubled by any serious concern for proof of previous parental failure that was likely to continue until the children reached the age of eighteen. There are arguments in favour of adoption of children, whether born within or outside marriage, once their parents freely consent. There are arguments against such a broad swathe of consensual adoption. It is worth recalling that legislation authorising adoption in any circumstances was for long opposed by members of the Catholic hierarchy precisely on the basis that it could encourage parents to abandon their children.

The 1988 Act speaks only in terms of authorising adoption on the basis of parental failure, not parental consent. It is pressing the policy of that legislation too far to interpret it as authorising consensual adoption in the circumstances of the instant case. The self-sacrifice and altruism of the father are precisely the qualities that refute any hypothesis of parental failure. One could imagine cases where a parental disposition to have the children adopted could be evidence of a neglectful disposition, capable of being characterised as amounting to parental failure but that seems far from the factual circumstances of the instant case.

Adoption eligibility and the injunctive power   Important issues of principle and policy arose in *P.F. and V.F. v An Bord Uchtála, L.G. and I.C.* [1994] 3 IR 500. Under present law children are in principle eligible for adoption, regardless of the marital status of their parents, under the provisions of the Adoption Act 1988 (provided, of course, the rigorous conditions prescribed by their Act are fulfilled). Otherwise eligibility to be adopted is restricted to orphans, children formerly designated as 'illegitimate' by the law and children who have been legitimated by the subsequent marriage of their parents but whose birth has not been re-registered under the Legitimacy Act 1931.

P.F. involved injunctive proceedings relating to an eleven-year-old girl, born outside marriage, who had not seen her natural parents for over ten years. She had been all that time in the custody of the applicants, whom Costello J described as 'an admirable couple'. Proceedings were taken under s. 3 of the Adoption Act 1974 to dispense with the mother's consent for the adoption. Costello J was quite satisfied that it was in the best interests of the child to make the necessary order. An obstacle loomed forth, however. The girl's parents sought to marry and to re-register her birth. The effect of doing so would have been to render the child ineligible for adoption (save possibly under the 1988 Act, though it is entirely speculative whether a court would have held that they were guilty of parental 'failure' which was likely to continue until the child reached full age).

Costello J originally made an order restraining the marriage and re-registration of birth until the instant hearing. On appeal to the Supreme Court by the parents, who undertook that they would not seek an order for custody of the child, the Supreme Court reversed Costello J's order. The parents in the meantime married but did not re-register their daughter's birth. Costello J, considering himself free to make another interlocutory order, granted a new injunction restraining the parents from re-registering the birth.

Costello J did not dwell on the circumstances that had led to the child's separation from her parents; he observed that the evidence of a psychiatrist made it 'abundantly clear that it would be most disadvantageous to the child for an adoption order not to be made.' He considered it his statutory and constitutional duty, in the best interests of the child, to make the order sought.

The parents had again given an undertaking not to seek custody of their daughter. Costello J was quite satisfied from the order made in the Supreme Court that 'no Court would allow custody or visits unless there was very clear and strong psychiatric evidence to justify it'. He was equally satisfied that it was in the interest of the child that an adoption order be made rather than that she merely remain in the custody of the applicants.

Costello J concluded that he had authority to enjoin the parents from applying to re-register the birth and to order the registrar not to register it. He observed:

> I would only do so, of course, if I thought that such an order was in the best interests of the child. The situation seems to me to be this. If the birth is re-registered then I cannot authorise the adoption. However, as I am satisfied that adoption is in the best interest of the child, I think that I should grant the injunction pursuant to the general duty which I have in relation to the child's welfare.

Two questions arise particularly from the case. The first is whether a court has a power to injunct a party or parties from marrying. *Pace* Kingsmill Moore J in *Donovan v Minister for Justice* (1951) 85 ILTR 134, the constitutional right to marry is surely not capable of limitation save for very serious reasons. It is tempting to formulate the basis of such limitation in constitutional terms. Thus, for example, most of the grounds for nullity of marriage, such as nonage, prior subsisting marriage and mental incapacity, could relatively easily be justified in terms of the constitutional rights of one or both of the parties (or of the spouse of a bigamous party) or in terms of protecting the Family under Article 41.

Does the range of necessary or permissible limitation on the right to marry go so far as to include cases where the welfare of a child would be damaged as a result of the marriage of his or her parents? That simple question surely does not admit of a simple answer. It must depend, in part at least, on the gravity and likelihood of the potential damage to the child. It has not previously been widely suggested that a court could injunct the mother of a child born outside marriage from marrying an undesirable suitor (in a case where no issue relating to the child's eligibility for adoption arises) merely because the court forms the view that the child's welfare will not best be served by the marriage. If the man were proven to be a paedophile, for example, the court would perhaps seriously contemplate doing so, but each case would need to be regarded on its special facts. The right to marry, no less than the right to liberty, should not be compromised by mere apprehensions about its possible future abuse.

The concept of a child's welfare is extremely broad. At one extreme, it is clear that a child's welfare may be *seriously damaged* in certain contexts. Where a proposed course of action is likely to be damaging to a child, the court should understandably be disposed to prevent it. At the other extreme, the issue of the child's welfare can be discussed in the context of whether a particular course of action is likely to be *the very best of several beneficial options*. For example, in the educational context, of several excellent schools one in particular may be considered the best from the standpoint of the child's welfare. If a mother of a child born outside marriage is contemplating marrying a particular person and the likely effect, financially, of her doing so is that the child will be educated in the second-best rather than the best school in the country, no court will injunct the marriage on the basis that it is not in the child's best interests.

The second question arising from the instant case relates to the policy underlying the rule that a child born outside marriage whose parents have subsequently married but whose birth has not been re-registered should be eligible for adoption on account of that failure to re-register. There is nothing hugely important about the bureaucratic act of re-registration: why should it have such a crucial effect?

Perhaps the Oireachtas took the view that a child formally designated as 'illegitimate' (prior to the Status of Children Act 1987) should be considered still eligible for adoption, in spite of the marriage of his or her parents, because the Oireachtas regarded the effects of legitimation *per subseqens matrimonium* to be weaker, constitutionally-speaking, than the courts later held to be the case. The parents' decision to re-register the child might have been considered the appropriate indication of their intent to integrate the child fully into their legal relationship. This perception seems terribly dated. Perhaps the Oireachtas considered it desirable that the mother should be entitled to preserve her right to have the child adopted even after she had married. Marriage would not in every case give her the economic security to rear her child.

It can be argued that the policy rationale for retaining eligibility for adoption until re-registration of the child's birth is so incoherent that there is no fundamental objection in public policy to the result achieved by Costello J. The means will remain a matter for debate.

FAMILY SUPPORT OBLIGATIONS

In *C.M. v J.M.*, High Court, June 3, 1994 (Circuit Appeal), the defendant sought to be relieved of liability for over £4,000 maintenance arrears. He had agreed that the plaintiff, his wife, should be paid £50,000 out of the proceeds of sale of the family home on the basis of a valuation of the house at £120,000 when it was later sold for £106,500. He contended that, on account of the default of his solicitor and of the plaintiff in the purchase of the family home some years previously, nearly £4,000 stamp duty, unknown to him, was due and unpaid until after he had made the agreement to pay the plaintiff £50,000. Finally, the delay in selling the house for nearly three years had added an extra £13,500 on the mortgage. The defendant argued that each of these three sums should be shared between the plaintiff and the defendant.

Lynch J rejected this contention. It was 'manifest', he said, that the plaintiff was in no way responsible for the stamp duty problem. The plaintiff had not been dilatory in efforts to effect a sale of the family home at an economic price as early as possible. The delay had been 'due to market conditions and difficulties generally in the property and financial markets'.

The form of settlement that the parties had made guaranteed that the plaintiff was paid £50,000 out of the proceeds and 'left to the defendant the hazards of the property market.' In these circumstances the defendant could benefit in boom times but in fact had lost out in slump times. In the absence of any default on the plaintiff's part, there was no basis for reducing her right to the £50,000, whether by reducing the arrears of maintenance by setting off some of the shortfall in relation to the family home or otherwise.

In the section on Judicial Separation, later in the Chapter, (below, 264), we note Costello J's decision in *K.D. v E.D.*, High Court, December 1, 1994, relating to the quantum of an order for maintenance following a decree of judicial separation.

Lurking under the surface of this case is the troublesome question of the relationship between spousal autonomy and the entitlement to obtain judicial relief, inconsistent with what one has agreed by contract. The Family Law (Maintenance of Spouses and Children) Act 1976 favoured the principle of paternalism over spousal autonomy. Thus a wife who has defined her maintenance entitlements in a contract with her husband, by way of separation agreement, for example, is always free to resort to the court seeking a maintenance order under s. 5 of the Act, where her husband has failed to provide her with 'proper' maintenance. The fact, and terms, of the maintenance agreement will naturally be taken into account by the court when deciding whether to make a maintenance order in favour of the wife and, if so, its amount, but the existence of the maintenance agreement cannot, of itself, block the wife's eligibility to apply for the maintenance order and the court's obligation to consider whether it should grant one. S. 28 of the 1976 Act renders void any provision in a maintenance agreement purporting to exclude a spouse's eligibility to seek from the court a maintenance order. Cf. *J.H. v R.H.*, High Court, July 27, 1995, *F. v F.*, Supreme Court, November 30, 1995.

The courts have interpreted the 1976 Act, wrongly, as protecting wives but not husbands. Thus a husband who, having undertaken by way of maintenance agreement to support his wife to a certain level, falls on hard times without any fault on his part – by suddenly being made redundant, for example – is not permitted to obtain a court order for maintenance against his wife under s. 5. There is of course something curiously circular about one spouse obtaining by court order money from the other that amounts in effect to a judicially-decreed set-off, but family relationships often generate legal curiosities: witness the spouses in *B. v B.*, High Court, January 24, 1995 who apparently managed to marry each other *twice*, lawfully, without having divorced in the meantime. The 1976 legislation self-consciously broke with gender discrimination of the previous law of maintenance: see Binchy (1976) 25 Int & Comp LQ 901, at 901-5. It is formulated exclusively in gender neutral terms. It clearly embraced the policy that husbands as well as wives should be entitled to apply for maintenance under s. 5. No doubt the inspiration for s. 28 was probably exclusively based on a concern that some wives were at risk of being coerced by their husbands into signing away their legal right to apply to the court for maintenance but, even if this is so, that is not a reason why husbands, whose wives' access to the courts is protected by s. 28, should themselves be *denied* similar access to the courts. A court hearing an application, by husband or wife, under s. 5 is not obliged to grant a maintenance order in favour of the applicant. All the concerns relating to an imbalance of economic power between husbands and wives, generally or in particular cases, may freely affect the court's deliberations in responding to the application.

JUDICIAL SEPARATION

Grounds In *F. v F.* [1994] 2 ILRM 401 Murphy J rejected a challenged to the constitutional validity of certain provisions of the Judicial Separation and Family Law Reform Act 1989 relating to the grounds for a decree of judicial separation and the ancillary orders that may be made on or after granting a decree. The Supreme Court affirmed: [1995] 2 ILRM 321. We shall examine this important decision in detail in the 1995 Review.

In *J.D. v P.D.*, High Court, August 9, 1994. Lynch J granted a decree of judicial separation on the basis of ground (f), that a normal marital relationship had not existed between the parties for at least a year preceding the date of issue of the Special Summons, on November 26, 1993. The respondent had left the family home on December 31, 1992, but Lynch J was satisfied that a normal marital relationship had not existed between the parties 'for some time before that'. There is no suggestion in the judgment that the absence of such a normal marital relationship had existed for a period of at least a year *before the respondent left the home*. The effect of the decision is that one year's separation, certainly if preceded by the absence of a normal marital relationship for some time when the parties were living together, and perhaps even if not, will be a good basis for a decree under ground (f).

In this case the respondent did not contest the granting of the decree. In principle, that should not have any effect on the outcome of a ground (f) application, in contrast to grounds (d) and (e), where it is crucial. Ground (d) authorises the court to grant a decree on the basis of one year's separation where the respondent does not object to the granting of a decree and ground (e) delays the granting of a decree, where the respondent does not consent, to *three* years.

Nothing in *J.D. v P.D.* suggests that the entitlement was conditioned on the fact that it was the respondent who had left the home. There is no finding of desertion (or of constructive desertion); in harmony with the no-fault philosophy of ground (f), Lynch J was silent on this question.

If, therefore, a deserting spouse is entitled to invoke his or her separation for a period of one year as the basis of a decree under ground (f), does this not conflict with the policy underlying the distinction between grounds (d) and (e) and does it not subvert the *three*-year requirement of ground (e)? It would be hard for a court to deny that separation (even if caused by the desertion of the applicant) terminates the 'normality' of the marital relationship of the spouses. This is surely a context crying out for application of the *noscitur a sociis* principle of statutory interpretation.

Maintenance In *K.D. v E.D.*, High Court, December 1, 1994, Costello J observed that, very frequently, an aspect not adverted to by the spouses, 'particularly by the husbands of broken marriages who have a duty to maintain their wives and children', is that a broken marriage 'invariably means a lowering of the standards of living of both parties, which can be very considerable in some instances.' In this case the husband had agreed to pay £1,000 per month for mortgage and electricity charges, as well as college and school fees for two of his five children; he contended that he could pay no more. His tax accounts indicated a nett income of £48,000 in the previous year. The husband, a doctor, did not work on Wednesday afternoons or on Saturdays, preferring to employ a locum at an annual cost of £5,162. He had, in the latter part of 1993, joined one of the most expensive golf clubs in the country, paying a membership of £4,000, and had joined a leisure club, with a membership fee of £400.

Costello J doubted the reliability of the tax accounts since the husband had engaged in other expenditure in 1993 which was not easy to reconcile with them. In view of the husband's failure to exploit his full earning capacity and his extravagant life style, Costello J concluded that it was proper to require the husband to pay £1,000 per month for the maintenance of his wife and children.

Family Home In *A.S. v G.S.* [1994] 1 IR 407, Geoghegan J held that proceedings for a property transfer order under s. 15 of the Judicial Separation and Law Reform Act 1989 constituted a *lis pendens*. In the instant case, this meant that a bank wishing to register a judgment mortgage against a family home where the husband was 'hopelessly in debt' was required to stay its hand. The wife's difficulty was to show that, although she had no estate or interest in the property sought to be transferred and had merely a claim to it, this was sufficient. 'With some hesitation', Geoghegan J concluded that an application under s. 15 for a property adjustment order relating to a specific property was a registerable *lis* for the purposes of s. 10 of the Judgments (Ireland) Act 1844. Later in his judgment, that hesitation appeared to be diluted. Geoghegan J stated:

At the time of the 1844 Act claims to land would have been based on alleged estates or interests in the land at the commencement of the action. But, having regard to the general purpose of the pre-1844 common law and chancery rules as to the binding nature of a *lis pendens*, I see no reason why a claim for a property adjustment order should not be included even though the claim is contingent on the court deciding to make such an order.

Were the legal position otherwise, the consequences would be 'most unfortunate'; if, for example, the hearing of an application for an adjustment order had to be adjourned for a fortnight because of not being reached in the list, it could be totally defeated by registration of a judgment mortgage in the meantime.

Geoghegan J accepted that notice by the bank of proceedings under s. 11(c) of the 1989 Act amounted to notice of the wife's claim under s. 15. Since the bank was seeking to register a judgment mortgage, however, it had no entitlement to notice under the 1844 Act which gave protection only to those acquiring an interest *for value*. A judgment mortgagee had long been held to be a volunteer: *Murphy v McCormack* [1930] IR 322, *Re Strong* [1940] IR 382.

Geoghegan J's observations on s. 11(c) are worth recording. He regarded an order made under that provision as analogous to an interlocutory injunction in that it was open to a party affected at the final hearing to establish that the applicant had never in fact been entitled to an order under it. In that event the court should as far as possible undo the damage caused by the preliminary order. S. 11(c) permits the court to make an order 'for the protection of the family home or of any monies realised from the conveyance of any interest in the family home pursuant to s. 5 of the Family Home Protection Act 1976'. Geoghegan J made it plain that, if there had been no *lis pendens* and it transpired that the husband had not had the requisite intention of depriving his wife of her residence in the family home under s. 5(1), he would have lifted the s. 11 order and permitted the bank to register its judgment mortgage before considering whether to make a property adjustment order.

In *J.D. v P.D.*, High Court, August 9, 1994, Lynch J, on granting a decree of judicial separation, ordered the sale of the family home, which was a large five-bedroomed house, standing on three-quarters of an acre, worth at least £200,000. He considered that '[t]he practicalities and common sense' indicated a sale as soon as possible rather than have the wife, her six year-old daughter and two-year-old son remaining there. He disposed of the wife's suggestion, tentatively supported by a clinical psychologist, that the added stress of moving house might affect the daughter by noting that, at the age of two, she had moved from London to Ireland without any adverse effects. He added:

Moving house can be portrayed as an adventure to a young child and it is up to the wife so to portray it to the daughter. *Inter alia* the psychologist described the daughter as being mall-adaptive with her peers in that she was bossy with them. I cannot help thinking that it is more likely that this trait of the daughter is not due to any stress or abnormality but is rather inherited from or imitative of her mother. . . .

NULLITY OF MARRIAGE

Grounds

Duress   Several cases on the question of vitiation of consent through duress fell for consideration during 1994. In *A.C. v P.J.* [1995] 2 IR 253, in defended proceedings, the facts were as follows. The petitioner was born in 1952. Her father was a small farmer and part-time postman. Her mother managed the home, which Barron J described as 'very strict, religious and pious'. The parents had a very strong wish to see their children succeed in life and were prepared to and did make sacrifices so that they might have the necessary education. The knowledge of this desire inhibited the petitioner. She felt under stress at exam time and resorted to anti-depressant tablets. She failed to get into a teacher training college, and failed her first year examination in Arts at a university. She realised by so doing she had let her parents down.

After leaving college the petitioner obtained jobs in the Dublin area. While working in a hospital in September 1972, she met the respondent who was doing similar work. They started going out together. Her relationship with her parents, based on her belief that she had let them down, inhibited her from telling them that she had a boyfriend and from going home that autumn. When she went home that Christmas she did not tell her parents that she was going out with a boy. She became engaged in January 1973. She met the respondent's parents who came from a different part of the country but she still did not tell her parents.

In February 1973, she wanted to break off the engagement but the respondent forced her to continue. At the end of the St Patrick's day week-end, on his persuasion, she went down with him to her parent's home. The petitioner was sure that her parents would not approve and the whole manner in which she acted made such disapproval more likely. Barron J observed in his judgement that 'the visit was not a success'. They then returned to Dublin and on the same evening had sexual intercourse for the first time.

The following month the petitioner found that she was pregnant. Barron J's judgment records that the petitioner:

was devastated. Her circumstances were such that she had no one to turn to. She knew her parents would be equally devastated and was totally unable to tell them. Her only solution was to agree to get married. This agreement was dependent solely upon the existence of her pregnancy. She made efforts to abort which were unsuccessful. She ultimately went to a general practitioner who had her admitted to a psychiatric hospital.

The consultant psychiatrist under whose care she came said that she was suffering from acute anxiety. Barron J was satisfied from her evidence that the petitioner saw marriage as the only means of escape from the situation in which she found herself. She remained afraid that she might take steps to end her pregnancy and asked the hospital staff to deprive her of anything which she could use to this end.

No one was told of her pregnancy save the respondent and the medical staff. She left all the arrangements for her wedding to her mother. She was discharged from hospital the day before the wedding and travelled down with the respondent to her home that night.

Her father described the petitioner on her wedding day before the ceremony as shaking all over, trembling and chain-smoking. He said that she did not seem happy. Barron J had no doubt that the petitioner's feelings on that day sprang from two main factors: her fear of how her parents would react if they realised that she was pregnant; and her wish not to marry the respondent because she felt dominated by him.

In Barron J's view, the petitioner had been motivated solely to bring her unhappy situation to an end. Her fear of her parents was 'genuine and justifiable'. This was later borne out by their reaction, after she was married, to the news of her pregnancy and in their failure to come to see her for some eighteen months after her marriage. In her mind, there was no way she could have continued to term without getting married. Barron J was satisfied also that she had tried to break off her relationship with the respondent before her pregnancy and that, if it had terminated, she would not have gone through a ceremony of marriage with him.

The subsequent history of the relationship between the petitioner and the respondent was fairly predictable. The respondent had no true understanding of her feelings at any time. The parties' first child was born in December 1973. There were five children in all, whose ages ranged at the time of the judgement from twenty-one to ten.

The question that Barron J had to consider was whether the petitioner's consent to the marriage had been a full and free exercise of an independent will. In the present case Barron J is quite satisfied that the circumstances surrounding her pregnancy and the attitude which her parents would have adopted to such pregnancy were of a character which the petitioner had been constitutionally unable to withstand and which had led her inexorably to her marriage.

Much the same circumstances had arisen in *N. (orse. K.) v. K.* [1985] IR 733. In that case it was found that the shock of discovering that she was pregnant had put the petitioner into a state where she could not think clearly and where the only outcome which she contemplated was that of marriage. There, as in the instant case, the petitioner had received no advice on alternative options. Even closer to the facts of the instant case were those in *D.B. (orse. O'R.) v. O'R.* [1991] 1 IR 536, which we analysed in the 1991 Review, 207. In that case also the duress had arisen from the circumstances themselves which the petitioner was not able to withstand, as a result of which her apparent consent to the marriage was not a true consent.

Barron J was satisfied that the petitioner's case came within the principles enunciated in these cases and that her apparent consent to be married was not such as was required by the law. Accordingly he granted a decree of nullity upon this ground.

Barron J's approach in this decision reflects his particular vision, apparent in several earlier decisions, of the way in which duress can eclipse a full and free consent. This approach favours the granting of a decree of annulment where the decision to marry is a short-term solution to an immediate pressure. If there is any hint from the evidence that the person, while buckling under the pressure, nonetheless is willing to contemplate marriage for other reasons as well as that of the pressure, a decree will not be forthcoming.

An unusual feature of the judgment, which makes it a difficult case to compare, on its facts, with other cases is the manner in which Barron J's narrative merges his account of the factual history of events with his perception of the petitioner's decisionmaking capacity at crucial moments.

In *B.C. v O'F. (otherwise known as L.C.)*, High Court, November 25, 1994, Morris J dismissed a petition for nullity based on duress. The parties had had a sexual relationship in the summer of 1981. At that time the petitioner was working as a technician; the respondent was a student. (The judgment does not mention the parties' ages.) In October 1982, the respondent contacted the petitioner to tell him that she had given birth to a baby boy and that the petitioner was the father. The petitioner took the initiative in locating the respondent. It transpired that the baby had been ill and was in hospital. The petitioner formed the clear impression (which in the event proved false) that the respondent's parents were applying pressure on her to have the baby adopted.

The parties had continuing contact with each other, though the petitioner found it difficult to have access to the baby. In June 1983, at the respondent's initiative, the parties agreed to marry. The petitioner was aware that this is what the petitioner's parents earnestly desired.

The baby was returned to the hospital in May 1983; again the petitioner apprehended that this was a preliminary step to placing the baby for adoption. On 11 July 1983, the petitioner told his mother, who was not enjoying good health, that he intended to marry the respondent. When he informed the respondent afterwards by telephone that his mother had taken the news well but needed a little time for the position to 'sink in', the respondent, after speaking to someone in the background, gave what the petitioner described in evidence as an ultimatum to present himself the following day at a certain hotel at a stated time as the respondent's father wanted to see him.

At this meeting the respondent's father said to the plaintiff, in clear terms, that if he did not marry the respondent, he would never see the respondent or the baby again. At this the petitioner stood up and said 'I do not have to take this'. The respondent's father replied that he had one hour to decide. When the petitioner left the hotel, the respondent begged him tearfully to marry her and gave him a guarantee that her father would never again interfere with their affairs. On the basis of this guarantee, the petitioner decided to go ahead with the wedding. He took no part in the arrangements. All the time he felt under pressure. On one occasion, when he suggested that the child be taken out of the hospital, the respondent's father had said: 'The child remains where he is until you are married and after that you can do what you like with it'. The parties were married on August 27, 1983. The petitioner collected the child from the hospital four days later. No further details of the parties' life together are given in the judgment.

The essence of the petitioner's case was that he had not been a free agent in giving his consent because the conduct of the respondent and her family had been such as to deprive him of the opportunity of doing his duty by the child unless he married and that, in effect, they had held the child over him as a weapon to force him to marry.

Morris J approached the matter on the basis of the test set out by Finlay CJ in *N. (Otherwise K.) v K.* [1985] IR 733. He dismissed the petition. He focused on several minute aspects of the evidence as offering indications that the petitioner's perception of the facts was not entirely reliable. In June 1983, the parties had exchanged presents of a silver watch and a lighter in return for an ingot. Morris J found the exchange of presents in this way completely out of harmony with the petitioner's description of the state of the relationship at that time. Morris J did not believe that the parties were standing apart from each other in the manner suggested by the petitioner.

Morris J accepted that, at the hotel meeting, the respondent's father had attempted to dictate terms to the petitioner but he considered it clear that the petitioner had been well able to resist this pressure. It was 'the pleas and tears' of the respondent and her undertaking that her father would not interfere in the future that had pressurised the petitioner into marrying. Morris J considered that the petitioner's visits to his son had not been as controlled as he had suggested; the petitioner's failure to visit the child in hospital was the result of the application of the hospital rules, common to all single-parent babies, rather than of any conduct on the respondent's part.

In Morris J's view, if the petitioner had been compelled against his will to marry for the sake of his son, under threat that he would not otherwise see his son again, it was 'singularly unlikely' that he would not have mentioned his problem to the priest before the marriage or to his family doctor. Morris J considered that the petitioner had been genuinely concerned for his son's welfare and anxious to do his duty by him at all times. He did not accept that this concern had been so heavy as to overbear his free will and force him into a marriage against his will. Had it been of such weight, the petitioner would not have allowed the child to remain for three or four days in the hospital during the honeymoon. (It has to be observed that this last point is perhaps less than convincing, since the petitioner's sense of urgency and anxiety would have been eased by the fact that the marriage had taken place.)

Morris J had no doubt whatever that the parties were at all times unsuited to each other and that probably the marriage had been a mistake from the start. He dismissed the petition, however, because he did not accept that the petitioner had discharged the onus of proof of establishing the absence of consent on the basis of duress.

In *K.W. v M.W.*, High Court, July 19, 1994, Lynch J dismissed a petition for nullity based on duress and relational incapacity. The parties had gone through a ceremony of marriage twenty-one years previously in England, where they both had been reared. The petitioner was then aged twenty three, the respondent seventeen years and ten months. The respondent was pregnant at the time. The parties had four children. They came to live in Ireland in 1978.

Lynch J had little hesitation in rejecting the ground of duress. The petitioner had proposed marriage on learning that the respondent was pregnant. His widowed mother had been happy with the idea of the marriage and, a week later, when he began to have doubts about the marriage, she suggested to him that the parties live together without getting married until the baby was born. The respondent was not willing to do this. The respondent's parents expected the parties to get married but put no pressure on the petitioner to do so. The petitioner had taken an active part in the preparations for the marriage; he had bought the respondent an engagement ring and commented that they would have as many children as there were small stones in the ring. Lynch J considered that the wedding photographs did not portray the miserable occasion suggested by the petitioner in evidence but rather a perfectly normal and happy one. (One has to wonder about the weight to be attached to this type of evidence; although other judges have also relied upon it, it surely is marginal at best.)

Lynch J noted that both parties, being Catholics, had a clear understanding at the time of the ceremony of the meaning and commitment of marriage as a lifelong union. Applying Finlay CJ's test expressed in *N. (Otherwise K.) v K.* [1985] IR 733, Lynch J was satisfied that the petitioner's decision to marry had been a full, free and informed one, involving a full, free exercise of his independent will. The husband had failed to establish the ground of duress on the balance of probabilities, 'assuming that to be the onus of proof in nullity cases'.

Lynch J went on to reject the petitioner's claim that the respondent lacked the capacity to enter into and sustain 'a normal functional and lifelong marital relationship'. (The addition of the expression 'functional' to 'normal', which was the expression used originally by Costello J in *D. v C.* [1984] ILRM 17 did not give rise to any discussion by Lynch J). While the respondent was young at the time of the wedding and was of rather a quiet disposition, she was also 'observant and intelligent and a thinking rather than a flighty person.'

The petitioner's claim that he himself lacked such capacity also foundered. His upbringing had been troubled by the fact that his father, who sustained head injuries in a traffic accident, had behaved violently, resulting in the petitioner and his siblings having to spend a couple of weeks in an orphanage. The stress in his childhood had given rise to physical symptoms and required investigation in hospital including interviews with a psychologist (who gave evidence in the case). The petitioner's father had left home to live with another woman when the petitioner was thirteen years old. His mother, however, was a 'devoted and capable' person. The petitioner had been in trouble with the police about three times and was violent on occasions but 'he never became what one would describe as a juvenile delinquent'. He had been successful educationally, training to be a pilot and ultimately obtaining good employment in another area of life. Lynch J considered that the petitioner was a very intelligent man who fully appreciated the obligations he was undertaking by marrying the respondent.

During the marriage the petitioner had failed to control a quick temper. He was guilty of occasional physical violence towards the respondent but more frequent verbal harassment. On the other hand, he could be charming and courteous and he provided pleasant surprises, such as unexpected holidays. In the early 1980s, he had formed an association with another woman, which had prompted the respondent to return to England and initiate judicial separation proceedings. Some months later he persuaded her to withdraw the proceedings and make a new start. Matters continued thereafter 'at first successfully but gradually less so'. The petitioner began an association with a different woman in the early 1990s, which led to a separation in 1992. The petitioner commenced the proceedings for annulment thereafter.

Lynch J held that the petitioner had failed to satisfy him, 'even on the balance of probabilities if that and not a higher standard of proof [was] all that was required of him', that he lacked the capacity at the date of the ceremony to enter into or sustain a normal functional and lifelong marital relationship with the respondent 'by reason of his state of mind, mental condition, emotional development and personality.'

Relational incapacity In *C.M. v E.L. (otherwise known as E.M.)*, High Court, July 27, 1994, Barr J granted a decree of nullity of marriage where the ceremony had taken place twenty-three years previously. The petitioner claimed that the respondent was suffering from a personality disorder that prevented her from being able to enter into and sustain 'a meaningful marriage contract and marital relationship' with him (*per* Barr J at p. 2; see also pp. 6 and 9). This rendition of the *R.S.J. v J.S.J.* grounds is unusual and might be considered to be more wide-ranging than the concept of 'a caring or considerate relationship' (*R.S.J.*) or 'normal marriage relationship' (*D. v C.* [1984] ILRM 17). Nothing appears to hinge on this distinction, however, since Barr J quoted extensively from *R.S.J.* and raised no question about its proper scope.

The instant case was one essentially of evidence rather than law. The respondent who was aged twenty-seven when she went through the ceremony of marriage with the petitioner, aged twenty-five, formally denied that she suffered from the alleged lack of capacity but she adduced no evidence.

The petitioner testified that the respondent had failed to tell him before the ceremony that she had required psychiatric treatment. On the honeymoon it transpired that the respondent was taking medication, for the purpose of facilitating sexual activity. A psychotherapist and general practitioner gave evidence that the respondent had explained to him that she had had sexual problems throughout her marriage; it had been 'alright' for a short time after the marriage but not subsequently. She was not sexually attracted to the petitioner and she said that she felt herself to be unemotional, unable to contend with touch and feeling; this was a problem going back to her childhood, when she 'could not tolerate the simple embrace of her father'. This witness expressed the view that the respondent had had difficulty in maintaining a normal marriage relationship.

Two psychiatrists who gave evidence were agreed that the respondent lacked the capacity to enter into and sustain a meaningful marriage relationship on account of her personality disorder. It is interesting to note how hearsay communications culminating in opinion evidence are capable of generating acceptable testimony. Thus we find one of the psychiatrists (who had examined both parties) stated in evidence that he had had interviews with the petitioner's sister-in-law and had been provided with reports from a doctor. It has become normal for courts to accept opinion evidence based in part on communications to the person forming the opinion where that person would not be permitted to give evidence of those communications but is permitted to give evidence on the basis of his or her acceptance of the truth of those communications.

In *O'R. v B.* [1995] 2 ILRM 57 (which we discuss below, 275), Kinlen J granted a decree of nullity on the ground of the petitioner's incapacity to enter into and sustain a normal, functional, lifelong marital relationship with the respondent. The petitioner had been aged twenty six, the respondent nearly thirty one, when they went through a ceremony of marriage in 1981. They had one child, born three years later. They separated in 1988. The evidence disclosed that the petitioner's immaturity well into adulthood had been a source of serious concern to those who knew him well. His childhood had been affected by a dominant mother and uncle, a parish priest, who lived in the family home. The petitioner's ambivalent attitude towards his mother persisted into adulthood. His relationship with the respondent lacked intensity. He was affected by a strong sense of guilt.

Kinlen J, granting the decree, noted that:

> the petitioner had entered into this marriage under the duress displayed by the distress of the respondent whenever he tried to break off the engagement. I am satisfied that there was no full, free and informed consent on his part.

This might appear to be a holding that the marriage was invalid on the ground of duress. Reading the judgment as a whole, however, it seems that the decree is based, not on the absence of consent resulting from duress, but rather on the petitioner's incapacity to enter into and sustain a normal, functional lifelong marital relationship with the respondent.

When discussing *R.S.J. v J.S.J.* and its progeny, Kinlen J made it plain that he agreed with 'the worries' that Keane J had expressed in *F. (otherwise known as C.) v C.* [1991] ILRM 65, at p. 79 regarding the 'elusive and impalpable area of emotions' that underlies the ground of relational incapacity. (Cf. our comments in the 1990 Review, 291-7.)

O.M. (Otherwise O.C.) v O.C., High Court, May 5, 1994 is a considerably more interesting case than a casual reading might suggest. The facts were not unprecedented: a former priest, with elements of immaturity, looking for a mother-figure in his wife but finding that he had married a woman, less yielding than he had expected, who was concerned to fulfil herself in her career. After five years of marriage the wife sought an annulment on the basis of both parties' incapacity to enter into and sustain 'a normal functional life-long marital relationship with each other by reason of their respective states of mind, mental condition, emotional development and personalities at the date of the marriage'. (She also invoked the ground of the failure of both parties to give a full, free and informed consent to the marriage; since no substantial evidence was given in support of this ground, Kinlen J rejected it summarily.)

What is fascinating about the case is the difference in philosophical premises among the psychiatric and psychological witnesses. The psychiatrist who gave evidence on behalf of the wife considered that she was a person who was fully capable of sustaining a valid marriage relationship with a suitable partner but that the respondent, at least at the time the wife consulted him, did not have a similar capacity to sustain a valid marriage relationship with her. This witness thought that 'the relationship had ceased to exist' after the birth of their second child and that 'nothing could have been done to restore it because of their different lifestyles, educational backgrounds and vocational training'. On account of these differences, they were incapable of sustaining a true valid marriage relationship with each other.

The philosophical assumptions here come from the determinist model, which views personal relationships as reducible to the inevitable intermingling of attitudes and emotions with no sense of autonomous moral capacity as an element in the process. On this approach, there can be no true distinction between capacity and incapacity, contrary to the basis of the ground first recognised in *R.S.J. v J.S.J.* [1981] ILRM 263.

The second psychiatrist, who had looked after the respondent during his laicisation process, appeared to come from a directly opposite philosophical school. Responding to the terms of the petition for annulment, he stated that the grounds set out in it would apply to the vast majority of people. He opined that:

> personality complex as a ground for nullity results in chaos. If the parties here had worked at their marriage, they mightn't be here today. . . .

Perhaps this does not go to the point of suggesting that *every* person is capable of contracting a valid marriage, so far as its relationship element is concerned; on one view, this psychiatrist is merely cautioning against the danger, from a practical point of view, of permitting an *R.S.J.*-type ground for annulment. At all events, his approach is entirely hostile to the determination favoured by the first psychiatrist.

Finally, a clinical psychologist quoted as part of his argument Gelder, Gath & Mayou's *Oxford Textbook of Psychiatry* (2nd ed., 1989), p. 139, which counsels the avoidance of the terms 'inadequate personality' and 'immature personality', on the basis that both tend to be used when a doctor has not thought clearly enough about the precise nature of the patient's difficulties. A clear description of the patient's problem, in these authors' view, is more likely to lead to a constructive approach than the mere labeling of the personality by the use of these two terms. Perhaps this does not constitute a frontal assault on the *R.S.J.* ground, which undoubtedly involves a label for the type of incapacity that invalidates a marriage. A decree of nullity of marriage is designed to serve a legal rather than a therapeutic function.

In the section on Duress, earlier in the Chapter (above, 270-2), we discuss in *K.W. v M.W.*, High Court, July 19, 1994 where Lynch J, as well as rejecting the petition for nullity based on duress, also rejected the petitioner's claim that he was incapable of forming a normal marital relationship with the respondent.

Standard of Proof In *O'R. v B.* [1995] 2 ILRM 57 (which we discuss above, 273), Kinlen J quoted the precedents on the issue of standard of proof, observing that he 'would be inclined to work on the basis of the balance of probabilities.' In *K.W. v M.W.*, High Court, July 19, 1994 (discussed above, 270-2), Lynch J rejected a petition for nullity, applying the balance of probabilities, 'assuming that to be the onus of proof in nullity cases.' Of course the outcome would have to be the same, a *fortiori*, if Lynch J had applied the standard of proof beyond reasonable doubt or some other intermediate standard.

Bars to a decree In *O'R. v B.* [1995] 2 ILRM 57 where Kinlen J granted an argument on the basis of the petitioner's incapacity to enter into and sustain a normal marital relationship (see above, 273), the respondent had opposed the granting of the decree, arguing, *inter alia*, that the petitioner had been guilty of unconscionable delay and that he had approbated the marriage. Kinlen J stated that he was satisfied that there was no unconscionable delay 'but w[ould] leave until a time when it is fully argued as to whether the maxim *ignorantia juris, quod quisque scire tenatur, neminem excusat* applies in matrimonial cases.' The answer would appear to be that it does: the courts have accepted that a petitioner who had no way of knowing of the possibility of taking annulment proceedings should not be held to have approbated the marriage.

In *C.M. v E.L. (otherwise known as E.M.)*, High Court, July 27, 1994, which we discuss above, 272-3, in relation to grounds for annulment, Barr J granted a decree of nullity over twenty-three years after the parties had gone through a ceremony of marriage. Earlier family law proceedings, not further identified in the judgment, had taken place between the parties in which both had had full legal representation. All of their differences had been settled to their mutual satisfaction. The settlement included a separation agreement, appropriate financial provisions and arrangements as to the custody of their three children.

Barr J held that the petitioner had established the ground for a decree emanating from the *R.S.J.* line of authority. He was satisfied that the petitioner had not become aware of the legal implications of the respondent's psychiatric incapacity until shortly before the nullity proceedings were instituted, when the matter was investigated by his solicitors and he was advised by them. There was no evidence that he had approbated the marriage or was guilty of unconscionable delay.

Representation of parties In *O'R. v B.* [1995] 2 ILRM 57, Kinlen J expressed the hope that, in nullity cases:

> particularly where there are children . . . [the parties] should be represented, if the trial Judge requires it. In cases where one or other party is not before the court, it would be eminently desirable at public expense to have a *legitimus contradictor*, an *amicus curiae* or 'devil's advocate' to argue in favour of the existence of the marriage.

One must agree with this sentiment, while admitting the formidable difficulty for any such person in gainsaying the evidence of a petitioner as to facts and feelings of the most intimate human kind, often incapable of corroboration or refutation.

Fisheries and Harbours

REGULATION OF FISHERIES

The Fisheries (Amendment) Act 1994 involved a number of significant further updating of the statutory regulation of the fishing industry, in particular sea fisheries. The Act came into force on August 1, 1994: Fisheries (Amendment) Act 1994 (Commencement) Order 1994 (SI No. 243 of 1994).

Registration of fishing boats S. 4 of the 1994 Act amended s. 373(5) of the Merchant Shipping Act 1894 to empower the Minister for the Marine to make Regulations governing the registration of fishing boats and their removal from the Register of Fishing Boats, and provided for the increase of penalties for breaches of such Regulations. Of particular importance in this context are ss. 5 and 6 of the 1994 Act, which amend s. 222B of the Fisheries (Consolidation) Act 1959 in order to accord equal treatment for the licensing of fishing boats to nationals of, and bodies corporate registered in any Member State of, the European Union. This provision was a belated recognition that existing statutory provisions did not comply with EC law. In this respect the State had followed the lead of the UK Merchant Shipping Act 1988, whose provisions were found incompatible with EC law in the long-running *Factortame* case, which culminated in the decision of the Court of Justice in *Brassiere du Pecheur; Factortame (No. 3)* [1996] 2 WLR 162.

Enforcement S. 8 of the 1994 Act amended s. 231(1) of the Fisheries (Consolidation) Act 1959 in order to extend the scope for the seizure of fish and nets in respect of which it is suspected that an offence is being or has been committed. S. 9 also amended s. 231(1) of the 1959 Act and provided for a statutory requirement to furnish information relating to the catching or sale of fish. Ss. 10 to 12 of the 1994 Act amended and clarified ss. 233, 233A and 234 of the 1959 Act concerning the detention and prosecution of fishing boats suspected of operating in breach of fisheries legislation. S. 14 of the 1994 Act amended s. 4 of the Fisheries (Amendment) Act 1978 to provide for the confiscation and forfeiture in certain circumstances of boats convicted of certain fisheries offences, while s. 16 amended s. 2 of the 1978 Act in order to apply the provision for statutory forfeiture of fish and fishing gear on conviction on a charge of illegal fishing under section 223A of the

Fisheries (Consolidation) Act 1959 to offences not involving the use of a boat.

Assault or obstruction of fishery protection officers   S. 15 of the 1995 Act increased the penalties for assaults on, or obstruction of, fisheries officers in the exercise of their functions under the 1959 Act, as amended. This increase arose from recommendations contained in the 1991 Report of the Formal Investigation Into the 1990 Shipping Casualty Off Ballycotton, Co Cork, conducted by District Court judge O'Reilly under s. 465 of the Merchant Shipping Act 1894.

Eel fishing   The 1994 Act brought the statutory arrangements for eel fishing into line with existing comparable provisions. S. 18 of the 1994 Act amended s. 95(1) of the Fisheries (Consolidation) Act 1959 in order to clarify the conditions under which a net can be used for the capture of eels. S. 19 amended s. 100 of the 1959 Act to provide for fines and forfeitures for breach of conditions of an eel fishing authorisation and increased the penalties for illegal use of a fishing weir, fishing mill dam or fixed engine. S. 20 consists of a completely updated text of Part X of the 1959 Act (ss. 154 to 163A of the 1959 Act) and extends the restrictions that were in place on the sale of salmon, trout and molluscan shellfish to the sale of eels. Significantly, the changes effected to the 1959 Act by s. 20 of the 1994 Act also ended the requirement for a special licence to export salmon and trout. S. 21 of the 1994 amended s. 182 of the 1959 Act by providing for certain controls on selling, purchasing or being in possession of eels. Finally, s. 22 of the 1994 Act amended s. 183 of the 1959 Act by requiring the marking of all packages or containers containing eels in the course of transit in the State: s. 183 of the 1959 Act had already required this for packages and containers containing salmon, trout and molluscan shellfish. The Licensed Salmon, Eel and Molluscan Shellfish Dealers' Register Regulations 1994 (SI No. 461 of 1994), the Fisheries (Salmon, Eel and Molluscan Shellfish Dealers' Licences) Regulations 1994 (SI No. 462 of 1994) and the Salmon, Eel and Molluscan Shellfish Dealers' Licences (Alteration of Duties) Order 1994 (SI No. 463 of 1994) give effect to the detailed provisions required under this aspect of the 1994 Act, effective from January 1, 1995.

Driftnets   The Sea Fisheries (International Waters) (Driftnet) Order 1994 (SI No. 201 of 1994) gave effect to Regulation (EEC) No. 345/92 which restricted the use of one or more driftnets for tuna fishing to a total of not more than 2.5 kilometres. Infringements may be prosecuted under s. 233 of the Fisheries (Consolidation) Act 1959, as amended.

Fisheries co-ops   The Fisheries (Amendment) Act 1991 (Fisheries Co-

Operative Societies) (Amendment) Rules 1994 (SI No. 54 of 1994) amended the 1992 Rules of the same title so that the closing date for application by angling clubs for annual corporate membership of fishery co-operatives (see the 1991 Review, 253) is May 1.

Licensing The Licensing of Sea Fishing Boats (Exemption) (Revocation) Regulations 1994 (SI No. 444 of 1994) removed from fishing vessels under 65 feet the exemption from obtaining a sea fishing boat licence under s. 222B of the Fisheries (Consolidation) Act 1959, as amended. This was achieved by the revocation of the Licensing of Sea-Fishing Boats (Exemption) Regulations 1983.

Shellfish waters quality The Quality of Shellfish Waters Regulations 1994 (SI No. 200 of 1994) are referred to in the Safety and Health chapter, 400, below.

Strict liability nature of fisheries offences In *Maguire v Shannon Regional Fisheries Board* [1994] 2 ILRM 253, Lynch J held that certain offences under the Fisheries (Consolidation) Act 1959 constituted offences of strict liability in respect of which it was not necessary to establish mens rea: see the discussion in the Criminal Law chapter, 228-31, above.

HARBOURS

Cork harbour The Cork Harbour Works Order 1994 (SI No. 254 of 1994) authorised Cork Harbour Commissioners to carry out certain works at Ringaskiddy Ferry Terminal, Cork.

Drogheda harbour The Harbour Rates (Drogheda Harbour) Order 1994 (SI No. 10 of 1994) authorised Drogheda Harbour Commissioners to charge goods, tonnage and service rates at Drogheda harbour.

Dún Laoghaire harbour The Dún Laoghaire Harbour Act 1994 established a funding mechanism for harbour development works at Dún Laoghaire harbour, County Dublin. As the Explanatory Memorandum published with the Bill that led to the Act pointed out, the purpose of the Act was to create a vehicle to fund development works at the harbour, pending the establishment outside the Exchequer framework of a semi-State commercial body to manage and operate Dún Laoghaire harbour The funding involved was envisaged not to exceed £20 million and the intention at the time the Act was passed was that the funding would be serviced from the revenue generated by the harbour's considerable commercial activity.

S. 3 of the Act provided for the establishment of a body corporate called the Dún Laoghaire Harbour (Finance) Board. S. 5 of the Act provides that it shall be the duty of the Board, on the direction of the Minister for the Marine, to secure the necessary moneys to defray the expenses incurred or to be incurred by the Minister in carrying out, or procuring the carrying out of, development works at Dún Laoghaire harbour. The Board is empowered top borrow moneys from commercial sources up to a limit of £20 million and the Minister for Finance may in certain circumstances make loans to the Board. S. 5 also provides that the Minister for the Marine may by Order appropriate to the Dún Laoghaire Harbour Development Fund (which the Board is required to establish under s. 6 of the 1994 Act) a proportion of the revenues payable from the harbour operations at Dun Laoghaire and, with the consent of the Minister for Finance, make non-repayable grants to the Board.

Tralee and Fenit pier and harbour   The Harbour Rates (Tralee and Fenit Pier and Harbour) Order 1994 (SI No. 192 of 1994) authorised Tralee and Fenit Pier and Harbour Commissioners to charge increased goods and tonnage rates at the pier and harbour.

Garda Síochána

ASSOCIATIONS

Sergeants and inspectors   The Garda Síochána (Associations) (Amendment) Regulations 1994 (SI No. 366 of 1994) involved amendments to the Garda Síochána (Associations) (Superintendents and Chief Superintendents) Regulations 1978 to 1991 concerning the election of the National Executive of the Association of Garda Sergeants and Inspectors.

Superintendents   The Garda Síochána (Associations) (Superintendents and Chief Superintendents) (Amendment) Regulations 1994 (SI No. 92 of 1994) involved minor amendments to the Garda Síochána (Associations) (Superintendents and Chief Superintendents) Regulations 1987 concerning Garda divisions for the purposes of the 1987 Regulations.

DISCIPLINE

Delay   In *McNeill v Garda Commissioner* [1995] 1 ILRM 321, the applicant was unsuccessful in seeking to have quashed a disciplinary decision made under the Garda Síochána (Discipline) Regulations 1989, the main ground for objection being the delay in having a disciplinary hearing under the 1989 Regulations.

In December 1989, the applicant, a member of An Garda Síochána was interviewed in connection with alleged false claims made for overtime. The applicant explained that the claims were in relation to work he had taken home. The matter was referred to the Director of Public Prosecutions who decided that the applicant should be prosecuted. In June 1991 he was suspended from duty with pay and in July 1991 was served with 87 District Court summonses. He elected for trial on indictment, but the trial did not go ahead as the applicant's explanatory statements had been made without caution and were felt to be presumptively inadmissible. All summonses against the applicant were withdrawn.

In February 1992 the applicant was served with a notice under Regulation 40 of the Garda Síochána (Discipline) Regulations 1989, the 'fast track' procedure which empowers the Garda Commissioner in specified circumstances to dismiss certain members from the Garda Síochána. The Regulation

40 power may only be exercised where the Commissioner has decided that dismissal is merited and that the holding of an inquiry could not affect his decision. The consent of the Minister for Justice must be obtained in order to proceed under Regulation 40. In May 1992 the Regulation 40 notice was withdrawn, the Minister advising that the Regulation 40 procedure was inappropriate and that the holding of an inquiry could affect the Commissioner's decision. In July 1992 the applicant's suspension was lifted and he resumed full duties.

Later in July 1992, procedures under Regulation 8 of the Garda Síochána (Discipline) Regulations 1989, which provides that an alleged breach of discipline shall be inspected 'as soon as practicable' by a Garda not below the rank of inspector, were commenced. The investigation commenced in September 1992 and in October 1992 the applicant was served with a notice indicating that an Inspector had been appointed to investigate the alleged breaches, which mirrored the summonses originally served on the applicant. The applicant's solicitor wrote three letters requesting time to prepare the defence and subsequently notified the Inspector of his intention to apply for judicial review. In January 1993, notice of witnesses to be called was served on the applicant, but it proved necessary to alter some of the charges and a new notice was served on the applicant in October 1993.

In January 1994 the applicant was granted leave to apply for judicial review but, as already indicated, Morris J ultimately refused the relief sought and held that the delays involved in the case did not preclude the holding of the disciplinary inquiry.

In relation to the period between June 1989, when the applicant was first interviewed, and July 1991, when the District Court summonses were served upon him, Morris J held that the investigating authorities had been justified in refraining from proceeding with the inquiry not only up to the time when the District Court summonses were served, but also up to the date when the summonses were withdrawn. Distinguishing the applicant's case from that in *Flynn v An Post* [1987] IR 68 (1987 Review, 228-9), he stated that different considerations might apply if the applicant had indicated a wish that the case should proceed notwithstanding the existence of criminal proceedings, or if the applicant had been suspended without pay.

In relation to the period of time between October 1991 and May 1992, when the Regulation 40 notice was withdrawn, Morris J again held that there had been no unconscionable delay on the part of the investigating authorities. He noted that the Commissioner had considered the case to be an appropriate one to proceed under Regulation 40 and it was only on seeking the consent of the Minister that it was found to be inappropriate. In those circumstances, he felt that it would be unreal to suggest that the Commissioner was not moving toward a resolution of the case during this period.

As for the period of time between May 1992 and January 1993, and from then up to the date of his judgment, Morris J concluded that the authorities had moved with all due expedition. He held that it was entirely reasonable that between January 1993 and September 1993 they should have had an opportunity to consider the implication of the Supreme Court decision in the McGrath case and obtain advice.

Looking at the overall delay of approximately four and a half years since the time when the matters were first brought to the notice of the applicant, Morris J referred to *Gallagher v Revenue Commissioners* [1991] ILRM 632 (1991 Review, 8-10) and *McGowan v Wren* [1988] ILRM 744 (1988 Review, 12) and concluded that it had not established that the authorities had been guilty of any conduct for which they could reasonably be criticised and that the case fell into the category of cases where the onus clearly rested on the applicant to establish to the satisfaction of the Court, on the balance of probabilities, that prejudice will arise in the conduct of his defence to the allegations made against him.

Finally, as to prejudice, Morris J held that the death of one of the applicant's material witnesses, who had been due to give evidence concerning work procedures in the Garda Síochána, could not affect the fairness of the proposed hearing, since that witness' knowledge was likely to have been shared by other members of the Garda Síochána. Thus, his death could not have prejudiced the applicant's position. On this basis, as already indicated, the applicant's claim was dismissed.

PAY

The Garda Síochána Pay Order 1994 (SI No. 441 of 1994) revised the rates of pay for all ranks of the force. Thus, the salary of the Garda Commissioner was increased to £58,594, with effect from January 1, 1993. The salary for a Garda trainee was fixed at £11,122.

Health Services

ELIGIBILITY

Disabled persons maintenance allowances   The Disabled Persons Maintenance Allowances Regulations 1994 (SI No. 237 of 1994) consolidated the regime for the granting of disabled persons maintenance allowances under s. 69 of the Health Act 1970 and replaced the Disabled Persons (Maintenance Allowances) Regulations 1991 to 1993 (see the 1993 Review, 344).

In-patient charges   The Health (In-Patient Charges) (Amendment) Regulations 1994 (SI No. 38 of 1994) amended the 1987 Regulations of the same title by eliminating the charge on the last day for in-patient hospital services. The £20 daily charge (1993 Review, 343) remained unchanged. The 1994 Regulations came into effect on March 1, 1994. On this area generally, see the 1991 Review, 258.

Out-patient charges   The Health (Out-Patient Charges) Regulations 1994 (SI No. 37 of 1994) provided that, in place of the £6 charge for out-patient services introduced by the Health (Out-Patient Charges) (Amendment) Regulations 1993 (1993 Review, 343), a charge of £12 per visit was introduced from March 1, 1994. The Health Services (Out-Patient) Regulations 1993 provided for the manner in which a person may avail of entitlement to consultant out-patient services under s. 56 of the Health Act 1970 and also provided for the first time for charges for 'private patients' who avail of this entitlement. The 1994 Regulations revoked the Health (Out-Patient Charges) Regulations 1987.

HEALTH INSURANCE

The Health Insurance Act 1994 was enacted to pave the way for competition in the private health insurance market and to regulate that market in accordance with the Third EC Directive on Non-Life Insurance, 92/49/EEC. The 1994 Act must be seen against the background of the virtual monopoly of the health insurance market in Ireland enjoyed by the Voluntary Health Insurance Board (VHI), which had been established by the Voluntary Health Insurance Act 1957. While competition in this market has been provided for in the 1994 Act, substantial statutory regulation remains in place particularly with a view to ensuring that those entering the market for the first time are prevented from 'cherry picking' the most lucrative end of the market. The 1994 Act came into effect on July 1, 1994: Health Insurance Act 1994 (Commencement) Order 1994 (SI No. 191 of 1994). We also note that the 1994 Act should be seen in conjunction with the coming into force of the Voluntary Health Insurance (Amendment) Act 1996, by which the monopoly of the VHI was removed. While we will return to the 1996 Act in the 1996 Review, we note here that, arising from the latter Act, the full terms of the 1994 Act became effective in 1996 when other health insurance providers entered the Irish market.

To this end, the 1994 Act requires health insurance undertakings to comply with the following major principles: (a) community rating (by which the same rate of premium must be charged for a given level of benefits irrespective of the age, sex or health status of the insured person); (b) open enrolment (by which, with certain qualifications, cover must be provided to any individual who wishes to take out a policy); and (c) lifetime cover (by which, again with certain qualifications, renewal cover may not be refused once an individual has enrolled).

As we will see, the 1994 Act underpinned the principle of community rating by requiring all health insurance undertakings offering cover for hospital in-patient services (as defined in the Health Act 1970) to provide a minimum level of benefits. It also provided for the introduction of a Risk Equalisation Scheme whereby certain adverse risk factors arising from the operation of community rating, open enrolment and life-time cover would be shared amongst the various insurance undertakings opting to provide health insurance. If such a Scheme were introduced, its implementation would be a matter for the Health Insurance Authority envisaged by the 1994 Act and, in that event, the Authority would also assume the regulatory functions assigned to the Minister for Health under the 1994 Act and also those of the Minister for Enterprise and Employment under the Insurance Acts and the various Regulations concerning the insurance industry. However, even if the Risk Equalisation Scheme were not introduced, the 1994 Act empowers the Minister to establish the Authority if it is considered appropriate to so in the light of market developments.

Community rating S. 7 of the 1994 Act prohibits the making of non-community rated health insurance contracts, which means that an undertaking may not vary the premium charged for a level of benefits regardless of the age, sex or health status of the individual. However, s. 7 does allow for the provision of discounts for children, persons between the age of 18 and 21 years who are in full-time education, and dependent on the subscriber, pensioners who are members of existing restricted membership schemes and groups of persons. A group scheme discount may not be more than 10% of the standard rate. In addition, cover for long term care will not be community rated.

Open enrolment   S. 8 of the 1994 Act obliges health insurance undertakings, with certain qualifications, to provide cover to any individual who wishes to enrol regardless of age, sex or health status. One exception is that an undertaking is not obliged to offer cover to an individual aged 65 years or over.

Lifetime cover   S. 9 of the 1994 Act prohibits health insurance undertakings from refusing to renew or terminate cover once an individual has enrolled, save in such circumstances as the Minister may prescribe in Regulations.

Minimum level of benefits   S. 10 of the 1994 Act requires that all health insurance contracts, other than those relating solely to a ancillary health benefits, must provide a minimum level of benefits, as may be prescribed by the Minister in Regulations. This is further underpinned by s. 11, which prohibits health insurance undertakings from offering 'no claims bonuses', cash payments or other inducements to individuals to forego their insured entitlements or to avail of public hospital services or to terminate, not to enrol or not to renew their cover with that undertaking.

Risk Equalisation Scheme   S. 12 of the 1994 Act empowers the Minister for Health to make Regulations prescribing a risk equalisation scheme, which shall apply to each registered health insurance undertaking subject to certain exclusions until June 30, 1999. As already indicated the Scheme is implemented by the Health Insurance Authority.

Registration of health insurance undertakings   S. 13 of the 1994 Act provides that every undertaking engaged in the business of health insurance in Ireland must have its name entered on a register of health benefits undertakings before it can engage in the business of health insurance. The register must be maintained by the Health Insurance Authority. Under the Third EC Directive on Non-Life Insurance, 92/49/EEC, insurance companies with head offices in other EU Member States but trading either directly or through branch offices established in Ireland are regulated by their Home State authorities. In the case of insurance companies from EU Member States, entry on the register of health benefits undertakings will be automatic, once they are duly authorised by their home state regulatory authorities to engage in health insurance business in Ireland. Any other health benefits undertaking, including the VHI, lawfully engaged in the business of health insurance in Ireland immediately prior to the 1994 Act is also be entitled to registration. Other undertakings wishing to engage in health insurance business in Ireland will have to apply to have their names entered on the register and will be required to satisfy certain conditions before registration will be granted.

Health Insurance Authority   S. 20 provides for the establishment of the Health Insurance Authority, which is in effect a State body. S. 21 provides that the principal functions of the Authority are to supervise and monitor compliance with the regulatory provisions of this Act and implement the Risk Equalisation Scheme. S. 22 envisages the possible conferring on the Authority of additional functions in relation to insurance and related matters, including the relevant functions now discharged by the Minister for Enterprise and Employment under the Insurance Acts and various Insurance Regulations. S. 26 provides for the appointment and lays down the functions of a chief executive officer of the Authority to be known as the Registrar, while s. 27 provides for the appointment of the staff of the Authority and the terms and conditions of employment of such staff.

MEDICAL PREPARATIONS

Further updating of the statutory regime for the manufacture, labelling and retail supply of medical preparations intended for human use in accordance with the Health Act 1947 and the Misuse of Drugs Act 1977 occurred in 1994 (see further the 1993 Review, 344-5).

Labelling and package leaflets   The Medical Preparations (Labelling and Package Leaflets) Regulations (Amendment) 1994 (SI No. 440 of 1994) amended the Medical Preparations (Labelling and Package Leaflets) Regulations 1993 (1993 Review, 344) to give effect to certain provisions of Directive 92/73/EEC on homeopathic medicines.

Licensing of products   The Medical Preparations (Licensing, Advertisement and Sale) (Amendment) Regulations 1994 (SI No. 439 of 1994) further amended the 1984 Regulations of the same title in order to give effect to certain provisions of Directive 92/73/EEC on homeopathic medicines as well as Regulation (EEC) No. 2309/93.

PHARMACY

Young v Pharmaceutical Society of Ireland and Ors [1994] 2 ILRM 262
involved an unsuccessful challenge to the legislation concerning restrictions
on the recognition of pharmacy qualifications. The case revolved around the
implementation of EC Directives on recognition of such qualifications.

S. 30 of the Pharmacy Act (Ireland) 1875 provides it is unlawful for any
person to sell or keep open a shop for retailing, dispensing or compounding
certain poisons unless he has been registered as a pharmaceutical chemist,
chemist or druggist under the Act. S. 2 of the Pharmacy Act 1962 provides
that the dispensing and compounding of medical prescriptions in a shop
operated by a body corporate must be personally supervised by a registered
pharmaceutical chemist, a registered dispensing chemist or druggist, or a
licentiate of the Apothecaries Hall employed in a whole-time capacity by the
particular body corporate.

Article 57 of the EC Treaty provides for the making of Directives on the
mutual recognition of diplomas, certificates and other evidence of formal
qualifications. It appears that the making of such Directives in respect of
pharmacy qualifications was problematic because Belgium, Denmark,
France and Luxembourg had statutory licensing regimes for pharmacies
intended to encourage the establishment of pharmacies in remote rural areas
and prevent excessive competition in urban areas which might lower standards. It was accepted that a Member State without such a licensing system
might be faced with an influx of pharmacists if a Directive on mutual
recognition was made. Working papers of the European Parliament indicated
that, as a temporary solution, it was intended to deal with this by restricting
pharmacists from one Member State to taking over existing pharmacies in
another Member State and precluding them from establishing new pharmacies.

This was acknowledged in the seventh recital to Council Directive
85/433/EEC on the recognition of qualifications in pharmacy, which indicated that it would be premature to provide that the recognition of diplomas,
certificates and other evidence of formal qualifications in pharmacy should
also extend to the activities of a pharmacist as the controller of a pharmacy
opened to the public for less than three years. The recital went on to state that
this problem would have to be re-examined by the Commission and the
Council within a certain period. Article 2(1) of the 1985 Directive required
each Member State to recognise certain diplomas, certificates and other
formal qualifications awarded to nationals of Member States by other Member States in accordance with Directive 85/432/EEC, by giving such qualifications the same effect in its territory as those diplomas, certificates and
other formal qualifications which it itself awarded. However, Article 2(2)

provided that Member States need not give effect to the diplomas, certificates and other formal qualifications with respect to the establishment of new pharmacies open to the public, and for the purposes of the Directive pharmacies which have been in operation for less than three years would be regarded as new.

The European Communities (Recognition of Qualifications in Pharmacy) Regulations 1987 were made by the Minister for Health in order to comply with Directive 85/433/EEC. The Regulations amended s. 22 of the 1875 Act by giving a national of a Member State who holds any qualification in pharmacy awarded in accordance with Article 2 of Directive 85/432/EEC a right to be registered. The 1987 Regulations also inserted s. 2(3A) into the 1962 Act. S. 2(3A) was subsequently amended by the European Communities (Recognition of Qualifications in Pharmacy) Regulations 1991 so as to provide that the expressions 'authorised person' and 'registered pharmaceutical chemist' in s. 2 do not include a person registered by virtue of s. 22A of the Pharmacy Act 1875 acting in respect of a shop for the dispensing or compounding of medical prescriptions or for the sale of poisons where such shop has been in operation for less than three years.

The plaintiff was an Irish citizen who had qualified as a pharmaceutical chemist in England in 1991. The qualification which she obtained was one of the recognised certificates specified in Directive 85/433/EEC and the 1875 Act, as amended by the 1987 and 1991 Regulations. The plaintiff was subsequently registered by the Pharmaceutical Society of Ireland. The certificate which was issued to her was expressed to have been granted in accordance with s. 22A of the 1875 Act. This meant that she was subject to the limitation that she could not carry on business in respect of a shop which had been in operation for less than three years. The plaintiff commenced proceedings in which she claimed that the limitation contained in s. 2(3A) was invalid because it was inconsistent with the right of establishment in Article 57 of the EC Treaty. In particular it was claimed that while Directive 85/433/EEC permitted derogations on the basis of public health considerations, it could not justify a general restraint or one designed to protect commercial interests. Murphy J refused the relief sought.

Having reviewed the background to the 1985 Directive, Murphy J stated that the reference to public health in Directive 85/433/EEC was a reference to public health in those Member States which operate geographical distribution of pharmacy licensing systems and there was nothing in the seventh recital to the 1985 Directive to suggest that public health considerations in Member States which do not operate licensing systems for new pharmacies had any bearing on the operation of the Directive. He went on that it would be impossible to derogate from the provisions of the EC Treaty except on the basis of the grounds specified therein, but in this respect there was no derogation. Rather, subject to review by the Commission or the Council, Directive 85/433/EEC allowed the Member States to refrain from recognising the specified diplomas in relation to a particular range of pharmacies. The seventh recital made it clear that to give such recognition would be premature. However, while the working documents of the European Parliament demonstrated how recognition as between Member States which operated licensing systems and those which do not could work an injustice, there was nothing to imply that this injustice would have any detrimental effect on the public health of the Member State affording recognition.

Murphy J reached the important conclusion that Directive 85/433/EEC did not grant, withdraw or limit the right of establishment. Like all other Directives made under Article 57(1) of the EC Treaty, he stated that it was designed to facilitate or make it easier for persons to take up and pursue activities as self-employed persons, but it was not a substantive provision. By excluding pharmacies which have been in existence for less than three years, the Directive had limited the facility conferred, but without prejudicing the basic right. The restriction on the recognition of pharmacy qualifications obtained in other member states was, he held, not to guarantee a particular measure of experience but was simply an artificial counterbalance to the licensing system operated in certain Member States. As such licensing systems were indefinite in duration, it was not illogical that the embargo on opening new pharmacies should likewise be indefinite, although subject to review by the Commission. In those circumstances, he concluded that there was no fundamental inconsistency in Directive 85/433/EEC or in the 1987 and 1991 Regulations which gave effect to it in Irish law.

Murphy J added that, in any event, the validity of the Directive could not be challenged in a national court, though it is curious that he did not go on to suggest that an application to the Court of Justice under the EC Treaty would be appropriate.

Further amendments to the legislation in question in the *Young* case were effected by the European Communities (European Economic Area) (Recognition of Qualifications in Pharmacy) Regulations 1994 (SI No. 438 of 1994): see the Education chapter, 238, above.

REGISTRATION OF BIRTHS AND DEATHS

Amalgamation of Registrars' Districts In 1994, a further series of statutory instruments were made to amalgamate certain Superintendent Registrars' Districts and, where applicable, Registrars' Districts in different administrative counties so as to reduce the number of such districts in each county, continuing a process begun in 1993: see the 1993 Review, 348. The relevant Orders were the Registration of Births and Deaths (Ireland) Act 1863 (sections 17 and 18) (Waterford) Order 1994 (SI No. 39 of 1994), the Registration of Births and Deaths (Ireland) Act 1863 (sections 17 and 18) (Wexford) Order 1994 (SI No. 68 of 1994), the Registration of Births and Deaths (Ireland) Act 1863 (sections 17 and 18) (Kilkenny) Order 1994 (SI No. 69 of 1994), the Registration of Births and Deaths (Ireland) Act 1863 (sections 17 and 18) (Clare) Order 1994 (SI No. 185 of 1994), the Registration of Births and Deaths (Ireland) Act 1863 (sections 17 and 18) (Louth) Order 1994 (SI No. 270 of 1994), the Registration of Births and Deaths (Ireland) Act 1863 (sections 17 and 18) (Meath) Order 1994 (SI No. 271 of 1994), the Registration of Births and Deaths (Ireland) Act 1863 (sections 17 and 18) (Dublin) Order 1994 (SI No. 296 of 1994) and the Registration of Births and Deaths (Ireland) Act 1863 (sections 17 and 18) (Dublin) (No. 2) Order 1994 (SI No. 296 of 1994).

Registration of stillbirths The Stillbirths Registration Act 1994 provides for the first time for the registration of stillbirths. The Act came into effect on January 1, 1995: Stillbirths Registration Act 1994 (Commencement) Order 1994 (SI No. 97 of 1994). In the case of stillbirths occurring on or after the commencement of the Act, the parents of the stillborn child now have an option to notify the local registrar of the stillbirth. If they do not exercise that option, the relevant hospital or, where no hospital is involved, the relevant medical practitioner, must notify the local registrar of the stillbirth. Stillbirths which occurred before the commencement of the Act may also be registered, but only at the request of either parent. Stillbirth certificates are available to bereaved parents, but entries in the stillbirths registers are not publicly accessible.

S. 3 of the Act brings stillbirths registration within the organisational structure for births and deaths under the Births and Deaths Registration Acts 1863 to 1987. It extends the functions of an tArd-Chlaraitheoir (the Registrar-General), superintendent-registrars and registrars in relation to stillbirths registration and enables an tArd-Chlaraitheoir to give directions to, and require the performance of duties by superintendent-registrars and registrars in relation to stillbirths registration. The Schedule to the Act outlines the details to be recorded in stillbirths registers. S. 8 deals with entries in the stillbirths registers. S. 8(1) provides for transmission of register entries from local level to an tArd-Chlaraitheoir. S. 8(2) provides that where such an entry is forwarded, no copy is retained at local level; this differs from the position in relation to live births registers. S. 10 applies to offences relating to stillbirths registration the penalties for corresponding offences relating to births registration. The offences include failing to notify a registrar in the case of a person whose duty it is to do so, giving false information and breaches of duty by registrars. The fees are also similar to those for a birth certificate. Detailed provisions concerning the registration arrangements are contained in the Registration of Stillbirths Regulations 1994 (SI No. 426 of 1994) and the Vital Statistics (Stillbirths) Regulations 1994 (SI No. 427 of 1994).

Irish Language and Gaeltacht

Various legislative provisions impact only on those areas in the State (referred to as Gaeltacht areas) which contain a significant population using the Irish language on a regular basis. In addition to specific grant-aiding schemes for these areas, a number of administrative bodies operate to encourage development generally.

ÚDARAS NA GAELTACHTA

Elections The Údaras Na Gaeltachta Elections (Amendment) Regulations 1994 (SI No. 103 of 1994) amended the 1979 Regulations of the same title to bring the electoral arrangements for Údaras Na Gaeltachta into line with amendments to the general electoral law made by the Electoral Act 1992 (1992 Review, 141-4). The Údaras Na Gaeltachta (Polling Day) Order 1994 (SI No. 104 of 1994) specified that the 1994 election to An tÚdaras would coincide with that for the European Parliament.

Labour Law

CATEGORIES OF EMPLOYEE

In *Simon v The Dublin Institute of Technology* [1994] ELR 188, Morris J held that the applicant, an eligible part-time teacher employed by the respondent Institute, was a member of the academic staff of the Institute within the meaning of s. 6(4)(b) of the Dublin Institute of Technology Act 1992, so as to entitle him to vote at the election for membership of the governing body of the Institute. The respondent relied on s. 12(4) of the Act in support of its claim that the applicant was not entitled to vote. That provision empowers the Institute to 'appoint suitable persons to research fellowships, research assistantships and other support posts in relation to the offering of services on a temporary part-time or contract basis . . .' The argument here was that, being employed on this basis, such a teacher would not qualify to be regarded as a member of the academic staff.

Morris J considered that s. 12(4) envisaged that from time to time in the offering of services the need for extra personnel would be identified on a temporary basis. In passing that subsection, the Oireachtas had never envisaged that a significant part of the entire teaching staff would be employed under the terms of the subsection. Of 898 teachers, 198 were eligible part-time teachers, the other 700 comprising permanent whole-time teachers and temporary whole-time teachers. As a result of an agreement between the City of Dublin Vocational Education Committee and the Teachers Union of Ireland, the contract under which the applicant was employed was of a category which entitled him to the renewal of his contract subject to two conditions: that he had given a satisfactory performance during the previous year and that his hours of teaching were available for the forthcoming year. Morris J could not accept that the employment of teachers under the terms of such a contract was ever contemplated by the legislature in passing s. 12(2). He could not identify any significant feature as between the status of an eligible part-time teacher and a permanent part-time teacher such as would disqualify the former from membership of the academic staff of the Institute and yet qualify the latter. The conclusion that the applicant was a member of the academic staff was strengthened by the fact that he was, by virtue of s. 13(1)(a) of the Act, clearly an officer or servant of the Institute.

CONTRACT OF EMPLOYMENT

In *Marine Port and General Workers Union v Pandoro Ltd* [1994] ELR 244, Geoghegan J refused to grant a mandatory injunction restraining the defendant company from employing personnel to work on its 'ro-ro' operation in the deep-sea section of Dublin port other than from the register of workers kept by the plaintiff union in that regard. The practice that only workers registered with the union were employed by stevedores and shippers operating in the area was long-established and sanctioned by s. 62 of the Harbour Act 1946 which provides that:

> [a] harbour authority may, either alone or in co-operation with any other body or bodies, take such steps as they think proper to improve conditions of employment of casual workers at their harbour and, in particular, may institute a system of registration of such workers and of confinement of employment to registered workers, but the harbour authority shall not exercise any of their powers under this section where such workers and their employers have themselves instituted any such system.

The defendant company had formerly operated a service between Dublin and Britain. When it transferred to the deep-sea section, it claimed that it was not a party to any agreement requiring it to employ only registered personnel.

In his judgment Geoghegan J reviewed the history of Dublin Port and Docks, which was one of 'clearly ongoing problems and grievances.' The register had been maintained largely unchanged since 1971, because there was not enough work available to give a living to the established dockers, let alone new employees. The practical result was that no one on the register was younger than the age of forty five.

Prescinding from the merits of the case from an industrial relations standpoint, Geoghegan J interpreted s. 62 as meaning that no system of registration could have *statutory* force unless it had been created by the harbour authority under their powers pursuant to the section. The powers were conditional on the non-existence of a system of agreement between the workers and the employers. Such a system was of a contractual character and did not become a statutory system simply because it was the type of system that a harbour authority might institute if no such system had in fact been instituted.

Geoghegan J considered that the position regarding s. 62 was:

> quite simple. If a system exists it must be a system importing some concept of reasonableness whereby people can be added. In effect it

must be an ongoing system and not a dead register. If there is such a system then the harbour authority cannot institute its own system.

The action had to fail because nothing is s. 62 gave rights to the plaintiff union. If the union was correct, this would have the 'astonishing' effect that the defendant was precluded from employing anyone under the age of forty-five because the register had never been altered since 1971. Geoghegan J was satisfied that the section did not have this effect. The argument on behalf of the union that the contractual system became a statutory system if it was of the type of system that the harbour authority might have instituted if there was no system had a two- edged character. It was in Geoghegan J's view, 'inconceivable' that the port authority would have been entitled under the section to institute a system with such effect.

EMPLOYMENT EQUALITY

Adoptive leave   In the 1993 Review, 349-50, we discussed the subject of adoptive leave for men. In *Telecom Éireann v A Worker* [1994] ELR 195, the Labour Court held that the employer had discriminated against the claimant contrary to s. 3 of the Employment Equality Act 1977 in denying him adoptive leave under its adoptive leave scheme, which applied only to women.

It will be recalled that s. 16 of the 1977 Act differs from Article 2.3 of the Equal Treatment Directive in an important respect. Under s. 16, nothing in the legislation makes it unlawful for an employer 'to arrange for or provide special treatment to women in connection with pregnancy or childbirth'. Article 2.3, in contrast, allows exemption from equal treatment for provisions 'concerning the protection of women, particularly as regards pregnancy and maternity.'

The employer cited *Commission of the European Communities v Italian Republic* [1983] ELR 3273 in its support. There the Court of Justice had upheld legislation providing for adoptive leave for women only. It found that the distinction between men and women was justified by the legitimate concern to assimilate the conditions of entry of the child into the adoptive family with those of the arrival of a newborn child in the family during the very delicate initial period. The distinction did not amount to discrimination under the Directive since the exceptions in Article 2.3 were wide enough to cover maternity, as understood in relation to an adopting family.

The Labour Court understood this decision as permitting a state in its legislation, if it chose to do so, to interpret its right to discriminate positively in favour of women in a wide sense, as long as that discrimination came within the ambits of pregnancy and maternity; but it followed that, if a state chose to address its positive discrimination in favour of women in a narrower sense, it must also have the discretion to do that. It was a matter for the state to fix those parameters. In Ireland, s. 16, which set those parameters, had limited them to 'the purely biological circumstances of a woman with a new child in the family.'

In the view of the Labour Court, the only way the employer could rely on its right to discriminate in favour of women was to show that the 1977 Act permitted it to do so. To show that Italian law was in conformity with the Directive did not help because the Directive referred to pregnancy and maternity, whereas the Irish law was much narrower.

The employer could gain no assistance from cases where a state's legislation was broader than in Ireland because its adoptive leave scheme was not a statutory one. Such a scheme had to come within the 'saver' provision of s. 16 of the 1977 Act if it was to survive legal scrutiny. It did not do this. It seemed to the Labour Court that:

> if the Irish legislature has chosen a strict construction to the exceptions in Article 2.3, it is not for this Court to extend such construction. If, then, an employer voluntarily chooses to give favourable treatment to employees which goes outside the strict exceptions to the 1977 Act, he [*sic*] must do so without discrimination.

In reaching its conclusion the Labour Court expressed itself unable to agree with its earlier decision in *Aer Rianta v IDATU*, DEE 390.

Equal pay In the 1993 Review, 357, we discuss Lynch J's judgment in *Irish Crown Cork Co. v Desmond* [1993] ELR 180, a case raising the issue of whether the claimants were performing like work with a comparator. Lynch J remitted the case to the Labour Court as he concluded that it had misdirected itself in law in relation to s. 2(3) of the Anti-Discrimination (Pay) Act 1974. When the case came back to the Labour Court (*sub nom. Irish Crown Cork Co. Ltd v Services Industrial Professional Technical Union* [1994] ELR 193) the company claimed that the comparator merited a higher grade of pay because of his availability to perform certain multi-die work and other replacement work associated with the higher grade, as well as cleaning duties associated with a still higher grade. In essence, it was the comparator's economic value to the company that induced it to pay him at a higher rate, it said.

The Labour Court rejected this argument on the evidence. It was satisfied that the actual reason for the change in the comparator's employment, involving a higher level of pay, was 'to accommodate his personal preference.' The pay policy of the company had been one where men occupied the more remunerative posts. The company had pointed out that only very few women had applied for these positions. The Labour Court opined that the reason for this 'could well be that the culture in the company was to identify certain jobs as "men's jobs" and other jobs as "women's jobs".'

The Labour Court explained that it had been guided by the decision of the Court of Justice in Case 170/84, *Bilka Kaufhaus v Weber von Hartz* [1986] ELR 1607, to the effect that the national court must determine whether and to what extent grounds put forward by an employer to explain the adoption of a pay practice, which applies independently of a worker's sex but in fact affects more women than men, might be regarded as objectively justified on economic grounds and whether the measures chosen by the employer corresponded to a real need on the part of the undertaking. In the instant case, the company had not proved that its action in paying the comparator at a higher rate for the short-term reliefs on the multi-die machine corresponded to a real need on part of the undertaking or that it could be regarded as objectively justified on economic grounds.

It is clear that the Anti-Discrimination (Pay) Act 1974 does not permit class actions. This was agreed by all the parties in *Verbatim Ltd v Duffy* [1994] ELR 159. It nonetheless arose as an issue on the facts. The applicant for judicial review employed six hundred persons. An equal pay claim was launched, originally listing twenty-two names. The union representing the claimants later attached a list of forty-five more employees who wished to be added to the original claimants. It sought subsequently to add a further twenty claimants.

The applicant's solicitor, Dr Mary Redmond, protested to the Equality Officer about the difficulties flowing from the ever-growing number of claimants. She observed that:

> [t]here is no such thing as a class action in Ireland's equal pay law. An equal pay claim is based on a legal fiction, namely, the presence of an equality clause in the individual contract of employment. The term is implied when a man and a woman are employed on like work. The section dealing with like work is s. 3, which begins:
>
> 'two persons shall be regarded as employed on like work. . . .'
>
> As you are aware, work which is of (i) a similar nature and (ii) work which is of equal value are distinguishable species of like work, with different criteria applying to each. In the present claim we do not know whether the X women are alleged to be employed on the same work, similar work, or work of equal value — to say nothing about the

differences between them in terms of the time of their claim. Obviously the case cannot proceed on the basis of assumptions; and . . . the onus is on the claimants to make out what the work equation is *inter se*.

The same difficulty applies to the comparators. What is the position *inter se*? Is it alleged — or not — that each of the comparators performs the same work/similar work/work of equal value? Or is it alleged that some of the comparators perform the same work etc. with each other, so that there are, as it were, some groups. We do not know what is alleged. Perhaps it is alleged that all the comparators are doing the same work, etc. *inter se*.

It is permissible to make a further point. In equal pay claims the work/wages equation, if successful, results in an entitlement to equal pay. Suppose that one comparator receives Z £ per week; and that another receives Z plus £ and a third comparator receives Z £ plus plus and so on. It is blatantly ridiculous to allege equal pay as against all three. . . .

Kinlen J was struck by the force of these arguments. He made a declaration that the union's application for redress on behalf of the claimants, as then formulated, comprised a multiplicity of class actions both in respect of these claimants and the several individuals nominated as comparators of the 1974 Act. There had been considerable delay in the prosecution of the claim. This had been compounded by a refusal to co-operate with the requirements of the Equality Officer originally assigned to hear the application as well as a persistent failure to provide the applicant with proper information relating to the claims. Kinlen J held that these factors constituted an abuse of process. He made an order of *mandamus* directed at the union, requiring it to withdraw its application on behalf of the claimants.

In the 1993 Review, 357-8, we discussed Murphy J's decision in *Faulkner v Minister for Industry and Commerce* [1994] ELR 187, to the effect that, whilst it is desirable that equality officers and the Labour Court should state in an unambiguous fashion the facts that form the basis of their determinations, it was not as a matter of law necessary to comply with this counsel of excellence. In taking this view, Murphy J was reflecting the language of Finlay CJ in *North Western Health Board v Martyn* [1987] IR 565, at 579.

The same issue arose in *Golding v The Labour Court and Cahill May Roberts Ltd* [1994] ELR 153. The applicants had taken equal pay proceedings under the Anti-Discrimination (Pay) Act 1974. An Equality Officer, in a detailed analysis of the facts of the application, had recommended against them on the basis that their work was not 'like work' to that performed by a male comparator. The Labour Court upheld that recommendation in a determination which recited the conclusions of the Equality Officer and stated that it was satisfied that they were well-founded. The applicants took proceedings for judicial review, claiming that the Labour Court's determination was so laconic that they were incapable of appealing on a question of law to the High Court in the absence of a clear statement of reasons for the determination.

Keane J rejected this contention. In view of the lengthy nature of the Equality Officer's recommendation, involving a number of findings of facts from which she drew her conclusions, coupled with the holding of the Labour Court that her conclusions were well founded, it followed inevitably that the Labour Court was upholding the material findings of fact which had been put in issue by the applicants on appeal and was also upholding her conclusions. Having regard to the Labour Court's specific incorporation in its determination of the Equality Officer's recommendations and the letter of appeal and its unqualified acceptance that her conclusions were well founded, there was not 'the slightest difficulty' in elaborating the reasons for the Labour Court's decision, which were clearly in substance the same as those which had led to the recommendation of the Equality Officer. What was essential was not that the determination of the Labour Court should, as a matter of law, take any particular form, but rather that the manner in which it was expressed should leave no grounds for doubt as to the reasons that led to the decision, thus ensuring that neither the supervisory nor appellate jurisdiction of the High Court was frustrated by an inadequate indication of reasons.

Pregnancy   In *Fox v National Council for the Blind* [1995] ELR 74, the Equality Officer rejected a claim that the respondent had discriminated against the claimant because of her sex when it withdrew its offer of employment on a fixed-term contract on discovering that she was pregnant. The Employment Equality Agency had alleged that there had been both direct discrimination, on the ground of the claimant's sex under s. 2(a) of the Employment Equality Act 1977, and indirect discrimination, on grounds of sex and marital status, in terms of s. 2(c), on the basis that unfavourable treatment because of pregnancy can only adversely impact on women and never on men.

The position in question was that of trainer of people with limited vision or no sight. The claimant had sought maternity leave for a period when the respondent had organised an essential training programme for the trainers, which involved some foreign travel. The Equality Officer concluded that the withdrawal of the offer of employment had been caused by the claimant's inability to fulfil an essential part of the contract rather than because of her sex or marital status.

The Equality Officer distinguished the instant case from the Court of Justice's judgments in cases involving pregnancy e.g. Case No. C/32/93 *Webb v Emo Cargo (UK) Ltd* and Case No. C.41/92 *Habermann/Beltermann v Arbeiterwohlfahrt, Bezirksverband*, on the basis that in these judgments the Court had referred to the fact that the contracts of employment were for an *indefinite* duration. The contract in the instant case was for a fixed term and the training was an essential part of it.

Sexual harassment In an important decision in *The Health Board v B.C. and the Labour Court* [1994] ELR 27, Costello J held that, as a matter of law, the Labour Court had been in error in holding that the appellant Health Board had discriminated against the claimant, in a claim for compensation for discrimination under s. 22 of the Employment Equality Act 1977, because the Labour Court had wrongly concluded that the appellant was vicariously liable for its employees' wrongful acts. Accordingly he overruled the award of £3,500 compensation.

The claimant had been employed for fifteen years by the appellant before she was transferred to the area where her assailants were working. For a period of six weeks, she was subjected to 'lewd and course remarks' by them. They touched her without her consent and generally harassed her. She threatened them that she would report them to her superiors and the union if they did not resist. They ignored her complaints. One day, when she was working alone, they both violently assaulted her in a grossly indecent way. She complained to her superiors. An investigation took place. Both assailants admitted what they had done and wrote letters of regret. One was dismissed; the other was suspended without pay for five weeks. The assailants were subsequently prosecuted unsuccessfully for indecent assault; Costello J noted that prosecutions fail for many reasons and that the verdict in no way affected the undoubted fact that the claimant had suffered a violent sexual assault at the hands of her attackers. It had such a devastating effect on her that she was out of work for nearly a year afterwards.

The essence of the claimant's case was that the Health Board had been guilty of discrimination in relation to conditions of employment. S. 3 of the 1977 Act includes discrimination in relation to conditions of employment as one form of discrimination that is prohibited by s. 2.

The Labour Court proceeded on the basis that the issue was whether the Health Board had taken *all reasonable steps to prevent the actions on which the complaint was based.* It stated that:

in dealing with cases of sexual harassment, it does and will take into account steps taken by employers to eliminate and prevent sexual harassment in the work place. Whilst accepting that an employer cannot guarantee total prevention of harassment, the Court will look for and take note of what steps have been taken. The adoption of a Code of Practice, the adoption of a policy statement on the prevention of sexual harassment, the existence of guidelines as to how all staff should behave and the establishment of clear grievance procedures, all constitute the kind of 'reasonable steps' which employers should adopt and which will be accepted by the Court as evidence of the employer's *bona fides* in this type of dispute. Clearly, information about steps must be widely circulated in the place of work and information on the employer's attitude to acts of sexual harassment made available to all staff.

The Health Board, prior to the assault, had distributed guidelines to its supervisors on how to deal with complaints of discrimination, but the guidelines did not indicate any steps to be taken to ensure that acts of sexual harassment did not occur, nor were employees informed of the procedures to be adopted if they were the victims of sexual harassment. The Labour Court did not consider that this degree of action by the Health Board constituted 'reasonable steps.'

The Labour Court went on to hold that the assailants' acts had been 'sexually offensive and . . . a form of harassment directly related to the claimant's sex and constituted less favourable treatment of her because of her sex'. This was contrary to s. 2(a) of the 1977 Act. Recalling that, in an earlier determination (Order N 2/1988), it had held that employers have a duty to ensure that employees enjoy working conditions free from sexual harassment, the Labour Court stated that it was reasonable to interpret s. 3 of the Act in a manner that was consistent with the overall policy of the Act. It noted that it had already set out its views on the reasonable steps employers should take and that it had concluded that in the instant case those steps had not been taken. Accordingly it upheld the Equality Officer's conclusion that the Health Board was guilty of discrimination in relation to the claimant.

On appeal to the High Court, Costello J placed considerable emphasis on the fact that the 1977 Act had not followed the same approach as its British counterpart, the Sex Discrimination Act 1975, in that it had not included a provision equivalent to s. 41 of the 1975 Act, subs. (1) of which provides that anything done by a person in the course of employment is to be treated as done by the employer as well as that employee, whether or not it was done with the employer's knowledge or approval; this principle is qualified by subs. (2), giving the employer a defence where he or she took such steps as were reasonably practicable to prevent the employee from doing that act or from doing in the course of his or her employment acts of that description. Costello J noted that the absence of a similar provision in the Irish Act of

1977 meant that the law of vicarious liability in this field was significantly different in the two jurisdictions.

Costello J's analysis proceeded as follows. The conduct of the assailants towards the claimant *prior* to the day of the assault constituted sexual harassment and clearly had a detrimental effect on the conditions in which she worked. The special problem presented by the facts of the case was the conduct of the assailants on the day in question:

> If an employee suddenly rapes a fellow employee, it seems to me that it would be a most imprecise use of language to describe him as having 'harassed' her — his conduct would have amounted to an act different in kind to what is meant by that term. And there may be other acts of sexual assault not amounting to rape which likewise are more serious in kind (and not merely in degree) than the conduct which that term connotes. But there are special features in this case which need to be noted. This is a case of a period of sexual harassment which culminated in a violent assault. . . . I will assume for the purpose of the case the assault on the [day in question] can be regarded as part of a course of conduct of which each part can reasonably be regarded as amounting to an act of sexual harassment.

The analysis here conflates two separate issues. The first is whether a violent sexual assault is capable of coming within the scope of the concept of sexual harassment. The second is whether such conduct falls outside the net of liability (vicarious or otherwise) on the part of an employer for an employee's conduct. The answer to the first question may seem a curious one: it is that the question is not the most appropriate one to ask. The crucial question is whether the conduct constitutes *discrimination* for the purposes of s. 3. If it does, it matters not that it is conduct other than sexual harassment. One might, in any event, have considered that, if sexual harassment constitutes discrimination, more seriously intrusive conduct such as rape would do so, *a fortiori*.

As to the second issue, relating to the employer's liability for violent sexual assault, it is clear that, in tort law, an employer would not normally be vicariously liable for conduct of this kind, since it could not be considered to have occurred within the course of the employee's employement. Two points should, however, be noted. First, an employer may indeed be liable in tort law, *personally* rather than vicariously, if he or she does not take reasonable steps to protect an employee from such violent sexual assault. Second, the employment environment may be one in which it is known that sexual harassment, at times of a very serious kind, has been condoned and 'institutionalised' to such a degree that it is not preposterous to speak of serious acts of sexual assault falling within the range of vicarious liability in tort. It may be that, in relation to a particular employer, it could not be said that sexual harassment had been an institutionalised feature of the work environment but in determining the parameters of vicarious liability in tort, the courts have not limited their focus to the practices of the particular employer.

At all events Costello J went on to argue that, although the *employees'* acts had amounted to discrimination within the meaning of s.2, s.3 prohibited acts by *employers*, and the Board:

> did not itself commit the acts of which complaint is made. The Board only infringed the section if it was vicariously liable for what its employees did on [the day in question]. It is at this point that I think the Labour Court's determination fell into error.

Costello J considered that, in the absence of express statutory provision, Irish law in relation to the liability of an employer for the tortious acts (including statutory torts) of an employee was 'perfectly clear': that vicarious liability would attach only where the act was committed by the employee within the scope of his or her employment. But, said Costello J,

> this is not the test in which the Labour Court applied in this case. Instead of considering whether in committing the assault on the claimant on [the day in question] the Board's employees were acting within the scope of their employment, the Labour Court applied in effect the statutory test of vicarious liability contained in s. 41 of the British Sex Discrimination Act 1975. . . . This has no counterpart in the Irish 1977 Act, and it erred in doing so.

> What the Labour Court should have done was to consider whether the employees were acting within the scope of their employment when they committed the violent sexual assault on the claimant. . . . This question admits to only one answer. An employer may, of course, be vicariously liable when his employee is acting negligently, or even criminally. It has not been shown either in the Equality Officer's Report or the Labour Court's determination what was the nature of employment in which the claimant's fellow-workers were engaged on [the day in question]. But I cannot envisage any employment in which they were engaged in respect of which a sexual assault would be regarded as so connected with it as to amount to an act within its scope. The Board is not therefore vicariously liable for what occurred.

Costello J found support for this conclusion in the fact that a Discussion Document published by the Department of Labour in 1987 had raised the question whether the legislation should be amended to include a provision specifying the extent of an employer's liability for acts of sexual harassment by an employee and the fact that Dr Déirdre Curtin, in *Irish Employment Equality Law*, p. 286 had described the absence of such an express provision as the major lacuna of the 1977 Act.

Reading the Labour Court's determination carefully it may be argued that it was seeking to impose liability, not on the basis of *vicarious* responsibility but rather on the basis of a broad duty resting on the employer to establish a system of work that reduces the potential for sexual harassment in the workplace. Under such an approach, the employer would not be liable *automatically* for one employee's sexual harassment of another (which is the position under vicarious liability, once the appropriate nexus has been established between the employment and the conduct in question). Similarly an employer would not *automatically* be exempt from liability, which is the position following from Costello J's rejection of vicarious liability and his failure to consider the possibility of non-vicarious liability attaching to the employer, provided the employer had failed to establish a reasonable system for reducing the potential for sexual harassment. This is akin to employers' liability for the negligent failure to provide a safe system of work for their employees (or to provide safe co-workers).

It is interesting to note that s. 41 of the British Act of 1975 does not in fact impose vicarious liability on an employer. It establishes a presumption of negligence on the part of the employer, capable of being rebutted by proof (on the balance of probabilities) that the employer took '*such steps as were reasonably practicable*' to prevent the act giving rise to the complaint.

In *A Company v A Worker* [1994] ELR 202, the claimant had worked as a kitchen help in the kitchen of the Company's restaurant. She was continually sexually harassed by her immediate supervisor, the head chef. This was of such intensity that she was obliged to resign. She took proceedings under s. 27 of the Employment Equality Act 1977; the dispute therefore was about whether there had been a contravention of s. 3(4) of the Act.

The company argued that Costello J's decision in *The Health Board v BC and the Labour Court* [1994] ELR 27 governed the case and that no vicarious liability arose. The claimant had made no complaint to the company director, who visited the premises several times a week and, the company claimed, the conduct of the head chef had been outside the scope of this employment.

The Labour Court rejected this argument, being satisfied that the company was indeed vicariously liable for the behaviour of the head chef:

He was responsible for the hiring and direction of staff; he had authority to dismiss staff. He had control over what occurred in the work-place, and that control had been given to him by the company; he represented the company *vis-à-vis* the other employees. The company must therefore taken responsibility if he abuses his position of power which, in his case, he did.

The Court was satisfied that the workers, including the claimant, had been too intimidated by the head chef to complain about his behaviour to the director of the company. It stated:

It was the company which had placed the head chief in the position of power which he held, and from which he carried out his intimidation. It must therefore be liable for his actions while exercising that power, even though it was not aware of those actions at the relevant time. The actions committed by the head chef were clearly committed within the scope of his employment, in that he was responsible for the supervision and management of the staff, and he chose to exercise those responsibilities in such manner as the Court has found amounted to sexual harassment. It was in the performance of his own duties that he harassed the employee, and that harassment amounted to discrimination within the meaning of s. 3(4) of the Act.

The contrast between these two approaches to the position of an employer in relation to acts of sexual harassment by an employee is striking. On the one hand, Costello J was unwilling to contemplate any non-vicarious basis of liability; on the other hand, the Labour Court extended the scope of vicarious liability very far – further, indeed, than the approach it had favoured in the earlier case where Costello J held that it had been mistaken. There is much to be said in favour of that approach. The absence of a legislative equivalent to the English legislation should not prevent the development of the rigorous, but not unduly strict, test that the earlier approach of the Labour Court incorporated.

For a comprehensive analysis of Costello J's decision in the *B.C.* case, see Noel Harvey and Adrian Twomey, *Sexual Harassment in the Workplace* (1995), 55-73.

FAIR PROCEDURES

In *Healy v Minister for Defence*, High Court, July 7, 1994, Barron J held that fair procedures had not been adopted in the decision (on more than one occasion), not to give the plaintiff, an army corporal, a posting that had been promised him. The plaintiff's claim, as we noted, was not based on promissory estoppel or legitimate expectation but rather on the right to fair procedures guaranteed by the Constitution.

Barron J regarded *Meskell v Córas Iompair Éireann* [1973] IR 121 as the authority for the plaintiff's right of action. His brief reference to Walsh J's holding in that case indicated that he considered that it warranted the awarding of damages for breach of fair procedures, with no serious argument to the contrary. Barron J accepted that an award of exemplary damages was in principle possible for an unconstitutional breach of fair procedures. Having regard, however, to the principles set out in the judgments of Finlay CJ and Griffin J in *Conway v Irish National Teachers Organisation* [1991] 2 IR 205 (analysed in the 1991 Review, 448-53), it seemed to Barron J that exemplary damages should not be awarded, since the plaintiff had not established any conscious or willful disregard of his constitutional rights.

STRIKES

In *Nolan Transport (Oaklands) Ltd v Halligan* [1995] ELR 1, Barron J gave some important guidance on the meaning and scope of a number of provisions in Part II of the Industrial Relations Act 1990, analysed in the 1990 Review, 347-55. In view of the small number of written judgments that have been given on this legislation, it is worth quoting *in extenso* what Barron J had to say. He considered that:

> A number of basic principles emerge from the provisions of this Act. First, it seems to me, that it is the policy of the Act that industrial relations should primarily be dealt with by the Labour Court and the other tribunals set up by the Act for mediating and conciliating and determining industrial relations disputes. Secondly, it seems to me that, so far as the law is to be applied to industrial relations disputes, the right to take industrial action including the right to picket has been restricted essentially to a right to workers to take action against their own employer and no one else. An exception to that does exist in Section 11 but is only intended to permit secondary picketing when the person being picketed has acted out of its ordinary course of business and solely for the purpose of making the primary picketing ineffective. . . . The right which emerges is that workmen may take action against their employer in relation to a dispute between others. In other words, workmen may picket their own employer in order to urge that employer to bring pressure to bear on the employer involved in the primary

dispute. Finally, it is essential before any industrial action is taken that those who are taking the industrial action shall first have had a secret ballot on the issue. If a majority is in favour of industrial action then that is a matter for the union concerned to determine whether or not the industrial action should take place. Where more than one union is concerned the Act provides that the majority of those voting is to be the guide and that the fact that there may be a majority in one union but not a majority overall would not entitle that union to commence industrial action.

Where workers are not in a union they do not have the right to be consulted as to whether or not industrial action should take place involving their workplace. In the ordinary course where all the workmen are a member of one or more unions the matter doesn't arise. However, in a case like the present, where there were a large number who were not members of the union at the time of the ballot . . . the Act does not give them any direct say in whether or not there should be industrial action.

The Act also protects acts done by two or more persons in contemplation or furtherance of a trade dispute provided that such acts done by one person would not be unlawful: ss. 10, 11 and 12. However, this protection is lost when the action is in disregard of or contrary to the outcome of a secret ballot relating to the issue or issues involved in he dispute: s. 17. These latter words are significant and suggest that the validity of the secret ballot is dependent upon proof that those voting were aware of the issue or issues involved.

In the instant case a union had sought to represent all the employees of the plaintiff's business. It also expressed concern at incidents which, it claimed, amounted to the dismissal of two of these employees. It involved itself in a strike against the plaintiff (professedly preceded by a valid secret ballot authorising industrial action) and it circulated publications casting aspersions on the plaintiff's employment practices.

The strike was protracted; the plaintiff's losses were very substantial. The plaintiff sought damages and an injunction, claiming that it was the victim of defamation and malicious falsehood.

Two crucial issues needed to be resolved. The first was whether the requirements of the 1990 Act regarding the holding of a secret ballot had been fulfilled. Barron J held that they had not. Several employees testified that they had not voted in favour of industrial action, contrary to the declared result. After a detailed review of the evidence, Barron J concluded:

> Having regard to all the circumstances and in particular to my belief that they gave fair and honest evidence I am satisfied that the declared result did not reflect the votes actually cast and was deliberately false.

The ballot papers produced in court could not therefore have been those actually used. When and in what manner all or some of them had been substituted for real ones, Barron J could not say.

The defendants contended, first, that the declared result of the secret ballot could not be contested by the plaintiff, but by the members themselves. Barron J rejected this argument. In his view, the secrecy of the ballot was 'a matter for the individual member who voted'. He could see no ground of public policy upon which such evidence should be disallowed. The obligation to hold a secret ballot was one imposed by rules of the union. S. 14(3) provided that the rights conferred by these rules were conferred on the union members and no one else. This did not mean that a secret ballot could be investigated only at the instance of the members. In so far as rights were conferred upon the members voting 'and no other person', the members by giving sworn evidence were availing themselves of such rights, there being no proviso in the subsection that such rights could be availed of only in proceedings to which they were parties. Nor could the union avoid the obligation imposed on it regarding the manner in which the ballot should be conducted. Furthermore, the allegation that the result had been not properly declared was an allegation of fraud. In Barron J's view, a section in an enactment could 'not be used as an instrument of fraud so that the defendants would not be entitled in refuting the allegation of fraud to rely solely upon subs. (3).'

The second major issue related to the definition of a trade dispute. Barron J noted that, since the enactment of the 1990 Act, it was clear that as between employers and employees everything pertaining to the terms and conditions of employment might be the subject of a trade dispute. Disputes between employees, however, were no longer capable of forming the basis of a trade dispute. One of the grounds upon which the plaintiff had submitted that there was no trade dispute in existence in the instant case was that the real dispute lay between those drivers who did not wish to be represented by the union and those who did. Barron J rejected this argument. In his view, the real dispute was between the company and the union, in relation to which the drivers at work supported the company and the drivers on strike supported the union.

In the instant case, the issue whether the two employees had been dismissed had been hotly contested. Barron J accepted the evidence on behalf of the plaintiff, to the effect that then no one had in fact been dismissed. There had been 'no more than a series of rows [one] evening . . . followed by a refusal to work on the part of the first two defendants on the [following] morning.' Nevertheless, if the union *bona fide* believed that they had been dismissed, a trade dispute would have existed until such time as the company had unequivocally made it clear to the men and to the union that there was no impediment to their return to work.

If the dismissals stood alone, there were factors which supported both sides of the issue. These dismissals, however, could not be isolated from the other events taking place at that time. It seemed to Barron J that the union had been following one overall strategy and that was to represent the entire workforce. Barron J did not believe that the union had ever regarded the issue of dismissals as more than an event to use to its advantage. Although the rows which had led to the allegations were not contrived, this aspect of the dispute had not been pursued *bona fide* to get the two men back to work but as part of the policy to take all of the drivers into membership. This was the real dispute between the parties.

Barron J stated:

> A claim to represent its own members is a trade dispute since it relates to a condition of their employment: see *Becton Dickinson v Lee* [1973] IR 1. But a claim to negotiate on behalf of all the workmen in a particular employment is an attempt to deprive those who are not members of their right of free association. On the basis of [*Educational Company of Ireland v Fitzpatrick* [1961] IR 365] this cannot form the basis of a trade dispute. Further, where what would be a trade dispute is put forward as a cloak for the real dispute, the element of *bona fides* is lacking and so even what would otherwise have been a genuine dispute ceases to be such. To find otherwise would as in the case of the false ballot be to allow s. 13 to be used as an instrument of fraud. The situation is analogous to that where the wrongful use of a power invalidates its exercise.

Counsel for the defendants submitted that the union was protected from liability in the proceedings by virtue of the provisions of s. 13 of the 1990 Act. In relation to s. 13(1) counsel for the union relied upon the decision in *Corry v National Union of Vintners, Grocers and Allied Trades Assistants* [1950] IR 315. That case held, on the authority of *Vacher and Sons Ltd v London Society of Compositors* [1913] AC 107, that no case lay against the union. However, *Corry* had been based on s. 4 of the Trade Disputes Act, 1906 which had barred all actions in tort against a union. The protection granted by s. 13(1) was limited to cases where a trade dispute existed. It did not avail the union in the present case. In Barron J's view, once there was no *bona fide* trade dispute in existence, such protection was lost.

Barron J then addressed s. 13(2), which provides as follows:

> In an action against a trade union or person referred to in subs. (1) in respect of any tortious act alleged or found to have been committed by or on behalf of a trade union it shall be a defence if the act was done in the reasonable belief that it was done in contemplation of furtherance of a trade dispute.

He observed:

> The defence under s. 13(2) lies in two different circumstances. There may be doubt as to whether acts done in furtherance or contemplation of a trade dispute are in fact so done. If there is a reasonable belief that they are so done, then the defence will prevail. Equally, where there is no trade dispute, the issue arises as to whether in relation to the acts done there is a reasonable belief that such a dispute existed. In the present case the fact that the creation of the dispute and the commencement of the industrial action was not *bona fide* does not of itself mean subsequent actions by the union or by other branches of the union were necessarily *mala fide*. Nevertheless the provision of s. 13(2) must be established as a matter of defence. It is therefore a matter for the union to establish such belief.

No witnesses had in fact given evidence on this issue. There was no evidence of any belief that the wider issue of recognition as opposed to the narrower issue was also a trade dispute. As a result the union was liable for the tortious activity established to the same extent as the other defendants.

UNFAIR DISMISSAL

Misconduct In *The Commissioners of Irish Lights v Sugg* [1994] ELR 97, Morris J affirmed the finding of the Circuit Court Judge that the applicant had not been unfairly dismissed from his employment as steward and assistant chef on board of one of the Commissioners' tenders. The applicant had failed to report for duty after the termination of the period of his shore leave. He delayed in reporting sick for over a day and he failed to supply a medical certificate for a further six days. The background to the case was that on previous occasions, when the applicant had 'a problem with alcoholism', he had failed to return promptly from shore leave and had been given a sharply-drafted ultimatum by his employers that, if he failed to comply with service regulations over the following two years, he would be discharged. The applicant's alcohol problem had been resolved satisfactorily. His failure to return from shore leave on the occasion in question was attributable to an ankle injury, which first gave the applicant trouble shortly before he went on shore leave.

Morris J emphasised the fact that the applicant had been aware that each member of the crew was essential to the smooth running of the vessel and that a relief crew had to be provided if any member of the regular crew was not available. Any conscientious or reasonable employee would have taken the fundamental step of warning his employer before leaving the vessel or at least made an effort to do so during the period of shore leave.

Illness   The illness of an employee can naturally generate controversy as to whether it is of sufficient seriousness and duration to constitute a frustration of the employment contract. In *Boyle v Marathon Petroleum (Ireland) Ltd* [1995] ELR 200, the claimant had been employed as an offshore production operator since 1997. He had been injured in an accident in January 1990 and remained unfit to return to work until the autumn of that year. He had declared a willingness to return at that time, supported by medical reports. His employer did not authorise his return and formally terminated his employment in June 1993 on the basis that his pre-accident position had been filled and there was no work available for him.

The Tribunal held that the claimant's contract of employment had been frustrated at a date *earlier* than he had informed his employer of his fitness to return. The doctrine of frustration terminated the contract and there had therefore been no onus on the employer to inform the claimant that the contract was at an end.

Redundancy   In *St. Ledger v Frontline Distribution Ireland Ltd* [1995] ELR 160, the Tribunal gave important guidance on the nature of redundancy. Definitions (d) and (e) of s. 7(2) of the Redundancy Payments Act 1967 (as amended by the Redundancy Payments Act 1971) provide as follows:

> (d) the fact that the employer has decided that the work for which the employee had been employed (or had been doing before his dismissal) should henceforward be done in a different manner for which the employee is not sufficiently qualified or trained,
>
> (e) the fact that his employer has decided that the work for which the employee had been employed (or had been doing before his dismissal) should henceforward be done by a person who is also capable of doing other work for which the employee is not sufficiently qualified or trained.

The claimant was a warehouse supervisor who had been dismissed and replaced by a person with no better qualifications. The employer argued that the new person had greater ability than the claimant. Invoking definition (e), it claimed that, though the nature of the work remained the same, the volume had increased and the new person was better able to handle the increase. It contended that the words 'other work' in definition (e) include an increase in the volume of the work.

The Tribunal could not accept this argument. It stated:

> Redundancy had two characteristics which are of importance in this case. It is impersonal and it involves change.

> Impersonality runs throughout the five definitions in the Act. Redundancy impacts on the job and only as a consequence of the redundancy does the person involved lose his job. It is worthy of note that the E.C. Directive on Collective Redundancies uses a shorter and simpler definition: 'one or more reasons not related to the individual workers concerned'.

> Change also runs through all five definitions. This means change in the workplace. The most dramatic change of all is a complete close down. Change may also mean a reduction in needs for employees, or a reduction in numbers. Definitions (d) and (e) involve change in the way the work is done or some other form of change in the nature of the job. Under these two definitions change in the job must mean qualitative change. Definition (e) must involve, partly at least, work of a different kind, and that is the only meaning we can put on the words 'other work'. More work or less work of the same kind does not mean 'other work' and is only quantitative change. In any event the quantitative change in this case is in the wrong direction. A downward change in the volume of work might imply redundancy under another definition, (b), but an upward change would not.

For redundancy to arise in the instant case the employer would have to satisfy the Tribunal that the nature of the job had changed and that, in connection with the change, and only in connection with the change, the person replacing the claimant had certain training which the claimant had not. The Tribunal was satisfied that the nature of the work had not changed, nor had the manner in which it was done. Therefore there was no redundancy within the meaning of either definition (d) or (e).

There was a further reason why redundancy did not arise in the case. There had been no evidence that the person replacing the claimant had any special training, either in the formal sense or related to work experience. The employer stated that he had more ability. But, observed the Tribunal,

> Ability is not the same as training. It is irrelevant whether the person
> replacing the claimant is better able to do the work previously done by
> the claimant. To hold otherwise would be to deny the essential imper-
> sonality of redundancy.

In *McElroy v Floraville Nurseries Ltd* [1994] ELR 91, the Tribunal held
that the claimant's dismissal had been unfair on the basis that a genuine
redundancy situation had not existed. While it was true that there had been
a diminution in the particular service which was part of her duties (in the
preparation of dried and silk flower arrangements), the remaining areas of
work where she was employed, in loading, unloading and customer assistance, for which other employees were recruited on a part-time basis,
continued.

In *Loscher v Mount Temple Comprehensive School* [1990] ELR 84, the
Tribunal rejected on the evidence the contention that the respondent school's
failure to re-employ the claimant was because of his religious and political
views. The Tribunal found that, as a result of the recruitment of a full-time
teacher, the teaching hours at the school had been re-organised, a genuine
redundancy situation existed and the claimant had not been unfairly selected
for redundancy. The evidence before the Tribunal had clearly indicated that
eligible part-time teachers were vulnerable in this type of situation.

The Tribunal was satisfied that there had been 'no evidence whatever' to
support the claimant's contention that he had been dismissed as a result of
religious or political discrimination. The claimant had submitted twenty
suggested timetables to the Tribunal which were designed to show that he
could have been retained by the school. The Tribunal, in its determination,
noted that it had examined one of them and did 'not dispute that those
timetables could be drawn up by a competent person.' It considered, however, that this was not the issue before the Tribunal.

Transfer of undertakings   In *Grady v Irish Society for the Prevention of
Cruelty to Animals* [1994] ELR 225, the Tribunal held that Dublin Corporation, in originally arranging for the ISPCA to provide a dog warden service
and in subsequently putting it up for tender, accepted by the second defendant
Mr Prendeville, had not involved itself in a transfer of undertakings. Under
the Control of Dogs Act 1986, the Corporation was under a duty to provide
this service. The Tribunal accepted the Corporation's argument that it had
never been the employer of the claimants but had merely entered into an
arrangement whereby its obligations under the Act would be fulfilled.

The Tribunal held, however, that there had been a transfer of undertakings when its functions had passed to Mr Prendeville and that the claimants were entitled to be employed by him on the same terms and conditions as with the ISPCA. It considered that Mr Prendeville's attempt to require the claimants to apply in writing for the position as a pre-condition of employing them 'was an attempt to put the onus on the employees to apply, while as we understand the Directive the onus is on the transferee to approach the employees.'

Inability to obtain insurance cover   In *Brennan v Bluegas Ltd* [1994] ELR 941, the Tribunal held that the claimant had not been dismissed unfairly where he had been involved in three traffic accidents within the period of six months and his employer unsuccessfully had sought insurance cover for the claimant from six insurance companies. The company's underwriters in Britain had greatly increased the premium. The Tribunal did not address the claimant's argument that regard should be had to the circumstances of each accident. The first had been minor, liability for the second had been disputed and a report on the third had identified mechanical problems as its cause. It was not clear whether the insurance companies were aware of this report. It is unfortunate that this aspect of the case was not addressed. It would seem unfortunate if an employee who had the misfortune to be involved, without any fault on his or her part, in several accidents could be dismissed because of an insurance company's increase of premium or refusal of cover as a result of this misfortune.

Fair procedures   In *Williams v St James Hospital Board* [1995] ELR 180, the Tribunal, by a majority, held that the procedures adopted in investigating alleged sexual harassment and intimidation, culminating in the dismissal of the claimants, had not been unfair. A female employee had complained to her father, also an employee, that two porters had intimidated her at work. Her father had spoken to her supervisor about these complaints over a period of twelve months. The father made a formal complaint, which was referred to the personnel department. Sexual harassment was mentioned by her to her father in October of 1993. The chief technologist, after he had received the complaints, interviewed all the porters individually and outlined to them the nature of the complaints. All of them denied any knowledge of them. He warned them about their behaviour in the future. During November 1993 items of graffiti were brought to the attention of the chief technologist. In evidence to the Tribunal he said that he might have spoken to the porters collectively but none of them accepted responsibility for any of the graffiti mentioned. He later circulated a memo indicating that graffiti had been found in the laboratory and warned that all staff should be vigilant in this matter.

One of the female porters at around the end of November approached the chief technologist and told him that two of her colleagues were annoying her and that she found it difficult to report for work. She told the personnel officer that she was being intimidated and treated badly by her two male colleagues. When she was asked if she wished to make a statement on the matter she did so.

The industrial relations officer was involved in the formal investigation into the allegations and complaints. The claimants were informed that they were being suspended with pay pending a full investigation in the matter. Their trade union representative was told what was happening. The personnel officer interviewed the complainant, the claimants and some other employees. The father of the original complainant was also interviewed and he gave a statement. Following the completion of the investigation, meetings were held separately with the claimants. The trade union representative was also in attendance. It was confirmed to them at the meetings that an investigation had been completed and statements had been taken from the three complainants. Copies of the three statements were given to the claimants, and they were given an opportunity of putting their case. Having discussed the matter at length it was confirmed verbally (and later in writing) to the claimants that management were left with no option but to recommend their dismissal. The decision to dismiss was appealed to the chief executive officer.

The chief executive officer was given copies of all the relevant documentation and he interviewed the industrial relations officer to satisfy himself that all procedures had been adhered to properly. He also interviewed the two male porters individually. He concluded that intimidation had gone on for some time. He was satisfied that the chief technologist had cautioned the porters but no attempt had been made by them to change their behaviour. He considered the possibility of lengthy suspension or re-assignment elsewhere in the hospital but was satisfied that there was no other area in the hospital to which he could assign them. He felt that the harassment was sufficient to warrant their dismissal. He had decided not to interview the original complainant on the basis, as he later said in evidence, that 'nothing good would come out of it'. He had before him a letter from her specialist.

One of the two claimants told the Tribunal that he had seen the statements made by the three complainants and that he was denying all the allegations contained in them. He was also denying the allegations in relation to the drawing of graffiti which he said were there before he commenced working in the hospital. He said that he had not in the past been involved in any disciplinary matter and even though the chief technologist had spoken to himself and his male colleagues he had not realised that the matter was serious and he did not take it seriously. The chief technologist had spoken about graffiti only and did not mention sexual harassment. His view was that the whole matter stemmed from the fact that he and another colleague were asked to do certain duties being carried out at the time by one of the female porters. The other claimant did not attend the Tribunal to give evidence.

The majority finding was that the employer had acted fairly and reasonably in making its decision to dismiss the claimants, given the information available to it at the time of making the decision to dismiss.

The dissent was based on the failure of the chief executive to interview the original complainant and her failure to attend the Tribunal hearing.

Jurisdiction   In *The Commissioners of Irish Lights v Sugg* [1994] ELR 97, which we discuss above, 311-2, in relation to grounds for dismissal, Morris J was satisfied that there was 'ample precedent' for an appeal to the High Court from a decision of the Circuit Court on appeal from the Employment Appeals Tribunal. The appeal to the High Court took the form of a full rehearing of the case.

In *Martin v PDFORRA* [1995] ELR 159 the claimant had been employed as General Secretary of the Permanent Defence Force Other Ranks Representative Association (PDFORRA) up to the time of termination of employment. As a preliminary issue it was submitted to the Tribunal by counsel for the respondent that the claimant had been in employment which is an excluded category under section 2(1)(d) of the Unfair Dismissals Act 1977. Prior to his secondment to PDFORRA the claimant had been a warrant officer in the naval section of the defence forces and remained at all times under the control of the Minister for Defence. While on secondment to PDFORRA the claimant received his military pay as a warrant officer in addition to his salary as general secretary and, on occasions, he wore his military uniform. It was also a condition that the person to be appointed to the position of general secretary would be a serving member of the defence forces. It was therefore contended that the claimant was at all times a member of the defence forces, a category excluded under the Act.

It was submitted on behalf of the claimant that during his secondment from the naval service to PDFORRA he was not a member of the defence forces. The constitution of PDFORRA stipulated that the general secretary would be a full time employee of the Association and would be employed on a contractual basis. The claimant argued that the fact that his contract of employment excluded the terms of the Act from its termination demonstrated that the contract was premised on acceptance that the Act applied during the period of the contract.

The Tribunal held that the position of general secretary of PDFORRA was so integrated into employment in the defence forces that it was impossible to separate the two. It was a qualifying condition of the position of general secretary that candidates be members of the defence forces. It was also a condition that the person appointed as general secretary should remain a member of the defence forces during the tenure of the office. The Tribunal was therefore satisfied that the claimant was excluded under section (1)(d) of the 1977 Act. Accordingly the Tribunal had no jurisdiction to hear the claim.

In *Concannon v St Grellan's Boys National School Ballinasloe, Co. Galway* [1994] ELR 229, the case had been part heard and then settled, the settlement being reduced to a written agreement. When the case came before the Tribunal, the claimant applied to have the case adjourned to a date after a specific date eleven months thereafter. The respondent applied to have the case struck out.

The Tribunal held that a claim or appeal could be removed from the jurisdiction of the Tribunal was either by way of a withdrawal pursuant to Regulation No. 4 of the Unfair Dismissals (Claims and Appeals) Regulations 1977 (SI No. 286 of 1977) or under s. 8 of the Act itself. It was of opinion that the Tribunal did not have jurisdiction to strike out a claim or appeal on the application of the respondent. Because the claimant was unwilling to withdraw his application prior to the end of the eleven-month period, it necessarily followed that his case could not be struck out by the Tribunal before then. Since neither party had sought the resumption of the hearing of the case in the meantime, the only option was for the Tribunal to adjourn the proceedings, as provided for in Regulation No. 14 of the Redundancy (Redundancy Appeals Tribunal) Regulations 1968 (SI No. 24 of 1968). The Tribunal considered that it did not have jurisdiction to adjourn from 'time to time', which it construed as meaning to adjourn to a definitive time in the future. Accordingly, it adjourned the matter until a specific date just over eleven months thereafter.

Limitation period In *Brady v Panwels Trafco (Ireland) Ltd* [1995] ELR 202, the Tribunal dismissed a claim for unfair dismissal served more than six months after the date of dismissal, and too soon for the discretionary extension of time under the amending legislation of 1993 (cf. the 1993 Review 367). The Tribunal could not accept the fact that the employer had allowed the claimant's application to go forward for consideration under the employer's permanent health insurance scheme 'as in any way rendering the letter of dismissal null and void or re-activating his employee status. . . .'

WRONGFUL DISMISSAL

In *Shortt v Data Packaging Ltd* [1994] ELR 251, the plaintiff, who had been dismissed from his position as managing director, with 'immediate effect', on the ground of redundancy, sought an interlocutory injunction restraining his employer from appointing anyone else to the position and continuing to pay his salary and other benefits. He contended that the dismissal had not been in conformity with the employer's Memorandum and Articles of Association, which provided that he could be dismissed only for stated reasons of incompetence, misconduct or infirmity, and that he had not been given a fair opportunity to correct any opinion relied on by the employer in determining his dismissal.

The employer disagreed with the plaintiff's interpretation of the Memorandum and Articles of Association. It argued that, if the plaintiff considered his dismissal unfair, he could always take a claim under the Unfair Dismissals Acts 1977 to 1993. The reliefs he sought would, in the employer's submission, amount to an order for the specific performance of a contract of employment, which is not legally permissible.

Keane J granted the interlocutory injunction, on the basis that the plaintiff had made out a fair issue. He was satisfied that damages would not be an adequate remedy where the plaintiff would have to await the trial of the action in circumstances where he was totally without remuneration. The balance of convenience also was in favour of granting the injunction. Any loss sustained by the defendant would be adequately met by the plaintiff's undertakings as to damages and to perform such duties on behalf of the employer as were reasonably appropriate pending the trial of the action.

In the Administrative Law Chapter, in the section on Judicial Review, above, 9-10, we discuss Morris J's judgment in *Gallagher v Revenue Commissioners* [1994] ELR 231 relating to fair procedures in the dismissal process.

Land Law

Paul Coughlan, School of Law, Trinity College Dublin

CO-OWNERSHIP

Legislative attempt to impose co-ownership of family homes   By means of the Matrimonial Home Bill 1993 the Oireachtas attempted to introduce a statutory right of co-ownership in favour of spouses. Under s. 4 of the Bill, where a dwelling had at any time since June 25, 1993 been occupied by a married couple and either or both of the spouses had an interest in the dwelling, the equitable interest in that dwelling was to vest in both spouses as joint tenants. S. 5 provided that s. 4 did not apply to an interest in a matrimonial home which was vested in spouses as joint tenants or tenants in common in equal shares. S. 6 empowered the court, on an application by the spouse who was not the spouse in whose favour s. 4 operated, to declare that the provisions of s. 4 should not apply to the matrimonial home as and from a specified date. By virtue of s. 7, a spouse who would otherwise benefit from the operation of s. 4 could, after obtaining independent legal advice, make a declaration in writing to the effect that s. 4 should not apply to the matrimonial home. In the absence of an agreement to the contrary, s. 14 provided that household chattels owned by either or both of the spouses would belong to both spouses as joint owners.

The President referred the Bill to the Supreme Court under Article 26 of the Constitution where it was found to be repugnant to Article 41 of the Constitution (*In re Article 26 and the Matrimonial Home Bill 1993* [1994] 1 IR 305; [1994] 1 ILRM 241). It was accepted that the encouragement by appropriate means of joint ownership in family homes was conducive to the stability of marriage and the general protection of the institution of the family. However, the right of a married couple to make a joint decision as to the ownership of a matrimonial home was one of the rights of the family recognised in Article 41.1.1 as being inalienable and imprescriptible, and antecedent and superior to all positive law. The exercise of this right was an important part of the authority of the family which the State guaranteed to protect in Article 41.1.2. The Bill's application of automatic ownership as joint tenants to every instance of a dwelling occupied by a married couple on or after June 25, 1993 interfered with decisions which may have been jointly made with regard to the ownership of the matrimonial home. This application was universal and was not dependent on the decision being injurious or oppressive in respect of a spouse or members of the family or the failure by a spouse to discharge his or her family obligations. The mandatory creation of joint equal interests also applied to every family home irrespective of when it was first acquired by the married couple and irrespective of the time at which a freely reached decision between the spouses may have been made as to the nature of the ownership and in whom it should vest. If a joint decision that ownership should vest in only one of the spouses had been made, after the coming into force of the Bill this could only continue if the non-owning spouse made a declaration in accordance with s. 7. The non-owning spouse, on grounds which could be reasonable or unreasonable, might refuse to make such a declaration and this could lead a couple who may have been content but not enthusiastic about the arrangements which they had made, and by which a substantial part of their married life had been governed, to become involved in the litigation contemplated in s. 6. The Bill could result in the automatic cancellation of a joint decision freely made by both spouses and its substitution with a wholly different decision unless the spouses could agree to a new joint decision confirming the earlier agreement or the owning spouse could obtain an order under s. 6. According to the court, this did not constitute reasonably proportionate intervention by the State with the rights of the family and amounted to a failure by the State to protect the authority of the family guaranteed by Article 41. The fact that joint ownership of the matrimonial home can be conducive to the stability of marriage could not justify such potentially indiscriminate alteration of joint decisions validly made within the authority of the family.

While it is arguable that an Act providing for the joint ownership of any matrimonial home acquired in the future would not attract the same objections as the 1993 Bill, as it would not interfere with decisions already reached by spouses, the government declined to engage in any further attempt to legislate for a general principle of co-ownership. At present the Oireachtas merely encourages the creation of joint tenancies as between married couples with the aid of modest financial incentives. In this regard s. 14 of the Family Home Protection Act 1976 provides that no stamp duty, land registration fee, Registry of Deeds fee or court fee shall be payable on any transaction creating a joint tenancy between spouses in respect of a family home where the home was immediately prior to such transaction owned by either spouse or by both spouses otherwise than as joint tenants.

FAMILY HOME PROTECTION ACT 1976

When does a house become a family home? Where a property is being purchased in the name of one spouse with the aid of a loan secured by a mortgage, it is commonplace for the mortgagee to require the consent of the non-owning spouse to the mortgage even though the married couple have not yet taken possession of the property. Prior to its amendment by s. 54(1)(a) of the Family Law Act 1995, s. 2(1) of the Family Home Protection Act 1976 provided that the term 'family home' meant:

> primarily, a dwelling in which a married couple ordinarily reside. The expression comprises, in addition, a dwelling in which a spouse whose protection is in issue ordinarily resides, or if that spouse has left the other spouse, ordinarily resided before so leaving.

In *National Irish Bank Ltd v Graham* [1994] 2 ILRM 109 the Supreme Court was called upon to decide whether premises can constitute a family home within the meaning of s. 2(1) at a point in time before a married couple begin to reside there. On August 29, 1989 the first, third and fifth named defendants purchased a large estate of approximately 3,000 acres with the aid of a loan granted by the plaintiff. The loan was secured by a deed of mortgage dated August 9, 1989 which had been executed by the first, second, third and fifth named defendants, along with their solicitor who had purchased the property in trust for them. At this time the first and second named defendants were married to each other, the third and fourth named defendants were married to each other and the fifth named defendant was unmarried. However, the latter got married on November 17, 1990. None of the mortgagors obtained possession of the land until after completion of the purchase and execution of the mortgage. On February 21, 1991 the mortgagors, with the consent of the plaintiff, transferred some of the land between themselves and executed three further mortgages in favour of the plaintiff. The mortgagors defaulted in repayment of the loan and the plaintiff sought an order of possession so that it could exercise its power of sale under the first mortgage. An affidavit filed on behalf of the plaintiff stated that the the third and fourth named defendants had been in possession of the land prior to August 9, 1989 and that the fourth named defendant had given her prior consent to the mortgage. This statement was subsequently corrected by means of later affidavits which averred that the third and fourth named defendants had not been in occupation before that date and that the fourth named defendant had not given any prior consent to the mortgage. The defendants claimed that the four mortgages were void under s. 3 of the 1976 Act.

In a judgment delivered on November 8, 1993 (reported at [1994] 1 ILRM 372) Costello J made an order of possession in favour of the plaintiff which excluded certain parts of the land which were already subject to contracts of sale which had been entered into with the plaintiff's consent. The defendants appealed to the Supreme Court which dismissed their appeal on May 4, 1994. Finlay CJ (with whom Egan and Blayney JJ concurred) held that the use of the word 'primarily' in the first sentence of s. 2(1) meant that the definition of a family home as a dwelling in which a married couple ordinarily reside was in the first place the appropriate definition under the 1976 Act. The second sentence, which refers to a dwelling in which a spouse whose protection is in issue ordinarily resides, provided an additional or subsidiary definition. Both definitions were expressed in complete terms and so left no room for the addition of any other subsidiary definition by means of judicial interpretation.

Finlay CJ concluded his judgment by observing that in reality a joint conveyancing transaction had taken place whereby the land was conveyed to the purchasers who immediately executed a mortgage in favour of the bank which had advanced a substantial portion of the purchase money. By virtue of this transaction the purchasers acquired an equity of redemption. It would be inconsistent with both the purposes and the provisions of the 1976 Act if the consent of the wife to the mortgage which was part of this transaction was required. Finlay CJ was careful to point out that different considerations would apply where land was acquired under a conveyance and was then, within a short time, subsequently mortgaged so as to provide the purchase price which up to then had been supplied by means of a bridging loan. The substantive approach taken by Finlay CJ echoes that adopted by the House of Lords in *Abbey National Building Society v Cann* [1991] 1 AC 56. The purchaser acquires nothing more than an equity of redemption because from the outset the property is bound by the mortgage securing the loan without which it would not have been transferred in the first place. Insofar as it concentrates on what is perceived as the substance of the successive transactions rather than the legal form which they have to adopt, it may be explained as an attempt to protect mortgagees who have, by insisting on execution of the mortgage at the same time as the conveyance in favour of the mortgagor, done all in their power to prevent the creation of intervening rights or interests.

PRIORITIES

Operation of application for property adjustment order as *lis pendens*
In *S. v S.* [1994] 1 IR 407; [1994] 2 ILRM 68 the applicant wife instituted proceedings against the respondent husband seeking a decree of judicial separation, together with various ancillary orders including an order pursuant to s. 15 of the Judicial Separation and Family Law Reform Act 1989 directing the respondent to transfer his entire estate and interest in the family home to her. Following the commencement of these proceedings, it came to the applicant's attention that Allied Irish Banks plc ('the bank') was about to

register a judgment mortgage against the property. The applicant obtained an interlocutory order pursuant to s. 11(c) of the 1989 Act preventing the registration of the judgment mortgage pending the hearing of the judicial separation proceedings. The bank subsequently sought the lifting of the s. 11 order so as to enable it to register its judgment mortgage before the court considered the applicant's claim to a property adjustment order.

Geoghegan J refused to lift the s. 11 order. To be affected by a *lis pendens* land must be connected with or constitute the subject-matter of the legal proceedings. Geoghegan J held, albeit reluctantly, that a claim for a property adjustment order under s. 15 of the Judicial Separation and Family Law Reform Act 1989 was a registrable *lis pendens* even though the property right at issue was contingent upon the court exercising its discretion so as to make an order in favour of the applicant spouse.

Geoghegan J regarded the system established by the Judgments (Ireland) Act 1844 as being specifically for the protection of purchasers and mortgagees. Under s. 10 of the 1844 Act, a *lis pendens* is binding upon a purchaser or mortgagee if he has actual notice of the litigation or the proceedings have been registered under the Act. Accordingly, a person whose claim to the land has not been acquired for value (i.e. a volunteer) will be bound by the *lis pendens*, regardless of whether he had notice of it and irrespective of whether it has been registered pursuant to the 1844 Act. In this case the pending application under the 1989 Act had not been registered as a *lis pendens*, but the bank had been given prior notice of the proceedings. Such notice on the part of the bank was in any event irrelevant. A judgment mortgagee is treated as a volunteer because no consideration is given for the security rights over the judgment debtor's land which are obtained through registration under the Judgment Mortgage (Ireland) Acts 1850–58. Thus even if the order under s. 11 of the 1989 Act had not been made, a property adjustment order made by the court would have priority over any judgment mortgage which the bank might have registered beforehand. Hence Geoghegan J concluded that it would be prejudicial to the applicant and ultimately pointless for the court to permit the bank to register a judgment mortgage prior to the making of the property adjustment order.

LANDLORD AND TENANT

Forfeiture of leasehold interest   In *Bank of Ireland Finance v McSorley*, unreported, June 24, 1994, Mr and Mrs Macari were assigned the interest under a 1959 lease in 1981. The lease was held from Cork Corporation and was registered as an incumbrance on the folio pertaining to the freehold. In 1981 Bank of Ireland Finance Ltd advanced £20,000 to Mr and Mrs Macari on the security of the leasehold interest. The premises were damaged by fire in 1983 and in February 1987 the Corporation served a notice under s. 14 of the Conveyancing Act 1881 on Mr Macari requiring the repair of the premises. In June 1987 the Corporation purported to re-enter the premises. By a contract dated October 11, 1988, the Corporation agreed to sell the fee simple estate in the premises to Mr McSorley. The contract referred to the folio in which the premises were registered and contained a special condition which provided that the vendor would furnish evidence of the surrender or forfeiture or other evidence as to the termination of any lease affecting the premises. On January 19, 1989 the Corporation wrote to Mr McSorley's solicitors and indicated that it was in a position to furnish all documents necessary to have the 1959 lease cancelled as a burden. The sale was completed on March 13, 1991 and on the same date Mr McSorley executed a document which acknowledged that he held the premises on trust for his wife. On April 3, 1991 Mrs McSorley was registered as owner of the premises subject to the 1959 lease. Mrs McSorley then entered into a contract to sell the premises and applied to the Land Registry for the discharge of the 1959 lease as a burden. However, problems were identified by the Chief Examiner of Titles in that the assignment to Mr and Mrs Macari had not been duly stamped, a forfeiture notice served under s. 14 of the 1881 Act on only one of two lessees was insufficient and the re-entry to the premises effected by the Corporation was not made on foot of the notice requiring repairs. It was then discovered that Bank of Ireland Finance Ltd claimed to have an equitable mortgage over the leasehold interest and it objected to the discharge of the lease as a burden on the folio. In 1991 the Corporation and Mrs McSorley purported to re-enter the premises for non-payment of rent. Bank of Ireland Finance Ltd instituted proceedings seeking to enforce its security and Mr and Mrs McSorley counterclaimed seeking damages on the grounds that the bank had maliciously abused the process of the court.

Murphy J held that while the bank might have found it difficult to persuade the court to grant relief against forfeiture, it could not be said that it would have been impossible to do so. Even if relief had been granted on the basis of all arrears of rent being paid and the lessee reconstructing the premises, there may have been some money left over after a sale of the leasehold interest by the bank which could have reduced the debt owed by Mr and Mrs Macari to the bank. Accordingly, Murphy J found that it had been reasonable for the bank to institute the proceedings and there had been no improper purpose.

As Mr and Mrs Macari were joint tenants of the leasehold interest and the forfeiture notice under s. 14 of the 1881 Act was neither addressed to nor served upon Mrs Macari, it followed that the lease had not been validly forfeited. The Corporation attempted to rely upon the case of *Pollok v Kelly*

(1856) 6 ICLR 367 as authority for the proposition that service of a notice to quit on one of several tenants is sufficient service on all of the tenants. Murphy J observed at p. 16 of the transcript:

> That case is merely authority for the proposition that service of a notice to quit on a person who is admittedly a tenant on the premises is some evidence of service on all the tenants. In that case the issue arose on the admissibility of the notice to quit and it was held that at the stage the document was tendered it should be admitted as there was some evidence that by serving at least one tenant all of the tenants had been served. The logic of that approach, as I understand it, is that where at the end of the day the evidence establishes that in fact only one of several joint tenants have been served that the notice to quit would be defective. I see no reason why the service of a forfeiture notice should be any different.

MORTGAGES

Mortgagee as trustee of surplus proceeds of sale   In *Murphy v Allied Irish Banks Ltd* [1994] 2 ILRM 220 the plaintiff's mother, who held shares in a company called Royal Candy Ltd ('the company'), created a charge over her house in favour of the defendant bank on February 13, 1957. The plaintiff's mother died on December 26, 1962. On November 4, 1965 the bank sold the house for £4,081 and, after deducting debts which had been secured by the charge (including an amount owed by the company) and the costs of realisation, credited a demand deposit account in the name of the plaintiff's mother with the balance of £1,980. On a number of subsequent occasions the bank informed members of the deceased's family that it had sold the house and that there had been a surplus. However, neither the plaintiff nor any of the deceased's other children required the bank to hand over this surplus. On October 15, 1984 the plaintiff instituted proceedings against the bank in respect of its failure to invest the surplus and on February 18, 1987 he extracted letters of administration in respect of his mother's estate. While conceding that the bank had been entitled to sell the house, the plaintiff claimed that it had no right to satisfy debts owed by the company out of the proceeds of sale.

Murphy J held that it was highly probable that the plaintiff's mother had given a guarantee to the defendant in respect of the company's debts. Accordingly, the bank had been entitled to discharge the debts due to it by the company out of the proceeds of sale. On the sale of the house the bank became an express trustee in respect of the balance of the proceeds remaining after discharge of the debts and costs. However, placing this balance in an account did not discharge the bank's obligations as a trustee as it did not constitute payment of these moneys. Instead it was merely a procedure by which payment could be made conveniently when sought by the personal representative of the deceased.

Murphy J observed that a mortgagee who is a trustee by virtue of the retention of surplus moneys following the sale of mortgaged property can be obliged to pay interest on those moneys to the person who is entitled to them. As an alternative to the payment of interest on trust moneys, a trustee may be required to pay the profits of a business successfully carried on by him with trust moneys. Here the plaintiff had not proved what profits earned by the bank during the relevant period were attributable to the balance retained by it. Hence the plaintiff was prima facie entitled to interest on the surplus. The appropriate rate of interest could not be determined, as had been claimed by the plaintiff, by reference to the amount which would have been earned if the surplus had been invested in a building society. Where a trustee is empowered and required to invest trust moneys within any range of investments authorised by the deed of trust or statute and neglects to do so, the extent of his liability can only be determined on the basis of the yield which would have accrued to the trust fund by investment in the security least beneficial to the trust fund. There was no basis for assuming that the trustee would have exercised his discretion in a more effective manner. The rate of interest payable by a trustee should be determined either by reference to the court rate of interest or to the yield on a deposit account payable on demand in a licensed bank. As the bank had identified the rate of interest payable on deposit accounts since April 1981, interest should be calculated at this rate for that period and, having regard to disparities between the court rate of 4% and market rates, at 8% from the date of realisation to April 1981.

The bank had sought to resist the plaintiff's claim by reference to the Statute of Limitations 1957, s. 43 of which provides that an action in respect of a breach of trust cannot be brought against a trustee or any person claiming through him after the expiration of six years from the date on which the right of action accrued. Murphy J was satisfied that the bank had not recognised at any time that it might be liable for a breach of trust. In any event, the rules as to acknowledgement contained in Chapter III of the Statute of Limitations 1957 do not apply to actions for breach of trust. The fact that a trustee admits liability for the trust money itself does not prevent time from running in respect of an action for breach of trust in which interest on that money might be sought. Accordingly, as there had been no fraud on the part of the bank, any claim to interest on the surplus for the period up to October 15, 1978 (i.e. six years prior to the initiation of the plaintiff's action) was barred.

Validity of lease over mortgaged premises In *ICC Bank plc v Verling* [1995] ILRM 123 the first named defendant executed a mortgage of premises used as an off-licence in favour of the plaintiff on May 31, 1991. Clause 15 of the mortgage provided that the statutory and other powers of leasing should not be exercisable by the borrower in respect of the mortgaged premises, nor should the borrower part with possession or grant any licence to occupy the premises, without the prior consent in writing of the lender. The reference to statutory powers of leasing relates to s. 18 of the Conveyancing Act 1881 which gives a mortgagor in possession of mortgaged premises the power to grant a lease of the premises without the mortgagee having to join in the lease. This power is subject various provisos, including that contained in s. 18(13), which states that the section applies only if and as far as a contrary intention is not expressed by the mortgagor and the mortgagee in the mortgage deed or otherwise in writing. The mortgage was registered in the Registry of Deeds on August 14, 1991. On March 23, 1993 the first named defendant purported to let the premises to the third named defendant for a term of two years and nine months from January 1, 1993. The licences pertaining to the premises were transferred into the name of the second named defendant as the nominee of the third named defendant and a notice to this effect was published in the Irish Press on March 29, 1993. On July 20, 1993 the plaintiff's solicitors wrote to the solicitors acting for the second and third named defendants and informed them that as it had not consented to the granting of the lease it was void. On April 27, 1994 the plaintiff instituted proceedings in which it sought possession and an order that the sums due by the first named defendant were well charged on the premises. It also applied for mandatory and prohibitory interlocutory injunctions requiring the defendants to vacate the premises. On July 19, 1994 the first named defendant wrote to the plaintiff indicating that he wished to return the keys to the premises. The plaintiff argued that the lease in favour of the third named defendant was null and void having regard to s. 18 of the 1881 Act. The second and third named defendants argued that by virtue of the plaintiff's delay and acquiescence, they had been allowed to expend money and so the plaintiff was estopped from claiming that the lease was void. In particular, it was argued that the plaintiff had been put on notice of the lease by the newspaper advertisement of March 29, 1993 which announced the transfer of the licence.

Lynch J held that clause 15 of the mortgage constituted an indication of a contrary intention within the meaning of s. 18(13) and so the lease was null and void. As to the estoppel argument, Lynch J pointed out that mortgagees are under no obligation to scrutinise every newspaper in the country to see if there are any notices of dealings purporting to affect mortgaged property. On the contrary, mortgagees are entitled to expect that mortgagors will not flagrantly ignore and breach covenants such as that contained in clause 15 of the mortgage in this case. The second and third named defendants had to be regarded as having notice of the mortgage as it was registered in the Registry of Deeds and they could have discovered its existence by means of a simple search. Furthermore, the plaintiff had not acquiesced in or recognised the lease by any express or positive conduct, such as demanding or accepting rent in place of the first named defendant. The fact that the plaintiff did not immediately engage in litigation was hardly blameworthy, especially as such delay as had occurred did not cause detriment to the defendants but rather left them enjoying the premises without the payment of rent. Any expenditure on stock made by the defendants would have been recouped through profits made on the sale of such stock, and in any event the stock had been purchased with full knowledge of the plaintiff's objection to the lease. In these circumstances Lynch J concluded that the plaintiff was entitled to the interlocutory relief which it had sought.

REGISTERED LAND

Effect of *lis pendens* as against person with actual notice   In *S. v S.* [1994] 1 IR 407; [1994] 2 ILRM 68 Geoghegan J expressed the view that a *lis pendens* pertaining to registered land which had not been registered as a burden under s. 69(1)(i) of the Registration of Title Act 1964 would bind either a volunteer or a person who had actual notice. But the clear import of the Act is that the only matters which can bind a registered transferee for value without appearing on the register are the burdens which, by virtue of s. 72, are specifically deemed to affect registered land without registration. S. 31 excludes the equitable doctrine of notice by providing that in the absence of actual fraud, the registered title of a person is not affected by notice of any deed, document or matter relating to the land. Accordingly, a person who is registered as the owner of land in the context of a *bona fide* transaction supported by valuable consideration cannot be bound by an interest which does not appear on the register. It is irrelevant that either he or his agent knew of this interest, or would have found out about it if they had made inquiries.

VENDOR AND PURCHASER

Vendor's obligations as regards incumbrances   In *Bank of Ireland Finance Ltd v McSorley*, unreported, June 24, 1994, the facts of which are outlined above, Mr and Mrs McSorley claimed that as Cork Corporation had conveyed the premises to Mr McSorley as 'beneficial owner' they were entitled to rely upon the covenant for quiet enjoyment implied into the conveyance by virtue of s. 7 of the Conveyancing Act 1881 and the continued existence of the 1959 lease as a burden on the folio breached that covenant. However, the folio mentioned in the contract of sale revealed the existence of the 1959 lease and so Murphy J rejected this argument at p. 13 of the transcript in the following terms:

> In my view the combination of the standard form of transfer in conjunction with a folio disclosing a particular estate or interest is equivalent to a conveyance made expressly subject to such estates and interests.

Murphy J held that the terms of the letter of January 19, 1989 were an amplification of the special condition to the effect that the vendor would furnish evidence of the surrender, forfeiture or termination of any lease affecting the premises. That special condition, as clarified, did not merge in the subsequent transfer of the premises on March 13, 1991 because of the presumed intention of the parties. If the transfer dealt solely with the freehold estate subject to and with the benefit of the 1959 lease, it was reasonable to infer or presume that the parties intended that their obligations and rights in relation to the leasehold interest would continue to be dealt with and be governed by the contract of sale.

Even if the forfeiture notice served on Mr Macari alone had been effective, there would still have been a breach of contract by the Corporation because the absence of a properly stamped assignment would have meant that the vendor could not prove the identity of the tenants. The informal surrender or assignment of the leasehold interest by Mr and Mrs Macari on June 24, 1991 remedied this breach of contract, as did Mrs McSorley's re-entry of the premises for non-payment of rent in August 1991. However, the fact remained that there was insufficient evidence to secure the discharge of the lease as a burden from the folio and that Bank of Ireland Finance Ltd might apply for relief against the forfeiture of the lease over which it held an equitable mortgage. Murphy J concluded that the Corporation was in breach of its contract from the date on which the application was made to discharge the burden until the date on which the bank announced in court that it was abandoning its claim for relief against forfeiture. Murphy J proceeded to award Mr and Mrs McSorley damages of £22,700 as against the Corporation.

In *Cadden v McCaffrey*, unreported, January 19, 1994, the defendants agreed to sell The Hibernian Hotel, Clones, to the plaintiffs under a contract dated June 14, 1988. The property was subsequently conveyed to the plaintiffs. However, it transpired that at the time of the contract the hotel was subject to two mortgages and a judgment mortgage. The defendants had sold the hotel as beneficial owners and so the covenants for title implied by s. 7 of the Conveyancing Act 1881 applied. By virtue of this provision a vendor is obliged to discharge mortgages prior to completion and if he does not and the land is conveyed subject to any mortgages, the purchaser is entitled to sue for any loss which he suffers as a consequence. Here the amounts due on foot of the two mortgages and the judgment mortgage had mounted since the date of completion and Costello J held that the plaintiffs were entitled to recover damages equal to those sums from the defendants. One final point which is worth noting is Costello J's criticism of the fact that in this case the same solicitor acted for both the plaintiffs and the defendants in relation to the sale. However, Costello J accepted that this had not contributed to the difficulties which had resulted in the litigation.

Law Reform

In 1994, the Law Reform Commission published three Reports and a Consultation Paper. We examine the Commission's *Report on Non-Fatal Offences Against the Person* (LRC 45–1994) and its *Report on Contempt of Court* (LRC 47-1994) in the Criminal Law Chapter above, 192-200 and 158-67. The Commission's *Report on Occupiers' Liability* (LRC 46–1994) led to legislation in 1995 which was based largely on the recommendations of the Commission but which differed from them in some important respects. We shall examine this Report in the context of that legislation in the 1995 Review. For analysis of the legislation, see Binchy, 'The Occupiers' Liability Act 1995', Law Society's Continuing Legal Education lecture series, March 13, 1996.

The Commission published a *Consultation Paper on Family Courts* in 1994. We shall examine that paper in the context of our analysis of the Commission's *Report on Family Courts* (LRC 52–1996), published in March 1996.

Limitation of Actions

At the beginning of the chapters we are happy to welcome publication of the second edition of James Brady and Tony Kerr's *Limitation of Actions in the Republic of Ireland* (1994). This work provides a comprehensive and penetrating analysis of the subject.

BREACH OF TRUST

In *Murphy v Allied Irish Banks Ltd* [1994] 2 ILRM 20, Murphy J addressed the matter, rarely litigated, of the limitation period for proceedings for breach of trust. S. 43 of the Statute of Limitations 1957 provides that an action of this type is not to be brought against a trustee (or any person claiming through the trustee) after the expiration of six years from the date on which the right of action accrued. This limitation is subject to s. 44, which provides that the limitation period does not apply where there was a fraudulent breach of trust to which the trustee was party or privy or the claim is to recover trust property or its proceeds still retained by the trustee and converted to his or her own use. The 'fraud' envisaged by s. 44 must amount to dishonesty: *Collings v Wade* [1896] 1 IR 340. In the instant case, there was no question of the circumstances being governed by s. 44.

The plaintiff sought to ensure that the limitation period might be extended by virtue of an acknowledgment allegedly given by the bank. Murphy J did not consider that an *acknowledgment* within the meaning and for the purposes of Chapter III of the 1957 Act had any application otherwise than in respect of a recognition of the title of a claimant to certain lands, mortgages, property and, more particularly, to a 'debt'. No convincing argument had been made to the effect that the doctrine of acknowledgment had any application to an action for breach of trust. The fact that a trustee admitted liability for trust monies and was accountable therefor did not prevent the statute running. The six-year limitation period accordingly applied.

DISMISSAL FOR WANT OF PROSECUTION

In *Primor plc (formerly PMPA Insurance plc) (Under Administration) v Stokes Kennedy Crowley (a firm)*, High Court, February 11, 1994, O'Hanlon

J, reversing the decision of the Master of the High Court, refused the defendants' application to strike out an action for breach of contract and negligence against them. The case arose from the debacle in which the PMPA Group had been placed under administration in 1983. The defendants had been appointed as statutory auditors for the plaintiff company in 1978. They acted in that capacity for one year only, with another firm of auditors. They had also acted as statutory auditors of one company within the PMPA Group. The gravamen of the plaintiff's case was that the defendants had failed to discharge their obligations as auditors in a prudent manner, resulting in loss to the plaintiff.

The case had proceeded at a snail's pace. The plenary summons had been issued at the end of 1984 but not served for a year. The statement of claim was issued in early 1986. It was met by a notice for particulars to which the plaintiff replied two years later. The defence did not emerge until January 1991.

O'Hanlon J accepted that the plaintiff had been guilty of delay but in his view the defendants had also been lethargic. He quoted from a wide range of Irish and English authorities which recognised that a defendant's delay is a factor to be taken into account in the exercise of the court's discretion as to whether to dismiss a case for want of prosecution. He considered that the defendants' failure to complain about the plaintiff's delay in making discovery and their failure to comply with the discovery order before bringing their application for dismissal were features of the case that were fatal to their application. A further factor was the relative lack of prejudice that they would suffer by being obliged to defend the case so long after the events in issue:

> A long delay in bringing a claim to a hearing may be much more prejudicial in certain types of action than in others. Where a claim and the defence to the claim have to be based largely on oral evidence, and the availability and recollection of particular witnesses, as in cases of injury caused by accident, or other personal injuries cases, the reliability of the witness evidence is bound to be diminished by the passage of time.

> The death of essential witnesses may make it impossible to have a fair hearing of the case for and against the plaintiff. So also may the destruction of essential documentation or the non-availability of witnesses. . . .

> On the other hand, a claim made in a commercial case may be based largely or entirely on documentation which has been preserved and which is still available for production in evidence years after the transaction to which it relates has been finalised.

While O'Hanlon J considered that he should not dismiss the action, he acknowledged that the defendants should be given a further opportunity to raise again the wholly exceptional lapse of time between *the completion of the audit* (in 1979) and the hearing of the claim. A much clearer picture might emerge, when the action came to trial, of the extent of prejudice caused to the defendants by the delay. He regarded this ground for dismissal as worthy of distinct characterisation, separate from that of dismissal for want of prosecution, since it is not premised on any default on the part of the plaintiff. O'Hanlon J regarded the decisions of *Toal v Duignan (Nos. 1 and 2)* [1991] ILRM 135, 140 as falling within this distinct 'no-fault' category. There is much to be said for this approach, which has yet to find clear endorsement by the Supreme Court.

The Supreme Court reversed O'Hanlon J on December 21, 1995. We shall discuss the Supreme Court decision in the 1995 Review. We need merely note that there appears to be a great deal of strength in O'Hanlon J's analysis.

The failure of the defendant to bring a motion to dismiss the proceedings will not *always* be a factor tilting against him or her. In *Kerrigan v Massey Brothers (Funerals) Ltd*, High Court, March 15, 1994, Geoghegan J held that it naturally could not tilt against a plaintiff whose inaction was attributable to the fact that he or she was unaware that a plenary summons had been issued because it had not yet been served on the plaintiff. He observed that:

> [t]here cannot be an obligation on a defendant to search in the Central Office to ascertain whether a plenary summons had been issued or not before treating the case as closed.

Kerrigan involved an application for extending the time for leave to renew the plenary summons. Geoghegan J cautioned that the principles and case law relating to dismissing actions on grounds of delay were 'quite different'. Nevertheless, it is surely a desirable principle of law that one should not be penalised for failure to act when one could not reasonably have been aware of the need to do so.

SURVIVAL OF ACTIONS

S. 9 of the Civil Liability Act 1961 requires that litigation against the estate of a deceased person be taken within two years from the date of the death of the deceased. In *Bus Éireann v Insurance Corporation of Ireland plc* [1994] 2 ILRM 444, the deceased had been killed in an accident in 1987 in which his vehicle had crashed into a bus. Proceedings launched on behalf of his estate proved unsuccessful as the deceased was held to have been the cause of the accident. The plaintiff company, whose bus received £17,000 worth of damage in the accident, took proceedings in 1990 against the defendant corporation, pursuant to s. 76(1)(d) of the Road Traffic Act 1961 (as amended), claiming the sum of £17,000, as the insurance cover held by the deceased did not indemnify him in respect of the driving of the vehicle on the occasion of the accident.

Morris J held that the plaintiff's proceedings were statute-barred under s. 9. He did not accept the submission by counsel for the plaintiff that s. 76 created a new cause of action in respect of which a separate limitation period would be applicable. All that the section did was to enable an injured party to substitute for a deceased defendant the insurance company holding cover at the relevant time, attaching to the insurance company whatever responsibility the deceased owner had.

TORT LITIGATION

In the 1992 Review, 430-2, we examined Lynch J's decision in *Tuohy v Courtney*, High Court, September 3, 1992, upholding the constitutional validity of s. 11 of the Statute of Limitations 1957. Briefly, the plaintiff's claim was one for negligence against his solicitors in failing to have warned him of the true nature of the title to the premises that he had bought. Lynch J held, on the evidence, that the proceedings were out of time. The plaintiff appealed against Lynch J's holding on the constitutional issue and the first and second defendants appealed, challenging Lynch J's holding that the plaintiff had *locus standi*: [1994] 2 ILRM 503.

The Supreme Court had little hesitation in dismissing the *locus standi* point. It was 'quite satisfied' that Lynch J's findings and conclusions constituted 'clear evidence' of the plaintiff's *locus standi*.

Finlay CJ, delivering the judgment of the Court, approached the substantive constitutional issue relating to s. 11 as follows. The first task was to determine the precise nature of the constitutional right which the plaintiff claimed had been wrongfully invaded. The Court was not satisfied that it was the constitutional right of access to the courts. Following Henchy J's analysis in *Ó Domhnaill v Merrick* [1984] IR 151, at 158, [1985] ILRM 40, at 45, Finlay CJ characterised the limitation of actions as affecting, not the plaintiff's *right to sue*, but rather his or her *right to succeed* if the action is brought after the relevant period of limitation has passed and the defendant invokes the Statute.

As regards the right to litigate, the Court took a neutral stance on the debate in earlier Supreme Court decisions as to whether it should be characterised exclusively as an unenumerated personal right, an exclusively property right or a hybrid. The Chief Justice observed that '[i]t may well indeed be that this controversy may remain academic as is suggested at p. 1064 of the third edition (1994) edition of Kelly on *The Irish Constitution.*'

It was agreed on all sides that the Oireachtas in legislating for time limits for litigation was engaged in a *balancing* of constitutional rights and duties:

> What has to be balanced is the constitutional right of the plaintiff to litigate against two other contesting rights or duties, firstly, the constitutional right of the defendant in his property to be protected against unjust or burdensome claims and secondly, the interest of the public constituting an interest or requirement of the common good which is involved in the avoidance of stale or delayed claims.

The role of the courts was not to impose their view of the correct or desirable balance in substitution for the view of the legislature but rather to determine 'from an objective stance' whether the balance contained in the impugned legislation was so contrary to reason and fairness as to constitute an unjust attack on some individuals' constitutional rights.

It could not be disputed that a person whose right to seek a legal remedy for a wrong was barred by a statutory time limit before he could have become aware of its existence had suffered a severe apparent injustice and would be entitled reasonably to entertain a major sense of grievance. To say this did not, however, of itself solve the question whether a statute permitting it to occur was by the fact inconsistent with the Constitution.

Statutes of limitation had been part of the legal system in Ireland for very many years, even before the Act of Union. The *primary* purpose appeared to be to *protect defendants against stale claims* and avoid injustices that might occur to them were they asked to defend themselves from claims that had not been notified to them within a reasonable time. *Secondly*, they were designed to promote as far as possible *expeditious trials of action* so that a court might have before it oral evidence that had the accuracy of recent recollection and documentary proof that was complete, 'features which must make a major contribution to the correctness and justice of the decision arrived at.' *Thirdly*, they were designed to promote as far as possible *finality in potential claims* which would permit individuals to arrange their affairs whether on a domestic, commercial or professional level in reliance to the maximum extent possible upon the absence of unknown or unexpected liabilities.

The counterbalance to these objectives was the necessity as far as was practicable for the State to ensure that such time limits did not unreasonably or unjustly impose hardship. Any time limit statutorily imposed upon the bringing of actions was potentially going to impose some hardship on some individual. The question therefore, was whether the extent that hardship was so undue unreasonable having regard to the proper objectives of the legislation as to make it constitutionally flawed.

The plaintiff sought to make a connection between the entitlement of the court to dismiss proceedings brought *within* the statutory limitation period, under the principles laid down in *Ó Domhnaill v Merrick* [1984] IR 151, [1985] ILRM 40 and *Toal v Duignan (Nos. 1 and 2)* [1991] 1 ILRM 135 and 140, and the courts' entitlement, asserted by the plaintiff, to *extend* the period in appropriate cases. In both instances a 'saver' would ensure justice without significantly diminishing the certainty or finality of the time limit. The Supreme Court rejected the argument as lacking sufficient strength to render an inflexible time limit of six years for breach of contract and tort causing damage other than personal injuries clearly unconstitutional.

The period of six years was objectively viewed as a substantial period. Historically, it had remained unchanged for this type of action since the Common Law Procedure (Ireland) Act 1853 and no shortening of it had been legislatively created 'notwithstanding the very significant increase in literacy, understanding of legal rights and sophistication which has as a matter of common knowledge occurred in the years since that time.' The Act of 1957 contained in Part III extensions of the periods of limitation in cases of disability, acknowledgment, part payment, fraud and mistake. These extensions constituted a significant inroad on the certainty of finality provided by the Act.

These were but some of the matters that the Oireachtas could properly consider in reaching a decision as to whether it should add to the grounds of extension of limitation periods already contained in the Act of 1957 a ground of discoverability of the cause of action. Together with those factors, of course, the courts should have regard to the consideration of examples of injustice such as appeared to have occurred in the instant case. For the Oireachtas to reach a decision either to add or not to add to the extensions of limitation periods contained in Part III of the Act of 1957 an extension relating to discoverability with regard to this particular time limit imposed by that Act, was a matter which in the view of the Supreme Court could be supported by just and reasonable policy decisions and was not accordingly a proper matter for judicial intervention.

This holding was entirely predictable after *Hegarty v O'Loughran* [1990] ILRM 403; [1990] 1 IR 148, where the Supreme Court made it plain that it did not perceive itself as having a function in fine-tuning legislation on limitation of actions where the issue was one of broad discretionary judgment. Cf. the 1990 Review, 389-94.

Local Government

BUILDING CONTROL

Building standards   The Building Regulations (Amendment) Regulations 1994. (SI No. 154 of 1994) amended the Building Regulations 1991 (1991 Review, 307-8), which concern the design standards required in the construction of certain buildings. A number of significant amendments to the 1991 Regulations were effected: see the discussion by Byran O'Rourke in (1994) 1 *IPELJ*. The 1994 Regulations came into operation on August 1, 1994. See also the European Communities (Construction Products) (Amendment) Regulations 1994 (SI No. 210 of 1994), discussed in the Safety and Health chapter, 402, below and which also concern building standards.

Fire control   The Building Control (Amendment) Regulations 1994. (SI No. 153 of 1994) amended the Building Control Regulations 1991(1991 Review, 307), which concern primarily the requirement to obtain a fire certificate when building or altering certain buildings. They exempt from compliance with the 1991 Regulations, *inter alia*, buildings for the use of local authorities, the Garda Síochána or the Defence Forces, a courthouse, buildings in the occupation of the Oireachtas and certain Government departments. Buildings may also be exempted for reasons of national security: included here might be prison buildings. The 1994 Regulations came into force on 1 August 1994 and revoked the Building Control (Amendment) Regulations 1993 (1993 Review, 418).

SURCHARGE IMPOSED BY AUDITOR

In *Downey v O'Brien* [1994] 2 ILRM 130, Costello J (as he then was) dismissed an application for an order of *certiorari* under s. 12 of the Local Government (Ireland) Act 1871 seeking to quash a charge made by a local government auditor. S. 20 of the Local Government (Ireland) Act 1902 empowers a local government auditor to charge against any member or officer of a local authority the amount of any deficiency or loss incurred by virtue of negligence or misconduct. A person aggrieved by such a charge may apply for an order of *certiorari* under s. 12 of the 1871 Act. In 1983 a particular company, Hellebore Ltd was incorporated in order to perform dredging in Waterford Harbour. The Waterford Harbour Commissioners owned 10,002 shares and one William O'Hanlon 10,000 shares. Both the commissioners and Mr O'Hanlon made interest free loans to the company.

The company purchased a dredger at a cost of £185,000. It also effected two policies of life assurance on the life of Mr O'Hanlon's son at a cost of £40,000 as an investment which, on maturity, would provide the necessary funds for the replacement of the dredger. The policies were entered on the company's balance sheet at their cost price of £40,000. In 1986 the commissioners decided to sell their shares to Mr O'Hanlon. Negotiations were conducted on their behalf by the general manager and the plaintiff, who was the chairman of the commissioners and a chartered accountant. By letter, Mr O'Hanlon offered to purchase the shares for £54,348 and three quarters of the surrender value of the life assurance policies, provided that the company was given a five-year dredging contract by the commissioners. The board of the commissioners passed a resolution accepting this offer and a formal agreement was signed on behalf of the board by the plaintiff and the general manager.

It transpired that the terms of this agreement did not correspond with what had actually been agreed between Mr O'Hanlon, the general manager and the plaintiff. In fact they had agreed that the consideration for the shares should merely be three quarters of the surrender value of the life assurance policies, together with the dredging contract. The sum of £54,348 was the outstanding balance on the loan which the commissioners had made to the company. Mr O'Hanlon, the general manager and the plaintiff had simply agreed that this loan should be repaid to the commissioners by the company. As a result, the commissioners actually received a sum of £19,960 for their shares. This sum constituted three quarters of the surrender value of the life assurance policies. While investigating the commissioners' accounts the defendant, a local government auditor, discovered that the consideration mentioned in the documents pertaining to the sale of the shares was incorrect. He sought information as to why an incorrect figure was mentioned and why the shares were sold for only £19,960.

In a letter written with the knowledge and approval of the plaintiff, the general manager indicated that the shares in the company were worth £58,639 given the net asset value of the company as revealed by its balance sheet dated 31 December 1985. Accordingly, as the commissioners had a 51% shareholding, their shares were worth £29,905. The letter also pointed to commercial considerations which justified the acceptance of a lower figure for the shares. The defendant did not accept these figures. In valuing the shares he deducted from the balance sheet net asset figure of £228,917 the figure of £106,838 in respect of shareholders' loans to the company. This meant that shareholders funds amounted to £122,079 and, as the commissioners were entitled to 51% of the shareholding, their shares were worth £62,260. According to the defendant, the figure for shareholders' funds consisted of the share capital (£20,002), the revenue reserves (£52,577) and a provision for deferred tax (£49,500). In calculating the figure for fixed assets the defendant had valued the life assurance policies at their cost of £40,000, whereas the plaintiff had valued them at their surrender value of £26,000. Furthermore, the plaintiff had deducted the provision for deferred taxation of £49,500 in ascertaining the net asset value of the company. The relevant Standard Statement of Accounting Practice (SSAP) required that accounts should contain a provision for deferred taxation. This provided for future tax liability which can arise as a result of capital allowances being used up in respect of an asset while the profit and loss account continues to make a deduction in respect of depreciation relating to that asset. The effect of the provision for deferred taxation is to reduce the profits which would otherwise be available for distribution to shareholders.

In a further letter, the defendant indicated his concern that the shares had been sold at an undervalue and that an incorrect figure for consideration had been inserted into the contract documents. He also pointed to the possibility that he would have to impose a surcharge on the commissioners if a loss had been occasioned by negligence or misconduct on their part. After the exchange of further correspondence, the board's solicitors indicated in a letter that there had been confusion concerning the consideration and that the correct sale price was £19,960. As he was not satisfied with the replies which he had received, the defendant imposed a charge of £42,300 (i.e. the difference between £62,260 and £19,960) jointly and severally on the plaintiff and the general manager on the grounds that they had been negligent in selling the commissioners' shares at an undervalue. This was done by a certificate of charge made under s. 20 of the 1902 Act and a document setting out the reasons for the charge was appended to the certificate. The defendant did not impose charges on the other commissioners as there was no evidence that the plaintiff or the general manager had informed them that the consideration mentioned in the written contract was incorrect. The plaintiff appealed against the charge by means of an application for an order of *certiorari* under s. 12 of the Local Government Act 1871 but, as already indicated, Costello J refused the relief sought.

As to the standard of negligence required, Costello J approved the view expressed in *Pentecost v London District Auditor* [1951] 2 KB 759 that ordinary principles of the law of negligence apply to the making of a charge under s. 20 of the 1902 Act and that there does not have to be any element of moral culpability or gross negligence on the part of the person against whom the charge is made.

In the instant case, he held that there had been no justification for the plaintiff's valuation of the life assurance policies according to their surrender value. He did not think it correct that, when considering the reasonableness of an offer to purchase the shares, or in justifying the acceptance of that offer at a later date, to ascertain their value according to their net asset value as revealed by the balance sheet dated December 31, 1985 and then reduce that figure because of a term agreed in negotiations in June 1986. To do so, he held, would produce a post-negotiation and not a pre-negotiation valuation of the shares.

He went on to hold that there was no reason why the figure for deferred taxation should have been deducted in calculating the figure for net assets as this valuation was not on an on-going concern basis. He noted that, if the company had gone into liquidation on January 1, 1986 and the assets had been sold at their book values, the shareholders would have received sums calculated by reference to the net asset figure calculated by the defendant and not that produced by the plaintiff. While he accepted that the Schedules to the Companies (Amendment) Act 1986 prescribed the format in which balance sheets and profit and loss accounts should be presented, he did not consider that they indicated the correct method for valuing shares by reference to balance sheet figures.

Costello J concluded that the two errors which the plaintiff had made resulted in the shares being sold at a serious undervalue. This amounted to a breach of the duty of care owed by him and so the conclusions reached by the defendant had been correct. He also rejected suggestions that the defendant had not complied with the rules of natural justice. Costello J noted that he had informed all the commissioners of his concerns as to what had happened, explained in great detail the complaints of wrongdoing which he had advanced, warned each commissioner of the possibility that a charge might be imposed, and gave each an opportunity to answer the complaints.

LOCAL GOVERNMENT REORGANISATION

The Local Government Act 1994 contained a number of provisions having a short-term objective, namely the holding of elections in 1994 to five Borough Corporations, 49 Urban District Councils and 26 Town Commissioners. However, on a more long-term footing, the 1994 Act is part of the strategy to engage in fundamental reform of local government in Ireland, which began in earnest with the Local Government Act 1991 (1991 Review, 310-3).

In this respect, the 1994 Act provided for the establishment of a Local Government Reorganisation Commission to make proposals for the modernisation of town local government, including future classification of town local authorities, functions, finances and procedures for the establishment of new local authorities. The Act also included a wide range of other reform measures, including updating and consolidation of provisions relating to local authority membership, local elections, local authority cathaoirleach and leas-chathaoirleach, and meetings and procedures of local authorities. The Act provided that elections to all local authorities would be held in 1998 and at five-yearly intervals thereafter. The 1994 Act also restated the law relating to local authority library services and local authority powers in relation to the provision of various types of amenities, facilities and services. In keeping with the move to decentralise some decision-making powers, the 1994 Act empowered local authorities to make bye-laws generally without the need for consent from the Minister for the Environment. Aspects of the law relating to local authority estimates and rates, personnel, local authority associations, local archives and certain other matters were also updated and unnecessary controls removed. A number of obsolete or outdated statutory provisions in various Local Government Acts were also repealed by s. 4 of the 1994 Act and the First Schedule to the Act. Various provisions of the 1994 Act came into force between on May 3, 1994 and December 9, 1994: Local Government Act 1994 (Commencement) Order 1994 (SI No. 113 of 1994); Local Government Act 1994 (Commencement) (No. 2) Order 1994 (SI No. 171 of 1994); Local Government Act 1994 (Commencement) (No. 3) Order 1994 (SI No. 315 of 1994); Local Government Act 1994 (Commencement) (No. 4) Order 1994 (SI No. 413 of 1994); Local Government Act 1994 (Section 53(1)) Order 1994 (SI No. 414 of 1994). However, we note that a number of sections of the Act will not come into force until after the 1998 local elections, and we refer to some of these below.

Local Authority Membership Part II of the 1994 Act (ss. 3 to 12) updated and consolidated the law in relation to local authority membership, including eligibility, disqualification, term of office, resignation and filling of casual vacancies.

S. 5 states the general eligibility criteria for local authority membership. S. 6 provides the grounds for disqualification for membership of a local authority. New disqualifications under the 1994 Act include disqualifications in respect of the Ceann Comhairle of the Dáil, the Cathaoirleach of the Seanad, chairpersons of Oireachtas select committees (other than committees specified in the 1994 Act or others which may be designated by Order), the Comptroller and Auditor General, judges appointed to courts established under the Constitution, members of the Commission of the European Communities and other EU office-holders. Disqualification also arises for failure to comply with a court judgment for payment of money due to a local authority and on conviction for fraudulent or dishonest dealings affecting a local authority or corrupt practice. S. 6 does not come into operation until the elections to all local authorities due in 1998. S. 7 provides that it is an offence to act or vote as a local authority member when disqualified and provides for a maximum penalty of £1,000 for such offence. S. 8 provides that where a person becomes disqualified under s. 6, that person ceases to be a member of the local authority and any body to which he or she was appointed by a local authority. S. 9 of the 1994 Act provides that the term of office of local authority members will continue until the seventh day after polling day at the next local elections whereupon the newly elected members come into office. S. 10 provides for the resignation of a local authority member.

S. 11 provides for the filling of casual vacancies on local authorities through co-option by the local authority. S. 13 validates any acts, decisions or proceedings of a local authority notwithstanding possible participation by a disqualified person.

Local elections   Part III of the 1994 Act (ss. 13 to 24) provides for the holding in 1994 of elections to borough councils, urban district councils and town commissioners (which were postponed by the Local Government Act 1991) and for consequential matters. Provision is made for the alteration of the boundaries of certain boroughs, urban districts and towns so that electors resident in their environs will have the right to vote at local elections. Part III also restates, with amendments, the law in relation to the conduct of local elections — which had prior to the 1994 Act been contained primarily in Part VI of the Electoral Act 1963.

S. 22 of the 1994 Act provides for the detailed rules for the conduct of local elections, including the counting of votes, to be set out in Regulations under the section which must be approved in draft by a resolution of each House of the Oireachtas before they are made. Pending the making of Regulations under s. 22, the existing procedures contained in the Local Elections Regulations 1965, as amended, continue to have effect. S. 23 restates the general provision regarding the right to vote at local elections. S. 20 provides that the year in which local elections are to be held may be altered by Order, rather than by Act as was required prior to the 1994 Act, but such an Order will not come into force unless and until it has been confirmed by resolution of each House of the Oireachtas. S. 24 of the 1994 Act consolidated the law on the alteration of local electoral areas (that is, local authority constituencies). Under Part V of the Local Government Act 1991 a division into local electoral areas may only be made following consideration of a report made under that Act by a statutorily-established Boundary Committee.

Cathaoirleach And Leas-Chathaoirleach   Part IV of the 1994 Act (ss. 25

to 29) provides for the offices of local authority cathaoirleach and leas-chathaoirleach and ancillary matters. S. 25 provides that each local authority shall have a cathaoirleach and a leas-chathaoirleach to be elected at every annual meeting of the authority, but provides for the continuation of existing titles of mayor and lord mayor. The cathaoirleach is empowered to nominate a deputy, to represent him or her at particular events or ceremonies. A person who is a member of either House of the Oireachtas is disqualified from election as cathaoirleach or leas-chathaoirleach but this disqualification does not come into effect until after the local elections due in 1998. S. 26 provides for the procedure to be followed in electing the cathaoirleach of a local authority to be prescribed. The 1994 Act continued the existing system of successive ballots to elect the cathaoirleach. S. 27 provides for the term of office of the cathaoirleach and leas-chathaoirleach of a local authority. S. 29 provides for the filling of a casual vacancy in the office of cathaoirleach or leas-chathaoirleach.

Meetings and Procedures of Local Authorities   Part V of the 1994 Act, consisting of s. 30 alone, allows for the introduction by Regulations of a comprehensive, updated and uniform code relating to local authority meetings and procedures in place of what was described in the Explanatory Memorandum as the 'existing inconsistent and fragmented provisions'.

Amenity, Recreation, Library and Other Functions   Part VI of the 1994 Act (ss. 31 to 35) provides for local authority functions in relation to the provision of facilities for amenity, recreation and library activities, allowing for the repeal of a large body of outdated and restrictive enactments. S. 31 contains a general provision empowering local authorities to undertake activities in the provision of amenities, facilities, services and related matters. These powers will be exercisable pursuant to s. 6 of the Local Government Act 1991, which provides a general competence for local authorities to take action in the interests of their areas and local communities and which largely was intended to remove the difficulties associated with the *ultra vires* rule. S. 31 is, in effect, a restatement of various existing amenity and miscellaneous powers of local authorities in a modern format which involves the removal of outmoded controls and allows for greater local authority discretion. S. 32 provides that county and county borough councils are library authorities, as was the case prior to the 1994 Act, and it also provided for the continuation of joint library committees. S. 33 restated the role of library authorities in modern form and removed an anomaly which prohibited the compulsory acquisition of land for library purposes. S. 34 provided for the continued operation of An Chomhairle Leabharlanna (the Library Council). S. 35 of the 1994 Act confirms that s. 8(1) of the Local Government Act 1991 (which conferred a general power on local authorities to do things ancillary to the performance of specific statutory functions) applies to all functions conferred on local authorities acting in any capacity.

Bye-Laws   In Part VII of the 1994 Act (ss. 36 to 43), s. 37 conferred a broad reserved-function power on local authorities (that is, one exercisable by the elected members only) to make bye-laws governing the operation of various facilities (such as parks and libraries) provided by them and a general power to control or regulate any matter which in the opinion of the local authority should, in the interests of the common good of the local community, be so regulated or controlled, provided such matter or thing is not the subject of existing law. As a result local authorities have greater discretion than prior to the 1994 Act in the making of bye-laws. In addition, the general require-ment that bye-laws be confirmed by the relevant Minister was removed, though a particular Minister may provide by Order that consent or confirma-tion is still required for certain bye-laws. S. 40 provides that it is an offence to contravene a bye-law, and allows for fines to be specified, subject to a maximum fine of £1,000. S. 41 provides that bye-laws may include provision for a system of fixed payment notices, that is 'on the spot fines', payment of which will preclude prosecution for a contravention of a bye-law.

Local Authority Estimates and Rates   Part VIII of the Act (ss. 44 to 47) made provision for some technical amendments to rating law, including provisions dealing with a situation where an insufficient estimate is adopted by a local authority. S. 44 restates in modern form the position where an insufficient estimate of expenses is adopted by a local authority and sets out the procedures which will apply in that respect. S. 45 removes the technical necessity for local authorities to strike rates on domestic dwellings, the payment of which was abolished by the Local Government (Financial Provisions) Act 1978. S. 46 updates the basis for the payment of general grants to rating authorities.

Local Authority Personnel   Part IX of the 1994 Act (ss. 48 to 52) contains provisions relating to local authority personnel matters. Ss. 48 and 49 amended existing law so as to confirm regulatory powers for the making of ex-gratia payments to local authority officers suspended from the perform-ance of their duties. These amendments arose from a 1986 report of the Oireachtas Joint Committee on Legislation. S. 50 provides for the activation of a request to the Local Appointments Commissioners seeking the recom-mendation of a person to fill the office of manager six months before the expiry of the manager's term of office in the case of managers appointed for a fixed term. S. 51 provides that when a manager is temporarily unable to act, an officer of a local authority may be appointed to be deputy manager for the duration of such inability and removes Ministerial controls in that regard. S. 52 provides that the manager may delegate any function to any officer of the local authority, without the need to obtain the consent of the relevant Minister.

Town Local Government   Part X of the 1994 Act (ss. 53 to 60) provided for the establishment of a Reorganisation Commission to carry out a review and make proposals for the reorganisation of local government in towns and for the implementation of such proposals. S. 56 requires the Commission to submit a reorganisation report containing proposals for town local government, including such matters as the number of classes of town local authority, their functions, finances, and other matters in relation to each class and implications for county councils, the appropriate class for each existing town local authority, procedures for the creation of local authorities for non-municipal towns and measures and arrangements for the implementation of the proposals for town local government.

Miscellaneous   Part XI of the 1994 Act (ss. 61 to 68) contains a number of other significant changes. Thus, s. 62 provides that separate estimates need not be prepared nor town charges levied in respect of specified towns in which town commissioners have not existed for many years.

S. 63 provides that areas hitherto known as 'wards' in county boroughs and 'district electoral divisions' in counties will, in future, be known as 'electoral divisions' and that the boundary or name of a division can be altered by Regulations.

S. 65 provides for the keeping of local records and archives by local authorities. These provisions are generally similar to those applying to national archives. S. 67 of the 1994 Act amended the provisions of the Local Government Act 1946 relating to the changing of place names. At future plebiscites on this question, all local government electors will be entitled to vote. To take account of situations (for example commercial streets) where there may be few, if any, local government electors the rated occupier of a hereditament which is subject to rates will also be entitled to vote, unless he or she already qualifies for the vote by virtue of being a resident local government elector. S. 67 also reduced the majority required for change from four-sevenths to a simple majority of the electorate concerned.

HOUSING

In *Meath Vocational Education Committee v Joyce and Ors (Meath County Council, Third Party)* [1994] 2 ILRM 210, Flood J directed Meath County

Council to comply with its statutory obligations under the Housing Act 1988 to provide suitable sites to house members of the travelling community. The case arose against the increasingly common background of travellers locating on unauthorised sites in the absence of local authority facilities (see also *University of Limerick v Ryan and Ors*, High Court, February 21, 1991, discussed in the 1991 Review, 309-10).

S. 111 of the Housing Act 1966 provides that whenever the Minister for the Environment is of the opinion that a housing authority has failed to perform any of its functions under the Act, he may by order require the authority to perform that function and may set a time limit for its perform-ance. If the authority fails to comply with this order the minister may then perform such of their functions as may be necessary to remedy the failure. S. 2 of the Housing Act 1988 provides that a person shall be regarded as homeless if there is no accommodation available which in the opinion of the housing authority he, with any other person who normally resides with him, can reasonably occupy or remain in occupation of, or if he is unable to provide accommodation from his own resources. S. 9 of the 1988 Act provides that in assessing the housing requirements in their functional area, a housing authority shall have regard to the need for housing of homeless persons, persons who traditionally pursue a nomadic way of life and persons who live in accommodation that is unfit for human habitation. S. 11 of the 1988 Act provides that in making up a scheme of priorities for letting, the authority shall have regard to persons who are unable to provide accommodation from their own resources and whose need for accommodation is included in the assessments made under s. 9. S. 13 of the Act applies to persons who traditionally pursue or have pursued a nomadic way of life and provides that a 'housing authority may provide, improve, manage and control sites for caravans used by these persons and may carry out works incidental to such provision, improvement, management or control, including the provision of services for such sites'.

The applicants were the owners and managers of a community school in Co. Meath. A number of families from the travelling community had been encamped on the roadside near the school. The applicants sought an order under s. 27 of the Local Government (Planning and Development) Act 1976, as amended, restraining an unauthorised use of the roadside at or near the community school by the respondents and other families at the camp site. They claimed that the unauthorised camp site constituted a nuisance as members of the travelling community who frequented the site had trespassed on the school grounds, caused serious disruption to classes by playing loud music and engaging in rowdy behaviour, and had intimidated teachers, pupils and parents. It was also claimed that rubbish, including human excrement, had been thrown around the school grounds and that the camp site itself constituted a public health hazard. The respondents denied responsibility for the matters complained of and issued third party proceedings against Meath County Council. They claimed an indemnity against the applicants' claim, or alternatively a contribution to such an extent as the court might direct, on the grounds that the Council owed them a duty to provide serviced camp sites pursuant to s. 13 of the Housing Act 1988 and that the applicants' complaint had arisen by reason of the Council's breach of these statutory provisions. Flood J ultimately granted an injunction against the respondents but he also made an order directing the Council to take steps to acquire suitable locations for camp sites and to equip them, subject to the parameters laid down by the Minister, within one year of the perfection of the order or such longer period as the Court might allow.

On the appropriateness of the procedures, he held that the third party procedure was an adequate vehicle to bring the issues as to whether the Council owed a statutory duty to the respondents to provide them with a serviced camp site. He added that rules of procedure should always be regarded as the servants and not the masters of justice.

Turning to the substantive issues in the case, Flood J stated that Housing Act 1966 was intended to deal with the persistent problem of bad and inadequate housing throughout the country. Although the 1966 Act was amended by the Housing Act 1988, its objectives of replacing unfit houses, eliminating overcrowding and providing new houses for those unable to provide for themselves were still applicable.

While there was no direction in the 1988 Act to build or provide halting sites, Flood J stated that it must be assumed that it was the intention of the legislature that the objectives of the 1966 Act, as amended, would be carried out by the local authorities and that the housing problem would be dealt with in accordance with the scheme of priorities which had to be compiled under s. 11. This view of the legislature's intention was borne out by s. 111 of the 1966 Act, referred to above.

He went on that it was clearly one of the functions of a housing authority to eliminate in a realistic manner over a period of time the lack of accommodation of persons in the order of priority as given to them pursuant to the assessment carried out under s. 11 of the 1988 Act. In this regard, the housing authority had a duty to perform its functions under the Housing Acts in a rational and reasonable manner and to provide accommodation for persons defined as homeless in the 1988 Act. The respondents undoubtedly came within the definition of homeless persons. The obligation was a statutory one and the importance attaching to it in relation to persons belonging to the travelling community was clearly set out in ss. 9 and 10 of the 1988 Act, also referred to above. However, irrespective of the scheme of priorities which may be in operation at any time, Flood J concluded that each housing authority must have regard to those persons who at any particular time were in its functional area and were in need of housing. It was on this basis that, as already indicated, he made the order against the Council referred to above. Nonetheless, this must be balanced against the more immediate order granted against the respondents.

PLANNING

Consolidated and updated Planning Regulations   The Local Government (Planning and Development) Regulations 1994 (SI No. 86 of 1994) comprise a comprehensive consolidation as well as updating of the previous regulations in this area. The 1994 Regulations came into effect on various dates between May 16 and June 15, 1994 and revoked the Local Government (Planning and Development) Regulations 1977 to 1993. Containing 168 Regulations and Seven Schedules, the scope and complexity of the 1994 Regulations render it impossible to provide an analysis of their contents here. For a detailed and informative assessment, see Scannell, Environmental and Planning Law (Round Hall Press, 1995).

Compensation for refusal   In *J. Wood & Co Ltd v Wicklow County Council* [1995] 1 ILRM 51, Costello J (as he then was) held that the applicant company was not precluded from receiving compensation under the Local Government (Planning and Development) Act 1990 in respect of the refusal of planning permission made by the respondent Council. The case turned on whether the 1990 Act had retrospective effect and on the impact of s. 21(1)(c) of the Interpretation Act 1937, which provides that when a portion of a statute is repealed, such repeal shall not affect any right acquired under the portion so repealed unless there appears to be a contrary intention. The Local Government (Planning and Development) Act 1990 came into operation on 10 June 1990. S. 3 of the 1990 Act repealed Part VI of the Local Government (Planning and Development) Act 1963, including s. 55 of the 1963 Act, the provision dealing with the right to compensation in the event of a refusal of planning permission: see the 1990 Review, 414-5.

In June 1989, an application for planning permission to build houses on certain land was made to Wicklow County Council by a company called Shalebrook Ltd. In March 1990 Shalebrook Ltd sold the land to the applicant. Further information as to the application for planning permission was sought by the Council and the application was re-advertised in June 1990. In July 1990 the Council decided to grant planning permission subject to conditions. An appeal was made and in July 1991 An Bord Pleanála refused planning permission. In October 1991 the applicant made a claim for compensation under s. 55 of the 1963 Act on the assumption that the compensation provisions of that Act applied and later that month a claim for compensation under s. 11 of the 1990 Act was made on the basis that compensation should be assessed under the later Act.

The applicant's claim for compensation went to arbitration and the arbitrator submitted a number of questions to the High Court. Costello J held that the applicant's claim for compensation fell to be determined under the 1990 Act. He held that any decision refusing planning permission made after June 10, 1990, when the 1990 Act came into operation, was subject to the compensation provisions of the 1990 Act, irrespective of whether the application to which the decision relates was made before or after the 1990 Act came into force. Since no statutory right to compensation can arise until a decision is made and as no decision had been made in respect of the applicant's application when the 1990 Act came into operation and repealed s. 55 of the 1963 Act, it followed that the applicant had not acquired any rights within the meaning of s. 21 (1)(c) of the 1937 Act.

Turning to the compensation payable, Costello J held that in deciding whether there has been a reduction in value for the purposes of s. 55(1) of the 1963 Act, regard must be had to the provisions relating to reduction in value contained in s. 55(2). Applying the views expressed in *Dublin County Council v Eighty-five Developments Ltd (No. 1)* [1993] 2 IR 378 (1992 Review, 453-5), he held that in determining whether there has been a reduction in value, and the amount of the reduction in value, s. 55 should be construed as providing that each determination should be made on the basis that the permission had been granted but subject to conditions relating to matters referred to in s. 26(2)(e), (g) and (h) and s. 56(1), and the land's value without this permission. Accordingly, in determining the reduction (if any) in the value of the applicant's interest in the lands under the 1963 Act, the open market value of the lands should be ascertained as if the planning permission applied for had been granted, and the arbitrator should then ascertain the open market value of the lands after the planning decision. Costello J also rejected a number of suggestions that the wording of the various elements of the decision of An Bord Pleanála could be construed as refusing permission on non-compensatable grounds under the 1963 Act.

Compliance with conditions: appropriate relief In *White v McInerney Construction Ltd* [1995] 1 ILRM 374, the Supreme Court refused injunctive relief notwithstanding there had been non-compliance with certain conditions in a planning permission. In November 1989 Lardner J had declined to grant the applicant an injunction under s. 27 of the Local Government (Planning and Development) Act 1976 although the respondent was in breach of a condition of his planning permission concerning the screening of the area around the development in question. However he had ordered that an undertaking by the respondent should be continued and varied to allow the respondent to comply with the relevant condition of the permission. The applicant appealed against the refusal to grant injunctive relief, but the Supreme Court (Hamilton CJ, O'Flaherty and Blayney JJ) dismissed the appeal and confirmed Lardner J's decision.

Delivering the only reasoned judgment, Blayney J held that the order made in November 1989 had been a final determination of the motion for relief, having been made in accordance with the procedure in s. 27 of the 1976 Act. The appellant had made no application for a direction that evidence should be given otherwise than on affidavit and there was no ground for suggesting that the application should have been on oral evidence. He noted that Lardner J had found that while there might not have been strict compliance with condition 6 of the planning permission, the planning authority had allowed this state of affairs to continue. Referring with approval to *Avenue Properties Ltd v Farrell Homes Ltd* [1982] ILRM 21, Blayney J held that, since orders under s. 27 of the 1976 Act were discretionary in character, and since the refusal of relief by Lardner J had been properly made in the exercise of his discretion, his decision should be upheld.

In any event, Blayney J also opined at the end of his judgment that even if there had been grounds for setting aside the orders made, it would not be possible to do so as the development had been substantially completed since 1989. The factual situation was therefore totally altered and would render unreal any order intended to deal with the situation as it was when the motions were heard. However, he noted that if the development had not been carried out in conformity with the permission, the appellant could bring a new motion under s. 27 to obtain an order requiring the respondent to do whatever was necessary to ensure that the development was in accordance with the permission.

Consent of adjoining landowners: mining   In *Scott and Ors v An Bord Pleanála (Arcon Mines Ltd and Ors, Notice Parties)* [1995] 1 ILRM 424, the Supreme Court rejected a claim that it was necessary to obtain the consent of the owner of lands under which a mine was to be located prior to applying for planning permission.

S. 12 of the provides that the exclusive right of working minerals in the State is vested in the Minister. In November 1992 the Minister for Transport, Energy and Communications, acting under s. 12 of the Minerals Development Act 1979, formally consented to the making of an application for planning permission by the first named notice party in relation to the development of a mine. In April 1994 the respondent Planning Board decided to grant planning permission to the first named notice party for a development comprising the operation of a lead and zinc mine which involved underground workings in accordance with plans lodged with Kilkenny County Council. The first named applicant was the owner of lands which adjoined the lands under which the ore body was situated. A small portion of the ore body was located under the first named applicant's land. The applicants sought an order of *certiorari* of the decision to grant planning permission. In the High Court, Costello J (as he then was) refused leave to apply for judicial review. However, he granted leave to the applicants to appeal to the Supreme Court under s. 29 of the Local Government (Planning and Development) Act 1992 (see generally the 1992 Review, 448-50), but the Supreme Court (Hamilton CJ, Egan and Blayney JJ) dismissed the applicant's appeal.

Delivering the only judgment, Egan J held that in order to obtain leave to apply for judicial review the applicants had to satisfy the court that there were substantial grounds for contending that the decision of the respondent was invalid or ought to be quashed. He held that the mere fact that the developer did not have any interest or estate in part of the lands to be developed and had not obtained that landowner's consent to the development did not constitute a substantial ground for contending that the decision was invalid because the Minister had given the necessary approval in relation to the development pursuant to s. 12 of the 1979 Act. Since for the purposes of the 1963 Act a development meant the carrying out of works on lands and not merely the consequences of those works on other lands, the argument that the consent of the owners of adjoining lands, who claimed that their lands would be adversely affected by the development, did not constitute a substantial ground for challenging the decision to grant planning permission.

Consultation process In *Keogh and Ors (Lower Salthill Residents Association) v Galway Corporation* [1995] 1 ILRM 141, Carney J held that a Council acted *ultra vires* in failing to consult local residents about the development of halting sites at a particular location even though such developments had been referred to generally in its Development Plan.

The Galway County Borough Development Plan 1991 provided, as a specific objective, for halting sites for travellers at four named locations. The Plan also allowed for particular objectives to be modified or deleted and the initiation of new works not included as specific objectives. In February 1994 Galway Corporation decided to develop a halting site on lands known as the 'Bishop's field'. In June 1994 the Galway county Manager was advised by his senior planning executive that the development plan was not exclusive of other works considered desirable or necessary and in accordance with the plan and with the proper planning and development of the area. Thus, he advised that the proposed development of the 'Bishop's field' was not contrary to the plan.

The applicants challenged the proposed development as being *ultra vires* by reason of its not having been notified to them in the development plan. They argued that this deprived them of their statutory right to make representations at the draft plan stage in relation to a development which affected them in a material and substantial way. Carney J granted the relief sought.

In his judgment, he stated that it was central to the scheme of the Local Government (Planning and Development) Act 1963 that a citizen to be given notice of a development which might affect him in a substantial way and have the opportunity of stating his case. Having put their citizenry on notice in their draft development plan that halting sites were proposed for four specific locations, the Corporation could not develop one at the Bishop's field without engaging in the appropriate consultation process. Carney J concluded that the proposed development sought to by-pass the mandatory consultation process provided for in the Act and materially contravene the development plan.

County manager's powers In *East Wicklow Conservation Community Ltd v Wicklow County Council* [1995] 2 ILRM 16, Costello J considered the validity of a refusal by a county manager to comply with a resolution passed by the elected local authority representatives to authorise approval for a municipal dump. The case arose against the following background.

Wicklow County Council had engaged consultants to investigate possible waste disposal sites and prepare an environmental impact statement in respect of the chosen site. The consultants recommended that certain land be developed as a dump. The elected members of the Council passed a resolution which rejected the proposed site and directed that further investigations should be carried out in order to find other land where the dump could be located. The county manager refused to regard this resolution as having any legal effect and directed that work should continue in the preparation of an environmental impact statement pertaining to the proposed site. The applicants were local residents who sought an order of *certiorari* quashing the decision of the county manager to ignore the resolution and to proceed with the consultants' proposals.

The statutory provisions involved in the case were as follows. S. 52 of the Public Health (Ireland) Act 1878 provides that every sanitary authority may themselves undertake or contract for the removal of house refuse from premises. S. 55 of the 1878 Act provides that a sanitary authority shall provide fit buildings or places for the deposit of any matters collected by them pursuant to the 1878 Act. S. 2(7) of the City and County Management (Amendment) Act 1955 provides that the city or county manager shall inform the members of the local authority before any works (other than works of maintenance or repair) of the local authority are undertaken, or before committing the local authority to any expenditure in connection with proposed works (other than works of maintenance or repair). S. 3 of the 1955 Act provides that where the members of a local authority are informed pursuant to s. 2 of the 1955 Act of any works (not being works which the local authority are required by or under statute or by order of a court to undertake), the local authority may by resolution direct that the works shall not be proceeded with, and the manager shall comply with the resolution. Costello J refused the relief sought by the applicants. He held that the proposed development of the site constituted 'works' within the meaning of s. 2(7) of the 1955 Act. While the county manager had taken a decision that the land should be developed as a waste disposal site, it was conditional on its suitability being established by the environmental impact statement and the Minister for the Environment approving that statement. In conveying this conditional decision to the elected members of the county council the manager fulfilled the requirements of s. 2(7). He went on to state that a local authority which has exercised its statutory power under s. 52 of the 1878 Act to remove house refuse is placed under a statutory duty to provide a fit place to deposit it by s. 55. In the instant case, the Council had exercised the power under s. 52 and so was subject to the duty contained in s. 55. As the development of a waste disposal site was work which the Council was required to undertake under s. 55, the elected members had no power under s. 3 of the 1955 Act to direct that it should be pursued. He thus concluded that the resolution was *ultra vires* in so far as it purported to be a direction under s. 3 and the county manager was not obliged to comply with it.

Error in planning register In *Schwestermann v An Bord Pleanála and Ors* [1995] 1 ILRM 269, O'Hanlon J rejected a challenge to a planning permission where an error concerning the company named as the applicant and freehold owner of the land had been corrected by the planning authority.

A company named Glenmoy Ltd had applied for planning permission for a development comprising the conversion, extension and alteration of a stud and stables into a hotel. The application stated that Glenmoy Ltd was the freehold owner of the site of the proposed development. However, at all relevant times the freehold owner was Glenmoy Developments Ltd. The shares in both Glenmoy Ltd and Glenmoy Developments Ltd were owned by a married couple. Glenmoy Developments Ltd had been formed in 1985 and it was intended that it should carry out the proposed development of the hotel. Glenmoy Ltd was formed in 1992 for the purpose of managing the hotel. The main shareholder in the two companies had instructed solicitors and architects to submit the application for planning permission in respect of the hotel, but due to an oversight Glenmoy Ltd was named on the application form as the freehold owner instead of Glenmoy Developments Ltd. Although Glenmoy Ltd was named as applicant, the main shareholder had signed the application form. After an initial refusal to grant planning permission for the development, An Bord Pleanála granted the permission.

The applicants sought an order of *certiorari* quashing the decision of An Bord Pleanála, but O'Hanlon J refused the relief sought. He held that the failure to give the correct name of the company which, as freehold owner, was the intended applicant did not invalidate the grant of planning permission by the respondent Board. The application had to be regarded as one made on behalf of, or with the knowledge and approval of, the freehold owner of the lands. In any event, it could be said that Glenmoy Ltd, Glenmoy Developments Ltd or the main shareholder in the companies had a sufficient interest in and connection with the lands and the proposed development to maintain an application for planning permission made in the name of any one of the three parties. In addition, O'Hanlon J noted that the error in question could be corrected by the planning authority under s. 8 of the Local Government (Planning and Development) Act 1963 which entitled them to make corrections in the planning register.

Finally, applying the decision of the Supreme Court in *O'Keeffe v An Bord Pleanála* [1993] 1 IR 39 (1991 Review, 16-18), he concluded that the applicants had failed to discharge the heavy onus on them of establishing that there had been no relevant material before the respondent which could support its decision.

State bodies *Howard and Ors v Commissioners of Public Works in Ireland and Ors (No. 2)* [1994] 2 ILRM 301 was a sequel to the decision in *Howard and Ors v Commissioners of Public Works in Ireland and Ors* [1994] 1 IR 101; [1993] ILRM 665 and the consequent enactment of the State Authorities (Development and Management) Act 1993, discussed in the 1993 Review, 4, 430-2.

It will be recalled that the plaintiffs had sought judicial review of the decision of the Commissioners of Public Works in Ireland, the Office of Public Works, to build a visitor centre in the Burren National Park near Mullaghmore, County Clare. In the wake of the Supreme Court decision in *Howard (No. 1)*, s. 2(1) of the State Authorities (Development and Management) Act 1993 provided, *inter alia*, that a state authority shall have, and be deemed always to have had, power to carry out, or procure the carrying out of development, and to maintain, manage, repair, improve, alter, enlarge, reduce in size, remove or otherwise deal with buildings or structures or other works of property of a state authority. S. 2(2) provides that a state authority shall have, and be deemed always to have had, all such incidental, supplemental, ancillary and consequential powers as, in the opinion of the authority, are necessary or expedient for the purposes of the exercise by it of the powers conferred by s. 2(1). S. 2(3) provides that if s. 2(1) or s. 2(2) conflict with the constitutional rights of any person, the provisions of those subsections shall be subject to such limitations as are necessary to secure that they do not so conflict, but shall otherwise be of full force and effect.

The plaintiffs instituted new proceedings claiming that by virtue of s. 2(3), the 1993 Act did not apply to the site of the proposed visitor centre because if the 1993 Act gave the Commissioners the power to develop the site, it would amount to an unconstitutional invasion of the exclusive domain of the courts in the administration of justice, an attack on the plaintiffs' rights of access to the courts and their property rights, and an injustice done to the plaintiffs. Lynch J rejected this argument.

He held that the decision in *Howard (No. 1)* did not find that an injustice had been done to anyone, but simply indicated that none of the statutes creating or relating to the Commissioners conferred on them the power to carry out the impugned development. The Oireachtas could not alter or reverse that finding, or the judgment and order made on foot of it, because this would amount to a trespass by the legislature on the judicial domain and thus contravene the constitutional separation of powers between the various organs of state. In an informal severing of legislative language, Lynch J held that s. 2(1) and s. 2(2) of the 1993 Act had to be read, in so far as the development of the visitor centre at Mullaghmore was concerned, as if the words 'and be deemed always to have had' were omitted.

He went on to say that there was nothing in the decision in *Howard (No. 1)* to suggest that the Oireachtas could not confer the power to effect developments on the commissioners by means of appropriate legislation. Indeed, he noted that the High Court judgment in that case had adverted to the possibility of this being done. While the declaration in the High Court order in *Howard (No. 1)* remained valid as of that date, the change in circumstances effected by the 1993 Act, which supplied the missing powers, meant that the original absence of power was no longer a valid basis upon which to support the injunction granted in the order. The basis of the second declaration as to illegality because of the absence of planning permission remained and would support the injunction as long as there was no such permission.

Lynch J considered that the injunction granted in *Howard (No. 1)* had been worded in excessively absolute terms without reference to the two declarations on which it was founded and although the orders were of a final and not an interim or interlocutory nature, they could be vacated or amended. In this respect, he distinguished the instant case from the circumstances considered by the Supreme Court in *Attorney General (Society for the Protection of Unborn Children) v Open Door Counselling Ltd (No. 2)* [1994]

1 ILRM 256 (discussed in the 1993 Review, 160-5).

Ultimately, Lynch J held that an injunction requiring the return of the site to its original condition would be refused even though the works currently on the site had been unlawfully executed and concluded that the proper forum to determine whether the existing works should remain and whether the visitor centre could be completed was the planning authority.

Substantial works   In the 1993 Review, 429, we adverted to the decision of the Supreme Court in *Garden Village Construction Co. Ltd v Wicklow County Council* [1994] 1 ILRM 354 (HC); [1994] 2 ILRM 527 (SC). The case involved whether the applicant company had carried out 'substantial works' on foot of a permission which would entitle it to an extension of time pursuant to s. 4 of the Local Government (Planning and Development) Act 1982. In the instant case, the Supreme Court held that works effected outside the boundaries of the planning permission could not be regarded as 'substantial works' for the purposes of s. 4 of the 1982 Act.

S. 4(1) of the Local Government (Planning and Development) Act 1982 provides that a planning authority shall extend the period of a planning permission if there has been compliance with certain requirements, which include the requirement that the planning authority must be satisfied that 'the development to which such permission relates commenced before the expiration of the appropriate period sought to be extended' and 'substantial works were carried out pursuant to such permission during such period.' In June 1986 the respondent Council had granted the applicant planning permission for the building of 287 houses on a particular site. The Council had already granted planning permission in respect of adjoining lands and some works, such as the laying of roads, water mains, electricity and telephone cables, had been carried out pursuant to these permissions. The June 1986 permission expired on 19 June 1991 without any works being carried out on the site in question. Applications for the extension of the June 1986 permission and the adjoining lands were made in which it was claimed that they should be considered together as a single development project. In July 1991 the respondents refused to extend the period of the permission.

The applicant instituted judicial review proceedings and, in the High Court [1994] 1 ILRM 354), Geoghegan J granted it an order of *certiorari* quashing the refusal, but on appeal by the Council the Supreme Court (Egan, Blayney and Denham JJ) allowing the appeal.

Delivering the sole judgment, Blayney J accepted that all the works which had been carried out outside the site to which the June 1986 permission related constituted development within the meaning of s. 3(1) of the Local Government (Planning and Development) Act 1963 and had been carried out 'under and in accordance with' a planning permission obtained in respect of the lands on which they were carried out and pursuant to such permission.

He concluded that it could not be said that the works carried out outside the site to which the June 1986 permission related were also carried out pursuant to that planning permission. Approving the decision in *The State (McCoy) v Dun Laoghaire Corporation* [1985] ILRM 533 he stated that s. 4 of the 1982 Act made it clear that a planning authority may look at only the actual permission which they are being asked to extend. In those circumstances, the relief was refused.

Time limits In *K.S. K. Enterprises Ltd v An Bord Pleanála* [1994] 2 ILRM 1, the Supreme Court (Finlay CJ, O'Flaherty, Egan, Blayney and Denham JJ) considered the time limit attaching to a notice seeking leave to apply for judicial review of a planning permission. It will be recalled that s. 19(3) of the Local Government (Planning and Development) Act 1992, amended s. 82 of the Local Government (Planning and Development) Act 1963, to provide that challenges to planning permissions shall be by judicial review and be made within two months from the date on which the planning decision is given: see the 1992 Review, 448.

In the instant case, in December 1993 An Bord Pleanála had dismissed an appeal by the applicant against a decision by Dublin Corporation granting planning permission to the second named respondent, and decided to grant such permission subject to conditions. On January 31, 1994 the applicant filed a notice of motion (dated January 29) in the High Court, which the Central Office made returnable for February 14, 1994. The notice of motion was accompanied by the statement required to ground an application for judicial review and a supporting affidavit, as required by O. 84 of the Rules of the Superior Courts 1986.

In the High Court the respondents argued, as a preliminary point, that the application was time barred. Flood J held that the application was time barred on the grounds that the section required that the application actually be moved in court, or at least be available in the court list to be heard if the court can deal with it, within the two month period. On further appeal, although the Supreme Court dismissed the appeal it took a different view on the interpretation placed on s. 82 of the 1963 Act as inserted by s. 19 of the 1992 Act.

Delivering the only reasoned judgment, Finlay CJ stated that the general scheme of s. 82 of the 1963 Act, as inserted by s. 19 of the Act of 1992, was to confine firmly and strictly the possibility of judicial review challenging or impugning a planning decision made either by a planning authority or by An Bord Pleanála. He stated that it was the intention of the legislature to ensure that, within a short interval, the recipient of a planning permission should be in a position to act with safety upon the basis of that decision and be legally protected against a subsequent challenge to the decision.

Because of the importance of notification to the recipient of a planning permission and the planning authorities, he stated that an application could not be made within two months merely by the filing of a notice of motion in the court offices. However, if within the period of two months from the date of the decision, a notice of motion was filed in court and served on the mandatory parties, this would constitute compliance with the time limit. He noted that the alternative, which was to require that the application actually be moved in court, or at least have been listed in the court lists was too imprecise a cut-off time for the making of an important application.

Urban renewal: Custom House Docks The Urban Renewal (Amendment) Act 1987 (Transfer of land) (No. 1) Order 1994 (SI No. 73 of 1994) and the Urban Renewal (Amendment) Act 1987 (Transfer of Land) (No. 2) Order 1994 (SI No. 74 of 1994) transferred certain lands in the Dublin Port area to the Custom House Docks Development Authority with a view to further urban renewal development of that area. The Urban Renewal (Amendment) Act 1987 (Extension of Custom House Docks Area) Order 1994 (SI No. 180 of 1994) extended the area of the Custom House Docks Area, while the Urban Renewal Act 1986 (Remission of Rates) (Custom House Docks Area) (Amendment) Scheme 1994 (SI No. 181 of 1994) extended the closing date for applications for the rate remission scheme in the area (as extended) to January 1997. On the urban renewal regime generally, see the 1992 Review, 461-3.

Urban renewal: general Further significant extensions of the urban renewal regime were effected in 1994. The Finance Act 1987 (Designation of Urban Renewal Areas) Order 1994 (SI No. 284 of 1994), the Finance Act 1987 (Designation of Urban Renewal Areas) (No. 2) Order 1994 (SI No. 285 of 1994), the Finance Act 1987 (Designation of Urban Renewal Areas) (No. 3) Order 1994 (SI No. 286 of 1994) and the Finance Act 1987 (Designation of Urban Renewal Areas) (No. 4) Order 1994 (SI No. 287 of 1994) extended the urban renewal status, with the connected taxation reliefs associated with such status, for a number of different areas on which that status had been conferred by Orders of 1993 (1993 Review, 434). The 1993 Orders were also revoked by the 1994 Orders. The Urban Renewal Act 1986 (Designated Areas) (Dublin) Order 1994 (SI No. 407 of 1994) further extended the regime to certain street areas in Dublin, while the Urban Renewal Act 1986 (Remission of Rates) (Amendment) Scheme 1994 (SI No. 418 of 1994) extended the period in respect of which remission of rates could be claimed for urban renewal schemes.

A series of Orders made in 1994 also significantly extended the scope of the regime outside the Dublin area. These were: the Urban Renewal Act 1986 (Designated Areas) (Tralee) Order 1994 (SI No. 361 of 1994), the Urban

Renewal Act 1986 (Designated Areas) (Cork) Order 1994 (SI No. 362 of 1994), the Urban Renewal Act 1986 (Designated Areas) (Wexford) Order 1994 (SI No. 363 of 1994), the Urban Renewal Act 1986 (Designated Areas) (Limerick) Order 1994 (SI No. 364 of 1994), the Urban Renewal Act 1986 (Designated Areas) (Sligo) Order 1994 (SI No. 365 of 1994), the Urban Renewal Act 1986 (Designated Areas) (Wicklow) Order (SI No. 367 of 1994), the Urban Renewal Act 1986 (Designated Areas) (Roscommon) Order 1994 (SI No. 368 of 1994), the Urban Renewal Act 1986 (Designated Areas) (Galway) Order 1994 (SI No. 369 of 1994), the Urban Renewal Act 1986 (Designated Areas) (Waterford) Order 1994 (SI No. 370 of 1994), the Urban Renewal Act 1986 (Designated Areas) (Tullamore) Order 1994 (SI No. 371 of 1994), the Urban Renewal Act 1986 (Designated Areas) (Athlone) Order 1994 (SI No. 372 of 1994), the Urban Renewal Act 1986 (Designated Areas) (Athlone) (No. 2) Order 1994 (SI No. 422 of 1994), the Urban Renewal Act 1986 (Designated Areas) (Ballinasloe) Order (SI No. 373 of 1994), the Urban Renewal Act 1986 (Designated Areas) (Bray) Order 1994 (SI No. 374 of 1994), the Urban Renewal Act 1986 (Designated Areas) (Clonmel) Order 1994 (SI No. 375 of 1994), the Urban Renewal Act 1986 (Designated Areas) (Dundalk) Order 1994 (SI No. 376 of 1994), the Urban Renewal Act 1986 (Designated Areas) (Enniscorthy) Order, (SI No. 377 of 1994), the Urban Renewal Act 1986 (Designated Areas) (Dungarvan) Order 1994 (SI No. 378 of 1994), the Urban Renewal Act 1986 (Designated Areas) (Kilkenny) Order 1994 (SI No. 379 of 1994), the Urban Renewal Act 1986 (Designated Areas) (Killarney) Order 1994 (SI No. 380 of 1994), the Urban Renewal Act 1986 (Designated Areas) (Letterkenny) Order 1994 (SI No. 381 of 1994), the Urban Renewal Act 1986 (Designated Areas) (Longford) Order 1994 (SI No. 382 of 1994), the Urban Renewal Act 1986 (Designated Areas) (Mallow) Order 1994 (SI No. 383 of 1994), the Urban Renewal Act 1986 (Designated Areas) (Monaghan) Order 1994 (SI No. 384 of 1994), the Urban Renewal Act 1986 (Designated Areas) (Navan) Order 1994 (SI No. 385 of 1994), the Urban Renewal Act 1986 (Designated Areas) (Nenagh) Order 1994 (SI No. 386 of 1994), the Urban Renewal Act 1986 (Designated Areas) (Mullingar) Order 1994 (SI No. 387 of 1994), the Urban Renewal Act 1986 (Designated Areas) (Newbridge) Order 1994 (SI No. 388 of 1994), the Urban Renewal Act 1986 (Designated Areas) (Portlaoise) Order 1994 (SI No. 389 of 1994) and the Urban Renewal Act 1986 (Designated Areas) (Carlow) Order 1994 (SI No. 390 of 1994). Each Order had attached to it a map indicating the boundary of the area in the town or city involved which was designated for urban renewal status.

RATING (VALUATION)

Agricultural v industrial In *International Mushrooms Ltd v Commissioner of Valuation* [1994] 2 ILRM 121, the respondent company produced mushroom spawn in premises which were situated in an industrial estate. A portion of the premises, which comprised an office section together with an area covered by a cladded roof supported upon steel and concrete trusses, was given a valuation by the Commissioner of Valuation. The company appealed to the Valuation Tribunal which held that the premises were not rateable. S. 12 of the Valuation (Ireland) Act 1852 provides that all lands and buildings shall be deemed to be rateable hereditaments. S. 2 of the Valuation Act 1986 provides that property falling within any of the categories of fixed property specified in the Schedule of the 1852 Act, as inserted by s. 3 of the 1986 Act, shall be deemed to be rateable hereditaments in addition to those specified in s. 12 of the 1852 Act. Reference No. 1 of the Schedule refers to 'all constructions affixed to lands or tenements'. On a case stated to the High Court the company submitted that its premises were exempt from rateability by virtue of s. 1 of the 1852 Act, which provides that 'a hereditament or tenement is not liable to be rated in respect of any increase in its value from the erection of farm, outhouse or office buildings or any permanent agricultural improvement.' Alternatively, it argued that they were exempt by virtue of reference No. 2 of the Schedule to the 1852 Act, which provides that lands developed for the purposes of agriculture or horticulture are not rateable, irrespective or whether or not such land is surfaced and includes any constructions affixed thereto which pertain to the development. Keane J overturned the decision of the Valuation Tribunal, thus upholding the original decision of the Commissioner.

He held that the intention of the legislature in enacting s. 14 of the 1852 Act had been to ensure that agricultural lands improved by the carrying out of works such as the erection of farm buildings should not attract an increased valuation. He considered that farm buildings meant buildings on a farm used in connection with the farming operations of the farm; that as the respondent's building was located in an industrial estate, it could not be considered a building on a farm used in connection with a farm; and the fact that the spawn produced would ultimately be used elsewhere in the cultivation of mushrooms was irrelevant.

Keane J considered that it was the clear intention of s. 2 of the Valuation Act 1986, which provides that property falling within any of the categories of fixed property specified in the schedule to the 1852 Act shall be deemed to be rateable hereditaments, to extend the scope of rateability to structures which failed to meet the criteria of a building for the purposes of s. 12 of the 1852 Act. He accepted that reference No. 2 of the Schedule to the 1852 Act provided an exemption from rateability for lands developed for the purposes of agriculture, horticulture, forestry or sport and constructions which are affixed to such lands which pertain to the development. However, he held that s. 2 of the 1986 Act and the Schedule to the 1852 Act did not afford an exemption to buildings which had hitherto been deemed to be rateable hereditaments. Keane J concluded that the respondent's building could properly be regarded as coming within the category of buildings deemed by s. 12 of the 1852 Act to be a rateable hereditament. It therefore remained a rateable hereditament.

Towards the end of his judgment, Keane J stated that there was an undoubted inconsistency in the language used in reference Nos. 1 and 2 of the Schedule to the 1852 Act (as amended) which might have to be resolved in favour of an occupier of property. However, in the instant case, that issue did not arise for consideration since he pointed out that the Commissioner was not seeking to avail of an ambiguity to bring within the additional categories of rateable hereditaments a construction which was obviously intended to be exempted. Despite this outcome, therefore, the decision raises once again the spectre that the 1986 Act has not provided the clarity in this area of the law which other judges had hoped it might (as to which see the 1990 Review, 423-7).

Marina *Trustees of Kinsale Yacht Club v Commissioner of Valuation* [1994] 1 ILRM 457 also concerned the interpretation of s. 2 of the Valuation Act 1986 and the associated Schedules in the context of a marina. The trustees of Kinsale Yacht Club were the owners of a marina which comprised a floating wooden platform attached to piles which were partially driven into the sea-bed. The platform could be detached from the piles and moved to another location. In 1989 the Commissioner of Valuation placed a valuation of £120 on the marina. The trustees appealed and in September 1990 the commissioner upheld the validity of the valuation but reduced it to £60. The trustees appealed to the Valuation Tribunal which held that the marina did not fall for exemption under reference No. 2 of the Schedule to the 1986 Act (see the *International Mushrooms* case, above) because, although there was a sporting element in the construction of the marina, it did not constitute a development of land. However, the Tribunal held that the marina was not a fixed mooring within the meaning of reference No. 4 to the 1986 Act (which refers to 'all fixed moorings, piers and docks') because the piles to which it was attached could be removed from the sea-bed and replaced in another location. Accordingly it adjudicated that there was a rateable easement within the meaning of s. 12 of the 1852 Act and it was valued at £2.50. On a case stated, Barr J held in the High Court ([1993] ILRM 393) that the Tribunal had erred (1992 Review, 465). However, on further appeal, the Supreme

Court (Finlay CJ, O'Flaherty and Blayney JJ) allowed the appeal.

Delivering the leading judgment, Finlay CJ held that while the 1986 Act was not a taxing or penal statute, by deeming the categories of fixed properties referred to in the Schedule to be rateable hereditaments in addition to those mentioned in s. 12 of the 1852 Act, s. 2 constituted a platform or necessary statutory precondition intended to lead to the fresh imposition of liability and thus had to be given a strict interpretation in accordance with the principles set out in *Inspector of Taxes v Kiernan* [1981] IR 117; [1982] ILRM 13.

The then Chief Justice went on to state that s. 2 of the 1986 Act provided without any ambiguity that property falling within any of the categories of fixed property specified in the Schedule was deemed to be a rateable hereditament. If a particular property fell within one of these categories of fixed property, no further enquiry had to be made as to whether it fell into any of the other categories. Finlay CJ concluded that the decision of the High Court that the marina was a fixed mooring was a determination of a mixed question of fact and law which had not been challenged on appeal. In the light of this finding it was inevitable that the marina fell within one of the categories of fixed property listed in the Schedule.

Finlay CJ did not consider it illogical or capricious that the 1986 Act should make all forms of fixed mooring rateable hereditaments by virtue of reference No. 4 while preventing certain constructions affixed to land developed for the purpose of sport from being rateable hereditaments by virtue of reference no. 2.

As in the *International Mushrooms* case, above, the Court noted there was an inconsistency as between the wording of reference No. 1 and reference No. 2 in the Schedule to the 1986 Act insofar as it was unclear whether something which would be deemed to be a rateable hereditament under reference No. 1 would still be rateable even though it appeared to be capable of being exempted under reference No. 2. In light of the views expressed in these two decisions of the courts, it is to be hoped that amending legislation could be brought forward to clarify this important area. Indeed, as with many other rating cases, a firm conclusion from these cases is that there is a pressing need for consolidation of the law.

Toll booths occupied by private company　In *Dublin County Council v West Link Toll Bridge Ltd* [1994] 2 ILRM 204, Geoghegan J held that toll booths operated by a private company were rateable hereditaments. The case arose as follows.

The plaintiff Council, the rating authority for the Dublin County, had entered into an agreement with the defendant for the establishment of a toll road pursuant to s. 9 of the Local Government (Toll Roads) Act 1979. The

agreement provided, *inter alia*, for the establishment, operation and maintenance of the road and for the defendant to dedicate the road to the public as
a public road. It was provided that the defendant would occupy the road and
operate a toll system for 30 years. It stated that the proceeds were to be applied
towards a payment of gross toll revenue to the plaintiff, towards the costs
and charges involved in its operation and towards the recovery of construction and associated costs. It also contained a recital referring to the delegation
of the council's right to collect tolls to the toll company. The Council sought
£348,559.20 in respect of rates for the year 1992 on the basis that the
defendant was the rated occupier of hereditaments comprising a toll road,
toll offices, stores and car parks. The defendant denied that it was in
occupation of a rateable hereditament. Geoghegan J found in the Council's
favour.

He held that the recital to the agreement did not reflect its true nature.
Subject to certain obligations, the defendant was entitled to profit from the
tolls and as it was entitled to the tolls for the period of 30 years it could not
be said that it was in occupation of the tolls and ancillary offices as an agent
of the plaintiff. Referring to the decision in *Telecom Éireann v Commissioner
of Valuation* [1994] 1 IR 66 (1992 Review, 465), he held that the effect of
the agreement was to oust the power of the plaintiff to collect tolls and to
confer the power on the defendant for a period of 30 years. It was immaterial
in this respect whether the benefit was in the nature of a lease, licence or
franchise since it conferred paramount occupation of the tolls and the
ancillary buildings on the defendant. He took the view that the tolls were in
the nature of a specific property right vested in the defendant for the period
of 30 years: they were a separate and privately occupied incorporeal hereditament and not merely ancillary to the public road. As to the toll offices,
store and car parks, he considered these where corporeal hereditaments
ancillary to the tolls, rather than the public road, and were therefore rateable.

Finally, distinguishing the case from *Guardians of Londonderry Union
v Londonderry Bridge Commissioners* (1868) IR 2 CL 577, Blayney J held
that as the tolls were not exclusively for public purposes and the defendant
derived a private use therefrom, the exemption provided for in the Poor Relief
(Ireland) Act 1838 did not apply.

Practice and Procedure

AFFIDAVITS

Leave to adduce evidence by affidavit *Phonographic Performance (Ireland) Ltd v Cody and Princes Investments Ltd* [1994] 2 ILRM 241 was a case on the enforcement of performing rights pursuant to the Copyright Act 1963. In the instant case, Keane J considered whether certain evidence alleging infringement could be adduced by affidavit. Ss. 7 and 17(4)(b) of the Copyright Act 1963 provide that unless the copyright owner has given consent, it is an act of copyright infringement to cause a published sound recording to be heard in public without the payment of equitable remuneration to the copyright owner. Disputes as to what constitutes 'equitable remuneration' can be resolved by the Controller of Industrial and Commercial Property under either s. 31 or s. 32 of the 1963 Act. The procedure under s. 32 is appropriate where the copyright owner already operates a licence scheme and a determination by the Controller that the amount of remuneration is reasonable binds all persons whose activities fall within that particular licence scheme. The membership of the plaintiff, PPI, consisted of various record companies. It collected revenue from the public performance, broadcasting and diffusion of the sound recordings made by its members. The second named defendant was the owner of a hotel in which there was a discotheque. The first named defendant was the holder of the intoxicating liquor licence and the public music and dance licence in respect of the premises. PPI claimed that since 1987 the defendants had caused sound recordings to be heard in public in the premises without paying it equitable remuneration and it sought an injunction restraining the defendants from causing the sound recordings to be heard in public, damages for infringement of copyright and an account of profits. In their defence the defendants put in issue the plaintiff's claim that copyright subsisted in the sound recordings and questioned whether the plaintiff was the owner or exclusive licensee of any copyright which might subsist. They also claimed that the remuneration sought by the plaintiff was not equitable and that the dispute should be resolved by the controller under s. 31 of the 1963 Act and not s. 32 as claimed by the plaintiff.

By a notice of motion, the plaintiff sought an order dismissing the defendants' defence because of their failure to comply with a previous order for discovery. Alternatively, it sought an order striking out so much of the defence as put in issue the plaintiff's ownership of copyright. As a further alternative, it sought an order pursuant to O.39, r.1 of the Rules of the Superior Courts 1986 permitting the plaintiff to establish certain matters by affidavit. An affidavit of discovery was then sworn on behalf of the defendants, but the plaintiff submitted this was inadequate as it failed to discover certain documents which were undoubtedly in existence, such as lists of sound recordings, accounts showing the level of turnover, documents relating to the purchase or hire of equipment for playing sound recordings, documents showing arrangements with disc jockeys, and receipts concerning the purchase or acquisition of copies of sound recordings. The defendants submitted that this material could only be relevant to the issue of damages or an account of profits and thus such discovery would be premature.

Keane J held that the claim should not be struck out, but he permitted PPI to adduce certain evidence on affidavit.

While the case primarily involved procedural matters, Keane J also made some important comments on the constitutional dimension to the case and on the effect of s. 60(4) of the Copyright Act 1963, which provides that no right in the nature of copyright shall subsist otherwise than by virtue of the Act or some other similar enactment. This would appear to suggest that the 1963 Act amounts to an entire code on the subject, and indeed this is supported by English authority. However, Keane J took a different view when he commented thus:

> The right of the creator of a literary, dramatic, musical or artistic work not to have his or her creation stolen or plagiarised is a right of private property within the meaning of Articles 40.3.2° and 43.1 of the Constitution, as is the similar right of a person who has employed his or her technical skills and/or capital in the sound recording of a musical work. As such, they can hardly be abolished in their entirety, although it was doubtless within the competence of the Oireachtas to regulate their exercise in the interests of the common good. In addition and even in the absence of any statutory machinery, it is the duty of the organs of the State, including the courts, to ensure, as best they may, that these rights are protected from unjust attack and, in the case of injustice done, vindicated. The statements in some English authorities that copyright other than by statutory provision ceased to exist with the abolition of common law copyright are not necessarily applicable in Ireland.

This passage may prove of some importance in the context of intellectual property law generally, underlining that the Constitution establishes a general umbrella that appears even over existing statutory commercial law in much the same way as, for example, the many provisions of the EC Treaty.

Turning to the precise issues raised in the motion before him, Keane J held that while the plaintiff might at some later stage in the action be entitled to an order requiring the defendants to make further and better discovery, he agreed with the defendants that the circumstances in which such an order would be appropriate had not yet arisen. Moreover, it would be inappropriate to give the plaintiff the more drastic remedy of striking out the defendants' defence.

He considered that the defendants were, in line with well accepted methods of pleading, entitled to raise alternative defences which denied the subsistence of copyright in favour of the plaintiff, while at the same time disputing the amount of remuneration which the plaintiff claimed by virtue of copyright in the sound recordings and seeking a resolution of the dispute under s. 31 of the 1963 Act and that this. did not of itself cause prejudice, embarrassment or delay to the plaintiff within the meaning of O.19, r.27 of the Rules of the Superior Courts 1986.

As to the plaintiff's claim to be permitted to prove facts by affidavit, he stated that the making of an order under O.39, r.1 of the 1986 Rules to permit that was a matter within the discretion of the court, subject to 'sufficient reason' being shown and where justice required that such an order should be made. In this respect he stated that the rule that witnesses at the trial of any action must be examined *viva voce* and in open court was of central importance and should not be departed from lightly. However, he stated that an order under O.39, r.1 of the 1986 Rules should be made where the following conditions were met:

(1) The facts sought to be proved do not relate to issues significantly in dispute between the parties;

(2) The court is not satisfied that the other party *bona fide* requires the production of the deponent for cross-examination;

(3) The difficulty or expense of producing the deponent in court is such that there is a serious risk of injustice to the party seeking to adduce the evidence on affidavit;

(4) The application is made as a preliminary application before the trial of the action.

On the first of these factors, he stated that if the defendants considered that the remuneration sought by the plaintiff was reasonable, it would be unlikely that they would involve themselves in expensive litigation merely in order to obtain proof of the plaintiff's entitlement to copyright. While the defendants were perfectly entitled to require the plaintiff to prove the existence of copyright in each of the sound recordings and its rights as owner or exclusive licensee of the copyright, as a matter of common sense it could not be said that these matters were pleas going to the gist of the present action. The gist of the action was the reasonableness of the remuneration sought by the plaintiff and the appropriate machinery by which any dispute as to the level of such remuneration was to be resolved.

On the second issue, Keane J noted that the defendants had not indicated in respect of any of the averments of fact which the plaintiff proposed to adduce by affidavit that there was any serious doubt as to the correctness of the averment or that they were in possession of material on the basis of which they would wish to cross-examine any of the proposed deponents. It followed that the attendance of the witnesses for cross-examination was not *bona fide* required by the defendants.

On the third factor, Keane J stated that as most of the affidavits would be from witnesses outside the jurisdiction who could not be compelled by the process of the court to attend the hearing, and there was evidence in the case of all the witnesses that they would find it difficult to attend, it followed that the plaintiff had succeeded in establishing a degree of difficulty and impracticality in the calling of witnesses leading to a serious risk of injustice if the application under O.39, r.1 was refused.

Since the instant case also satisfied the fourth requirement that the application be made at a preliminary stage, it followed that this was an appropriate case in which to allow the evidence to be given on affidavit without the necessity of producing the deponents for cross-examination. However, Keane J noted at the end of his judgment that this order did not prevent the defendants from putting the plaintiff on proof both of the existence of copyright in the sound recordings and its rights as owner or exclusive licensee of the copyright.

APPEALS

Fresh evidence In *Fitzgerald v Kenny* [1994] 2 ILRM 8, the Supreme Court (Finlay CJ, O'Flaherty, Egan, Blayney and Denham JJ) permitted the plaintiff to introduce additional evidence in an application under O.58, r.8 of the Rules of the Superior Courts 1986. The background was that the plaintiff had been injured in two accidents in 1983 and 1985. In July 1987, he was awarded £17,500 general damages to the date of trial and £12,500 general damages for the future for injuries sustained to his left arm and back in his action against the first defendant and £5,000 general damages for a whiplash injury in his action against the second defendant. On his appeal to the Supreme Court, the plaintiff claimed that his circumstances had altered dramatically since the date of assessment. In particular, he had lost his job as a Garda because of his injuries, and this had not been contemplated by either side at the trial. In addition, he claimed that his physical and mental injuries had greatly increased since 1987. The Supreme Court agreed.

The Court held that, under O.58, r.8 of the 1986 Rules, the plaintiff could introduce new evidence on an appeal as to matters which occurred after the date of the 1987 decision, in particular the loss of his job, subject to the Supreme Court's discretion. The discretion as to whether to admit fresh evidence by either a plaintiff or a defendant must be exercised in a fair and just manner.

Unlike in previous decisions of the Court on this topic in recent years, the Court referred to English authority on the subject, notably *dicta* of Lord Wilberforce in *Mulholland v Mitchell* [1971] AC 666. Indeed, the Court distinguished its own decision in *O'Connor v O'Shea*, Supreme Court, July 24, 1989 (1989 Review, 342-3) in stating that, although it was desirable to have finality in litigation, the Court should exercise its discretion and admit fresh evidence where a serious injustice would be suffered by the plaintiff such as where, for example, basic assumptions, common to both sides, have clearly been falsified by subsequent events; and when to refuse fresh evidence would be an affront to common sense or a sense of justice. However, its discretion should not be exercised so as to admit fresh evidence when such evidence bears upon matters falling within the field or area of uncertainty in respect of which the trial judge's estimate has previously been made, or where there has simply been a dramatic alteration in the circumstances on which the decision in the High Court was based.

Applying these principles, the Court concluded that fresh evidence relating to the plaintiff's loss of employment should be admitted as otherwise there was a possibility that the plaintiff would suffer a serious injustice. In addition, since the evidence relating to the plaintiff's physical and mental condition was connected with the evidence relating to his loss of employment, it also held that fresh evidence on these matters should be admitted. The Court made it clear that, without this connection, the evidence would not have been admitted as it would otherwise have fallen squarely within the area of uncertainty in which the trial judge's estimate of damages had been made.

Review of trial court's findings   In *Tuohy v Courtney and Ors* [1994] 2 ILRM 503 (discussed in the Limitations of Actions chapter, 336-8, above, the Supreme Court applied its decisions in *Hay v O'Grady* [1992] 1 IR 210 (1992 Review, 470-3) and *Best v Wellcome Foundation Ltd* [1993] 3 IR 421 (1992 Review, 610-11) in confirming that the jurisdiction of the Supreme Court to review findings of primary fact made by a trial judge is confined to determining whether those findings were supported by credible evidence; in the instant case there were no grounds for interfering with the trial judge's findings.

BIAS

Three Supreme Court decisions in 1994 raised issues concerning alleged judicial bias: see *O'Reilly v Cassidy (No. 2)* [1995] 1 ILRM 311 and *McNally v Martin* [1995] 1 ILRM 350, both discussed in the Administrative Law chapter, 6-8, above, and *Dublin Wellwoman Centre and Ors v Ireland and Ors* [1995] 1 ILRM 408, discussed in the Constitutional Law chapter, 109-111, above.

COSTS

Security for costs In *Malone v Brown Thomas & Co. Ltd and Federal Security Services Ltd* [1995]1 ILRM 369, the Supreme Court considered well-established principles concerning security for costs.

The plaintiff had instituted proceedings against the defendants for damages for wrongful arrest, false imprisonment and defamation. Because the plaintiff was resident outside the jurisdiction in Australia (although she had been born in Ireland and intended to return home in June 1995) the first named defendant brought an application before the High Court seeking security for costs, which was furnished by the plaintiff in the form of a lodgment for £7,500. In July 1991 the plaintiff's claim against the respondents was dismissed and the she was ordered to pay the defendants' costs. A notice of appeal was served by the plaintiff and the defendants then applied to have her furnish security for costs in relation to the appeal. In the absence of a response, the first named defendant brought an application to the Supreme Court for an order for security for costs and a stay on the appellant's appeal pending the furnishing of such security for costs. The Supreme Court (Hamilton CJ, Egan and Denham JJ) refused the application.

Delivering the leading judgment, Hamilton CJ referred to *dicta* from the Supreme Court decisions in *Perry v Stratham Ltd* [1928] IR 580 and *Midland Bank Ltd v Crossley Cooke* [1969] IR 56 and to the High Court decision of Finlay P (as he then was) in *Collins v Doyle* [1982] ILRM 495 (while it is unfortunate that the Chief Justice did not refer to the more recent decisions of the Court itself in *Fallon v An Bord Pleanála* [1992] 2 IR 380; [1991] ILRM 799 (1991 Review, 333-4) or *Fares v Wiley* [1994] 1 ILRM 465 (1993 Review, 441-2), it must also be said that these cases are entirely consistent with and approved of the earlier line of authority).

Applying the principles in these cases, Hamilton CJ noted that ordering of security for costs is a matter for the discretion of the court, and in the exercise of its discretion, the court must consider all the circumstances of the case. In that respect, neither mere residence outside the jurisdiction or the poverty of the plaintiff is a sufficient justification for compelling a lodgment of security for costs. He stated that the onus was on the applicant to establish reasonable grounds for an entitlement to the order of security for costs and he added that access to the courts, including the Supreme Court, was the constitutional right of every citizen and no unnecessary monetary obstacle should be placed in the path of those who seek access to the courts.

Having considered all the circumstances of the case, namely, that the plaintiff intended to return permanently to Ireland in June 1995 (just seven months after the judgment of the Supreme Court), the lodgment of £7,500, that the plaintiff's grounds of appeal included some issues relating to the adequacy of the questions left to the jury and the judge's charge to the jury and the plaintiff's constitutional right of access to the court, the court's discretion was exercised in favour of the plaintiff.

In *Irish Press plc v Ingersoll Irish Publications Ltd (No. 3)* [1995] 1 ILRM 117, the Supreme Court, in an *ex tempore* decision, declined to order security for costs for an appeal in a complex commercial dispute, the substantive issues in which are discussed in the 1993 Review, 86 and in the Company Law chapter, 60, above. The security for costs point is discussed below, 387.

DELAY

In *Hogan and Others (Irish Rugby Football Union) v Jones and Ors* [1994] 1 ILRM 512, Murphy J considered the question of dismissing a claim on grounds of delay in the context of a building contract relating to a well-known sports stadium. The plaintiffs had commenced proceedings in 1982 in relation to the alleged negligent design and construction of the West Stand at the Irish Rugby Football Union (IRFU) headquarters at Lansdowne Road in Dublin. The first, second and third named defendants were respectively the architects, the engineers and the builders for the stand. The contract was signed in June 1977 and a certificate of practical completion of the works was issued in March 1978. The plenary summons in the matter was issued in October 1982 and the plaintiffs' statement of claim delivered in January 1984. The third named defendants, the builders, delivered their defence in February 1988 and between 1988 and 1992 the plaintiffs delayed for somewhere in the region of two years on two separate occasions in replying to notices for particulars. A notice of trial was issued in November 1989 and a certificate of readiness in respect of the matter was granted in June 1993.

In July 1993 the third named defendants issued a motion to dismiss the plaintiffs' claim as against them for want of prosecution. In their affidavits the third named defendants referred to the dimmed recollection of some of their witnesses, the death of one witness and the alleged non-availability of other witnesses. The plaintiffs alleged that much of the case would turn upon the existing structure and plans and drawings which were available. In the end, Murphy J refused to dismiss the claim.

He referred to the existing case law on the topic, notably the decision of the Supreme Court in *Dowd v Kerry County Council* [1970] IR 27, the judgment of Finlay P (as he then was) in *Rainsford v Limerick Corporation* [1995] 2 ILRM 561 (decided in 1979), and the decision in *Celtic Ceramics Ltd v Industrial Development Authority* [1994] ILRM 248. He relied in particular on the judgment in *Rainsford* to the effect that the Court must consider the following:

(i) whether the delay is inordinate, and if so, whether it has been inexcusable, the onus being on the party seeking the dismissal of the proceedings;

(ii) if a delay is both inordinate and inexcusable, whether the balance of justice is in favour of, or against, the proceeding of the case, taking account of the failure of the party seeking dismissal for want of prosecution to apply for such dismissal at an earlier stage; and

(iii) the extent of the litigant's personal blameworthiness for delay.

Referring with approval to the decision of the House of Lords in *Birkett v James* [1978] AC 297, Murphy J was of the view that time elapsed prior to the commencement of proceedings within the relevant limitation period cannot of itself constitute inordinate delay but that a late start within this period makes it more incumbent on a plaintiff to proceed with expedition.

Murphy J stated that the dismissal of proceedings is not an order made to punish a party, but will be made only where it is necessary to protect the legitimate interests of the party sued and in particular his constitutional right to a trial in accordance with fair procedures. In the instant case, he felt that on the one hand the plaintiffs were guilty of inordinate delay in taking 14 months to deliver a statement of claim, but that, on the other hand the defendants were responsible for the four year delay between January 1984 and February 1988 prior to the delivery of their defence. He considered that the delay by the plaintiffs in taking two years to reply to each of the notices for particulars served by the defendant was both inordinate and inexcusable. As to the defendants supposed difficulties concerning witnesses, he noted that these had not been adverted to prior to July 1993. If the defendants had been concerned by the effect of the outstanding litigation on their professional and financial reputation he considered that they could have pressed the plaintiffs to proceed with the action. On this basis, he concluded, as already indicated that the claim should be allowed the proceed, notwithstanding the inordinate delays on both sides.

DISCOVERY

Discovery sought to plead cause of action   In *Galvin v Graham-Twomey*
[1994] 2 ILRM 315, O'Flaherty J (sitting as a High Court judge) declined to
allow discovery be used to plead a cause of action which hitherto had not
been pleaded.

The plaintiff was the vice-principal of a primary school. The defendant
was a teacher at the same school. In 1992 the plaintiff commenced proceedings against the defendant in the Circuit Court in which she claimed damages
for libel, slander, misrepresentation, negligence and wrongful interference
with her constitutional right to her good name. The plaintiff's civil bill
alleged that the defendant had sent letters which contained allegations that
defamed the plaintiff to the chairman of the school's board of management,
a schools' inspector, various public representatives and the Department of
Education. It was also claimed that the chairman of the board of management
had shown the letter which had been sent to him to the parish priest. The
plaintiff never saw any of the alleged letters. The Circuit Court refused to
make an order for discovery against the parish priest, the board of management or its chairman. While the Minister of Education was willing to make
discovery, the Circuit Court also refused to make an order for inspection of
documents against the Minister. In January 1993 the Circuit Court struck out
that part of the plaintiff's civil bill which claimed that she had been defamed
by the alleged letters. The plaintiff appealed, but O'Flaherty J in dismissing
the appeal.

He pointed out that the purpose of the procedural remedy of discovery
(leaving to one side, as he noted, the *action* for discovery, discussed in
Megaleasing UK Ltd v Barrett [1992] 1 IR 219; [1993] ILRM 497 and the
1992 Review, 479-80) is to aid a party in the progress of litigation: it was not
to be invoked so as to enable a person to plead a cause of action which he is
not otherwise in a position to plead. Counsel for the defendant had relied, in
particular, on the decision of the Court of Appeal in England in *Collins v
Jones* [1955] 1 QB 564 in support of the argument that as the plaintiff had
made out a *prima facie* case that the letters probably contained defamatory
matter and that she had been given leave to amend the civil bill, it would be
much better that discovery should also be ordered. O'Flaherty J rejected this
suggestion in the following passage:

> [J]ust as it is essential for a plaintiff to be able to prove publication of
> a defamatory matter, so he must set forth with some particularity in his
> pleadings the details of his complaint. He cannot be permitted to launch
> his proceedings and then hope by discovery to be able to amend his
> pleadings and thereby make his case. In my judgment that is not the

purpose of discovery and would be a quite wrong use of the procedural remedy of discovery.

In the circumstances, he dismissed the plaintiff's appeal and affirmed the orders of the Circuit Court.

Privilege: UN Board of Inquiry In *O'Brien v Ireland and Ors* [1995] 1 ILRM 22, O'Hanlon J declined to order discovery of a United Nations UNIFIL Board of Inquiry Report. The case involved the borders between domestic law on privilege and diplomatic immunity.

The plaintiff's husband, a member of the Irish Defence Forces, had been killed in Lebanon while serving with the United Nations Peace-Keeping Force, UNIFIL. An official inquiry into the death was held by the United Nations and a further inquiry was held by a court of inquiry pursuant to the Defence Act 1954, the Rules of Procedure (Defence Forces) 1954 and the Defence Force Regulations 1982. The plaintiff instituted proceedings in negligence and breach of duty against the defendants, their servants and agents. The plaintiff obtained an order of discovery against the defendants and the affidavit of discovery sworn on behalf of the defendants claimed privilege in respect of the United Nations UNIFIL board of inquiry report, the United Nations contingent book of inquiry report and the court of inquiry report.

The statutory background to the claim for privilege was that Rule 121 of the Rules of Procedure (Defence Forces) 1954 provides that the proceedings of a court of inquiry and any confession, statement or answer to any question made or given at a court of inquiry shall not be admissible in evidence against any person subject to military law, nor shall any evidence respecting the proceedings of a court of inquiry be given against any such person except upon his trial for committing the civil offence of perjury. Rule 122 provides that a finding of a court of inquiry shall not be admissible in evidence nor shall any question be asked of any witness in relation thereto. Regulation 11(2) of the Defence Forces Regulations 1982 provides that the findings and recommendations of all courts of inquiry shall be treated as confidential and shall not be disclosed to interested parties except as provided in s. 181(2) of the Defence Act 1954, the Rules of Procedure (Defence Forces) 1954 and the Defence Forces Regulations themselves. Article II.4 of the Convention on the Privileges and Immunities of the United Nations 1946 provides that the archives of the United Nations, and in general all documents belonging to it or held by it shall be inviolable, irrespective of where they are located. Under s. 9 of the Diplomatic Relations and Immunities Act 1967, the United Nations Organisation and its property, and a person to whom the convention applies and the property of that person, enjoy inviolability, exemptions, facilities, immunities, privileges and rights in such manner, to such extent and subject to such extent, and subject to such limitations (including the waiver thereof) as are provided for in each case by the Convention.

As already indicated, O'Hanlon J held that the documents were privileged and refused to order discovery. Indeed, he quoted from what appeared to be an ex tempore and previously uncirculated judgment of Barrington J in *O'Mahony v Ireland*, High Court, June 27, 1989 in which he had ruled that such documents were privileged. In addition, O'Hanlon J surveyed the case law on discovery in general, including the most recent re-statement of the applicable principles in *Ambiorix Ltd v Minister for the Environment (No. 1)* [1992] 1 IR 277; [1992] ILRM 209 (1991 Review, 338-9). Notwithstanding that these cases indicated that the courts in general adjudicate on conflicting claims based on the public interest between compelling the production of documents and exempting them from production, O'Hanlon J accepted that the legislature retained the power to intervene and confer the privilege of exemption from production on specified categories of documentary or other evidence. This power was not curtailed or restricted in any way save that any such legislation must not conflict with the overriding provisions of the Constitution.

He considered that the relevant provisions of the Defence Act 1954, the Rules of Procedure (Defence Forces) 1954, the Defence Force Regulations 1982 and the Diplomatic Relations and Immunities Act 1967 protected the documents in respect of which the defendants had claimed privilege from disclosure. Finally, in line with what Finlay CJ had said in the *Ambiorix* case, he did not think that the Court had to examine any particular document before deciding that it was exempt from production: it was entitled to make this determination on the basis of a description of the document's nature and contents, which he was prepared to accept.

Third party: extradition In *Fusco v O'Dea* [1994] 2 ILRM 389, the Supreme Court declined to order third party discovery under O.31, r.29 of the Rules of the Superior Courts 1986 against a party outside the jurisdiction in the context of an extradition case. The plaintiff had been convicted in Northern Ireland in 1981 on various charges, including murder and sentenced to imprisonment for life. However, prior to the imposition of the sentence he escaped from prison in Northern Ireland and entered the State. In 1982 he was arrested in the State and was convicted of escaping from lawful custody in Northern Ireland and sentenced to ten years' imprisonment. Prior to the due date for his release in 1991, he was brought before the District Court, pursuant to the Extradition Act 1965, on foot of warrants which were issued by the Northern Ireland authorities and supported by the defendant, an Assistant Garda Commissioner. In January 1992 an order was made in the

District Court for the extradition to Northern Ireland. He then instituted proceedings under s. 50 of the 1965 Act seeking his release. An application was also brought seeking to have the government of Great Britain and Northern Ireland joined as a co-defendant in the proceedings and discovery as against the Secretary of State for Northern Ireland of certain documents and the giving of answers to certain interrogatories. In the High Court it was admitted that the only reason that an order was being sought joining the government of Great Britain and Northern Ireland as a defendant was so as to obtain the discovery of documents from it. The plaintiff indicated that alternatively he would be content to obtain an order for third party discovery pursuant to O.31, r.29 of the Rules of the Superior Courts 1986 as against the government of Great Britain and Northern Ireland. In the High Court, an order for discovery was made against the defendant and the Director of Public Prosecutions, but was refused as against the government of Great Britain and Northern Ireland. The plaintiff appealed, but the Supreme Court (Finlay CJ, Egan and Blayney JJ) dismissed the appeal.

Delivering the sole judgment, Egan J stated that O.31, r.29 of the 1986 Rules was an unusual provision in that it required a stranger to an action to make discovery and thus should be construed strictly. Citing with approval the approach of Costello J (as he then was) in *Allied Irish Banks plc v Ernst & Whinney* [1993] 1 IR 375 (1992 Review, 483-4), he agreed that the onus was on the applicant to satisfy the court that such documents were in the third party's power or possession and, in addition, whether such an order should be granted was a matter for the court's discretion and it was not available as of right. Egan J might also have added that this approach had already been stated by the Supreme Court itself in the Allied Irish Banks case (see the 1992 Review, 484).

He pointed out that the categories of cases specified in O.11 of the 1986 Rules in which an order granting liberty to serve out of the jurisdiction could be obtained were exhaustive. Egan J was of the view that the principle underlying O.11, that parties outside the jurisdiction were only amenable to the court's jurisdiction in specified circumstances, would be circumvented to a certain extent if an order for discovery was granted against a third party outside the jurisdiction because the order would subject such a party to the jurisdiction of the Irish courts in circumstances other than those provided for in O.11. Since O.31, r.29 was silent as to its possible application to third parties outside the jurisdiction, in the absence of an express provision it should not be read as conferring an extra-territorial jurisdiction on the Irish courts in addition to that conferred by O.11.

Finally, he held that it was well established that where a foreign state had submitted itself to the jurisdiction of the Irish courts by, for example, initiating proceedings with itself as plaintiff, it must be prepared to make discovery. However, to allow discovery in any other circumstance against a foreign state would undermine the principle that sovereign states are generally immune from the jurisdiction of the courts of another state. This principle was based on the perfect equality and absolute independence of sovereign states and therefore to order discovery would be to subject a foreign government to the jurisdiction of the Irish courts. In those circumstances, discovery was refused.

EXECUTION OF JUDGMENTS

Fieri facias **order** In *National Irish Bank Ltd v Graham and Ors (No. 2)*, High Court, January 10, 1994 Keane J dealt with the enforcement by means of a fieri facias order of a judgment for possession.

The general background to the case have been described in the 1993 Review, 388-90: *National Irish Bank Ltd v Graham and Ors* [1994] 1 ILRM 372 (HC); [1994] 2 ILRM 109 (SC). Briefly, the first and second named defendants had executed a chattel mortgage over a herd of cattle in favour of the plaintiff bank as security for a loan. A herd of milking cattle on the defendants' farm was not brought within the scope of this mortgage. The defendants failed to make the agreed repayments and the bank appointed a receiver and manager in respect of the herd which was subject to the chattel mortgage. An order was later made in the High Court restraining the defendants from disposing of any interest in the herd which was subject to the chattel mortgage except with the consent of the receiver and/or the court. In September 1993 the defendants gave an undertaking to the court to the effect that they would not attempt to frustrate the activities of the receiver in respect of the herd which was subject to the chattel mortgage. In November 1993 the bank obtained judgment in the High Court (later upheld by the Supreme Court) against the defendants for the sum of £3,543,840.96 with interest: *National Irish Bank Ltd v Graham and Ors* [1994] 1 ILRM 372 (HC); [1994] 2 ILRM 109 (SC) (1993 Review, 388-90).

The bank then sued out an order of *fieri facias* in respect of this amount. While an inventory of the herd subject to the mortgage taken on behalf of the first named plaintiff in January 1993 revealed a total of 657, a count taken in December 1993 showed only 397 cattle. It was also discovered that identification tags on the cattle had been removed and replaced. The defendants disclaimed all knowledge of these events. The bank sought orders for the attachment and/or committal of each of the defendants for contempt of court in failing to obey the order of Lardner J and breaching the undertaking given to the court. They also sought an order appointing the second named plaintiff as receiver in respect of the milking herd. However, Keane J refused the relief sought.

He stated that before the court would take the serious step of depriving a person of his or her liberty for failure to comply with an order of the court, it must be satisfied beyond reasonable doubt that he or she has in fact committed the alleged contempt. Although the defendants lived on the farm where the herd subject to the chattel mortgage was kept, and it was remarkable that they were totally unaware of the significant and unexplained reduction in its numbers and the interference with the tags, he did not consider that their complicity in these events had not been established beyond a reasonable doubt. Accordingly, he refused the application for attachment.

Turning to the application for the appointment of a receiver to the milking herd, Keane J stated that while the milking herd could be seized and sold on foot of the order of *fieri facias*, in the meantime it remained the exclusive property of the defendants. As the bank had no proprietary interest, vested or contingent, there was no ground upon which the court could appoint a receiver in respect of that herd. He added that the jurisdiction to appoint a receiver by way of equitable execution was confined to cases in which a debtor enjoys an equitable interest in property which cannot be reached by legal process. The defendants were the legal owners of the milking herd, and not merely the owners in equity. Thus there was no impediment to the execution of the order of *fieri facias* arising from the defendants' interest in the herd and no grounds for the appointment of a receiver by way of equitable execution.

JUDGMENT IN DEFAULT

Setting aside In *Maher v Dixon, Truck Dismantlers (Dublin) Ltd and Commercial Vehicle Dismantlers Ltd* [1995] 1 ILRM 218, Budd J set aside a judgment obtained in default against an 'off the shelf' company. The plaintiff had obtained judgment in default of appearance against all three defendants in respect of personal injuries he alleged occurred when he was employed by the third named defendant. In 1989 damages were assessed at £90,000 and the judgment was registered against the defendants. In January 1993, one James McCarthy purchased the third named defendant as an 'off the shelf' company from a company which specialised in company formations. Mr McCarthy then arranged for the third named defendant to become the owner of a commercial property, but when an attempt was made to sell the property a search revealed the judgment of £90,000 in the name of the plaintiff that had been entered and so the purchaser was reluctant to complete the transaction. It was in that context that the third named defendant then brought a motion to set aside the judgment granted against it. In one of the affidavits on which the motion was grounded, Mr McCarthy claimed that he had no knowledge of the plaintiff or the other two defendants. In addition, the person from whom the third named defendant had been purchased averred that the third named defendant had been incorporated in 1982, that it had never traded, that its directors had never authorised anyone to act on its behalf and that there was no recollection of any service of documents in the claim that had been brought by the plaintiff.

While Budd J evinced every sympathy for the plaintiff, who he pointed out had 'not recovered a farthing in damages', the judgment against the third named defendant was set aside. Budd J relied on the decision of the House of Lords in *Evans v Bartlam* [1937] AC 473 as the 'bedrock authority' in this area. He stated that where a judgment has been obtained by default, an application to set it aside must be supported by an affidavit setting out the merits of the defence to the plaintiff's claim and that the onus is on the applicant who is seeking to have the judgment set aside. If the affidavit dealing with the merits of the defence discloses a defence and these matters are averred to in the affidavit, O.13, r.11 of the Rules of the Superior Courts 1986 gives the court an untrammelled discretion. In the instant case, he concluded that a fair case had been provisionally made out that the third named defendant only 'came off the shelf' in January 1993 and if this contention was correct, the plaintiff could not have been employed by the third named defendant. This was a stateable defence to the plaintiff's claim and the third named defendant should be given an opportunity to make it. He gave the third named defendant two weeks within which to file a defence confined to the matters referred to in the affidavits filed in support of the motion to set aside the judgment.

JUDICIAL SALARIES

The Courts (Supplemental Provisions) Act 1961 (Section 46) Order 1994 (SI No. 273 of 1994) gave effect to Report No. 35 of the Review Body on Higher Remuneration in the Public Sector of January 1992. The 1994 Order provided for a 50% increase over that contained in the Courts (Supplemental Provisions) Act 1961 (section 46) Order 1989 (1989 Review, 356) with effect from April 1994 and a further 50% increase from May 1995. This produced the following scales in 1995: Chief Justice: £95,920; President of the High Court: £86,109; Supreme Court judges: £82,840; High Court judges (and President of the Circuit Court): £76,300; Circuit Court judges (and President of the

District Court): £56,680; District Court judges: £46,870. The Explanatory Note to the 1994 Order also stated that these figures would be further uprated in 1996 and 1997 to take account of the Programme for Competitiveness and Work, agreed by the social partners in 1994.

INTERROGATORIES

Two High Court judgments in 1994 dealt with the provisions of the Rules of the Superior Courts 1986 concerning interrogatories. O.31, r.1 of the 1986 Rules provides that parties may deliver interrogatories 'which relate to any matters in question in the cause or matter.' Where the leave of the court is required for the delivery of interrogatories, of O. 31, r. 2 provides that such leave shall be given to deliver 'such only of the interrogatories as shall be considered necessary either for disposing fairly of the cause or matter or for saving costs.'

In the first case in this area, *Mercantile Credit Company of Ireland Ltd and Highland Finance (Ireland) Ltd v Heelan and Ors* [1994] 1 ILRM 406, the plaintiffs had instituted proceedings in which it was claimed that they had been induced to make various loans as a result of the fraud of the defendants. The third named defendant was a solicitor who had acted for the second and fourth named defendants in respect of the transactions which gave rise to the proceedings. The plaintiffs furnished interrogatories to be answered by him in relation to 33 loan transactions which took place between May 1988 and June 1990. They related to various documents, including copies of cheques, journal entries, bank drafts and letters, which, according to the plaintiffs, pertained to the loan transactions. The interrogatories asked the third named defendant to identify the documents and to confirm that the particular journal entries related to the relevant loan transaction so as to establish what had happened to the loan moneys. They also asked him to establish certain facts about the security given in respect of the loans, and to give information concerning his instructions regarding the loan, information as to the knowledge of the second named defendant concerning the loan and information as to the movement of the sums represented by the loans. When the third named defendant refused to answer these interrogatories the plaintiffs brought a motion under O. 31 seeking an order of the court requiring him to answer. Costello J (as he then was) refused the relief sought.

He stated that, in considering the fair disposal of an action commenced by plenary summons, the court must bear in mind that such actions are, in principle at least, to be heard on oral evidence and that the use of evidence on affidavit given in reply to interrogatories is an exception which must be justified by some special exigency in the case which, in the interest of doing justice, requires that the exception should be allowed. He gave as an example a situation where a person suffers memory loss after a road traffic accident: in such a case interrogatories and affidavit evidence would be permitted concerning the issue of negligence and damages so that justice could be done.

Referring to *Attorney General v Gaskill* (1882) 20 Ch D 519 and *Marriott v Chamberlain*, he pointed out that interrogatories may be delivered either to obtain information from the interrogated party about the issues that arise in the action or to obtain admissions from the interrogated party and that if interrogatories seek information they must relate to the issues raised in the pleadings and not to the evidence which a party wishes to adduce in order to establish his case.

Costello J went on that when an interrogating party seeks admissions from an opposing party, he should first of all either request them informally by letter or under O. 32, rr.1-9. If the admissions are refused an application under O. 31 may then be brought. In considering whether it is fair to ask the interrogated party to make the admissions, the court will have to consider whether there are any special features of the case which might produce unfairness. Ordinarily, he felt that where admissions are sought merely for the purpose of formally proving documents which have been identified in an affidavit of discovery and are in the possession and power of the interrogated party, the court will grant the order unless there are special reasons why in the interests of justice an order should not be made. He noted that to refuse such an order would not only add unnecessary costs, but also bring about a possible injustice as an interrogating party might have to call the deponent at the trial in order to prove the relevant documents orally and, in doing so, would deprive himself of the right to cross-examine that deponent.

He stated that although O.31, r.2 of the 1986 Rules allows interrogatories to be served for the purpose of saving costs, the interest of doing justice between the parties was the paramount consideration in applications made under it. Accordingly, he held that an order should be refused if a fair hearing of the issues between the parties might be prejudiced by it, even if the costs of the proceedings could be reduced by making such an order.

In the instant case, he stated that while some of the interrogatories furnished by the plaintiffs required information relating to issues raised in the pleadings and were thus allowable, most related to information which the plaintiffs sought so as to obtain evidence for the purpose of proving their case against the defendant and thus liberty to deliver them would be denied. In respect of those interrogatories which sought admissions, he held that in a number of situations this went beyond the admission of documents and signatures to documents, and evidence about the documents and admissions about the facts surrounding the documents had been sought. Costello J held that interrogatories of this type may not be allowable as they may relate to the evidence to be adduced and not to the issues raised in the pleadings. Finally, he concluded that rather than attempting to identify those of the plaintiffs' interrogatories which were permissible, he felt that the order would be denied but the plaintiffs would have liberty to re-apply in the light of the guidelines he had laid down.

The second case on interrogatories arose in the long-running litigation, *Bula Ltd and Ors v Tara Mines Ltd and Ors (No. 9)* [1995] 1 ILRM 401. The case concerned the exploitation and ownership of a large zinc ore deposit in Navan, County Meath and for a general outline of the proceedings, see the 1991 Review, 336. In this aspect of the case, the first, second, fifth and sixth named plaintiffs brought an application seeking liberty to deliver a large number of interrogatories for answer by the first, second, fifteenth and sixteenth named defendants. In November 1993 Murphy J declined to accede to the application on the basis that it was unfair to expect the defendants to answer extensive interrogatories when they were completely preoccupied with preparing for the trial which was due to commence in December 1993. The application was adjourned to the hearing of the action. However, when the trial eventually commenced before Lynch J in December 1993 the application was not renewed, the defendants having made extensive discovery at the instance of the plaintiffs. The first fourteen defendants by a letter of December 16, 1993 expressly admitted a vast range of documents and also stated that these documents were *prima facie* evidence of their contents insofar as they recorded statements made by any servant of the first or second named defendants. The fifteenth and sixteenth named defendants also admitted a large number of documents. The trial continued until January 1994 when it was adjourned to enable other proceedings involving some of the parties to be litigated before another judge.

In July 1994 an application was made by the plaintiffs to fix a date for the hearing of the application for interrogatories. However, Lynch J indicated that the process of opening the case would have to be completed before the hearing of this application. The trial resumed in October 1994 and, after the process of the opening of the case had been completed, the application for interrogatories was made. Lynch J allowed some of the interrogatories as against the first, second and fifteenth named defendants and disallowed those sought as against the sixteenth named defendant.

Lynch J reiterated the view expressed by Costello J in the *Mercantile Credit* case, above (though he was not referred to it) that in proceedings commenced by plenary summons the primary manner of proving disputed facts was by oral evidence, so that the use of affidavit evidence at the trial was exceptional and usually required the leave of the court. Interrogatory evidence was also in this category as interrogatories could not be delivered without leave first being obtained from the court. Again, he reiterated that the basic purpose of interrogatories was to avoid injustice where one party had the knowledge and ability to prove facts which were important to the opposing party's case in circumstances where such party did not have the knowledge or ability to prove these facts either at all or without undue difficulty. He also pointed out that interrogatories must be as to facts in issue or facts reasonably relevant to establishing facts in issue and thus interrogatories as to mere evidence, opinions or matters of law, such as the meaning or effect of documents, statements or conduct, were not permissible. He added that it was also inappropriate that unnecessary interrogatories should be put relating to facts which were within the knowledge of and were readily capable of proof by the interrogating party.

Turning to the instant case, he stated that it appeared that the plaintiffs did not take account of the extensive discovery or the vast amount of documents admitted by the defendants when they were settling and/or pruning the interrogatories before the application was brought. In these circumstances it was not surprising that a large number of the interrogatories against the defendants were quite unnecessary and that others were impermissible for vagueness or for asking for opinions or evidence as distinct from facts. He felt that the Court was not required to go through interrogatories which were prolix, oppressive or unnecessary to ascertain which, if any, were admissible and could disallow them as a whole even though some of them were proper. However, referring to *dicta* of Myers J in *American Flange Manufacturing Co. Inc. v Rheem (Australia) Pty Ltd* [1965] NSW 193, he was prepared to accept that because of the costs involved in an application for leave to deliver interrogatories and in order to ensure that the case should continue to a conclusion without any further interruptions due to interlocutory applications, he would go through the interrogatories to determine which of them ought to be allowed. Before doing this, he cited the views of Murphy J in a previous interlocutory application in the proceedings, *Bula Ltd (in Receivership) v Tara Mines Ltd* [1987] IR 85; [1988] ILRM 149 (1987 Review, 282), in order to emphasise that the making of an order granting leave to deliver interrogatories did not lend credence, respect or support of any description to the plaintiffs' claim. It was a purely procedural relief and was ancillary to the institution of the proceedings themselves.

RULES OF COURT

Circuit Court: family   The Circuit Court Rules (No. 1) 1994 (SI No. 225 of 1994) specified the procedures to be followed in the Family Circuit Court under the Judicial Separation and Family Law Reform Act 1989 and replaced the Circuit Court Rules (No. 1) 1991 (1991 Review, 350). The 1994 Rules came into effect on August 22, 1994.

Circuit Court: labour The Circuit Court Rules (No. 2) 1994 (unfair Dismissals Acts 1977-1993 and Payment of Wages Act 1991) (SI No. 279 of 1994) specified the procedures to be followed in the Circuit Court under the Acts referred to in their title and came into operation on September 30, 1994. They replaced the Circuit Court Rules (No. 2) 1981 (Unfair Dismissals Act 1977).

Compensation orders The District Court (Compensation Order) Rules 1994 (SI No. 63 of 1994), which came into effect on April 11, 1994, prescribe the procedures to be followed in the District Court in relation to applications for compensation orders and applications for the adjustment of such orders under the Criminal Justice Act 1993 (as to which see the 1993 Review, 216). They also prescribe the forms to be used in relation to such orders.

District Court areas The District Court Districts and Areas (Amendment) Order 1994 (SI No. 187 of 1994) abolished the District Court Area of Causeway, amalgamating it with the District Court Area of Tralee.

Extradition The District Court (Extradition) Rules 1994 (SI No. 266 of 1994) amend the practice and procedure of the District Court with regard to extradition proceedings, to take account of changes arising from the entry into force of the Extradition (Amendment) Act 1994, discussed in the Criminal Law chapter, 178-81, above). The 1994 Rules also prescribe the forms to be used in the District Court in connection with extradition proceedings and came into force on August 24, 1994.

Service abroad: Hague Convention on Civil and Commercial Matters The Rules of the Superior Courts (No. 3) 1994 (SI No. 101 of 1994), which came into operation on June 4, 1994, regulate the practice and procedure of the Superior Courts with respect to the 1965 Hague Convention on the Service Abroad of Judicial and Extrajudicial Documents in Civil or Commercial Matters. Similarly, the District Court (Service Abroad of Documents in Civil or Commercial Matters) Rules 1994 (SI No. 120 of 1994) regulate the practice and procedure of the District Court for the purposes of the 1965 Hague Convention. They amend the Rules of 1962, 1963 and 1988 and prescribe forms to be used in the service abroad of documents and also came into operation on June 4, 1994.

SERVICE OF PROCEEDINGS

The decisions concerning service out of the jurisdiction under O.11 of the Rules of the Superior Courts 1986 are considered in the Conflict of Laws chapter, 101, above.

SOLICITORS

Coming off record *Ó Fearail v McManus* [1994] 2 ILRM 81 is an important (albeit *ex tempore*) decision of the Supreme Court concerning the circumstances in which a solicitor may come off record pursuant to O.7, r.3 of the Rules of the Superior Courts 1986. The case was an unusual road traffic accident in the sense that the plaintiff had initiated proceedings alleging that the defendant had got out of his car, dragged the plaintiff form his bicycle and had caused him to fall and suffer injuries. The insurance company which provided cover to the defendant in respect of the driving of his car instructed a solicitor to act in the matter and he subsequently delivered a defence in relation to the claim. However, the insurance company then took the view that the alleged incident was not covered by the defendant's policy of motor insurance and that it should no longer be involved in the matter. As O'Flaherty J summarised the position, the solicitor was effectively without instructions. The solicitor then applied under O.7, r.3 to come off record. In the High Court, Johnson J refused the application on the grounds that there had been no fraud or impropriety on the part of the defendant and the difficulties which had arisen were attributable to the insurance company failing to carry out a sufficient investigation before it instructed the applicant solicitor. However, on appeal the Supreme Court (O'Flaherty, Egan and Denham JJ) reversed.

Delivering the only judgment, O'Flaherty J stated that O.7, r.3 gave the court a wide discretion in deciding whether or not a solicitor should be permitted to come off record. In the instant case, he considered that irrespective of whether the repudiation of liability by the insurance company was correct, the fact remained that it no longer wanted the applicant to act for the defendant. He considered that the question of whether the repudiation was valid was a matter for another day, and the Court had to deal with the reality as it presented itself to the Court. He went on:

> The present situation, as it has unfolded before us, is that the insurance company, rightly or wrongly, has repudiated. It says that it does not want Mr O'Brien to act any longer and I think in those circumstances it would be a forced form of liaison to say to Mr O'Brien that he should continue to act for this defendant and I would in the circumstances allow him to come off record. . . .

We should also note that the Supreme Court ordered the insurance company to pay the costs of the applications in both the High Court and Supreme Court.

SUPREME COURT

Stay of execution pending appeal In *Irish Press plc v Ingersoll Irish Publications Ltd (No. 3)* [1995] 1 ILRM 117, the Supreme Court, in an *ex tempore* decision, granted a partial stay on a High Court order in an appeal in a complex commercial dispute, the substantive issues in which are discussed in the 1993 Review, 86 and in the Company Law chapter, 60, above. The Court also dealt with an application for security for costs.

To put these procedural applications in context, it will be recalled that the petitioner and the respondent were each entitled to 50% of the shareholdings in two companies, Irish Press Newspapers Ltd and Irish Press Publications Ltd. The petitioner brought proceedings under s. 205 of the Companies Act 1963 against the respondent in which it was claimed that the latter had engaged in oppression. In the High Court, Barron J held in the petitioner's favour and the respondent was ordered to pay £6,000,000 to Irish Press Newspapers Ltd and Irish Press Publications Ltd, and £2,750,000 to Irish Press plc. The respondent was also ordered to transfer all shares which it held in Irish Press Newspapers Ltd and Irish Press Publications Ltd to the petitioner in return for £2,250,000, which was not to be paid until all moneys which the court had ordered the respondent to pay had been transferred. Finally, it was ordered that two loans which had been made by the respondent to Irish Press Newspapers Ltd and Irish Press Publications Ltd would not be repayable until all moneys which the court had ordered the respondent to pay had been transferred. The High Court placed a stay on these orders which was due to expire in July 1994.

The respondent appealed against the order of the High Court and sought a stay on its operation. It argued that if it made the payments which had been ordered its appeal would become a moot. The petitioner argued that unless it could secure the injection of funds into the company by an outside investor and have shares for such an investor to acquire, the company would not survive until the hearing of the appeal. The petitioner also sought an order for security for costs against the respondent. An affidavit filed on behalf of the respondent claimed that in the event of the respondent losing the appeal and an order for costs being made in favour of the petitioner, the respondent would be unable to pay such costs. The respondent did not own any assets of substance apart from its interest in the company which was the subject matter of the petition and thus on this 'poverty' argument no order requiring security for costs should be made. The Supreme Court (Finlay CJ, Egan and

Blayney JJ) refused the application for security for costs, granted a stay on the order requiring the respondent to pay the sums totalling £6,000,000 but it also ordered the immediate transfer by he respondent of the shares involved in the case.

Delivering *ex tempore* the leading judgment, Finlay CJ dealt first with the application for security for costs. Accepting that the case was to be determined applying the principles it had stated in *Fallon v An Bord Pleanála* [1992] 2 IR 380; [1991] ILRM 799 (1991 Review, 333-4), he stated that the question as to whether a court hearing a petition under s. 205 of the Companies Act 1963 has the power to award damages to petitioning share-holders who have been oppressed, or to any other associated body or company, constituted a point of law of public importance which transcended the individual facts of the case. Accordingly the discretion of the Court would be exercised against the making of any order for security for costs.

Turning to the question of a stay, Finlay CJ rejected the *dictum* he himself had, in his own words 'inadvertently stated' in *Corish v Hogan*, Supreme Court, Irish Times LR, May 21, 1990 (noted briefly in the 1990 Review, 454) to the effect that a defendant raising the issue of liability on appeal is required to prove a probability that his appeal on that issue would succeed. As we had already pointed out in discussing the Court's later decision in *Redmond v Ireland* [1992] ILRM 291 (1991 Review, 351), the *dicta* of Finlay CJ in the *Corish* case had proved difficult to apply and their formal disapproval by their author certainly deprives them of any authority. Thus, in keeping with the Court's decision in *Redmond*, an applicant for a stay is required, in effect, to raise an arguable case that they may succeed rather than establish this as a matter of probability (though we note here also that other factors will come into play also: see the other matters referred to in the *Redmond* case, referred to in the 1991 Review, 352).

Applying the correct test in the instant case, Finlay CJ stated that the respondent had raised an arguable case as to whether the sum of £6,000,000 damages, both as to the amount and parties to whom it is directed to be given, was something which came within s. 205, as to the valuation of the shares and the date on which they should have been valued, and as to the propriety and legal correctness of directing the payment of £2,750,000 damages. However, the respondent had not established an arguable case that the finding of oppression made in the High Court was in error or that the order requiring the transfer of shares from the respondent to the petitioner was not a remedy which was available given the findings of fact made in the High Court.

Finally, the Court concluded that the balance of convenience favoured the immediate transfer of the shares to the petitioner. On delivery of the executed share transfers, a stay on the payment of the sums of £6,000,000 and £2,750,000 was given until the determination of the appeal. Pending the share transfer, the Court ordered that no payment on foot of the loans would be made. Finally, the payment of £2,250,000 to the respondent in respect of the transferred shares would be restrained or delayed until a further order of the court was made.

By way of completeness, we note here that, on the substantive appeal, the Supreme Court (Hamilton CJ, Egan and Blayney JJ) held that, in an application under s. 205 of the Companies Act 1963, the Court had no general power to order damages for oppression. Since the share transfer already effected had brought the oppression to an end, the Court reversed the High Court order concerning the payment of the sum of £6,000,000 by the respondent: *Irish Press plc v Ingersoll Irish Publications Ltd (No. 4)* [1995] 2 ILRM 270 (see Company Law chapter, 60, above).

Prisons

REMISSION

In *Dempsey v Minister for Justice* [1994] 1 ILRM 401, Morris J applied the principles of legitimate expectation in the context of a prisoner who had been transferred to a prison where his entitlement to remission on his sentence of imprisonment was proportionately less than that of the prison from which he had been transferred.

The case was considered against the background of the following statutory provisions. First, s. 17(3) of the Criminal Justice Administration Act 1914, as adapted, provides that:

Prisoners shall be committed to such prisons as the [Minister for Justice] may from time to time direct; and may on the like direction be removed therefrom during the term of their imprisonment to any other prison.

Second, Rule 38(1) of the Rules for the Government of Prisons 1947, made pursuant to s. 1 of the Prisons (Ireland) Act 1907, provides that a prisoner sentenced to a term of imprisonment:

shall be eligible, by industry and good conduct, to earn a remission of a portion of his imprisonment, not exceeding one- fourth of the whole sentence, provided that the remission so granted does not result in the prisoner being discharged before he has served one month.

(We may note parenthetically that, in *The State (Carney) v Governor of Portlaoise Prison* [1957] IR 25, the Supreme Court held that Rule 38(2) of the 1947 Rules, which applied to sentences of penal servitude only, was *ultra vires* the 1907 Act: see Byrne, Hogan and McDermott, *Prisoners' Rights: A Study in Irish Prison Law* (1981), p.105).

In July and August 1988 the applicant had been sentenced to terms of imprisonment for periods of six and eight years respectively. Between August 1988 and April 1993 he was transferred to a number of different prisons, the last of which were Portlaoise Prison and Shelton Abbey, before being finally transferred to Wheatfield Prison. Both Portlaoise Prison and Shelton Abbey operated a non-statutory scheme whereby a prisoner could earn a remission of up to one half of his sentence, as opposed to the statutory scheme operated by the other prisons which only allowed for an eligibility for a remission of one-quarter of the total sentence. With his transfer from Shelton Abbey to Wheatfield Prison, the applicant lost his opportunity to gain the 50% remission on his sentence. The applicant sought an order of *certiorari* quashing the decision of the respondent transferring him to Wheatfield Prison claiming that he had a legitimate expectation not to be transferred from a prison where a more favourable scheme of remission operated to one where a less favourable scheme was in operation and that in consequence, the respondent was wrongfully depriving him of his liberty. Morris J dismissed the application.

He accepted that it might have been reasonable for the applicant to expect that for such periods as he was detained in either Portlaoise Prison or Shelton Abbey he would be entitled to benefit from such rights to remission as would flow from being detained in these establishments. In the instant case, the applicant was in fact credited with 50% remission in relation to the period in which he was detained in these prisons. However, Morris J did not consider there was any basis on which the applicant could establish a legitimate expectation that he would never be moved from these institutions.

Applying the principles laid down in the leading Irish decision *Webb v Ireland* [1988] IR 353 (see the 1987 Review, 162-4), he held that for a legitimate expectation to arise there must be either a direct assurance which was an integral part of the transaction or the expectation must be based upon conduct which was so well established and regular that the expectation of a reward in this case was so well founded that the courts should give effect to it. As far as the applicant was concerned, no case had been made that any assurance was given to him that he would not be moved from Portlaoise Prison or Shelton Abbey nor had he shown that there was a well established or regular practice whereby prisoners were not moved from these institutions.

In any event, applying the 'four corners' principle considered in *Devitt v Minister for Education* [1989] ILRM 639 (1988 Review, 26-8) and *Tara Prospecting Ltd v Minister for Energy* [1993] ILRM 771 (1993 Review, 23-5) Morris J concluded that even if the applicant could establish a legitimate expectation to this effect it must fail as the doctrine of estoppel could not be used to fetter the exercise of the discretionary statutory power conferred on the Minister by s. 17(3) of the Criminal Justice Administration Act 1914.

Safety and Health

CHEMICAL SAFETY

Manufacture and labelling of single chemicals   The European Communities (Classification, Packaging, Labelling and Notification of Dangerous Substances) Regulations 1994 (SI No. 77 of 1994) consolidated and updated the statutory regime concerning the manufacture and placing on the market of dangerous substances. The 1994 Regulations apply to most chemical substances, that is, single chemicals rather than mixtures of chemicals, and impose obligations on manufacturers and others who place such chemicals on the market to ensure that they have been tested, packaged and labelled in accordance with criteria laid down in Directive 67/548/EEC, as amended. The 1967 Directive, and hence the 1994 Regulations, do not apply to certain chemicals, such as pesticides and cosmetics, which are governed by separate Regulations, based on other EC Directives. The 1967 Directive introduced the orange and black labelling system that applies to virtually all chemical substances, from the proprietary brands such as Tippex and Domestos to large quantities of chemicals used in an industrial context. The 1967 Directive has been amended on numerous occasions, the most recent significant amendment being the 7th Amendment Directive, 92/32/EEC. The 1994 Regulations implement the terms of the 7th Amendment Directive, together with no fewer than 8 Adaptations to Technical Progress (ATP) Directives in this area. While the 1967 Directive and 1994 Regulations apply to single chemicals, it may be noted that chemical preparations, that is, mixtures of chemicals, are regulated separately, the most recent such Regulations being the European Communities (Classification, Packaging, Labelling and Notification of Dangerous Preparations) Regulations 1995 (SI No. 272 of 1995), which implemented complementary requirements for such chemical mixtures and which we will consider in the 1995 Review. Further restrictions on the manufacture and sale of dangerous substances and preparations are also contained in the European Communities (Dangerous Substances and Preparations) (Marketing and Use) Regulations 1994 (SI No. 79 of 1994), discussed below. In addition, certain other categories of chemicals are regulated under special statutory regimes: see for example the European Communities (Classification, Packaging and Labelling of Pesticides) Regulations 1994 (SI No. 138 of 1994), 394, below.

SI No. 77 of 1994 applies to existing chemicals in terms of testing and labelling. Significantly, the Regulations also require those placing chemicals on the market to provide users, including industrial users, with a standardised Material Safety Data Sheet (MSDS) containing the information required to use the chemical safely and without risk to health of persons or the environment. New substances being placed on the market for the first time in Ireland must be notified to the National Authority for Occupational Safety and Health, established by the Safety, Health and Welfare at Work Act 1989.

The 1994 Regulations revoked the European Communities (Dangerous Substances) (Classification, Packaging and Labelling) Regulations 1979 (SI No. 383 of 1979), the European Communities (Dangerous Substances) (Classification, Packaging, Labelling and Notification) Regulations 1982 (SI No. 258 of 1982), the European Communities (Dangerous Substances) (Classification, Packaging, Labelling and Notification) (Amendment) Regulations 1985 (SI No. 89 of 1985) and the European Communities (Dangerous Substances) (Classification, Packaging, Labelling and Notification) Regulations 1992 (SI No. 426 of 1992). The 1994 Regulations came into effect on April 7, 1994 on their signing by the Minister for Enterprise and Employment.

Restrictions and bans on chemicals The European Communities (Dangerous Substances and Preparations) (Marketing and Use) Regulations 1994 (SI No. 79 of 1994) consolidated and updated the statutory regime that imposes restrictions and, in some cases, bans outright the placing on the market and use of certain dangerous substances and preparations, that is single chemicals and mixtures of chemicals. These Regulations are therefore complementary to the terms of SI No. 77 of 1994, discussed above. SI No. 79 of 1994 implemented a number of Directives which are based on the original Directive in this area, 76/769/EEC. Among the substances and preparations covered by the Regulations are PCB, PCT, VCM, 'Tris', Benzene, different categories of asbestos, lead, mercury, cadmium and arsenic compounds as well as items containing such dangerous substances. Labelling requirements for asbestos substances and preparations, where they are still permitted under the Regulations, were also laid down. The National Authority for Occupational Safety and Health is the enforcement body for the 1994 Regulations.

The 1994 Regulations revoked the following previous Regulations in this area: the European Communities (Dangerous Substances and Preparations). (Marketing and Use) Regulations 1979 (SI No. 382 of 1979), the European Communities (Dangerous Substances and Preparations) (Marketing and Use) Regulations 1981 (SI No. 149 of 1981), the Industrial Research and Standards (Section 44) (Children's Toys) Order 1985 (SI No. 44 of 1985), the European Communities (Dangerous Substances and Preparations) (Marketing and Use) Regulations 1985 (SI No. 244 of 1985), the European Communities (Dangerous Substance and Preparations) (Marketing and Use) Regulations 1986 (SI No. 47 of 1986), the European Communities (Dangerous Substances and Preparations) (Marketing and Use) Regulations 1987 (SI No. 204 of 1987) and the European Communities (Dangerous Substances and Preparations) (Marketing and Use) Regulations 1988 (SI No. 294 of 1988). The 1994 Regulations came into effect on April 6, 1994 on their signing by the Minister for Enterprise and Employment.

Explosives   The Import of Explosives Order 1994 (SI No. 449 of 1994), requires that the forms of explosives covered by the Order may not be imported into the State unless they meet certain standards laid down in 1993 by the United Nations Committee of Experts on the Transport of Dangerous Goods. The Classification and Labelling of Explosives Order 1994 (SI No. 450 of 1994) requires that explosives must be labelled in accordance with the classification system also laid down in 1993 by the United Nations Committee of Experts on the Transport of Dangerous Goods. The latter Order also revoked three Orders in Council on the classification of explosives, dated August 5, 1875, December 12, 1891 and April 11, 1913. This indicates the radical updating of the law effected by the 1994 Order. Both 1994 Orders were made under the Explosives Act 1875 and came into effect on December 30, 1994. They are enforced through the Department of Justice. It may be noted that Part II of the Dangerous Substances Act 1972, which envisages the repeal of the 1875 Act and a transfer of responsibility for the civil use of explosives from the Department of Justice to the Department of Enterprise and Employment and the Health and Safety Authority, has never been brought into force, so that the 1875 Act continues to be the relevant Act in this area.

Pesticides   The European Communities (Classification, Packaging and Labelling of Pesticides) Regulations 1994 (SI No. 138 of 1994) consolidated and updated the statutory regime concerning the manufacture and placing on the market of pesticides, in order to implement the most recent amendments to the Principal Directive in this area, 78/631/EEC. Similar requirements apply for pesticides as apply to chemicals in general under the terms of SI No. 77 of 1994, discussed above, 392-3. The 1994 Regulations came into force on June 1, 1994 and revoked the European Communities (Classification, Packaging and Labelling of Pesticides) Regulations 1985 to 1992 (SI No. 370 of 1985, SI No. 207 of 1987, SI No. 149 of 1989, SI No. 88 of 1991 and SI No. 416 of 1992). See also the European Communities (Authorization, Placing on the Market, Use and Control of Plant Protection Products) Regulations 1994 (SI No. 139 of 1994), discussed in the Agriculture chapter, 19, above.

Manufacture and disposal of batteries containing dangerous substances
The European Communities (Batteries and Accumulators) Regulations 1994
(SI No. 262 of 1994) implemented Directive 91/157/EEC and 93/86/EEC
and laid down requirements concerning the manufacture and disposal of
certain batteries and accumulators containing specified quantities of cadmium, lead or mercury.

ENVIRONMENTAL SAFETY

An indispensable addition to the literature on environmental law is Dr
Yvonne Scannell's, *Environmental and Planning Law* (Round Hall Press,
1995). Although this a fast-moving area, Dr Scannell's text anticipates many
developments that were merely in train when the text was published as well
as providing a comprehensive view of developments to the end of 1994.

Air pollution: emission standards and civil liability The Environmental
Protection Agency Act 1992 (Commencement) (No. 2) Order 1994 (SI No.
178 of 1994) brought into effect the Third Schedule to the Environmental
Protection Agency Act 1992, which amended a number of provisions of the
Air Pollution Act 1987. Principal among these are (a) that compliance with
emission standards must be taken into account by a local authority in granting
a licence under s. 32 of the 1987 Act; (b) improved remedies for unauthorised
emissions are included in a new s. 28A of the 1987 Act; and (c) civil liability
for pollution is provided for in a new s. 28B of the 1987 Act. The 1994 Order
brought these provisions into effect on July 1, 1994.

Air pollution: fossil fuels The Air Pollution Act 1987 (Marketing, Sale
and Distribution of Fuels) (Cork) Regulations 1994 (SI No. 403 of 1994)
brought into effect a prohibition on the marketing, sale and distribution of
bituminous coals within the restricted area of Cork and set certain standards
for allowable fuels within that area. The prohibition does not apply to certain
operations involving the storage of prohibited fuels within the area and their
transport or delivery through the area. The Regulations also make provision
for their enforcement by Cork Corporation and Cork County Council within
their respective functional areas and provide controls in that regard (such as
the keeping and examination of records). The Regulations also revoke the
Air Pollution Act 1987 (Marketing, Sale and Distribution of Fuels) (Cork)
Regulations 1993 (SI No. 294 of 1993) (see the 1993 Review, 474) which
prohibited the sale of slack and required retailers to have a supply of
smokeless or low-smoke fuel for sale in the designated area of Cork. The
Regulations, which came into effect on February 13, 1995, replicate a similar

regime as has applied in the Dublin area for a number of years: see the 1990 Review, 470.

Air pollution: gas oil   The Air Pollution Act 1987 (Sulphur Content of Gas Oil) Regulations 1994 (SI No. 256 of 1994) implemented Directive 93/12/EEC on the permissible sulphur content of gas fuels and replace the Air Pollution Act 1987 (Sulphur Content of Gas Oil) Regulations 1989.

Asbestos waste   The European Communities (Asbestos Waste) Regulations 1994 (SI No. 90 of 1994) impose requirements in addition to those in the European Communities (Asbestos Waste) Regulations 1990 concerning activities producing asbestos waste in order, as far as reasonably practicable, to reduce at source or prevent such waste. The activities involved must comply with the BATNEEC principle (see the 1992 Review, 531).

Disposal of batteries   The European Communities (Batteries and Accumulators) Regulations 1994 (SI No. 262 of 1994) are referred to above, 395.

EPA: declaration of interests   The Environmental Protection Agency (Declaration of Interests) Regulations 1994 (SI No. 205 of 1994) prescribed the classes, descriptions and grades of employees of the Environmental Protection Agency (EPA) and persons whose services are availed of by the Agency to whom s. 37 of the Environmental Protection Agency Act 1992 applies. S.37 of the 1992 Act requires that certain persons must declare their interests in real property, land development and any profession, business or occupation related to dealing or developing land. The form of such declaration is also prescribed and the Regulations came into effect on July 18, 1994. See also the Environmental Protection Agency Act 1992 (section 36(4)) Order 1994 (SI No. 204 of 1994) which prescribed the classes, descriptions and grades of employees of the EPA to whom s. 36(2) and (3) of the 1992 Act does not apply.

EPA: fees   The Environmental Protection Agency (Licensing Fees) Regulations 1994 (SI No. 130 of 1994) set out the schedule of fees payable to the EPA for various licensing applications and connected matters.

EPA: Integrated Pollution Control (IPC)   The Environmental Protection Agency Act 1992 (Commencement) Order 1994 (SI No. 82 of 1994) brought into effect a number of paragraphs of the First Schedule to the Environmental Protection Agency Act 1992 (see generally the 1992 Review, 529-34). This Commencement Order produced a number of consequential Regulations concerning the Integrated Pollution Control (IPC) system operated by the

Environmental Protection Agency (EPA) in respect of scheduled industrial activities under the 1992 Act. The most detailed of these were the Environmental Protection Agency (Licensing) Regulations 1994 (SI No. 85 of 1994), which provide for various procedural matters concerning the IPC system. The Regulations provide for applications for licences, reviews of licences or revised licences, consideration by the EPA of objections, including the holding of oral hearings and the contents of the register of licences.

The Regulations also prescribe the day on or after which specified classes of activity in the First Schedule to the 1992 Act will require an integrated licence in accordance with s. 82(1) of the Act. The Regulations also specify the 'relevant day' for the purposes of the definition of 'established activity' in s. 3 of the 1992 Act in respect of specified classes of activity in the First Schedule to the 1992 Act.

The Environmental Protection Agency Act 1992 (Established Activities) Order 1994 (SI No. 83 of 1994), which should be read in conjunction with s. 82(3) of the 1992 Act and also SI No. 85 of 1994, above, specifies dates on or after which the established activities concerned must have applied for an integrated licence from the EPA. The European Communities (Environmental Impact Assessment) (Amendment) Regulations 1994 (SI No 84 of 1994) amended the Local Government (Planning and Development) Acts 1963 to 1993; the European Communities (Environmental Impact Assessment) Regulations 1989 and the Environmental Protection Agency Act 1992 for the purpose of giving effect to Council Directive 85/337/EEC on the assessment of the effects of certain public and private projects on the environment. The amendments arise principally from the coming into operation of the IPC function of the EPA which includes a role in relation to environmental impact statements for licensable activities concerned and thus should also be seen in conjunction with SI No. 85 of 1994, above.

EPA: Water pollution   The Environmental Protection Agency (Extension of Powers) Order 1994 (SI No. 206 of 1994) applies certain sections of the Local Government (Water Pollution) Acts 1977 to 1990 and the Air Pollution Act 1987 to the Environmental Protection Agency and has the effect of transferring certain functions previously exercisable by local authorities under those Acts to the EPA. These include entry and inspection powers, service of notices requiring measures to be taken to prevent air or water pollution, application to the High Court for remedial orders and the prosecution of offences. The Order came into force on August 1, 1994.

Genetically Modified Organisms (GMOs)   The Genetically Modified Organisms Regulations 1994 (SI No. 345 of 1994) gave effect to Directive 90/219/EEC on the contained use of genetically modified micro-organisms

(GMOs) and Directive 90/220/EEC on the deliberate release of genetically modified organisms into the environment. The Regulations provide for various procedural matters in relation to the contained use, deliberate release and placing on the market of GMOs. They provide for notifications for consent, application of good microbiological practice, risk assessment, review of consents, accident procedures and the contents of a register of notifications. Users of genetically modified organisms are required under the Regulations to ensure that all appropriate measures are taken to avoid adverse effects on human health and the environment. A consent to place a product, containing or consisting of a GMO, on the market must include conditions relating to the labelling and packaging of the product. These Regulations were made under s. 111 of the Environmental Protection Agency Act 1992; see Scannell, *op. cit.*, 509-10.

Noise   The Environmental Protection Agency Act 1992 (Noise) Regulations 1994 (SI No. 179 of 1994), which came into effect on July 1, 1994, prescribed the form to be served under s. 108 of the 1992 Act where a complaint is made to the District Court concerning noise pollution.

Sea pollution   The Sea Pollution (Prevention of Oil Pollution) Regulations 1994 (SI No. 44 of 1994), the Sea Pollution (Prevention of Pollution by Garbage from Ships) Regulations 1994 (SI No. 45 of 1994) and the Sea Pollution (Prevention of Pollution by Noxious Liquid Substances in Bulk) Regulations 1994 (SI No. 46 of 1994), each made under the Sea Pollution Act 1991 (1991 Review, 366) and which came into force on 1 June 1994, gave legislative effect to the detailed elements of the MARPOL Convention, that is, the International Convention for the Prevention of Pollution from Ships of 1973 and a 1978 Protocol to that Convention. Failure to comply with the detailed requirements of the Regulations constitute offences for which the penalties are prescribed in s. 29 of the 1991 Act. As a result of the coming into effect of SI No. 44 of 1994 in particular, the Sea Pollution Act 1991 (section 8) (Commencement) Order 1994 (SI No. 123 of 1994) brought s. 8 of the 1991 Act into effect on June 1, 1994. S.8 of the 1991 Act provided for the repeal in full of the Oil Pollution of the Sea Acts 1956 to 1977, which became obsolete. As a result of the 1994 Regulations and the Commencement Order, all provisions of the 1991 became fully effective (for commencement of other provisions, see the 1992 Review, 536). The Sea Pollution Act 1991 (Survey Fees) Order 1994 (SI No. 195 of 1994) prescribe the fees payable to certify compliance with the 1991 Act.

Strict liability offences   In *Maguire v Shannon Regional Fisheries Board* [1994] 2 ILRM 253, Lynch J held that certain offences under the Local

Government (Water Pollution) Act 1977 constituted offences of strict liability in respect of which it was not necessary to establish *mens rea*: see the discussion in the Criminal Law chapter, 228-9, above.

Urban waste water treatment The Environmental Protection Agency Act 1992 (Urban Waste Water Treatment) Regulations 1994 (SI No. 419 of 1994), made under s. 59 of the Environmental Protection Agency Act 1992, gave effect to Directive 91/271/EEC and lay down standards concerning the treatment of urban waste water and in particular the standards to which waste treatment plants must conform.

Waste shipment The European Communities (Transfrontier Shipment of Waste) Regulations 1994 (SI No. 121 of 1994), which came into effect on May 6, 1994, laid down the administrative arrangements required to give full effect to Regulation (EEC) No. 259/93 on the supervision and control of shipments of waste within, into and out of the European Community. While the 1993 Regulation is, of course, directly applicable in Member States, it was necessary to provide for certain administrative details, in particular those relating to the environment. The Regulations provide, *inter alia*, for the designation of competent authorities for the purpose of controlling waste transhipments, the powers of the competent authorities, the imposition of certain requirements in relation to the shipment of waste into or out of the State and the prohibition of waste imports by the Environmental Protection Agency. Subject to certain transitional arrangements, the 1994 Regulations revoked the European Communities (Transfrontier Shipment of Hazardous Waste) Regulations 1988, which had given effect to Directive 84/631/EEC.

Water pollution The Local Government (Water Pollution) Acts 1977 and 1990 (Control of Carbon Tetrachloride, DDT and Pentachlorophenol Discharges) Regulations 1994 (SI No. 43 of 1994) and the Local Government (Water Pollution) Acts 1977 and 1990 (Control of EDC, TRI, PER and TCB Discharges) Regulations 1994 (SI No. 43 of 1994) prescribe quality standards to be applied by local and sanitary authorities when licensing discharges of effluents containing the substances referred to in their title and were made under the provisions of the Local Government (Water Pollution) Acts 1977 and 1990. The Regulations gave effect to Directive 86/280/EEC and 90/415/EEC, respectively, on limit values and quality objectives for discharges of certain dangerous substances included in List I of the Annex to Council Directive 76/464/EEC, the Principal Directive in this area.

Water quality: bathing waters The Quality of Bathing Waters (Amendment) Regulations 1994. (SI No. 145 of 1994) amended the Quality of

Bathing Waters Regulations 1992 (1992 Review, 534) which gave effect to Directive 76/160/EEC, as amended, on the quality of bathing water. The effect of the 1994 Regulations is to add 22 bathing areas to the 94 areas listed in the First Schedule of the 1992 Regulations.

Water quality: shellfish waters   The Quality of Shellfish Waters Regulations 1994. (SI No. 200 of 1994) gave effect to Directive 79/923/EEC, as amended, on the quality of shellfish waters.

FOOD SAFETY

Emulsifiers, stabilisers etc.   The Health (Emulsifiers, Stabilisers, Thickeners and Gelling Agents in Food) Regulations 1994 (SI No. 78 of 1994) consolidated the protective measures and restrictions concerning the use as food ingredients of emulsifiers, stabilisers, thickeners and gelling agents (most of which carry 'E numbers') as well as imposing restrictions on advertisements concerning such items. The 1994 Regulations gave effect to a large number of EC Directives on this area, deriving from Directive 74/329/EEC. The 1994 Regulations came into effect on April 11, 1994 and revoked the Health (Emulsifiers, Stabilisers, Thickeners and Gelling Agents in Food) Regulations 1980 to 1992.

Extraction solvents in foodstuffs   The European Communities (Extraction Solvents in Foodstuffs) (Revocation) Regulations 1994 (SI No. 81 of 1994) formally revoked the European Communities (Extraction Solvents in Foodstuffs) Regulations 1991 as these had been superseded by the European Communities (Extraction Solvents in Foodstuffs) Regulations 1993 (1993 Review, 480).

Flavourings   The European Communities (Labelling, Presentation and Advertising of Foodstuffs) (Amendment) Regulations 1994 (SI No. 95 of 1994) gave effect to Directive 91/72/EEC which had amended Council Directive 79/112/EEC, the Principal Directive on the labelling, presentation and advertising of foodstuffs for sale to the ultimate consumer. The effect of the 1994 Regulations is to add a further Annex (Annex III) to the Principal Directive. The Annex sets out the rules for the designation of flavourings when used as ingredients in other foodstuffs. Flavouring must be described by the word 'flavouring(s)' or by a more specific name or description of the flavouring. The word 'natural' or any word having substantially the same meaning may be used only when the flavouring component exclusively contains flavouring substances and/or flavouring preparations as defined in

Directive 88/388/EEC on flavourings. Where the name of the flavouring contains a reference to the vegetable or animal nature of origin of the incorporated substances, the word 'natural', or any other word having substantially the same meaning, may not be used unless the flavouring component has been isolated by appropriate physical processes, enzymatic or microbiological processes or traditional food preparation processes, solely or almost solely from the foodstuff or the flavouring source concerned. The Regulations came into effect on August 1, 1994.

Fruit juices and fruit nectars The Food Standards (Fruit Juices and Fruit Nectars) (European Communities) (Amendment) Regulations 1994 (SI No. 203 of 1994) amended the Food Standards (Fruit Juices and Fruit Nectars) (European Communities) Regulations 1978 to 1992 to implement Directive 93/45/EEC, which had in turn amended the Principal Directive in this area, 75/726/EEC.

Infant formulae The European Communities (Infant Formulae) Regulations 1994 (SI No. 459 of 1994) gave effect to Directives 91/321/EEC and 92/52/EEC and compositional, labelling and marketing requirements for infant formulae. They came into effect on January 3, 1995.

Labelling, presentation and advertising of foodstuffs The European Communities (Labelling, Presentation and Advertising of Foodstuffs) (Amendment) Regulations 1994 (SI No. 95 of 1994) amended the 1982 Regulations of the same title to give effect to Directive 91/72/EEC, which further regulates the labelling requirements for flavourings on foodstuffs and the circumstances in which the word 'natural' may be used on labels in connection with flavourings.

Materials coming into contact with foodstuffs The European Communities (Materials and Articles intended to come into Contact with Foodstuffs) (Amendment) Regulations 1994 (SI No. 7 of 1994) and the European Communities (Materials and Articles intended to come into Contact with Foodstuffs) (Amendment) (No. 2) Regulations 1994 (SI No. 93 of 1994) amended the 1991 Regulations of the same title (1991 Review, 366) (and see also the 1993 Regulations of the same title, 1993 Review, 480) in order to give effect to Directives 92/15/EEC, 93/8/EEC, 93/9/EEC, 93/10/EEC, 93/11/EEC and 93/111/EEC concerning the protective measures required for materials intended to come into contact with foodstuffs. The 1994 Regulations deal with cellulose and also teats and soothers.

Minced meat and meat preparations The European Communities

(Minced Meat) Regulations 1994 (SI No. 215 of 1994) implemented Directive 88/657/EEC, as amended by Directives 89/662/EEC and 92/110/EEC. They laid down requirements for the production of and trade in minced meat, meat in pieces of less than 100 grams and meat preparations for human consumption. Provision is made for the approval of production plants by the Minister for Agriculture and hygiene standards are also laid down both for production and transport of the meat.

MANUFACTURING STANDARDS

In previous Reviews (1991 Review, 368, 1992 Review, 538 and 1993 Review, 480, we noted the increased number of EC 'New Approach' or 'Approximation' Directives which establish minimum safety and health criteria for various products and which are linked to detailed technical standards, or European Norms (EN), developed by the European Standards bodies such as CEN and CENELEC. In 1994, a number of Regulations gave effect to Directive 93/68/EEC, which had amended a number of previous 'New Approach' Directives. The 1993 Directive imposed a standardised 'CE' marking requirement in place of the mixture of 'CE' and 'EC' marking provisions in the earlier Directives: clearly a case of standardising the standards laws. Other Directives in this area were also implemented in 1994 and we also refer to these.

Construction products The European Communities (Construction Products) (Amendment) Regulations 1994 (SI No. 210 of 1994) amended the European Communities (Construction Products) Regulations 1992 (1992 Review, 538) to implement Directive 93/68/EEC, referred to above. The 1993 Directive had amended Directive 89/106/EEC, the Construction Products Directive, requiring the placing of a 'CE' mark rather than a 'EC' mark on construction products to indicate compliance with the technical standards laid down in the 1989 Construction Products Directive. The Regulations came into effect on January 1, 1995. See also the Building Regulations (Amendment) Regulations 1994 (SI No. 154 of 1994) discussed in the Local Government chapter, 339, above, which also concern construction design standards.

Electrical equipment As with SI No. 210 of 1994, above, the European Communities (Low Voltage Electrical Equipment) (Amendment) Regulations 1994 (SI No. 307 of 1994) amended the European Communities (Low Voltage Electrical Equipment) Regulations 1992 (SI No. 428 of 1992) (1992 Review, 538) to implement Directive 93/68/EEC on the 'CE' mark. The 1994

Regulations require the manufacturer, or his authorised representative within the European Community, to affix on the electrical equipment the CE mark and to draw up a written declaration of conformity to the provisions of the Regulations. They also require that a technical file be established and kept on Community territory, enabling assessment by the appropriate authorities of the conformity of the electrical equipment to the safety objectives of the relevant Directives on this matter. The Regulations came into effect on January 1, 1995 but electrical equipment complying with the marking arrangements in force before that date shall continue to be allowed to be placed on the market until January 1, 1997.

Machinery The European Communities (Machinery) Regulations 1994 (SI No. 406 of 1994) implemented Directive 89/392/EEC, as amended by Directive 91/368/EEC, on the approximation of the laws of the Member States relating to machinery. The amendments effected by the 1991 Directive primarily concern requirements for machinery by which persons may be lifted as well as provisions on safety components. In addition, the 1994 Regulations also implemented the 'CE' mark provisions of Directive 93/68/EEC in so far as that Directive applied to machinery. The Regulations apply to machinery and safety components which are first placed on the market or put into service in the Community on or after January 1, 1995. They also revoked and replaced the European Communities (Machinery) Regulations 1992 (SI No. 246 of 1992) (1992 Review, 539). The 1994 Regulations also revoked the European Communities (Wire-Ropes, Chains and Hooks) Regulations 1979 with effect from January 1, 1995. The European Communities (Roll Over and Falling Object Protective Structures for Construction Plant) Regulations 1990 (SI No. 202 of 1990) and the European Communities (Self-Propelled Industrial Trucks) Regulations 1991 (SI No. 12 of 1991) were also revoked with effect from January 1, 1996.

Medical devices The European Communities (Medical Devices) Regulations 1994 (SI No. 252 of 1994) implemented Directive 93/42/EEC on the standards applicable to medical devices generally. The European Communities (Active Implantable Medical Devices) Regulations 1994 (SI No. 253 of 1994). implemented Directive 90/385/EEC, as amended by 93/42/EEC, on active implantable medical devices, a term which includes heart pacemakers.

Motor vehicles The Regulations governing the type approval for motor vehicles are referred to in the Transport chapter, 469, below.

Non-automatic weighing instruments The European Communities (Non-automatic Weighing Instruments) (Amendment) Regulations 1994 (SI

No. 447 of 1994), which came into effect on January 1, 1995, amended the European Communities (Non-automatic Weighing Instruments) Regulations 1992 in order to implement Directive 93/68/EEC in so far as it had amended Directive 90/384/EEC on the approximation of the laws of the Member State relating to non-automatic weighing instruments.

Personal protective equipment The European Communities (Personal Protective Equipment) (Amendment) Regulations 1994 (SI No. 13 of 1994), which came into effect on January 28, 1994, implemented Directive 93/95/EEC in so far as it had amended Directive 89/686/EEC on the approximation of the laws of the Member State relating to personal protective equipment (PPE). The 1989 Directive had been implemented by the European Communities (Personal Protective Equipment) Regulations 1993 (SI No. 272 of 1993) (1993 Review, 480). The 1994 Regulations amended the 1993 Regulations and provided that PPE may continue to be placed on the market and brought into service until July 1, 1995 provided it is in conformity with the law of the State in force on June 30, 1992. Another effect of the 1994 Regulations was that helmets and visors indicated for users of two or three-wheeled motor vehicles were excluded from the scope of 1993 and 1994 Regulations. Finally, the European Communities (Personal Protective Equipment) (CE Marking) Regulations 1994 (SI No. 457 of 1994), which came into effect on January 1, 1995, amended the 1993 and 1994 PPE Regulations in order to implement Directive 93/68/EEC in so far as it had amended Directive 89/686/EEC.

Toys The European Communities (Safety of Toys) (Amendment) Regulations 1994 (SI No. 458 of 1994) amended the 1990 Regulations of the same title in order to implement Directive 93/68/EEC in so far as it had amended Directive 88/378/EEC on the safety of toys. The 1994 Regulations, which came into force on January 1, 1995, provided for certain transitional arrangements for toys carrying the 'EC' mark rather than the new 'CE' mark until January 1, 1997.

OCCUPATIONAL SAFETY AND HEALTH

Biohazards and infection The Safety, Health and Welfare at Work (Biological Agents) Regulations 1994 (SI No. 146 of 1994) implemented Directive 90/679/EEC, as amended by Council Directive 93/88/ EEC, on the protection of workers from risks associated with biological agents at work. They prescribe protective and preventive measures which all employers must take in order to protect employees from the risks connected with exposure to any micro-organism (whether bacteria, viruses, parasites or fungi) that might cause any infection, allergy or toxicity to employees. The Regulations lay down detailed mandatory requirements and certain recommendations concerning, for example, vaccination. The Regulations also include a very extensive list of 145 bacteria, 113 viruses, 67 parasites and 22 fungi covered by the Regulations. The list includes the bacteria connected with brucellosis and Legionnaires Disease and the viruses for Hepatitis B, HIV and Creuzfeld-Jacob Disease (CJD). The Regulations were made under the Safety, Health and Welfare at Work Act 1989, apply to all places of work and came into effect on May 23, 1994.

Chemical hazards The Safety, Health and Welfare at Work (Chemical Agents) Regulations 1994 (SI No. 445 of 1994) implemented Directive 88/642/EEC and Directive 91/322/EEC on the protection of workers from the risks related to any chemical agents at work. The 1994 Regulations define a chemical agent as being any chemical substance hazardous to health. This appears to include chemical substances in whatever form, whether solid (for example, asbestos), liquid (for example, sulphuric acid) or gaseous (for example, chlorine gas). It is estimated that there over 100,000 known chemical agents on the market in the European Community, so that the scope of the 1994 Regulations is extremely wide, by contrast with previous Regulations in this area which either covered a single chemical, such as asbestos, or else a discrete group of chemicals, such as carcinogenic chemicals (see the 1993 Review, 504). The 1994 Regulations outline the duties of employers in relation to the prevention and limitation of exposure of employees to chemical agents in the workplace, the assessment of risks to employees and monitoring of exposure levels. There are also requirements in relation to information, training and consultation of employees The Regulations require employers to comply with any Occupational Exposure Limits (OELs) contained in an Approved Code of Practice (ACoP) published by the National Authority for Occupational Safety and Health under s. 50 of the Safety, Health and Welfare at Work Act 1989. An ACoP containing OELs for over 600 chemical agents which come within the scope of the 1994 Regulations was published by the Authority in December 1995. The contents of this ACoP correspond with a similar document published by the British Health and Safety Commission in connection with the British Control of Substances Hazardous to Health Regulations 1994 (COSHH), to which the Irish Regulations correspond. The Regulations were made under the Safety, Health and Welfare at Work Act 1989, apply to all places of work and came into effect on January 25, 1995.

Employer's liability The case law from 1994 on employer's liability is discussed in the Torts chapter, 443, below.

Merchant shipping The Regulations made in 1994 under the Merchant Shipping Acts are discussed in the Transport chapter, 467-8, below.

Pregnant employees, recent mothers and breastfeeding mothers The Safety, Health and Welfare at Work (Pregnant Employees Etc.) Regulations 1994 (SI No. 446 of 1994) implemented the occupational safety and health provisions of Directive 92/85/EEC on the introduction of measures to encourage improvements in the safety and health at work of pregnant workers and workers who have recently given birth or are breastfeeding. The 1994 Regulations require employers to assess the risks involved in exposing pregnant employees, employees who have recently given birth and those who are breastfeeding to a list of chemical agents (such as lead and its compounds), physical agents (such as radiation), and biological agents (such as rubella) which are specified in the Regulations. While the 1994 Regulations do not impose an outright ban in respect of any of the matters referred to in the Regulations, the employer must ensure that the three categories of employees concerned be removed from situations of risk to their health or the health of the foetus or new born child. A progressive series of preventive measures is laid down in the Regulations, from re-arrangement of work patterns, to removal from certain work areas, to restrictions on night work and ultimately (if all other steps fail to reduce the risks) paid health and safety leave for three weeks. The 1994 Regulations were made under the Safety, Health and Welfare at Work Act 1989, apply to all places of work and came into effect on December 30, 1994. Other elements of the 1992 Directive, concerning maternity leave, were implemented in the Maternity Protection Act 1994.

Radiological protection We discuss separately the provisions of the European Communities (Protection of Outside Workers from Ionising Radiation) Regulations 1994 (SI No. 144 of 1994), below.

RADIOLOGICAL PROTECTION

Employees working away from employer's premises The European Communities (Protection of Outside Workers from Ionising Radiation) Regulations 1994 (SI No. 144 of 1994), which came into force on May 31, 1994, implemented Directive 90/641/Euratom. The 1994 Regulations provide for protection against radiological exposure for employees likely to receive high levels of exposure while working away from their employers' premises, including where they work in another EC Member State. The 1994 Regulations refer to the general protective measures required by the European Communities (Ionising Radiation) Regulations 1991 (1991 Review, 375-6). They also expressly amend the 1991 Regulations by the insertion of a new Regulation 30 into the 1991 Regulations in order to provide that the Radiological Protection Institute of Ireland (RPII) be the enforcement body for the 1991 Regulations. We had drawn attention to this lacuna in the 1991 Review, 375.

Shipments of radioactive waste   The European Communities (Supervision and Control of Certain Shipments of Radioactive Waste) Regulations 1994 (SI No. 276 of 1994) implemented Directive 92/3/Euratom on the supervision and control of shipments of radioactive waste.

TOBACCO PRODUCTS

The Tobacco Products (Control of Advertising, Sponsorship and Sales Promotion) (Amendment) Regulations 1994 (SI No. 28 of 1994) amended the Tobacco Products (Control of Advertising, Sponsorship and Sales Promotion) Regulations 1991 (SI No. 28 of 1991) and implemented Directive 92/41/EEC on the approximation of the laws, regulations and administrative provisions of the Member States concerning the labelling of tobacco products and their advertisement. The 1994 Regulations update the existing requirements specifying that packages of tobacco products display in rotation a number of health warnings by extending these to products other than cigarettes The Regulations came into effect on March 1, 1994.

Social Welfare Law

CONTRACT FOR SERVICES

In *McAuliffe v Minister for Social Welfare* [1995] 1 ILRM 189, a dispute arose as to whether two people who worked for the appellant were employed by him pursuant to contracts of service or were in contracts for services. The appellant's claim was by way of appeal pursuant to s. 271 of the Social Welfare (Consolidation) Act 1993 against a decision of an appeals officer that the relationship was that of contract of service.

The appellant was a wholesale distributor of newspapers. The two people whose contracts were in question had responsibility for the province of Leinster. One worked six or seven days per week, the other five days. They were paid monthly against invoices they submitted. The agreed rates of remuneration were between £34 and £50 per day. The two each owned their delivery vehicles and were responsible for all out goings, including tax, insurance repairs, fuel and depreciation. While the contracts envisaged that the two would act as drivers, they had a right to provide substitute drivers acceptable to the appellant when necessary, in that event, payment of the relief drivers was a matter for them rather than the appellant. The appellant was not obliged to provide them with any particular deliveries on particular days, in fact there were regular deliveries. The pair were free to carry goods for any other person, both when not engaged on deliveries for the appellant and in conjunction with the delivery of newspapers for him, subject only to an embargo on the delivery of newspapers for any other supplier while engaged in deliveries for the appellant.

One of the two registered for value added tax and invoiced the appellant for and was paid and remitted value added tax on his charges. The other was not registered for such tax as his turnover was less than the statutory threshold. Both made income tax returns as self-employed persons. The two were responsible for damage, destruction or loss of goods carried for the appellant and for losses caused by any delays.

The relationship between the appellant and the two men was initially regulated orally and later by agreements in writing which confirmed the terms of the oral arrangements.

The contract of one of the pair was in due course terminated. As has been mentioned, the appeals officer decided that he had been employed by the appellant pursuant to a contract of service. The appellant claimed that that decision was erroneous in point of law and sought a determination that at all times both men had been engaged by the appellant as independent contractors pursuant to contracts for services.

In considering the law on this issue, Barr J observed that, having regard to the wide range of particular circumstances from case to case, it was not possible to devise any hard and fast rule as to what constitutes a servant and what constitutes an independent contractor. Each case had to be considered on its own special facts in the light of the broad guidelines which case law provided. Many of the authorities in the area related to whether or not the employer was liable for the negligence of the employed person and most turned upon the degree of control exercised over the latter by the former. In the case under review there was a special circumstance which touched upon the element of control. The appellant being a wholesale distributor of newspapers over a wide area, time and reliability were of the essence in the performance of that service and, whatever the nature of the contract between the distributor and the deliverer, one would expect to find stringent terms regarding the time factor.

A wholesale newspaper distributor such as the appellant might decide to employ an independent haulage company to perform the service for him. Conversely, he might decide to operate the service himself and provide vehicles and personnel from within his own organisation. If a haulage company were employed by the wholesaler then, undoubtedly, it would be a contract for services and not of service. In Barr J's view one would expect it to contain the following distinctive features:

(a) The carrier company would provide and maintain its own transport.

(b) It would be remunerated on the basis of a sum per vehicle per run, or perhaps a mileage charge would be agreed. In either case the remuneration would be structured to cover the wages of the company driver together with cost of fuel, maintenance, insurance and depreciation of the vehicle, and also to provide an acceptable net profit.

(c) The carrier would not be inhibited by contract from delivering for reward goods from other suppliers to the employer's customers or to other outlets in the area served though a restriction on delivery of newspapers to the employer's customers from rival suppliers might form part of the contract.

(d) It would be usual for such contracts to provide an indemnity to the employer in respect of any loss he might sustain through the negligence or breach of contract of the carrier.

On the other hand, if the wholesaler decided to provide a delivery service from within his own organisation, the following major differences would arise as to employer's contract with his driver:

(a) The driver's employment would be a contract of service with the employer.

(b) The employer would provide the requisite vehicle and pay for all overheads relating to it.

(c) The driver might be remunerated on the basis of a sum per run, but more likely he would receive a weekly wage and overtime.

(d) The employer would be liable to pay his share of the worker's PRSI contributions and also would have an obligation to collect and remit to the State the driver's PAYE income tax.

(e) The driver would have a statutory entitlement to holiday remuneration from his employer and other benefits such as redundancy and pension rights.

(f) The driver would not be allowed to use his employer's vehicle for carrying on a delivery business of his own with the employer's customers or others.

(g) In the ordinary course it would be for the employer to provide a substitute driver if the regular person was not available.

None of the distinguishing features of the postulated contract of service were to be found in the contracts in the instant case, but both had much in common with the form of delivery contract which the appellant probably would have entered into with a haulage company if he had taken that course. Barr J accepted that there was the practical distinction that the contracts were with individuals and it was envisaged that in the ordinary course the delivery vehicles were to be driven by them, with a right to substitute an acceptable relief driver. It seemed to him that such a provision did not affect the nature of the contracts. All in all he had no hesitation in concluding that they were both contracts for services and that the appeal should be allowed.

THE FAMILY

In the Constitutional Law Chapter, above, 112-4, we analyse the decision of the Supreme Court in *Mhic Mhathúna v Ireland and the Attorney General* [1995] 1 ILRM 69, in which the plaintiff unsuccessfully challenged the constitutional validity of the distinctions drawn in the legislation relating to tax and social welfare between married parents and parents who were separated or unmarried.

In the Conflicts of Law chapter, above, 83-6, we discuss Budd J's decision in *Clancy v Minister for Social Welfare*, High Court, February 18,

1994, which addressed the issue of whether recognition should be given to a divorce obtained in England when the husband was domiciled in Ireland. The grant of a widow's pension to the woman who had married the man after the dissolution of the marriage in England was conditional on the divorce being recognised under Irish Law.

LEGISLATION

The Social Welfare Act 1994 The Social Welfare Act 1994 gives effect to the social welfare insurance and assistance payment increases announced in the 1993 Budget: Part II of the Act reduces the PRSI contributions of employers in relation to lower-paid workers (s. 7), marginally raises the earnings ceiling for self-employment contributions (s. 8), encourages employees to take on new workers by giving them a PRSI moratorium of two years (s. 10), replaces the widows contributory pension scheme and survivor's benefit by a gender-neutral survivor's pension scheme (Part IV), amends the means test for lone parents allowance (s. 15) and carer's allowance (s. 16) to encourage lone parents to re-enter the work force and families to assume the burden of looking after their elderly parents: see Professor Robert Clarke, *Annotation* [1994] ICLSA, General notes to ss. 15 and 16. Professor Clark's *Annotation*, as always, provides a comprehensive, accessible and scholarly analysis of this complex area of legislation.

Statutory instruments There were several statutory instruments on social welfare in 1994 which dealt with aspects of the Social Welfare Code. We summarise them below, using, for the most part, the language of the explanatory notes appended to them.

The Social Welfare (No. 2) Act 1993 (Part II) (Commencement) Order 1994 (SI No. 52 of 1994) brings Part II of the Social Welfare (No. 2) Act 1993 into effect from February 23, 1994. Part II of the Social Welfare (No. 2) Act 1993 provides for the introduction of a scheme of social insurance for persons in share fishing.

The Social Welfare (Optional Contributions) Regulations 1994 (SI No. 53 of 1994) provide for certain matters in connection with the payment of optional contributions under the scheme of social insurance for share fisherman provided for in the Social Welfare (No. 2) Act 1993.

The Regulations also provide that where a person applies to become an optional contributor in the contribution year in which he or she became insured as a self-employed contributor, the optional contribution payable will be £250.

The Social Welfare (Agreement with New Zealand on Social Security)

Order 1994 (SI No. 57 of 1994) gives effect to the Bilateral Agreement on Social Security made between Ireland and New Zealand, which comes into effect from March 1, 1994. The Order provides that the Social Welfare Acts and relevant regulations will be modified to take account of the provisions of the Agreement. The primary purpose of the Agreement is to allow social insurance contributions paid in Ireland to count towards satisfying the contributions for certain Irish benefits. In the case of Ireland the Agreement covers old age (contributory) pension, retirement pension, widow's (contributory) allowance.

The agreement also deals with the liability for Irish social insurance contributions (PRSI) of 'detached' workers who are seconded to work in New Zealand for a temporary period by an employer who has business in Ireland. Such workers will continue to remain attached to the Irish PRSI system for periods of absences up to two years.

The Social Welfare (Employment of Inconsiderable Extent) (Amendment) Regulations 1994 (SI No. 76 of 1994) increases from £25 to £30, the weekly earnings ceiling below which employment is regarded as employment of inconsiderable extent (i.e. part-time employment).

The Social Welfare (Unemployment Benefit) Regulations 1994 (SI No. 128 of 1994) provide that a person under the age of 55 who receives money in respect of redundancy in excess of a prescribed amount may be disqualified for receiving unemployment benefit for a period of up to nine weeks. The Regulations increase from £12,000 to £15,000 the amount prescribed for the purpose of this disqualification.

The Social Welfare (Treatment Benefit) (Amendment) Regulations 1994 (SI No. 129 of 1994) increase the earnings limit used to determine entitlement to treatment benefit from £30,000 to £35,000 and increase from £60,000 to £70,000 the earnings of a couple below which a dependent spouse can qualify for treatment benefit.

The Social Welfare (Treatment Benefit) (Amendment) (No. 2) Regulations 1994 (SI No. 211 of 1994) provide that, where an insured person satisfies the qualifying conditions for entitlement to Treatment Benefit at the age 60, he or she shall remain entitled for life.

The Social Welfare (Supplementary Welfare Allowance) Regulations 1994 (SI No. 214 of 1994) provide that the blind welfare allowance will not be taken into account in calculating means for the purpose of asserting a person's entitlement to supplementary welfare allowance.

The Social Welfare (Deserted Wife's Benefit) Regulations 1994 (SI No. 229 of 1994) provide for increases in the reduced rates of deserted wife's benefit from July 28, 1994.

The Social Welfare (Maternity Benefit) (Amendment) Regulations 1994 (SI No. 230 of 1994) provide for a new minimum weekly payment of maternity benefit of £74.20 with effect from July 25, 1994.

The Social Welfare (Supplementary Welfare Allowance) (Amendment) Regulations 1994 (SI No. 231 of 1994) provide for an increase from £5 to £6 in the minimum rents which must be paid by claimants for rent supplements under the supplementary welfare allowance scheme and an increase from £3.50 to £4.50 in the minimum rent applying in the case of certain claimants. The increases come into effect from July 25, 1994.

The Social Welfare (Miscellaneous Social Insurance Provisions) Regulations 1994 (SI No. 232 of 1994) provide for increases in the reduced rates of unemployment benefit and disability benefit with effect from the end of July 1994.

The Social Welfare (Amendment of Miscellaneous Social Insurance Provisions) Regulations 1994 (SI No. 233 of 1994) provide for increases in the reduced rates of various social insurance payments from the end of July 1994. Part II of the Regulations provides for certain increases in the rates of benefit payable under the Occupational Injuries Benefits Scheme Part III provides for increase in the reduced rates of the old age (contributory) pension, widow's (contributory) pension and retirement pension where the contribution for receipt of the maximum rates are not satisfied.

Part IV provides for increases in the reduced rate of the old age (contributory) pension and widows (contributory) pension payable to certain people who came back into insurance on the abolition of the earnings limit for liability for social insurance contributions in April 1974, but who did not have sufficient contributions paid to entitle them to maximum rate pensions.

The Social Welfare (Old Age (Contributory) Pension) Regulations 1994 (SI No. 235 of 1994), relate to one of the qualifying conditions for the old age (contributory) pension, which is that the person has a minimum yearly average number of contributions since entering social insurance to reaching pension age. The Regulations provide that contributions in the years spent working in the home while caring in a full-time basis for a child, up to six years of age, or an incapacitated person, will be disregarded in calculating a person's yearly average number of contributions.

The Social Welfare (Social Assistance) (Amendment) Regulations, 1994 (SI No. 239 of 1994) relate to s. 15 of the Social Welfare Act 1994, which provides that a prescribed amount of a person's earnings, from employment or self-employment can be disregarded in the assessment of means for the lone parent's allowance. The Regulations provide that the amount to be disregarded will be £24 per week.

S. 16 of the Social Welfare Act 1994 provides that where a carer's spouse is in employment or self-employment, a prescribed amount of their earnings can be disregarded in the assessment of means for the career's allowance. The Regulations provide that the amount to be disregarded will be £100 per week.

The Social Welfare (Rent Allowance) (Amendment) Regulations 1994 (SI No. 241 of 1994) provide for a reduction, from six to four weeks, in the period over which a person's income comprising earnings from employment as employee is assessed in the case of family income supplement for the purpose of calculating the weekly family income. Under existing provisions, people participating in a social employment scheme are not regarded as being in remunerative full-time employment for family income supplement purposes. The Regulations make similar provisions for people participating in community employment, which incorporates the former social employment scheme.

The Social Welfare (Miscellaneous Social Insurance Provisions) (No. 2) Regulations, 1994 (SI No. 282 of 1994) relate to s. 19 of the Social Welfare Act 1994, which exempts people engaged in casual employment from the qualifying condition for unemployment benefit of having to have sustained a substantial loss of employment. The Regulations set out the circumstances in which a person will be regarded as being engaged in casual employment.

The Social Welfare (Claims and Payments) (Amendment) Regulations, 1994 (SI No. 310 of 1994), relate to s. 12(2) of the Social Welfare (Consolidation) Act 1993, which provides that social welfare inspectors may investigate all matters in relation to social welfare payments. Inspectors can require a wide range of specified persons to provide such information and documents as they may reasonably require within a prescribed period.

The Social Welfare (Health and Safety Benefit) Regulations 1994 (SI No. 313 of 1994) prescribe the amount of reckonable weekly earnings a claimant must have to qualify for health and safety benefit at the standard rate and provide for payment of reduced rated of benefit to claimants whose reckonable weekly earnings are below this amount. The Regulations also contain general provisions relating to claims and payments.

The Social Welfare (Social Assistance) (Amendment) (No. 2) Regulations 1994 (SI No. 316 of 1994) provide that an income of up to £1,000 a year derived from the harvesting of seaweed is to be disregarded in the assessment of means for unemployment assistance.

The Social Welfare (Overlapping Benefits) (Amendments), Regulations 1994 (SI No. 320 of 1994) provide for a number consequential amendments arising from the introduction of the survivor's pension and extend the existing provisions which apply to widows in receipt of the widow's (contributory) pension to both widows and widowers who receive survivors pension.

The Social Welfare Act 1994 (Part IV) (Commencement) Order 1994 (SI No. 321 of 1994) brings part IV of the 1994 Act into effect from October 28, 1994. Part IV provides for the introduction of a new survivor's pension scheme under which widowers will become entitled to a pension scheme on the basis of the existing conditions applied in deterring entitlement to widow's (contributory) pension.

The Social Welfare (Contributions) (Amendment) Regulations 1994 (SI No. 352 of 1994) deal with the provision where social insurance contributions are paid in error. Previously, an application for the return of these payments had to be made within a prescribed period, which was normally three years from the end of the contribution year in respect of which the contributions were paid. The Regulations abolish the time limit and provide for off-setting an amount due to an employer's contribution against outstanding liability.

The Social Welfare (Survivor's Pension) Regulations 1994 (SI No. 322 of 1994) consolidate the existing provisions relating to widow's (contributions) pension and extend them to the survivor's pension. They provide for reduced rate pensions whereby the yearly average is between 24 and 48 and for the special reduce rate pensions payable to people, affected by the abolition of the earnings limit for social insurance in 1974, who gave a yearly average between 5 and 24.

The Social Welfare (Consolidated Payments Provisions) Regulations 1994 (SI No. 417 of 1994) consolidate the regulatory provisions relating to:

— all of the social insurance payments, other than occupational injuries benefits and treatment benefit (Part II);

— all of the social assistance payments, other than supplementary welfare allowance (Part II);

— child benefit (Part IV);

— family income supplement (Part V); and

— related provisions governing the making of claims and payments and the overlapping benefits provisions which set out the circumstances in which a person may receive more than one social welfare payment at the same time (Part VI).

In addition to consolidating the existing provisions, the Regulations also provide:

— that the acceptance of a late claim, heretofore a Ministerial function, will be a matter for decision by a deciding officer, thereby giving the client the right of appeal;

— for an extension of the categories exempted from having to have thirteen paid contributions in the governing contributions year (or certain other years) in order to qualify for disability benefit, to include people who immediately before making their claim for disability benefit were in receipt of invalidity pension;

— an increase from £24 to £33.30 in a weekly amount which a person in receipt of disability benefit may earn from work which he or she may engage in under the prescribed Rules of Behaviour; and

— a change in the method of calculating the yearly average number of contributions for deserted wife's benefit purposes under which a fraction of a contribution will be rounded to the nearest whole number, thereby bringing these provisions into line with those applying in the case of other social welfare payments.

The Social Welfare (Temporary Provisions) Regulations, 1994 (SI No. 437 of 1994) provide for the payment of a Christmas bonus to long-term social welfare recipients, equivalent to 70% of their normal weekly payment, subject to a minimum payment bonus of £20.

Solicitors

SOLICITORS (AMENDMENT) ACT 1994

The Solicitors (Amendment) Act 1994 amended the Solicitors Acts 1954 and 1960 and effected some major reforms in the law relating to solicitors, producing the collective citation the Solicitors Acts 1954 to 1994. Among its more significant provisions, the 1994 Act altered the title of the Incorporated Law Society of Ireland to the Law Society of Ireland, laid down new procedures by which the Law Society deals with complaints against solicitors and increased its powers to intervene in solicitors' practices with a view to giving greater protection to solicitors' clients. The 1994 Act also extended the High Court's supervisory functions over the profession. The 1994 Act updated and amended the Society's functions in relation to the education and training of solicitors. The Act also aimed at promoting competition in the provision of certain legal services, though its provisions concerning what had been the conveyancing 'monopoly' of solicitors was substantially altered from what had originally been proposed. Many, though not all of the provisions of the 1994 Act can be traced to the former Fair Trade Commission (now the Competition Authority) Report of Study into Restrictive Practices in the Legal Profession, published in 1990 (see the 1990 Review, 437). The vast majority of the 1994 Act came into effect on November 4, 1994 on its signature by the President. The limited exceptions to this were as follows: in accordance with s. 1(3) of the 1994 Act, s. 68 of the Act (on charges to clients) came into effect on February 4, 1995, three months after the Act's signing; in accordance with s. 1(4) of the 1994 Act, ss. 16, 17, 18, 22, 23 and 58(3) of the Act (which concern the new disciplinary arrangements for solicitors) require a Commencement Order.

Name and membership of Law Society of Ireland   Part II of the 1994 Act (ss. 4 to 7) deals with a number of connected issues concerning the name and membership of the Law Society of Ireland. S. 4 of the 1994 Act provides for a change in the Society's name from the 'Incorporated Law Society of Ireland' to the 'Law Society of Ireland'. S. 5 inserts a new s. 78 into the Solicitors Act 1954 (hereinafter the 1954 Act) and obliges the Society to amend its bye-laws to bring them into conformity with the provisions of the Solicitors Acts 1954 to 1994 or any Regulations made under them and empowered the Society to make regulations providing for membership of

and elections or appointments to the Council of the Society, and for the
admission of honorary or associate members of the Society. S. 6 of the 1994
Act defines the categories of persons who may be admitted as honorary and
associate members. S. 7 amended s. 73 of the 1954 Act regarding membership of committees of the Council of the Society. S. 73 of the 1954 Act
empowered the Council to appoint committees and to delegate the exercise
of its functions to such committees and the changes effected by s. 7 of the
1994 Act enabled up to one-third of the membership of committees discharging functions of the Society to include solicitors who are not members of the
Council of the Society and persons who are not solicitors; it also provides
that committees of the Council may sit in divisions.

Investigation of complaints   Part III of the 1994 Act (ss. 8 to 25) deals with
the investigation of complaints by the Law Society. S. 8 of the 1994 Act
empowers the Society to deal with complaints by solicitors' clients alleging
that the services provided were inadequate and were not of a quality that
could reasonably have been expected of a solicitor. The Society is required
to investigate a complaint (unless they are satisfied that it is frivolous or
vexatious) and to attempt to resolve the matter by agreement between the
parties. Following the investigation of a complaint the Society may impose
on a solicitor the various sanctions and requirements set out in the section,
including refunding client funds and limits on costs. S. 8 also sets out certain
matters which the Society must have regard to in considering whether to
impose sanctions on a solicitor. We should also note that s. 8 provides that
the Society shall not investigate complaints relating to legal services provided more than five years before the date on which the complaint was made.
S. 22 of the 1994 Act requires the Society to publish annual information in
the Gazette of the Society, and in any other manner that the Society may
direct, on complaints received about solicitors, and on complaints referred
to the Disciplinary Tribunal (see below) for investigation and the outcome
of such investigations.

Excessive charges   S. 9 of the 1994 Act empowers the Society to impose
sanctions on a solicitor where a client complains that a solicitor has charged
an excessive amount in respect of services provided to that client. The Society
is required to investigate any complaint of overcharging received (unless they
are satisfied that it is frivolous or vexatious) and to attempt to resolve the
matter by agreement between the parties. If the Society are satisfied that the
solicitor's bill of costs is grossly excessive they may direct the solicitor to
refund in whole or in part any amount paid by the client, or require the
solicitor to waive in whole or in part the right to recover costs. The right of
a person to have a bill of costs taxed by a Taxing Master of the High Court

is not be affected by the section. As with s. 8, complaints concerning services of more than five years previously shall not be investigated.

Production of documents   S. 10 empowers the Society to require a solicitor to produce any documents in his or her possession or under his or her control relating to a complaint which the Society is investigating.

High Court appeals and offences   S. 11 provides for appeals to the High Court arising from the exercise by the Society of their powers under ss. 8, 9 and 10 of the 1994 Act. In addition, s. 11 provides that failure to comply with a determination or direction of the Society under ss. 8 or 9 or to comply with a notice to produce or deliver up documents under s. 10 without reasonable excuse is an offence carrying, on summary conviction, a maximum fine of £1,500. S. 12 empowers the Society, where they impose a sanction following the investigation of a complaint under ss. 8 or 9, to require a solicitor to make a payment not exceeding £1,000 as a contribution towards the Society's costs of investigating the complaint. The Society may recover any such sum as a liquidated debt. S. 13 provides that the Society may adjourn the taking of any action relating to a complaint against a solicitor made under ss. 8 or 9 where connected civil or criminal proceedings have not been finally determined, and the Society consider that those proceedings would be likely to determine an issue relevant to the conduct alleged in the complaint. S. 14 provides that the Society may authorise a person to inspect documents at a solicitor's place of business for the purposes of investigating alleged misconduct.

Independent adjudication of Law Society's procedures   S. 15 provides for a system of independent adjudication of complaints concerning the Society's handling of complaints made to the Society by members of the public about solicitors. The Minister for Justice may, by Regulations, require the Society to establish and fund a scheme for the investigation of such complaints by an independent adjudicator. The section provides for a right of appeal to the High Court against a requirement of the adjudicator and it confers the same immunities and privileges on a person required to attend before the adjudicator as if that person was a witness before the High Court. The obstruction of an adjudicator in the performance of his or her functions is an offence carrying a maximum fine on summary conviction of £1,500.

Disciplinary Tribunal of High Court   S. 16 of the 1994 Act inserted a new s. 6 of the Solicitors Act 1960 (hereinafter the 1960 Act), which concerned the Disciplinary Committee of the High Court. The 1994 Act provides for a new Disciplinary Tribunal with, for the first time, the appointment of up to

5 'lay members' to the Disciplinary Tribunal to represent the interests of the general public. S. 17 of the 1994 Act inserted a new s. 7 of the 1960 Act concerning the powers of the Disciplinary Tribunal to inquire into allegations of misconduct by solicitors. Prior to the 1994 Act, the Disciplinary Committee (as it was then known) could recommend to the High Court the removal of a solicitor's name from the roll of solicitors or else advise, admonish or censure that solicitor. S. 17 of the 1994 Act gives the new Disciplinary Tribunal power, where they have found a solicitor has been guilty of misconduct, to advise, admonish or censure that solicitor, to order him or her to pay a sum not exceeding £5,000 to the Compensation Fund, and/or to pay a sum not exceeding £5,000 as restitution to any aggrieved party. S. 25 of the 1994 Act inserted a new s. 15 into the 1960 Act (which deals with the powers of the Disciplinary Tribunal as to the taking of evidence in the course of an inquiry into alleged misconduct by a solicitor, and in the consideration of an application by a solicitor to have his/her name removed from the roll). In particular, a person who refuses to obey a direction of the Disciplinary Tribunal or wilfully gives false evidence or otherwise obstructs or hinders the Disciplinary Tribunal, shall be guilty of an offence. An offence under the amended s. 15 of the 1960 Act may be tried on indictment and in such a case carries a maximum fine of up to £10,000 and/or 2 years imprisonment. When the offence is tried summarily the maximum penalties are a fine of £1,500 and/or 12 months imprisonment. Appeals may be brought, both by the solicitor in question and the complainant, to the High Court against orders made by the Disciplinary Tribunal under its extended powers. The new provisions do not apply to any application to the Disciplinary Committee made before s. 17 came into operation.

Powers of High Court S. 18 of the 1994 Act inserted a new s. 8 of the 1960 Act concerning the powers of the High Court in relation to a report by the Disciplinary Tribunal on a finding of misconduct against a solicitor. The amended s. 8 of the 1960 Act extended the previous powers of the High Court to limit such a solicitor's practice (for example by placing restrictions on the areas of work which he/she may undertake). It also empowers the High Court to direct a financial institution to furnish information in its possession relating to the financial affairs of a solicitor's practice to the Society, and to direct a solicitor to swear an affidavit disclosing information relating to accounts held with any financial institution. In addition, the amended s. 8 of the 1960 Act empowers the High Court to direct a solicitor to swear an affidavit disclosing all information as to his or her assets and to examine a solicitor in relation to the contents of the affidavit. The High Court may also direct a solicitor not to reduce his or her assets below a specified value in cases where the conduct of that solicitor is likely to give rise to the Society making a grant out of the

Compensation Fund. The maximum fine in summary conviction for reducing the assets below the specified limit was increased from £100 to £1,500. Again the new provisions do not apply to any report to the High Court made before this section came into operation. S. 23 of the 1994 Act provides for the publication of orders of the Disciplinary Tribunal and of the High Court.

Restoration of name to roll of solicitors   S. 19 of the 1994 Act amended s. 10 of the 1960 Act regarding the restoration of a solicitor's name to the roll of solicitors. The amended s. 10 of the 1960 Act provides that, where a solicitor's name has been struck off the roll because of dishonesty relating to his or her practice or a criminal conviction, the High Court shall not restore the name to the roll unless it is satisfied that the person is a fit and proper person to practise as a solicitor and that the restoration would not adversely affect public confidence in the solicitor's profession or in the administration of justice.

Restriction on employment of person struck off   S. 20 of the 1994 Act inserted a new s. 60 of the 1954 Act relating to the prohibitions on any person employing a person in connection with the provision of legal services, who he or she knows has been struck off the roll of solicitors, or who has been suspended, or who has been refused a practising certificate, or who has given an undertaking to the High Court not to practise as a solicitor, without the Society's permission. The amended s. 60 of the 1954 Act provides that where a person continues to employ a person in contravention of that section the Society may apply to the High Court for an injunction to restrain the employer from continuing the employment. S. 21 of the 1994 Act inserted a new s. 63 of the 1954 Act. The amended s. 63 prohibits a person who has been struck off, suspended, has had a practising certificate refused or suspended, or who has given an undertaking to the High Court not to practise as a solicitor from seeking employment connected with the provision of legal services from any person, without previously informing the person that he or she is an unqualified person.

The maximum fine on summary conviction for a breach of this section was increased from £50 to £1,500.

Definition of misconduct   S. 24 of the 1994 Act amended the definition of misconduct in s. 3 of the 1960 Act of 1960 to include a contravention of a provision contained in the Solicitors Acts 1954 to 1994, or of any Regulation made thereunder. This is an addition to, *inter alia*, the commission of treason, felony or a misdemeanour or 'conduct tending to bring the solicitors profession into disrepute'.

Protection of clients Part IV of the 1994 Act (ss. 26 to 39) deal with the general protection of clients.

Professional indemnity insurance S. 26 of the 1994 Act contains provision for professional indemnity cover. The Law Society may, with the concurrence of the President of the High Court, make Regulations for indemnity against losses arising from civil liability claims in connection with a solicitor's practice, either through the existing Solicitors' Mutual Defence Fund or the establishment of any other indemnity fund by the Society, or through an indemnity insurance policy.

Production of documents S. 27 inserted a new s. 19 into the 1960 Act, which empowers the Society to require the production of documents in cases where they believe that a solicitor (or his/her clerk or servant) has been guilty of dishonesty. The amended s. 19 of the 1960 Act provides that, in addition to cases of dishonesty, the Society may require a sole practitioner who has abandoned his or her practice or ceased to practise, to produce any documents relating to the practice where the Society are of the opinion that he or she has not made adequate arrangements to make available documents to clients. The maximum fine on summary conviction for refusing or failing to produce or deliver up documents under the section was increased from £50 to £1,500.

Control of banking accounts or assets S. 28 of the 1994 Act inserted a new s. 20 into the 1960 Act, which is concerned with the control of banking accounts of solicitors who the Society believe have been guilty of dishonesty in connection with their practice. The Society is empowered by the amended provision to apply to the High Court for the equivalent of a Mareva injunction to 'freeze' any moneys which may be in a bank account in the name of a solicitor or of a sole practitioner who has abandoned his or her practice or ceased to practise. A 'freezing order' may also apply to assets held by a solicitor. The maximum fine that may be imposed for attempting to frustrate any such court order was increased from £100 to £1,500.

Payments from the Compensation Fund S. 29 of the 1994 Act inserted a new s. 21 into the 1960 Act which established the Compensation Fund from which losses sustained due to the dishonesty of solicitors, or their employees, may be recouped. Prior to the 1994 Act, there was no limit of the amounts that could be recouped from the Fund, and the Law Society had pressed for a 'cap' on the maximum amount that could be claimed, largely because enormously increased claims had been made on the Fund during the 1980s and early 1990s arising from claims by clients against a number of solicitors who had either been struck off or whose deaths had revealed, in some instances, substantial shortfalls in client accounts. The 1994 Act effected a number of limits to the level of claims that can be made against the Fund. Crucially, the 1994 Act placed a 'cap' of £350,000 on a grant from the Fund in any particular case (a cap of £250,000 had appeared in the Bill as published). The Minister for Justice is empowered to vary this amount by Regulations to take account of changes in the value of money. The Law Society is also empowered to make a grant in excess of £250,000 in cases of 'grave hardship'. The new s. 21 of the 1960 Act also limits the operation of the Fund to clients of solicitors practising in the State, although the Society may, by means of Regulations, extend the provisions of the section to a solicitor's practice outside the State. For the first time the payment of interest on losses sustained by a client is also expressly provided for. The Law Society has a discretion to make or refuse to make a grant in certain cases including where they are of the opinion that the loss was not due to misappropriation or conversion of clients' moneys entrusted to a solicitor or where the loss arose from the provision of services other than services of a legal nature. Finally, the Society is also empowered to make grants to clients of a dishonest solicitor in cases where there has been no dishonesty or negligence on the part of a partner who would otherwise be vicariously liable to the clients of the dishonest solicitor.

Contributions to and minimum level of Compensation Fund   S. 30 of the 1994 Act inserted a new s. 22 into the 1960 Act which governs the contributions payable by solicitors to the Compensation Fund. The new section provides that before a practising certificate can be issued to a solicitor, he or she must pay the annual contribution to the Fund. The Society may specify different rates of contribution to the Fund in relation to any class of solicitor. In exercising its powers under the section, the Society must have regard to the principle that the total amount standing to the credit of the Fund on the specified date should be at least £1 million, or such greater amount as the Society may determine. Prior to the 1994 Act, the Fund had to be maintained at a minimum level of £25,000.

Death, bankruptcy and abandonment of practice   S. 31 of the 1994 Act inserted a new s. 61 into the 1954 Act concerning arrangements to carry on the practice of a sole practitioner in case of death, incapacity or bankruptcy. A new provision was included for the appointment of a solicitor by the High Court to carry on the practice of a sole practitioner who has abandoned the practice. S. 32 of the 1994 Act empowers the Society to intervene in the practice of a sole practitioner who has died, where another solicitor has not been appointed by the personal representative to carry on the practice within 4 weeks of the death of the sole practitioner. In such circumstances, the right to operate client accounts shall vest in the Society and the Society may appoint a solicitor to operate the client accounts for a specified period, and take any further action in relation to the practice as they deem necessary in the interests of the clients. Of some interest is that, in contrast with other sections of the 1994 Act already discussed, this new power extends to the affairs of a sole practitioner who died before the section came into effect. S. 33 of the 1994 Act enables the Society to apply to the High Court for authority to sell the practice of an incapacitated or deceased solicitor, or the practice of a solicitor who has abandoned it, where the solicitor's conduct has given or is likely to give rise to the Society making a grant out of the Compensation Fund. S. 34 of the 1994 Act contains ancillary provisions in relation to documents taken into the possession of the Society under the Solicitors Acts 1954 to 1994, and expenses incurred by the Society in connection with powers of intervention in a solicitor's practice. S. 35 of the 1994 Act provides that notice of any application to a court under the provisions of the Solicitors Acts shall be given to the Society, unless a court otherwise orders.

Defence to proceedings S. 36 provides that is shall be a defence to an action for damages against the in relation to the exercise of any of their powers under the Solicitors Acts 1954 to 1994 that they acted in good faith and reasonably having regard to all the circumstances.

Restrictions on becoming sole practitioner after admission S. 37 of the 1994 Act introduced a new restriction on a solicitor practising as a sole practitioner or as a partner for a period of up to three years after admission, without the consent of the Society, unless in the case of a partnership, another partner has been in continuous practice for a period of at least three years. This provision was inserted in the 1994 Act because of the fears that the increased number of young sole practitioners in recent years might lead to increased calls on the Compensation Fund.

High Court and Supreme Court S. 38 of the 1994 Act conferred a general power on the High Court on an application coming before it under the Solicitors Acts 1954 to 1994 to make any order that it thinks fit in relation to a solicitor's practice to protect the interests of a client, the public or the profession. S. 39 inserted a new s. 12 into the 1960 Act and empowers the Society or the solicitor concerned to appeal to the Supreme Court against decisions of the High Court made under ss. 8, 9 or 10 of the 1954 Act (as amended by the 1994 Act).

Qualifying for admission as a solicitor Part V of the 1994 Act (ss. 40 to 53) deals with the process of qualifying as a solicitor. S. 40 of the 1994 Act inserted a new s. 24 into the 1954 Act which sets out the requirements for admission as a solicitor. The amended s. 24 empowers the Society to exempt persons from serving apprenticeships and from the prescribed examinations. It also prohibits a person from being admitted as a solicitor unless he or she satisfies the Society that they are a fit and proper person to be admitted, subject to an appeal against that decision to the High Court.

Admission to apprenticeship   S. 41 of the 1994 Act inserts a new s. 25 into the 1954 Act, which sets out the requirements for admission to apprenticeship. The new s. 25 empowers the Society to require intending apprentices to attend education and training courses. S. 42 of the 1994 Act inserted a new s. 26 of the 1954 Act concerning the terms of indentures of apprenticeship to practising solicitors. The new s. 26 provides that the Society may prescribe, by Regulations, terms of indentures of apprenticeships not exceeding two years. Prior to the 1994 Act, terms of indentures of up to 5 years might apply, depending on qualifications and experience. S. 43 inserted a new s. 27 into the 1954 Act concerning the production of evidence of good character for intending solicitors' apprentices. Under the amended s. 27 of the 1954 Act, Society may require a person to furnish evidence as to his or her previous education and employment record and as to health, in addition to evidence of good character. S. 44 of the 1994 Act inserted a new s. 29 into the 1954 Act on the restrictions on a solicitor taking or retaining an apprentice. The principal change effected was to reduce from seven to five years the period of continuous practice required before a solicitor may take on an apprentice. S. 45 of the 1994 Act inserted a new s. 32 into the 1954 Act, requiring the written consent of the Society to be obtained where an apprentice wishes to become bound by indentures to another solicitor following the termination of indentures. S. 46 of the 1994 Act inserted a new s. 33 of the 1954 Act, setting out arrangements for the discharging of indentures of apprenticeship, and the Society is required under the amended s. 33 to notify each party to the indentures where they decide to discharge the indentures of apprenticeship. This is also subject to an appeal to the High Court. S. 47 of the 1994 Act inserted a new s. 36 into the 1954 Act on the number of apprentices that a solicitor may have, limiting this in general to not more than two apprentices at the same time. S. 48 of the 1994 Act inserted a new s. 37 into the 1954 Act. By providing that an apprentice must serve 'in the prescribed manner' a bona fide apprenticeship the new s. 37 empowered the Society to make Regulations relating to this matter. S. 53 of the 1994 Act empowers the Society to prescribe by Regulations the conditions under which an apprenticeship may be served in Northern Ireland, England or Wales.

Provision of education by the Law Society   S. 49 of the 1994 Act amended

s. 40 of the 1954 Act concerning the Society's obligations and functions in relation to the education of persons seeking to be admitted as solicitors and well as the continuing education of solicitors. Under the amended s. 40 of the 1954 Act, the Society may provide, either on its own or in association with other institutions, educational courses for its own students and for students of other educational and training institutions. Under the amended s. 40 of the 1954 Act, the Society may join with other institutions in providing joint or common courses leading to a joint or common qualification. These provisions would appear to encompass, for example, joint courses with the Honourable Society of King's Inns, the educational establishment for the Bar. The amended section also empowers the Society to require in Regulations that attendance apprentices or intending apprentices at education or training courses may extend to persons seeking to be admitted as solicitors. This empowered the Society to require, for example, foreign lawyers to attend such courses. Regulations made by the Society pursuant to this section can be made only with the concurrence of the Minister for Justice and they must be laid before both Houses of the Oireachtas, subject to annulled within 21 sitting days.

Exemptions from Law Society's examinations S. 50 of the 1994 Act amended s. 41 of the 1954 Act as to general exemptions from the Society's preliminary examination. No major changes were effected by the 1994 Act in this area, but there is no doubt that this has proved to be a particularly contentious matter. The decision in *Bloomer and Ors v Law Society of Ireland* [1995] 2 ILRM 13, which we will discuss in the 1995 Review, is the latest in a line of cases concerning the Law Society's examinations and the Society's difficulties in regulating the numbers entering the solicitor's branch of the legal profession. S. 51 of the 1994 Act inserted a new s. 43 into the 1954 Act on exemptions from the Society's examinations for barristers who propose to become solicitors. The new s. 43 facilitates easier interchange between the branches of the legal profession and reduced the period of practice at the Bar required of barristers who propose to become solicitors to a maximum of three years (during any period of time which may be specified in regulations prescribed by the Society). Subject to this requirement, a barrister who procures himself/herself to be disbarred, who obtains a certificate that he or she is in good standing as a barrister, who satisfies the Society that he or she is a fit and proper person to be admitted as a solicitor and who attends any courses and passes any examinations (other than examinations in substantive law subjects) prescribed by the Society, shall be entitled to be enrolled as a solicitor. The former requirement in the original s. 43 of the 1954 for former barristers to pass the Society's second examination in the Irish language was removed by the 1994 Act, where such barristers have passed or have been exempted from the statutory Irish language examination for barristers. It is also provided that service as a member of the judiciary or in State bodies or as a barrister in full-time employment will be deemed to be practice as a barrister.

Reciprocal recognition of qualifications S. 52 of the 1994 Act inserted a new s. 44 into the 1954 Act, which contained an enabling provision to grant exemptions from the Society's examinations to solicitors in Northern Ireland wishing to be admitted to practise in the State. The new s. 44 provides for wider exemptions from the Society's examinations for members of professions corresponding to the profession of solicitor in States, other than EC Member States, who wish to practise in this jurisdiction, subject to a reciprocal recognition arrangements for Irish solicitors. We should also note here that s. 80 of the 1994 Act expressly disapplies the provisions in the Solicitors Acts 1954 to 1994 concerning the requirements for admission as a solicitor, including educational requirements, to lawyers from EC states who are entitled to practise in this jurisdiction under the terms of Directive 89/48/EEC, implemented by the European Communities (General System for the Recognition of Higher Education Diplomas) Regulations 1991 (1991 Review, 187).

Practising certificates and practice Part VI of the 1994 Act (ss. 54 to 64) deals with a number of matters concerning the granting of practising certificates and practice in general.

Applications and the Register S. 54 of the 1994 Act inserted a new s. 47 into the 1954 Act. The new s. 47 empowers the Society to make Regulations regarding applications for, and the issue of, practising certificates and obliges the Society to make Regulations requiring a solicitor to provide evidence of indemnity cover under s. 26 of the 1994 Act. On the making of these Regulations, the Third and Fourth Schedules to the 1954 Act, which prescribed the form of declaration for obtaining a practising certificate and the form of the certificate, were repealed. The new s. 47 also provides that the register of solicitors may be kept in an electronic (including computer) or other non-written form. The previously stated provisions in the original s. 47 of the 1954 requiring the registrar to issue a practising certificate on an application being made in accordance with the requirements of the Solicitors Acts, and for the right for a person to apply to the High Court where a practising certificate is refused, are repeated in the amended s. 47. S. 55(1) of the 1994 Act provides that a practising certificate shall remain in force until the end of the practice year following the coming into operation of Regulations made under s. 47 of the 1954 Act, as inserted by s. 54 of the

1994 Act. S. 55(2) of the 1994 Act amended s. 48 of the 1954 Act to provide that, from January 1, 1996, the commencement date for practising certificates shall be January 1 rather than January 5. These sections should be seen in conjunction with s. 65 of the 1994 Act which inserted a new s. 9 into the 1954 Act, which provided that the registrar of solicitors shall maintain a roll of solicitors which shall be available for inspection during office hours without payment. The new s. 9 of the 1954 Act provides in addition that the roll may be kept in an electronic (such as computer) or other non-written form, but that it must be kept in such form as it will be available in written form for inspection. They should also be seen in conjunction with s. 81 of the 1994 Act, which amended s. 53(1) of the 1954 Act with effect from 1 January 1996 by providing that the list published by the Law Society of the names of the solicitors who have obtained practising certificates for the current practice year shall, until the contrary is proved, be evidence that the persons named on the list are solicitors holding such certificates.

Prohibition of practising without practice certificate   S. 56 of the 1994 Act provides that, in general, no solicitor shall practice as a solicitor without a practising certificate which is in force. This general rule does not apply to solicitors in the full-time service of the State. In addition, a solicitor who is full-time engaged in the provision of conveyancing services to his or her employer is not required to hold a practising certificate. This latter provision should be seen in the context of s. 77 of the 1994, below, which provides that non-practising barristers may provide conveyancing services to their employer. S. 57 of the 1994 Act provides that a solicitor in practice who does not hold a practising certificate shall be guilty of misconduct. This is stated to be without prejudice to other specific provisions in the Solicitors Acts 1954 to 1994.

Suspension of certificates   S. 58 of the 1994 Act empowers the Law Society to apply to the High Court in any case where the Society consider that there has been a serious by a solicitor to comply with any provision of the Solicitors Acts 1954 to 1994 or any Regulations made under the Acts. The powers of the High Court on the hearing of an application include suspending a solicitor's practising certificate and directing the solicitor to remedy any consequences of his or her failure to comply with the Acts.

Imposition of conditions on certificate   S. 61 of the 1994 Act inserted a new s. 49 into the 1954 Act as to the circumstances in which the Society may direct the registrar of solicitors to refuse to issue a practising certificate, or to issue a practising certificate subject to conditions. S. 49 of the 1954 Act provided that the Society may refuse to issue a practising certificate or may issue a certificate subject to conditions in certain circumstances, for example, where a solicitor has been adjudicated a bankrupt or has failed to give a satisfactory explanation regarding his or her conduct. These provisions are repeated in the 1994 Act, but among the new provisions are those which empower the Society to require an applicant for a practising certificate to take specified steps, which they consider necessary for carrying on an efficient practice, even where these may involve expenditure for that person. Such directions may be appealed to the High Court. In tandem with this amendment to s. 49 of the 1954 Act, s. 59 of the 1994 Act empowers the Society to impose conditions on the current practising certificate of a solicitor if circumstances arise which, had they arisen at the time when the person applied for the practising certificate, would have entitled the Society to refuse to issue the practising certificate or to impose conditions. Again, a solicitor may appeal the conditions imposed to the High Court. S. 60 of the 1994 Act provides that a certificate issued by the registrar of solicitors to the effect that an unqualified person has been acting as a solicitor maybe admitted in any proceedings as *prima facie* evidence of the facts stated thereon.

Qualifications for acting as solicitor S. 62 of the 1994 Act inserted a new s. 54 into the 1954 Act concerning the qualifications needed to practise as a solicitor. The previous qualifications, primarily that the person is on the roll of solicitors and is not suspended therefrom that the person is in the full-time service of the State or that a practising certificate in respect of the person is in force, are repeated in the amended s. 54. However, an additional provision to the effect that a solicitor is not qualified to act as a solicitor if he or she has given an undertaking to the High Court not to practise was added.

Penalties S. 63 of the 1994 Act amended s. 55 of the 1954 Act to increase the maximum penalties for the offences committed when an unqualified person acts as a solicitor. On a summary conviction, the maximum fine was increased from £50 to £1,500 (the maximum sentence of imprisonment remaining at six months), while on indictment the maximum fine was increased from £200 to £10,000 (the maximum sentence again remaining unchanged from two years). S. 64 of the 1994 Act amended s. 56 of the 1954 Act to increase the maximum penalty for the offence committed where a person who is not a solicitor holds himself or herself out to be so or implies by certain actions that he or she is a solicitor. On a summary conviction, the maximum fine was increased from £50 to £1,500; this offence is not indictable.

Miscellaneous provisions Part VII of the 1994 Act (ss. 65 to 82), which is headed 'Miscellaneous Provisions' contains a number of very important provisions, some of which have been discussed above.

Fees S. 66 of the 1994 Act provides that the Sixth Schedule to the 1954 Act, which contains a list of applications for which fees may be charged by the Society (for example, an application for the consent of the Society to entry into indentures, or to attend any examination) may be extended by Regulations made with the concurrence of the President of the High Court.

Register of solicitors prepared to act in certain civil cases S. 67 of the 1994 Act obliges the Society to maintain a register of solicitors who are prepared to act for any person who is unable to engage the services of a solicitor to take civil proceedings against another solicitor, in a case arising from the conduct of that other solicitor. The Society must make the information on the register available to a person requesting it and take all reasonable measures to assist that person. This register would be of particular relevance in the context of negligence actions.

Charges to clients S. 68 of the 1994 Act places new obligations and restrictions on a solicitor concerning solicitor and client costs. S. 68(1) provides that, on the taking of instructions, a solicitor must provide a client with particulars in writing of the actual charges or, where this is not possible, an estimate or if neither is possible, the basis for the charges for legal services. If the work involves litigation, the solicitor must provide the client in writing with particulars of the circumstances in which the client may be required to pay costs to another party and the circumstances, if any, where costs recovered from another party may not discharge the client's liability to the solicitor. S. 68(2) of the 1994 Act prohibits a solicitor in litigation work from charging a client on the basis of a percentage or proportion of any damages awarded to the client, except in cases relating to recovery of a debt or a liquidated demand. Any costs charged on basis will be unenforceable as against the client in any action to recover them. S. 68(3), (4) and (5) prohibit a solicitor from deducting any sum in respect of costs from the amount of any damages that may awarded to a client, except by agreement with the client. Any such agreement with a client must be in writing to be enforceable against the client. The agreement must include an estimate by the solicitor of the costs recoverable from the other party in the event of the client recovering damages. S. 68(6) requires a solicitor who conducts contentious business on behalf of a client to show on a bill of costs a summary of the legal services provided, the total amount of damages recovered, details of costs recovered and amounts charged in respect of fees, outlays, disbursements and expenses incurred arising out of the provision of legal services. S. 68(7) provides that the provisions of the section shall not affect a person's right to have a bill of costs taxed. Finally, s. 68(8) requires a solicitor to inform a client of his or her right to have a bill of costs taxed and of his or her right to make a complaint to the Law Society under s. 9 of the 1994 Act.

Professional practice Regulations and advertising   S. 69 of the 1994 Act amended s. 71 of the 1954 Act, which empowers the Society to make Regulations with respect to the professional practice, conduct and discipline of solicitors. Of the changes involved, we may note that the Law Society may not prohibit solicitors from charging less for a service than any fee specified for that service in any statutory or other scale of fees. In addition, the Society may not in general prohibit advertising by solicitors, except in the case of advertising which is likely to bring the profession into disrepute, is in bad taste, reflects unfavourably on other solicitors, is false or misleading, is contrary to public policy or consists of unsolicited approaches to individuals for business. It is specifically provided that the Law Society's powers to prohibit the types of advertising listed does not extend to prohibiting the advertising of fees by solicitors.

Incorporated practices   S. 70 of the 1994 Act provides for the first time, notwithstanding the general rule in s. 64 of the 1954 Act, for the incorporation of solicitors practices, that is the use of the corporate body as a vehicle for carrying on the practice of the profession. It is hardly surprising that this innovation is hedged around with a number of restrictions. S. 70 of the 1994 Act enables the Society, with the concurrence of the Minister for Justice, following consultation with the Minister for Enterprise and Employment, to make Regulations providing for the incorporation of solicitors practices, and prescribing the circumstances in which incorporated practices may be recognised by the Society as being suitable to provide legal services and the conditions which they must satisfy if they are to remain recognised. At the time of writing (September 1996) no Regulations have been made under s. 70.

Fee-sharing   S. 71 of the 1994 Act empowers the Society to make Regulations, with the concurrence of the Minister for Justice following consultation with the Minister for Enterprise and Employment, to provide for fee-sharing between solicitors and non-solicitors. These are sometimes referred to as multi-disciplinary arrangements) In addition, similar Regulations may be made for fee-sharing between multi-national practices between solicitors and lawyers in other countries.

Commissioners for Oaths   S. 72 of the 1994 Act provides that every solicitor who holds a current practising certificate shall have all the powers of a commissioner for oaths. It prohibits a solicitor from using powers as a commissioner for oaths in proceedings in which that solicitor has an interest In accordance with long-established practice, it is also required that the solicitor must state in the jurat or attestation at which place and on what date the oath or affidavit is taken or made. It is also provided that where a solicitor signs or seals a document in accordance with the requirements of s. 72, the document may be admitted in evidence without further proof of the signature or seal, or that the person is a solicitor. S. 72 does not affect the provisions concerning the appointment of commissioners for oaths under s. 73 of the Supreme Court of Judicature (Ireland) Act 1877.

Withdrawal from criminal cases S. 74 of the 1994 Act prohibits a solicitor from withdrawing from a criminal case where the client is in custody, without having obtained permission from the court.

Client accounts S. 76 of the 1994 Act substituted a new s. 66 of the 1954 Act as to accounting requirements for solicitors. The new s. 66 empowers the Law Society to make Regulations, with the consent of the President of the High Court, prescribing the responsibilities and duties of a solicitor, as to opening and maintaining bank accounts for clients' moneys, the lodgement of clients' moneys, the keeping of accounting records and the appointment of persons to enforce compliance with the Regulations. The new s. 66 provides it is an offence for a solicitor to lodge clients' moneys in an account other than in an approved bank or financial institution. In this respect, s. 75 of the 1994 Act amended the definition of bank or financial institution for the purposes of the Solicitors Acts and provided that the definition may be extended to other financial institutions by Ministerial Order. S. 75 of the 1994 Act requires solicitors to maintain clients accounts only at a bank or financial institution as defined in the section itself or as extended by Order. To revert to s. 66 of the 1954 Act, as amended by s. 76 of the 1994 Act, it is also provided that it is an offence for a solicitor to fail to lodge clients' moneys in a bank account, to fail to maintain accounting records, to fail to record the receipt of clients' money, to fail to record the lodgement of clients' moneys to a bank account in accordance with Regulations made by the Law Society or to make a false or misleading entry in accounting records. The Law Society may also authorise a person (such as an accountant) to attend at a solicitor's place of business and to inspect accounting records. here a solicitor, or an employee of the solicitor, fails to comply with a requirement of an authorised person in regard to the inspection of accounting records, the High Court may order the solicitor or employee e to comply with the requirements of s. 66, as amended by the 1994 Act.

Interest on clients' money S. 73 of the 1994 Act obliges the Law Society, without prejudice to s. 66 of the 1954 Act, as amended by s. 76 of the 1994 Act, above, to make Regulations, with the concurrence of the President of the High Court, to require solicitors, in general, to maintain clients' moneys in deposit accounts for the benefit of clients or to pay to clients a sum equivalent to the interest which would have accrued if the money had been kept on deposit. The Regulations define the obligations of solicitors in this regard by reference to the sum held, or the length of time the sum is held by a solicitor on behalf of a client, and enable a client to require the Society to determine any question arising under the Regulations. The Regulations cannot affect any written agreement between a solicitor and client as to how the client's money or interest should be applied, nor can they apply to money received by a solicitor which is the subject of a trust of which the solicitor is trustee.

Restrictions on conveyancing, will making and probate work Ss. 77 to 79 of the 1994 Act concern certain legal work which traditionally has been the province of solicitors. It had originally been proposed that the long-standing 'monopoly' enjoyed by solicitors in conveyancing would be opened up to financial institutions under Regulations to be made by the Minister for Justice. However, this proposal was dropped from the final version of the 1994 Act, but some 'liberalisation' of will making and probate work was included in s. 78 of the 1994 Act. By way of introduction to this aspect of the 1994 Act, s. 77 amended ss. 58(2) and (3) of the 1954 Act and increased the maximum penalties where an unqualified person carries out any of the conveyancing, will making and probate work functions normally restricted to solicitors under section 58 of the 1954 Act, from £100 to £1,500 on summary conviction and to £10,000 on conviction on indictment. S. 58(3) of the 1954 Act creates certain exemptions from various prescribed legal activities which are normally restricted to solicitors under s. 58(1) (such as the drawing or preparing of a document relating to real or personal estate). S. 77 of the 1994 Act added to the list of exemptions in s. 58(3) of the 1954 Act any act done by a lawyer to whom Directive 77/249/EEC, which concerns lawyers from EC Member States providing particular legal services in Ireland, applies. Finally, in keeping with a corresponding provision in s. 56 for solicitors in employment, 428, above, s. 77 also amended s. 58 of the 1954 Act by providing that non-practising barristers in employment are empowered to act as conveyancers for their employers. Prior to the changes effected by ss. 56 and 77 of the 1994 Act, these acts could only be performed by practising barristers and solicitors.

S. 78 of the 1994 Act provides that the Minister for Justice may make Regulations authorising banks, building societies, wholly owned subsidiaries of insurance companies and credit unions (referred to as authored bodies) to prepare wills, take instructions for a grant of probate or of letters of administration or draw papers on which to found or oppose such grants. As already indicated, prior to the 1994 Act, these were functions reserved generally to practising solicitors and barristers S. 78 lists various matters which may be covered in Regulations made under the section, including the protective measures for clients that are applicable where solicitors provide such services. S. 79 of the 1994 Act enables the Minister for Justice to prescribe by Regulations that the bodies authorised to provide the services under s. 78 to establish a scheme for the investigation of complaints about the provision of those services.

As already indicated, it had originally been proposed that the Minister for Justice would be empowered to make Regulations authorising banks and wholly owned subsidiaries of insurance companies to provide conveyancing services. These proposed provisions were similar to those in s. 31 the Building Societies Act 1989, which enabled building societies to provide conveyancing services to the public. However, this proposal was not proceeded with.

Laying of Regulations before the Oireachtas S. 82 of the 1994 Act requires that, save where otherwise provided in the 1994 Act, the Law Society must lay Regulations made by it under the Act before each House of the Oireachtas as soon as may be after they have been made.

NEGLIGENCE

Cases involving solicitors' liability in negligence are discussed in the Torts chapter, 456, below.

PRACTICE AND PROCEDURE

The circumstances in which a solicitor may come off record are discussed in *Ó Fearail v McManus* [1994] 2 ILRM 81, see the Practice and Procedure chapter, 386-7, above.

REGULATIONS

In addition to the highly significant 1994 Act, the following Regulations were promulgated in 1994.

Practising certificates   The Solicitors Acts 1954 and 1960 (Fees) Regulations 1994 (SI No. 1 of 1994) prescribed revised fees for obtaining practising certificates. The Solicitors (Practising Certificate 1995/96) Regulations 1994 (SI No. 436 of 1994) prescribed the arrangements for obtaining practising certificates for the period January 1995 to January 1996, including the relevant fees.

Sport and the Law

In *Clancy v Irish Rugby Football Union* [1995] 1 ILRM 193, Morris J considered a number of important issues in a situation where a rugby player had been precluded from playing for new club for a specified. For a comprehensive discussion of the case, see Paul McCutcheon's article, 'Judicial Scrutiny of Sports Administration' (1995) 13 *ILT* 171.

The plaintiff had represented Ireland as a member of the Irish international rugby team on nine occasions between 1987 and 1989. During the 1993-94 rugby season he had played in six matches prior to the end of February 1994 in the Insurance Corporation of Ireland All-Ireland League for the De La Salle/Palmerston Rugby Club. He then transferred to Blackrock College Rugby Football Club for the 1994-95 season. Pursuant to regulation 7 of the Irish Rugby Football Union (IRFU) Regulations introduced for the year 1994-95, the plaintiff was precluded from playing for Blackrock College RFC until after December 31, 1994 because he had played in three or more league matches in the 1993-94 season for another club. The result of this was that the plaintiff would miss an opportunity to be a substitute for the next match in the league and an opportunity to be picked as a member of the team for the last remaining match in the league. The plaintiff felt that it was essential for him to play in the league matches to be considered as a member of the Irish rugby team for the (then imminent) 1994 Rugby World Cup.

An application was made on behalf of the plaintiff to the IRFU under regulation 7(c), which provides that 'any player or club wishing to appeal for special circumstances on registration must do so in writing to the IRFU who will consider each case on its merits'. A reply was received at the end of August 1994 refusing to lift the bar. That decision had been made by a two-member sub-committee. A second application was made by Blackrock College RFC. At a meeting in September 1994, the IRFU 'declined to alter the earlier decision' and by letter wrote saying the IRFU 'confirmed the decision' on the plaintiff's ineligibility. The plaintiff then applied to the High Court seeking, *inter alia*, an order removing the prohibition against his playing in the league on the basis of its retrospective effect, a declaration that he should be eligible for participation in the league matches, and an order requiring the reconsideration of the application made on his behalf under regulation 7(c). Morris J granted the relief sought.

Morris J began his discussion of the issues raised in the case by stating that it was not open to the plaintiff to blame the prohibition against his playing for his new club solely upon retrospective regulations: he had chosen to transfer clubs when he knew the likelihood that under regulation 7 he would be ruled out of selection until after December 31, 1994. As a result, he was not in the position of being prejudiced by retrospective legislation through no fault of his own. Therefore the regulations were not of retrospective effect to the plaintiff, nor were they an improper or unlawful interference with his right to freedom of association. However, even if the regulations were retrospective, Morris J noted that regulation 7 contained a provision for an appeal procedure to the IRFU who would be obliged to deal with such appeals on their merits and, in a proper case, to remove the prohibition against playing, thereby altering the complexion of a rule which might otherwise be unduly and improperly harsh.

Furthermore, applying the principles in *Chestvale Properties Ltd v Glackin* [1993] 3 IR 35 (1992 Review, 68-73), he held that as regards the degree to which the plaintiff's rights were encroached upon by the regulation, the possibility of his being chosen as a substitute and then as a team member was minimal. He thus concluded that regulation 7 was fully justifiable as a means of reconciling the exercise of the individual's rights with the exigencies of the common good.

However, the plaintiff was more successful when it came to the application of regulation 7(c), which Morris J noted was intended to provide for circumstances where a player who would in the ordinary course be barred until after 31 December might make an application to the IRFU to have that bar removed. As he had already pointed out, Morris J stated that the IRFU was required to consider such an application on its merits and rule upon it. In the instant case, the first decision on the application made on behalf of the plaintiff was made not by the IRFU but by a two-person sub-committee. Since there was no provision for such a committee to decide on an application under regulation 7(c), so that the IRFU in full had to consider each case on its merits, the decision of the two-person committee was not a valid determination of the application made to the IRFU on behalf of the plaintiff.

As to the second application which came before the IRFU in September 1994, Morris J concluded that this too required fair procedures. Thus, the IRFU should have considered the application *de novo* and not on the basis of approving or disapproving of the decision of the two-person sub-committee to which the matter should not have been delegated in the first place.

In those circumstances, he granted an injunction requiring the IRFU to consider, on their merits, the plaintiff's special circumstances for registering with Blackrock College RFC, such consideration to include consideration of submissions made by or on behalf of the plaintiff. He added that, as the IRFU had failed to comply with their obligations under regulation 7(c), a proper determination of the application should be made without delay and that any delay would reflect on the quantum of damages that might be awarded in the future. However, of some interest is that Morris J opined that, in reconsidering the matter, the IRFU would be under no obligation to give reasons for any decisions which they might make. In this context, Morris J expressly followed the approach in *Rajah v Royal College of Surgeons in Ireland* [1994] 1 IR 384 (1993 Review, 17-18) to the effect that the giving of reasons is not an indispensable element of fair procedures. In his article referred to above, Paul McCutcheon noted that a hearing was held within a matter of days after the judgment of Morris J in the case, but the plaintiff was unsuccessful in having his ban lifted and remained ineligible to play for his new club until the beginning of 1995: see (1995) 13 *ILT* 171, at 175.

Statutory Interpretation

Duplicity of charges In *O'B. v Pattwell* [1994] 2 ILRM 465, the Supreme Court upheld a decision of the O'Hanlon J [1993] ILRM 614 to the effect that no duplicity of charges within the meaning of s. 14 of the Interpretation Act 1937 was involved where a person is charged with both common law rape and unlawful carnal knowledge of girl under 15 years of age: see the Criminal Law chapter, 206-8, above.

Repeal not affecting existing rights In *J. Wood & Co. Ltd v Wicklow County Council* [1995] 1 ILRM 51, Costello J considered s. 21(1)(c) of the Interpretation Act 1937, which provides that the repeal of a statute shall not affect any right acquired under the repealed provision unless there appears to be a contrary intention: see the Local Government chapter, 350-1, above.

Strict construction: extradition In *Aamand v Smithwick and Attorney General* [1995] 1 ILRM 612, discussed in the Criminal Law chapter, 184-6, above, the Supreme Court held that the Extradition Act 1965, being a statute that affected people's rights, must be strictly construed.

Teleological approach In *Bosphorus Hava Yollari Turizm Ve Ticaret Anonim Sirketi v Minister for Transport, Energy and Communications and Ors* [1994] 2 ILRM 551 (discussed in the Commercial Law chapter, 42-4, above), Murphy J considered the application of the teleological approach to interpretation in the context of the European Communities (Prohibition of Trade with the Federal Republic of Yugoslavia (Serbia and Montenegro)) Regulations 1993.

Torts

DAMAGES

Collateral Benefits In *O'Sullivan v Iarnród Éireann — Irish Rail*, High Court, 14 March 1994, where the plaintiff had received serious personal injuries to his back, the defendant submitted that deductions fell to be made under s. 75(1) of the Social Welfare (Consolidation) Act 1993, which requires that, in the assessment of damages, account is to be taken, against any loss or damage, of 'the value of any rights which have accrued or will probably accrue to [the plaintiff] therefrom in respect of injury benefit . . . or disablement benefit . . . for the five years beginning with the time when the cause of action accrued'. See further McMahon & Binchy, *op cit.*, 795. Counsel for the plaintiff argued that there was no evidence before the court as to what might happen to disablement benefit into the future, on the conclusion of the litigation, and therefore the most that should be taken into account was the amount of the benefits that had accrued to date. Morris J rejected this approach. He noted that the plaintiff was then in receipt of disablement benefits and had been so since his occupational injury benefit had run out four years previously. He was not aware of an indication of any intention of the part of the Department of Social Welfare to alter this status. During the course of the evidence, reference had been made to the rule of the Department as to the plaintiff's disability and incapacity for work. In Morris J's view, the onus, in the circumstances of the case, lay on the plaintiff to show that there was in the Department's contemplation an intention to alter the *status quo*.

Pain and suffering In *Furlong v Waterford Co-operative Society Ltd* [1995] 1 ILRM 148 Budd J awarded £60,000 damages, for pain and suffering in relation to a plaintiff whom a medical witness on behalf of the defendant characterised as that 'rare bird, the true maliingerer' but whose evidence Budd J nonetheless believed. The Supreme Court dismissed the defendant's appeal: *id.*, at 157ff.

In an *ex tempore judgment*, with which Egan and Blayney JJ concurred, O'Flaherty J considered it 'understandable' that he plaintiff should not want to face an operation in regard to his thigh injuries since, on a previous occasion, after the anaesthetic had been administered, his blood pressure had dropped and the operation had had to be abandoned because of fear that he might not survive it. O'Flaherty J regarded the award, while it might be 'at the very extremity of the higher end of the scale', as still being within that scale.

Unlawful arrest Below, we discuss *Walsh v Ireland and the Attorney General*, Supreme Court, November 30, 1994, where the Supreme Court upheld the imposition of liability on the State for unlawful arrest. The plaintiff had claimed damages for breach of his constitutional rights, unlawful arrest, false imprisonment and negligence. By the time the case was going to the jury, Lavan J had held that the arrest was unlawful. Hamilton CJ's judgment does not make it clear what was the precise status of the other claims. Certainly the claim for breach of constitutional rights was still active. No further mention was made of the claims for false imprisonment and negligence. At all events the jury appears to have been asked merely to assess damages as a single sum of money, so far as general damages were concerned.

The jury awarded the plaintiff £50,000. The Supreme Court reduced this to £25,000. Hamilton CJ (Egan, Blayney, Denham and Carroll JJ concurring) acknowledged that the case was one of mistaken identity and that the members of the Garda Síochána had at all times behaved in a courteous and considerate manner. The Gardaí had, however, been 'rather dilatory' in clearing up the matter. Moreover, there had been a clear breach of the plaintiff's constitutional right to liberty; he had been obliged to delay the start of his holidays so that he could appear in the District Court in accordance with his recognisance and his wife and niece had to travel abroad on their own. He had been subjected to the worry and concern caused by his arrest and court appearances and was 'entitled to substantial damages in respect of such breach of his constitutional right to liberty and to his good name'. (There is no mention in the judgment of a claim for defamation, but perhaps the claim for breach of constitutional rights could be considered to embrace the plaintiff's right to a good name.)

Taking all the factors into account, the Chief Justice considered that the award of £50,000 was so excessive as to justify intervention. Since it would not be in the interests of the parties to refer the case back to the High Court, the sum of £25,000 was sustituted.

Exemplary damages There is still confusion about exemplary damages, in spite of several recent Supreme Court decisions. In *Walsh v Ireland and the Attorney General*, Supreme Court, November 30, 1994, which we have discussed above, the jury was invited to assess damages under three headings: general, punitive and expemplary. As matters transpired, the jury made an award under the first heading only, the plaintiff did not appeal against this and Hamilton CJ offered the view, on appeal, that '[t]his [was] not a case for the award of punitive or exemplary damages'. He gave no indication that he saw anything wrong with a threefold category.

This is unfortunate. The distinction between punitive and exemplary damages defies discription. Certainly, the Supreme Court has never undertaken the task. There is no way that a trial judge, in the light of the complete confusion on the issue at appellate level, could guide a group of lay persons as to the law on the matter. In truth, there is no distinction between exemplary and punitive damages. Other courts throughout the common law world are aware of this fact. Our judges have allowed themselves to be confused by the inclusion in the Civil Liability Act 1961 of the two terms in separate sections. We have sought to trace the explanation for this differentation in drafting and a convincing explanation seems to present itself: see the 1991 Review, 448-53.

DEFAMATION

In *Nolan Transport (Oaklands) Ltd v Halligan* [1995] ELR 1, Barron J held that the defendant union had defamed the plaintiff in publishing allegations as to the plaintiff's work practices that held the plaintiff up to the hatred and contempt of right-minded people. The union had not been justified in alleging that violence had been used against picketers and had been unfair in its comments about certain sackings and alleged victimisations.

DUTY OF CARE

In *Downey v O'Brien*, High Court, April 12, 1994, which we examine in detail in the Local Government Chapter, above, 339-42, Costello J analysed the meaning of s. 20 of the Local Government (Ireland) Act 1902, under which a charge had been levied by a local government auditor against the appellant, the Chairman of the Waterford Harbour Commissioners, for loss incurred by his negligence in the sale of the Commissioners' shares. Costello J, following the lead of the English decision of *Pentecost v London District Auditor* [1951] 2 KB 759, considered that:

> negligence which gives rise to a charge under the section does not involve any element of moral culpability or gross negligence and . . . the ordinary principles of the law of negligence apply when a claim under the section against a member of a local authority is made. This means that the auditor was, and now this Court is, required to consider

whether the . . . appellant . . . owed a duty of care to the Harbour Commissioners, the nature of that duty (if it existed) and whether the Harbour Commissioners thereby suffered loss.

It had not been suggested that the appellant had owed no duty of care when negotiating the sale of the Commissioners' shares. Costello J thought it 'perfectly clear that he did so.'

One may perhaps doubt the wisdom of incorporating into this statutory provision the elaborate and uncertain jurisprudence of the common law doctrine of the duty of care. Cf. Mahon & Binchy, *op. cit.*, chapter 6. S. 20 was enacted long before Lord Atkin in *Donoghue v Stevenson* [1932] AC 562, at 580 sowed together the disparate strands of negligence to create the generic concept of a duty of care. What s. 20 probably envisaged was carelessness, pure and simple; the requirements of neighbourhood, proximity and policy could not have entered the minds of the legislators at the turn of the century.

EMPLOYERS' LIABILITY

Safe System of Work To what extent may an employer rely on an employee to go to some lengths to ensure his or her own safety? Lord Oaksey's answer in *General Cleaning Contractors v Christmas* [1952] AC 737, has a freshness even today:

In my opinion, it is the duty of an employer to give such general safety instructions as a reasonably careful employer who has considered the problem presented by the work would give to his workmen. It is, I think, well known to employers, and there is evidence in this case that it was well known to the appellants, that their work people are very frequently, if not habitually, careless about the risks which their work may involve. It is, in my opinion, for that very reason that the common law demands that employers should take reasonable care to lay down a reasonably safe system of work. Employers are not exempted from this duty by the fact that their men are experienced and might, if they were in the position of an employer, be able to lay down a reasonably safe system of work themselves. Workmen are not in the position of employers. Their duties are not performed in the calm atmosphere of a board room with the advice of experts. They have to make their decisions on narrow window sills and other places of danger and in circumstances in which the dangers are obscured by repetition.

In *Hanratty v Drogheda Web Offset Printers Ltd*, Supreme Court, June 2, 1994 (*ex tempore*) Finlay CJ quoted this passage and adopted it as representing the law here. The plaintiff, a master printer employed by the defendant for about twenty years in its printing works in Ireland, went to Greece to teach the employees of a Greek company how to use a major piece of printing machinery that the defendant had sold to the Greek company. The plaintiff had worked with that machine for many years previously.

The plaintiff was injured when he fell from the machine as he was descending from it, having carried out an adjustment to the webbing. The essence of his claim was that the whole method of getting up on, and climbing down from, the machine was unsafe and that a platform or steps ought to have been provided. Whilst he had space to jump from the machine onto an open floor in the defendant's own premises in Ireland, there was no similar space in the Greek premises as there was a plate glass window in his way. Even the system in Ireland had not been satisfactory: there had been a number of 'near misses' there, two of which were known to the management. An engineer gave evidence in relation to a virtually identical machine that was unsafe in that there were very significant potential hazards 'in working somewhat over the head and trying to stand on a narrow ledge. . . .'

The trial judge dismissed the case on the basis that the defendant was entitled to rely on the Greek company to look after the plaintiff and on the plaintiff to look after his own welfare by reporting to the defendant the different conditions that prevailed in Greece. The Supreme Court reversed Finlay CJ (Egan and Blayney JJ concurring) considered that there was 'a continuing obligation positively to take reasonable steps' for the plaintiff's safety, which had not been discharged or terminated by the relocation of the machine in Greece. The issues of the plaintiff's contributory negligence and the possible liability in negligence of the Greek company were remitted to the High Court's rehearing.

In *O'Sullivan v Iarnród Éireann – Irish Rail*, High Court, March 14, 1994, Morris J imposed liability on the defendant employer where the plaintiff, a plate-layer, fell when carrying a heavy sleeper for storage, in a station yard full of scrap metal and wire that had been left lying on the ground. This breached the defendants' obligation to take reasonable care to provide its employee with a safe place and safe system of work.

Employee's obligation of due care   Courts set a high standard of care in employers' liability litigation but eventually the point is reached where they deny a claim on the basis that the employer has done sufficient in the discharge of his or her duty to relieve him or her of liability, essentially because the accident is attributable exclusively to the plaintiff's failure to take care. The dividing line between characterising the plaintiff's lack of care as totally causative of his or her injuries or as merely contributory negligence can be a narrow one. It reduces itself to a consideration of what a reasonable employer can assume the employee will do in self-protection and in obedience to the employer's directions.

In *O'Mahony v John Sisk & Son Ltd*, High Court, December 16, 1994, the plaintiff, a labourer employed by the defendant, was injured when he fell from a ladder while using a kanga hammer. He claimed that the defendant had been negligent in allowing him to carry out his work in this way rather than on a scaffold. The defendant accepted that a scaffold should have been used but contended that the plaintiff had failed to avail himself of one that was accessible and that he had been instructed to use. He had actually used it the previous evening.

Barron J held that the defendant was not liable in negligence. Although the plaintiff had been left to carry out the work on his own, the foreman had no reason to anticipate that he would not do what he had been told to do. *Ginty v Belmont Building Supplies Ltd* [1959] 1 All ER 414 supported the holding; this was another case where the employee had acted contrary to instructions as to his safety.

INFRINGEMENT OF CONSTITUTIONAL RIGHT

In *Parsons v Kavanagh* [1990] ILRM 560, O'Hanlon J held that it was proper to grant an injunction in order to protect the plaintiff's constitutional right to earn his living from violation by criminal breach of a statutory provision. What was striking about the case was the fact that the plaintiff would not have been entitled to sue for damages in tort for breach of statutory duty because the statutory provision had not been enacted with the view to providing him with civil remedy of damages.

That case involved a claim by one bus coach service provider against another where the other was providing a service without the requisite licence, in breach of provisions of the Road Transport Act 1932. A somewhat similar situation arose in *Lovett t/a Lovett Transport v Gogan t/a P.S. Travel*, Supreme Court, 11 May 1994. In the High Court, on March 18, 1993, Costello J had granted an injunction in favour of the plaintiff. The Supreme Court affirmed.

Finlay CJ (Egan and Denham JJ concurring) considered that *Parsons v Kavanagh* had been correctly decided. He rejected the defendants' contention that the plaintiff should be obliged to frame his proceedings within one of the common law actions such as breach of contract, inducing a breach of contract or conspiracy. Walsh J's judgment in *Meskell v Coras Iompair Éireann* [1973] IR 121 at 132 provided the answer to such a suggestion. The plaintiff was entitled to the injunction if he could establish that it was 'the only way of protecting him from the threatened invasion of his constitutional rights.' Having regard to the statutory limitations on the fine that might be imposed on a person running a road passenger service without a licence and in particular the minimal figure of £5 in respect of a continued offence, there was, in the Chief Justice's view, no doubt that, if the plaintiff was entitled to an injunction, it was the only remedy that could protect him.

The defendants sought to argue that, since the plaintiff had been in breach of the licence under which he operated his road passenger service, an injunction should not be granted. Finlay CJ was:

> not satisfied that the right of the plaintiff to an injunction . . . deriving . . . from an invasion and threatened continued invasion of his constitutional rights must be approached in the same manner as may generally apply to the discretion of a court to grant the equitable relief of injunction and the doctrine that a plaintiff seeking that must come to the court with clean hands. Where the court is . . . prepared to grant to a plaintiff an injunction in order to protect his constitutional right, the enquiry must rather be as to whether he has got a constitutional right and whether it is that right which is being threatened.

Having regard to that consideration, the test in the case should be whether the plaintiff's conduct and any established breaches by him of one or more conditions of his licence under the Act of 1932 transformed his conduct in operating the road passenger service into the category of an unlawful method of earning his living. Quite clearly there could be no constitutional right to earn one's living by an unlawful method and therefore no right to earn a living in that manner could ever be protected. Looked at from that view it seemed to the Chief Justice quite clear that the evidence with regard to individual breaches of individual conditions in the licence fell 'far short indeed' of establishing the plaintiff was not a person who in the running of the passenger service way earning this living by lawful means. The Supreme Court therefore dismissed the appeal.

One may wonder whether this reluctance to confront the possibility of an injection of equity into the jurisprudence relating to infringement of constitutional rights is wise. The Chief Justice's alternative solution offers courts in future cases an unsophisticated linguistic cloak rather than a sensitive yardstick.

NEGLIGENT MISSTATEMENT

In *Donnellan v Dungoyne Ltd* [1995] 1 ILRM 388, the plaintiffs took a lease of a shoe retailing shop in the defendant's new shopping centre after the defendant's selling agent had represented that most of the remaining units would be let within a short time. This was not the case. Subsequently the plaintiff's business failed. They sought, *inter alia*, rescission of the lease, damages for negligent misrepresentation. They succeeded in both claims in the Circuit Court, the damages award being for £320,000.

On appeal, O'Hanlon J awarded £12,000 and declined to order rescission. In a detailed judgment, he reviewed the commercial realities of the development of shopping centres. He concluded from the evidence that, if the misrepresentation had not been made, the plaintiffs would still have been prepared to go ahead with the lease, but would in all probability have held out for greater inducements than the five-month rent-free period which they had actually achieved. On that basis he considered that a case had not been made out for rescission of the lease, but merely for damages for breach of warranty, and negligent misrepresentation, as happened in the case of *Esso Petroleum Co. Ltd v Mardon* [1976] QB 801, and *McAnarney v Hanrahan* [1993] 3IR 492; [1994] 1 ILRM 210. See the 1993 Review, 547, O'Hanlon J considered that a further seven months' rent would adequately compensate the plaintiffs. The failure to their business was attributable only in part to the misrepresentation; other factors such as the youth and inexperience of one of the plaintiff's, 'a certain lack of effort' on his part, and a major down-turn in the shoe retailing business had also contributed to it.

OCCUPIER'S LIABILITY

In *O'Toole v Dublin Corporation*, High Court, February 18, 1994, a seven year old boy, living with his family in the defendant's flat complex, was injured when scaling a wall seven feet nine inches high around a playground in the flat complex. The playground contained a football pitch. A game was in progress and the ball had gone over the wall. The plaintiff was seeking to retrieve the ball which had landed in an enclosed area, access to which required unlocking a door. The area was enclosed for security reasons to prevent the area from providing an easy escape root for thieves, especially handbag snatchers. The key was in the possession of the defendant's employees.

The plaintiff's case was essentially one of the occupier's liability. He invoked the Supreme Court decision of *Foley v Musgrave Cash & Carry Ltd*, December 20, 1985 (extracted in McMahon & Binchy's *Casebook on the*

Irish Law of Torts (2nd ed., 1991), p. 164), where the Court showed a willingness to extend to all entrants the negligence criterion, first recognised in *Purtill v Athlone UDC* [1968] IR 205 and *McNamara v Electricity Supply Board* [1975] IR 1 in relation to *trespassers*. The plaintiff contended that the defendant had been negligent in attaching a metal pole to mesh wire fencing near the wall, which was accessible to young children such as the plaintiff. Lynch J noted that counsel for the defendant had not contested the application of *Foley*, so that there was no need to consider whether the plaintiff was an invitee or licensee. The test to be applied, therefore, was whether the defendant had taken reasonable care for the safety of the plaintiff in all the circumstances of the case.

Lynch J rejected the plaintiff's case. The premises were in good order; the pole did not amount to an allurement or trap; nor would it be reasonable to expect the defendant 'to create a prison-like area' by enclosing the whole play area in a high mesh wire fence The only basis on which the defendant could be liable was if it had been asked by the organisers of the football game to provide a key to give access to the amenity area and it had refused. This had not been the case. If the organisers had considered such a strategy too onerous, they should have helped a couple of youngsters over the fence to stay in the amenity area to retrieve balls, so as to avoid the danger of such a young child as the plaintiff trying to retrieve the ball ahead of other boys.

One can only speculate as to how this case would have been decided under the Occupiers' Liability Act 1995. Two crucial questions would be whether the plaintiff was a 'recreational user' and whether there was any damage arising from the state of the premises.

MALICIOUS FALSEHOOD

In *Nolan Transport (Oaklands) Ltd v Halligan* [1995] ELR 1, Barron J held that the defendant union had been guilty of malicious falsehood where, in an ongoing strike, it had claimed falsely that the strike was having a greater economic impact on the employer than it was in fact.

PASSING OFF

In the Chapter on Equitable Remedies, above, 242, Hilary Delany discusses in *An Post v The Irish Permanent plc*, High Court, November 18, 1994, where Kinlen J granted an interlocutory injunction against the use by the defendant of the phrase 'Savings Certificates' to describe its system of investment bonds. The essential question was whether the plaintiff could establish that it had such a strong association in the public mind with the phrase used to describe its investment bond system, that the adoption of the same phrase, albeit precedent by the distinguishing phrase 'Irish Permanent', would be likely to confuse some would-be purchasers into believing that the defendant's system was the plaintiff's.

Recognising that the plaintiff had only to establish a *prima facie* case, Kinlen J was of the view that it had done this. He referred to several English dictionaries in which the phrase was said to connote a Governmental dimension.

Perhaps it can be argued that, while it is undoubtedly the case that the public, in Britain and in Ireland, should make an association between the phrase 'savings certificates' and the Government for as long as the Government remained the sole provider of savings certificates, that association would not necessarily continue if some other agency became a provider. The crucial question was not how the public understood the phrase during the period of Governmental monopoly but rather how it understood, and was likely in the future to understand, that phrase once that monopoly was broken. In this context, the use by the defendant of the identification 'Irish Permanent' in conjunction with the phrase 'savings certificates' may, or may not have been sufficient to remove the inevitable initial potential confusion resulting from the inevitable association with the Government (and An Post as its successor) during the period of monopoly.

PRODUCT LIABILITY

In *Ryan v Dan Dooley Rent a Car, Topcar Ltd and Rover (Ireland) Ltd*, High Court, May 19, 1994 (Circuit Appeal) the plaintiff had bought a car from the first defendant which had been obtained from the second defendant, the Munster main dealers for Rover cars, who were the third defendants. The vehicle turned out to have a number of problems, notably its propensity to cut out periodically.

Affirming the Circuit Court decision in favour of the plaintiff, Kinlen J was satisfied from the evidence of three different people who had driven the car that the problem regarding cutting out indicated that the vehicle was defective in design, manufacture or assembly. It could 'not be just a defective driver'. He held that the first defendant was liable in contract and the second and third defendants were liable in negligence. The fact that the third defendants had sent out bulletins to their dealers alerting them of the problem was significant in establishing the existence of the problem and of their knowledge of it. These defendants had also been negligent in failing to inform the plaintiff of the problem and in not informing the second defendant after they had eliminated the problem. The second defendant was negligent in failing to enquire from the third defendants what was the cure for the problem and in failing to have absorbed the relevance of the information it received in the third defendant's bulletin. It had thus failed to inform itself fully of the problem and its eradication. Kinlen J held, that, as between the second and third defendants, the liability should be apportioned on the basis that the second defendant was one-third responsible and the third defendants two-thirds.

PROFESSIONAL NEGLIGENCE

Medical Negligence

Medical Examination   In *Goonan v Dooley*, High Court, March 23, 1994, the plaintiff, who was born in 1977, was found in 1979 to have a very seriously dislocated left hip. She sued the hospital where she was born, arguing that those who treated her at that time should have discovered the condition. Had they done so, she claimed, the condition could have been ameliorated to a significant degree. The essential issue was whether in fact there had been a congenital condition capable of being identified at the time of the birth.

Lynch J concluded on the evidence that there had not. The plaintiff had been given the Ortolani Barlo examination, a standard test as to whether there was abnormality in her hips at the time of her birth, by two junior house doctors and a public health nurse. The public health nurse had given the examination again some weeks afterwards.

Lynch J observed that one could readily accept as a reasonable probability that a medical examiner might slip up and culpably failed to diagnose a present and ascertainable dislocation of the hip but this did 'not so readily follow as a probability' when three separate medical persons had examined the plaintiff on four occasions within two months of her birth and concluded that there was no abnormality. The evidence of one of the medical experts in the case was to the effect that the Ortolani Barlo examination was not a very sensitive test and would not show up abnormalities in 20% to 30% of cases that emerged later. Two experts were of the view that the condition might not be congenital but might develop later.

Lynch J acquitted the defendants of negligence in failing to detect the abnormality in the plaintiff's hips. He was, moreover, of the view that the abnormality was probably not present in the first few months following birth and had developed later.

Treatment   In *Edwards v Southern Health Board*, Supreme Court, July 26, 1994, the Supreme Court affirmed O'Hanlon J's dismissal, on January 20, 1989, of proceedings for negligence based on the claim that the defendants had failed to provide the correct treatment for a post-operative infection. The essence of the plaintiff's case was that, with proper treatment, the infection would have been cured earlier.

O'Hanlon J, applying the principles laid down by Walsh J in *O'Donovan v Cork County Council* [1967] IR 173, held that the conservative treatment adopted by the defendants, in providing antibiotics and draining the wound had the support of a substantial body of medical practitioners and did not have inherent defects which ought to have been obvious to any medical practitioner caring for the plaintiff at the time. Accordingly he dismissed the proceedings.

The Supreme Court affirmed. Finlay CJ (Egan and Denham JJ concurring) rejected specific legal inferences which the plaintiff proposed should be drawn from the evidence.

Informed Consent   In the 1992 Review, 558-68, we analysed the troublesome decision of *Walsh v Family Planning Services Ltd* [1992] 1 IR 496, where the Supreme Court was divided on the proper test to apply to the question of informed consent for medical treatment. Finlay CJ and McCarthy J, and perhaps Egan J too, favoured an embodiment of the test adopted in *Dunne v National Maternity Hospital* [1989] IR 91 in respect of medical treatment generally, to the effect that, whilst compliance with customary practice would normally discharge a medical practitioner's duty of care to patients, liability would attach to practices which, although customary, were obviously wanting in care. In the context of the disclosure issue, the question became one of whether in the circumstances, in spite of a customary practice of non-disclosure, disclosure should obviously have been made. The other two judges in the case, O'Flaherty J, with Hederman J concurring, specifically rejected the idea that the court should even tentatively defer to medical practice in this area. The test they preferred was essentially an unqualified one of whether disclosure of material risks had been made. For comprehensive analysis of the *Walsh* decision, see Tomkin and Hanafin, *Irish Medical Law* (1994), 68-77, Healy (1995) 12 *ILT* 196, Symmons (1994) 10 *Professional Negligence* 134 and Donnelly (1995) 2 *Medico-Legal J of Ireland* 3.

The matter arose in *Farrell v Varian*, High Court, September 19, 1994. The plaintiff had consulted the defendant, a specialist in hand surgery, in relation to a condition of bilateral Dupuytren's contracture affecting both hands. It was agreed to operate first on the right hand. The operation was not successful. A rare progressive and incapacitating condition developed, known as reflex sympathetic dystrophy syndrome; this affected, not only the plaintiff's hand, but also his arm and shoulder. His hand was contracted, discoloured and covered with scaly skin; he was in constant serious pain and, he said in evidence, he had lost his employment as a result of the condition.

O'Hanlon J rejected the plaintiff's claim for professional negligence in the defendant's post-operative treatment of the plaintiff. After an extensive review of the evidence, taking well over forty pages, O'Hanlon J was satisfied that, on crucial issues of fact, the defendant's evidence was more reliable.

The plaintiff's other claim was that the defendant had failed to give him sufficient information as to the risks involved in the operation to enable him to make an informed decision whether he wished to undergo it. O'Hanlon J rejected this also. He accepted the defendant's evidence that he had an invariable practice to explain briefly to the patient the nature of Dupuytren's contracture, to convey the information that the appropriate treatment to alleviate the condition was by surgery, to explain that the cause of the condition was unknown and that the condition tended to recur in a significant number of cases after surgery and to stress that no guarantee could be given of full correction of the contracture, particularly where the proximal inter-phalangeal joint was involved.

In O'Hanlon J's opinion, this represented an adequate warning of what the operation involved so as to enable the plaintiff to make an informed decision on the matter. The plaintiff said in evidence that, had he known of the risks involved, he would not have undergone the operation, but O'Hanlon J believed he was making this assertion with hindsight, influenced by the terrible misfortune that had befallen him in the aftermath of the operative treatment. In view of his earlier medical history, before he had consulted the defendant, he already had first-hand knowledge that it was not possible to guarantee the lasting success of the treatment by operation and that the condition was liable to recur.

As regards the nature and extent of the warning which should be given to a patient contemplating an operation, O'Hanlon J was of opinion that:

> the doctor's obligation does not extend to enumerating all the possible risks, however remote, which are involved. Such a procedure could only subject many patients to unnecessary fears and worries, and possibly have the effect of deterring many patients from submitting to treatment which it was obviously in their best interests to undergo.

If there was some significant danger of serious consequence the patient would have an entitlement to be warned of it. O'Hanlon J noted that in *Sidaway v Bethlem Royal Hospital* [1985] AC 871, it had been suggested, by way of example that, if there was an operation involving a substantial risk of grave adverse consequences, such as a ten *per cent* risk of a stroke, a judge would be entitled to conclude that, in the absence of some cogent clinical reason why the patient should not be informed, a doctor could hardly fail to appreciate the necessity for an appropriate warning.

All the expert evidence in the present case was to the effect that the onset of reflex sympathetic dystrophy was a rare phenomenon. The plaintiff's case had been described by all the doctors as the worst they had ever seen; the general incidence of the condition in a severe form had been put at lower than one *per cent* of cases arising from operative treatment. O'Hanlon J observed that:

> in view of the extremely small number of actual cases seen by these medical gentlemen of great experience in their field, their evidence would suggest a much smaller incidence than one *per cent*.

There appeared also to be an incidence 'of a much less serious character', which cleared up within a relatively short period, even without remedial treatment, in a significantly larger number of cases.

In a crucial passage, O'Hanlon J said that he agreed with:

> the view expressed by the House of Lords in the *Sidaway* case that 'the decision what degree of disclosure of risks is best calculated to assist a particular patient to make a rational choice as to whether or not to undergo a particular treatment must primarily be a matter of clinical judgment', although, as also observed by their Lordships, a case might arise where a judge could conclude that disclosure of a particular risk was so obviously necessary to an informed choice on the part of the patient that no reasonably prudent medical man would fail to make it.

O'Hanlon J was satisfied that the warning given by the defendant in the instant case had been 'adequate in all the circumstances to meet his obligation in this respect.'

O'Hanlon J's approach merits two observations. *First*, the failure to mention the Supreme Court judgment in *Walsh v Family Planning Services* [1992] 1 IR 496 is striking. The list of authorities included as an appendix to the judgment makes it plain that the case was cited by counsel. Why should it not have been considered worthy of discussion, especially since the High Court is bound by the Supreme Court precedent? Perhaps the answer is that O'Hanlon J regarded the divisions among the Judges in *Walsh* as so great as to neutralise the decision's precedential influence.

Secondly, O'Hanlon J's discussion of *Sidaway* gives little impression of the internal divisions in that case. It seems that O'Hanlon J preferred the approach favoured by Lord Bridge but he has no word of criticism for the competing approaches of Lords Diplock, Scarman and Bridge.

The issue of informed consent arose again in two months in *Bolton v Blackrock Clinic Ltd*, High Court, December 20, 1994. The plaintiff, who had undergone bronchial and lung surgery on two occasions, with permanent distressing and incapacitating *sequelae*, sought to impugn the treatment she had been given by her cardiac physician and her cardio-thoracic surgeon. Part of her case was that the cardio-thoracic surgeon had failed to obtain her informed consent to a sleeve resection of her left main bronchus.

Geoghegan J dismissed the plaintiff's claim against both specialists. On the specific issue of the consent to the sleeve resection, he accepted that the surgeon had 'told [the plaintiff] that there would be a 1% risk of death but that in reality chances of survival were better than 99%'.

He had explained to her where the narrowing of the bronchus was and warned her that if no surgery was carried out it could get slowly worse, affecting the function of her left lung and her whole lung could become destroyed ultimately. He had advised that sleeve resection was the most appropriate procedure, particularly having regard to her cardiac condition. He had told the plaintiff he would remove the cylinder of the left main bronchus and join the root of the lung back up to the origin of the left main bronchus. He had further told her that the success rate was 95% but that there was a 5% risk of restenosis. The plaintiff had apparently been somewhat alarmed by this and wondered why he would not do a full pneumonectomy. With the help of diagrams the surgeon had explained to her that sleeve resection was more appropriate. He had advised her of wound pain.

Geoghegan J stated that he had 'noted the view' of O'Flaherty J in *Walsh v Family Planning Services Ltd*, with which Hederman J had concurred. He applied this test to the facts of the case and concluded that the information imparted had been 'adequate' and that it had represented a reasonable exercise of care on the part of the surgeon. He also held that the consultant thoracic physician had not been in any way negligent in this communication with the plaintiff who had 'quite clearly' given an informed consent to both operations.

Geoghegan J made no reference to the other approaches in *Walsh*, which were quite opposed to that favoured by O'Flaherty and Hederman JJ. Nor did he discuss O'Hanlon J's judgment in *Farrell v Varian*. It seems clear that the plaintiff would have fared no better if the other approaches in *Walsh* had been applied to the facts of the case.

A third case, decided earlier in 1994, is *O'Keeffe v Cody*, High Court, March 11, 1994, also raised the issue of consent. In this case Lynch J dismissed the plaintiff's action for negligence in relation to the administration of an epidural injection when she was giving birth. The plaintiff claimed that this had damaged her spinal cord, causing her an incomplete paralysis. Lynch J, on the evidence, concluded that the plaintiff was in fact suffering from multiple sclerosis, even before the time of this injection. He also addressed the issue of informed consent, which was clearly moot, in view of his holding as to the nature of the plaintiff's medical condition. He held that the consultant anaesthetist, before administering the injection, had warned the plaintiff of its possible side effects. That warning 'was the customary [one] given by anaesthetists and was adequate and proper in the absence of any inquiry as to the possibility of other adverse effects'. The anaesthetist had not mentioned the rare possibility of paralysis but, having regard to the plaintiff's anxiety to have an epidural injection when giving birth previously and her similar, 'if not greater', anxiety to have an epidural injection on the instant occasion, Lynch J was satisfied that she would have opted to have the injection even if she had received this warning.

Lynch J's failure to discuss *Walsh* or even *Sidaway* makes it difficult to assess with confidence his precise view on the best approach to the issue of informed consent. What he had to say on the subject suggests a position somewhere between Lord Diplock and Lord Bridge. This is not at all unlike the approach adopted by the Supreme Court in the old case of *Daniels v Heskin* [1954] IR 73.

1994 was thus not a very satisfactory year for clarifying the issue of informed consent to treatment. One factor is striking, however, regardless of which approach is formally adopted, the judges are reluctant to hold that there has been a *failure* of informed consent. No Irish case has yet so concluded. But these may be early days.

Nurses   In *Firth v South Eastern Health Board*, High Court, July 27, 1994, the plaintiff, a ward attendant in a hospital that catered primarily for long-term geriatric and psychiatric patients, received injuries to her back when assisting a staff nurse lift a patient who weighed eleven stone. Uncontradicted expert evidence was given by a nursing consultant who was a Health and Safety Adviser to hospitals and a former executive member of the Irish Nurses Organisation with over twenty years experience as a state registered nurse. She referred to a book published by the Back Pain Association in collaboration with the Royal College of Nursing, entitled *The Handling of Patients — A Guide for Nurses* (2nd ed., 1987). She also referred to a detailed pamphlet on the same subject published by the Cork Regional Hospital, which stated that the cradle-lift should be avoided whenever possible because it induces excessive stresses in the spine and trunk.

The expert witness condemned the lifting technique adopted in the instant case on two grounds. First, it was a combination of two lifts, a drag lift used to move the patient towards the pillows, which had been totally banned by the Royal College of Nursing in 1981 and the cradle lift which had been totally banned since 1987 because it involved bending over the patient and the lifting fulcrum was moved away from the lifter's body. The proper cause would have been to sue the draw-sheet for the purpose. This would have enabled the staff nurse and the plaintiff to adjust the patient's position in the bed effectively.

Secondly, the expert witness expressed the opinion that the plaintiff ought to have had retraining in lifting techniques from time to time as the instructions she had received in 1970 had become obsolete.

Barr J, in imposing liability, held, not only that the draw-sheet should have been used, but also that the defendant had been negligent in failing to have *all* nursing staff at the hospital retrained and kept up to date in lifting techniques prior to the accident. He observed that:

> [a] health authority has a clear duty to keep itself abreast of developments in nursing practices so as to ensure that procedures adopted in hospitals under their control do not involve the nursing staff in risks of injury which could and should be avoided.

Solicitors' Negligence   In the 1992 Review, 545-5, we analysed Barron J's decision in *McMullen v Farrell*, High Court, February 18, 1992. The Supreme Court, on February 9, 1994 reversed the award of £2,210 against the second defendant in relation to fees for planning applications, which came into operation in 1983. In the circumstances of the case, the Supreme Court found that the second defendant's negligence had not been causative of this expenditure.

In *Tuohy v Courtney* [1994] 2 ILRM 503, the Supreme Court unanimously rejected the plaintiff's appeal against Lynch J's decision (High Court, October 5, 1992) that the third and fourth named defendants had not been negligent. We analyse Lynch J's decision in the 1992 Review, 430-2. The essence of the plaintiff's case was that these defendants, solicitors of the vendor of property, had given him inaccurate information as regards the title. Far from there being any doubt about Lynch J's entitlement to prefer the evidence of the solicitor to that of the plaintiff, the surrounding circumstances 'overwhelmingly' pointed to the correctness of his finding, having regard in particular to a number of matters corroborating the solicitor's testimony.

PUBLICANS' LIABILITY

In *Hall v Kennedy*, High Court, December 20, 1993, Morris J held that proprietors of a public house had not been guilty of negligence in failing to prevent an assault on the plaintiff, a customer, by another customer. The violent customer had shown 'none of the signs or manifestations of drunk such as should have alerted a reasonable publican or his staff to the prospect that he might assault another customer.' The assailant's 'hot-tempered, spontaneous' response to what he had regarded as an insult by the plaintiff could not have been foreseen by the publican.

Morris J set out with commendable succinctness the relevant principles of law:

> The obligation of the [publican] at law is to take all reasonable care for the safety of the [customer] while on the premises. This would include in this case ensuring that [another] customer in the premises did not assault him. The necessary steps would include, in an appropriate case, removing such a customer from the premises, refusing to serve him drink [and] staffing the bar with sufficient barmen or security staff so as to ensure the safety of the [customer].

REMOTENESS OF DAMAGE

Drivers are obliged to park their vehicles so as not to be an inconvenience and obstruction or danger to other traffic. Bye-law 26(1) of the Road Traffic (General Bye-Laws) 1964 provides that:

when parking, a driver shall ensure that the vehicle —

(a) is not likely to cause inconvenience, to obstruct or endanger other traffic, or to obstruct the view of another driver at or near a road junction, corner or bend or at or near a brow of a hill, or to prevent another driver from seeing a traffic sign; . . .
(c) will not interfere with the normal flow of traffic.

See further Robert Pierse, *Road Traffic Law* (2nd ed., 1995), para. 5.8.

In *Quinn v Kennedy Brothers Construction Ltd*, High Court, March 4, 1994, the plaintiff, a twelve-year-old cyclist, was injured by a cyclist coming in the other direction when the plaintiff and a school friend of the same age, also on a bicycle, were passing outside the second defendant's van which was parked at the side of the road. The weather at the time was very bad: wind and rain were beating into the plaintiff's face.

Barron J was satisfied that the plaintiff had not been looking where he was going, his schoolfriend had blocked the available thoroughfare for traffic coming towards the pair by riding parallel with the plaintiff, and the cyclist who struck the plaintiff had been driving without any proper control. Barron J accepted that there was no doubt that, if one parked a car on a thoroughfare on which two cars could pass freely so that only one could do so, there was an interference with the normal flow of traffic, contrary to Regulation 26(1)(c). That was not the end of the matter since the plaintiff had to show that the parked van in some way contributed to the accident.

Undoubtedly, if the van had not been parked where it was, the accident might not have happened or might have happened in some other manner but that was not to say that the person who parked the van was liable: a distinction should be drawn between a *causa causans* and a *causa sine qua non*, as *Conole v Redbank Oyster Co. Ltd* [1976] IR 191 established. That case had involved a vessel that had been constructed with a safety defect, which foundered when it was put out to sea with far too large a complement of passengers when it was known to be unseaworthy. Those who constructed the vessel were relieved of liability on the basis of *novus actus interveniens*: the direct and proximate cause of the accident was the decision of the boat-owners, knowing its unsafe condition, to put the boat to sea with passengers. See McMahon & Binchy, *op. cit.*, 47-8; cf. *Crowley v AIB* [1988] ILRM 225, analysed in the 1987 Review, 328-9.

Barron J identified the combined failures of care of the three cyclists as 'the real cause of the accident'. In his view the van had been 'parked sufficiently far from the crest of the hill to absolve it from liability for the circumstances which accrued.'

ROAD TRAFFIC ACCIDENTS

Highway authorities In *Rowe v Bus Éireann/Irish Bus and Wicklow County Council*, High Court, March 3, 1994, Carroll J imposed liability on the defendant council for its failure to give adequate warning to motorists of the dangerous state of the surface of the Dublin-Rosslare road which was in the process of being repaired. The accident took place in the summertime, shortly after a thunderstorm. The surface dressing that had been used on the stretch of the road where the accident occurred was cut-back bitumen binding. On account of the hot weather conditions, the bitumen became lower in viscosity and was forced up to the surface by the expansion of the stones. This process is known among road engineers as 'fatting up'. A road that has been fatted up is shiny; in dry weather it is safe but in wet weather, driving a vehicle in excess of 40 mph on it is 'like traveling on ice'.

The Council had put a series of signs on the road. These indicted that major road works were ahead, that machinery would be crossing, that there were loose chippings (counselling a speed of 20 mph); among the signs were three permanent slippy road signs consisting of a drawing of a car with skid marks in a yellow square mounted as a diamond. In fact there were no on-going road works in the sense that men were working there and there were no loose chippings on the stretch of the carriageway where the accident took place. The bus driver traveled the route several times a week and had already passed the spot twice that day.

Carroll J considered that, since the road was 'exceptionally dangerous' in hot, wet conditions, a sign that failed to give this information to the general public was inadequate. Since the condition was temporary, she did not accept the Council's argument that it could only put up approved statutory road signs:

> It was a special and, I hope, unique situation where, given heat and rain, a situation akin to black ice could arise in a matter of hours. In a situation like that, if the statutory signs are inadequate, the County Council should have made up a temporary sign describing the hazard e.g. 'extremely dangerous when wet, speed limit 30 m.p.h.'

The statutory slippy road sign, which was permanent and did not even indicate aquaplaning as the hazard, was 'an inadequate warning for the general public, though it went part of the way by indicating the existence of some hazard.'

Carroll J went on to hold that the bus driver had misunderstood the sign when he interpreted it as being limited to a warning of slippiness in the context of materials falling from heavy trucks engaged in road works. A professional driver should have reduced speed on encountering the slippy road signs. Whether he would necessarily have gone as low as 30-35 mph was an open question. She divided liability equally between the defendants on the basis of the driver's excessive speed and the deficiency of the signs, which had gone 'part of the way but not enough'.

Collisions In *McKenna v Wall*, High Court, July 27, 1994, O'Hanlon J had to determine the issue of liability for a traffic accident in circumstances of considerable sadness. The plaintiff, a young man at the time of the accident, had received serious injuries, resulting in very severe brain injury as well as confinement to a wheelchair. He had been unconscious for several months after the accident.

After a most detailed review of the evidence, over twenty-one pages, O'Hanlon J dismissed the action. He thought that it would be unsafe to rely on the plaintiff's evidence in view of his serious intellectual impairment. The evidence suggested to him that, even during the months while he remained unconscious, the plaintiff's family had come to their own conclusion about what he must in all probability have been doing immediately prior to the accident and that, in discussions with the plaintiff later, a version of events had become fixed in his mind which did not originally emanate from himself but the well-meaning efforts of other persons to help him recollect what had happened.

Earlier in the chapter, above 457-8, in the section on remoteness of damage, we have discussed Barron J's judgment in *Quinn v Kennedy Brothers Construction Ltd*, High Court, March 4, 1994, which involved a collision between cyclists passing a parked van.

Insurance   In *Bus Éireann v Insurance Corporation of Ireland plc* [1994] 2 ILRM 444, Morris J had to interpret s. 56 of the Road Traffic Act 1961, as amended. This provides that insurance cover is compulsory for a mechanically propelled vehicle to the extent only of £40,000 in respect of injury to property. At the relevant time in the instant litigation the appropriate maximum was £1,000 rather than £40,000. S. 76 of the Act enables a person who has suffered damage caused tortiously by the owner of a mechanically propelled vehicle where there was in place a policy of insurance covering the use of the vehicle at the relevant time, to recover from that owner's insurer any sum he would have been entitled to recover from the owner. In the instant case the insurance cover held by the owner did not indemnify him in respect of the driving on the occasion of the accident.

The plaintiff company's bus had been damaged to the extent of £17,000 loss by a person whose insurance cover did not indemnify him in respect of his driving on the occasion of the accident. On behalf of the plaintiff, it was submitted that, if a claimant suffered property damage in a sum in excess of £1,000 and if in fact the driver had cover in excess of that amount, nothing in the 1961 Act prohibited the claimant from pursuing his claim against the insurance company in lieu of the driver to *the full extent* of his damage.

Morris J rejected this argument. It was clear from the terms of s. 56 that the requirement to insure for injury to property was limited to £1,000 in respect of injury caused by any one act of negligence or any one series of acts of negligence collectively constituting one event. It was equally clear from s. 76(3) that the section applied only to claims against the liability for which an approved policy of insurance was required by the Act to be effected. Accordingly, if the plaintiff's action had not been statute-barred, it would not have been entitled to recover damages in excess of £1,000.

UNLAWFUL ARREST

A man is arrested for an offence. He says that he is Kevin Walsh, of 30 South Brown Street. He is duly charged and released on bail. He fails to turn up in the District Court, contrary to the conditions of bail and the District Judge issues a bench warrant, authorising the arrest of Kevin Walsh of that address. If the Gardaí go to that house and arrest a person named Kevin Walsh, should the State be found liable for the false arrest if it transpires that the case is one of mistake as to identity, induced by the lies of the person who originally claimed to be Kevin Walsh, and that the real Kevin Walsh is entirely innocent?

The Supreme Court apparently thinks that it should. The facts of *Walsh v Ireland and the Attorney General*, Supreme Court, November 30, 1994 were somewhat different from those posited in the hypothetical, above, since the Gardaí never in fact went to Number 30; instead they visited No. 32, where the plaintiff's mother lived. She told them that her son lived at another address in the city, to which they repaired and arrested the plaintiff, who at all times naturally protested his complete innocence and contended that a mistake had been made. The plaintiff had to undergo the indignity of being charged with the offence of breach of bail recognisances, detention in a Garda station and remand on continuing bail for over two months.

The plaintiff claimed damages against Ireland and the Attorney General for breach of his constitutional rights (notably the right of liberty), unlawful arrest, false imprisonment and the negligence of their servants and agents. The jury awarded £50,000 (reduced to £25,000 on appeal).

As regards the issue of the defendants' liability, counsel for the defendants contended that the arrest had been lawful in that it had been made pursuant to a warrant issued by the District Court, that that warrant had been validly issued pursuant to the provisions of the District Court Rules 1948, in particular Order 41, which states that:

> when a defendant who is charged with an offence and who has been arrested and admitted to bail to appear before a Justice at any court fails to appear at the time and place at which he was bound by his recognisance to appear, the Justice sitting at the court before which the defendant was bound to appear may, on production to the Justice of the said recognizance, issue a warrant (Form 3B) for the defendant's arrest on the said charge, and when the defendant is arrested he shall be dealt with in the manner provided either by Rule 38 or Rule 39 hereof.

Hamilton CJ (Egan, Blayney, Denham and Carroll JJ concurring) considered that:

[t]he person whose arrest was authorised by this warrant was the person who had previously been arrested, who had been admitted to bail on his recognisance to appear before the District Court and who had failed to appear in accordance with such recognisance and who was described in the said warrant as Kevin Walsh of 30, South Brown Street, Dublin 8. Such person was not [the plaintiff] herein. . . . This was not an arrest in accordance with the terms of the said warrant. The respondent was not the person referred to in the . . . warrant and did not reside at the address given in the . . . warrant.

Reliance cannot be placed on the . . . warrant to render lawful the arrest of any person other than the person referred to and named in the warrant.

Neither could the State shelter behind the immunity afforded members of the Garda Síochána by s. 6 and s. 50 of the Constabulary (Ireland) Act 1836. These provisions protected Gardaí from civil liability 'for any act done in obedience to the warrant of any magistrate'. The Chief Justice considered that this did not apply to the instant case because the arrest of the plaintiff had not been done in obedience to the warrant since the wrong person had been arrested.

The Chief Justice's judgment does not resolve whether the crucual basis for the holding is the fact of the disparity between the identity of the plaintiff and the person to whom the warrant referred or the disparity in regard to the addresses. If it is the former, the Garda Síochána is exposed to liability without fault.

VICARIOUS LIABILITY

Hospitals In *Bolton v Blackrock Clinic Ltd*, High Court, December 20, 1994, Geoghegan J dismissed proceedings against a cardio-thoracic surgeon and a consultant thoracic physician for alleged negligence in the plaintiff's treatment and the failure to obtain an informed consent from her. See above 454. The plaintiff had also sued the hospital where these specialists worked, on the basis of direct and vicarious liability.

Having dismissed the claim against the specialists, Geoghegan J observed:

That being so there cannot be any question of vicarious liability on the part of the first named defendant for medical negligence. Indeed at any rate as the plaintiff was a private patient of the doctors in a private hospital, the question of vicarious liability may not arise.

There being no evidence of negligence by the hospital itself or its staff, Geoghegan J dismissed the claim for direct negligence also.

The issue of the possible basis of a hospital's liability deserves detailed analysis.

Contract of service or for services?   In the Social Welfare chapter, above 408-10, we disscuss *McAuliffe v Minister for Social Welfare* [1995] 1 ILRM 189, where Barr J addressed the question whether a wholesale distributor of newspapers who engaged a number of persons to deliver the papers to retail shops and similar outlets was their employer or a person who had entered into a contract for their services. The issue arose in the context of s. 271 of the Social Welfare (Consolidation) Act 1993.

Barr J observed that many of the authorities in this area related to 'whether or not the employer is liable for the negligence of the employed person' and that most of the cases turned on the degree of control exercised over the latter by the former. He appeared happy to apply the principles developed in the context of negligence litigation to a consideration of s. 271 of the 1993 Act.

The State   In *Deighan v Ireland* [1995] 1 ILRM 88; [1995] 2 IR 56, the plaintiff and another party had been attached by Costello J for contempt in the face of the court in proceedings taken under s. 297 of the Companies Act 1963. The count on which the attachment was based was the alleged inducement of a witness under subpoena to leave the court and its precincts so as to prevent his then being called on to give evidence. Having heard the evidence, including that of the plaintiff and the other party attached, Costello J, in a summary trial without a jury, convicted the plaintiff and ordered his imprisonment for six months without hard labour. He refused bail pending appeal. The Supreme Court, in proceedings that are reported *sub nom. In the matter of the trial of Matthew Kelly and Michael J. Deighan for contempt of court* [1984] ILRM 424, allowed the appeals. O'Higgins CJ stated:

> This Court is satisfied that in cases of contempt in the face of the court a High Court judge has jurisdiction to deal with the matter summarily and to impose punishment where it is necessary to do so to protect the administration of justice. Assuming for the purpose of this appeal that the allegations made in the present case would, if proved, amount to contempt in the face of the court, this Court is of opinion that, having regard to the sequence in which witnesses gave their evidence and adverting in particular to the fact that [the witness] had completed his evidence in the Companies Act matter, the necessity for the judge to hear and determine the issue did not exist.

> In these circumstances, these appeals will be allowed. The court will
> make an order for the release of the appellants.

The plaintiff, in the instant case, issued a plenary summons claiming damages
for assault and battery, unlawful imprisonment an malicious prosecution. The
defendants — Ireland, the Attorney General and the Ministers for Justice and
Finance — sought the dismissal of the proceedings for failure to disclose any
cause of action.

The plaintiff sought to place emphasis on the Chief Justice's statement
that: '. . . the necessity for the judge to hear and determine the contempt issue
did not exist.' He contended that this amounted to the proposition that he had
not in fact been in contempt of court and he argued that Costello J had been
in error in acting as he had done in charging and incarcerating him and
refusing bail.

The plaintiff also contended that he did not in fact commit the acts alleged
to constitute the contempt. Flood J was of opinion that this was 'not relevant
to a consideration of the preliminary point in issue. . . .'

Flood J noted that the Supreme Court had made it clear that Costello J
had at all material times been acting within jurisdiction. He was of the view
that the inferences the plaintiff sought to draw from the quoted part of the
judgment were unduly wide. Even if this was not so, no action was maintainable for anything said or done by a trial judge in the exercise of a jurisdiction
belonging to and exerciseable by him. Flood J invoked Lord Denning MR's
observations in *Sirros v Moore* [1974] All ER 776 in this context.

In Flood J's opinion it followed that if the trial judge was not liable in
damages for any erroneous decision made by him, the juridical body 'Ireland'
could not in any circumstances be rendered liable if the only basis upon which
such a proposition could be founded was vicarious liability.

> Vicarious liability cannot arise unless there is a primary liability. Again
> vicarious liability is a concept related to the law of torts and it is certainly
> arguable whether the event in this case could ever be regarded as a tort.

It was quite clear that the Governor of Mountjoy had been acting correctly
on foot of a warrant which on its face empowered him to do what he was
directed to do and, in Flood J's view, he 'certainly could not be made liable
in damages.' The Minister for Finance and the Minister for Justice who were
not servants of the judiciary, could not have vicarious liability for any act of
the judiciary.

Flood J dismissed summarily the plaintiff's claim to compensation under
s. 9 of the Criminal Procedure Act 1993. He observed that the section 'clearly
does not apply to the plaintiff's case.' The Convention for the Protection of

Human Rights and Fundamental Freedoms was not part of the domestic law of this country and accordingly was not a ground which could give rise to an action in this country. (On this subject generally, see further Byrne & McCutcheon, *The Irish Legal System* (3rd ed., 1996), 724-8.)

For the foregoing reasons Flood J was satisfied that the plaintiff had not shown a maintainable cause of action in his pleadings nor did the facts upon which he founded the pleadings give rise to a maintainable cause of action. Accordingly he acceded to the defence application on this preliminary point and dismissed the plaintiff's case.

Transport

AIR TRANSPORT

Airport bye-laws The Airport Bye-Laws 1994 (SI No. 425 of 1994) consolidated with amendments the bye-laws for the three State airports at Dublin, Shannon and Cork and revoked the Airport Bye-Laws 1978, the Airport Bye-Laws 1980 and the Shannon Airport (Small Public Service Vehicles) Bye-Laws 1980. Bye-laws 4, 5 and 6 deal with various offences by persons in airports, including smoking in prohibited areas, being intoxicated, releasing birds within an airport, failing to drive with due care for other users of an airport as well as matters specifically connected with aircraft, such as precautions concerning re-fuelling. Bye-law 7 deals with the control of animals at airports, while Bye-law 8 lists those activities for which permission must be granted by Aer Rianta, the Airports Management Authority. These include selling of items, grazing of animals and the use of any electrical devices. Bye-laws 9 and 10 deal with speed limits and vehicles generally, including 'wheel clamping' of vehicles. Bye-law 11 concerns the regulation of taxis and hackney cab services at airports. Bye-law 12 requires those in contravention of any Bye-law to indemnify Aer Rianta in respect of any expenditure incurred by it arising therefrom. Bye-law 13 requires persons to comply with directions from safety and security personnel. Finally, Bye-law 14 requires contractors to carry personal injuries insurance in connection with such work at an airport.

Eurocontrol route charges The Irish Aviation Authority (Eurocontrol) (Route Charges) Regulations 1994 (SI No. 456 of 1994) amended the Air Navigation (Eurocontrol) (Route Charges) Regulations 1989 to 1990 by imposing an interest payment where route charges are not paid by the due date and also altering the categories of flights exempt from route charges. The 1994 Regulations also produced a new collective citation, the Irish Aviation Authority (Eurocontrol) (Route Charges) Regulations 1989 to 1994, taking account of the establishment of the Irish Aviation Authority (1993 Review, 584).

MERCHANT SHIPPING

As in previous Reviews, we note a number of Regulations which give effect to amendments to the 1974 IMO Convention for the Safety of Lives at Sea (SOLAS). The essential requirements of SOLAS were incorporated into Irish law by the Merchant Shipping Act 1981 and many Regulations have been made since 1981 to give effect to detailed requirements of, and amendments to, SOLAS. S.3 of the 1981 Act also empowers the Minister for the Marine to amend any provision of the Merchant Shipping Acts 1894 to 1994 in order to give effect to SOLAS requirements. Thus, the Merchant Shipping Act 1947 (Section 11) (Amendment) Order 1994 (SI No. 346 of 1994) amended s. 11 of the 1947 Act to provide that Regulations made under its terms may involve the implementation of SOLAS. SI No. 347 of 1994, discussed below, followed from this amendment of the 1947 Act by Ministerial Order.

Cargo ships: construction and survey The Merchant Shipping (Cargo Ship Construction and Survey) Rules 1983 (Amendment) Rules 1994 (SI No. 30 of 1994) amended the 1983 Rules of the same title to give effect to 1989 amendments to SOLAS.

   The Merchant Shipping (Cargo Ship Construction and Survey) Rules 1985 (Amendment) Rules 1994 (SI No. 31 of 1994) amended the 1985 Rules of the same title to give effect to 1983 amendments to SOLAS.

Cargo ships: safety equipment survey The Merchant Shipping (Cargo Ship Safety Equipment Survey) (Amendment) Rules 1994 (SI No. 29 of 1994) amended the 1983 Rules of the same title to give effect to 1981 amendments to SOLAS.

Certification of officers and shipping operations The Merchant Shipping (Certification of Deck Officers) (Amendment) Regulations 1994 (SI No. 264 of 1994) and the Merchant Shipping (Certification of Marine Engineer Officers and Marine Engine Operators) (Amendment) Regulations 1994 (SI No. 265 of 1994) amended manning requirements in the respective 1988 Regulations of the same titles and also authorised certain ships to operate within the entire Gulf of Finland.

Passenger ships: construction and survey The Merchant Shipping (Passenger Ship Construction and Survey) (Amendment) Rules 1994 (SI No. 12 of 1994) and the Merchant Shipping (Passenger Ship Construction and Survey) (Amendment No. 2) Rules 1994 (SI No. 131 of 1994) amended the Merchant Shipping (Passenger Ship Construction) Rules 1983 and the Merchant Shipping (Passenger Ship Construction and Survey) Rules 1985 to give effect to 1988 and 1989 amendments to SOLAS. SI No. 12 of 1994 also revoked the Merchant Shipping (Passenger Ship Construction) (Amendment) Rules 1989.

Radioactive waste The European Communities (Supervision and Control of Certain Shipments of Radioactive Waste) Regulations 1994 (SI No. 276 of 1994) are referred to in the Safety and Health chapter, 407, above.

Ro-Ro passenger ships: survivability The Merchant Shipping (Ro-Ro Passenger Ship Survivability) Rules 1994 (SI No. 251 of 1994) implemented the 'Agreement Concerning the Stability of Existing Ro-Ro Passenger Ships Operating Services To or From Ports Within a Designated Area of North West Europe' dated July 27, 1994. This international agreement arose from the sinking of the passenger ferry Estonia in the Baltic Sea in 1994, and the 1994 Rules specify updated survivability standards for all ro-ro passenger ships built on or after April 29, 1990.

Safe manning document The Merchant Shipping (Safe Manning Document) Regulations 1994 (SI No. 347 of 1994) require certain ships to possess a Safe Manning Level Document, in accordance with certain amendments to SOLAS.

Salvage and Wrecks The Merchant Shipping (Salvage and Wreck) Act 1993 (discussed in the 1993 Review, 587-8) came into effect on 1 March 1994: see the Merchant Shipping (Salvage and Wreck) Act 1993 (Commencement) Order 1994 (SI No. 32 of 1994).

Tonnage The Merchant Shipping (Tonnage Regulations 1984) (Amendment) Regulations 1994 (SI No. 4 of 1994) amended the 1984 Regulations to permit vessels under 24 metres in length have their tonnage measured in accordance with Part II of the 1984 Regulations.

ROAD TRAFFIC

Road Traffic Act 1994 The terms of the Road Traffic Act 1994 are considered in the Criminal Law chapter, 217-222, above.

Combined transport of goods: EC The European Communities (Combined Transport of Goods Between Member States) Regulations 1994 (SI No. 60 of 1994) gave effect to Directive 92/106/EEC on the establishment of common rules for certain types of combined transport of goods, primarily road and rail transport, between EC Member States. The effect to abolish quota systems and authorisation systems which might otherwise be required under the various Transport Acts 1933 to 1986. The 1994 Regulations also revoked the European Communities (International Carriage of Goods By Road and Rail) Regulations 1975, the European Communities (Combined Road/Rail Carriage of Goods Between Member States) Regulations 1979 and the European Communities (Combined Road/Rail Carriage of Goods Between Member States) Regulations 1982.

Construction Standards The European Communities (Motor Vehicles Type Approval) Regulations 1994 (SI No. 71 of 1994), which came into effect on March 23, 1994 on their signing by the Minister for Enterprise and Employment, further amended the European Communities (Motor Vehicles Type Approval) Regulations 1978 to take account of 13 Directives agreed in 1993, all of which lay down technical specifications for the construction of motor vehicles. The 1994 Regulations now contain the most updated listing of the Directives to which manufacturers must comply. The result is that the list of Directives in the European Communities (Motor Vehicles Type Approval) (Amendment) Regulations 1993 (1993 Review, 589) became obsolete.

Emission levels The European Communities (Mechanically Propelled Vehicle Emission Control) Regulations 1994 (SI No. 194 of 1994) prohibit the issue of first licences for certain new vehicles from October 1, 1994, unless they comply with the air pollutant emission control requirements specified in Directives 91/441/EEC, as amended by Directive 93/59/EEC. Certain limited exemptions are provided for as well as penalties for non-compliance.

Declaration and designation of public roads The Roads Regulations 1994 (SI No. 119 of 1994)specify requirements as to public notice in respect of the declaration of public roads, prescribe the category of persons who must make a declaration of interests to the National Roads Authority, specify the types of vehicles which may use motorways, specify the types of road projects which require an environmental impact assessment, prescribe requirements as to public notice in respect of applications for consent to carry out works on motorways and protected roads, control access to service areas, specify the requirements as to public notice and other procedures relating to the temporary closure of roads, set down general requirements as to notice under the Roads Act 1993 (as to which see the 1993 Review, 588) and regulate the disposal of moneys accruing to local authorities and the National Roads Authority under the 1993 Act. The Regulations also prescribe the form to be used by local authorities in connection with the submission to the

Minister for the Environment of schemes for the provision of motorways, busways and protected roads and to notify the public and persons affected by such schemes and the forms to be used in relation to the environmental impact assessment of road projects. On the actual designation of roads, the Roads Act 1993 (Declaration of National Roads) Order 1994 (SI No. 209 of 1994) contains a full list of existing national primary roads (the 'N' roads), as well a short list of proposed national roads. The Order, which came into effect on August 1, 1994, revoked and replaced the Local Government (Roads and Motorways) Act 1974 (Declaration of National Roads) Orders 1977, 1980 and 1986. Similarly, the Roads Act 1993 (Declaration of Regional Roads) Order 1994 (SI No. 400 of 1994) contains a full list of existing regional roads (the 'R' roads). This Order came into effect on January 1, 1995.

Disabled drivers' and passengers' tax concessions   The Disabled Drivers and Disabled Passengers (Tax Concessions) Regulations 1994 (SI No. 353 of 1994) set out revised medical criteria, certification procedures, repayment limits, forms and other matters necessary for the purposes of giving effect to s. 92 of the Finance Act 1989 which provides for tax concessions for disabled drivers and disabled passengers. The Regulations came into effect on December 1, 1994.

Driving licence   The Road Traffic (Licensing of Drivers) (Amendment) Regulations 1994 (SI No. 56 of 1994) amended the Road Traffic (Licensing of Drivers) Regulations 1989 to 1993 to provide for changes in the administration of driving test applications and imposed a requirement that, in order to obtain a third or subsequent provisional driving licence, a person must have undergone a driving test within the previous two years. They also provided that the fee paid for a driving test will not be refundable except in exceptional circumstances.

Emergency vehicles: speed limit   The Road Traffic (Built-up Area Speed limit) Regulations 1994 (SI No. 224 of 1994) exempted ambulances, fire brigade vehicles and Garda Síochána vehicles, while being used in the course of duty, from the built-up area speed limit.

Fees   The Road Transport Acts (Fees) Regulations 1994 (SI No. 141 of 1994) prescribed updated fees for national and international road freight carriers' licences under s. 3(6) of the Road Transport Act 1986.

International carriage of goods: EC   The European Communities (International Carriage of Goods by Road) Regulations 1994 (SI No. 140 of 1994 and SI No. 188 of 1994) introduced the necessary administrative arrangements required to give full effect to Regulation (EEC) 881/92 on the international carriage of goods by road in the European Community. They provide, *inter alia*, that a Community authorisation issued by the competent authority of an EC Member State shall be deemed to be a restricted road freight licence for the purposes of s. 8 of the Road Transport Act 1971 as inserted by the Road Transport Act 1986.

Lighting of Customs and Excise vehicles   The Road Traffic (Lighting of Vehicles (Amendment) Regulations 1994 (SI No. 3 of 1994) permitted the fitting and use of amber flashing warning lights on Customs and Excise patrol cars.

Registration and licensing   The Road Vehicles (Registration and Licensing) (Amendment) Regulations 1994 (SI No. 277 of 1994) amended the definition of 'registered owner' of a mechanically propelled vehicle and 'licensing records' contained in Art. 1 of the 1992 Regulations of the same title (1992 Review, 630) in order to conform fully with the registration requirements of the Finance Act 1992 (1992 Review, 502-6).

Property damage insurance   The monetary limits concerning compulsory insurance for property damage under s. 56 of the Road Traffic Act 1961 was adverted to in *Bus Éireann v Insurance Corporation of Ireland plc* [1994] 2 ILRM 444: see the Limitation of Actions chapter, 353-6 above.

Road freight vehicle plate application form   The Road Transport Acts (Vehicle Plate Application Form) Regulations 1994 (SI No. 142 of 1994) amended the Road Transport Act 1933 (Part II) Regulations Order 1933 to alter the prescribed application form for a road freight vehicle plate.

SHANNON NAVIGATION

The Shannon Navigation (Amendment) Bye-Laws 1994 (SI No. 66 of 1994) amended the tolls payable under the Shannon Navigation Bye-Laws 1992 (1992 Review, 631-2) and were made pursuant to the Shannon Navigation Act 1990 (1990 Review, 585-6). The Shannon Navigation (Extension of Limits of Navigation) Bye-Laws 1994 (SI No. 314 of 1994), also made under the 1990 Act, brought a further stretch of river within the scope of the 1990 Act. The Shannon Navigation (Construction of Vessels) (Amendment) Bye-Laws 1994 (SI No. 421 of 1994) amended the Shannon Navigation (Construction of Vessels) Bye-Laws 1992 (1992 Review, 631-2) and laid down additional requirements concerning the prevention of pollution from toilets on vessels using the Shannon waterway.

Index